OLIVER TWIST

AUTHORITATIVE TEXT

BACKGROUNDS AND SOURCES

EARLY REVIEWS

CRITICISM

A NORTON CRITICAL EDITION

Charles Dickens
OLIVER TWIST

AUTHORITATIVE TEXT
BACKGROUNDS AND SOURCES
EARLY REVIEWS
CRITICISM

Edited by

FRED KAPLAN

QUEENS COLLEGE AND THE GRADUATE CENTER,
CITY UNIVERSITY OF NEW YORK

W • W • NORTON & COMPANY • *New York* • *London*

The text of this book is composed in Electra with the display set in Bernhard Modern. Composition by PennSet, Inc. Manufacturing by Courier. Book design by Antonina Krass.

Library of Congress Cataloging-in-Publication Data
Dickens, Charles, 1812–1870.
Oliver Twist : authoritative text, reviews, and essays in
criticism / Charles Dickens ; edited by Fred Kaplan. — A Norton
critical ed.
p.   cm.
Includes bibliographical references.
1. Dickens, Charles, 1812–1870. Oliver Twist. I. Kaplan, Fred,
1937–   II. Title.
PR4567.A2K35   1993
823'.8—dc20   92-34792

ISBN 0-393-96292-X (pa)

W. W. Norton & Company, Inc., 500 Fifth Avenue, New York, N.Y. 10110
W. W. Norton & Company Ltd., 10 Coptic Street, London WC1A 1PU

1   2   3   4   5   6   7   8   9   0

Contents

Early Reviews

Criticism

Preface

When first published in 1837, *Oliver Twist* struck the English and American reading public as a bold, powerful portrayal of aspects of early Victorian life that literature (let alone polite literature for a middle-class reading audience) had mostly kept away from. Having from childhood seen for himself the underside of London life, Dickens at the age of twenty-five was well-equipped to write about its ugliness and danger as well as about its energy and excitement. The novel pivots on an idealized vision of the possibility of virtue and beauty; but it also pivots on the powerful, almost pervasive horror of criminality, prostitution, child abuse, poverty, violence, and brutalization that urbanization has made a fulcrum of modern life. The conditions of personal and public criminality that Dickens dramatizes in *Oliver Twist* provide a historical mirror image of similar conditions in the great cities of our own contemporary world. *Oliver Twist* is the first and perhaps still the most powerful work of fiction to attempt to bring to the attention of those who read such books the misery that daily life is for large numbers of people caught up in generational cycles of poverty and despair and in the selfishness and stupidity of government and its agencies.

The themes and psychological patterns of *Oliver Twist* were to be those of all of Dickens' novels thereafter, more or less: the horrors of exploitation; the struggle between good and evil; the venality and hypocrisy of privilege and of corrupt government; the destructive force of materialism; the heavy burden of history; the search for lost parents and happy homes; the sacredness of children and of the moral sentiments; the need for energetic pursuit of social reform and literacy; the power of language and imagination to create structures of life and hope; and the redeeming potential of charity and love.

Like all Dickens' novels, *Oliver Twist* has a happy ending. Vice is punished and virtue is rewarded. But any satisfaction the modern reader may feel in the rescue of the small boy and the restoration of a moral balance is likely be undercut by the reader's sense throughout that what threatens Oliver is far more powerful and real than what saves him. What saves him is a Victorian novelist's and his culture's residual faith in the ultimate triumph of goodness on earth and in heaven. The novel's plot and its idealistic characterizations are instruments of that faith. For Dickens, coincidences of plot and other devices that run counter to the modern reader's sense of reality are the ways in which a narrative can express its creator's and its audience's belief that for individuals and for society as a whole things will work out well in the end. That Oliver is rescued from a life of criminality is an expression of Victorian optimism. For some modern readers, it seems an expression of Victorian hypocrisy. But Dickens genuinely hoped that, no matter how brutal the lives they led in the London slums, the little children would be saved.

A Note on the Text

The history of the text of *Oliver Twist* is unique in Dickens' career. Initially published as a serial in a weekly magazine, *Bentley's Miscellany*, from February 1837 to April 1839, it was published in three volumes in book form in November 1838; a second edition was published in early 1839, with a new reprinting in late 1839 and then again in 1840; the "Third edition" was published in 1841 and a new, substantially revised edition in 1846. This 1846 edition was first published in ten monthly parts and then in one volume. It is the ten monthly parts of the 1846 edition that serve as the copy-text for this Norton Critical Edition. It is the last edition that Dickens himself revised substantially, and it represents the author's final wishes in regard to the text.

Students interested in a detailed expository history of the text of *Oliver Twist* and a variorum account of the changes made from one edition to another may consult the excellent definitive edition of the novel, edited by Kathleen Tillotson for the Clarendon Dickens, published by Oxford University Press in 1966. I have gone directly to the 1846 edition for the text of the Norton Critical Edition. But I am indebted to the Clarendon *Oliver Twist* for a number of elements. As I agree with the small number of substantive emendations made by the Clarendon edition, I have adopted them without exception. I have also learned from the Clarendon edition's "Glossary of Thieves' Cant and Slang" and the "Glossary of Words and Phrases in Thieves' Slang" in the Penguin English Library edition, edited by Peter Fairclough, as well as the explanatory notes provided in the Penguin English Library edition and the World's Classics edition, edited by Kathleen Tillotson. As has Tillotson in the Clarendon edition, I have silently corrected all the obvious misprints I have noticed.

This edition, though, departs from the Clarendon edition on a number of points: (1) Since they are not properly a part of the 1846 edition, I have not included passages that appeared in an earlier version but were eliminated by Dickens from the 1846 edition; (2) I have retained the spelling of the 1846 edition, with the exception of eliminating extra spacing preceeding tall punctuation (regularization within the text or conformity to modern spelling seems to me undesirable); (3) I have not made uniform the spelling of contractions (*dont*, *do'nt*, *don't*, for example), though whenever a contraction has had an extra space, the space has been closed up; (4) I have retained Dickens' use of double rather than single quotations for dialogue (which is consistent with modern American but not modern British usage).

Backgrounds, Sources, and Criticism

The Poor Law Amendment Act of 1834 dominates the Backgrounds section. Like much "welfare reform," it made living conditions for the poor worse than they had been and made it even more difficult for the working poor to get assistance. Victorian wages for the vast number of low-paid workers often could not possibly support a family even at the lowest subsistence level. The debates from the *Annual Register* represent the variety of political and moral considerations that preoccupied the Victorian ruling class in regard to the new law. Then, as now, the burden to the state (the taxpaying public) of illegitimate children in one-parent households was an important aspect of the debate. The law eventually pronounced that the mothers of illegitimate children were solely financially responsible for them. Though fornication was a crime, it was a greater crime for the mother than for the father. In such a strongly patriarchal, Bible-driven culture, economics and morality neatly dovetailed: the distance between the fallen woman of the middle class, like Oliver's mother, and the street prostitute, like Nancy, was small. Regardless, the society took little to no responsibility. In *Oliver Twist*, Dickens paradoxically further narrows the distance. But he does so by elevating all women rather than by participating in total or even selective degradation. In "An Appeal to Fallen Women," Dickens demonstrates how difficult it was for even the "enlightened" Victorian male to find the right tone and approach.

Modern criticism of *Oliver Twist* is so fully represented in this edition that I can happily say that most of the best that has been written about the novel is included. There are a few exceptions, mostly because I had to choose between equally good essays or selections from books that covered essentially the same ground.

Acknowledgments

I have been ably assisted by Noah J. Kaplan in determining the copy-text and in creating the textual annotation. His professional expertise in the area of textual editing has made that aspect of the edition a happy collaboration. For the cover illustration, I have drawn on the rich resources of the Morgan Library. The Map of London in 1828 and the black-and-white Cruikshank illustrations are reproduced courtesy of the Huntington Library, San Marino, California. To the Huntington I owe special thanks for its hospitality and resources while I worked on this edition.

The Text of
OLIVER TWIST

The Author's Preface
to
the Third Edition (1841)

"Some of the author's friends cried, 'Lookee, gentlemen, the man is a villain; but it is Nature for all that;' and the young critics of the age, the clerks, apprentices, &c., called it low, and fell a groaning."—FIELDING.[1]

The greater part of this Tale was originally published in a magazine.[2] When I completed it, and put it forth in its present form three years ago, I fully expected it would be objected to on some very high moral grounds in some very high moral quarters. The result did not fail to prove the justice of my anticipations.

I embrace the present opportunity of saying a few words in explanation of my aim and object in its production. It is in some sort a duty with me to do so, in gratitude to those who sympathized with me and divined my purpose at the time, and who, perhaps, will not be sorry to have their impression confirmed under my own hand.

It is, it seems, a very coarse and shocking circumstance, that some of the characters in these pages are chosen from the most criminal and degraded of London's population; that Sikes is a thief, and Fagin a receiver of stolen goods; that the boys are pickpockets, and the girl is a prostitute.

I confess I have yet to learn that a lesson of the purest good may not be drawn from the vilest evil. I have always believed this to be a recognised and established truth, laid down by the greatest men the world has ever seen, constantly acted upon by the best and wisest natures, and confirmed by the reason and experience of every thinking mind. I saw no reason, when I wrote this book, why the very dregs of life, so long as their speech did not offend the ear, should not serve the purpose of a moral, at least as well as its froth and cream. Nor did I doubt that there lay festering in Saint Giles's as good materials towards the truth as any flaunting in Saint James's.[3]

In this spirit, when I wished to show, in little Oliver, the principle of Good surviving through every adverse circumstance, and triumphing at last; and when I considered among what companions I could try him best, having regard to that kind of men into whose hands he would most naturally fall; I bethought myself of those who figure in these volumes. When I came to discuss the subject more maturely with myself, I saw

---

1. From Henry Fielding's *Tom Jones* 8.1. Fielding (1707–54), who had himself been a London magistrate, defended the depictions of vice in his novels as essential for the assertion of the triumph of virtue.
2. *Bentley's Miscellany*, which Dickens edited from January 1837 until early 1839.
3. An area of London noted for its wealth and elegance. "Saint Giles's": an area notorious for its slums, criminals, and street crime.

many strong reasons for pursuing the course to which I was inclined. I had read of thieves by scores—seductive fellows (amiable for the most part), faultless in dress, plump in pocket, choice in horseflesh, bold in bearing, fortunate in gallantry, great at a song, a bottle, pack of cards or dice-box, and fit companions for the bravest. But I had never met (except in HOGARTH)[4] with the miserable reality. It appeared to me that to draw a knot of such associates in crime as really do exist; to paint them in all their deformity, in all their wretchedness, in all the squalid poverty of their lives; to show them as they really are, for ever skulking uneasily through the dirtiest paths of life, with the great, black, ghastly gallows closing up their prospect, turn them where they may; it appeared to me that to do this, would be to attempt a something which was greatly needed, and which would be a service to society. And therefore I did it as I best could.

In every book I know, where such characters are treated of at all, certain allurements and fascinations are thrown around them. Even in the Beggar's Opera, the thieves are represented as leading a life which is rather to be envied than otherwise; while MACHEATH, with all the captivations of command, and the devotion of the most beautiful girl and only pure character in the piece, is as much to be admired and emulated by weak beholders, as any fine gentleman in a red coat who has purchased, as VOLTAIRE says, the right to command a couple of thousand men, or so, and to affront death at their head.[5] Johnson's question, whether any man will turn thief because Macheath is reprieved, seems to me beside the matter.[6] I ask myself, whether any man will be deterred from turning thief because of his being sentenced to death, and because of the existence of Peachum and Lockit;[7] and remembering the captain's roaring life, great appearance, vast success, and strong advantages, I feel assured that nobody having a bent that way will take any warning from him, or will see anything in the play but a very flowery and pleasant road, conducting an honourable ambition in course of time, to Tyburn Tree.[8]

In fact, Gay's witty satire on society had a general object, which made him careless of example in this respect, and gave him other, wider, and higher aims. The same may be said of Sir Edward Bulwer's admirable and most powerful novel of Paul Clifford,[9] which cannot be fairly considered as having, or being intended to have, any bearing on this part of the subject, one way or other.

What manner of life is that which is described in these pages, as the

4. William Hogarth (1697–1764), British engraver and painter.
5. Dickens refers to chapter 4 of Voltaire's *Babouc*, which comments on the purchase of high-ranking army commands by the wealthy. John Gay's *The Beggar's Opera* was first produced in London in 1728; its main character is Captain Macheath.
6. In Samuel Johnson, *Lives of the English Poets* (1779–81).
7. Characters in *The Beggar's Opera*.
8. The gallows on which condemned criminals were hanged in eighteenth-century London.
9. Edward Bulwer's popular novel *Paul Clifford* (1830).

everyday existence of a Thief? What charms has it for the young and ill-disposed, what allurements for the most jolter-headed of juveniles? Here are no canterings upon moonlit heaths, no merry-makings in the snuggest of all possible caverns, none of the attractions of dress, no embroidery, no lace, no jack-boots, no crimson coats and ruffles, none of the dash and freedom with which "the road" has been, time out of mind, invested. The cold, wet, shelterless midnight streets of London; the foul and frowsy dens, where vice is closely packed and lacks the room to turn; the haunts of hunger and disease, the shabby rags that scarcely hold together: where are the attractions of these things? Have they no lesson, and do they not whisper something beyond the little-regarded warning of a moral precept?

But there are people of so refined and delicate a nature, that they cannot bear the contemplation of these horrors. Not that they turn instinctively from crime; but that criminal characters, to suit them, must be, like their meat, in delicate disguise. A Massaroni in green velvet is quite an enchanting creature; but a Sikes in fustian is insupportable.[1] A Mrs. Massaroni, being a lady in short petticoats and a fancy dress, is a thing to imitate in tableaux[2] and have in lithograph on pretty songs; but a Nancy, being a creature in a cotton gown and cheap shawl, is not to be thought of. It is wonderful how Virtue turns from dirty stockings; and how Vice, married to ribbons and a little gay attire, changes her name, as wedded ladies do, and becomes Romance.

Now, as the stern and plain truth, even in the dress of this (in novels) much exalted race, was a part of the purpose of this book, I will not, for these readers, abate one hole in the Dodger's coat, or one scrap of curl-paper[3] in the girl's dishevelled hair. I have no faith in the delicacy which cannot bear to look upon them. I have no desire to make proselytes among such people. I have no respect for their opinion, good or bad; do not covet their approval; and do not write for their amusement. I venture to say this without reserve; for I am not aware of any writer in our language having a respect for himself, or held in any respect by his posterity, who ever has descended to the taste of this fastidious class.

On the other hand, if I look for examples, and for precedents, I find them in the noblest range of English literature. Fielding, De Foe, Goldsmith, Smollett, Richardson, Mackenzie[4]—all these for wise purposes, and especially the two first, brought upon the scene the very scum and refuse of the land. Hogarth, the moralist, and censor of his age—in

---

1. Allesandro Massaroni, "the Italian Robin Hood," is a character in J. R. Planche's *The Brigand; a Romantic Drama* (1829).
2. A form of stage representation in which single set scenes without action or voice are presented.
3. Pieces of paper around which hair is rolled in order to set curls.
4. Henry MacKenzie (1745–1831), author of *The Man of Feeling* (1771) and *The Man of the World* (1773); Daniel Defoe (1660–1731), author of *Robinson Crusoe* (1719) and *Moll Flanders* (1722); Oliver Goldsmith (1730–74), author of *The Vicar of Wakefield* (1764); Tobias Smollett (1721–71), author of *The Adventures of Roderick Random* (1748); Samuel Richardson (1689–1761), author of *Pamela* (1741) and *Clarissa* (1747).

whose great works the times in which he lived, and the characters of every time, will never cease to be reflected—did the like, without the compromise of a hair's breadth; with a power and depth of thought which belonged to few men before him, and will probably appertain to fewer still in time to come. Where does this giant stand now in the estimation of his countrymen? And yet, if I turn back to the days in which he or any of these men flourished, I find the same reproach levelled against them every one, each in his turn, by the insects of the hour, who raised their little hum, and died, and were forgotten.

Cervantes laughed Spain's chivalry away, by showing Spain its impossible and wild absurdity. [5] It was my attempt, in my humble and fardistant sphere, to dim the false glitter surrounding something which really did exist, by showing it in its unattractive and repulsive truth. No less consulting my own taste, than the manners of the age, I endeavoured, while I painted it in all its fallen and degraded aspect, to banish from the lips of the lowest character I introduced, any expression that could by possibility offend; and rather to lead to the unavoidable inference that its existence was of the most debased and vicious kind, than to prove it elaborately by words and deeds. In the case of the girl, in particular, I kept this intention constantly in view. Whether it is apparent in the narrative, and how it is executed, I leave my readers to determine.

It has been observed of this girl, that her devotion to the brutal housebreaker does not seem natural, and it has been objected to Sikes in the same breath—with some inconsistency, as I venture to think— that he is surely overdrawn, because in him there would appear to be none of those redeeming traits which are objected to as unnatural in his mistress. Of the latter objection I will merely say, that I fear there are in the world some insensible and callous natures that do become, at last, utterly and irredeemably bad. But whether this be so or not, of one thing I am certain: that there are such men as Sikes, who, being closely followed through the same space of time, and through the same current of circumstances, would not give, by one look or action of a moment, the faintest indication of a better nature. Whether every gentler human feeling is dead within such bosoms, or the proper chord to strike has rusted and is hard to find, I do not know; but that the fact is so, I am sure.

It is useless to discuss whether the conduct and character of the girl seems natural or unnatural, probable or improbable, right or wrong. IT IS TRUE. Every man who has watched these melancholy shades of life knows it to be so. Suggested to my mind long ago—long before I dealt in fiction—by what I often saw and read of, in actual life around me, I have, for years, tracked it through many profligate and noisome ways, and found it still the same. From the first introduction of that poor

---

5. A paraphrase of Byron's reference to Miguel Cervantes' *Don Quixote* (1605) in *Don Juan* 13.11.

wretch, to her laying her bloody head upon the robber's breast, there is not one word exaggerated or over-wrought. It is emphatically God's truth, for it is the truth He leaves in such depraved and miserable breasts; the hope yet lingering behind; the last fair drop of water at the bottom of the dried-up weed-choked well. It involves the best and worst shades of our common nature; much of its ugliest hues, and something of its most beautiful; it is a contradiction, an anomaly, an apparent impossibility, but it is a truth. I am glad to have had it doubted, for in that circumstance I find a sufficient assurance that it needed to be told.

DEVONSHIRE TERRACE,
April, 1841.

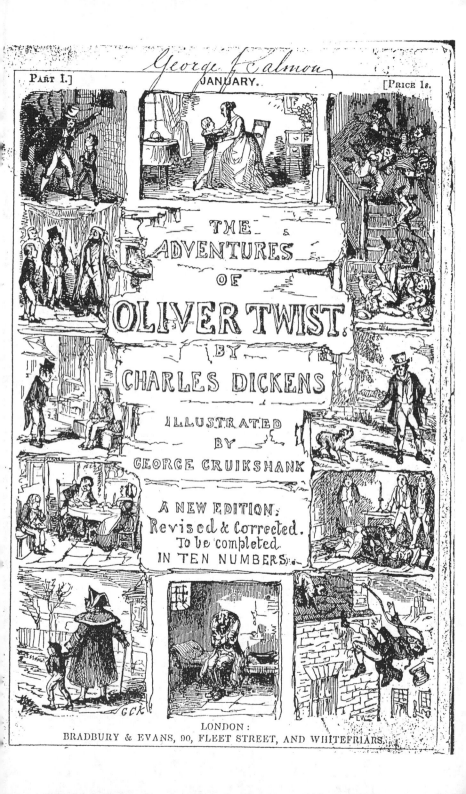

Part I.] JANUARY. [Price 1s.

THE & ADVENTURES OF OLIVER TWIST.

BY CHARLES DICKENS

ILLUSTRATED BY GEORGE CRUIKSHANK

A NEW EDITION. Revised & Corrected. To be completed IN TEN NUMBERS

LONDON: BRADBURY & EVANS, 90, FLEET STREET, AND WHITEFRIARS.

THE

ADVENTURES

OF

OLIVER TWIST;

OR,

The Parish Boy's Progress.

BY

CHARLES DICKENS.

WITH TWENTY-FOUR ILLUSTRATIONS ON STEEL, BY
GEORGE CRUIKSHANK.

A NEW EDITION, REVISED AND CORRECTED.

LONDON:
PUBLISHED FOR THE AUTHOR,
BY BRADBURY & EVANS, WHITEFRIARS.
MDCCCXLVI.

The Contents of *Oliver Twist*

Oliver Twist

Chapter I.

TREATS OF THE PLACE WHERE OLIVER TWIST WAS BORN;
AND OF THE CIRCUMSTANCES ATTENDING HIS BIRTH.

Among other public buildings in a certain town, which for many reasons it will be prudent to refrain from mentioning, and to which I will assign no fictitious name, there is one anciently common to most towns, great or small: to wit, a workhouse;[1] and in this workhouse was born: on a day and date which I need not trouble myself to repeat, inasmuch as it can be of no possible consequence to the reader, in this stage of the business at all events: the item of mortality whose name is prefixed to the head of this chapter.

For a long time after it was ushered into this world of sorrow and trouble, by the parish surgeon, it remained a matter of considerable doubt whether the child would survive to bear any name at all; in which case it is somewhat more than probable that these memoirs would never have appeared; or, if they had, that being comprised within a couple of pages, they would have possessed the inestimable merit of being the most concise and faithful specimen of biography, extant in the literature of any age or country.

Although I am not disposed to maintain that the being born in a workhouse, is in itself the most fortunate and enviable circumstance that can possibly befal a human being, I do mean to say that in this particular instance, it was the best thing for Oliver Twist that could by possibility have occurred. The fact is, that there was considerable difficulty in inducing Oliver to take upon himself the office of respiration,—a troublesome practice, but one which custom has rendered necessary to our

1. The Poor Law Amendment Act of 1834 divided England and Wales into twenty-four districts, each of which was responsible for creating large institutional homes called "workhouses" (which were not places of work) for the indigent poor of all ages and states of health. Parishes, which had been the smallest administrative subdivisions, were united into larger administrative units and governed by a local Board of Guardians and paid for by local taxpayers. The intent was to discourage the poor from living in the workhouses (also called "Unions") by providing a standard of living even lower than what the poorest paid worker outside the workhouse might achieve.

easy existence; and for some time he lay gasping on a little flock mattress,[2] rather unequally poised between this world and the next: the balance being decidedly in favour of the latter. Now, if, during this brief period, Oliver had been surrounded by careful grandmothers, anxious aunts, experienced nurses, and doctors of profound wisdom, he would most inevitably and indubitably have been killed in no time. There being nobody by, however, but a pauper old woman, who was rendered rather misty by an unwonted allowance of beer; and a parish surgeon who did such matters by contract; Oliver and Nature fought out the point between them. The result was, that, after a few struggles, Oliver breathed, sneezed, and proceeded to advertise to the inmates of the workhouse the fact of a new burden having been imposed upon the parish, by setting up as loud a cry as could reasonably have been expected from a male infant who had not been possessed of that very useful appendage, a voice, for a much longer space of time than three minutes and a quarter.

As Oliver gave this first proof of the free and proper action of his lungs, the patchwork coverlet which was carelessly flung over the iron bedstead, rustled; the pale face of a young woman was raised feebly from the pillow; and a faint voice imperfectly articulated the words, "Let me see the child, and die."

The surgeon had been sitting with his face turned towards the fire: giving the palms of his hands, a warm and a rub alternately. As the young woman spoke, he rose, and advancing to the bed's head, said, with more kindness than might have been expected of him:

"Oh you must not talk about dying yet."

"Lor bless her dear heart, no!" interposed the nurse, hastily depositing in her pocket a green glass bottle, the contents of which she had been tasting in a corner with evident satisfaction. "Lor bless her dear heart, when she has lived as long as I have, sir, and had thirteen children of her own, and all on 'em dead except two, and them in the wurkus[3] with me, she'll know better than to take on in that way, bless her dear heart! Think what it is to be a mother, there's a dear young lamb, do."

Apparently this consolatory perspective of a mother's prospects, failed in producing its due effect. The patient shook her head, and stretched out her hand towards the child.

The surgeon deposited it in her arms. She imprinted her cold white lips passionately on its forehead; passed her hands over her face; gazed wildly round; shuddered; fell back—and died. They chafed her breast, hands, and temples; but the blood had stopped for ever. They talked of hope and comfort. They had been strangers too long.

"It's all over, Mrs. Thingummy!" said the surgeon at last.

"Ah, poor dear, so it is!" said the nurse, picking up the cork of the

---

2. A mattress stuffed with small pieces of wool or cotton gathered from old clothes torn into shreds.
3. Workhouse.

green bottle which had fallen out on the pillow as she stooped to take up the child. "Poor dear!"

"You needn't mind sending up to me, if the child cries, nurse," said the surgeon, putting on his gloves with great deliberation. "It's very likely it *will* be troublesome. Give it a little gruel[4] if it is." He put on his hat, and, pausing by the bed side on his way to the door, added "She was a good-looking girl, too; where did she come from?"

"She was brought here last night," replied the old woman, "by the overseer's order. She was found lying in the street. She had walked some distance, for her shoes were worn to pieces; but where she came from, or where she was going to, nobody knows."

The surgeon leaned over the body, and raised the left hand. "The old story," he said, shaking his head: "no wedding-ring, I see. Ah! Good night!"

The medical gentleman walked away to dinner; and the nurse, having once more applied herself to the green bottle, sat down on a low chair before the fire, and proceeded to dress the infant.

What an excellent example of the power of dress, young Oliver Twist was! Wrapped in the blanket which had hitherto formed his only covering, he might have been the child of a nobleman or a beggar; it would have been hard for the haughtiest stranger to have assigned him his proper station in society. But now that he was enveloped in the old calico robes which had grown yellow in the same service, he was badged and ticketed, and fell into his place at once—a parish child—the orphan of a workhouse—the humble half-starved drudge—to be cuffed and buffeted through the world—despised by all, and pitied by none.

Oliver cried lustily. If he could have known that he was an orphan, left to the tender mercies of churchwardens and overseers, perhaps he would have cried the louder.

Chapter II.

TREATS OF OLIVER TWIST'S GROWTH, EDUCATION, AND BOARD.

For the next eight or ten months, Oliver was the victim of a systematic course of treachery and deception. He was brought up by hand.[1] The hungry and destitute situation of the infant orphan was duly reported by the workhouse authorities to the parish authorities. The parish authorities inquired with dignity of the workhouse authorities, whether there was no female then domiciled in "the house" who was in a situation to impart to Oliver Twist, the consolation and nourishment of which he stood in need. The workhouse authorities replied with humility, that

---

4. Cereal diluted with water.
1. Fed a mixture of water or milk and bread rather than suckled.

there was not. Upon this, the parish authorities magnanimously and humanely resolved, that Oliver should be "farmed," or, in other words, that he should be despatched to a branch-workhouse some three miles off, where twenty or thirty other juvenile offenders against the poor-laws,[2] rolled about the floor all day, without the inconvenience of too much food or too much clothing, under the parental superintendence of an elderly female, who received the culprits at and for the consideration of sevenpence-halfpenny per small head per week. Sevenpence-halfpenny's worth per week is a good round diet for a child; a great deal may be got for sevenpence-halfpenny: quite enough to overload its stomach, and make it uncomfortable. The elderly female was a woman of wisdom and experience; she knew what was good for children; and she had a very accurate perception of what was good for herself. So, she appropriated the greater part of the weekly stipend to her own use, and consigned the rising parochial generation to even a shorter allowance than was originally provided for them. Thereby finding in the lowest depth a deeper still;[3] and proving herself a very great experimental philosopher.

Everybody knows the story of another experimental philosopher, who had a great theory about a horse being able to live without eating, and who demonstrated it so well, that he got his own horse down to a straw a day, and would most unquestionably have rendered him a very spirited and rampacious animal on nothing at all, if he had not died, just four-and-twenty hours before he was to have had his first comfortable bait of air. Unfortunately for the experimental philosophy of the female to whose protecting care Oliver Twist was delivered over, a similar result usually attended the operation of *her* system; for at the very moment when a child had contrived to exist upon the smallest possible portion of the weakest possible food, it did perversely happen in eight and a half cases out of ten, either that it sickened from want and cold, or fell into the fire from neglect, or got half-smothered by accident; in any one of which cases, the miserable little being was usually summoned into another world, and there gathered to the fathers which it had never known in this.

Occasionally, when there was some more than usually interesting inquest upon a parish child who had been overlooked in turning up a bedstead, or inadvertently scalded to death when there happened to be a washing; though the latter accident was very scarce,—anything approaching to a washing being of rare occurrence in the farm—the jury would take it into their heads to ask troublesome questions, or the parishioners would rebelliously affix their signatures to a remonstrance.

2. The rules and regulations governing the administration of the workhouses established by the Poor Law Amendment Act of 1834.
3. Dickens is paraphrasing Milton's line "And in the lowest deep a lower deep" (*Paradise Lost* 4.76) to express satirically his horror that the workhouse authorities have created a place for children even worse than the workhouse.

But these impertinences were speedily checked by the evidence of the surgeon, and the testimony of the beadle; the former of whom had always opened the body and found nothing inside (which was very probable indeed), and the latter of whom invariably swore whatever the parish wanted; which was very self-devotional. Besides, the board made periodical pilgrimages to the farm, and always sent the beadle the day before, to say they were going. The children were neat and clean to behold, when *they* went; and what more would the people have!

It cannot be expected that this system of farming would produce any very extraordinary or luxuriant crop. Oliver Twist's ninth birth-day found him a pale thin child, somewhat diminutive in stature, and decidedly small in circumference. But nature or inheritance had implanted a good sturdy spirit in Oliver's breast. It had had plenty of room to expand, thanks to the spare diet of the establishment; and perhaps to this circumstance may be attributed his having any ninth birth-day at all. Be this as it may, however, it *was* his ninth birth-day; and he was keeping it in the coal-cellar with a select party of two other young gentlemen, who, after participating with him in a sound threshing, had been locked up therein for atrociously presuming to be hungry, when Mrs. Mann, the good lady of the house, was unexpectedly startled by the apparition of Mr. Bumble, the beadle,[4] striving to undo the wicket of the garden-gate.

"Goodness gracious! is that you, Mr. Bumble, sir?" said Mrs. Mann, thrusting her head out of the window in well-affected ecstacies of joy. "(Susan, take Oliver and them two brats up stairs, and wash 'em directly.)—My heart alive! Mr. Bumble, how glad I am to see you, sure-ly!"

Now, Mr. Bumble was a fat man, and a choleric; so, instead of responding to this open-hearted salutation in a kindred spirit, he gave the little wicket a tremendous shake, and then bestowed upon it a kick which could have emanated from no leg but a beadle's.

"Lor, only think," said Mrs. Mann, running out,—for the three boys had been removed by this time,—"only think of that! That I should have forgotten that the gate was bolted on the inside, on account of them dear children! Walk in sir; walk in, pray, Mr. Bumble, do sir."

Although this invitation was accompanied with a curtsey that might have softened the heart of a churchwarden, it by no means mollified the beadle.

"Do you think this respectful or proper conduct, Mrs. Mann," inquired Mr. Bumble, grasping his cane, "to keep the parish officers a waiting at your garden-gate, when they come here upon porochial business connected with the porochial orphans? Are you aweer, Mrs. Mann,

4. A low-ranking officer of the parish whose duty it was to implement and enforce the rules of the parish board in regard to local law and social services. The word was also used for a low-level official of private companies, law courts, and churches.

that you are, as I may say, a porochial delegate, and a stipendiary?"[5]

"I'm sure, Mr. Bumble, that I was only a telling one or two of the dear children as is so fond of you, that it was you a coming," replied Mrs. Mann with great humility.

Mr. Bumble had a great idea of his oratorical powers and his importance. He had displayed the one, and vindicated the other. He relaxed.

"Well, well, Mrs. Mann," he replied in a calmer tone; "it may be as you say; it may be. Lead the way in, Mrs. Mann, for I come on business, and have something to say."

Mrs. Mann ushered the beadle into a small parlour with a brick floor; placed a seat for him; and officiously deposited his cocked hat and cane on the table before him. Mr. Bumble wiped from his forehead the perspiration which his walk had engendered; glanced complacently at the cocked hat; and smiled. Yes, he smiled. Beadles are but men: and Mr. Bumble smiled.

"Now don't you be offended at what I'm a going to say," observed Mrs. Mann, with captivating sweetness. "You've had a long walk, you know, or I wouldn't mention it. Now, will you take a little drop of somethink, Mr. Bumble?"

"Not a drop. Not a drop," said Mr. Bumble, waving his right hand in a dignified, but placid manner.

"I think you will," said Mrs. Mann, who had noticed the tone of the refusal, and the gesture that had accompanied it. "Just a leetle drop, with a little cold water, and a lump of sugar."

Mr. Bumble coughed.

"Now, just a leetle drop," said Mrs. Mann persuasively.

"What is it?" inquired the beadle.

"Why, it's what I'm obliged to keep a little of in the house, to put into the blessed infants' Daffy,[6] when they ain't well, Mr. Bumble," replied Mrs. Mann as she opened a corner cupboard, and took down a bottle and glass. "It's gin. I'll not deceive you, Mr. B. It's gin."

"Do you give the children Daffy, Mrs. Mann?" inquired Bumble, following with his eyes the interesting process of mixing.

"Ah, bless 'em, that I do, dear as it is," replied the nurse. "I couldn't see 'em suffer before my very eyes, you know, sir."

"No," said Mr. Bumble approvingly; "no, you could not. You are a humane woman, Mrs. Mann." (Here she set down the glass.) "I shall take a early opportunity of mentioning it to the board, Mrs. Mann." (He drew it towards him.) "You feel as a mother, Mrs. Mann." (He stirred the gin-and-water.) "I—I drink your health with cheerfulness, Mrs. Mann;" and he swallowed half of it.

5. A person on the parish payroll. "Porochial delegate": someone representing the parish.
6. A children's medicine the main ingredient of which was gin. "Daffy" became a slang term for gin.

"And now about business," said the beadle, taking out a leathern pocket-book. "The child that was half-baptized[7] Oliver Twist, is nine year old to-day."

"Bless him!" interposed Mrs. Mann, inflaming her left eye with the corner of her apron.

"And notwithstanding a offered reward of ten pound, which was afterwards increased to twenty pound. Notwithstanding the most superlative, and, I may say, supernat'ral exertions on the part of this parish," said Bumble, "we have never been able to discover who is his father, or what was his mother's settlement, name, or con—dition."

Mrs. Mann raised her hands in astonishment; but added, after a moment's reflection, "How comes he to have any name at all, then?"

The beadle drew himself up with great pride, and said, "I inwented it."

"You, Mr. Bumble!"

"I, Mrs. Mann. We name our fondlins in alphabetical order. The last was a S,—Swubble, I named him. This was a T,—Twist, I named him. The next one as comes will be Unwin, and the next Vilkins. I have got names ready made to the end of the alphabet, and all the way through it again, when we come to Z."

"Why, you're quite a literary character, sir!" said Mrs. Mann.

"Well, well," said the beadle, evidently gratified with the compliment; "perhaps I may be. Perhaps I may be, Mrs. Mann." He finished the gin-and-water, and added, "Oliver being now too old to remain here, the board have determined to have him back into the house. I have come out myself to take him there. So let me see him at once."

"I'll fetch him directly," said Mrs. Mann, leaving the room for that purpose. Oliver, having had by this time as much of the outer coat of dirt, which encrusted his face and hands, removed, as could be scrubbed off in one washing, was led into the room by his benevolent protectress.

"Make a bow to the gentleman, Oliver," said Mrs. Mann.

Oliver made a bow, which was divided between the beadle on the chair, and the cocked-hat on the table.

"Will you go along with me, Oliver?" said Mr. Bumble in a majestic voice.

Oliver was about to say that he would go along with anybody with great readiness, when, glancing upwards, he caught sight of Mrs. Mann, who had got behind the beadle's chair, and was shaking her fist at him with a furious countenance. He took the hint at once, for the fist had been too often impressed upon his body not to be deeply impressed upon his recollection.

"Will *she* go with me?" inquired poor Oliver.

7. Baptized privately and without full rites, usually done for children who were in danger of dying.

"No, she can't," replied Mr. Bumble. "But she'll come and see you sometimes."

This was no very great consolation to the child. Young as he was, however, he had sense enough to make a feint of feeling great regret at going away. It was no very difficult matter for the boy to call the tears into his eyes. Hunger and recent ill-usage are great assistants if you want to cry; and Oliver cried very naturally indeed. Mrs. Mann gave him a thousand embraces, and, what Oliver wanted a great deal more, a piece of bread and butter, lest he should seem too hungry when he got to the workhouse. With the slice of bread in his hand, and the little brown-cloth parish cap on his head, Oliver was then led away by Mr. Bumble from the wretched home where one kind word or look had never lighted the gloom of his infant years. And yet he burst into an agony of childish grief, as the cottage-gate closed after him. Wretched as were the little companions in misery he was leaving behind, they were the only friends he had ever known; and a sense of his loneliness in the great wide world, sank into the child's heart for the first time.

Mr. Bumble walked on with long strides; little Oliver, firmly grasping his gold-laced cuff, trotted beside him: inquiring at the end of every quarter of a mile whether they were "nearly there." To these interrogations, Mr. Bumble returned very brief and snappish replies; for the temporary blandness which gin-and-water awakens in some bosoms had by this time evaporated: and he was once again a beadle.

Oliver had not been within the walls of the workhouse a quarter of an hour; and had scarcely completed the demolition of a second slice of bread; when Mr. Bumble, who had handed him over to the care of an old woman, returned; and, telling him it was a board night, informed him that the board had said he was to appear before it forthwith.

Not having a very clearly defined notion of what a live board was, Oliver was rather astounded by this intelligence, and was not quite certain whether he ought to laugh or cry. He had no time to think about the matter, however; for Mr. Bumble gave him a tap on the head, with his cane, to wake him up: and another on the back to make him lively: and bidding him follow, conducted him into a large whitewashed room, where eight or ten fat gentlemen were sitting round a table. At the top of the table, seated in an arm-chair rather higher than the rest, was a particularly fat gentleman with a very round, red face.

"Bow to the board," said Bumble. Oliver brushed away two or three tears that were lingering in his eyes; and seeing no board but the table, fortunately bowed to that.

"What's your name, boy?" said the gentleman in the high chair.

Oliver was frightened at the sight of so many gentlemen, which made him tremble; and the beadle gave him another tap behind, which made him cry; and these two causes made him answer in a very low and hesitating voice; whereupon a gentleman in a white waistcoat said he was a fool. Which was a capital way of raising his spirits, and putting him quite at his ease.

"Boy," said the gentleman in the high chair, "listen to me. You know you're an orphan, I suppose?"

"What's that, sir?" inquired poor Oliver.

"The boy *is* a fool—I thought he was," said the gentleman in the white waistcoat.

"Hush!" said the gentleman who had spoken first. "You know you've got no father or mother, and that you were brought up by the parish, don't you?"

"Yes, sir," replied Oliver, weeping bitterly.

"What are you crying for?" inquired the gentleman in the white waistcoat. And to be sure it was very extraordinary. What *could* the boy be crying for?

"I hope you say your prayers every night," said another gentleman in a gruff voice; "and pray for the people who feed you, and take care of you—like a Christian."

"Yes, sir," stammered the boy. The gentleman who spoke last was unconsciously right. It would have been *very* like a Christian, and a marvellously good Christian, too, if Oliver had prayed for the people who fed and took care of *him*. But he hadn't, because nobody had taught him.

"Well! You have come here to be educated, and taught a useful trade," said the red-faced gentleman in the high chair.

"So you'll begin to pick oakum[8] to-morrow morning at six o'clock," added the surly one in the white waistcoat.

For the combination of both these blessings in the one simple process of picking oakum, Oliver bowed low by the direction of the beadle, and was then hurried away to a large ward: where, on a rough hard bed, he sobbed himself to sleep. What a noble illustration of the tender laws of England! They let the paupers go to sleep!

Poor Oliver! He little thought, as he lay sleeping in happy unconsciousness of all around him, that the board had that very day arrived at a decision which would exercise the most material influence over all his future fortunes. But they had. And this was it:—

The members of this board were very sage, deep, philosophical men; and when they came to turn their attention to the workhouse, they found out at once, what ordinary folks would never have discovered—the poor people liked it! It was a regular place of public entertainment for the poorer classes; a tavern where there was nothing to pay; a public breakfast, dinner, tea, and supper all the year round; a brick-and-mortar elysium,[9] where it was all play and no work. "Oho!" said the board, looking very knowing; "we are the fellows to set this to rights; we'll stop it all, in no

8. Loose fibers obtained by untwisting old ropes; oakum was frequently used as caulking.
9. From Greek mythology, the place of ideal happiness that the blessed go to after death.

time." So, they established the rule, that all poor people should have the alternative (for they would compel nobody, not they,) of being starved by a gradual process in the house, or by a quick one out of it. With this view, they contracted with the water-works to lay on an unlimited supply of water; and with a corn-factor to supply periodically small quantities of oatmeal; and issued three meals of thin gruel a day, with an onion twice a week, and half a roll on Sundays. They made a great many other wise and humane regulations, having reference to the ladies, which it is not necessary to repeat; kindly undertook to divorce poor married people, in consequence of the great expense of a suit in Doctors' Commons;[1] and, instead of compelling a man to support his family, as they had theretofore done, took his family away from him, and made him a bachelor! There is no saying how many applicants for relief under these last two heads, might have started up in all classes of society, if it had not been coupled with the workhouse; but the board were long-headed men, and had provided for this difficulty. The relief was inseparable from the workhouse and the gruel; and that frightened people.

For the first six months after Oliver Twist was removed, the system was in full operation. It was rather expensive at first, in consequence of the increase in the undertaker's bill, and the necessity of taking in the clothes of all the paupers, which fluttered loosely on their wasted, shrunken forms, after a week or two's gruel. But the number of workhouse inmates got thin as well as the paupers; and the board were in ecstacies.

The room in which the boys were fed, was a large stone hall, with a copper at one end: out of which the master, dressed in an apron for the purpose, and assisted by one or two women, ladled the gruel at mealtimes. Of this festive composition each boy had one porringer,[2] and no more—except on occasions of great public rejoicing, when he had two ounces and a quarter of bread besides. The bowls never wanted washing. The boys polished them with their spoons till they shone again; and when they had performed this operation, (which never took very long, the spoons being nearly as large as the bowls,) they would sit staring at the copper, with such eager eyes, as if they could have devoured the very bricks of which it was composed; employing themselves, meanwhile, in sucking their fingers most assiduously, with the view of catching up any stray splashes of gruel that might have been cast thereon. Boys have generally excellent appetites. Oliver Twist and his companions suffered the tortures of slow starvation for three months; at last they got so voracious and wild with hunger, that one boy: who was tall for his age,

1. A college of lawyers, founded in the thirteenth century, whose members had the sole right to appear in ecclesiastical and probate courts and consequently had to be employed to obtain marriage licenses, divorces, and wills. "Ladies": The Poor Law Amendment Act of 1834 provided that unwed mothers were fully responsible for the support of their illegitimate children.
2. A small wooden or metal bowl. "Copper": a large cooking pot.

and hadn't been used to that sort of thing, (for his father had kept a small cook's shop): hinted darkly to his companions, that unless he had another basin of gruel *per diem*,[3] he was afraid he might some night happen to eat the boy who slept next him, who happened to be a weakly youth of tender age. He had a wild, hungry, eye; and they implicitly believed him. A council was held, lots were cast who should walk up to the master after supper that evening, and ask for more; and it fell to Oliver Twist.

The evening arrived; the boys took their places. The master, in his cook's uniform, stationed himself at the copper; his pauper assistants ranged themselves behind him; the gruel was served out; and a long grace was said over the short commons.[4] The gruel disappeared; the boys whispered each other, and winked at Oliver; while his next neighbours nudged him. Child as he was, he was desperate with hunger, and reckless with misery. He rose from the table; and advancing to the master, basin and spoon in hand, said: somewhat alarmed at his own temerity:

"Please, sir, I want some more."

The master was a fat, healthy man; but he turned very pale. He gazed in stupefied astonishment on the small rebel for some seconds; and then clung for support to the copper. The assistants were paralysed with wonder; the boys with fear.

"What!" said the master at length, in a faint voice.

"Please, sir," replied Oliver, "I want some more."

The master aimed a blow at Oliver's head with the ladle; pinioned him in his arms; and shrieked aloud for the beadle.

The board were sitting in solemn conclave, when Mr. Bumble rushed into the room in great excitement, and addressing the gentleman in the high chair, said,

"Mr. Limbkins, I beg your pardon, sir! Oliver Twist has asked for more!"

There was a general start. Horror was depicted on every countenance.

"For *more!*" said Mr. Limbkins. "Compose yourself, Bumble, and answer me distinctly. Do I understand that he asked for more, after he had eaten the supper allotted by the dietary?"[5]

"He did, sir," replied Bumble.

"That boy will be hung," said the gentleman in the white waistcoat. "I know that boy will be hung."

Nobody controverted the prophetic gentleman's opinion. An animated discussion took place. Oliver was ordered into instant confinement; and a bill was next morning pasted on the outside of the gate, offering a reward of five pounds to anybody who would take Oliver Twist off the

3. Each day (Latin).
4. The shared food.
5. The prescribed diet.

Oliver asking for more.

hands of the parish. In other words, five pounds and Oliver Twist were offered to any man or woman who wanted an apprentice to any trade, business, or calling.

"I never was more convinced of anything in my life," said the gentleman in the white waistcoat, as he knocked at the gate and read the bill next morning: "I never was more convinced of anything in my life, than I am, that that boy will come to be hung."

As I purpose to show in the sequel whether the white-waistcoated gentleman was right or not, I should perhaps mar the interest of this narrative (supposing it to possess any at all), if I ventured to hint, just yet, whether the life of Oliver Twist had this violent termination or no.

Chapter III.

RELATES HOW OLIVER TWIST WAS VERY NEAR GETTING A PLACE, WHICH WOULD NOT HAVE BEEN A SINECURE.

For a week after the commission of the impious and profane offence of asking for more, Oliver remained a close prisoner in the dark and solitary room to which he had been consigned by the wisdom and mercy of the board. It appears, at first sight, not unreasonable to suppose, that, if he had entertained a becoming feeling of respect for the prediction of the gentleman in the white waistcoat, he would have established that sage individual's prophetic character, once and for ever, by tying one end of his pocket-handkerchief to a hook in the wall, and attaching himself to the other. To the performance of this feat, however, there was one obstacle: namely, that pocket-handkerchiefs being decided articles of luxury, had been, for all future times and ages, removed from the noses of paupers by the express order of the board, in council assembled: solemnly given and pronounced under their hands and seals. There was a still greater obstacle in Oliver's youth and childishness. He only cried bitterly all day; and when the long, dismal night came on, he spread his little hands before his eyes to shut out the darkness, and crouching in the corner, tried to sleep: ever and anon waking with a start and tremble, and drawing himself closer and closer to the wall, as if to feel even its cold hard surface were a protection in the gloom and loneliness which surrounded him.

Let it not be supposed by the enemies of "the system," that, during the period of his solitary incarceration, Oliver was denied the benefit of exercise, the pleasure of society, or the advantages of religious consolation. As for exercise: it was nice cold weather, and he was allowed to perform his ablutions[1] every morning under the pump, in a stone yard, in the presence of Mr. Bumble, who prevented his catching cold, and

1. Washings.

caused a tingling sensation to pervade his frame, by repeated applications of the cane. As for society: he was carried every other day into the hall where the boys dined, and there sociably flogged as a public warning and example. And so far from being denied the advantages of religious consolation, he was kicked into the same apartment every evening at prayer-time, and there permitted to listen to, and console his mind with, a general supplication of the boys: containing a special clause, therein inserted by authority of the board, in which they entreated to be made good, virtuous, contented, and obedient, and to be guarded from the sins and vices of Oliver Twist: whom the supplication distinctly set forth to be under the exclusive patronage and protection of the powers of wickedness, and an article direct from the manufactory[2] of the very Devil himself.

It chanced one morning, while Oliver's affairs were in this auspicious and comfortable state, that Mr. Gamfield, chimney-sweeper, was wending his way down the High-street, deeply cogitating in his mind, his ways and means of paying certain arrears of rent, for which his landlord had become rather pressing. Mr. Gamfield's most sanguine estimate of his finances could not raise them within full five pounds of the desired amount; and, in a species of arithmetical desperation, he was alternately cudgelling his brains and his donkey, when, passing the workhouse, his eyes encountered the bill on the gate.

"Wo—o!" said Mr. Gamfield to the donkey.

The donkey was in a state of profound abstraction: wondering, probably, whether he was destined to be regaled with a cabbage-stalk or two, when he had disposed of the two sacks of soot with which the little cart was laden; so, without noticing the word of command, he jogged onward.

Mr. Gamfield growled a fierce imprecation on the donkey generally, but more particularly on his eyes; and, running after him, bestowed a blow on his head, which would inevitably have beaten in any skull but a donkey's. Then, catching hold of the bridle, he gave his jaw a sharp wrench, by way of gentle reminder that he was not his own master; and by these means turned him round. He then gave him another blow on the head, just to stun him till he came back again. Having completed these arrangements, he walked up to the gate, to read the bill.

The gentleman with the white waistcoat, was standing at the gate with his hands behind him, after having delivered himself of some profound sentiments in the board-room. Having witnessed the little dispute between Mr. Gamfield and the donkey, he smiled joyously when that person came up to read the bill, for he saw at once that Mr. Gamfield was exactly the sort of master Oliver Twist wanted. Mr. Gamfield smiled, too, as he perused the document, for five pounds was just the sum he had been wishing for; and, as to the boy with which it was encumbered,

2. Workshop.

Mr. Gamfield, knowing what the dietary of the workhouse was, well knew he would be a nice small pattern: just the very thing for register stoves.[3] So, he spelt the bill through again, from beginning to end; and then, touching his fur cap in token of humility, accosted the gentleman in the white waistcoat.

"This here boy, sir, wot the parish wants to 'prentis," said Mr. Gamfield.

"Aye my man," said the gentleman in the white waistcoat, with a condescending smile. "What of him?"

"If the parish vould like him to learn a light pleasant trade, in a good 'spectable chimbley-sweepin' bisness," said Mr. Gamfield, "I wants a 'prentis, and I'm ready to take him."

"Walk in," said the gentleman in the white waistcoat. Mr. Gamfield having lingered behind, to give the donkey another blow on the head, and another wrench of the jaw, as a caution not to run away in his absence: followed the gentleman with the white waistcoat into the room where Oliver had first seen him.

"It's a nasty trade," said Mr. Limbkins, when Gamfield had again stated his wish.

"Young boys have been smothered in chimneys before now," said another gentleman.

"That's acause they damped the straw afore they lit it in the chimbley to make 'em come down again," said Gamfield; "that's all smoke, and no blaze; veras smoke ain't o' no use at all in makin' a boy come down, for it only sinds him to sleep, and that's wot he likes. Boys is wery obstinit, and wery lazy, gen'lmen, and there's nothink like a good hot blaze to make 'em come down vith a run. It's humane too, gen'lmen, acause, even if they've stuck in the chimbley, roastin' their feet makes 'em struggle to hextricate theirselves."

The gentleman in the white waistcoat, appeared very much amused by this explanation; but his mirth was speedily checked by a look from Mr. Limbkins. The board then proceeded to converse among themselves for a few minutes, but in so low a tone, that the words "saving of expenditure," "look well in the accounts," "have a printed report published," were alone audible. These only chanced to be heard, indeed, on account of their being very frequently repeated with great emphasis.

At length the whispering ceased; and the members of the board, having resumed their seats and their solemnity, Mr. Limbkins said:

"We have considered your proposition, and we don't approve of it."

"Not at all," said the gentleman in the white waistcoat.

"Decidedly not," added the other members.

As Mr. Gamfield did happen to labour under the slight imputation of having bruised three or four boys to death already, it occurred to him

---

3. Stoves with metal plates to regulate the passage of air, heat, and smoke.

that the board had, perhaps, in some unaccountable freak, taken it into their heads that this extraneous circumstance ought to influence their proceedings. It was very unlike their general mode of doing business, if they had; but still, as he had no particular wish to revive the rumour, he twisted his cap in his hands, and walked slowly from the table.

"So you won't let me have him, gen'lmen?" said Mr. Gamfield, pausing near the door.

"No," replied Mr. Limbkins; "at least, as it's a nasty business, we think you ought to take something less than the premium we offered."

Mr. Gamfield's countenance brightened, as, with a quick step he returned to the table, and said,

"What'll you give, gen'lmen? Come! Don't be too hard on a poor man. What'll you give?"

"I should say three pound ten, was plenty," said Mr. Limbkins.

"Ten shillings too much," said the gentleman in the white waistcoat.

"Come!" said Gamfield; "say four pound, gen'lmen. Say four pound, and you've got rid on him for good and all. There!"

"Three pound ten," repeated Mr. Limbkins, firmly.

"Come! I'll split the difference, gen'lmen," urged Gamfield. "Three pound fifteen."

"Not a farthing more," was the firm reply of Mr. Limbkins.

"You're desperate hard upon me, gen'lmen," said Gamfield, wavering.

"Pooh! pooh! nonsense!" said the gentleman in the white waistcoat. "He'd be cheap with nothing at all, as a premium. Take him, you silly fellow! He's just the boy for you. He wants the stick, now and then: it'll do him good; and his board needn't come very expensive, for he hasn't been overfed since he was born. Ha! ha! ha!"

Mr. Gamfield gave an arch look at the faces round the table, and, observing a smile on all of them, gradually broke into a smile himself. The bargain was made. Mr. Bumble was at once instructed that Oliver Twist and his indentures were to be conveyed before the magistrate,[4] for signature and approval, that very afternoon.

In pursuance of this determination, little Oliver, to his excessive astonishment, was released from bondage, and ordered to put himself into a clean shirt. He had hardly achieved this very unusual gymnastic performance, when Mr. Bumble brought him, with his own hands, a basin of gruel, and the holiday allowance of two ounces and a quarter of bread. At this tremendous sight, Oliver began to cry very piteously: thinking, not unnaturally, that the board must have determined to kill him for some useful purpose, or they never would have begun to fatten him up in that way.

"Don't make your eyes red, Oliver, but eat your food and be thankful,"

---

4. Judge. "Indentures": binding contracts to tie an apprentice to a master, usually for seven years.

said Mr. Bumble, in a tone of impressive pomposity. "You're a going to be made a 'prentice of, Oliver."

"A'prentice, sir!" said the child, trembling.

"Yes, Oliver," said Mr. Bumble. "The kind and blessed gentlemen which is so many parents to you, Oliver, when you have none of your own: are a going to 'prentice you: and to set you up in life, and make a man of you: although the expense to the parish is three pound ten!— three pound ten, Oliver!—seventy shillin's—one hundred and forty sixpences!—and all for a naughty orphan which nobody can't love."

As Mr. Bumble paused to take breath, after delivering this address in an awful voice, the tears rolled down the poor child's face, and he sobbed bitterly.

"Come," said Mr. Bumble, somewhat less pompously, for it was gratifying to his feelings to observe the effect his eloquence had produced, "come, Oliver! Wipe your eyes with the cuffs of your jacket, and don't cry into your gruel; that's a very foolish action, Oliver." It certainly was, for there was quite enough water in it already.

On their way to the magistrate, Mr. Bumble instructed Oliver that all he would have to do, would be to look very happy, and say, when the gentleman asked him if he wanted to be apprenticed, that he should like it very much indeed; both of which injunctions Oliver promised to obey: the rather as Mr. Bumble threw in a gentle hint, that if he failed in either particular, there was no telling what would be done to him. When they arrived at the office, he was shut up in a little room by himself, and admonished by Mr. Bumble to stay there, until he came back to fetch him.

There the boy remained, with a palpitating heart, for half an hour. At the expiration of which time Mr. Bumble thrust in his head, unadorned with the cocked hat, and said aloud,

"Now, Oliver, my dear, come to the gentleman." As Mr. Bumble said this, he put on a grim and threatening look, and added in a low voice, "Mind what I told you, you young rascal!"

Oliver stared innocently in Mr. Bumble's face at this somewhat contradictory style of address; but that gentleman prevented his offering any remark thereupon, by leading him at once into an adjoining room: the door of which was open. It was a large room, with a great window. Behind a desk, sat two old gentlemen with powdered heads: one of whom was reading the newspaper: while the other was perusing, with the aid of a pair of tortoise-shell spectacles, a small piece of parchment which lay before him. Mr. Limbkins was standing in front of the desk on one side; and Mr. Gamfield, with a partially washed face, on the other; while two or three bluff-looking men, in top-boots, were lounging about.

The old gentleman with the spectacles, gradually dozed off, over the little bit of parchment; and there was a short pause, after Oliver had been stationed by Mr. Bumble in front of the desk.

"This is the boy, your worship," said Mr. Bumble.

The old gentleman who was reading the newspaper, raised his head for a moment, and pulled the other old gentleman by the sleeve; whereupon, the last-mentioned old gentleman woke up.

"Oh, is this the boy?" said the old gentleman.

"This is him, sir," replied Mr. Bumble. "Bow to the magistrate, my dear."

Oliver roused himself, and made his best obeisance. He had been wondering, with his eyes fixed on the magistrates' powder,[5] whether all boards were born with that white stuff on their heads, and were boards from thenceforth on that account.

"Well," said the old gentleman, "I suppose he's fond of chimney-sweeping?"

"He doats on it, your worship," replied Bumble: giving Oliver a sly pinch, to intimate that he had better not say he didn't.

"And he *will* be a sweep, will he?" inquired the old gentleman.

"If we was to bind him to any other trade to-morrow, he'd run away simultaneous, your worship," replied Bumble.

"And this man that's to be his master—you, sir—you'll treat him well, and feed him, and do all that sort of thing,—will you?" said the old gentleman.

"When I says I will, I means I will," replied Mr. Gamfield doggedly.

"You're a rough speaker, my friend, but you look an honest, open-hearted man," said the old gentleman: turning his spectacles in the direction of the candidate for Oliver's premium, whose villanous countenance was a regular stamped receipt for cruelty. But, the magistrate was half blind and half childish, so he couldn't reasonably be expected to discern what other people did.

"I hope I am, sir," said Mr. Gamfield with an ugly leer.

"I have no doubt you are, my friend," replied the old gentleman: fixing his spectacles more firmly on his nose, and looking about him for the inkstand.

It was the critical moment of Oliver's fate. If the inkstand had been where the old gentleman thought it was, he would have dipped his pen into it, and signed the indentures; and Oliver would have been straightway hurried off. But, as it chanced to be immediately under his nose, it followed, as a matter of course, that he looked all over his desk for it, without finding it; and happening in the course of his search to look straight before him, his gaze encountered the pale and terrified face of Oliver Twist: who, despite all the admonitory[6] looks and pinches of Bumble, was regarding the repulsive countenance of his future master: with a mingled expression of horror and fear, too palpable to be mistaken, even by a half-blind magistrate.

5. The magistrates wear powdered wigs. "Obeisance": bow.
6. Critical.

The old gentleman stopped, laid down his pen, and looked from Oliver to Mr. Limbkins: who attempted to take snuff with a cheerful and unconcerned aspect.

"My boy!" said the old gentleman, leaning over the desk. Oliver started at the sound. He might be excused for doing so; for the words were kindly said; and strange sounds frighten one. He trembled violently, and burst into tears.

"My boy!" said the old gentleman, "you look pale and alarmed. What is the matter?"

"Stand a little away from him, Beadle," said the other magistrate: laying aside the paper, and leaning forward with an expression of interest. "Now, boy, tell us what's the matter: don't be afraid."

Oliver fell on his knees, and clasping his hands together, prayed that they would order him back to the dark room—that they would starve him—beat him—kill him if they pleased—rather than send him away with that dreadful man.

"Well!" said Mr. Bumble, raising his hands and eyes with most impressive solemnity, "Well! of all the artful and designing orphans that ever I see, Oliver, you are one of the most bare-facedest."

"Hold your tongue, Beadle," said the second old gentleman, when Mr. Bumble had given vent to this compound adjective.

"I beg your worship's pardon," said Mr. Bumble, incredulous of his having heard aright. "Did your worship speak to me?"

"Yes. Hold your tongue."

Mr. Bumble was stupefied with astonishment. A beadle ordered to hold his tongue! A moral revolution!

The old gentleman in the tortoise-shell spectacles, looked at his companion; he nodded significantly.

"We refuse to sanction these indentures," said the old gentleman: tossing aside the piece of parchment as he spoke.

"I hope," stammered Mr. Limbkins: "I hope the magistrates will not form the opinion that the authorities have been guilty of any improper conduct, on the unsupported testimony of a mere child."

"The magistrates are not called upon to pronounce any opinion on the matter," said the second old gentleman sharply. "Take the boy back to the workhouse, and treat him kindly. He seems to want it."

That same evening, the gentleman in the white waistcoat most positively and decidedly affirmed, not only that Oliver would be hung, but that he would be drawn and quartered into the bargain. Mr. Bumble shook his head with gloomy mystery, and said he wished he might come to good; whereunto Mr. Gamfield replied, that he wished he might come to him; which, although he agreed with the beadle in most matters, would seem to be a wish of a totally opposite description.

The next morning, the public were once more informed that Oliver

Twist was again To Let; and that five pounds would be paid to anybody who would take possession of him.

Chapter IV.

OLIVER, BEING OFFERED ANOTHER PLACE, MAKES HIS FIRST ENTRY INTO PUBLIC LIFE.

In great families: when an advantageous place cannot be obtained, either in possession, reversion, remainder, or expectancy, for the young man who is growing up: it is a very general custom to send him to sea. The board, in imitation of so wise and salutary[1] an example, took counsel together on the expediency of shipping off Oliver Twist, in some small trading vessel bound to a good unhealthy port; which suggested itself as the very best thing that could possibly be done with him: the probability being, that the skipper would flog him to death, in a playful mood, some day after dinner; or would knock his brains out with an iron bar; both pastimes being, as is pretty generally known, very favourite and common recreations among gentlemen of that class. The more the case presented itself to the board, in this point of view, the more manifold the advantages of the step appeared; so they came to the conclusion, that the only way of providing for Oliver effectually, was to send him to sea without delay.

Mr. Bumble had been despatched to make various preliminary inquiries, with the view of finding out some captain or other who wanted a cabin-boy without any friends; and was returning to the workhouse to communicate the result of his mission; when he encountered, just at the gate, no less a person than Mr. Sowerberry, the parochial undertaker.

Mr. Sowerberry was a tall, gaunt, large-jointed man, attired in a suit of thread-bare black, with darned cotton stockings of the same colour, and shoes to answer. His features were not naturally intended to wear a smiling aspect, but he was in general rather given to professional jocosity. His step was elastic, and his face betokened inward pleasantry, as he advanced to Mr. Bumble, and shook him cordially by the hand.

"I have taken the measure of the two women that died last night, Mr. Bumble," said the undertaker.

"You'll make your fortune, Mr. Sowerberry," said the beadle, as he thrust his thumb and forefinger into the proffered snuff-box of the undertaker: which was an ingenious little model of a patent coffin. "I say you'll make your fortune, Mr. Sowerberry," repeated Mr. Bumble, tapping the undertaker on the shoulder, in a friendly manner, with his cane.

1. Healthy.

"Think so?" said the undertaker in a tone which half admitted and half disputed the probability of the event. "The prices allowed by the board are very small, Mr. Bumble."

"So are the coffins," replied the beadle: with precisely as near an approach to a laugh as a great official ought to indulge in.

Mr. Sowerberry was much tickled at this: as of course he ought to be; and laughed a long time without cessation. "Well, well, Mr. Bumble," he said at length, "there's no denying that, since the new system of feeding has come in, the coffins are something narrower and more shallow than they used to be; but we must have some profit, Mr. Bumble. Well-seasoned timber is an expensive article, sir; and all the iron handles come, by canal, from Birmingham."[2]

"Well, well," said Mr. Bumble, "every trade has its drawbacks. A fair profit is, of course, allowable."

"Of course, of course," replied the undertaker; "and if I don't get a profit upon this or that particular article, why, I make it up in the long-run, you see—he! he! he!"

"Just so," said Mr. Bumble.

"Though I must say," continued the undertaker, resuming the current of observations which the beadle had interrupted: "though I must say, Mr. Bumble, that I have to contend against one very great disadvantage: which is, that all the stout people go off the quickest. The people who have been better off, and have paid rates for many years, are the first to sink when they come into the house; and let me tell you, Mr. Bumble, that three or four inches over one's calculation makes a great hole in one's profits: especially when one has a family to provide for, sir."

As Mr. Sowerberry said this, with the becoming indignation of an ill-used man; and as Mr. Bumble felt that it rather tended to convey a reflection on the honour of the parish; the latter gentleman thought it advisable to change the subject. Oliver Twist being uppermost in his mind, he made him his theme.

"By the bye," said Mr. Bumble, "you don't know anybody who wants a boy, do you? A porochial 'prentis, who is at present a deadweight; a millstone, as I may say; round the porochial throat? Liberal terms, Mr. Sowerberry, liberal terms!" As Mr. Bumble spoke, he raised his cane to the bill above him, and gave three distinct raps upon the words "five pounds:" which were printed thereon in Roman capitals of gigantic size.

"Gadso!" said the undertaker: taking Mr. Bumble by the gilt-edged lappel of his official coat; "that's just the very thing I wanted to speak to you about. You know—dear me, what a very elegant button this is, Mr. Bumble! I never noticed it before."

"Yes, I think it is rather pretty," said the beadle, glancing proudly

---

2. A city northwest of London famous for its iron and steel mills.

downwards at the large brass buttons which embellished his coat. "The die is the same as the porochial seal—the Good Samaritan[3] healing the sick and bruised man. The board presented it to me on New-year's morning, Mr. Sowerberry. I put it on, I remember, for the first time, to attend the inquest on that reduced tradesman, who died in a doorway at midnight."

"I recollect," said the undertaker. "The jury brought in, 'Died from exposure to the cold, and want of the common necessaries of life,' didn't they?"

Mr. Bumble nodded.

"And they made it a special verdict, I think," said the undertaker, "by adding some words to the effect, that if the relieving officer had——"

"Tush! Foolery!" interposed the beadle. "If the board attended to all the nonsense that ignorant jurymen talk, they'd have enough to do."

"Very true," said the undertaker; "they would indeed."

"Juries," said Mr. Bumble, grasping his cane tightly, as was his wont when working into a passion: "juries is ineddicated,[4] vulgar, grovelling wretches."

"So they are," said the undertaker.

"They haven't no more philosophy nor political economy about 'em than that," said the beadle, snapping his fingers contemptuously.

"No more they have," acquiesced the undertaker.

"I despise 'em," said the beadle, growing very red in the face.

"So do I," rejoined the undertaker.

"And I only wish we'd a jury of the independent sort, in the house for a week or two," said the beadle; "the rules and regulations of the board would soon bring their spirit down for 'em."

"Let 'em alone for that," replied the undertaker. So saying, he smiled, approvingly: to calm the rising wrath of the indignant parish officer.

Mr. Bumble lifted off his cocked hat; took a handkerchief from the inside of the crown; wiped from his forehead, the perspiration which his rage had engendered; fixed the cocked hat on again; and, turning to the undertaker, said in a calmer voice:

"Well; what about the boy?"

"Oh!" replied the undertaker; "why, you know, Mr. Bumble, I pay a good deal towards the poor's rates."

"Hem!" said Mr. Bumble. "Well?"

"Well," replied the undertaker, "I was thinking that if I pay so much towards 'em, I've a right to get as much out of 'em as I can, Mr. Bumble; and so—and so—I think I'll take the boy myself."

---

3. Refers to the parable in Luke 10.30–37, in which Jesus tells the story, as an example of moral conduct, of a man from Samaria (a district in Judaea) who takes care of the wounds of and gives charity to a stranger.
4. Uneducated.

Mr. Bumble grasped the undertaker by the arm, and led him into the building. Mr. Sowerberry was closeted with the board for five minutes; and it was arranged that Oliver should go to him that evening "upon liking,"—a phrase which means, in the case of a parish apprentice, that if the master find, upon a short trial, that he can get enough work out of a boy without putting too much food into him, he shall have him for a term of years, to do what he likes with.

When little Oliver was taken before "the gentlemen" that evening; and informed that he was to go, that night, as general house-lad to a coffin-maker's; and that if he complained of his situation, or ever came back to the parish again, he would be sent to sea: there to be drowned, or knocked on the head, as the case might be; he evinced so little emotion, that they, by common consent, pronounced him a hardened young rascal, and ordered Mr. Bumble to remove him forthwith.

Now, although it was very natural that the board, of all people in the world, should feel in a great state of virtuous astonishment and horror at the smallest tokens of want of feeling on the part of anybody, they were rather out, in this particular instance. The simple fact was, that Oliver, instead of possessing too little feeling, possessed rather too much; and was in a fair way of being reduced, for life, to a state of brutal stupidity and sullenness by the ill usage he had received. He heard the news of his destination, in perfect silence; and, having had his luggage put into his hand—which was not very difficult to carry, inasmuch as it was all comprised within the limits of a brown paper parcel, about half a foot square by three inches deep—he pulled his cap over his eyes; and once more attaching himself to Mr. Bumble's coat cuff, was led away by that dignitary to a new scene of suffering.

For some time, Mr. Bumble drew Oliver along, without notice or remark; for the beadle carried his head very erect, as a beadle always should: and, it being a windy day, little Oliver was completely enshrouded by the skirts of Mr. Bumble's coat as they blew open, and disclosed to great advantage his flapped waistcoat and drab plush knee-breeches. As they drew near to their destination, however, Mr. Bumble thought it expedient to look down, and see that the boy was in good order for inspection by his new master: which he accordingly did: with a fit and becoming air of gracious patronage.

"Oliver!" said Mr. Bumble.

"Yes, sir," replied Oliver, in a low, tremulous voice.

"Pull that cap off of your eyes, and hold up your head, sir."

Although Oliver did as he was desired, at once; and passed the back of his unoccupied hand briskly across his eyes; he left a tear in them when he looked up at his conductor. As Mr. Bumble gazed sternly upon him, it rolled down his cheek. It was followed by another, and another. The child made a strong effort, but it was an unsuccessful one. Withdrawing his other hand from Mr. Bumble's, he covered his face with both; and wept until the tears sprung out, from between his thin and bony fingers.

"Well!" exclaimed Mr. Bumble, stopping short, and darting at his little charge a look of intense malignity. "Well! Of *all* the ungratefullest, and worst-disposed boys as ever I see, Oliver, you are the——"

"No, no, sir," sobbed Oliver, clinging to the hand which held the well-known cane; "no, no, sir; I will be good indeed; indeed, indeed I will, sir! I am a very little boy, sir; and it is so—so—"

"So what?" inquired Mr. Bumble in amazement.

"So lonely, sir! So very lonely!" cried the child. "Everybody hates me. Oh! sir, don't, don't pray be cross to me!" The child beat his hand upon his heart; and looked in his companion's face, with tears of real agony.

Mr. Bumble regarded Oliver's piteous and helpless look, with some astonishment, for a few seconds; hemmed three or four times in a husky manner, and, after muttering something about "that troublesome cough," bid Oliver dry his eyes and be a good boy. Then, once more taking his hand, he walked on with him in silence.

The undertaker, who had just put up the shutters of his shop, was making some entries in his day-book[5] by the light of a most appropriately dismal candle, when Mr. Bumble entered.

"Aha!" said the undertaker: looking up from the book, and pausing in the middle of a word; "is that you, Bumble?"

"No one else, Mr. Sowerberry," replied the beadle. "Here! I've brought the boy." Oliver made a bow.

"Oh! that's the boy, is it?" said the undertaker: raising the candle above his head, to get a better view of Oliver. "Mrs. Sowerberry! will you have the goodness to come here a moment, my dear?"

Mrs. Sowerberry emerged from a little room behind the shop, and presented the form of a short, thin, squeezed-up woman, with a vixenish countenance.

"My dear," said Mr. Sowerberry, deferentially, "this is the boy from the workhouse that I told you of." Oliver bowed again.

"Dear me!" said the undertaker's wife, "he's very small."

"Why, he *is* rather small," replied Mr. Bumble: looking at Oliver as if it were his fault that he was no bigger; "he *is* small. There's no denying it. But he'll grow, Mrs. Sowerberry,—he'll grow."

"Ah! I dare say he will," replied the lady pettishly, "on our victuals and our drink. I see no saving in parish children, not I; for they always cost more to keep, than they're worth. However, men always think they know best. There! Get down stairs, little bag o' bones." With this, the undertaker's wife opened a side door, and pushed Oliver down a steep flight of stairs into a stone cell, damp and dark: forming the ante-room

5. Daily account book.

to the coal-cellar, and denominated "the kitchen:" wherein sat a slatternly girl, in shoes down at heel, and blue worsted stockings very much out of repair.

"Here, Charlotte," said Mrs. Sowerberry, who had followed Oliver down, "give this boy some of the cold bits that were put by for Trip. He hasn't come home since the morning, so he may go without 'em. I dare say the boy isn't too dainty to eat 'em,—are you, boy?"

Oliver, whose eyes had glistened at the mention of meat, and who was trembling with eagerness to devour it, replied in the negative; and a plateful of coarse broken victuals was set before him.

I wish some well-fed philosopher, whose meat and drink turn to gall within him; whose blood is ice, whose heart is iron; could have seen Oliver Twist clutching at the dainty viands that the dog had neglected. I wish he could have witnessed the horrible avidity with which Oliver tore the bits asunder with all the ferocity of famine. There is only one thing I should like better; and that would be to see the Philosopher making the same sort of meal himself, with the same relish.

"Well," said the undertaker's wife, when Oliver had finished his supper: which she had regarded in silent horror, and with fearful auguries[6] of his future appetite: "have you done?"

There being nothing eatable within his reach, Oliver replied in the affirmative.

"Then come with me," said Mrs. Sowerberry: taking up a dim and dirty lamp, and leading the way up stairs; "your bed's under the counter. You don't mind sleeping among the coffins, I suppose? But it doesn't much matter whether you do or don't, for you can't sleep anywhere else. Come; don't keep me here all night!"

Oliver lingered no longer, but meekly followed his new mistress.

Chapter V.

OLIVER MINGLES WITH NEW ASSOCIATES. GOING TO A FUNERAL FOR THE FIRST TIME, HE FORMS AN UNFAVOURABLE NOTION OF HIS MASTER'S BUSINESS.

Oliver, being left to himself in the undertaker's shop, set the lamp down on a workman's bench, and gazed timidly about him with a feeling of awe and dread, which many people a good deal older than he will be at no loss to understand. An unfinished coffin on black tressels, which stood in the middle of the shop, looked so gloomy and deathlike that a cold tremble came over him, every time his eyes wandered in the direction of the dismal object: from which he almost expected to see some frightful form slowly rear its head, to drive him mad with terror. Against

6. Predictions.

the wall, were ranged, in regular array, a long row of elm boards cut into the same shape: looking, in the dim light, like high-shouldered ghosts with their hands in their breeches-pockets. Coffin-plates, elm-chips, bright-headed nails, and shreds of black cloth, lay scattered on the floor; and the wall behind the counter was ornamented with a lively representation of two mutes in very stiff neckcloths,[1] on duty at a large private door: with a hearse drawn by four black steeds, approaching in the distance. The shop was close and hot; and the atmosphere seemed tainted with the smell of coffins. The recess beneath the counter in which his flock mattress was thrust, looked like a grave.

Nor were these the only dismal feelings which depressed Oliver. He was alone in a strange place; and we all know how chilled and desolate the best of us will sometimes feel in such a situation. The boy had no friends to care for, or to care for him. The regret of no recent separation was fresh in his mind; the absence of no loved and well-remembered face sunk heavily into his heart. But his heart *was* heavy, notwithstanding; and he wished, as he crept into his narrow bed, that that were his coffin; and that he could be laid in a calm and lasting sleep in the churchyard ground: with the tall grass waving gently above his head: and the sound of the old deep bell to soothe him in his sleep.

Oliver was awakened in the morning, by a loud kicking at the outside of the shop-door: which, before he could huddle on his clothes, was repeated, in an angry and impetuous manner, about twenty-five times. When he began to undo the chain, the legs desisted and a voice began.

"Open the door, will yer?" cried the voice which belonged to the legs which had kicked at the door.

"I will, directly, sir," replied Oliver: undoing the chain, and turning the key.

"I suppose yer the new boy, a'n't yer?" said the voice, through the key-hole.

"Yes, sir," replied Oliver.

"How old are yer?" inquired the voice.

"Ten, sir," replied Oliver.

"Then I'll whop yer when I get in," said the voice; "you just see if I don't, that's all, my work'us brat!" and having made this obliging promise, the voice began to whistle.

Oliver had been too often subjected to the process to which the very expressive monosyllable just recorded bears reference, to entertain the smallest doubt that the owner of the voice, whoever he might be, would redeem his pledge, most honourably. He drew back the bolts with a trembling hand, and opened the door.

For a second or two, Oliver glanced up the street, and down the street, and over the way: impressed with the belief that the unknown, who had

1. Mutes were hired as professional attendants at funerals to add to the solemnity; they wore tight white collars to contrast with their black garments.

addressed him through the key-hole, had walked a few paces off, to warm himself; for nobody did he see but a big charity-boy,[2] sitting on a post in front of the house, eating a slice of bread and butter: which he cut into wedges, the size of his mouth, with a clasp-knife, and then consumed with great dexterity.

"I beg your pardon, sir," said Oliver, at length: seeing that no other visitor made his appearance; "did you knock?"

"I kicked," replied the charity-boy.

"Did you want a coffin, sir?" inquired Oliver, innocently.

At this, the charity-boy looked monstrous fierce; and said that Oliver would want one before long, if he cut jokes with his superiors in that way.

"Yer don't know who I am, I suppose, Work'us?" said the charity-boy, in continuation: descending from the top of the post, meanwhile, with edifying gravity.

"No, sir," rejoined Oliver.

"I'm Mister Noah Claypole," said the charity-boy, "and you're under me. Take down the shutters, yer idle young ruffian!" With this, Mr. Claypole administered a kick to Oliver, and entered the shop with a dignified air, which did him great credit. It is difficult for a large-headed, small-eyed youth, of lumbering make and heavy countenance, to look dignified under any circumstances; but it is more especially so, when superadded to these personal attractions are a red nose and yellow smalls.[3]

Oliver, having taken down the shutters, and broken a pane of glass in his efforts to stagger away beneath the weight of the first one to a small court at the side of the house in which they were kept during the day, was graciously assisted by Noah: who, having consoled him with the assurance that "he'd catch it," condescended to help him. Mr. Sowerberry came down soon after. Shortly afterwards, Mrs. Sowerberry appeared; and Oliver having "caught it," in fulfilment of Noah's prediction, followed that young gentleman down stairs to breakfast.

"Come near the fire, Noah," said Charlotte. "I saved a nice little bit of bacon for you from master's breakfast. Oliver, shut that door at Mister Noah's back, and take them bits that I've put out on the cover of the bread-pan. There's your tea; take it away to that box, and drink it there, and make haste, for they'll want you to mind the shop. D'ye hear?"

"D'ye hear, Work'us?" said Noah Claypole.

"Lor, Noah!" said Charlotte, "what a rum creature you are! Why don't you let the boy alone?"

"Let him alone!" said Noah. "Why everybody lets him alone enough, for the matter of that. Neither his father nor his mother will ever interfere with him. All his relations let him have his own way pretty well. Eh, Charlotte? He! he! he!"

2. A student at a free charity school for poor children; such children wore uniforms.
3. Pants.

"Oh, you queer soul!" said Charlotte, bursting into a hearty laugh, in which she was joined by Noah; after which, they both looked scornfully at poor Oliver Twist, as he sat shivering on the box in the coldest corner of the room: and ate the stale pieces which had been specially reserved for him.

Noah was a charity-boy, but not a workhouse orphan. No chance-child was he, for he could trace his genealogy all the way back to his parents, who lived hard by; his mother being a washerwoman, and his father a drunken soldier: discharged with a wooden leg, and a diurnal[4] pension of twopence-halfpenny and an unstateable fraction. The shop-boys in the neighbourhood had long been in the habit of branding Noah, in the public streets, with the ignominious epithets of "leathers," "charity," and the like; and Noah had borne them without reply. But, now that fortune had cast in his way a nameless orphan, at whom even the meanest could point the finger of scorn, he retorted on him with interest. This affords charming food for contemplation. It shows us what a beautiful thing human nature sometimes is; and how impartially the same amiable qualities are developed in the finest lord and the dirtiest charity-boy.

Oliver had been sojourning at the undertaker's some three weeks or a month. Mr. and Mrs. Sowerberry: the shop being shut up: were taking their supper in the little back-parlour, when Mr. Sowerberry, after several deferential glances at his wife, said,

"My dear—" He was going to say more; but, Mrs. Sowerberry looking up, with a peculiarly unpropitious aspect, he stopped short.

"Well," said Mrs. Sowerberry, sharply.

"Nothing, my dear, nothing," said Mr. Sowerberry.

"Ugh, you brute!" said Mrs. Sowerberry.

"Not at all, my dear," said Mr. Sowerberry humbly. "I thought you didn't want to hear, my dear. I was only going to say——"

"Oh, don't tell me what you were going to say," interposed Mrs. Sowerberry. "I am nobody; don't consult me, pray. I don't want to intrude upon your secrets." As Mrs. Sowerberry said this, she gave an hysterical laugh, which threatened violent consequences.

"But, my dear," said Sowerberry, "I want to ask your advice."

"No, no, don't ask mine," replied Mrs. Sowerberry, in an affecting manner: "ask somebody else's." Here, there was another hysterical laugh, which frightened Mr. Sowerberry very much. This is a very common and much-approved matrimonial course of treatment, which is often very effective. It at once reduced Mr. Sowerberry to begging, as a special favour, to be allowed to say what Mrs. Sowerberry was most curious to hear. After a short altercation of less than three quarters of an hour's duration, the permission was most graciously conceded.

4. Daily.

"It's only about young Twist, my dear," said Mr. Sowerberry. "A very good-looking boy that, my dear."

"He need be, for he eats enough," observed the lady.

"There's an expression of melancholy in his face, my dear," resumed Mr. Sowerberry, "which is very interesting. He would make a delightful mute, my love."

Mrs. Sowerberry looked up with an expression of considerable wonderment. Mr. Sowerberry remarked it; and, without allowing time for any observation on the good lady's part, proceeded.

"I don't mean a regular mute to attend grown-up people, my dear, but only for children's practice. It would be very new to have a mute in proportion, my dear. You may depend upon it, it would have a most superb effect."

Mrs. Sowerberry, who had a good deal of taste in the undertaking way, was much struck by the novelty of this idea; but, as it would have been compromising her dignity to have said so, under existing circumstances: she merely inquired, with much sharpness, why such an obvious suggestion had not presented itself to her husband's mind before. Mr. Sowerberry rightly construed this, as an acquiescence in his proposition; it was speedily determined, therefore, that Oliver should be at once initiated into the mysteries of the trade; and, with this view, that he should accompany his master on the very next occasion of his services being required.

The occasion was not long in coming. Half an hour after breakfast next morning, Mr. Bumble entered the shop; and supporting his cane against the counter, drew forth his large leathern pocket-book: from which he selected a small scrap of paper, which he handed over to Sowerberry.

"Aha!" said the undertaker, glancing over it with a lively countenance; "an order for a coffin, eh?"

"For a coffin first, and a porochial funeral afterwards," replied Mr. Bumble, fastening the strap of the leathern pocket-book: which, like himself, was very corpulent.

"Bayton," said the undertaker, looking from the scrap of paper to Mr. Bumble. "I never heard the name before."

Bumble shook his head, as he replied, "Obstinate people, Mr. Sowerberry; very obstinate. Proud, too, I'm afraid, sir."

"Proud, eh?" exclaimed Mr. Sowerberry with a sneer. "Come, that's too much."

"Oh, it's sickening," replied the beadle. "Antimonial,[5] Mr. Sowerberry!"

"So it is," acquiesced the undertaker.

"We only heard of the family the night before last," said the beadle;

5. Bitter-tasting, like a medicine containing the metal antimony, which was often added to wine as an emetic.

"and we shouldn't have known anything about them, then, only a woman who lodges in the same house made an application to the porochial committee for them to send the porochial surgeon to see a woman as was very bad. He had gone out to dinner; but his 'prentice: which is a very clever lad: sent 'em some medicine in a blacking-bottle,[6] off-hand."

"Ah, there's promptness," said the undertaker.

"Promptness, indeed!" replied the beadle. "But what's the consequence; what's the ungrateful behaviour of these rebels, sir? Why, the husband sends back word that the medicine won't suit his wife's complaint, and so she shan't take it—says she shan't take it, sir! Good, strong, wholesome medicine, as was given with great success to two Irish labourers and a coalheaver, only a week before—sent 'em for nothing, with a blackin-bottle in,—and he sends back word that she shan't take it, sir."

As the atrocity presented itself to Mr. Bumble's mind in full force, he struck the counter sharply with his cane, and became flushed with indignation.

"Well," said the undertaker, "I ne—ver—did——"

"Never did, sir!" ejaculated the beadle. "No, nor nobody never did; but, now she's dead, we've got to bury her; and that's the direction; and the sooner it's done, the better."

Thus saying, Mr. Bumble put on his cocked hat wrong side first, in a fever of parochial excitement; and flounced out of the shop.

"Why, he was so angry, Oliver, that he forgot even to ask after you!" said Mr. Sowerberry, looking after the beadle as he strode down the street.

"Yes, sir," replied Oliver, who had carefully kept himself out of sight, during the interview; and who was shaking from head to foot at the mere recollection of the sound of Mr. Bumble's voice. He needn't have taken the trouble to shrink from Mr. Bumble's glance, however; for that functionary, on whom the prediction of the gentleman in the white waistcoat had made a very strong impression, thought that now the undertaker had got Oliver upon trial, the subject was better avoided, until such time as he should be firmly bound for seven years: and all danger of his being returned upon the hands of the parish should be thus effectually and legally overcome.

"Well," said Mr. Sowerberry, taking up his hat, "the sooner this job is done, the better. Noah, look after the shop. Oliver, put on your cap, and come with me." Oliver obeyed, and followed his master on his professional mission.

They walked on, for some time, through the most crowded and densely inhabited part of the town; and then, striking down a narrow street more

---

6. A bottle that had contained black shoe polish, or blacking.

dirty and miserable than any they had yet passed through, paused to look for the house which was the object of their search. The houses on either side were high and large, but very old; and tenanted by people of the poorest class: as their neglected appearance would have sufficiently denoted, without the concurrent testimony afforded by the squalid looks of the few men and women who, with folded arms and bodies half doubled, occasionally skulked along. A great many of the tenements had shop-fronts; but these were fast closed, and mouldering away: only the upper rooms being inhabited. Some houses which had become insecure from age and decay, were prevented from falling into the street, by huge beams of wood reared against the walls, and firmly planted in the road; but even these crazy dens seemed to have been selected as the nightly haunts of some houseless wretches; for many of the rough boards, which supplied the place of door and window, were wrenched from their positions, to afford an aperture wide enough for the passage of a human body. The kennel[7] was stagnant and filthy. The very rats, which here and there lay putrefying in its rottenness, were hideous with famine.

There was neither knocker nor bell-handle at the open door where Oliver and his master stopped; so, groping his way cautiously through the dark passage, and bidding Oliver keep close to him and not be afraid, the undertaker mounted to the top of the first flight of stairs: and stumbling against a door on the landing, rapped at it with his knuckles.

It was opened by a young girl of thirteen or fourteen. The undertaker at once saw enough of what the room contained, to know it was the apartment to which he had been directed. He stepped in; and Oliver followed him.

There was no fire in the room; but a man was crouching, mechanically, over the empty stove. An old woman, too, had drawn a low stool to the cold hearth: and was sitting beside him. There were some ragged children in another corner; and in a small recess, opposite the door, there lay upon the ground, something covered with an old blanket. Oliver shuddered as he cast his eyes towards the place: and crept involuntarily closer to his master; for though it was covered up, the boy felt that it was a corpse.

The man's face was thin and very pale; his hair and beard were grizzly; and his eyes were bloodshot. The old woman's face was wrinkled; her two remaining teeth protruded over her under lip; and her eyes were bright and piercing. Oliver was afraid to look at either her or the man. They seemed so like the rats he had seen outside.

"Nobody shall go near her," said the man, starting fiercely up, as the undertaker approached the recess. "Keep back! d—n you, keep back, if you've a life to lose!"

---

7. The gutter or drain at the sides of streets.

"Nonsense, my good man," said the undertaker, who was pretty well used to misery in all its shapes. "Nonsense!"

"I tell you," said the man: clenching his hands, and stamping furiously on the floor,—"I tell you I won't have her put into the ground. She couldn't rest there. The worms would worry her: not eat her: she is so worn away."

The undertaker offered no reply to this raving; but, producing a tape from his pocket, knelt down for a moment by the side of the body.

"Ah!" said the man: bursting into tears, and sinking on his knees at the feet of the dead woman; "kneel down, kneel down—kneel round her, every one of you, and mark my words! I say she was starved to death. I never knew how bad she was, till the fever came upon her; and then her bones were starting through the skin. There was neither fire nor candle; she died in the dark—in the dark. She couldn't even see her children's faces, though we heard her gasping out their names. I begged for her in the streets: and they sent me to prison. When I came back, she was dying; and all the blood in my heart has dried up, for they starved her to death. I swear it before the God that saw it! They starved her!" He twined his hands in his hair; and, with a loud scream, rolled grovelling upon the floor: his eyes fixed: and the foam gushing from his lips.

The terrified children cried bitterly; but the old woman, who had hitherto remained as quiet as if she had been wholly deaf to all that passed, menaced them into silence; and having unloosed the man's cravat: who still remained extended on the ground: tottered towards the undertaker.

"She was my daughter," said the old woman, nodding her head in the direction of the corpse; and speaking with an idiotic leer, more ghastly than even the presence of death in such a place. "Lord, Lord! Well, it *is* strange that I who gave birth to her, and was a woman then, should be alive and merry now; and she lying there: so cold and stiff! Lord, Lord!—to think of it;—it's as good as a play—as good as a play!"

As the wretched creature mumbled and chuckled in her hideous merriment, the undertaker turned to go away.

"Stop, stop!" said the old woman in a loud whisper. "Will she be buried to-morrow, or next day, or to-night? I laid her out; and I must walk, you know. Send me a large cloak: a good warm one: for it is bitter cold. We should have cake and wine, too, before we go! Never mind; send some bread—only a loaf of bread and a cup of water. Shall we have some bread, dear?" she said eagerly: catching at the undertaker's coat, as he once more moved towards the door.

"Yes, yes," said the undertaker, "of course. Anything, everything!" He disengaged himself from the old woman's grasp; and, drawing Oliver after him, hurried away.

The next day, (the family having been meanwhile relieved with a half-quartern loaf and a piece of cheese: left with them by Mr. Bumble himself,) Oliver and his master returned to the miserable abode; where Mr. Bumble had already arrived, accompanied by four men from the workhouse: who were to act as bearers. An old black cloak had been thrown over the rags of the old woman and the man; and the bare coffin having been screwed down, was hoisted on the shoulders of the bearers, and carried into the street.

"Now, you must put your best leg foremost, old lady!" whispered Sowerberry in the old woman's ear; "we are rather late; and it won't do, to keep the clergyman waiting. Move on, my men,—as quick as you like!"

Thus directed, the bearers trotted on under their light burden; and the two mourners kept as near them, as they could. Mr. Bumble and Sowerberry walked at a good smart pace in front; and Oliver, whose legs were not so long as his master's, ran by the side.

There was not so great a necessity for hurrying as Mr. Sowerberry had anticipated, however; for when they reached the obscure corner of the churchyard in which the nettles grew, and where the parish graves were made, the clergyman had not arrived; and the clerk, who was sitting by the vestry-room fire, seemed to think it by no means improbable that it might be an hour or so, before he came. So, they put the bier[8] on the brink of the grave; and the two mourners waited patiently in the damp clay, with a cold rain drizzling down: while the ragged boys, whom the spectacle had attracted into the churchyard, played a noisy game at hide-and-seek among the tombstones: or varied their amusements by jumping backwards and forwards over the coffin. Mr. Sowerberry and Bumble, being personal friends of the clerk, sat by the fire with him, and read the paper.

At length, after the lapse of something more than an hour, Mr. Bumble, and Sowerberry, and the clerk, were seen running towards the grave. Immediately afterwards, the clergyman appeared: putting on his surplice[9] as he came along. Mr. Bumble then threshed a boy or two, to keep up appearances; and the reverend gentleman, having read as much of the burial service as could be compressed into four minutes, gave his surplice to the clerk, and walked away again.

"Now, Bill!" said Sowerberry to the grave-digger, "fill up."

It was no very difficult task; for the grave was so full, that the uppermost coffin was within a few feet of the surface. The grave-digger shovelled in the earth; stamped it loosely down with his feet; shouldered his spade; and walked off: followed by the boys: who murmured very loud complaints at the fun being over so soon.

8. A stand on which a coffin is placed. "Vestry-room": in England, the room in a church in which the local church governing board meets.
9. A loose-fitting white clerical gown.

"Come, my good fellow!" said Bumble, tapping the man on the back. "They want to shut up the yard."

The man: who had never once moved, since he had taken his station by the grave side: started; raised his head; stared at the person who had addressed him; walked forward for a few paces; and fell down in a swoon. The crazy old woman was too much occupied in bewailing the loss of her cloak (which the undertaker had taken off), to pay him any attention; so they threw a can of cold water over him; and when he came to, saw him safely out of the churchyard: locked the gate; and departed on their different ways.

"Well, Oliver," said Sowerberry, as they walked home, "how do you like it?"

"Pretty well, thank you, sir," replied Oliver, with considerable hesitation. "Not very much, sir."

"Ah, you'll get used to it in time, Oliver," said Sowerberry. "Nothing when you *are* used to it, my boy."

Oliver wondered, in his own mind, whether it had taken a very long time to get Mr. Sowerberry used to it. But he thought it better not to ask the question; and walked back to the shop: thinking over all he had seen and heard.

Chapter VI.

OLIVER, BEING GOADED BY THE TAUNTS OF NOAH, ROUSES INTO ACTION, AND RATHER ASTONISHES HIM.

The month's trial over, Oliver was formally apprenticed. It was a nice sickly season just at this time. In commercial phrase, coffins were looking up; and, in the course of a few weeks, Oliver had acquired a great deal of experience. The success of Mr. Sowerberry's ingenious speculation, exceeded even his most sanguine hopes. The oldest inhabitants recollected no period at which measles had been so prevalent, or so fatal to infant existence; and many were the mournful processions which little Oliver headed, in a hat-band reaching down to his knees: to the indescribable admiration and emotion of all the mothers in the town. As Oliver accompanied his master in most of his adult expeditions, too, in order that he might acquire that equanimity of demeanour and full command of nerve, which are so essential to a finished undertaker, he had many opportunities of observing the beautiful resignation and fortitude with which some strong-minded people bear their trials and losses.

For instance; when Sowerberry had an order for the burial of some rich old lady or gentleman, who was surrounded by a great number of nephews and nieces, who had been perfectly inconsolable during the previous illness, and whose grief had been wholly irrepressible even on the most public occasions; they would be as happy among themselves as need be—quite cheerful and contented: conversing together, with as much freedom and gaiety, as if nothing whatever had happened to disturb them. Husbands, too, bore the loss of their wives with the most heroic calmness. Wives, again, put on weeds for their husbands, as if, so far from grieving in the garb of sorrow, they had made up their minds to render it as becoming and attractive as possible. It was observable, too, that ladies and gentlemen who were in passions of anguish during the ceremony of interment, recovered almost as soon as they reached home; and became quite composed before the tea-drinking was over. All this, was very pleasant and improving to see; and Oliver beheld it with great admiration.

That Oliver Twist was moved to resignation by the example of these good people, I cannot, although I am his biographer, undertake to affirm with any degree of confidence; but I can most distinctly say, that for many months he continued meekly to submit to the domination and ill-treatment of Noah Claypole: who used him far worse than before, now that his jealousy was roused by seeing the new boy promoted to the black stick and hat-band, while he, the old one, remained stationary in the muffin-cap[1] and leathers. Charlotte treated him badly, because Noah did; and Mrs. Sowerberry was his decided enemy, because Mr. Sowerberry was disposed to be his friend; so, between these three on one side, and a glut of funerals on the other: Oliver was not altogether as comfortable as the hungry pig was, when he was shut up, by mistake, in the grain department of a brewery.

And now I come to a very important passage in Oliver's history; for I have to record an act: slight and unimportant perhaps in appearance: but which indirectly produced a most material change in all his future prospects and proceedings.

One day, Oliver and Noah had descended into the kitchen at the usual dinner-hour, to banquet upon a small joint of mutton[2]—a pound and a half of the worst end of the neck—when, Charlotte being called out of the way, there ensued a brief interval of time, which Noah Claypole, being hungry and vicious, considered he could not possibly devote to a worthier purpose than aggravating and tantalizing young Oliver Twist.

Intent upon this innocent amusement, Noah put his feet on the table-cloth; and pulled Oliver's hair; and twitched his ears; and expressed his opinion that he was a "sneak;" and furthermore announced his intention of coming to see him hung, whenever that desirable event should take place; and entered upon various other topics of petty annoyance, like a malicious and ill-conditioned charity-boy as he was. But, none of these taunts producing the desired effect of making Oliver cry, Noah attempted

---

1. A flat wool cap worn by charity-school boys.
2. The meat of a fully grown sheep.

to be more facetious still; and in this attempt, did what many small wits, with far greater reputations than Noah, sometimes do, to this day, when they want to be funny. He got rather personal.

"Work'us," said Noah, "how's your mother?"

"She's dead," replied Oliver; "don't you say anything about her to me!"

Oliver's colour rose as he said this; he breathed quickly; and there was a curious working of the mouth and nostrils, which Mr. Claypole thought must be the immediate precursor of a violent fit of crying. Under this impression he returned to the charge.

"What did she die of, Work'us?" said Noah.

"Of a broken heart, some of our old nurses told me," replied Oliver: more as if he were talking to himself, than answering Noah. "I think I know what it must be to die of that!"

"Tol de rol lol lol, right fol lairy,[3] Work'us," said Noah, as a tear rolled down Oliver's cheek. "What's set you a snivelling now?"

"Not *you*," replied Oliver, hastily brushing the tear away. "Don't think it."

"Oh, not me, eh?" sneered Noah.

"No, not you," replied Oliver, sharply. "There; that's enough. Don't say anything more to me about her; you'd better not!"

"Better not!" exclaimed Noah. "Well! better not! Work'us, don't be impudent. *Your* mother, too! She was a nice 'un, she was.[4] Oh, Lor!" And here, Noah nodded his head expressively; and curled up as much of his small red nose as muscular action could collect together, for the occasion.

"Yer know, Work'us," continued Noah; emboldened by Oliver's silence; and speaking in a jeering tone of affected pity: of all tones the most annoying: "Yer know, Work'us, it carn't be helped now; and of course yer couldn't help it then; and I'm very sorry for it; and I'm sure we all are: and pity yer very much. But yer must know, Work'us, yer mother was a regular right-down bad'un."

"What did you say?" inquired Oliver, looking up very quickly.

"A regular right-down bad 'un, Work'us," replied Noah, coolly. "And it's a great deal better, Work'us, that she died when she did, or else she'd have been hard labouring in Bridewell, or transported,[5] or hung: which is more likely than either, isn't it?"

Crimson with fury, Oliver started up; overthrew the chair and table; seized Noah by the throat; shook him, in the violence of his rage, till his teeth chattered in his head; and, collecting his whole force into one heavy blow, felled him to the ground.

3. Mocking nonsense words.
4. A sarcastic reference to Oliver's mother having borne an illegitimate child.
5. Convicted criminals were sometimes exiled (transported), mainly to Australia. "Bridewell": a generic name for a prison where the inmates usually had to do forced labor.

A minute ago, the boy had looked the quiet, mild, dejected creature that harsh treatment had made him. But his spirit was roused at last; the cruel insult to his dead mother had set his blood on fire. His breast heaved; his attitude was erect; his eye bright and vivid; his whole person changed, as he stood glaring over the cowardly tormentor who now lay crouching at his feet: and defied him with an energy he had never known before.

"He'll murder me!" blubbered Noah. "Charlotte! missis! Here's the new boy a murdering of me! Help! help! Oliver's gone mad! Char— lotte!"

Noah's shouts were responded to, by a loud scream from Charlotte, and a louder from Mrs. Sowerberry; the former of whom rushed into the kitchen by a side-door: while the latter paused on the staircase till she was quite certain that it was consistent with the preservation of human life, to come further down.

"Oh, you little wretch!" screamed Charlotte; seizing Oliver with her utmost force, which was about equal to that of a moderately strong man in particularly good training, "Oh, you little un-grate-ful, mur-de-rous, hor-rid vil-lain!" And between every syllable, Charlotte gave Oliver a blow with all her might: accompanying it with a scream, for the benefit of society.

Charlotte's fist was by no means a light one; but, lest it should not be effectual in calming Oliver's wrath, Mrs. Sowerberry plunged into the kitchen, and assisted to hold him with one hand, while she scratched his face with the other. In this favourable position of affairs, Noah rose from the ground: and pommelled him behind.

This was rather too violent exercise to last long. When they were all three wearied out, and could tear and beat no longer, they dragged Oliver, struggling and shouting, but nothing daunted, into the dust-cellar,[6] and there locked him up; this being done, Mrs. Sowerberry sunk into a chair, and burst into tears.

"Bless her, she's going off!" said Charlotte. "A glass of water, Noah, dear. Make haste."

"Oh! Charlotte," said Mrs. Sowerberry: speaking as well as she could, through a deficiency of breath, and a sufficiency of cold water, which Noah had poured over her head and shoulders. "Oh! Charlotte, what a mercy we have not all been murdered in our beds!"

"Ah! mercy indeed, ma'am," was the reply. "I only hope this'll teach master not to have any more of these dreadful creatures, that are born to be murderers and robbers from their very cradle. Poor Noah! He was all but killed, ma'am, when I come in."

"Poor fellow!" said Mrs. Sowerberry: looking piteously on the charity-boy.

---

6. A basement where garbage is stored.

Noah: whose top waistcoat-button might have been somewhere on a level with the crown of Oliver's head: rubbed his eyes with the inside of his wrists while this commiseration was bestowed upon him; and performed some affecting tears and sniffs.

"What's to be done!" exclaimed Mrs. Sowerberry. "Your master's not at home: there's not a man in the house; and he'll kick that door down, in ten minutes." Oliver's vigorous plunges against the bit of timber in question, rendered this occurrence highly probable.

"Dear, dear! I don't know, ma'am," said Charlotte, "unless we send for the police-officers."

"Or the millingtary,"[7] suggested Mr. Claypole.

"No, no," said Mrs. Sowerberry: bethinking herself of Oliver's old friend. "Run to Mr. Bumble, Noah; and tell him to come here directly, and not to lose a minute; never mind your cap! Make haste! You can hold a knife to that black eye, as you run along; and it'll keep the swelling down."

Noah stopped to make no reply, but started off at his fullest speed; and very much it astonished the people who were out walking, to see a charity-boy tearing through the streets pell-mell: with no cap on his head, and a clasp-knife at his eye.

Chapter VII.

OLIVER CONTINUES REFRACTORY.

Noah Claypole ran along the streets at his swiftest pace; and paused not once for breath, until he reached the workhouse-gate. Having rested here, for a minute or so, to collect a good burst of sobs and an imposing show of tears and terror, he knocked loudly at the wicket,[1] and presented such a rueful face to the aged pauper who opened it, that even he, who saw nothing but rueful faces about him at the best of times, started back in astonishment.

"Why, what's the matter with the boy!" said the old pauper.

"Mr. Bumble! Mr. Bumble!" cried Noah, with well-affected dismay: and in tones so loud and agitated, that they not only caught the ear of Mr. Bumble himself, who happened to be hard by, but alarmed him so much that he rushed into the yard without his cocked hat,—which is a very curious and remarkable circumstance: as showing that even a beadle, acted upon by a sudden and powerful impulse, may be afflicted with a momentary visitation of loss of self-possession, and forgetfulness of personal dignity.

"Oh, Mr. Bumble, sir!" said Noah: "Oliver, sir,—Oliver has——"

7. Soldiers.
1. A small door placed beside a large one, to be used when the large one is closed.

"What? What?" interposed Mr. Bumble: with a gleam of pleasure in his metallic eyes. "Not run away; he hasn't run away, has he, Noah?"

"No, sir, no. Not run away, sir, but he's turned wicious," replied Noah. "He tried to murder me, sir; and then he tried to murder Charlotte; and then missis. Oh! what dreadful pain it is! Such agony, please, sir!" And here, Noah writhed and twisted his body into an extensive variety of eel-like positions; thereby giving Mr. Bumble to understand that, from the violent and sanguinary[2] onset of Oliver Twist, he had sustained severe internal injury and damage, from which he was at that moment suffering the acutest torture.

When Noah saw that the intelligence he communicated, perfectly paralyzed Mr. Bumble, he imparted additional effect thereunto, by bewailing his dreadful wounds ten times louder than before; and, when he observed a gentleman in a white waistcoat crossing the yard, he was more tragic in his lamentations than ever: rightly conceiving it highly expedient to attract the notice, and rouse the indignation, of the gentleman aforesaid.

The gentleman's notice was very soon attracted; for he had not walked three paces, when he turned angrily round, and inquired what that young cur was howling for; and why Mr. Bumble did not favour him with something which would render the series of vocular exclamations[3] so designated, an involuntary process.

"It's a poor boy from the free-school, sir," replied Mr. Bumble, "who has been nearly murdered—all but murdered, sir—by young Twist."

"By Jove!" exclaimed the gentleman in the white waistcoat, stopping short. "I knew it! I felt a strange presentiment from the very first, that that audacious young savage would come to be hung!"

"He has likewise attempted, sir, to murder the female servant," said Mr. Bumble, with a face of ashy paleness.

"And his missis," interposed Mr. Claypole.

"And his master, too, I think you said, Noah?" added Mr. Bumble.

"No; he's out, or he would have murdered him," replied Noah. "He said he wanted to."

"Ah! said he wanted to: did he, my boy?" inquired the gentleman in the white waistcoat.

"Yes, sir," replied Noah. "And please, sir, missis wants to know whether Mr. Bumble can spare time to step up there, directly, and flog him: 'cause master's out."

"Certainly, my boy; certainly," said the gentleman in the white waistcoat: smiling benignly: and patting Noah's head, which was about three inches higher than his own. "You're a good boy—a very good boy. Here's a penny for you. Bumble, just step up to Sowerberry's with your cane, and see what's best to be done. Don't spare him, Bumble."

2. Bloodthirsty.
3. Loud howls.

"No, I will not, sir," replied the beadle: adjusting the wax-end which was twisted round the bottom of his cane, for purposes of parochial flagellation.

"Tell Sowerberry not to spare him either. They'll never do anything with him, without stripes and bruises," said the gentleman in the white waistcoat.

"I'll take care, sir," replied the beadle. And the cocked hat and cane having been, by this time, adjusted to their owner's satisfaction: Mr. Bumble and Noah Claypole betook themselves with all speed to the undertaker's shop.

Here, the position of affairs had not at all improved: as Sowerberry had not yet returned: and Oliver continued to kick, with undiminished vigour, at the cellar-door. The accounts of his ferocity, as related by Mrs. Sowerberry and Charlotte, were of so startling a nature, that Mr. Bumble judged it prudent to parley, before opening the door. With this view, he gave a kick at the outside, by way of prelude; and then, applying his mouth to the keyhole, said, in a deep and impressive tone

"Oliver!"

"Come; you let me out!" replied Oliver, from the inside.

"Do you know this here voice, Oliver?" said Mr. Bumble.

"Yes," replied Oliver.

"Ain't you afraid of it, sir? Ain't you a-trembling while I speak, sir?" said Mr. Bumble.

"No!" replied Oliver boldly.

An answer so different from the one he had expected to elicit, and was in the habit of receiving, staggered Mr. Bumble not a little. He stepped back from the keyhole; drew himself up to his full height; and looked from one to another of the three by-standers, in mute astonishment.

"Oh, you know, Mr. Bumble, he must be mad," said Mrs. Sowerberry. "No boy in half his senses could venture to speak so to you."

"It's not Madness, ma'am," replied Mr. Bumble, after a few moments of deep meditation. "It's Meat."

"What!" exclaimed Mrs. Sowerberry.

"Meat, ma'am, meat," replied Bumble, with stern emphasis. "You've overfed him, ma'am. You've raised a artificial soul and spirit in him, ma'am, unbecoming a person of his condition: as the board, Mrs. Sowerberry, who are practical philosophers, will tell you. What have paupers to do with soul or spirit? It's quite enough that we let 'em have live bodies. If you had kept the boy on gruel, ma'am, this would never have happened."

"Dear, dear!" ejaculated Mrs. Sowerberry, piously raising her eyes to the kitchen ceiling: "this comes of being liberal!"

The liberality of Mrs. Sowerberry to Oliver, had consisted in a profuse bestowal upon him of all the dirty odds and ends which nobody else would eat; so, there was a great deal of meekness and self-devotion in her voluntarily remaining under Mr. Bumble's heavy accusation; of which, to do her justice, she was wholly innocent, in thought, word, or deed.

"Ah!" said Mr. Bumble, when the lady brought her eyes down to earth again; "the only thing that can be done now, that I know of, is to leave him in the cellar for a day or so, till he's a little starved down; and then to take him out, and keep him on gruel all through his apprenticeship. He comes of a bad family. Excitable natures, Mrs. Sowerberry! Both the nurse and doctor said, that that mother of his made her way here, against difficulties and pain that would have killed any well-disposed woman weeks before."

At this point of Mr. Bumble's discourse, Oliver, just hearing enough to know that some further allusion was being made to his mother, recommenced kicking, with a violence that rendered every other sound inaudible. Sowerberry returned at this juncture; and Oliver's offence having been explained to him, with such exaggerations as the ladies thought best calculated to rouse his ire: he unlocked the cellar-door in a twinkling, and dragged his rebellious apprentice out, by the collar.

Oliver's clothes had been torn in the beating he had received; his face was bruised and scratched; and his hair scattered over his forehead. The angry flush had not disappeared, however; and when he was pulled out of his prison, he scowled boldly on Noah, and looked quite undismayed.

"Now, you are a nice young fellow, ain't you?" said Sowerberry: giving Oliver a shake, and a box on the ear.

"He called my mother names," replied Oliver.

"Well, and what if he did, you little ungrateful wretch?" said Mrs. Sowerberry. "She deserved what he said, and worse."

"She didn't," said Oliver.

"She did," said Mrs. Sowerberry.

"It's a lie!" said Oliver.

Mrs. Sowerberry burst into a flood of tears.

This flood of tears left Sowerberry no alternative. If he had hesitated for one instant to punish Oliver most severely, it must be quite clear to every experienced reader that he would have been, according to all precedents in disputes of matrimony established, a brute, an unnatural husband, an insulting creature, a base imitation of a man: and various other agreeable characters too numerous for recital within the limits of this chapter. To do him justice, he was, as far as his power went,—it was not very extensive,—kindly disposed towards the boy; perhaps because it was his interest to be so; perhaps because his wife disliked him. The flood of tears, however, left him no resource; so he at once gave him a drubbing, which satisfied even Mrs. Sowerberry herself; and rendered Mr. Bumble's subsequent application of the parochial cane, rather unnecessary. For the rest of the day, he was shut up in the back kitchen,

in company with a pump and a slice of bread; and, at night, Mrs.
Sowerberry, after making various remarks outside the door, by no means
complimentary to the memory of his mother, looked into the room:
and, amidst the jeers and pointings of Noah and Charlotte, ordered him
up stairs to his dismal bed.

It was not until he was left alone in the silence and stillness of the
gloomy workshop of the undertaker, that Oliver gave way to the feelings
which the day's treatment may be supposed likely to have awakened in
a mere child. He had listened to their taunts with a look of contempt;
he had borne the lash without a cry: for he felt that pride swelling in
his heart which would have kept down a shriek to the last, though they
had roasted him alive. But, now, when there were none to see or hear
him, he fell upon his knees on the floor; and, hiding his face in his
hands, wept such tears as, God send for the credit of our nature, few
so young may ever have cause to pour out before him!

For a long time, Oliver remained motionless in this attitude. The
candle was burning low in the socket when he rose to his feet. Having
gazed cautiously round him, and listened intently, he gently undid the
fastenings of the door, and looked abroad.

It was a cold, dark night. The stars seemed, to the boy's eyes, farther
from the earth than he had ever seen them before; there was no wind;
and the sombre shadows thrown by the trees upon the ground, looked
sepulchral[4] and death-like, from being so still. He softly reclosed the
door; and, having availed himself of the expiring light of the candle to
tie up in a handkerchief the few articles of wearing apparel he had; sat
himself down upon a bench, to wait for morning.

With the first ray of light that struggled through the crevices in the
shutters, Oliver rose, and again unbarred the door. One timid look
around,—one moment's pause of hesitation,—he had closed it behind
him, and was in the open street.

He looked to the right and to the left, uncertain whither to fly. He
remembered to have seen the waggons, as they went out, toiling up the
hill. He took the same route; and arriving at a footpath across the fields:
which he knew, after some distance, led out again into the road: struck
into it, and walked quickly on.

Along this same footpath, Oliver well remembered he had trotted
beside Mr. Bumble, when he first carried him to the workhouse from
the farm. His way lay directly in front of the cottage. His heart beat
quickly when he bethought himself of this; and he half resolved to turn
back. He had come a long way though, and should lose a great deal of
time by doing so. Besides, it was so early that there was very little fear
of his being seen; so he walked on.

4. Tomblike.

He reached the house. There was no appearance of its inmates stirring at that early hour. Oliver stopped, and peeped into the garden. A child was weeding one of the little beds; and as he stopped, he raised his pale face, and disclosed the features of one of his former companions. Oliver felt glad to see him, before he went; for, though younger than himself, he had been his little friend and playmate. They had been beaten, and starved, and shut up together, many and many a time.

"Hush, Dick!" said Oliver, as the boy ran to the gate, and thrust his thin arm between the rails to greet him. "Is any one up?"

"Nobody but me," replied the child.

"You mustn't say you saw me, Dick," said Oliver. "I am running away. They beat and ill-use me, Dick; and I am going to seek my fortune, some long way off. I don't know where. How pale you are!"

"I heard the doctor tell them I was dying," replied the child with a faint smile. "I am very glad to see you, dear; but don't stop, don't stop!"

"Yes, yes, I will, to say good-b'ye to you," replied Oliver. "I shall see you again, Dick; I know I shall. You will be well and happy!"

"I hope so," replied the child. "After I am dead, but not before. I know the doctor must be right, Oliver, because I dream so much of Heaven and Angels; and kind faces that I never see when I am awake. "Kiss me," said the child, climbing up the low gate, and flinging his little arms round Oliver's neck: "Good-b'ye, dear! God bless you!"

The blessing was from a young child's lips, but it was the first that Oliver had ever heard invoked upon his head; and through all the struggles and sufferings, and troubles and changes, of his after life, he never once forgot it.

Chapter VIII.

OLIVER WALKS TO LONDON. HE ENCOUNTERS ON THE ROAD, A STRANGE SORT OF YOUNG GENTLEMAN.

Oliver reached the style[1] at which the bypath terminated; and once more gained the high-road. It was eight o'clock now. Though he was nearly five miles away from the town, he ran, and hid behind the hedges, by turns, till noon: fearing that he might be pursued and over-taken. Then he sat down to rest by the side of a mile-stone; and began to think, for the first time, where he had better go and try to live.

The stone by which he was seated, bore, in large characters, an intimation that it was just seventy miles from that spot to London. The name awakened a new train of ideas in the boy's mind. London!—that great large place!—nobody—not even Mr. Bumble—could ever find

1. A pillar or post; the usual spelling is "stile."

him there! He had often heard the old men in the workhouse, too, say that no lad of spirit need want in London; and that there were ways of living in that vast city, which those who had been bred up in country parts had no idea of. It was the very place for a homeless boy, who must die in the streets, unless some one helped him. As these things passed through his thoughts, he jumped upon his feet, and again walked forward.

He had diminished the distance between himself and London by full four miles more, before he recollected how much he must undergo ere he could hope to reach his place of destination. As this consideration forced itself upon him, he slackened his pace a little, and meditated upon his means of getting there. He had a crust of bread; a coarse shirt; and two pairs of stockings in his bundle. He had a penny too—a gift of Sowerberry's, after some funeral in which he had acquitted himself more than ordinarily well—in his pocket. "A clean shirt," thought Oliver, "is a very comfortable thing, very; and so are two pairs of darned stockings; and so is a penny; but they are small helps to a sixty-five miles' walk in winter time." But Oliver's thoughts, like those of most other people, although they were extremely ready and active to point out his difficulties, were wholly at a loss to suggest any feasible mode of surmounting them; so, after a good deal of thinking to no particular purpose, he changed his little bundle over to the other shoulder, and trudged on.

Oliver walked twenty miles that day; and all that time tasted nothing but the crust of dry bread, and a few draughts of water, which he begged at the cottage-doors by the road-side. When the night came, he turned into a meadow; and, creeping close under a hay-rick, determined to lie there, till morning. He felt frightened at first; for the wind moaned dismally over the empty fields; and he was cold and hungry, and more alone than he had ever felt before. Being very tired with his walk, however, he soon fell asleep and forgot his troubles.

He felt cold and stiff, when he got up next morning: and so hungry that he was obliged to exchange the penny for a small loaf, in the very first village through which he passed. He had walked no more than twelve miles, when night closed in again; for his feet were sore: and his legs so weak that they trembled beneath him. Another night passed in the bleak damp air, made him worse; and, when he set forward on his journey next morning, he could hardly crawl along.

He waited at the bottom of a steep hill, till a stage-coach came up: and then begged of the outside passengers; but there were very few who took any notice of him; and even those told him to wait till they got to the top of the hill; and then let them see how far he could run for a halfpenny. Poor Oliver tried to keep up with the coach a little way, but was unable to do it, by reason of his fatigue and sore feet. When the outsides saw this, they put their halfpence back into their pockets again:

declaring that he was an idle young dog, and didn't deserve anything; and the coach rattled away, and left only a cloud of dust behind.

In some villages, large painted boards were fixed up: warning all persons who begged within the district, that they would be sent to jail. This frightened Oliver very much; and made him glad to get out of them with all possible expedition. In others, he would stand about the inn-yards, and look mournfully at every one who passed: a proceeding which generally terminated in the landlady's ordering one of the post-boys who were lounging about, to drive that strange boy out of the place, for she was sure he had come to steal something. If he begged at a farmer's house, ten to one but they threatened to set the dog on him; and when he showed his nose in a shop, they talked about the beadle: which brought Oliver's heart into his mouth,—very often the only thing he had there, for many hours together.

In fact, if it had not been for a good-hearted turnpike-man, and a benevolent old lady, Oliver's troubles would have been shortened by the very same process which put an end to his mother's; in other words, he would most assuredly have fallen dead upon the king's highway.[2] But the turnpike-man gave him a meal of bread and cheese; and the old lady, who had a shipwrecked grandson wandering barefooted in some distant part of the earth, took pity upon the poor orphan; and gave him what little she could afford—and more—with such kind and gentle words, and such tears of sympathy and compassion, that they sank deeper into Oliver's soul, than all the sufferings he had ever undergone.

Early on the seventh morning after he had left his native place, Oliver limped slowly into the little town of Barnet.[3] The window-shutters were closed; the street was empty; not a soul had awakened to the business of the day. The sun was rising in all his splendid beauty; but the light only served to show the boy his own lonesomeness and desolation, as he sat, with bleeding feet and covered with dust, upon a cold door-step.

By degrees, the shutters were opened; the window-blinds were drawn up; and people began passing to and fro. Some few stopped to gaze at Oliver for a moment or two, or turned round to stare at him as they hurried by; but none relieved him, or troubled themselves to inquire how he came there. He had no heart to beg. And there he sat.

He had been crouching on the step for some time: wondering at the great number of public houses (every other house in Barnet was a tavern, large or small): gazing listlessly at the coaches as they passed through: and thinking how strange it seemed that they could do, with ease, in a few hours, what it had taken him a whole week of courage and deter-mination beyond his years to accomplish: when he was roused by ob-serving that a boy, who had passed him carelessly some minutes before,

2. The main road to London.
3. On the northeast outskirts of London.

had returned, and was now surveying him most earnestly from the opposite side of the way. He took little heed of this at first; but the boy remained in the same attitude of close observation so long, that Oliver raised his head, and returned his steady look. Upon this, the boy crossed over; and, walking close up to Oliver, said,

"Hullo! my covey,[4] what's the row?"

The boy who addressed this inquiry to the young wayfarer, was about his own age: but one of the queerest-looking boys that Oliver had ever seen. He was a snub-nosed, flat-browed, common-faced boy enough; and as dirty a juvenile as one would wish to see; but he had about him all the airs and manners of a man. He was short of[5] his age: with rather bow-legs: and little, sharp, ugly eyes. His hat was stuck on the top of his head so lightly, that it threatened to fall off every moment; and would have done so, very often, if the wearer had not had a knack of every now and then giving his head a sudden twitch: which brought it back to its old place again. He wore a man's coat, which reached nearly to his heels. He had turned the cuffs back, halfway up his arm, to get his hands out of the sleeves: apparently with the ultimate view of thrusting them into the pockets of his corduroy trousers; for there he kept them. He was, altogether, as roystering and swaggering a young gentleman as ever stood four feet six, or something less, in his bluchers.[6]

"Hullo, my covey, what's the row?" said this strange young gentleman to Oliver.

"I am very hungry and tired," replied Oliver: the tears standing in his eyes as he spoke. "I have walked a long way. I have been walking these seven days."

"Walking for sivin days!" said the young gentleman. "Oh, I see. Beak's[7] order, eh? But," he added, noticing Oliver's look of surprise, "I suppose you don't know what a beak is, my flash com-pan-i-on."

Oliver mildly replied, that he had always heard a bird's mouth described by the term in question.

"My eyes, how green!" exclaimed the young gentleman. "Why, a beak's a madgst'rate; and when you walk by a beak's order, it's not straight forerd, but always agoing up, and nivir acoming down agin. Was you never on the mill?"[8]

"What mill?" inquired Oliver.

"What mill!—why, *the* mill—the mill as takes up so little room that it'll work inside a Stone Jug; and always goes better when the wind's low with people, than when it's high: acos then they can't get workmen. But come," said the young gentleman; "you want grub, and you shall have it. I'm at low-water-mark myself—only one bob and a magpie; but, *as*

4. Fellow
5. Short for.
6. Half-boots made of leather. "Roystering": blustering (usually spelled "roistering").
7. Magistrate's.
8. The treadmill; a circular machine worked by prisoners in British jails.

far *as* it goes, I'll fork out and stump. Up with you on your pins. There! Now then! Morrice!"[9]

Assisting Oliver to rise, the young gentleman took him to an adjacent chandler's shop:[1] where he purchased a sufficiency of ready-dressed ham and a half-quartern loaf: or, as he himself expressed it, "a fourpenny bran;" the ham being kept clean and preserved from dust, by the ingenious expedient of making a hole in the loaf by pulling out a portion of the crumb, and stuffing it therein. Taking the bread under his arm, the young gentleman turned into a small public-house: and led the way to a tap-room in the rear of the premises. Here, a pot of beer was brought in, by direction of the mysterious youth; and Oliver: falling to, at his new friend's bidding: made a long and hearty meal; during the progress of which, the strange boy eyed him from time to time with great attention.

"Going to London?" said the strange boy, when Oliver had at length concluded.

"Yes."

"Got any lodgings?"

"No."

"Money?"

"No."

The strange boy whistled; and put his arms into his pockets, as far as the big coat sleeves would let them go.

"Do you live in London?" inquired Oliver.

"Yes, I do, when I'm at home," replied the boy. "I suppose you want some place to sleep in to-night, don't you?"

"I do indeed," answered Oliver. "I have not slept under a roof since I left the country."

"Don't fret your eyelids on that score," said the young gentleman, "I've got to be in London to-night; and I know a 'spectable old genelman as lives there, wot'll give you lodgings for nothink, and never ask for the change; that is, if any genelman he knows interduces you. And don't he know me? Oh, no! Not in the least! By no means. Certainly not!"

The young gentleman smiled, as if to intimate that the latter fragments of discourse were playfully ironical; and finished the beer as he did so.

This unexpected offer of shelter, was too tempting to be resisted: especially as it was immediately followed up, by the assurance that the old gentleman already referred to, would doubtless provide Oliver with a comfortable place, without loss of time. This led to a more friendly and confidential dialogue; from which Oliver discovered that his friend's name was Jack Dawkins: and that he was a peculiar pet and *protégé* of the elderly gentleman before mentioned.

9. Make haste. "One bob and a magpie": a shilling and a halfpenny. "Fork out and stump": pay up.
1. A shop that sells candles and other household goods and foods.

Mr. Dawkins's appearance did not say a vast deal in favour of the comforts which his patron's interest obtained for those whom he took under his protection; but as he had a rather flighty and dissolute mode of conversing: and furthermore avowed that among his intimate friends he was better known by the *sobriquet*[2] of "The artful Dodger:" Oliver concluded that, being of a dissipated and careless turn, the moral precepts of his benefactor had hitherto been thrown away upon him. Under this impression, he secretly resolved to cultivate the good opinion of the old gentleman as quickly as possible; and, if he found the Dodger incorrigible, as he more than half suspected he should, to decline the honour of his farther acquaintance.

As John Dawkins objected to their entering London before nightfall, it was nearly eleven o'clock when they reached the turnpike at Islington. They crossed from the Angel into St. John's-road; struck down the small street which terminates at Sadler's Wells Theatre; through Exmouth-street and Coppice-row; down the little court by the side of the work-house; across the classic ground which once bore the name of Hockley-in-the-Hole; thence into Little Saffron-hill; and so into Saffron-hill the Great:[3] along which, the Dodger scudded at a rapid pace: directing Oliver to follow close at his heels.

Although Oliver had enough to occupy his attention in keeping sight of his leader, he could not help bestowing a few hasty glances on either side of the way, as he passed along. A dirtier or more wretched place he had never seen. The street was very narrow and muddy; and the air was impregnated with filthy odours. There were a good many small shops; but the only stock in trade appeared to be heaps of children, who, even at that time of night, were crawling in and out at the doors, or screaming from the inside. The sole places that seemed to prosper, amid the general blight of the place, were the public-houses; and in them, the lowest orders of Irish were wrangling with might and main. Covered ways and yards, which here and there diverged from the main street, disclosed little knots of houses, where drunken men and women were positively wallowing in the filth; and from several of the door-ways, great ill-looking fellows were cautiously emerging: bound, to all appearance, on no very well-disposed or harmless errands.

Oliver was just considering whether he hadn't better run away, when they reached the bottom of the hill. His conductor, catching him by the arm, pushed open the door of a house near Field-lane; and, drawing him into the passage, closed it behind them.

2. Nickname.
3. The route that Oliver and the Artful Dodger take is the most frequently used nineteenth-century route into London from the northeast; Islington is the terminus of the turnpike and Angel the main marker of the entry into London. From Angel, they descend through London streets southward into the slums of the East End. Saffron-hill was notorious for filth and criminality; the "classic ground" of Hockley-in-the-Hole refers to the old "bear-garden" on the site, a small arena used in the seventeenth and eighteenth centuries for cock-fighting, animal baiting, and boxing matches.

"Now, then!" cried a voice from below, in reply to a whistle from the Dodger.

"Plummy and slam!"[4] was the reply.

This seemed to be some watchword or signal that all was right; for the light of a feeble candle gleamed on the wall at the remote end of the passage; and a man's face peeped out, from where a balustrade of the old kitchen staircase had been broken away.

"There's two on you," said the man, thrusting the candle farther out, and shading his eyes with his hand. "Who's the t'other one?"

"A new pal," replied Jack Dawkins, pulling Oliver forward.

"Where did he come from?"

"Greenland. Is Fagin up stairs?"

"Yes, he's a sortin' the wipes.[5] Up with you!" The candle was drawn back; and the face disappeared.

Oliver, groping his way with one hand; and having the other firmly grasped by his companion; ascended with much difficulty the dark and broken stairs: which his conductor mounted with an ease and expedition that showed he was well acquainted with them. He threw open the door of a back-room, and drew Oliver in after him.

The walls and ceiling of the room were perfectly black, with age and dirt. There was a deal table[6] before the fire: upon which were a candle, stuck in a ginger-beer bottle: two or three pewter pots: a loaf and butter: and a plate. In a frying-pan which was on the fire, and which was secured to the mantelshelf by a string, some sausages were cooking; and standing over them, with a toasting-fork in his hand, was a very old shrivelled Jew, whose villanous-looking and repulsive face was obscured by a quantity of matted red hair. He was dressed in a greasy flannel gown, with his throat bare; and seemed to be dividing his attention between the frying-pan and a clothes-horse: over which a great number of silk handkerchiefs were hanging. Several rough beds made of old sacks, were huddled side by side on the floor; and seated round the table were four or five boys: none older than the Dodger: smoking long clay pipes, and drinking spirits, with the air of middle-aged men. These all crowded about their associate as he whispered a few words to the Jew; and then turned round and grinned at Oliver; as did the Jew himself: toasting-fork in hand.

"This is him, Fagin," said Jack Dawkins; "my friend Oliver Twist."

The Jew grinned; and, making a low obeisance to Oliver, took him by the hand; and hoped he should have the honour of his intimate acquaintance. Upon this, the young gentlemen with the pipes came round him, and shook both his hands very hard—especially the one in which he held his little bundle. One young gentleman was very anxious

4. A password meaning "all right."
5. Pocket handkerchiefs. "Greenland": the country of greenhorns, or rural innocents.
6. A table made of pinewood planks.

to hang up his cap for him; and another was so obliging as to put his hands in his pockets: in order that, as he was very tired, he might not have the trouble of emptying them, himself, when he went to bed. These civilities would probably have been extended much further, but for a liberal exercise of the Jew's toasting-fork on the heads and shoulders of the affectionate youths who offered them.

"We are very glad to see you, Oliver—very," said the Jew. "Dodger, take off the sausages; and draw a tub near the fire for Oliver. Ah, you're a-staring at the pocket-handkerchiefs! eh, my dear? There are a good many of 'em, ain't there? We've just looked 'em out, ready for the wash; that's all, Oliver; that's all. Ha! ha! ha!"

The latter part of this speech, was hailed by a boisterous shout from all the hopeful pupils of the merry old gentleman. In the midst of which, they went to supper.

Oliver ate his share; and the Jew then mixed him a glass of hot gin and water: telling him he must drink it off directly, because another gentleman wanted the tumbler. Oliver did as he was desired. Immediately afterwards, he felt himself gently lifted on to one of the sacks; and then he sunk into a deep sleep.

Chapter IX.

CONTAINING FURTHER PARTICULARS CONCERNING THE PLEASANT OLD GENTLEMAN, AND HIS HOPEFUL PUPILS.

It was late next morning when Oliver awoke, from a sound, long sleep. There was no other person in the room but the old Jew; who was boiling some coffee in a saucepan for breakfast; and whistling softly to himself as he stirred it round and round, with an iron spoon. He would stop every now and then to listen when there was the least noise below; and, when he had satisfied himself, he would go on, whistling and stirring again, as before.

Although Oliver had roused himself from sleep, he was not thoroughly awake. There is a drowsy state, between sleeping and waking, when you dream more in five minutes with your eyes half open, and yourself half conscious of everything that is passing around you, than you would in five nights with your eyes fast closed, and your senses wrapt in perfect unconsciousness. At such times, a mortal knows just enough of what his mind is doing, to form some glimmering conception of its mighty powers: its bounding from earth and spurning time and space: when freed from the restraint of its corporeal associate.[1]

Oliver was precisely in this condition. He saw the Jew with his half-closed eyes; heard his low whistling; and recognised the sound of the

1. Body.

spoon, grating against the saucepan's sides; and yet the self-same senses were mentally engaged, at the same time, in busy action with almost everybody he had ever known.

When the coffee was done, the Jew drew the saucepan to the hob;[2] and, standing in an irresolute attitude for a few minutes, as if he did not well know how to employ himself, turned round and looked at Oliver, and called him by his name. He did not answer; and was to all appearance asleep.

After satisfying himself upon this head, the Jew stepped gently to the door: which he fastened. He then drew forth: as it seemed to Oliver, from some trap in the floor: a small box, which he placed carefully on the table. His eyes glistened as he raised the lid, and looked in. Dragging an old chair to the table, he sat down, and took from it a magnificent gold watch, sparkling with jewels.

"Aha!" said the Jew: shrugging up his shoulders: and distorting every feature with a hideous grin. "Clever dogs! clever dogs! Staunch to the last! Never told the old parson where they were. Never peached upon old Fagin! And why should they? It wouldn't have loosened the knot: or kept the drop up, a minute longer. No, no, no! Fine fellows! Fine fellows!"

With these, and other muttered reflections of the like nature, the Jew once more deposited the watch in its place of safety. At least half a dozen more were severally drawn forth from the same box, and surveyed with equal pleasure; besides rings, brooches, bracelets, and other articles of jewellery: of such magnificent materials, and costly workmanship, that Oliver had no idea, even of their names.

Having replaced these trinkets, the Jew took out another: so small that it lay in the palm of his hand. There seemed to be some very minute inscription on it; for the Jew laid it flat upon the table: and shading it with his hand: pored over it, long and earnestly. At length he put it down, as if despairing of success; and, leaning back in his chair, muttered,

"What a fine thing capital punishment is! Dead men never repent; dead men never bring awkward stories to light. Ah, it's a fine thing for the trade! Five of 'em strung up in a row; and none left to play booty,[3] or turn white-livered!"

As the Jew uttered these words, his bright dark eyes, which had been staring vacantly before him, fell on Oliver's face; the boy's eyes were fixed on his in mute curiosity; and, although the recognition was only for an instant—for the briefest space of time that can possibly be conceived—it was enough to show the old man that he had been observed. He closed the lid of the box with a loud crash; and, laying his hand on a bread knife which was on the table, started furiously up. He

2. A shelf at the side or the back of a fireplace.
3. To betray their accomplices to the police.

trembled very much though; for, even in his terror, Oliver could see that the knife quivered in the air.

"What's that?" said the Jew. "What do you watch me for? Why are you awake? What have you seen? Speak out, boy! Quick—quick! for your life!"

"I wasn't able to sleep any longer, sir," replied Oliver, meekly. "I am very sorry if I have disturbed you, sir."

"You were not awake an hour ago?" said the Jew, scowling fiercely on the boy.

"No—no, indeed," replied Oliver.

"Are you sure?" cried the Jew: with a still fiercer look than before: and a threatening attitude.

"Upon my word I was not, sir," replied Oliver, earnestly. "I was not, indeed, sir."

"Tush, tush, my dear!" said the Jew, abruptly resuming his old manner, and playing with the knife a little, before he laid it down: as if to induce the belief that he had caught it up, in mere sport. "Of course I know that, my dear. I only tried to frighten you. You're a brave boy. Ha! ha! you're a brave boy, Oliver!" The Jew rubbed his hands with a chuckle, but glanced uneasily at the box, notwithstanding.

"Did you see any of these pretty things, my dear?" said the Jew, laying his hand upon it after a short pause.

"Yes, sir," replied Oliver.

"Ah!" said the Jew, turning rather pale. "They—they're mine, Oliver; my little property. All I have to live upon, in my old age. The folks call me a miser, my dear—only a miser; that's all."

Oliver thought the old gentleman must be a decided miser to live in such a dirty place, with so many watches; but, thinking that perhaps his fondness for the Dodger and the other boys, cost him a good deal of money, he only cast a deferential look at the Jew, and asked if he might get up.

"Certainly, my dear—certainly," replied the old gentleman. "Stay. There's a pitcher of water in the corner by the door. Bring it here; and I'll give you a basin to wash in, my dear."

Oliver got up; walked across the room; and stooped for one instant to raise the pitcher. When he turned his head, the box was gone.

He had scarcely washed himself: and made everything tidy, by emptying the basin out of the window, agreeably to the Jew's directions: when the Dodger returned; accompanied by a very sprightly young friend, whom Oliver had seen smoking on the previous night; and who was now formally introduced to him as Charley Bates. The four sat down, to breakfast on the coffee, and some hot rolls and ham, which the Dodger had brought home in the crown of his hat.

"Well," said the Jew, glancing slyly at Oliver, and addressing himself to the Dodger, "I hope you've been at work this morning, my dears?"

"Hard," replied the Dodger.

"As Nails," added Charley Bates.

"Good boys, good boys!" said the Jew. "What have you got, Dodger?"

"A couple of pocket-books," replied that young gentleman.

"Lined?" inquired the Jew, with eagerness.

"Pretty well," replied the Dodger, producing two pocket-books: one green: and the other red.

"Not so heavy as they might be," said the Jew, after looking at the insides carefully; "but very neat and nicely made. Ingenious workman, ain't he, Oliver?"

"Very, indeed, sir," said Oliver. At which Mr. Charles Bates laughed uproariously; very much to the amazement of Oliver, who saw nothing to laugh at, in anything that had passed.

"And what have you got, my dear?" said Fagin to Charley Bates.

"Wipes," replied Master Bates; at the same time producing four pocket-handkerchiefs.

"Well," said the Jew, inspecting them closely; "they're very good ones—very. You haven't marked them well, though, Charley; so the marks[4] shall be picked out with a needle, and we'll teach Oliver how to do it. Shall us, Oliver, eh? Ha! ha! ha!"

"If you please, sir," said Oliver.

"You'd like to be able to make pocket-handkerchiefs as easy as Charley Bates, wouldn't you, my dear?" said the Jew.

"Very much indeed, if you'll teach me, sir," replied Oliver.

Master Bates saw something so exquisitely ludicrous in this reply, that he burst into another laugh; which laugh, meeting the coffee he was drinking, and carrying it down some wrong channel, very nearly terminated in his premature suffocation.

"He is so jolly green!" said Charley when he recovered: as an apology to the company for his unpolite behaviour.

The Dodger said nothing, but he smoothed Oliver's hair down over his eyes, and said he'd know better by-and-bye; upon which the old gentleman, observing Oliver's colour mounting, changed the subject by asking whether there had been much of a crowd at the execution that morning.[5] This made him wonder more and more; for it was plain from the replies of the two boys that they had both been there; and Oliver naturally wondered how they could possibly have found time to be so very industrious.

When the breakfast was cleared away, the merry old gentleman and the two boys played at a very curious and uncommon game, which was performed in this way: The merry old gentleman: placing a snuff-box

---

4. The owner's identifying initials or personal code.
5. Executions were public events in England until 1868. Dickens supported capitol punishment but opposed public executions, which were attended by huge crowds and which attracted pickpockets and other criminals.

in one pocket of his trousers, a note-case in the other, and a watch in his waistcoat pocket: with a guard-chain round his neck: and sticking a mock diamond pin in his shirt: buttoned his coat tight round him, and putting his spectacle-case and handkerchief in his pockets, trotted up and down the room with a stick, in imitation of the manner in which old gentlemen walk about the streets any hour in the day. Sometimes he stopped at the fire-place, and sometimes at the door; making belief that he was staring with all his might into shop-windows. At such times, he would look constantly round him, for fear of thieves; and keep slapping all his pockets in turn, to see that he hadn't lost anything; in such a very funny and natural manner, that Oliver laughed till the tears ran down his face. All this time, the two boys followed him closely about: getting out of his sight, so nimbly, every time he turned round, that it was impossible to follow their motions. At last, the Dodger trod upon his toes, or ran upon his boot accidentally, while Charley Bates stumbled up against him behind; and in that one moment they took from him, with the most extraordinary rapidity, snuff-box, note-case, watch-guard, chain, shirt-pin, pocket-handkerchief; even the spectacle-case. If the old gentleman felt a hand in any one of his pockets, he cried out where it was; and then the game began all over again.

When this game had been played a great many times, a couple of young ladies called to see the young gentlemen; one of whom was named Bet, and the other Nancy. They wore a good deal of hair:[6] not very neatly turned up behind; and were rather untidy about the shoes and stockings. They were not exactly pretty, perhaps; but they had a great deal of colour in their faces; and looked quite stout and hearty. Being remarkably free and agreeable in their manners, Oliver thought them very nice girls indeed. As there is no doubt they were.

These visitors stopped a long time. Spirits were produced, in consequence of one of the young ladies complaining of a coldness in her inside; and the conversation took a very convivial and improving turn. At length, Charley Bates expressed his opinion that it was time to pad the hoof.[7] This, it occurred to Oliver, must be French for going out; for directly afterwards, the Dodger, and Charley, and the two young ladies, went away together, having been kindly furnished by the amiable old Jew with money to spend.

"There, my dear," said Fagin: "That's a pleasant life, isn't it? They have gone out for the day."

"Have they done work, sir?" inquired Oliver.

"Yes," said the Jew; "that is, unless they should unexpectedly come across any, when they are out; and they won't neglect it, if they do, my dear: depend upon it.

6. The amount and disarray of their hair would indicate to Victorian readers their low manners and profession.
7. To go out walking.

"Make 'em your models, my dear. Make 'em your models," said the Jew, tapping the fire-shovel on the hearth to add force to his words; "do everything they bid you, and take their advice in all matters: especially the Dodger's, my dear. He'll be a great man himself; and will make you one too, if you take pattern by him. Is my handkerchief hanging out of my pocket, my dear?" said the Jew, stopping short.

"Yes, sir," said Oliver.

"See if you can take it out, without my feeling it: as you saw them do, when we were at play this morning."

Oliver held up the bottom of the pocket with one hand, as he had seen the Dodger hold it; and drew the handkerchief lightly out of it with the other.

"Is it gone?" cried the Jew.

"Here it is, sir," said Oliver, showing it in his hand.

"You're a clever boy, my dear," said the playful old gentleman, patting Oliver on the head approvingly. "I never saw a sharper lad. Here's a shilling for you. If you go on, in this way, you'll be the greatest man of the time. And now come here; and I'll show you how to take the marks out of the handkerchiefs."

Oliver wondered what picking the old gentleman's pocket in play, had to do with his chances of being a great man. But thinking that the Jew, being so much his senior, must know best, he followed him quietly to the table; and was soon deeply involved in his new study.

Chapter X.

OLIVER BECOMES BETTER ACQUAINTED WITH THE CHARACTERS OF HIS NEW ASSOCIATES; AND PURCHASES EXPERIENCE AT A HIGH PRICE. BEING A SHORT, BUT VERY IMPORTANT CHAPTER, IN THIS HISTORY.

For many days, Oliver remained in the Jew's room, picking the marks out of the pocket handkerchiefs, (of which a great number were brought home,) and sometimes taking part in the game already described: which the two boys and the Jew played, regularly, every morning. At length, he began to languish for the fresh air; and took many occasions of earnestly entreating the old gentleman to allow him to go out to work, with his two companions.

Oliver was rendered the more anxious to be actively employed, by what he had seen of the stern morality of the old gentleman's character. Whenever the Dodger or Charley Bates came home at night, empty-handed, he would expatiate with great vehemence on the misery of idle and lazy habits; and would enforce upon them the necessity of an active life, by sending them supperless to bed. On one occasion, indeed, he

even went so far as to knock them both down a flight of stairs; but this
was carrying out his virtuous precepts to an unusual extent.

At length, one morning, Oliver obtained the permission he had so
eagerly, sought. There had been no handkerchiefs to work upon, for
two or three days; and the dinners had been rather meagre. Perhaps
these were reasons for the old gentleman's giving his assent; but, whether
they were or no, he told Oliver he might go; and placed him under the
joint guardianship of Charley Bates, and his friend the Dodger.

The three boys sallied out; the Dodger with his coat-sleeves tucked
up, and his hat cocked, as usual; Master Bates sauntering along with
his hands in his pockets; and Oliver between them: wondering where
they were going: and what branch of manufacture he would be instructed
in, first.

The pace at which they went, was such a very lazy, ill-looking saunter,
that Oliver soon began to think his companions were going to deceive
the old gentleman, by not going to work at all. The Dodger had a vicious
propensity, too, of pulling the caps from the heads of small boys and
tossing them down areas; while Charley Bates exhibited some very loose
notions concerning the rights of property, by pilfering divers apples and
onions from the stalls at the kennel sides, and thrusting them into pockets
which were so surprisingly capacious, that they seemed to undermine
his whole suit of clothes in every direction. These things looked so bad,
that Oliver was on the point of declaring his intention of seeking his
way back, in the best way he could; when his thoughts were suddenly
directed into another channel, by a very mysterious change of behaviour
on the part of the Dodger.

They were just emerging from a narrow court not far from the open
square in Clerkenwell,[1] which is yet called, by some strange perversion
of terms, "The Green:" when the Dodger made a sudden stop; and,
laying his finger on his lip, drew his companions back again, with the
greatest caution and circumspection.

"What's the matter?" demanded Oliver.

"Hush!" replied the Dodger. "Do you see that old cove at the book-
stall?"

"The old gentleman over the way?" said Oliver. "Yes, I see him."

"He'll do," said the Dodger.

"A prime plant," observed Master Charley Bates.

Oliver looked from one to the other, with the greatest surprise; but
he was not permitted to make any inquiries; for the two boys walked
stealthily across the road, and slunk close behind the old gentleman
towards whom his attention had been directed. Oliver walked a few
paces after them; and, not knowing whether to advance or retire, stood
looking on in silent amazement.

1. A London suburb close to the City, or main business area, known for its small jewelry and
   clock-making shops.

The old gentleman was a very respectable-looking personage, with a powdered head and gold spectacles. He was dressed in a bottle-green[2] coat with a black velvet collar; wore white trousers; and carried a smart bamboo cane under his arm. He had taken up a book from the stall; and there he stood: reading away, as hard as if he were in his elbow-chair, in his own study. It is very possible that he fancied himself there, indeed; for it was plain, from his utter abstraction, that he saw not the book-stall, nor the street, nor the boys, nor, in short, anything but the book itself; which he was reading straight through; turning over the leaf when he got to the bottom of a page; beginning at the top line of the next one; and going regularly on, with the greatest interest and eagerness.

What was Oliver's horror and alarm as he stood a few paces off, looking on with his eyelids as wide open as they would possibly go, to see the Dodger plunge his hand into the old gentleman's pocket; and draw from thence a handkerchief! To see him hand the same to Charley Bates; and finally to behold them, both, running away round the corner at full speed!

In an instant the whole mystery of the handkerchiefs, and the watches, and the jewels, and the Jew, rushed upon the boy's mind. He stood, for a moment, with the blood so tingling through all his veins from terror, that he felt as if he were in a burning fire; then, confused and frightened, he took to his heels; and, not knowing what he did, made off as fast as he could lay his feet to the ground.

This was all done in a minute's space. In the very instant when Oliver began to run; the old gentleman, putting his hand to his pocket, and missing his handkerchief, turned sharp round. Seeing the boy scudding away at such a rapid pace, he very naturally concluded him to be the depredator;[3] and, shouting "Stop thief!" with all his might, made off after him, book in hand.

But the old gentleman was not the only person who raised the hue-and-cry. The Dodger and Master Bates, unwilling to attract public attention by running down the open street, had merely retired into the very first doorway round the corner. They no sooner heard the cry, and saw Oliver running, than, guessing exactly how the matter stood, they issued forth with great promptitude; and, shouting "Stop thief!" too, joined in the pursuit like good citizens.

Although Oliver had been brought up by philosophers, he was not theoretically acquainted with the beautiful axiom that self-preservation is the first law of nature. If he had been, perhaps he would have been prepared for this. Not being prepared, however, it alarmed him the more; so away he went like the wind: with the old gentleman and the two boys, roaring and shouting behind him.

"Stop thief! Stop thief!" There is a magic in the sound. The tradesman

2. A dark green color, as in a standard glass used for bottles.
3. Plunderer.

leaves his counter; and the carman his waggon; the butcher throws down his tray; the baker his basket; the milk-man his pail; the errand-boy his parcels; the schoolboy his marbles; the paviour his pick-axe; the child his battledore.[4] Away they run, pell-mell, helter-skelter, slap-dash: tearing, yelling, and screaming: knocking down the passengers as they turn the corners: rousing up the dogs, and astonishing the fowls; and streets, squares, and courts, re-echo with the sound.

"Stop thief! Stop thief!" The cry is taken up by a hundred voices; and the crowd accumulate at every turning. Away they fly: splashing through the mud, and rattling along the pavements; up go the windows; out run the people; onward bear the mob; a whole audience desert Punch[5] in the very thickest of the plot; and, joining the rushing throng, swell the shout: and lend fresh vigour to the cry, "Stop thief! Stop thief!"

"Stop thief! Stop thief!" There is a passion *for hunting something* deeply implanted in the human breast. One wretched breathless child, panting with exhaustion; terror in his looks; agony in his eye; large drops of perspiration streaming down his face; strains every nerve to make head upon his pursuers; and as they follow on his track, and gain upon him every instant, they hail his decreasing strength with still louder shouts: and whoop and scream with joy. "Stop thief!" Ay, stop him for God's sake, were it only in mercy!

Stopped at last. A clever blow. He is down upon the pavement; and the crowd eagerly gather round him: each new comer, jostling and struggling with the others to catch a glimpse. "Stand aside!" "Give him a little air!" "Nonsense! he don't deserve it." "Where's the gentleman?" "Here he is, coming down the street." "Make room there for the gentleman!" "Is this the boy, sir!" "Yes."

Oliver lay, covered with mud and dust: and bleeding from the mouth, looking wildly round upon the heap of faces that surrounded him: when the old gentleman was officiously dragged and pushed into the circle by the foremost of the pursuers.

"Yes," said the gentleman, "I am afraid it is."

"Afraid!" murmured the crowd. "That's a good 'un."

"Poor fellow!" said the gentleman, "he has hurt himself."

"*I* did that, sir," said a great lubberly fellow, stepping forward; "and preciously I cut my knuckle agin' his mouth. *I* stopped him, sir."

The fellow touched his hat with a grin: expecting something for his pains; but the old gentleman, eyeing him with an expression of dislike, looked anxiously round, as if he contemplated running away himself: which it is very possible he might have attempted to do, and thus afforded another chase, had not a police officer (who is generally the last person to arrive in such cases) at that moment made his way through the crowd, and seized Oliver by the collar.

4. A small racket used in playing badminton. "Paviour": a workman who lays paving stones.
5. Punch and Judy outdoor puppet shows.

"Come, get up," said the man, roughly.

"It wasn't me indeed, sir. Indeed, indeed, it was two other boys," said Oliver: clasping his hands passionately, and looking round. "They are here somewhere."

"Oh no, they ain't," said the officer. He meant this to be ironical, but it was true besides; for the Dodger and Charley Bates had filed off down the first convenient court they came to. "Come, get up!"

"Don't hurt him," said the old gentleman, compassionately.

"Oh no, I won't hurt him," replied the officer, tearing his jacket half off his back, in proof thereof. "Come, I know you; it won't do. Will you stand upon your legs, you young devil?"

Oliver, who could hardly stand, made a shift to raise himself on his feet; and was at once lugged along the streets by the jacket-collar, at a rapid pace. The gentleman walked on with them by the officer's side; and as many of the crowd as could achieve the feat, got a little a-head, and stared back at Oliver from time to time. The boys shouted in triumph; and on they went.

Chapter XI.

TREATS OF MR. FANG THE POLICE MAGISTRATE; AND FURNISHES A
SLIGHT SPECIMEN OF HIS MODE OF ADMINISTERING JUSTICE.

The offence had been committed within the district, and indeed in the immediate neighbourhood of, a very notorious metropolitan police office. The crowd had only the satisfaction of accompanying Oliver through two or three streets, and down a place called Mutton-hill, when he was led beneath a low archway, and up a dirty court, into this dispensary of summary justice, by the back way. It was a small paved yard into which they turned; and here, they encountered a stout man with a bunch of whiskers on his face, and a bunch of keys in his hand.

"What's the matter now?" said the man carelessly.

"A young fogle-hunter,"[1] replied the man who had Oliver in charge.

"Are you the party that's been robbed, sir?" inquired the man with the keys.

"Yes, I am," replied the old gentleman; "but I am not sure that this boy actually took the handkerchief. I—I would rather not press the case."

"Must go before the magistrate now, sir," replied the man. "His worship will be disengaged in half a minute. Now, young gallows."

This was an invitation for Oliver to enter through a door which he unlocked as he spoke: and which led into a small stone cell. Here he was searched; and, nothing being found upon him, locked up.

---

1. A pocket-handkerchief thief.

This cell was in shape and size, something like an area cellar, only not so light. It was most intolerably dirty; for it was Monday morning; and it had been tenanted by six drunken people, who had been locked up elsewhere since Saturday night. But this is little. In our station-houses, men and women are every night confined on the most trivial *charges*—the word is worth noting—in dungeons, compared with which, those in Newgate,[2] occupied by the most atrocious felons: tried, found guilty, and under sentence of death: are palaces. Let any man who doubts this, compare the two.

The old gentleman looked almost as rueful as Oliver when the key grated in the lock. He turned with a sigh to the book, which had been the innocent cause of all this disturbance.

"There is something in that boy's face," said the old gentleman to himself as he walked slowly away: tapping his chin with the cover of the book, in a thoughtful manner; "something that touches and interests me. *Can* he be innocent? He looked like—. By the bye," exclaimed the old gentleman, halting very abruptly, and staring up into the sky, "Bless my soul!—where have I seen something like that look before?"

After musing for some minutes, the old gentleman walked, with the same meditative face, into a back ante-room opening from the yard; and there, retiring into a corner, called up before his mind's eye a vast amphitheatre of faces over which a dusky curtain had hung for many years. "No," said the old gentleman, shaking his head; "it must be imagination."

He wandered over them again. He had called them into view; and it was not easy to replace the shroud that had so long concealed them. There were the faces of friends, and foes: and of many that had been almost strangers: peering intrusively from the crowd; there were the faces of young and blooming girls that were now old women; there were faces that the grave had changed and closed upon, but which the mind, superior to its power, still dressed in their old freshness and beauty: calling back the lustre of the eyes, the brightness of the smile, the beaming of the soul through its mask of clay: and whispering of beauty beyond the tomb, changed but to be heightened, and taken from earth only to be set up as a light, to shed a soft and gentle glow upon the path to Heaven.

But the old gentleman could recall no one countenance of which Oliver's features bore a trace. So he heaved a sigh over the recollections he had awakened; and being, happily for himself, an absent old gentleman, buried them again in the pages of the musty book.

He was roused by a touch on the shoulder, and a request from the man with the keys to follow him into the office. He closed his book

2. The main prison in central London.

hastily; and was at once ushered into the imposing presence of the renowned Mr. Fang.[3]

The office was a front parlour, with a panelled wall. Mr. Fang sat behind a bar at the upper end; and on one side the door was a sort of wooden pen in which poor little Oliver was already deposited: trembling very much at the awfulness of the scene.

Mr. Fang was a lean, long-backed, stiff-necked, middle-sized man, with no great quantity of hair: and what he had, growing on the back and sides of his head. His face was stern, and much flushed. If he were really not in the habit of drinking rather more than was exactly good for him, he might have brought an action against his countenance for libel, and have recovered heavy damages.

The old gentleman bowed respectfully; and, advancing to the magistrate's desk, said, suiting the action to the word, "That is my name and address, sir." He then withdrew a pace or two; and, with another polite and gentlemanly inclination of the head, waited to be questioned.

Now, it so happened that Mr. Fang was at that moment perusing a leading article in a newspaper of the morning, adverting to some recent decision of his; and commending him, for the three hundred and fiftieth time, to the special and particular notice of the Secretary of State for the Home Department.[4] He was out of temper; and he looked up with an angry scowl."

"Who are you?" said Mr. Fang.

The old gentleman pointed, with some surprise, to his card.

"Officer!" said Mr. Fang, tossing the card contemptuously away with the newspaper, "who is this fellow?"

"My name, sir," said the old gentleman, speaking *like* a gentleman, "my name, sir, is Brownlow. Permit me to inquire the name of the magistrate who offers a gratuitous and unprovoked insult to a respectable person: under the protection of the bench." Saying this, Mr. Brownlow looked round the office as if in search of some person who would afford him the required information.

"Officer!" said Mr. Fang, throwing the paper on one side, "what's this fellow charged with?"

"He's not charged at all, your worship," replied the officer. "He appears against the boy, your worship."

His worship knew this perfectly well; but it was a good annoyance, and a safe one.

3. The model for Magistrate Fang was the notoriously severe Hatton Garden magistrate Allan Stewart Laing (1788–1862), who presided at the "very notorious metropolitan police office" at 54 Hatton Garden referred to at the beginning of the chapter. Dickens went anonymously to observe him. Laing was soon dismissed from the bench, though the precipitating factors had no connection to Dickens' portrayal of him in *Oliver Twist*.

4. The government department responsible for the judiciary system and internal security.

"Appears against the boy, does he?" said Fang, surveying Mr. Brownlow contemptuously from head to foot. "Swear him!"

"Before I am sworn, I must beg to say one word," said Mr. Brownlow: "and that is, that I really never, without actual experience, could have believed—"

"Hold your tongue, sir!" said Mr. Fang peremptorily.

"I will not, sir!" replied the old gentleman.

"Hold your tongue this instant, or I'll have you turned out of the office!" said Mr. Fang. "You're an insolent, impertinent fellow. How dare you bully a magistrate!"

"What!" exclaimed the old gentleman, reddening.

"Swear this person!" said Fang to the clerk. "I'll not hear another word. Swear him."

Mr. Brownlow's indignation was greatly roused; but, reflecting perhaps, that he might only injure the boy by giving vent to it, he suppressed his feelings, and submitted to be sworn at once.

"Now," said Fang, "what's the charge against this boy? What have you got to say, sir?"

"I was standing at a book-stall—" Mr. Brownlow began.

"Hold your tongue, sir!" said Mr. Fang. "Policeman! Where's the policeman? Here, swear this policeman. Now, policeman, what is this?"

The policeman with becoming humility related how he had taken the charge; how he had searched Oliver, and found nothing on his person; and how that was all he knew about it.

"Are there any witnesses?" inquired Mr. Fang.

"None, your worship," replied the policeman.

Mr. Fang sat silent for some minutes, and then, turning round to the prosecutor, said in a towering passion,

"Do you mean to state what your complaint against this boy is, fellow, or do you not? You have been sworn. Now, if you stand there, refusing to give evidence, I'll punish you for disrespect to the bench; I will, by—"

By what or by whom, nobody knows; for the clerk and jailer coughed very loud just at the right moment; and the former dropped a heavy book upon the floor: thus preventing the word from being heard— accidentally, of course.

With many interruptions, and repeated insults, Mr. Brownlow contrived to state his case; observing that, in the surprise of the moment, he had run after the boy because he saw him running away; and expressing his hope that, if the magistrate should believe him, although not actually the thief, to be connected with thieves; he would deal as leniently with him as justice would allow.

"He has been hurt already," said the old gentleman in conclusion.

"And I fear," he added, with great energy, looking towards the bar, "I really fear that he is very ill."

"Oh! yes; I dare say!" said Mr. Fang, with a sneer. "Come; none of your tricks here, you young vagabond; they won't do. What's your name?"

Oliver tried to reply, but his tongue failed him. He was deadly pale; and the whole place seemed turning round and round.

"What's your name, you hardened scoundrel?" demanded Mr. Fang. "Officer, what's his name?"

This was addressed to a bluff old fellow, in a striped waistcoat: who was standing by the bar. He bent over Oliver, and repeated the inquiry; but finding him really incapable of understanding the question; and knowing that his not replying would only infuriate the magistrate the more, and add to the severity of his sentence; he hazarded a guess.

"He says his name's Tom White, your worship," said this kind-hearted thief-taker.

"Oh, he won't speak out, won't he?" said Fang. "Very well, very well. Where does he live?"

"Where he can, your worship," replied the officer: again pretending to receive Oliver's answer.

"Has he any parents?" inquired Mr. Fang.

"He says they died in his infancy, your worship," replied the officer: hazarding the usual reply.

At this point of the inquiry, Oliver raised his head; and, looking round with imploring eyes, murmured a feeble prayer for a draught of water.

"Stuff and nonsense!" said Mr. Fang: "don't try to make a fool of me."

"I think he really is ill, your worship," remonstrated the officer.

"I know better," said Mr. Fang.

"Take care of him, officer," said the old gentleman, raising his hands instinctively; "he'll fall down."

"Stand away, officer," cried Fang; "let him, if he likes."

Oliver availed himself of the kind permission; and fell heavily to the floor in a fainting fit. The men in the office looked at each other, but no one dared to stir.

"I knew he was shamming," said Fang, as if this were incontestable proof of the fact. "Let him lie there; he'll soon be tired of that."

"How do you propose to deal with the case, sir?" inquired the clerk in a low voice.

"Summarily," replied Mr. Fang. "He stands committed for three months,—hard labour of course. Clear the office."

The door was opened for this purpose; and a couple of men were preparing to carry the insensible boy to his cell; when an elderly man of decent but poor appearance, clad in an old suit of black, rushed hastily into the office: and advanced towards the bench.

"Stop, stop! Don't take him away! For Heaven's sake stop a moment!" cried the new-comer: breathless with haste.

Although the presiding Genii in such an office as this, exercise a summary and arbitrary power over the liberties, the good name, the character, almost the lives of Her Majesty's subjects, especially of the poorer class; and although, within such walls, enough fantastic tricks are daily played to make the angels blind with weeping, they are closed to the public, save through the medium of the daily press. Mr. Fang was consequently not a little indignant to see an unbidden guest enter in such irreverent disorder.

"What is this? Who is this? Turn this man out. Clear the office!" cried Mr. Fang.

"I will speak," cried the man; "I will not be turned out. I saw it all. I keep the book-stall. I demand to be sworn. I will not be put down. Mr. Fang, you must hear me. You must not refuse, sir."

The man was right. His manner was bold and determined; and the matter was growing rather too serious to be hushed up.

"Swear the fellow," growled Fang with a very ill grace. "Now, man, what have you got to say?"

"This," said the man: "I saw three boys: two others and the prisoner here: loitering on the opposite side of the way, when this gentleman was reading. The robbery was committed by another boy. I saw it done; and I saw that this boy was perfectly amazed and stupified by it." Having by this time recovered a little breath, the worthy book-stall keeper proceeded to relate, in a more coherent manner, the exact circumstances of the robbery.

"Why didn't you come here before?" said Fang, after a pause.

"I hadn't a soul to mind the shop," replied the man. "Everybody who could have helped me, had joined in the pursuit. I could get nobody till five minutes ago; and I've run here all the way."

"The prosecutor was reading, was he?" inquired Fang, after another pause.

"Yes," replied the man. "The very book he has in his hand."

"Oh, that book, eh?" said Fang. "Is it paid for?"

"No, it is not," replied the man, with a smile.

"Dear me, I forgot all about it!" exclaimed the absent old gentleman, innocently.

"A nice person to prefer a charge against a poor boy!" said Fang, with a comical effort to look humane. "I consider, sir, that you have obtained possession of that book, under very suspicious and disreputable circumstances; and you may think yourself very fortunate that the owner of the property declines to prosecute. Let this be a lesson to you, my man, or the law will overtake you yet. The boy is discharged. Clear the office."

"D—n me!" cried the old gentleman, bursting out with the rage he had kept down so long, "d—me! I'll—"

"Clear the office!" said the magistrate. "Officers, do you hear? Clear the office!"

The mandate was obeyed; and the indignant Mr. Brownlow was conveyed out: with the book in one hand, and the bamboo cane in the other: in a perfect phrenzy of rage and defiance. He reached the yard; and it vanished in a moment. Little Oliver Twist lay on his back on the pavement, with his shirt unbuttoned, and his temples bathed with water; his face a deadly white; and a cold tremble convulsing his whole frame.

"Poor boy, poor boy!" said Mr. Brownlow, bending over him. "Call a coach, somebody, pray. Directly!"

A coach was obtained, and Oliver, having been carefully laid on one seat, the old gentleman got in and sat himself on the other.

"May I accompany you?" said the book-stall keeper, looking in.

"Bless me, yes, my dear friend," said Mr. Brownlow quickly. "I forgot you. Dear, dear! I have this unhappy book still. Jump in. Poor fellow! there's no time to lose."

The book-stall keeper got into the coach; and away they drove.

Chapter XII.

IN WHICH OLIVER IS TAKEN BETTER CARE OF, THAN HE EVER WAS
BEFORE. AND IN WHICH THE NARRATIVE REVERTS TO THE MERRY OLD
GENTLEMAN AND HIS YOUTHFUL FRIENDS.

The coach rattled away, down Mount Pleasant and up Exmouth-street, over nearly the same ground as that which Oliver had traversed when he first entered London in company with the Dodger; and, turning a different way when it reached the Angel at Islington, stopped at length before a neat house, in a quiet shady street near Pentonville.[1] Here, a bed was prepared, without loss of time, in which Mr. Brownlow saw his young charge carefully and comfortably deposited; and here, he was tended with a kindness and solicitude that knew no bounds.

But, for many days, Oliver remained insensible to all the goodness of his new friends. The sun rose and sunk, and rose and sunk again, and many times after that; and still the boy lay stretched on his uneasy bed: dwindling away beneath the dry and wasting heat of fever. The worm does not his work more surely on the dead body, than does this slow creeping fire upon the living frame.

Weak, and thin, and pallid, he awoke at last from what seemed to have been a long and troubled dream. Feebly raising himself in the bed, with his head resting on his trembling arm, he looked anxiously round.

1. A fashionable suburb in North London immediately north of Clerkenwell.

"What room is this? Where have I been brought to?" said Oliver. "This is not the place I went to sleep in."

He uttered these words in a feeble voice: being very faint and weak; but they were overheard at once; for the curtain at the bed's head was hastily drawn back: and a motherly old lady, very neatly and precisely dressed, rose as she undrew it, from an arm-chair close by, in which she had been sitting at needle-work.

"Hush, my dear," said the old lady softly, "You must be very quiet, or you will be ill again; and you have been very bad,—as bad as bad could be, pretty nigh. Lie down again; there's a dear!" With these words, the old lady very gently placed Oliver's head upon the pillow; and, smoothing back his hair from his forehead, looked so kindly and lovingly in his face, that he could not help placing his little withered hand on hers, and drawing it round his neck.

"Save us!" said the old lady, with tears in her eyes, "what a grateful little dear it is. Pretty creetur! what would his mother feel if she had sat by him as I have, and could see him now!"

"Perhaps she does see me," whispered Oliver, folding his hands together; "perhaps she has sat by me. I almost feel as if she had."

"That was the fever, my dear," said the old lady mildly.

"I suppose it was," replied Oliver, "because Heaven is a long way off; and they are too happy there, to come down to the bedside of a poor boy. But if she knew I was ill, she must have pitied me, even there; for she was very ill herself before she died. She can't know anything about me though," added Oliver after a moment's silence. "If she had seen me hurt, it would have made her sorrowful; and her face has always looked sweet and happy, when I have dreamed of her."

The old lady made no reply to this; but wiping her eyes first: and her spectacles, which lay on the counterpane, afterwards: as if they were part and parcel of those features; brought some cool stuff[2] for Oliver to drink; and then, patting him on the cheek, told him he must lie very quiet, or he would be ill again.

So, Oliver kept very still; partly because he was anxious to obey the kind old lady in all things; and partly, to tell the truth, because he was completely exhausted with what he had already said. He soon fell into a gentle doze, from which he was awakened by the light of a candle: which, being brought near the bed, showed him a gentleman, with a very large and loud-ticking gold watch in his hand: who felt his pulse, and said he was a great deal better.

"You *are* a great deal better, are you not, my dear?" said the gentleman.

"Yes, thank you, sir," replied Oliver.

2. A drink usually composed of wine, water, lemon, and spices. "Counterpane": bedspread.

"Yes, I know you are," said the gentleman: "You're hungry too, an't you?"

"No, sir," answered Oliver.

"Hem!" said the gentleman. "No, I know you're not. He is not hungry, Mrs. Bedwin," said the gentleman: looking very wise.

The old lady made a respectful inclination of the head, which seemed to say that she thought the doctor was a very clever man. The doctor appeared very much of the same opinion himself.

"You feel sleepy, don't you, my dear?" said the doctor.

"No, sir," replied Oliver.

"No," said the doctor with a very shrewd and satisfied look. "You're not sleepy. Nor thirsty. Are you?"

"Yes, sir, rather thirsty," answered Oliver.

"Just as I expected, Mrs. Bedwin," said the doctor. "It's very natural that he should be thirsty. You may give him a little tea, ma'am, and some dry toast without any butter. Don't keep him too warm, ma'am; but be careful that you don't let him be too cold—will you have the goodness?"

The old lady dropped a curtsey. The doctor, after tasting the cool stuff, and expressing a qualified approval thereof, hurried away: his boots creaking in a very important and wealthy manner as he went down stairs.

Oliver dozed off again, soon after this; and when he awoke, it was nearly twelve o'clock. The old lady tenderly bade him good-night shortly afterwards; and left him in charge of a fat old woman who had just come: bringing with her, in a little bundle, a small Prayer Book and a large nightcap. Putting the latter on her head, and the former on the table, the old woman, after telling Oliver that she had come to sit up with him, drew her chair close to the fire and went off into a series of short naps: chequered at frequent intervals with sundry tumblings forward, and divers moans and chokings: which, however, had no worse effect than causing her to rub her nose very hard, and then fall asleep again.

And thus the night crept slowly on. Oliver lay awake for some time, counting the little circles of light which the reflection of the rushlight-shade[3] threw upon the ceiling; or tracing with his languid eyes the intricate pattern of the paper on the wall. The darkness and deep stillness of the room were very solemn; and as they brought into the boy's mind the thought that death had been hovering there, for many days and nights, and might yet fill it with the gloom and dread of his awful presence, he turned his face upon the pillow, and fervently prayed to Heaven.

Gradually, he fell into that deep tranquil sleep which ease from recent

---

3. A candle made from tallow and the stalk of a rush plant.

suffering alone imparts; that calm and peaceful rest which it is pain to wake from. Who, if this were death, would be roused again to all the struggles and turmoils of life; to all its cares for the present; its anxieties for the future; more than all, its weary recollections of the past!

It had been bright day, for hours, when Oliver opened his eyes; and when he did so, he felt cheerful and happy. The crisis of the disease was safely past. He belonged to the world again.

In three days' time, he was able to sit in an easy-chair, well propped up with pillows; and, as he was still too weak to walk, Mrs. Bedwin had him carried down stairs into the little housekeeper's room, which belonged to her: where, having sat him up by the fireside, the good old lady sat herself down too; and, being in a state of considerable delight at seeing him so much better, forthwith began to cry most violently.

"Never mind me, my dear," said the old lady. "I'm only having a regular good cry. There; it's all over now; and I'm quite comfortable."

"You're very, very, kind to me, ma'am," said Oliver.

"Well, never you mind that, my dear," said the old lady; "that's got nothing to do with your broth; and it's full time you had it; for the doctor says Mr. Brownlow may come in to see you this morning: and we must get up our best looks, because the better we look, the more he'll be pleased." And with this, the old lady applied herself to warming up in a little saucepan a basin full of broth: strong enough to furnish an ample dinner, when reduced to the regulation strength: for three hundred and fifty paupers, at the very lowest computation.

"Are you fond of pictures, dear?" inquired the old lady, seeing that Oliver had fixed his eyes, most intently, on a portrait which hung against the wall: just opposite his chair.

"I don't quite know, ma'am," said Oliver, without taking his eyes from the canvas; "I have seen so few that I hardly know. What a beautiful, mild face that lady's is!"

"Ah!" said the old lady, "painters always make ladies out prettier than they are, or they wouldn't get any custom, child. The man that invented the machine for taking likenesses[4] might have known *that* would never succeed; it's a deal too honest. A deal!" said the old lady, laughing very heartily at her own acuteness.

"Is—is that a likeness, ma'am?" said Oliver.

"Yes," said the old lady, looking up for a moment from the broth; "that's a portrait."

"Whose, ma'am?" asked Oliver eagerly.

"Why, really, my dear, I don't know," answered the old lady in a good-humoured manner. "It's not a likeness of anybody that you or I know, I expect. It seems to strike your fancy, dear."

4. Images, created by a machine, prior to the invention of photography, that used the process of heliography (which involved a metallic plate and oil of lavender) to create a faint image after a long exposure. "Custom": business.

"It is so very pretty," replied Oliver.

"Why, sure you're not afraid of it?" said the old lady: observing, in great surprise, the look of awe with which the child regarded the painting.

"Oh no, no," returned Oliver quickly; "but the eyes look so sorrowful; and where I sit, they seem fixed upon me. It makes my heart beat," added Oliver in a low voice, "as if it was alive, and wanted to speak to me, but couldn't."

"Lord save us!" exclaimed the old lady, starting; "don't talk in that way, child. You're weak and nervous after your illness. Let me wheel your chair round to the other side; and then you won't see it. There!" said the old lady, suiting the action to the word; "you don't see it now, at all events."

Oliver *did* see it in his mind's eye as distinctly as if he had not altered his position; but he thought it better not to worry the kind old lady; so he smiled gently when she looked at him; and Mrs. Bedwin, satisfied that he felt more comfortable, salted and broke bits of toasted bread into the broth, with all the bustle befitting so solemn a preparation. Oliver got through it with extraordinary expedition: and had scarcely swallowed the last spoonful, when there came a soft tap at the door. "Come in," said the old lady; and in walked Mr. Brownlow.

Now, the old gentleman came in as brisk as need be; but he had no sooner raised his spectacles on his forehead, and thrust his hands behind the skirts of his dressing-gown to take a good long look at Oliver, than his countenance underwent a very great variety of odd contortions. Oliver looked very worn and shadowy from sickness: and made an ineffectual attempt to stand up, out of respect to his benefactor: which terminated in his sinking back into the chair again; and the fact is, if the truth must be told, that Mr. Brownlow's heart, being large enough for any six ordinary old gentlemen of humane disposition, forced a supply of tears into his eyes, by some hydraulic process[5] which we are not sufficiently philosophical to be in a condition to explain.

"Poor boy, poor boy!" said Mr. Brownlow, clearing his throat. "I'm rather hoarse this morning, Mrs. Bedwin. I'm afraid I have caught cold."

"I hope not, sir," said Mrs. Bedwin. "Everything you have had, has been well aired, sir."

"I don't know, Bedwin. I don't know," said Mr. Brownlow; "I rather think I had a damp napkin at dinner-time yesterday; but never mind that. How do you feel, my dear?"

"Very happy, sir," replied Oliver. "And very grateful indeed, sir, for your goodness to me."

"Good boy," said Mr. Brownlow, stoutly. "Have you given him any nourishment, Bedwin? Any slops, eh?"

"He has just had a basin of beautiful strong broth, sir," replied Mrs.

5. The use of water pressure to create movement.

Bedwin: drawing herself up slightly, and laying a strong emphasis on the last word: to intimate that between slops, and broth well compounded, there existed no affinity or connexion whatsoever.

"Ugh!" said Mr. Brownlow, with a slight shudder; "a couple of glasses of port wine would have done him a great deal more good. Wouldn't they, Tom White, eh?"

"My name is Oliver, sir," replied the little invalid: with a look of great astonishment.

"Oliver," said Mr. Brownlow; "Oliver what? Oliver White, eh?"

"No, sir, Twist, Oliver Twist."

"Queer name!" said the old gentleman. "What made you tell the magistrate your name was White?"

"I never told him so, sir," returned Oliver in amazement.

This sounded so like a falsehood, that the old gentleman looked somewhat sternly in Oliver's face. It was impossible to doubt him; there was truth in every one of its thin and sharpened lineaments.

"Some mistake," said Mr. Brownlow. But, although his motive for looking steadily at Oliver no longer existed, the old idea of the resemblance between his features and some familiar face came upon him so strongly, that he could not withdraw his gaze.

"I hope you are not angry with me, sir?" said Oliver, raising his eyes beseechingly.

"No, no," replied the old gentleman. "Why! what's this? Bedwin, look there!"

As he spoke, he pointed hastily to the picture above Oliver's head; and then to the boy's face. There was its living copy. The eyes, the head, the mouth; every feature was the same. The expression was, for the instant, so precisely alike, that the minutest line seemed copied with a startling accuracy.

Oliver knew not the cause of this sudden exclamation; for, not being strong enough to bear the start it gave him, he fainted away. A weakness on his part, which affords the narrative an opportunity of relieving the reader from suspense, in behalf of the two young pupils of the Merry Old Gentleman; and of recording

That when the Dodger, and his accomplished friend Master Bates, joined in the hue-and-cry which was raised at Oliver's heels, in consequence of their executing an illegal conveyance of Mr. Brownlow's personal property, as has been already described, they were actuated by a very laudable and becoming regard for themselves; and forasmuch as the freedom of the subject and the liberty of the individual are among the first and proudest boasts of a true-hearted Englishman; so I need hardly beg the reader to observe, that this action should tend to exalt them in the opinion of all public and patriotic men; in almost as great a degree as this strong proof of their anxiety for their own preservation and safety, goes to corroborate and confirm the little code of laws which certain profound and sound-judging philosophers have laid down as the mainsprings of all Nature's deeds and actions: the said philosophers very wisely reducing the good lady's proceedings to matters of maxim and theory: and, by a very neat and pretty compliment to her exalted wisdom and understanding, putting entirely out of sight any considerations of heart, or generous impulse and feeling. For these are matters totally beneath a female who is acknowledged by universal admission to be far above the numerous little foibles and weaknesses of her sex.

If I wanted any further proof of the strictly philosophical nature of the conduct of these young gentlemen in their very delicate predicament, I should at once find it in the fact (also recorded in a foregoing part of this narrative), of their quitting the pursuit, when the general attention was fixed upon Oliver; and making immediately for their home by the shortest possible cut. For although I do not mean to assert that it is usually the practice of renowned and learned sages, to shorten the road to any great conclusion; their course indeed being rather to lengthen the distance, by various circumlocutions and discursive staggerings, like unto those in which drunken men under the pressure of a too mighty flow of ideas, are prone to indulge; still I do mean to say, and do say distinctly, that it is the invariable practice of many mighty philosophers, in carrying out their theories, to evince great wisdom and foresight in providing against every possible contingency which can be supposed at all likely to affect themselves. Thus, to do a great right, you may do a little wrong;[6] and you may take any means which the end to be attained will justify; the amount of the right, or the amount of the wrong, or indeed the distinction between the two, being left entirely to the philosopher concerned: to be settled and determined by his clear, comprehensive, and impartial view of his own particular case.

It was not until the two boys had scoured, with great rapidity, through a most intricate maze of narrow streets and courts, that they ventured to halt, by one consent, beneath a low and dark archway. Having remained silent here, just long enough to recover breath to speak, Master Bates uttered an exclamation of amusement and delight; and, bursting into an uncontrollable fit of laughter, flung himself upon a door-step, and rolled thereon in a transport of mirth.

"What's the matter?" inquired the Dodger.

"Ha! ha! ha!" roared Charley Bates.

"Hold your noise," remonstrated the Dodger, looking cautiously round. "Do you want to be grabbed, stupid?"

"I can't help it," said Charley, "I can't help it. To see him splitting away at that pace; and cutting round the corners; and knocking up against the posts; and starting on again as if he was made of iron as well as them; and me with the wipe in my pocket, singing out arter him—oh,

6. A loose quotation from Shakespeare, *The Merchant of Venice* 4.1.216. Dickens may have been drawn to the words, spoken by Bassanio to Portia, by associating Fagin with Shylock.

my eye!" The vivid imagination of Master Bates, presented the scene before him in too strong colours. As he arrived at this apostrophe, he again rolled upon the door-step, and laughed louder than before.

"What'll Fagin say?" inquired the Dodger; taking advantage of the next interval of breathlessness on the part of his friend to propound the question.

"What!" repeated Charley Bates.

"Ah, what?" said the Dodger.

"Why, what should he say?" inquired Charley: stopping rather suddenly in his merriment; for the Dodger's manner was impressive. "What should he say?"

Mr. Dawkins whistled for a couple of minutes; then, taking off his hat, scratched his head, and nodded thrice.

"What do you mean?" said Charley.

"Toor rul lol loo, gammon and spinnage, the frog he wouldn't, and high cockolorum,"[7] said the Dodger: with a slight sneer on his intellectual countenance.

This was explanatory, but not satisfactory. Master Bates felt it so; and again said, "What do you mean?"

The Dodger made no reply; but putting his hat on again, and gathering the skirts of his long-tailed coat under his arm, thrust his tongue into his cheek, slapped the bridge of his nose some half-dozen times in a familiar but expressive manner; and turning on his heel, slunk down the court. Master Bates followed, with a thoughtful countenance.

The noise of footsteps on the creaking stairs, a few minutes after the occurrence of this conversation, roused the merry old gentleman as he sat over the fire with a saveloy and a small loaf in his left hand; a pocket knife in his right; and a pewter pot on the trivet.[8] There was a rascally smile on his white face as he turned round; and, looking sharply out from under his thick red eyebrows, bent his ear towards the door, and listened intently.

"Why, how's this?" muttered the Jew: changing countenance; "only two of 'em? Where's the third? They can't have got into trouble. Hark!"

The footsteps approached nearer; they reached the landing. The door was slowly opened; and the Dodger and Charley Bates entered: closing it behind them.

7. A series of nonsense words and idioms, with the exception of *gammon*, which means "nonsense."
8. A stand on which to place a pot or bottle over a fire for heating or cooking. "Saveloy": a highly seasoned cooked and dried sausage.

Chapter XIII.

SOME NEW ACQUAINTANCES ARE INTRODUCED TO THE INTELLIGENT
READER; CONNECTED WITH WHOM, VARIOUS PLEASANT MATTERS ARE
RELATED, APPERTAINING TO THIS HISTORY.

"Where's Oliver?" said the furious Jew, rising with a menacing look. "Where's the boy?"

The young thieves eyed their preceptor as if they were alarmed at his violence; and looked uneasily at each other. But they made no reply.

"What's become of the boy?" said the Jew, seizing the Dodger tightly by the collar, and threatening him with horrid imprecations.[1] "Speak out, or I'll throttle you!"

Mr. Fagin looked so very much in earnest, that Charley Bates, who deemed it prudent in all cases to be on the safe side; and who conceived it by no means improbable that it might be his turn to be throttled second; dropped upon his knees; and raised a loud, well-sustained, and continuous roar—something between a mad bull and a speaking trumpet.

"Will you speak?" thundered the Jew: shaking the Dodger so much that his keeping in the big coat at all, seemed perfectly miraculous.

"Why, the traps have got him, and that's all about it," said the Dodger, sullenly. "Come, let go o' me, will you!" And, swinging himself, at one jerk, clean out of the big coat: which he left in the Jew's hands: the Dodger snatched up the toasting fork, and made a pass at the merry old gentleman's waistcoat; which, if it had taken effect, would have let a little more merriment out, than could have been easily replaced in a month or two.

The Jew skipped back, in this emergency, with more agility than could have been anticipated in a man of his apparent decrepitude; and, seizing up the pot, prepared to hurl it at his assailant's head. But, Charley Bates, at this moment, calling his attention by a perfectly terrific howl, he suddenly altered its destination, and flung it full at that young gentleman.

"Why, what the blazes is in the wind now!" growled a deep voice. "Who pitched that 'ere at me? It's well it's the beer, and not the pot, as hit me, or I'd have settled somebody. I might have know'd, as nobody but an infernal, rich, plundering, thundering, old Jew, could afford to throw away any drink but water; and not that, unless he done the River Company every quarter.[2] Wot's it all about, Fagin? D—me, if my neckankercher an't lined with beer! Come in, you sneaking warmint;

1. Curses.
2. Unless he didn't pay his water company bill.

wot are you stopping outside for, as if you was ashamed of your master! Come in!"

The man who growled out these words, was a stoutly-built fellow of about five-and-thirty, in a black velveteen coat, very soiled drab breeches, lace-up half boots, and grey cotton stockings, which inclosed a very bulky pair of legs, with large swelling calves;—the kind of legs, that in such costume, always look in an unfinished and incomplete state without a set of fetters to garnish them. He had a brown hat on his head, and a dirty belcher handkerchief[3] round his neck: with the long frayed ends of which, he smeared the beer from his face as he spoke; disclosing, when he had done so, a broad heavy countenance with a beard of three days' growth: and two scowling eyes; one of which, displayed various parti-coloured[4] symptoms of having been recently damaged by a blow.

"Come in, d'ye hear?" growled this engaging ruffian.

A white shaggy dog, with his face scratched and torn in twenty different places, skulked into the room.

"Why didn't you come in afore?" said the man. "You're getting too proud to own me afore company, are you? Lie down!"

This command was accompanied with a kick, which sent the animal to the other end of the room. He appeared well used to it, however; for he coiled himself up in a corner very quietly, without uttering a sound; and winking his very ill-looking eyes about twenty times in a minute, appeared to occupy himself in taking a survey of the apartment.

"What are you up to? Ill-treating the boys, you covetous, avaricious, in-sa-ti-a-ble old fence?" said the man, seating himself deliberately. "I wonder they don't murder you; I would if I was them. If I'd been your 'prentice, I'd have done it long ago; and—no, I couldn't have sold you arterwards, though; for you're fit for nothing but keeping as a curiosity of ugliness in a glass bottle, and I suppose they don't blow glass bottles large enough."

"Hush! hush! Mr. Sikes," said the Jew, trembling; "don't speak so loud."

"None of your mistering," replied the ruffian; "you always mean mischief when you come that. You know my name: out with it! I shan't disgrace it when the time comes."

"Well, well, then—Bill Sikes," said the Jew with abject humility. "You seem out of humour, Bill."

"Perhaps I am," replied Sikes; "I should think *you* was rather out of sorts too, unless you mean as little harm when you throw pewter pots about, as you do when you blab and——"

"Are you mad?" said the Jew, catching the man by the sleeve, and pointing towards the boys.

Mr. Sikes contented himself with tying an imaginary knot under his

3. A multicolored scarf popularized by a well-known prizefighter, Jim Belcher (1781–1811).
4. Of two or more colors.

left ear, and jerking his head over on the right shoulder; a piece of dumb show which the Jew appeared to understand perfectly. He then in cant terms,[5] with which his whole conversation was plentifully besprinkled, but which would be quite unintelligible if they were recorded here, demanded a glass of liquor.

"And mind you don't poison it," said Mr. Sikes, laying his hat upon the table.

This was said in jest; but if the speaker could have seen the evil leer with which the Jew bit his pale lip as he turned round to the cupboard, he might have thought the caution not wholly unnecessary, or the wish (at all events,) to improve upon the distiller's ingenuity not very far from the old gentleman's merry heart.

After swallowing two or three glassfulls of spirits, Mr. Sikes condescended to take some notice of the young gentlemen; which gracious act led to a conversation, in which the cause and manner of Oliver's capture were circumstantially detailed; with such alterations and improvements on the truth, as to the Dodger appeared most advisable under the circumstances.

"I'm afraid," said the Jew, "that he may say something which will get us into trouble."

"That's very likely," returned Sikes with a malicious grin. "You're blowed upon,[6] Fagin."

"And I'm afraid, you see," added the Jew, speaking as if he had not noticed the interruption, and regarding the other closely as he did so, —"I'm afraid that, if the game was up with us, it might be up with a good many more; and that it would come out rather worse for you than it would for me, my dear."

The man started, and turned fiercely round upon the Jew. But the old gentleman's shoulders were shrugged up to his ears; and his eyes were vacantly staring on the opposite wall.

There was a long pause. Every member of the respectable coterie appeared plunged in his own reflections; not excepting the dog, who by a certain malicious licking of his lips seemed to be meditating an attack upon the legs of the first gentleman or lady he might encounter in the streets when he went out.

"Somebody must find out wot's been done at the office," said Mr. Sikes in a much lower tone than he had taken since he came in.

The Jew nodded assent.

"If he hasn't peached,[7] and is committed, there's no fear till he comes out again," said Mr. Sikes, "and then he must be taken care on. You must get hold of him, somehow."

Again the Jew nodded.

5. Slang.
6. Squealed on.
7. Turned informer.

The prudence of this line of action, indeed, was obvious; but unfortunately there was one very strong objection to its being adopted; and this was, that the Dodger, and Charley Bates, and Fagin, and Mr. William Sikes, happened, one and all, to entertain a most violent and deeply-rooted antipathy to going near a police-office, on any ground or pretext whatever.

How long they might have sat and looked at each other, in a state of uncertainty not the most pleasant of its kind, it is difficult to say. It is not necessary to make any guesses on the subject, however; for the sudden entrance of the two young ladies whom Oliver had seen on a former occasion, caused the conversation to flow afresh.

"The very thing!" said the Jew. "Bet will go; won't you, my dear?"

"Wheres?" inquired the young lady.

"Only just up to the office, my dear," said the Jew coaxingly.

It is due to the young lady to say that she did not positively affirm that she would not, but that she merely expressed an emphatic and earnest desire to be "blessed" if she would; a polite and delicate evasion of the request, which shows the young lady to have been possessed of that natural good breeding which cannot bear to inflict upon a fellow-creature, the pain of a direct and pointed refusal.

The Jew's countenance fell; and he turned from this young lady: who was gaily, not to say gorgeously attired, in a red gown, green boots, and yellow curl-papers;[8] to the other female.

"Nancy, my dear," said the Jew in a soothing manner, "what do *you* say?"

"That it won't do; so it's no use a-trying it on, Fagin," replied Nancy.

"What do you mean by that?" said Mr. Sikes, looking up in a surly manner.

"What I say, Bill," replied the lady collectedly.

"Why, you're just the very person for it," reasoned Mr. Sikes: "nobody about here knows anything of you."

"And as I don't want 'em to, neither," replied Nancy in the same composed manner, "it's rather more no than yes with me, Bill."

"She'll go, Fagin," said Sikes.

"No, she won't, Fagin," said Nancy.

"Yes she will, Fagin," said Sikes.

And Mr. Sikes was right. By dint of alternate threats, promises, and bribes, the lady in question was ultimately prevailed upon to undertake the commission. She was not, indeed, withheld by the same considerations as her agreeable friend; for, having very recently removed into the neighbourhood of Field-lane from the remote but genteel suburb of Ratcliffe, she was not under the same apprehension of being recognised by any of her numerous acquaintance.

8. See above, p. 5, n. 3.

Accordingly, with a clean white apron tied over her gown, and her curl-papers tucked up under a straw bonnet,—both articles of dress being provided from the Jew's inexhaustible stock,—Miss Nancy prepared to issue forth on her errand.

"Stop a minute, my dear," said the Jew, producing a little covered basket. "Carry that in one hand. It looks more respectable, my dear."

"Give her a door-key to carry in her t'other one, Fagin," said Sikes; "it looks real and genivine like."

"Yes, yes, my dear, so it does," said the Jew, hanging a large street-door key on the fore-finger of the young lady's right hand. "There; very good! Very good indeed, my dear," said the Jew, rubbing his hands.

"Oh, my brother! My poor, dear, sweet, innocent little brother!" exclaimed Nancy, bursting into tears, and wringing the little basket and the street-door key in an agony of distress. "What has become of him! Where have they taken him to! Oh, do have pity, and tell me what's been done with the dear boy, gentlemen; do, gentlemen, if you please, gentlemen!"

Having uttered these words in a most lamentable and heart-broken tone: to the immeasurable delight of her hearers: Miss Nancy paused, winked to the company, nodded smilingly round, and disappeared.

"Ah! she's a clever girl, my dears," said the Jew, turning to his young friends, and shaking his head gravely, as if in mute admonition to them to follow the bright example they had just beheld.

"She's a honour to her sex," said Mr. Sikes filling his glass, and smiting the table with his enormous fist. "Here's her health, and wishing they was all like her!"

While these, and many other encomiums,[9] were being passed on the accomplished Nancy, that young lady made the best of her way to the police-office; whither, notwithstanding a little natural timidity consequent upon walking through the streets alone and unprotected, she arrived in perfect safety shortly afterwards.

Entering by the back way, she tapped softly with the key at one of the cell-doors; and listened. There was no sound within: so she coughed and listened again. Still there was no reply: so she spoke.

"Nolly, dear?" murmured Nancy in a gentle voice; "Nolly?"

There was nobody inside but a miserable shoeless criminal, who had been taken up for playing the flute, and who: the offence against society having been clearly proved: had been very properly committed by Mr. Fang to the House of Correction for one month; with the appropriate and amusing remark that since he had so much breath to spare, it would be much more wholesomely expended on the treadmill than in a musical instrument. He made no answer: being occupied in mentally bewailing

9. Praises.

the loss of the flute, which had been confiscated for the use of the county; so Nancy passed on to the next cell, and knocked there.

"Well!" cried a faint and feeble voice.

"Is there a little boy here?" inquired Nancy, with a preliminary sob.

"No," replied the voice; "God forbid!"

This was a vagrant of sixty-five, who was going to prison for *not* playing the flute; or, in other words, for begging in the streets, and doing nothing for his livelihood. In the next cell, was another man, who was going to the same prison for hawking tin saucepans without a license; thereby doing something for his living, in defiance of the Stamp-office.[1]

But, as neither of these criminals answered to the name of Oliver, or knew anything about him, Nancy made straight up to the bluff officer in the striped waistcoat; and with the most piteous wailings and lamentations: rendered more piteous by a prompt and efficient use of the street-door key and the little basket: demanded her own dear brother.

"I haven't got him, my dear," said the old man.

"Where is he?" screamed Nancy, in a distracted manner.

"Why, the gentleman's got him," replied the officer.

"What gentleman? Oh, gracious heavens! what gentleman?" exclaimed Nancy.

In reply to this incoherent questioning, the old man informed the deeply affected sister that Oliver had been taken ill in the office, and discharged in consequence of a witness having proved the robbery to have been committed by another boy, not in custody; and that the prosecutor had carried him away, in an insensible condition, to his own residence: of and concerning which, all the informant knew was, that it was somewhere at Pentonville: he having heard that word mentioned in the directions to the coachman.

In a dreadful state of doubt and uncertainty, the agonised young woman staggered to the gate, and then: exchanging her faltering walk for a good, swift, steady run: returned by the most devious and complicated route she could think of, to the domicile of the Jew.

Mr. Bill Sikes no sooner heard the account of the expedition delivered, than he very hastily called up the white dog; and, putting on his hat, expeditiously departed: without devoting any time to the formality of wishing the company good-morning.

"We must know where he is, my dears; he must be found," said the Jew, greatly excited. "Charley, do nothing but skulk about, till you bring home some news of him! Nancy, my dear, I must have him found. I trust to you, my dear,—to you and the Artful for everything! Stay, stay," added the Jew, unlocking a drawer with a shaking hand; "there's money, my dears. I shall shut up this shop to-night. You'll know where to find me! Don't stop here a minute. Not an instant, my dears!"

1. The government department that marked paper to certify that the tax on paper had been paid and that provided legally necessary licenses, including those for peddling.

With these words, he pushed them from the room; and carefully double-locking and barring the door behind them, drew from its place of concealment the box which he had unintentionally disclosed to Oliver. Then, he hastily proceeded to dispose the watches and jewellery, beneath his clothing.

A rap at the door, startled him in this occupation. "Who's there?" he cried in a shrill tone.

"Me!" replied the voice of the Dodger, through the key-hole.

"What now?" cried the Jew impatiently.

"Is he to be kidnapped to the other ken,[2] Nancy says?" inquired the Dodger.

"Yes," replied the Jew, "wherever she lays hands on him. Find him, find him out, that's all! I shall know what to do next; never fear."

The boy murmured a reply of intelligence; and hurried down stairs after his companions.

"He has not peached so far," said the Jew as he pursued his occupation. "If he means to blab us among his new friends, we may stop his mouth yet."

Chapter XIV.

COMPRISING FURTHER PARTICULARS OF OLIVER'S STAY AT MR. BROWNLOW'S. WITH THE REMARKABLE PREDICTION WHICH ONE MR. GRIMWIG UTTERED CONCERNING HIM, WHEN HE WENT OUT ON AN ERRAND.

Oliver soon recovered from the fainting-fit into which Mr. Brownlow's abrupt exclamation had thrown him; and the subject of the picture was carefully avoided, both by the old gentleman and Mrs. Bedwin, in the conversation that ensued: which indeed bore no reference to Oliver's history or prospects, but was confined to such topics as might amuse without exciting him. He was still too weak to get up to breakfast; but, when he came down into the housekeeper's room next day, his first act was to cast an eager glance at the wall, in the hope of again looking on the face of the beautiful lady. His expectations were disappointed, however, for the picture had been removed.

"Ah!" said the housekeeper, watching the direction of Oliver's eyes. "It is gone, you see."

"I see it is, ma'am," replied Oliver, with a sigh. "Why have they taken it away?"

"It has been taken down, child, because Mr. Brownlow said, that, as it seemed to worry you, perhaps it might prevent your getting well, you know," rejoined the old lady.

2. Thieves' house.

"Oh, no, indeed. It didn't worry me, ma'am," said Oliver. "I liked to see it; I quite loved it."

"Well, well!" said the old lady, good-humouredly; "you get well as fast as ever you can, dear, and it shall be hung up again. There! I promise you that! Now let us talk about something else."

This was all the information Oliver could obtain about the picture at that time. As the old lady had been so kind to him in his illness, he endeavoured to think no more of the subject just then; so he listened attentively, to a great many stories she told him, about an amiable and handsome daughter of hers, who was married to an amiable and handsome man, and lived in the country; and about a son, who was clerk to a merchant in the West Indies; and who was, also, such a good young man: and wrote such dutiful letters home four times a year: that it brought the tears into her eyes, to talk about them. When the old lady had expatiated, a long time, on the excellences of her children, and the merits of her kind good husband besides, who had been dead and gone, poor dear soul! just six-and-twenty years, it was time to have tea; and after tea she began to teach Oliver cribbage:[1] which he learnt as quickly as she could teach: and at which game they played, with great interest and gravity, until it was time for the invalid to have some warm wine and water, with a slice of dry toast; and then to go cosily to bed.

They were happy days, those of Oliver's recovery. Everything was so quiet, and neat, and orderly; everybody so kind and gentle; that after the noise and turbulence in the midst of which he had always lived, it seemed like Heaven itself. He was no sooner strong enough to put his clothes on, properly, than Mr. Brownlow caused a complete new suit, and a new cap, and a new pair of shoes, to be provided for him. As Oliver was told that he might do what he liked with the old clothes, he gave them to a servant who had been very kind to him: and asked her to sell them to a Jew:[2] and keep the money for herself. This she very readily did; and, as Oliver looked out of the parlour window, and saw the Jew roll them up in his bag and walk away, he felt quite delighted to think that they were safely gone, and that there was now no possible danger of his ever being able to wear them again. They were sad rags, to tell the truth; and Oliver had never had a new suit before.

One evening, about a week after the affair of the picture, as he was sitting talking to Mrs. Bedwin, there came a message down from Mr. Brownlow, that if Oliver Twist felt pretty well, he should like to see him in his study, and talk to him a little while.

"Bless us, and save us! Wash your hands, and let me part your hair nicely for you, child," said Mrs. Bedwin. "Dear heart alive! If we had

---

1. A card game that can be played by up to four people and in which the cards each player discards to the dealer are called the "crib."
2. Jews dominated the used-clothing trade in London.

known he would have asked for you, we would have put you a clean collar on, and made you as smart as sixpence!"

Oliver did as the old lady bade him; and, although she lamented grievously, meanwhile, that there was not even time to crimp the little frill that bordered his shirt-collar; he looked so delicate and handsome, despite that important personal advantage, that she went so far as to say: looking at him with great complacency from head to foot: that she really didn't think it would have been possible, on the longest notice, to have made much difference in him for the better.

Thus encouraged, Oliver tapped at the study door. On Mr. Brownlow calling to him to come in, he found himself in a little back room, quite full of books: with a window, looking into some pleasant little gardens. There was a table drawn up before the window, at which Mr. Brownlow was seated reading. When he saw Oliver, he pushed the book away from him, and told him to come near the table, and sit down. Oliver complied; marvelling where the people could be found to read such a great number of books as seemed to be written to make the world wiser. Which is still a marvel to more experienced people than Oliver Twist, every day of their lives.

"There are a good many books, are there not, my boy?" said Mr. Brownlow: observing the curiosity with which Oliver surveyed the shelves that reached from the floor to the ceiling.

"A great number, sir," replied Oliver. "I never saw so many."

"You shall read them, if you behave well," said the old gentleman kindly; "and you will like that, better than looking at the outsides,— that is, in some cases; because there *are* books of which the backs and covers are by far the best parts."

"I suppose they are those heavy ones, sir," said Oliver, pointing to some large quartos, with a good deal of gilding about the binding.

"Not always those," said the old gentleman, patting Oliver on the head, and smiling as he did so; "there are other equally heavy ones, though of a much smaller size. How should you like to grow up a clever man, and write books, eh?"

"I think I would rather read them, sir," replied Oliver.

"What! wouldn't you like to be a book-writer?" said the old gentleman.

Oliver considered a little while; and at last said, he should think it would be a much better thing to be a bookseller; upon which the old gentleman laughed heartily, and declared he had said a very good thing. Which Oliver felt glad to have done, though he by no means knew what it was.

"Well, well," said the old gentleman, composing his features. "Don't be afraid! We won't make an author of you, while there's an honest trade to be learnt, or brick-making to turn to."

"Thank you, sir," said Oliver. At the earnest manner of his reply, the old gentleman laughed again; and said something about a curious instinct, which Oliver, not understanding, paid no very great attention to.

"Now," said Mr. Brownlow, speaking if possible in a kinder, but at the same time in a much more serious manner, than Oliver had ever known him assume yet, "I want you to pay great attention, my boy, to what I am going to say. I shall talk to you without any reserve; because I am sure you are as well able to understand me, as many older persons would be."

"Oh, don't tell me you are going to send me away, sir, pray!" exclaimed Oliver, alarmed at the serious tone of the old gentleman's commencement! "Don't turn me out of doors to wander in the streets again. Let me stay here, and be a servant. Don't send me back to the wretched place I came from. Have mercy upon a poor boy, sir!"

"My dear child," said the old gentleman, moved by the warmth of Oliver's sudden appeal; "you need not be afraid of my deserting you, unless you give me cause."

"I never, never will, sir," interposed Oliver.

"I hope not," rejoined the old gentleman. "I do not think you ever will. I have been deceived, before, in the objects whom I have endeavoured to benefit; but I feel strongly disposed to trust you, nevertheless; and I am more interested in your behalf than I can well account for, even to myself. The persons on whom I have bestowed my dearest love, lie deep in their graves; but, although the happiness and delight of my life lie buried there too, I have not made a coffin of my heart, and sealed it up, for ever, on my best affections. Deep affliction has but strengthened and refined them."

As the old gentleman said this, in a low voice: more to himself than to his companion; and as he remained silent for a short time afterwards; Oliver sat quite still.

"Well, well!" said the old gentleman at length, in a more cheerful tone, "I only say this, because you have a young heart; and knowing that I have suffered great pain and sorrow, you will be more careful, perhaps, not to wound me again. You say you are an orphan, without a friend in the world; all the inquiries I have been able to make, confirm the statement. Let me hear your story; where you come from; who brought you up; and how you got into the company in which I found you. Speak the truth; and you shall not be friendless while I live."

Oliver's sobs checked his utterance for some minutes; when he was on the point of beginning to relate how he had been brought up at the farm, and carried to the workhouse by Mr. Bumble, a peculiarly impatient little double-knock was heard at the street-door; and the servant, running up stairs, announced Mr. Grimwig.

"Is he coming up?" inquired Mr. Brownlow.

"Yes, sir," replied the servant. "He asked if there were any muffins in the house; and, when I told him yes, he said he had come to tea."

Mr. Brownlow smiled; and, turning to Oliver, said that Mr. Grimwig was an old friend of his, and he must not mind his being a little rough in his manners; for he was a worthy creature at bottom, as he had reason to know.

"Shall I go down stairs, sir?" inquired Oliver.

"No," replied Mr. Brownlow; "I would rather you remained here."

At this moment, there walked into the room: supporting himself by a thick stick: a stout old gentleman, rather lame in one leg, who was dressed in a blue coat, striped waistcoat, nankeen breeches and gaiters,[3] and a broad-brimmed white hat, with the sides turned up with green. A very small-plaited shirt frill, stuck out from his waistcoat; and a very long steel watch-chain, with nothing but a key at the end, dangled loosely below it. The ends of his white neckerchief were twisted into a ball about the size of an orange; the variety of shapes into which his countenance was twisted, defy description. He had a manner of screwing his head on one side when he spoke: and of looking out of the corners of his eyes at the same time: which irresistibly reminded the beholder of a parrot. In this attitude, he fixed himself, the moment he made his appearance; and, holding out a small piece of orange-peel at arm's length, exclaimed in a growling, discontented voice,

"Look here! do you see this? Isn't it a most wonderful and extraordinary thing that I can't call at a man's house but I find a piece of this poor surgeon's-friend on the stair-case? I've been lamed with orange-peel once, and I know orange-peel will be my death at last. It will, sir; orange-peel will be my death, or I'll be content to eat my own head, sir!"

This was the handsome offer with which Mr. Grimwig backed and confirmed nearly every assertion he made; and it was the more singular in his case, because, even admitting for the sake of argument, the possibility of scientific improvements being ever brought to that pass which will enable a gentleman to eat his own head in the event of his being so disposed; Mr. Grimwig's head was such a particularly large one, that the most sanguine man alive, could hardly entertain a hope of being able to get through it at a sitting—to put entirely out of the question, a very thick coating of powder.

"I'll eat my head, sir," repeated Mr. Grimwig, striking his stick upon the ground. "Hallo! what's that!" looking at Oliver, and retreating a pace or two.

"This is young Oliver Twist, whom we were speaking about," said Mr. Brownlow.

Oliver bowed.

"You don't mean to say that's the boy who had the fever, I hope?" said Mr. Grimwig, recoiling a little more. "Wait a minute! Don't speak!

3. Pants and ankle and leg coverings made of yellow cotton cloth.

Stop—" continued Mr. Grimwig, abruptly, losing all dread of the fever in his triumph at the discovery; "that's the boy who had the orange! If that's not the boy, sir, who had the orange, and threw this bit of peel upon the stair-case, I'll eat my head, and his too."

"No, no, he has not had one," said Mr. Brownlow, laughing. "Come! Put down your hat; and speak to my young friend."

"I feel strongly on this subject, sir," said the irritable old gentleman, drawing off his gloves. "There's always more or less orange-peel on the pavement in our street; and I *know* it's put there by the surgeon's boy at the corner. A young woman stumbled over a bit last night, and fell against my garden-railings; directly she got up I saw her look towards his infernal red lamp with the pantomime-light.[4] 'Don't go to him,' I called out of the window, 'he's an assassin! A man-trap!' So he is. If he is not——" Here the irascible old gentleman gave a great knock on the ground with his stick; which was always understood, by his friends, to imply the customary offer, whenever it was not expressed in words. Then, still keeping his stick in his hand, he sat down; and, opening a double eye-glass, which he wore attached to a broad black riband, took a view of Oliver: who, seeing that he was the object of inspection, coloured, and bowed again.

"That's the boy, is it?" said Mr. Grimwig, at length.

"That is the boy," replied Mr. Brownlow.

"How are you, boy?" said Mr. Grimwig.

"A great deal better, thank you, sir," replied Oliver.

Mr. Brownlow, seeming to apprehend that his singular friend was about to say something disagreeable, asked Oliver to step down stairs and tell Mrs. Bedwin they were ready for tea; which, as he did not half like the visitor's manner, he was very happy to do.

"He is a nice-looking boy, is he not?" inquired Mr. Brownlow.

"I don't know," replied Mr. Grimwig, pettishly.

"Don't know?"

"No. I don't know. I never see any difference in boys. I only know two sorts of boys. Mealy boys, and beef-faced boys."

"And which is Oliver?"

"Mealy. I know a friend who has a beef-faced boy; a fine boy, they call him; with a round head, and red cheeks, and glaring eyes; a horrid boy; with a body and limbs that appear to be swelling out of the seams of his blue clothes; with the voice of a pilot,[5] and the appetite of a wolf. I know him! The wretch!"

"Come," said Mr. Brownlow, "these are not the characteristics of young Oliver Twist; so he needn't excite your wrath."

"They are not," replied Mr. Grimwig. "He may have worse."

---

4. Surgeons used red lamps to identify their offices; Grimwig associates the red light with Christmas pantomime performances.
5. A ship's helmsman.

Here, Mr. Brownlow coughed impatiently; which appeared to afford Mr. Grimwig the most exquisite delight.

"He may have worse, I say," repeated Mr. Grimwig. "Where does he come from? Who is he? What is he? He has had a fever. What of that? Fevers are not peculiar to good people; are they? Bad people have fevers sometimes; haven't they, eh? I knew a man who was hung in Jamaica for murdering his master. He had had a fever six times; he wasn't recommended to mercy on that account. Pooh! nonsense!"

Now, the fact was, that, in the inmost recesses of his own heart, Mr. Grimwig was strongly disposed to admit that Oliver's appearance and manner were unusually prepossessing; but he had a strong appetite for contradiction: sharpened on this occasion by the finding of the orange-peel; and inwardly determining that no man should dictate to him whether a boy was well-looking or not, he had resolved, from the first, to oppose his friend. When Mr. Brownlow admitted that on no one point of inquiry could he yet return a satisfactory answer; and that he had postponed any investigation into Oliver's previous history until he thought the boy was strong enough to bear it; Mr. Grimwig chuckled maliciously. And he demanded, with a sneer, whether the housekeeper was in the habit of counting the plate at night; because, if she didn't find a table-spoon or two missing some sunshiny morning, why, he would be content to——and so forth.

All this, Mr. Brownlow, although himself somewhat of an impetuous gentleman: knowing his friend's peculiarities: bore with great good humour; as Mr. Grimwig, at tea, was graciously pleased to express his entire approval of the muffins, matters went on very smoothly; and Oliver, who made one of the party, began to feel more at his ease than he had yet done in the fierce old gentleman's presence.

"And when are you going to hear a full, true, and particular account of the life and adventures of Oliver Twist?" asked Grimwig of Mr. Brownlow, at the conclusion of the meal: looking sideways at Oliver, as he resumed the subject.

"To-morrow morning," replied Mr. Brownlow. "I would rather he was alone with me at the time. Come up to me to-morrow morning at ten o'clock, my dear."

"Yes, sir," replied Oliver. He answered with some hesitation, because he was confused by Mr. Grimwig's looking so hard at him.

"I'll tell you what," whispered that gentleman to Mr. Brownlow; "he won't come up to you to-morrow morning. I saw him hesitate. He is deceiving you, my good friend."

"I'll swear he is not," replied Mr. Brownlow, warmly.

"If he is not," said Mr. Grimwig, "I'll——" and down went the stick.

"I'll answer for that boy's truth with my life!" said Mr. Brownlow, knocking the table.

"And I for his falsehood with my head!" rejoined Mr. Grimwig, knocking the table also.

"We shall see," said Mr. Brownlow, checking his rising anger.

"We will," replied Mr. Grimwig, with a provoking smile; "we will."

As fate would have it, Mrs. Bedwin chanced to bring in, at this moment, a small parcel of books: which Mr. Brownlow had that morning purchased of the identical bookstall-keeper, who has already figured in this history; having laid them on the table, she prepared to leave the room.

"Stop the boy, Mrs. Bedwin!" said Mr. Brownlow; "there is something to go back."

"He has gone, sir," replied Mrs. Bedwin.

"Call after him," said Mr. Brownlow; "it's particular. He is a poor man, and they are not paid for. There are some books to be taken back, too."

The street-door was opened. Oliver ran one way; and the girl ran another; and Mrs. Bedwin stood on the step and screamed for the boy; but there was no boy in sight. Oliver and the girl returned, in a breathless state, to report that there were no tidings of him.

"Dear me, I am very sorry for that," exclaimed Mr. Brownlow; "I particularly wished those books to be returned to-night."

"Send Oliver with them," said Mr. Grimwig with an ironical smile; "he will be sure to deliver them safely, you know."

"Yes; do let me take them, if you please, sir," said Oliver. "I'll run all the way, sir."

The old gentleman was just going to say that Oliver should not go out on any account; when a most malicious cough from Mr. Grimwig determined him that he should; and that, by his prompt discharge of the commission, he should prove to him the injustice of his suspicions: on this head at least: at once.

"You *shall* go, my dear," said the old gentleman. "The books are on a chair by my table. Fetch them down."

Oliver, delighted to be of use, brought down the books under his arm in a great bustle; and waited, cap in hand, to hear what message he was to take.

"You are to say," said Mr. Brownlow, glancing steadily at Grimwig; "you are to say that you have brought those books back; and that you have come to pay the four pound ten I owe him. This is a five-pound note, so you will have to bring me back, ten shillings change."

"I won't be ten minutes, sir," replied Oliver, eagerly. Having buttoned up the bank-note in his jacket pocket, and placed the books carefully under his arm, he made a respectful bow, and left the room. Mrs. Bedwin followed him to the street-door, giving him many directions about the nearest way, and the name of the bookseller, and the name of the street: all of which Oliver said he clearly understood; and, having superadded many injunctions to be sure and not take cold, the old lady at length permitted him to depart.

"Bless his sweet face!" said the old lady, looking after him. "I can't bear, somehow, to let him go out of my sight."

At this moment, Oliver looked gaily round, and nodded before he turned the corner. The old lady smilingly returned his salutation, and, closing the door, went back to her own room.

"Let me see; he'll be back in twenty minutes, at the longest," said Mr. Brownlow, pulling out his watch, and placing it on the table. "It will be dark by that time."

"Oh! you really expect him to come back, do you?" inquired Mr. Grimwig.

"Don't you?" asked Mr. Brownlow, smiling.

The spirit of contradiction was strong in Mr. Grimwig's breast, at the moment; and it was rendered stronger, by his friend's confident smile.

"No," he said, smiting the table with his fist, "I do not. The boy has a new suit of clothes on his back; a set of valuable books under his arm; and a five-pound note in his pocket. He'll join his old friends the thieves, and laugh at you. If ever that boy returns to this house, sir, I'll eat my head."

With these words, he drew his chair closer to the table; and there the two friends sat, in silent expectation, with the watch between them.

It is worthy of remark: as illustrating the importance we attach to our own judgments, and the pride with which we put forth our most rash and hasty conclusions: that, although Mr. Grimwig was not by any means a bad-hearted man; and though he would have been unfeignedly sorry to see his respected friend, duped and deceived; he really did, most earnestly and strongly hope, at that moment, that Oliver Twist might not come back.

It grew so dark, that the figures on the dial-plate were scarcely discernible; but there the two old gentlemen continued to sit, in silence: with the watch between them.

Chapter XV.

SHOWING HOW VERY FOND OF OLIVER TWIST, THE MERRY OLD JEW AND MISS NANCY WERE.

In the obscure parlour of a low public-house, situate in the filthiest part of Little Saffron-Hill; a dark and gloomy den, where a flaring gas-light burnt all day in the winter-time: and where no ray of sun ever shone in the summer; there sat: brooding over a little pewter measure and a small glass, strongly impregnated with the smell of liquor: a man in a velveteen coat, drab shorts, half boots, and stockings, whom, even by that dim light, no experienced agent of police would have hesitated for one instant to recognise as Mr. William Sikes. At his feet, sat a white-coated, red-eyed dog; who occupied himself, alternately, in winking at his master with both eyes at the same time; and in licking a large, fresh cut on one side of his mouth, which appeared to be the result of some recent conflict.

"Keep quiet, you warmint! keep quiet!" said Mr. Sikes, suddenly breaking silence. Whether his meditations were so intense as to be disturbed by the dog's winking, or whether his feelings were so wrought upon by his reflections that they required all the relief derivable from kicking an unoffending animal to allay them, is matter for argument and consideration. Whatever was the cause, the effect was a kick and a curse bestowed upon the dog simultaneously.

Dogs are not generally apt to revenge injuries inflicted upon them by their masters; but Mr. Sikes's dog, having faults of temper in common with his owner: and labouring, perhaps, at this moment, under a powerful sense of injury: made no more ado but at once fixed his teeth in one of the half-boots. Having given it a hearty shake, he retired, growling, under a form; thereby just escaping the pewter measure which Mr. Sikes levelled at his head.

"You would, would you?" said Sikes, seizing the poker in one hand, and deliberately opening with the other a large clasp knife, which he drew from his pocket. "Come here, you born devil! Come here! D'ye hear?"

The dog no doubt heard; because Mr. Sikes spoke in the very harshest key of a very harsh voice; but, appearing to entertain some unaccountable objection to having his throat cut, he remained where he was, and growled more fiercely than before: at the same time grasping the end of the poker between his teeth, and biting at it like a wild beast.

This resistance only infuriated Mr. Sikes the more; who, dropping on his knees, began to assail the animal most furiously. The dog jumped from right to left, and from left to right: snapping, growling, and barking; the man, thrust and swore, and struck and blasphemed; and the struggle was reaching a most critical point for one or other, when, the door suddenly opening, the dog darted out; leaving Bill Sikes with the poker and the clasp-knife in his hands.

There must always be two parties to a quarrel, says the old adage. Mr. Sikes, being disappointed of the dog's participation, at once transferred his share in the quarrel to the new-comer.

"What the devil do you come in between me and my dog for?" said Sikes, with a fierce gesture.

"I didn't know, my dear, I didn't know," replied Fagin, humbly—for the Jew was the new-comer.

"Didn't know, you white-livered thief!" growled Sikes. "Couldn't you hear the noise?"

"Not a sound of it, as I'm a living man, Bill," replied the Jew.

"Oh no! You hear nothing, you don't," retorted Sikes with a fierce sneer. "Sneaking in and out, so as nobody hears how you come or go! I wish you had been the dog, Fagin, half a minute ago."

"Why?" inquired the Jew with a forced smile.

" 'Cause the government, as cares for the lives of such men as you, as haven't half the pluck of curs, lets a man kill a dog how he likes," replied Sikes, shutting up the knife with a very expressive look; "that's why."

The Jew rubbed his hands; and, sitting down at the table, affected to laugh at the pleasantry of his friend. He was obviously very ill at ease, however.

"Grin away," said Sikes, replacing the poker, and surveying him with savage contempt; "grin away. You'll never have the laugh at me, though, unless it's behind a night-cap.[1] I've got the upper hand over you, Fagin; and, d—me, I'll keep it. There! If I go, you go; so take care of me."

"Well, well, my dear," said the Jew, "I know all that; we—we—have a mutual interest, Bill,—a mutual interest."

"Humph," said Sikes, as if he thought the interest lay rather more on the Jew's side than on his. "Well, what have you got to say to me?"

"It's all passed safe through the melting-pot," replied Fagin, "and this is your share. It's rather more than it ought to be, my dear; but as I know you'll do me a good turn another time, and—"

"'Stow that gammon,"[2] interposed the robber, impatiently. "Where is it? Hand over!"

"Yes, yes, Bill; give me time, give me time," replied the Jew, sooth- ingly. "Here it is! All safe!" As he spoke, he drew forth an old cotton handkerchief from his breast; and untying a large knot in one corner, produced a small brown-paper packet. Sikes, snatching it from him, hastily opened it; and proceeded to count the sovereigns it contained.

"This is all, is it?" inquired Sikes.

"All," replied the Jew.

"You haven't opened the parcel and swallowed one or two as you come along, have you?" inquired Sikes, suspiciously. "Don't put on an injured look at the question; you've done it many a time. Jerk the tinkler."

These words, in plain English, conveyed an injunction to ring the bell. It was answered by another Jew: younger than Fagin, but nearly as vile and repulsive in appearance.

Bill Sikes merely pointed to the empty measure. The Jew, perfectly understanding the hint, retired to fill it: previously exchanging a re- markable look with Fagin, who raised his eyes for an instant, as if in expectation of it, and shook his head in reply; so slightly that the action would have been almost imperceptible to an observant third person. It

1. The blinders placed over the eyes of a condemned man about to be hanged.
2. Stop talking nonsense.

was lost upon Sikes, who was stooping at the moment to tie the boot-lace which the dog had torn. Possibly, if he had observed the brief interchange of signals, he might have thought that it boded no good to him.

"Is anybody here, Barney?" inquired Fagin; speaking: now that Sikes was looking on: without raising his eyes from the ground.

"Dot a shoul," replied Barney; whose words: whether they came from the heart or not: made their way through the nose.

"Nobody?" inquired Fagin, in a tone of surprise: which perhaps might mean that Barney was at liberty to tell the truth.

"Dobody but Biss Dadsy," replied Barney.

"Nancy!" exclaimed Sikes. "Where? Strike me blind, if I don't honor that 'ere girl, for her native talents."

"She's bid havid a plate of boiled beef id the bar," replied Barney,

"Send her here," said Sikes, pouring out a glass of liquor. "Send her here."

Barney looked timidly at Fagin, as if for permission; the Jew remaining silent, and not lifting his eyes from the ground, he retired; and presently returned, ushering in Nancy: who was decorated with the bonnet, apron, basket, and street-door key, complete.

"You are on the scent, are you, Nancy?" inquired Sikes, proffering the glass.

"Yes, I am, Bill," replied the young lady, disposing of its contents; "and tired enough of it I am, too. The young brat's been ill and confined to the crib; and—"

"Ah, Nancy, dear!" said Fagin, looking up.

Now, whether a peculiar contraction of the Jew's red eye-brows, and a half-closing of his deeply-set eyes, warned Miss Nancy that she was disposed to be too communicative, is not a matter of much importance. The fact is all we need care for here; and the fact is, that she suddenly checked herself: and with several gracious smiles upon Mr. Sikes, turned the conversation to other matters. In about ten minutes' time, Mr. Fagin was seized with a fit of coughing; upon which Nancy pulled her shawl over her shoulders, and declared it was time to go. Mr. Sikes, finding that he was walking a short part of her way himself, expressed his intention of accompanying her; and they went away together: followed, at a little distance, by the dog: who slunk out of a back-yard as soon as his master was out of sight.

The Jew thrust his head out of the room door when Sikes had left it; looked after him as he walked up the dark passage; shook his clenched fist; muttered a deep curse; and then, with a horrible grin, re-seated himself at the table: where he was soon deeply absorbed in the interesting pages of the Hue-and-Cry. [3]

3. An official weekly police magazine.

Meanwhile, Oliver Twist, little dreaming that he was within so very short a distance of the merry old gentleman, was on his way to the bookstall. When he got into Clerkenwell, he accidentally turned down a bye-street which was not exactly in his way; but not discovering his mistake until he had got half-way down it, and knowing it must lead in the right direction, he did not think it worth while to turn back; and so marched on, as quickly as he could, with the books under his arm.

He was walking along; thinking how happy and contented he ought to feel; and how much he would give for only one look at poor little Dick: who, starved and beaten, might be weeping bitterly at that very moment; when he was startled by a young woman screaming out very loud, "Oh, my dear brother!" And he had hardly looked up, to see what the matter was, when he was stopped by having a pair of arms thrown tight round his neck.

"Don't," cried Oliver, struggling. "Let go of me. Who is it? What are you stopping me for?"

The only reply to this, was a great number of loud lamentations from the young woman who had embraced him; and who had a little basket and a street-door key in her hand.

"Oh my gracious!" said the young woman, "I've found him! Oh! Oliver! Oliver! Oh you naughty boy, to make me suffer sich distress on your account! Come home, dear, come, Oh, I've found him. Thank gracious goodness heavins, I've found him!" With these incoherent exclamations, the young woman burst into another fit of crying, and got so dreadfully hysterical, that a couple of women who came up at the moment asked a butcher's boy with a shiny head of hair anointed with suet, who was also looking on, whether he didn't think he had better run for the doctor. To which, the butcher's boy: who appeared of a lounging, not to say indolent disposition: replied, that he thought not.

"Oh, no, no, never mind," said the young woman, grasping Oliver's hand; "I'm better now. Come home directly, you cruel boy! Come!"

"What's the matter, ma'am?" inquired one of the women.

"Oh, ma'am," replied the young woman, "he ran away, near a month ago, from his parents, who are hard-working and respectable people; and went and joined a set of thieves and bad characters; and almost broke his mother's heart."

"Young wretch!" said one woman.

"Go home, do, you little brute," said the other.

"I'm not," replied Oliver, greatly alarmed. "I don't know her. I haven't any sister, or father and mother either. I'm an orphan; I live at Pentonville."

"Oh, only hear him, how he braves it out!" cried the young woman.

"Why, it's Nancy!" exclaimed Oliver; who now saw her face for the first time; and started back, in irrepressible astonishment

"You see he knows me!" cried Nancy, appealing to the bystanders. "He can't help himself. Make him come home, there's good people, or he'll kill his dear mother and father, and break my heart!"

"What the devil's this?" said a man, bursting out of a beer-shop, with a white dog at his heels; "young Oliver! Come home to your poor mother, you young dog! Come home directly."

"I don't belong to them. I don't know them. Help! help!" cried Oliver, struggling in the man's powerful grasp.

"Help!" repeated the man. "Yes; I'll help you, you young rascal! What books are these? You've been a stealing 'em, have you? Give 'em here." With these words, the man tore the volumes from his grasp, and struck him on the head.

"That's right!" cried a looker-on, from a garret-window. "That's the only way of bringing him to his senses!"

"To be sure!" cried a sleepy-faced carpenter, casting an approving look at the garret-window.

"It'll do him good!" said the two women.

"And he shall have it, too!" rejoined the man, administering another blow, and seizing Oliver by the collar. "Come on, you young villain! Here, Bull's-eye, mind him boy! Mind him!"

Weak with recent illness; stupified by the blows and the suddenness of the attack; terrified by the fierce growling of the dog, and the brutality of the man; and overpowered by the conviction of the bystanders that he really was the hardened little wretch he was described to be; what could one poor child do! Darkness had set in; it was a low neighbourhood; no help was near; resistance was useless. In another moment, he was dragged into a labyrinth of dark narrow courts: and forced along them, at a pace which rendered the few cries he dared to give utterance to, wholly unintelligible. It was of little moment, indeed, whether they were intelligible or no; for there was nobody to care for them, had they been ever so plain.

The gas-lamps were lighted; Mrs. Bedwin was waiting anxiously at the open door; the servant had run up the street twenty times to see if there were any traces of Oliver; and still the two old gentlemen sat, perseveringly, in the dark parlour: with the watch between them.

Chapter XVI.

RELATES WHAT BECAME OF OLIVER TWIST, AFTER HE HAD BEEN
CLAIMED BY NANCY.

The narrow streets and courts, at length terminated in a large open space; scattered about which, were pens for beasts: and other indications of a cattle-market. Sikes slackened his pace when they reached this spot: the girl being quite unable to support, any longer, the rapid rate at which they had hitherto walked. Turning to Oliver, he roughly commanded him to take hold of Nancy's hand.

"Do you hear?" growled Sikes, as Oliver hesitated, and looked round.

They were in a dark corner, quite out of the track of passengers. Oliver saw, but too plainly, that resistance would be of no avail. He held out his hand, which Nancy clasped tight in hers.

"Give me the other," said Sikes, seizing Oliver's unoccupied hand. "Here, Bull's-eye!"

The dog looked up, and growled.

"See here, boy!" said Sikes, putting his other hand to Oliver's throat; "if he speaks ever so soft a word, hold him! D'ye mind?"

The dog growled again; and, licking his lips, eyed Oliver as if he were anxious to attach himself to his windpipe without delay.

"He's as willing as a Christian, strike me blind if he isn't!" said Sikes, regarding the animal with a kind of grim and ferocious approval. "Now, you know what you've got to expect, master, so call away as quick as you like; the dog will soon stop that game. Get on, young'un!"

Bull's-eye wagged his tail in acknowledgment of this unusually endearing form of speech; and, giving vent to another admonitory growl for the benefit of Oliver, lead the way onward.

It was Smithfield that they were crossing, although it might have been Grosvenor-square,[1] for anything Oliver knew to the contrary. The night was dark and foggy. The lights in the shops could scarcely struggle through the heavy mist, which thickened every moment and shrouded the streets and houses in gloom; rendering the strange place still stranger in Oliver's eyes; and making his uncertainty the more dismal and depressing.

They had hurried on a few paces, when a deep church-bell struck the hour. With its first stroke, his two conductors stopped: and turned their heads in the direction whence the sound proceeded.

"Eight o'clock, Bill," said Nancy, when the bell ceased.

"What's the good of telling me that; I can hear, can't I?" replied Sikes.

---

1. A fashionable upper-class residential area in the West End of London. "Smithfield": a district on the northeastern boundary of the City of London, dominated by its cattle market.

"I wonder whether *they* can hear it," said Nancy.

"Of course they can," replied Sikes. "It was Bartlemy time when I was shopped;[2] and there warn't a penny trumpet in the fair, as I couldn't hear the squeaking on. Arter I was locked up for the night, the row and din outside, made the thundering old jail so silent, that I could almost have beat my head against the iron plates of the door."

"Poor fellows!" said Nancy, who still had her face turned towards the quarter in which the bell had sounded. "Oh, Bill, such fine young chaps as them!"

"Yes; that's all you women think of," answered Sikes. "Fine young chaps! Well, they're as good as dead, so it don't much matter."

With this consolation, Mr. Sikes appeared to repress a rising tendency to jealousy; and, clasping Oliver's wrist more firmly, told him to step out again.

"Wait a minute!" said the girl: "I wouldn't hurry by, if it was you that was coming out to be hung, the next time eight o'clock struck, Bill. I'd walk round and round the place till I dropped, if the snow was on the ground, and I hadn't a shawl to cover me."

"And what good would that do?" inquired the unsentimental Mr. Sikes. "Unless you could pitch over a file and twenty yards of good stout rope, you might as well be walking fifty mile off, or not walking at all, for all the good it would do me. Come on, will you, and don't stand preaching there."

The girl burst into a laugh; drew her shawl more closely round her; and they walked away. But Oliver felt her hand tremble; and, looking up in her face as they passed a gas-lamp, saw that it had turned a deadly white.

They walked on, by little-frequented and dirty ways, for a full half-hour: meeting very few people: and those appearing from their looks to hold much the same position in society as Mr. Sikes himself. At length they turned into a very filthy narrow street, nearly full of old-clothes shops; the dog, running forward, as if conscious that there was now no further occasion for his keeping on guard, stopped before the door of a shop that was closed and apparently untenanted. The house was in a ruinous condition; and on the door was nailed a board, intimating that it was to let: which looked as if it had hung there, for many years.

"All right," said Sikes, glancing cautiously about.

Nancy stooped below the shutters; and Oliver heard the sound of a bell. They crossed to the opposite side of the street: and stood for a few moments under a lamp. A noise, as if a sash-window were gently raised, was heard; and soon afterwards the door softly opened. Mr. Sikes then seized the terrified boy by the collar with very little ceremony; and all three were quickly inside the house.

---

2. Imprisoned. "Bartlemy time": late August, the time of the Feast of St. Bartholomew.

The passage was perfectly dark. They waited, while the person who had let them in, chained and barred the door.

"Anybody here?" inquired Sikes.

"No," replied a voice, which Oliver thought he had heard before.

"Is the old'un here?" asked the robber.

"Yes," replied the voice; "and precious down in the mouth he has been. Won't he be glad to see you? Oh, no!"

The style of this reply, as well as the voice which delivered it, seemed familiar to Oliver's ears; but it was impossible to distinguish even the form of the speaker in the darkness.

"Let's have a glim,"[3] said Sikes, "or we shall go breaking our necks, or treading on the dog. Look after your legs if you do! That's all."

"Stand still a moment, and I'll get you one," replied the voice. The receding footsteps of the speaker were heard; and, in another minute, the form of Mr. John Dawkins, otherwise the artful Dodger, appeared. He bore in his right hand, a tallow candle stuck in the end of a cleft stick.

The young gentleman did not stop to bestow any other mark of recognition upon Oliver than a humorous grin; but, turning away, beckoned the visitors to follow him down a flight of stairs. They crossed an empty kitchen; and, opening the door of a low earthy-smelling room, which seemed to have been built in a small back-yard, were received with a shout of laughter.

"Oh, my wig, my wig!" cried Master Charles Bates, from whose lungs the laughter had proceeded; "here he is! oh, cry, here he is! Oh, Fagin, look at him; Fagin, do look at him! I can't bear it; it is such a jolly game, I can't bear it. Hold me, somebody, while I laugh it out."

With this irrepressible ebullition[4] of mirth, Master Bates laid himself flat on the floor: and kicked convulsively, for five minutes, in an ecstacy of facetious joy. Then, jumping to his feet, he snatched the cleft stick from the Dodger: and, advancing to Oliver, viewed him round and round; while the Jew, taking off his nightcap, made a great number of low bows to the bewildered boy. The Artful meantime, who was of a rather saturnine[5] disposition, and seldom gave way to merriment when it interfered with business, rifled Oliver's pockets with steady assiduity.

"Look at his togs, Fagin!" said Charley, putting the light so close to his new jacket as nearly to set him on fire. "Look at his togs!—superfine cloth, and the heavy-swell cut! Oh, my eye, what a game! And his books, too; nothing but a gentleman, Fagin!"

"Delighted to see you looking so well, my dear," said the Jew, bowing with mock humility. "The Artful shall give you another suit, my dear, for fear you should spoil that Sunday one. Why didn't you write, my

3. A light.
4. Boiling over.
5. Gloomy.

Oliver's reception by Fagin and the boys.

dear, and say you were coming? We'd have got something warm for supper."

At this, Master Bates roared again; so loud, that Fagin himself relaxed: and even the Dodger smiled; but as the Artful drew forth the five-pound note at that instant, it is doubtful whether the sally or the discovery awakened his merriment.

"Hallo! what's that?" inquired Sikes, stepping forward as the Jew seized the note. "That's mine, Fagin."

"No, no, my dear," said the Jew. "Mine, Bill, mine. You shall have the books."

"If that ain't mine!" said Bill Sikes, putting on his hat with a determined air; "mine and Nancy's, that is: I'll take the boy back again."

The Jew started. Oliver started too, though from a very different cause; for he hoped that the dispute might really end in his being taken back.

"Come! Hand over, will you?" said Sikes.

"This is hardly fair, Bill; hardly fair, is it, Nancy?" inquired the Jew.

"Fair, or not fair," retorted Sikes, "hand over, I tell you! Do you think Nancy and me has got nothing else to do with our precious time but to spend it in scouting arter, and kidnapping, every young boy as gets grabbed through you? Give it here, you avaricious old skeleton; give it here!"

With this gentle remonstrance, Mr. Sikes plucked the note from between the Jew's finger and thumb; and, looking the old man coolly in the face, folded it up small, and tied it in his neckerchief.

"That's for our share of the trouble," said Sikes; "and not half enough, neither. You may keep the books, if you're fond of reading. If you a'n't, sell 'em."

"They're very pretty," said Charley Bates: who, with sundry grimaces, had been affecting to read one of the volumes in question; "beautiful writing, isn't it, Oliver?" At sight of the dismayed look with which Oliver regarded his tormentors, Master Bates, who was blessed with a lively sense of the ludicrous, fell into another ecstasy, more boisterous than the first.

"They belong to the old gentleman," said Oliver, wringing his hands; "to the good, kind, old gentleman who took me into his house, and had me nursed, when I was near dying of the fever. Oh, pray send them back; send him back the books and money. Keep me here all my life long; but pray, pray send them back. He'll think I stole them; the old lady: all of them who were so kind to me: will think I stole them. Oh, do have mercy upon me, and send them back!"

With these words, which were uttered with all the energy of passionate grief, Oliver fell upon his knees at the Jew's feet; and beat his hands together, in perfect desperation.

"The boy's right," remarked Fagin, looking covertly round, and knitting his shaggy eyebrows into a hard knot. "You're right, Oliver, you're right; they *will* think you have stolen 'em. Ha! ha!" chuckled the Jew, rubbing his hands; "it couldn't have happened better, if we had chosen our time!"

"Of course it couldn't," replied Sikes; "I know'd that, directly I see him coming through Clerkenwell, with the books under his arm. It's all right enough. They're soft-hearted psalm-singers, or they wouldn't have taken him in at all; and they'll ask no questions after him, fear they should be obliged to prosecute, and so get him lagged.[6] He's safe enough."

Oliver had looked from one to the other, while these words were being spoken, as if he were bewildered, and could scarcely understand what passed; but when Bill Sikes concluded, he jumped suddenly to his feet, and tore wildly from the room: uttering shrieks for help, which made the bare old house echo to the roof.

"Keep back the dog, Bill!" cried Nancy, springing before the door, and closing it, as the Jew and his two pupils darted out in pursuit; "keep back the dog; he'll tear the boy to pieces."

"Serve him right!" cried Sikes, struggling to disengage himself from the girl's grasp. "Stand off from me, or I'll split your head against the wall."

"I don't care for that, Bill; I don't care for that," screamed the girl, struggling violently with the man: "the child shan't be torn down by the dog, unless you kill me first."

"Shan't he!" said Sikes, setting his teeth fiercely. "I'll soon do that, if you don't keep off."

The housebreaker flung the girl from him to the further end of the room; just as the Jew and the two boys returned: dragging Oliver among them.

"What's the matter here?" said Fagin, looking round.

"The girl's gone mad, I think," replied Sikes, savagely.

"No, she hasn't," said Nancy, pale and breathless from the scuffle; "no, she hasn't, Fagin; don't think it."

"Then keep quiet, will you?" said the Jew, with a threatening look.

"No, I won't do that, neither," replied Nancy, speaking very loud. "Come! What do you think of that?"

Mr. Fagin was sufficiently well acquainted with the manners and customs of that particular species of humanity to which Nancy belonged, to feel tolerably certain that it would be rather unsafe to prolong any conversation with her, at present. With the view of diverting the attention of the company, he turned to Oliver.

"So you wanted to get away, my dear, did you?" said the Jew, taking up a jagged and knotted club which lay in a corner of the fireplace; "eh?"

6. Transported.

Oliver made no reply. But he watched the Jew's motions; and breathed quickly.

"Wanted to get assistance; called for the police; did you?" sneered the Jew, catching the boy by the arm. "We'll cure you of that, my young master."

The Jew inflicted a smart blow on Oliver's shoulders with the club; and was raising it for a second, when the girl, rushing forward, wrested it from his hand. She flung it into the fire, with a force that brought some of the glowing coals whirling out into the room.

"I won't stand by and see it done, Fagin," cried the girl. "You've got the boy, and what more would you have? Let him be—let him be, or I shall put that mark on some of you,[7] that will bring me to the gallows before my time."

The girl stamped her foot violently on the floor as she vented this threat; and with her lips compressed, and her hands clenched, looked alternately at the Jew and the other robber: her face quite colourless from the passion of rage into which she had gradually worked herself.

"Why, Nancy!" said the Jew, in a soothing tone; after a pause, during which he and Mr. Sikes had stared at one another in a disconcerted manner; "you—you're more clever than ever to-night. Ha! ha! my dear, you are acting beautifully."

"Am I!" said the girl. "Take care I don't overdo it. You will be the worse for it, Fagin, if I do; and so I tell you in good time to keep clear of me."

There is something about a roused woman: especially if she add to all her other strong passions, the fierce impulses of recklessness and despair: which few men like to provoke. The Jew saw that it would be hopeless to affect any further mistake regarding the reality of Miss Nancy's rage; and, shrinking involuntarily back a few paces, cast a glance, half imploring and half cowardly, at Sikes: as if to hint that he was the fittest person to pursue the dialogue.

Mr. Sikes, thus mutely appealed to; and possibly feeling his personal pride and influence interested in the immediate reduction of Miss Nancy to reason; gave utterance to about a couple of score of curses and threats, the rapid production of which reflected great credit on the fertility of his invention. As they produced no visible effect on the object against whom they were discharged, however, he resorted to more tangible arguments.

"What do you mean by this?" said Sikes; backing the inquiry with a very common imprecation concerning the most beautiful of human features:[8] which, if it were heard above, only once out of every fifty thousand times that it is uttered below, would render blindness as com-

7. I'll inform on you to the police.
8. Damn your eyes!

mon a disorder as measles; "what do you mean by it? Burn my body! Do you know who you are, and what you are?"[9]

"Oh, yes, I know all about it," replied the girl, laughing hysterically; and shaking her head from side to side, with a poor assumption of indifference.

"Well, then, keep quiet," rejoined Sikes, with a growl like that he was accustomed to use when addressing his dog, "or I'll quiet you for a good long time to come."

The girl laughed again: even less composedly than before; and, darting a hasty look at Sikes, turned her face aside and bit her lip till the blood came.

"You're a nice one," added Sikes, as he surveyed her with a contemptuous air, "to take up the humane and gen—teel side! A pretty subject for the child, as you call him, to make a friend of!"

"God Almighty help me, I am!" cried the girl passionately; "and I wish I had been struck dead in the street, or had changed places with them we passed so near to-night, before I had lent a hand in bringing him here. He's a thief, a liar, a devil: all that's bad, from this night forth. Isn't that enough for the old wretch without blows?"

"Come, come, Sikes," said the Jew, appealing to him in a remonstratory tone, and motioning towards the boys, who were eagerly attentive to all that passed; "we must have civil words; civil words, Bill."

"Civil words!" cried the girl, whose passion was frightful to see. "Civil words, you villain! Yes; you deserve 'em from me. I thieved for you when I was a child not half as old as this!" pointing to Oliver. "I have been in the same trade, and in the same service, for twelve years since. Don't you know it? Speak out! don't you know it?"

"Well, well," replied the Jew, with an attempt at pacification; "and, if you have, it's your living!"

"Aye, it is!" returned the girl; not speaking, but pouring out the words in one continuous and vehement scream. "It is my living; and the cold, wet, dirty streets are my home; and you're the wretch that drove me to them long ago; and that'll keep me there, day and night, day and night, till I die!"

"I shall do you a mischief!" interposed the Jew, goaded by these reproaches; "a mischief worse than that, if you say much more!"

The girl said nothing more; but, tearing her hair and dress in a transport of frenzy, made such a rush at the Jew as would probably have left signal marks of her revenge upon him, had not her wrists been seized by Sikes at the right moment; upon which, she made a few ineffectual struggles: and fainted.

"She's all right now," said Sikes, laying her down in a corner. "She's uncommon strong in the arms, when she's up in this way."

9. Sikes alludes to Nancy being a prostitute.

The Jew wiped his forehead: and smiled, as if it were a relief to have the disturbance over; but neither he, nor Sikes, nor the dog, nor the boys, seemed to consider it in any other light than a common occurrence incidental to business.

"It's the worst of having to do with women," said the Jew, replacing his club; "but they're clever, and we can't get on, in our line, without 'em. Charley, show Oliver to bed."

"I suppose he'd better not wear his best clothes to-morrow, Fagin, had he?" inquired Charley Bates.

"Certainly not," replied the Jew, reciprocating the grin with which Charley put the question.

Master Bates, apparently much delighted with his commission, took the cleft stick: and led Oliver into an adjacent kitchen, where there were two or three of the beds on which he had slept before; and here, with many uncontrollable bursts of laughter, he produced the identical old suit of clothes which Oliver had so much congratulated himself upon leaving off at Mr. Brownlow's; and the accidental display of which, to Fagin, by the Jew who purchased them, had been the very first clue received, of his whereabout.

"Pull off the smart ones," said Charley, "and I'll give 'em to Fagin to take care of. What fun it is!"

Poor Oliver unwillingly complied. Master Bates, rolling up the new clothes under his arm, departed from the room; leaving Oliver in the dark; and locking the door behind him.

The noise of Charley's laughter; and the voice of Miss Betsy, who opportunely arrived to throw water over her friend, and perform other feminine offices for the promotion of her recovery; might have kept many people awake under more happy circumstances than those in which Oliver was placed. But he was sick and weary; and he soon fell sound asleep.

Chapter XVII.

OLIVER'S DESTINY, CONTINUING UNPROPITIOUS, BRINGS A GREAT MAN TO
LONDON TO INJURE HIS REPUTATION.

It is the custom on the stage: in all good, murderous melodramas: to present the tragic and the comic scenes, in as regular alternation, as the layers of red and white in a side of streaky, well-cured bacon. The hero sinks upon his straw bed, weighed down by fetters and misfortunes; and, in the next scene, his faithful but unconscious squire regales the audience with a comic song. We behold, with throbbing bosoms, the heroine in the grasp of a proud and ruthless baron: her virtue and her life alike in danger; drawing forth her dagger to preserve the one at the cost of the other; and, just as our expectations are wrought up to the highest pitch, a whistle is heard: and we are straightway transported to the great hall of the castle: where a grey-headed seneschal[1] sings a funny chorus with a funnier body of vassals, who are free of all sorts of places from church vaults to palaces, and roam about in company, carolling perpetually.

Such changes appear absurd; but they are not so unnatural as they would seem at first sight. The transitions in real life from well-spread boards to death-beds, and from mourning weeds to holiday garments, are not a whit less startling; only, there, we are busy actors, instead of passive lookers-on; which makes a vast difference. The actors in the mimic life of the theatre, are blind to violent transitions and abrupt impulses of passion or feeling, which, presented before the eyes of mere spectators, are at once condemned as outrageous and preposterous.

As sudden shiftings of the scene, and rapid changes of time and place, are not only sanctioned in books by long usage, but are by many considered as the great art of authorship: an author's skill in his craft being, by such critics, chiefly estimated with relation to the dilemmas in which he leaves his characters at the end of every chapter: this brief introduction to the present one may perhaps be deemed unnecessary. If so, let it be considered a delicate intimation on the part of the historian that he is going back, directly, to the town in which Oliver Twist was born; the reader taking it for granted that there are good and substantial reasons for making the journey, or he would not be invited to proceed upon such an expedition, on any account.

Mr. Bumble emerged at early morning from the workhouse gate; and walked, with portly carriage and commanding steps, up the High-street. He was in the full bloom and pride of beadlehood; his cocked hat and coat were dazzling in the morning sun; and he clutched his cane with the vigorous tenacity of health and power. Mr. Bumble always carried his head high; but this morning it was higher than usual. There was an abstraction in his eye, an elevation in his air, which might have warned an observant stranger that thoughts were passing in the beadle's mind, too great for utterance.

Mr. Bumble stopped not to converse with the small shopkeepers and others who spoke to him, deferentially, as he passed along. He merely returned their salutations with a wave of his hand; and relaxed not in his dignified pace, until he reached the farm where Mrs. Mann tended the infant paupers with parochial care.

"Drat that beadle!" said Mrs. Mann, hearing the well-known shaking at the garden gate. "If it isn't him at this time in the morning! Lauk, Mr. Bumble, only think of its being you! Well, dear me, it *is* a pleasure, this is! Come into the parlour, sir, please."

---

1. A medieval word for the chief servant or steward in charge of an aristocratic household.

The first sentence was addressed to Susan; and the exclamations of delight were uttered to Mr. Bumble: as the good lady unlocked the garden gate: and showed him, with great attention and respect, into the house.

"Mrs. Mann," said Mr. Bumble; not sitting upon, or dropping himself into a seat, as any common jackanapes would: but letting himself gradually and slowly down into a chair; "Mrs. Mann, ma'am, good morning."

"Well, and good morning to *you*, sir," replied Mrs. Mann, with many smiles; "and hoping you find yourself well, sir?"

"So-so, Mrs. Mann," replied the beadle. "A porochial life is not a bed of roses, Mrs. Mann."

"Ah, that it isn't indeed, Mr. Bumble," rejoined the lady. And all the infant paupers might have chorussed the rejoinder with great propriety, if they had heard it.

"A porochial life, ma'am," continued Mr. Bumble, striking the table with his cane, "is a life of worrit, and vexation, and hardihood; but all public characters, as I may say, must suffer prosecution."

Mrs. Mann, not very well knowing what the beadle meant, raised her hands with a look of sympathy: and sighed.

"Ah! You may well sigh, Mrs. Mann!" said the beadle.

Finding she had done right, Mrs. Mann sighed again: evidently to the satisfaction of the public character: who, repressing a complacent smile by looking sternly at his cocked hat, said,

"Mrs. Mann, I am a going to London."

"Lauk,[2] Mr. Bumble!" cried Mrs. Mann, starting back.

"To London, ma'am," resumed the inflexible beadle, "by coach. I and two paupers, Mrs. Mann! A legal action is a coming on, about a settlement; and the board has appointed me—me, Mrs. Mann—to depose to the matter before the quarter-sessions at Clerkinwell.[3] And I very much question," added Mr. Bumble, drawing himself up, "whether the Clerkinwell Sessions will not find themselves in the wrong box before they have done with me."

"Oh! you mustn't be too hard upon them, sir," said Mrs. Mann, coaxingly.

"The Clerkinwell Sessions have brought it upon themselves, ma'am," replied Mr. Bumble; "and if the Clerkinwell Sessions find that they come off rather worse than they expected, the Clerkinwell Sessions have only themselves to thank."

There was so much determination and depth of purpose about the menacing manner in which Mr. Bumble delivered himself of these words, that Mrs. Mann appeared quite awed by them. At length, she said:

2. An exclamation of surprise.
3. The quarterly meeting of the magistrate's court in the borough of Clerkenwell.

"You're going by coach, sir? I thought it was always usual to send them paupers in carts."

"That's when they're ill, Mrs. Mann," said the beadle. "We put the sick paupers into open carts in the rainy weather, to prevent their taking cold."

"Oh!" said Mrs. Mann.

"The opposition coach contracts for these two; and takes them cheap," said Mr. Bumble. "They are both in a very low state, and we find it would come two pound cheaper to move 'em than to bury 'em—that is, if we can throw 'em upon another parish, which I think we shall be able to do, if they don't die upon the road to spite us. Ha! ha! ha!"

When Mr. Bumble had laughed a little while, his eyes again encountered the cocked hat; and he became grave.

"We are forgetting business, ma'am," said the beadle; "here is your porochial stipend for the month."

Mr. Bumble produced some silver money rolled up in paper, from his pocket-book; and requested a receipt: which Mrs. Mann wrote.

"It's very much blotted, sir," said the farmer of infants; "but it's formal enough, I dare say. Thank you, Mr. Bumble, sir. I am very much obliged to you, I'm sure."

Mr. Bumble nodded, blandly, in acknowledgment of Mrs. Mann's curtsey; and inquired how the children were.

"Bless their dear little hearts!" said Mrs. Mann with emotion, "they're as well as can be, the dears! Of course, except the two that died last week. And little Dick."

"Isn't that boy no better?" inquired Mr. Bumble.

Mrs. Mann shook her head.

"He's a ill-conditioned, wicious, bad-disposed porochial child that," said Mr. Bumble angrily. "Where is he?"

"I'll bring him to you in one minute, sir," replied Mrs. Mann. "Here, you Dick!"

After some calling, Dick was discovered. Having had his face put under the pump, and dried upon Mrs. Mann's gown, he was led into the awful presence of Mr. Bumble, the beadle.

The child was pale and thin; his cheeks were sunken; and his eyes large and bright. The scanty parish dress: the livery of his misery: hung loosely on his feeble body; and his young limbs had wasted away, like those of an old man.

Such was the little being who stood trembling beneath Mr. Bumble's glance; not daring to lift his eyes from the floor; and dreading even to hear the beadle's voice.

"Can't you look at the gentleman, you obstinate boy?" said Mrs. Mann.

The child meekly raised his eyes, and encountered those of Mr. Bumble.

"What's the matter with you, porochial Dick?" inquired Mr. Bumble with well-timed jocularity.

"Nothing, sir," replied the child faintly.

"I should think not," said Mrs. Mann, who had of course laughed very much at Mr. Bumble's humour. "You want for nothing, I'm sure."

"I should like—" faltered the child.

"Hey-day!" interposed Mrs. Mann, "I suppose you're going to say that you *do* want for something, now? Why, you little wretch——"

"Stop, Mrs. Mann, stop!" said the beadle, raising his hand with a show of authority. "Like what, sir; eh?"

"I should like," faltered the child, "if somebody that can write, would put a few words down for me on a piece of paper: and fold it up and seal it. and keep it for me, after I am laid in the ground."

"Why, what does the boy mean?" exclaimed Mr. Bumble, on whom the earnest manner and wan aspect of the child had made some impression: accustomed as he was, to such things. "What do you mean, sir?"

"I should like," said the child, "to leave my dear love to poor Oliver Twist; and to let him know how often I have sat by myself and cried to think of his wandering about in the dark nights with nobody to help him. And I should like to tell him," said the child, pressing his small hands together, and speaking with great fervour, "that I was glad to die when I was very young; for, perhaps, if I had lived to be a man, and had grown old, my little sister, who is in Heaven, might forget me, or be unlike me; and it would be so much happier if we were both children there together."

Mr. Bumble surveyed the little speaker, from head to foot, with indescribable astonishment; and, turning to his companion, said, "They're all in one story, Mrs. Mann. That out-dacious Oliver has demogalized[4] them all!"

"I couldn't have believed it, sir?" said Mrs. Mann, holding up her hands, and looking malignantly at Dick. "I never see such a hardened little wretch!"

"Take him away, ma'am!" said Mr. Bumble imperiously. "This must be stated to the board, Mrs. Mann."

"I hope the gentlemen will understand that it isn't my fault, sir?" said Mrs. Mann, whimpering pathetically.

"They shall understand that, ma'am; they shall be acquainted with the true state of the case," said Mr. Bumble. "There; take him away. I can't bear the sight on him."

Dick was immediately taken away, and locked up in the coal-cellar. Mr. Bumble shortly afterwards took himself off, to prepare for his journey.

---

4. Demoralized. "Out-dacious": audacious.

At six o'clock next morning, Mr. Bumble: having exchanged his cocked hat for a round one, and encased his person in a blue great-coat with a cape to it: took his place on the outside of the coach, accompanied by the criminals whose settlement was disputed; with whom, in due course of time, he arrived in London. He experienced no other crosses, on the way, than those which originated in the perverse behaviour of the two paupers, who persisted in shivering, and complaining of the cold, in a manner which, Mr. Bumble declared, caused his teeth to chatter in his head, and made him feel quite uncomfortable; although he had a great-coat on.

Having disposed of these evil-minded persons for the night, Mr. Bumble sat himself down in the house at which the coach stopped: and took a temperate dinner of steaks, oyster-sauce, and porter. Putting a glass of hot gin-and-water on the chimney-piece, he drew his chair to the fire; and, with sundry moral reflections on the too-prevalent sin of discontent and complaining, composed himself to read the paper.

The very first paragraph upon which Mr. Bumble's eyes rested, was the following advertisement.

"FIVE GUINEAS REWARD.

"WHEREAS a young boy, named Oliver Twist, absconded, or was enticed, on Thursday evening last, from his home, at Pentonville; and has not since been heard of. The above reward will be paid to any person who will give such information as will lead to the discovery of the said Oliver Twist, or tend to throw any light upon his previous history, in which the advertiser is, for many reasons, warmly interested."

And then followed a full description of Oliver's dress, person, appearance, and disappearance: with the name and address of Mr. Brownlow at full length.

Mr. Bumble opened his eyes; read the advertisement, slowly and carefully, three several times; and in something more than five minutes was on his way to Pentonville: having actually, in his excitement, left the glass of hot gin-and-water, untasted.

"Is Mr. Brownlow at home?" inquired Mr. Bumble of the girl who opened the door.

To this inquiry the girl returned the not uncommon, but rather evasive reply of "I don't know; where do you come from?"

Mr. Bumble no sooner uttered Oliver's name, in explanation of his errand, than Mrs. Bedwin, who had been listening at the parlour door, hastened into the passage in a breathless state.

"Come in—come in," said the old lady: "I knew we should hear of him. Poor dear! I knew we should! I was certain of it. Bless his heart! I said so, all along."

Having said this, the worthy old lady hurried back into the parlour again; and seating herself on a sofa, burst into tears. The girl, who was not quite so susceptible, had run up-stairs meanwhile; and now returned with a request that Mr. Bumble would follow her immediately: which he did.

He was shown into the little back study, where sat Mr. Brownlow and his friend Mr. Grimwig, with decanters and glasses before them. The latter gentleman at once burst into the exclamation:

"A beadle! A parish beadle, or I'll eat my head."

"Pray don't interrupt just now," said Mr. Brownlow. "Take a seat, will you?"

Mr. Bumble sat himself down: quite confounded by the oddity of Mr. Grimwig's manner. Mr. Brownlow moved the lamp, so as to obtain an uninterrupted view of the Beadle's countenance; and said, with a little impatience,

"Now, sir, you come in consequence of having seen the advertisement?"

"Yes, sir," said Mr. Bumble.

"And you *are* a beadle, are you not?" inquired Mr. Grimwig.

"I am a porochial beadle, gentlemen," rejoined Mr. Bumble, proudly.

"Of course," observed Mr. Grimwig aside to his friend, "I knew he was. A beadle all over!"

Mr. Brownlow gently shook his head to impose silence on his friend, and resumed:

"Do you know where this poor boy is now?"

"No more than nobody," replied Mr. Bumble.

"Well, what *do* you know of him?" inquired the old gentleman. "Speak out, my friend, if you have anything to say. What *do* you know of him?"

"You don't happen to know any good of him, do you?" said Mr. Grimwig, caustically; after an attentive perusal of Mr. Bumble's features.

Mr. Bumble catching at the inquiry very quickly, shook his head with portentous solemnity.

"You see?" said Mr. Grimwig, looking triumphantly at Mr. Brownlow.

Mr. Brownlow looked apprehensively at Mr. Bumble's pursed-up countenance; and requested him to communicate what he knew regarding Oliver, in as few words as possible.

Mr. Bumble put down his hat; unbuttoned his coat; folded his arms; inclined his head in a retrospective manner; and, after a few moments' reflection, commenced his story.

It would be tedious if given in the beadle's words: occupying, as it did, some twenty minutes in the telling; but the sum and substance of it was, That Oliver was a foundling, born of low and vicious parents. That he had, from his birth, displayed no better qualities than treachery, ingratitude, and malice. That he had terminated his brief career in the place of his birth, by making a sanguinary and cowardly attack on an unoffending lad; and running away in the night-time from his master's house. In proof of his really being the person he represented himself, Mr. Bumble laid upon the table the papers he had brought to town: and, folding his arms again, awaited Mr. Brownlow's observations.

"I fear it is all too true," said the old gentleman sorrowfully, after looking over the papers. "This is not much for your intelligence; but I would gladly have given you treble the money, if it had been favourable to the boy."

It is not at all improbable that if Mr. Bumble had been possessed of this information at an earlier period of the interview, he might have imparted a very different colouring to his little history. It was too late to do it now, however; so he shook his head gravely: and, pocketing the five guineas, withdrew.

Mr. Brownlow paced the room to and fro for some minutes; evidently so much disturbed by the beadle's tale, that even Mr. Grimwig forbore to vex him further.

At length he stopped, and rang the bell violently.

"Mrs. Bedwin," said Mr. Brownlow, when the housekeeper appeared; "that boy, Oliver, is an impostor."

"It can't be, sir. It cannot be," said the old lady energetically.

"I tell you he is," retorted the old gentleman. "What do you mean by can't be? We have just heard a full account of him from his birth; and he has been a thorough-paced little villain, all his life."

"I never will believe it, sir," replied the old lady, firmly. "Never!"

"You old women never believe anything but quack-doctors, and lying story-books," growled Mr. Grimwig. "I knew it all along. Why didn't you take my advice in the beginning; you would, if he hadn't had a fever, I suppose, eh? He was interesting, wasn't he? Interesting! Bah!" And Mr. Grimwig poked the fire with a flourish.

"He was a dear, grateful, gentle child, sir," retorted Mrs. Bedwin, indignantly. "I know what children are, sir; and have done these forty years; and people who can't say the same, shouldn't say anything about them. That's my opinion!"

This was a hard hit at Mr. Grimwig, who was a bachelor. As it extorted nothing from that gentleman but a smile, the old lady tossed her head, and smoothed down her apron preparatory to another speech, when she was stopped by Mr. Brownlow.

"Silence!" said the old gentleman, feigning an anger he was far from feeling. "Never let me hear the boy's name again. I rang to tell you that. Never. Never, on any pretence, mind! You may leave the room, Mrs. Bedwin. Remember! I am in earnest."

There were sad hearts at Mr. Brownlow's that night.

Oliver's heart sank within him, when he thought of his good kind friends; it was well for him that he could not know what they had heard, or it might have broken outright.

Chapter XVIII.

HOW OLIVER PASSED HIS TIME, IN THE IMPROVING SOCIETY OF HIS REPUTABLE FRIENDS.

About noon next day, when the Dodger and Master Bates had gone out to pursue their customary avocations, Mr. Fagin took the opportunity of reading Oliver a long lecture on the crying sin of ingratitude: of which he clearly demonstrated he had been guilty, to no ordinary extent, in wilfully absenting himself from the society of his anxious friends; and, still more, in endeavouring to escape from them after so much trouble and expense had been incurred in his recovery. Mr. Fagin laid great stress on the fact of his having taken Oliver in, and cherished him, when, without his timely aid, he might have perished with hunger; and he related the dismal and affecting history of a young lad whom, in his philanthropy, he had succoured under parallel circumstances, but who, proving unworthy of his confidence, and evincing a desire to communicate with the police, had unfortunately come to be hanged at the Old Bailey[1] one morning. Mr. Fagin did not seek to conceal his share in the catastrophe, but lamented with tears in his eyes that the wrong-headed and treacherous behaviour of the young person in question, had rendered it necessary that he should become the victim of certain evidence for the crown: which, if it were not precisely true, was indispensably necessary for the safety of him (Mr. Fagin) and a few select friends. Mr. Fagin concluded by drawing a rather disagreeable picture of the discomforts of hanging; and, with great friendliness and politeness of manner, expressed his anxious hope that he might never be obliged to submit Oliver Twist to that unpleasant operation.

Little Oliver's blood ran cold, as he listened to the Jew's words, and imperfectly comprehended the dark threats conveyed in them. That it was possible even for justice itself to confound the innocent with the guilty when they were in accidental companionship, he knew already; and that deeply-laid plans for the destruction of inconveniently knowing, or over-communicative, persons, had been really devised and carried out by the old Jew on more occasions than one, he thought by no means unlikely, when he recollected the general nature of the altercations between that gentleman and Mr. Sikes: which seemed to bear reference to some foregone conspiracy of the kind. As he glanced timidly up, and

1. The central criminal court for the City of London and for Middlesex County.

met the Jew's searching look, he felt that his pale face and trembling limbs were neither unnoticed, nor unrelished by, that wary old gentleman.

The Jew smiled hideously; and, patting Oliver on the head, said, that if he kept himself quiet, and applied himself to business, he saw they would be very good friends yet. Then, taking his hat; and covering himself with an old patched great-coat; he went out, and locked the room-door behind him.

And so Oliver remained all that day, and for the greater part of many subsequent days; seeing nobody, between early morning and midnight; and left, during the long hours, to commune with his own thoughts: which, never failing to revert to his kind friends, and the opinion they must long ago have formed of him, were sad indeed.

After the lapse of a week or so, the Jew left the room-door unlocked; and he was at liberty to wander about the house.

It was a very dirty place. The rooms up stairs, had great high wooden chimney-pieces and large doors, with paneled walls and cornices to the ceilings: which, although they were black with neglect and dust, were ornamented in various ways; from all of which tokens Oliver concluded that a long time ago, before the old Jew was born, it had belonged to better people, and had perhaps been quite gay and handsome: dismal and dreary as it looked now.

Spiders had built their webs in the angles of the walls and ceilings; and sometimes, when Oliver walked softly into a room, the mice would scamper across the floor, and run back terrified to their holes. With these exceptions, there was neither sight nor sound of any living thing; and often, when it grew dark, and he was tired of wandering from room to room, he would crouch in the corner of the passage by the street-door, to be as near living people as he could; and would remain there, listening and counting the hours, until the Jew or the boys returned.

In all the rooms, the mouldering shutters were fast closed: and the bars which held them were screwed tight into the wood; the only light which was admitted, stealing its way through round holes at the top: which made the rooms more gloomy, and filled them with strange shadows. There was a back-garret window, with rusty bars outside, which had no shutter; and out of this, Oliver often gazed with a melancholy face for hours together; but nothing was to be descried from it but a confused and crowded mass of house-tops, blackened chimneys, and gable-ends. Sometimes, indeed, a ragged grizzly head might be seen, peering over the parapet-wall of a distant house: but it was quickly withdrawn again; and as the window of Oliver's observatory was nailed down, and dimmed with the rain and smoke of years, it was as much as he could do to make out the forms of the different objects beyond, without making any attempt to be seen or heard—which he had as much chance of being, as if he had lived inside the ball of St. Paul's Cathedral.[2]

One afternoon: the Dodger and Master Bates being engaged out that evening: the first-named young gentleman took it into his head to evince some anxiety regarding the decoration of his person (which, to do him justice, was by no means an habitual weakness with him;) and, with this end and aim, he condescendingly commanded Oliver to assist him in his toilet, straightway.

Oliver was but too glad to make himself useful; too happy to have some faces, however bad, to look upon; and too desirous to conciliate those about him when he could honestly do so; to throw any objection in the way of this proposal. So he at once expressed his readiness; and, kneeling on the floor, while the Dodger sat upon the table so that he could take his foot in his lap, he applied himself to a process which Mr. Dawkins designated as "japanning his trotter-cases." Which phrase, rendered into plain English, signifieth, cleaning his boots.

Whether it was the sense of freedom and independence which a rational animal may be supposed to feel when he sits on a table in an easy attitude, smoking a pipe, swinging one leg carelessly to and fro, and having his boots cleaned all the time, without even the past trouble of having taken them off, or the prospective misery of putting them on, to disturb his reflections; or whether it was the goodness of the tobacco that soothed the feelings of the Dodger, or the mildness of the beer that mollified his thoughts, he was evidently tinctured, for the nonce,[3] with a spice of romance and enthusiasm, foreign to his general nature. He looked down on Oliver, with a thoughtful countenance, for a brief space; and then, raising his head, and heaving a gentle sigh, said, half in abstraction, and half to Master Bates:

"What a pity it is he isn't a prig!"[4]

"Ah!" said Master Charles Bates; "he don't know what's good for him."

The Dodger sighed again, and resumed his pipe: as did Charley Bates. They both smoked, for some seconds, in silence.

"I suppose you don't even know what a prig is?" said the Dodger mournfully.

"I think I know that," replied Oliver, looking up. "It's a th—; you're one, are you not?" inquired Oliver, checking himself.

"I am," replied the Dodger. "I'd scorn to be anythink else." Mr. Dawkins gave his hat a ferocious cock, after delivering this sentiment; and looked at Master Bates, as if to denote that he would feel obliged by his saying anything to the contrary.

"I am," repeated the Dodger. "So's Charley. So's Fagin. So's Sikes.

---

2. St. Paul's Cathedral, in central London, has as its pinnacle at the top of the dome a hollow golden ball.
3. For the time being.
4. A thief.

So's Nancy. So's Bet. So we all are, down to the dog. And he's the downiest one of the lot!"

"And the least given to peaching," added Charley Bates.

"He wouldn't so much as bark in a witness-box, for fear of committing himself; no, not if you tied him up in one, and left him there without wittles for a fortnight," said the Dodger.

"Not a bit of it," observed Charley.

"He's a rum dog. Don't he look fierce at any strange cove that laughs or sings when he's in company!" pursued the Dodger. "Won't he growl at all, when he hears a fiddle playing! And don't he hate other dogs as ain't of his breed!—Oh, no!"

"He's an out-and-out Christian," said Charley.

This was merely intended as a tribute to the animal's abilities, but it was an appropriate remark in another sense, if Master Bates had only known it; for there are a great many ladies and gentlemen, claiming to be out-and-out Christians, between whom, and Mr. Sikes' dog, there exist very strong and singular points of resemblance.

"Well, well," said the Dodger, recurring to the point from which they had strayed: with that mindfulness of his profession which influenced all his proceedings. "This has'nt got anything to do with young Green[5] here."

"No more it has," said Charley. "Why don't you put yourself under Fagin, Oliver?"

"And make your fortun' out of hand?" added the Dodger, with a grin.

"And so be able to retire on your property, and do the gen-teel: as I mean to, in the very next leap-year but four that ever comes, and the forty-second Tuesday in Trinity-week,"[6] said Charley Bates.

"I don't like it," rejoined Oliver timidly; "I wish they would let me go. I—I—would rather go."

"And Fagin would *rather* not!" rejoined Charley.

Oliver knew this too well; but, thinking it might be dangerous to express his feelings more openly, he only sighed, and went on with his boot-cleaning.

"Go!" exclaimed the Dodger. "Why, where's your spirit? Don't you take any pride out of yourself? Would you go and be dependent on your friends?"

"Oh, blow that!" said Master Bates: drawing two or three silk hand-kerchiefs from his pocket, and tossing them into a cupboard, "that's too mean; that is."

"*I* couldn't do it," said the Dodger, with an air of haughty disgust.

5. Innocent.
6. The week beginning the first Sunday after Pentecost, eight weeks after Easter; Charley means that the day when he will be able to retire as a gentleman will never come. "Do the gen-teel": live like a gentleman.

"You can leave your friends, though," said Oliver with a half smile; "and let them be punished for what you did."

"That," rejoined the Dodger, with a wave of his pipe, "That was all out of consideration for Fagin, 'cause the traps[7] know that we work together, and he might have got into trouble if we hadn't made our lucky; that was the move, wasn't it, Charley?"

Master Bates nodded assent, and would have spoken; but the recollection of Oliver's flight came so suddenly upon him, that the smoke he was inhaling got entangled with a laugh; and went up into his head, and down into his throat: and brought on a fit of coughing and stamping, about five minutes long.

"Look here," said the Dodger, drawing forth a handful of shillings and halfpence. "Here's a jolly life! What's the odds where it comes from? Here, catch hold; there's plenty more where they were took from. You won't, won't you? Oh, you precious flat!"[8]

"It's naughty, ain't it, Oliver?" inquired Charley Bates. "He'll come to be scragged,[9] won't he?"

"I don't know what that means," replied Oliver.

"Something in this way, old feller," said Charley. As he said it, Master Bates caught up an end of his neckerchief; and, holding it erect in the air, dropped his head on his shoulder, and jerked a curious sound through his teeth: thereby indicating, by a lively pantomimic representation, that scragging and hanging were one and the same thing.

"That's what it means," said Charley. "Look how he stares, Jack! I never did see such prime company as that 'ere boy; he'll be the death of me, I know he will." Master Charles Bates, having laughed heartily again, resumed his pipe with tears in his eyes.

"You've been brought up bad," said the Dodger, surveying his boots with much satisfaction when Oliver had polished them. "Fagin will make something of you, though, or you'll be the first he ever had that turned out unprofitable. You'd better begin at once; for you'll come to the trade long before you think of it; and you're only losing time, Oliver."

Master Bates backed this advice with sundry moral admonitions of his own: which, being exhausted, he and his friend Mr. Dawkins launched into a glowing description of the numerous pleasures incidental to the life they led, interspersed with a variety of hints to Oliver that the best thing he could do, would be to secure Fagin's favour without more delay, by the means which they themselves had employed to gain it.

"And always put this in your pipe, Nolly," said the Dodger, as the Jew was heard unlocking the door above, "if you don't take fogles and tickers——"

7. Policemen.
8. Simpleton.
9. Hanged.

"What's the good of talking in that way?" interposed Master Bates: "he don't know what you mean."

"If you don't take pocket hankechers and watches," said the Dodger, reducing his conversation to the level of Oliver's capacity, "some other cove will; so that the coves that lose 'em will be all the worse, and you'll be all the worse too, and nobody half a ha'p'orth[1] the better, except the chaps wot gets them—and you've just as good a right to them as they have."

"To be sure, to be sure!" said the Jew, who had entered, unseen by Oliver. "It all lies in a nutshell, my dear; in a nutshell, take the Dodger's word for it. Ha! ha! He understands the catechism of his trade."

The old man rubbed his hands gleefully together, as he corroborated the Dodger's reasoning in these terms; and chuckled with delight at his pupil's proficiency.

The conversation proceeded no farther at this time, for the Jew had returned home accompanied by Miss Betsy, and a gentleman whom Oliver had never seen before, but who was accosted by the Dodger as Tom Chitling; and who, having lingered on the stairs to exchange a few gallantries with the lady, now made his appearance.

Mr. Chitling was older in years than the Dodger: having perhaps numbered eighteen winters; but there was a degree of deference in his deportment towards that young gentleman which seemed to indicate that he felt himself conscious of a slight inferiority, in point of genius and professional acquirements. He had small twinkling eyes, and a pock-marked face; wore a fur cap, a dark corduroy jacket, greasy fustian[2] trousers, and an apron. His wardrobe was, in truth, rather out of repair; but he excused himself to the company by stating that his "time" was only out an hour before; and that, in consequence of having worn the regimentals[3] for six weeks past, he had not been able to bestow any attention on his private clothes. Mr. Chitling added, with strong marks of irritation, that the new way of fumigating clothes up yonder was infernal unconstitutional, for it burnt holes in them, and there was no remedy against the County. The same remark he considered to apply to the regulation mode of cutting the hair: which he held to be decidedly unlawful. Mr. Chitling wound up his observations by stating that he had not touched a drop of anything for forty-two mortal long hard-working days; and that he "wished he might be busted if he warn't as dry as a lime-basket."

"Where do you think the gentleman has come from, Oliver?" inquired the Jew with a grin, as the other boys put a bottle of spirits on the table.

"I—I—don't know, sir," replied Oliver.

1. Halfpenny.
2. A coarse cloth made of cotton and flax.
3. Prison uniform.

"Who's that?" inquired Tom Chitling, casting a contemptuous look at Oliver.

"A young friend of mine, my dear," replied the Jew.

"He's in luck then," said the young man, with a meaning look at Fagin. "Never mind where I came from, young 'un; you'll find your way there, soon enough, I'll bet a crown!"[4]

At this sally, the boys laughed. After some more jokes on the same subject, they exchanged a few short whispers with Fagin; and withdrew.

After some words apart between the last comer and Fagin, they drew their chairs towards the fire; and the Jew, telling Oliver to come and sit by him, led the conversation to the topics most calculated to interest his hearers. These were, the great advantages of the trade, the proficiency of the Dodger, the amiability of Charley Bates, and the liberality of the Jew himself. At length these subjects displayed signs of being thoroughly exhausted; and Mr. Chitling did the same: for the house of correction[5] becomes fatiguing after a week or two. Miss Betsy accordingly withdrew; and left the party to their repose.

From this day, Oliver was seldom left alone; but was placed in almost constant communication with the two boys, who played the old game with the Jew every day: whether for their own improvement or Oliver's, Mr. Fagin best knew. At other times, the old man would tell them stories of robberies he had committed in his younger days: mixed up with so much that was droll and curious, that Oliver could not help laughing heartily, and showing that he was amused in spite of all his better feelings.

In short, the wily old Jew had the boy in his toils; and, having prepared his mind, by solitude and gloom, to prefer any society to the companionship of his own sad thoughts in such a dreary place, was now slowly instilling into his soul the poison which he hoped would blacken it, and change its hue for ever.

Chapter XIX.

IN WHICH A NOTABLE PLAN IS DISCUSSED AND DETERMINED ON.

It was a chill, damp, windy night, when the Jew: buttoning his great-coat tight round his shrivelled body, and pulling the collar up over his ears so as completely to obscure the lower part of his face: emerged from his den. He paused on the step as the door was locked and chained

4. Five shillings.
5. Coldbath Fields, the Middlesex House of Correction in Clerkenwell, was the prison of designation for minor offenders with prison sentences up to three years. It was run on the silent system, which Dickens favored, in contrast to the solitary system. Prisoners had one another's company but could not speak.

behind him; and having listened while the boys made all secure, and until their retreating footsteps were no longer audible, slunk down the street as quickly as he could.

The house to which Oliver had been conveyed, was in the neighbourhood of Whitechapel.[1] The Jew stopped for an instant at the corner of the street; and, glancing suspiciously round, crossed the road, and struck off in the direction of Spitalfields.

The mud lay thick upon the stones: and a black mist hung over the streets; the rain fell sluggishly down: and everything felt cold and clammy to the touch. It seemed just the night when it befitted such a being as the Jew, to be abroad. As he glided stealthily along, creeping beneath the shelter of the walls and doorways, the hideous old man seemed like some loathsome reptile, engendered in the slime and darkness through which he moved: crawling forth, by night, in search of some rich offal[2] for a meal.

He kept on his course, through many winding and narrow ways, until he reached Bethnal Green;[3] then, turning suddenly off to the left, he soon became involved in a maze of the mean and dirty streets which abound in that close and densely-populated quarter.

The Jew was evidently too familiar with the ground he traversed, however, to be at all bewildered, either by the darkness of the night, or the intricacies of the way. He hurried through several alleys and streets; and at length turned into one, lighted only by a single lamp at the farther end. At the door of a house in this street, he knocked; and having exchanged a few muttered words with the person who opened it, walked up stairs.

A dog growled as he touched the handle of a room-door; and a man's voice demanded who was there.

"Only me, Bill; only me, my dear," said the Jew, looking in.

"Bring in your body then," said Sikes. "Lie down, you stupid brute! Don't you know the devil when he's got a great-coat on?"

Apparently, the dog had been somewhat deceived by Mr. Fagin's outer garment; for as the Jew unbuttoned it, and threw it over the back of a chair, he retired to the corner from which he had risen: wagging his tail as he went, to show that he was as well satisfied as it was in his nature to be.

"Well!" said Sikes.

"Well, my dear," replied the Jew. "Ah! Nancy."

The latter recognition was uttered with just enough of embarrassment to imply a doubt of its reception; for Mr. Fagin and his young friend had not met, since she had interfered in behalf of Oliver. All doubts

---

1. A district just east of the City.
2. The waste parts of a slaughtered animal.
3. A suburb of London; Fagin is traveling northeast.

upon the subject, if he had any, were speedily removed by the young lady's behaviour. She took her feet off the fender; pushed back her chair; and bade Fagin draw up his, without saying more about it: for it was a cold night, and no mistake.

"It *is* cold, Nancy dear," said the Jew, as he warmed his skinny hands over the fire. "It seems to go right through one," added the old man, touching his side.

"It must be a piercer, if it finds its way through *your* heart," said Mr. Sikes. "Give him something to drink, Nancy. Burn my body, make haste! It's enough to turn a man ill, to see his lean old carcase shivering in that way, like a ugly ghost just rose from the grave."

Nancy quickly brought a bottle from a cupboard, in which there were many: which, to judge from the diversity of their appearance, were filled with several kinds of liquids. Sikes, pouring out a glass of brandy, bade the Jew drink it off.

"Quite enough, quite, thankye, Bill," replied the Jew, putting down the glass, after just setting his lips to it.

"What! you're afraid of our getting the better of you, are you?" inquired Sikes, fixing his eyes on the Jew. "Ugh!"

With a hoarse grunt of contempt, Mr. Sikes seized the glass, and threw the remainder of its contents into the ashes: as a preparatory ceremony to filling it again for himself: which he did at once.

The Jew glanced round the room, as his companion tossed down the second glassful; not in curiosity: for he had seen it often before; but in a restless and suspicious manner which was habitual to him. It was a meanly furnished apartment, with nothing but the contents of the closet to induce the belief that its occupier was anything but a working man; and with no more suspicious articles displayed to view than two or three heavy bludgeons which stood in a corner, and a "life-preserver" that hung over the chimney-piece.

"There," said Sikes, smacking his lips, "Now I'm ready."

"For business?" inquired the Jew.

"For business," replied Sikes; "so say what you've got to say."

"About the crib at Chertsey,[4] Bill?" said the Jew, drawing his chair forward, and speaking in a very low voice.

"Yes. Wot about it," inquired Sikes.

"Ah! you know what I mean, my dear," said the Jew. "He knows what I mean, Nancy; don't he?"

"No, he don't," sneered Mr. Sikes. "Or he won't; and that's the same thing. Speak out, and call things by their right names; don't sit there, winking and blinking, and talking to me in hints: as if you warn't the very first that thought about the robbery. Wot d'ye mean?"

---

4. The house in Chertsey, a town on the river Thames in Surrey, about twenty miles southwest of London.

"Hush, Bill, hush!" said the Jew, who had in vain attempted to stop this burst of indignation; "somebody will hear us, my dear. Somebody will hear us."

"Let 'em hear!" said Sikes; "I don't care." But as Mr. Sikes *did* care, upon reflection, he dropped his voice as he said the words, and grew calmer.

"There, there," said the Jew coaxingly. "It was only my caution—nothing more. Now, my dear, about that crib at Chertsey; when is it to be done, Bill, eh? When is it to be done? Such plate,[5] my dears, such plate!" said the Jew: rubbing his hands, and elevating his eyebrows in a rapture of anticipation.

"Not at all," replied Sikes coldly.

"Not to be done at all!" echoed the Jew, leaning back in his chair.

"No, not at all," rejoined Sikes. "At least it can't be a put-up job, as we expected."

"Then it hasn't been properly gone about," said the Jew, turning pale with anger. "Don't tell me."

"But I will tell you," retorted Sikes. "Who are you that's not to be told? I tell you that Toby Crackit has been hanging about the place for a fortnight; and he can't get one of the servants into a line."[6]

"Do you mean to tell me, Bill," said the Jew: softening as the other grew heated: "that neither of the two men in the house can be got over?"

"Yes, I do mean to tell you so," replied Sikes. "The old lady has had 'em these twenty year; and, if you were to give 'em five hundred pound, they wouldn't be in it."

"But do you mean to say, my dear," remonstrated the Jew, "that the women can't be got over?"

"Not a bit of it," replied Sikes.

"Not by flash[7] Toby Crackit?" said the Jew incredulously. "Think what women are, Bill."

"No; not even by flash Toby Crackit," replied Sikes. "He says he's worn sham whiskers, and a canary waistcoat, the whole blessed time he's been loitering down there; and it's all of no use."

"He should have tried mustachios and a pair of military trousers, my dear," said the Jew.

"So he did," rejoined Sikes, "and they warn't of no more use than the other plant."

The Jew looked very blank at this information. After ruminating for some minutes with his chin sunk on his breast, he raised his head, and said, with a deep sigh, that if flash Toby Crackit reported aright, he feared the game was up.

"And yet," said the old man, dropping his hands on his knees, "it's

5. Silver objects.
6. To cooperate with the robbers.
7. Dashing.

a sad thing, my dear, to lose so much when we had set our hearts upon it."

"So it is," said Mr. Sikes. "Worse luck!"

A long silence ensued; during which, the Jew was plunged in deep thought: with his face wrinkled into an expression of villany perfectly demoniacal. Sikes eyed him furtively from time to time; Nancy, apparently fearful of irritating the housebreaker, sat with her eyes fixed upon the fire, as if she had been deaf to all that passed.

"Fagin," said Sikes, abruptly breaking the stillness that prevailed, "is it worth fifty shiners[8] extra, if it's safely done from the outside?"

"Yes," said the Jew, as suddenly rousing himself.

"Is it a bargain?" enquired Sikes.

"Yes, my dear, yes," rejoined the Jew; his eyes glistening, and every muscle in his face working, with the excitement that the enquiry had awakened.

"Then," said Sikes, thrusting aside the Jew's hand, with some disdain, "let it come off as soon as you like. Toby and I were over the garden-wall the night afore last, sounding the panels of the doors and shutters. The crib's barred up at night like a jail; but there's one part we can crack, safe and softly."

"Which is that, Bill?" asked the Jew eagerly.

"Why," whispered Sikes, "as you cross the lawn——"

"Yes, yes," said the Jew, bending his head forward, with his eyes almost starting out of it.

"Umph!" cried Sikes, stopping short, as the girl: scarcely moving her head: looked suddenly round, and pointed for an instant to the Jew's face. "Never mind which part it is. You can't do it without me, I know; but it's best to be on the safe side when one deals with you."

"As you like my dear, as you like," replied the Jew. "Is there no help wanted, but yours and Toby's?"

"None," said Sikes. "'Cept a centre-bit[9] and a boy. The first we've both got; the second you must find us."

"A boy!" exclaimed the Jew. "Oh! then it's a panel,[1] eh?"

"Never mind wot it is!" replied Sikes. "I want a boy; and he musn't be a big un. Lord!" said Mr. Sikes, reflectively, "if I'd only got that young boy of Ned, the chimbley-sweeper's! He kept him small on purpose, and let him out by the job. But the father gets lagged; and then the Juvenile Delinquent Society comes, and takes the boy away from a trade where he was arning money: teaches him to read and write: and in time makes a 'prentice of him. And so they go on," said Mr. Sikes, his wrath rising with the recollection of his wrongs, "so they go on; and, if they'd got money enough (which it's a Providence they have not,) we

8. Gold coins worth one pound and five pence.
9. An instrument for making cylindrical holes, commonly used by housebreakers.
1. A small door set into a larger door.

shouldn't have half-a-dozen boys left in the whole trade, in a year or two."

"No more we should," acquiesced the Jew, who had been considering during this speech, and had only caught the last sentence. "Bill!"

"What now?" inquired Sikes.

The Jew nodded his head towards Nancy, who was still gazing at the fire; and intimated, by a sign, that he would have her told to leave the room. Sikes shrugged his shoulders impatiently, as if he thought the precaution unnecessary; but complied, nevertheless, by requesting Miss Nancy to fetch him a jug of beer.

"You don't want any beer," said Nancy, folding her arms, and retaining her seat very composedly.

"I tell you I do!" replied Sikes.

"Nonsense," rejoined the girl coolly. "Go on, Fagin. I know what he's going to say, Bill; he need'nt mind me."

The Jew still hesitated. Sikes looked from one to the other in some surprise.

"Why, you don't mind the old girl, do you, Fagin?" he asked at length. "You've known her long enough to trust her, or the Devil's in it. She ai'nt one to blab. Are you, Nancy?"

"*I* should think not!" replied the young lady: drawing her chair up to the table, and putting her elbows upon it.

"No, no, my dear, I know you're not," said the Jew; "but——" and again the old man paused.

"But wot?" inquired Sikes.

"I did'nt know whether she mightn't p'r'aps be out of sorts, you know, my dear, as she was the other night," replied the Jew.

At this confession, Miss Nancy burst into a loud laugh; and, swallowing a glass of brandy, shook her head with an air of defiance, and burst into sundry exclamations of "Keep the game a-going!" "Never say die!" and the like. These seemed at once to have the effect of re-assuring both gentlemen; for the Jew nodded his head with a satisfied air, and resumed his seat: as did Mr. Sikes likewise.

"Now, Fagin," said Nancy with a laugh. "Tell Bill at once, about Oliver!"

"Ah! you're a clever one, my dear; the sharpest girl I ever saw!" said the Jew, patting her on the neck. "It *was* about Oliver I was going to speak, sure enough. Ha! ha! ha!"

"What about him?" demanded Sikes.

"He's the boy for you, my dear," replied the Jew in a hoarse whisper; laying his finger on the side of his nose; and grinning frightfully.

"He!" exclaimed Sikes.

"Have him, Bill!" said Nancy. "I would, if I was in your place. He mayn't be so much up, as any of the others; but that's not what you want, if he's only to open a door for you. Depend upon it he's a safe one, Bill."

"I know he is," rejoined Fagin. "He's been in good training these last few weeks; and it's time he began to work for his bread. Besides, the others are all too big."

"Well, he is just the size I want," said Mr. Sikes, ruminating.

"And will do everything you want, Bill, my dear," interposed the Jew; "he can't help himself. That is, if you frighten him enough."

"Frighten him!" echoed Sikes. "It'll be no sham frightening, mind you. If there's anything queer about him when we once get into the work; in for a penny, in for a pound. You won't see him alive again, Fagin. Think of that, before you send him. Mark my words!" said the robber, poising a crowbar: which he had drawn from under the bedstead.

"I've thought of it all," said the Jew with energy. "I've—I've had my eye upon him, my dears, close—close. Once let him feel that he is one of us; once fill his mind with the idea that he has been a thief; and he's ours! Ours for his life! Oho! It couldn't have come about better!" The old man crossed his arms upon his breast; and, drawing his head and shoulders into a heap, literally hugged himself for joy.

"Ours!" said Sikes. "Yours, you mean."

"Perhaps I do, my dear," said the Jew, with a shrill chuckle. "Mine, if you like, Bill."

"And wot," said Sikes, scowling fiercely on his agreeable friend, "wot makes you take so much pains about one chalk-faced kid, when you know there are fifty boys snoozing about Common Garden[2] every night, as you might pick and choose from?"

"Because they're of no use to me, my dear," replied the Jew with some confusion, "not worth the taking. Their looks convict 'em when they get into trouble; and I lose 'em all. With this boy, properly managed, my dears, I could do what I couldn't with twenty of them. Besides," said the Jew, recovering his self-possession, "he has us now if he could only give us leg-bail[3] again; and he *must* be in the same boat with us. Never mind how he came there; it's quite enough for my power over him that he was in a robbery; that's all I want. Now, how much better this is, than being obliged to put the poor leetle boy out of the way: which would be dangerous: and we should lose by it besides."

"When is it to be done?" asked Nancy, stopping some turbulent exclamation on the part of Mr. Sikes, expressive of the disgust with which he received Fagin's affectation of humanity.

"Ah, to be sure," said the Jew, "when is it to be done, Bill?"

"I planned with Toby, the night after to-morrow," rejoined Sikes in a surly voice, "if he heerd nothing from me to the contrairy."

2. Probably Covent Garden, the London produce and flower market.
3. The slip.

"Good," said the Jew; "there's no moon."

"No," rejoined Sikes.

"It's all arranged about bringing off the swag,[4] is it?" asked the Jew.
Sikes nodded.

"And about—"

"Oh, ah, it's all planned," rejoined Sikes, interrupting him. "Never
mind particulars. You'd better bring the boy here, to-morrow night; I
shall get off the stones an hour arter day-break. Then you hold your
tongue, and keep the melting-pot[5] ready; and that's all you'll have to
do."

After some discussion, in which all three took an active part, it was
decided that Nancy should repair to the Jew's next evening when the
night had set in: and bring Oliver away with her; Fagin craftily observing,
that, if he evinced any disinclination to the task, he would be more
willing to accompany the girl who had so recently interfered in his behalf,
than anybody else. It was also solemnly arranged that poor Oliver should,
for the purposes of the contemplated expedition, be unreservedly consigned to the care and custody of Mr. William Sikes; and further, that
the said Sikes should deal with him as he thought fit; and should not
be held responsible by the Jew for any mischance or evil that might
befall the boy, or any punishment with which it might be necessary to
visit him: it being understood that, to render the compact in this respect
binding, any representations made by Mr. Sikes on his return should
be required to be confirmed and corroborated, in all important particulars, by the testimony of flash Toby Crackit.

These preliminaries adjusted, Mr. Sikes proceeded to drink brandy
at a furious rate; and to flourish the crowbar in an alarming manner;
yelling forth, at the same time, most unmusical snatches of song, mingled with wild execrations. At length, in a fit of professional enthusiasm,
he insisted upon producing his box of housebreaking tools: which he
had no sooner stumbled in with, and opened for the purpose of explaining the nature and properties of the various implements it contained, and the peculiar beauties of their construction: than he fell over
it upon the floor, and went to sleep where he fell.

"Good night, Nancy," said the Jew, muffling himself up as before.

"Good night."

Their eyes met; and the Jew scrutinised her, narrowly. There was no
flinching about the girl. She was as true and earnest in the matter as
Toby Crackit himself could be.

The Jew again bade her good night; and, bestowing a sly kick upon
the prostrate form of Mr. Sikes, while her back was turned, groped down
stairs.

"Always the way!" muttered the Jew to himself as he turned home-

4. Booty [Dickens' note].
5. The pot in which to melt down the stolen silver objects. "Get off the stones": be out of London.

wards. "The worst of these women is, that a very little thing serves to call up some long-forgotten feeling; and the best of them is, that it never lasts. Ha! ha! The man against the child, for a bag of gold!"

Beguiling the time with these pleasant reflections, Mr. Fagin wended his way, through mud and mire, to his gloomy abode: where the Dodger was sitting up, impatiently awaiting his return.

"Is Oliver a-bed? I want to speak to him," was his first remark as they descended the stairs.

"Hours ago," replied the Dodger, throwing open a door. "Here he is!"

The boy was lying, fast asleep, on a rude bed upon the floor; so pale with anxiety, and sadness, and the closeness of his prison, that he looked like death; not death as it shows in shroud and coffin, but in the guise it wears when life has just departed; when a young and gentle spirit has, but an instant, fled to Heaven: and the gross air of the world has not had time to breathe upon the changing dust it hallowed.

"Not now," said the Jew, turning softly away. "To-morrow. To-morrow."

Chapter XX.

WHEREIN OLIVER IS DELIVERED OVER TO MR. WILLIAM SIKES.

When Oliver awoke in the morning, he was a good deal surprised to find that a new pair of shoes, with strong thick soles, had been placed at his bedside; and that his old ones had been removed. At first, he was pleased with the discovery: hoping that it might be the forerunner of his release; but such thoughts were quickly dispelled, on his sitting down to breakfast alone with the Jew, who told him, in a tone and manner which increased his alarm, that he was to be taken to the residence of Bill Sikes that night.

"To—to—stop there, sir?" asked Oliver, anxiously.

"No, no, my dear. Not to stop there," replied the Jew. "We should'nt like to lose you. Don't be afraid, Oliver, you shall come back to us again. Ha! ha! ha! We wont be so cruel as to send you away, my dear. Oh no, no!"

The old man, who was stooping over the fire toasting a piece of bread, looked round as he bantered Oliver thus; and chuckled, as if to shew that he knew he would still be very glad to get away if he could.

"I suppose," said the Jew, fixing his eyes on Oliver, "you want to know what you're going to Bill's for—eh, my dear?"

Oliver coloured, involuntarily, to find that the old thief had been reading his thoughts; but boldly said, Yes, he did want to know.

"Why, do you think?" inquired Fagin, parrying the question.

"Indeed I don't know, sir," replied Oliver.

"Bah!" said the Jew, turning away with a disappointed countenance from a close perusal of the boy's face. "Wait till Bill tells you, then."

The Jew seemed much vexed by Oliver's not expressing any greater curiosity on the subject; but the truth is, that, although he felt very anxious, he was too much confused by the earnest cunning of Fagin's looks, and his own speculations, to make any further inquiries just then. He had no other opportunity; for the Jew remained very surly and silent till night: when he prepared to go abroad.

"You may burn a candle," said the Jew, putting one upon the table. "And here's a book for you to read, till they come to fetch you. Good night!"

"Good night!" replied Oliver, softly.

The Jew walked to the door: looking over his shoulder at the boy as he went. Suddenly stopping, he called him by his name.

Oliver looked up; the Jew, pointing to the candle, motioned him to light it. He did so; and, as he placed the candlestick upon the table, saw that the Jew was gazing fixedly at him, with lowering and contracted brows, from the dark end of the room.

"Take heed, Oliver! take heed!" said the old man, shaking his right hand before him in a warning manner. "He's a rough man, and thinks nothing of blood when his own is up. Whatever falls out, say nothing; and do what he bids you. Mind!" Placing a strong emphasis on the last word, he suffered his features gradually to resolve themselves into a ghastly grin; and, nodding his head, left the room.

Oliver leaned his head upon his hand when the old man disappeared; and pondered, with a trembling heart, on the words he had just heard. The more he thought of the Jew's admonition, the more he was at a loss to divine its real purpose and meaning. He could think of no bad object to be attained by sending him to Sikes: which would not be equally well answered by his remaining with Fagin; and after meditating for a long time, concluded that he had been selected to perform some ordinary menial offices for the housebreaker, until another boy, better suited for his purpose, could be engaged. He was too well accustomed to suffering, and had suffered too much where he was, to bewail the prospect of change very severely. He remained lost in thought for some minutes; and then, with a heavy sigh, snuffed the candle: and taking up the book which the Jew had left with him, began to read.

He turned over the leaves. Carelessly at first; but, lighting on a passage which attracted his attention, he soon became intent upon the volume. It was a history of the lives and trials of great criminals; and the pages were soiled and thumbed with use. Here, he read of dreadful crimes that made the blood run cold; of secret murders that had been committed by the lonely wayside: and bodies hidden from the eye of man in deep pits and wells: which would not keep them down, deep as they were, but had yielded them up at last, after many years, and so maddened the murderers with the sight, that in their horror they had confessed their guilt, and yelled for the gibbet[1] to end their agony. Here, too, he read of men who, lying in their beds at dead of night, had been tempted (as they said) and led on, by their own bad thoughts, to such dreadful bloodshed as it made the flesh creep, and the limbs quail, to think of. The terrible descriptions were so real and vivid, that the sallow pages seemed to turn red with gore; and the words upon them, to be sounded in his ears, as if they were whispered, in hollow murmurs, by the spirits of the dead.

In a paroxysm of fear, the boy closed the book, and thrust it from him. Then, falling upon his knees, he prayed Heaven to spare him from such deeds; and rather to will that he should die at once, than be reserved for crimes, so fearful and appalling. By degrees, he grew more calm; and besought, in a low and broken voice, that he might be rescued from his present dangers; and that if any aid were to be raised up for a poor outcast boy, who had never known the love of friends or kindred, it might come to him now: when, desolate and deserted, he stood alone in the midst of wickedness and guilt.

He had concluded his prayer, but still remained with his head buried in his hands, when a rustling noise aroused him.

"What's that!" he cried, starting up, and catching sight of a figure standing by the door. "Who's there?"

"Me. Only me," replied a tremulous voice.

Oliver raised the candle above his head: and looked towards the door. It was Nancy.

"Put down the light," said the girl, turning away her head. "It hurts my eyes."

Oliver saw that she was very pale; and gently inquired if she were ill. The girl threw herself into a chair, with her back towards him: and wrung her hands; but made no reply.

"God forgive me!" she cried after a while, "I never thought of this."

"Has anything happened?" asked Oliver. "Can I help you? I will if I can. I will, indeed."

She rocked herself to and fro; caught her throat; and, uttering a gurgling sound, struggled and gasped for breath.

"Nancy!" cried Oliver, "What is it?"

The girl beat her hands upon her knees, and her feet upon the ground; and, suddenly stopping, drew her shawl close round her: and shivered with cold.

Oliver stirred the fire. Drawing her chair close to it, she sat there, for a little time, without speaking; but at length she raised her head, and looked round.

1. Gallows.

"I don't know what comes over me sometimes," said she, affecting to busy herself in arranging her dress; "it's this damp, dirty room, I think. Now, Nolly, dear, are you ready?"

"Am I to go with you?" asked Oliver.

"Yes; I have come from Bill," replied the girl. "You are to go with me."

"What for?" said Oliver, recoiling.

"What for!" echoed the girl, raising her eyes, and averting them again, the moment they encountered the boy's face. "Oh! for no harm."

"I don't believe it," said Oliver: who had watched her closely.

"Have it your own way," rejoined the girl, affecting to laugh. "For no good, then."

Oliver could see that he had some power over the girl's better feelings; and, for an instant, thought of appealing to her compassion for his helpless state. But, then, the thought darted across his mind that it was barely eleven o'clock; and that many people were still in the streets: of whom surely some might be found to give credence to his tale. As the reflection occurred to him, he stepped forward: and said, somewhat hastily, that he was ready.

Neither his brief consideration, nor its purport, was lost on his companion. She eyed him narrowly, while he spoke; and cast upon him a look of intelligence which sufficiently showed that she guessed what had been passing in his thoughts.

"Hush!" said the girl, stooping over him, and pointing to the door as she looked cautiously round. "You can't help yourself. I have tried hard for you, but all to no purpose. You are hedged round and round; and if ever you are to get loose from here, this is not the time."

Struck by the energy of her manner, Oliver looked up in her face with great surprise. She seemed to speak the truth; her countenance was white and agitated; and she trembled with very earnestness.

"I have saved you from being ill-used once: and I will again: and I do now," continued the girl aloud; "for those who would have fetched you, if I had not, would have been far more rough than me. I have promised for your being quiet and silent: if you are not, you will only do harm to yourself and me too: and perhaps be my death. See here! I have borne all this for you already, as true as God sees me shew it."

She pointed, hastily, to some livid bruises on her neck and arms; and continued, with great rapidity.

"Remember this! And don't let me suffer more for you, just now. If I could help you, I would; but I have not the power. They don't mean to harm you; and whatever they make you do, is no fault of yours. Hush! every word from you is a blow for me. Give me your hand. Make haste! Your hand!"

She caught the hand which Oliver instinctively placed in hers; and, blowing out the light, drew him after her up the stairs. The door was opened, quickly, by some one shrouded in the darkness; and was as quickly closed, when they had passed out. A hackney-cabriolet[2] was in waiting; with the same vehemence which she had exhibited in addressing Oliver, the girl pulled him in with her; and drew the curtains close. The driver wanted no directions, but lashed his horse into full speed, without the delay of an instant.

The girl still held Oliver fast by the hand; and continued to pour into his ear, the warnings and assurances she had already imparted. All was so quick and hurried, that he had scarcely time to recollect where he was, or how he came there, when the carriage stopped at the house to which the Jew's steps had been directed on the previous evening.

For one brief moment, Oliver cast a hurried glance along the empty street; and a cry for help hung upon his lips. But the girl's voice was in his ear: beseeching him in such tones of agony to remember her: that he had not the heart to utter it. While he hesitated, the opportunity was gone; for he was already in the house; and the door was shut.

"This way," said the girl, releasing her hold for the first time. "Bill!"

"Hallo!" replied Sikes: appearing at the head of the stairs, with a candle. "Oh! that's the time of day. Come on!"

This was a very strong expression of approbation: an uncommonly hearty welcome: from a person of Mr. Sikes's temperament. Nancy, appearing much gratified thereby, saluted him cordially.

"Bullseye's gone home with Tom," observed Sikes, as he lighted them up. "He'd have been in the way."

"That's right," rejoined Nancy.

"So you've got the kid," said Sikes, when they had all reached the room: closing the door as he spoke.

"Yes, here he is," replied Nancy.

"Did he come quiet?" inquired Sikes.

"Like a lamb," rejoined Nancy.

"I'm glad to hear it," said Sikes, looking grimly at Oliver; "for the sake of his young carcase: as would otherways have suffered for it. Come here, young un; and let me read you a lectur', which is as well got over at once."

Thus addressing his new pupil, Mr. Sikes pulled off Oliver's cap and threw it into a corner; and then, taking him by the shoulder, sat himself down by the table, and stood the boy in front of him.

"Now, first: do you know wot this is?" inquired Sikes, taking up a pocket-pistol which lay on the table.

Oliver replied in the affirmative.

"Well then, look here," continued Sikes. "This is powder; that 'ere's a bullet; and this is a little bit of a old hat for waddin'."[3]

Oliver murmured his comprehension of the different bodies referred

2. A two-wheeled horsedrawn carriage.
3. Wadding, a soft mass of cotton or woolen fabric used to stuff a lead ball in a gun.

to; and Mr. Sikes proceeded to load the pistol, with great nicety and deliberation.

"Now it's loaded," said Mr. Sikes, when he had finished.

"Yes, I see it is, sir," replied Oliver.

"Well," said the robber, grasping Oliver's wrist tightly: and putting the barrel so close to his temple that they touched; at which moment the boy could not repress a start; "if you speak a word when you're out o'doors with me, except when I speak to you, that loading will be in your head without notice. So, if you *do* make up your mind to speak without leave; say your prayers first."

Having bestowed a scowl upon the object of this warning, to increase its effect, Mr. Sikes continued.

"As near as I know, there isn't anybody as would be asking very partickler arter you, if you *was* disposed of; so I needn't take this devil-and-all of trouble to explain matters to you, if it warn't for your own good. D'ye hear me?"

"The short and the long of what you mean," said Nancy: speaking very emphatically: and slightly frowning at Oliver as if to bespeak his serious attention to her words, "is, that if you're crossed by him in this job you have on hand, you'll prevent his ever telling tales afterwards by shooting him through the head; and will take your chance of swinging for it, as you do for a great many other things in the way of business, every month of your life."

"That's it!" observed Mr. Sikes, approvingly; "women can always put things in fewest words. Except when it's blowing up;[4] and then they lengthens it out. And now that he's thoroughly up to it, let's have some supper, and get a snooze before starting."

In pursuance of this request, Nancy quickly laid the cloth; and, disappearing for a few minutes, presently returned with a pot of porter and a dish of sheep's heads: which gave occasion to several pleasant witticisms on the part of Mr. Sikes: founded upon the singular coincidence of "jemmies"[5] being a cant name, common to them: and also to an ingenious implement much used in his profession. Indeed, the worthy gentleman, stimulated perhaps by the immediate prospect of being in active service, was in great spirits and good humour; in proof whereof, it may be here remarked, that he humorously drank all the beer at a draught; and did not utter, on a rough calculation, more than four-score oaths during the whole progress of the meal.

Supper being ended—it may be easily conceived that Oliver had no great appetite for it—Mr. Sikes disposed of a couple of glasses of spirits and water: and threw himself upon the bed; ordering Nancy, with many imprecations in case of failure, to call him at five precisely. Oliver stretched himself in his clothes, by command of the same authority, on

4. Except when they're upset.
5. A short crowbar.

a mattress upon the floor; and the girl mending the fire, sat before it, in readiness to rouse them at the appointed time.

For a long time Oliver lay awake: thinking it not impossible that Nancy might seek that opportunity of whispering some further advice; but the girl sat brooding over the fire, without moving, save now and then to trim the light. Weary with watching and anxiety, he at length fell asleep.

When he awoke, the table was covered with tea things; and Sikes was thrusting various articles into the pockets of his great-coat, which hung over the back of a chair: while Nancy was busily engaged in preparing breakfast. It was not yet daylight; for the candle was still burning; and it was quite dark outside. A sharp rain, too, was beating against the window-panes; and the sky looked black and cloudy.

"Now, then!" growled Sikes, as Oliver started up; "half-past five! Look sharp, or you'll get no breakfast; for it's late as it is."

Oliver was not long in making his toilet; and, having taken some breakfast, replied to a surly inquiry from Sikes, by saying that he was quite ready.

Nancy, scarcely looking at the boy, threw him a handkerchief to tie round his throat; and Sikes gave him a large rough cape to button over his shoulders. Thus attired, he gave his hand to the robber, who, merely pausing to shew him, with a menacing gesture, that he had the pistol in a side pocket of his great-coat, clasped it firmly in his; and, exchanging a farewell with Nancy, led him away.

Oliver turned, for an instant, when they reached the door: in the hope of meeting a look from the girl. But she had resumed her old seat in front of the fire; and sat, perfectly motionless, before it.

Chapter XXI.

THE EXPEDITION.

It was a cheerless morning when they got into the street; blowing and raining hard; and the clouds looking dull and stormy. The night had been very wet: for large pools of water had collected in the road: and the kennels were overflowing. There was a faint glimmering of the coming day in the sky; but it rather aggravated than relieved the gloom of the scene: the sombre light only serving to pale that, which the street-lamps afforded: without shedding any warmer or brighter tints upon the wet housetops, and dreary streets. There appeared to be nobody stirring in that quarter of the town; for the windows of the houses were all closely shut: and the streets through which they passed, were noiseless and empty.

By the time they had turned into the Bethnal Green-road,[1] the day had fairly begun to break. Many of the lamps were already extinguished; a few country waggons were slowly toiling on, towards London; and now and then, a stagecoach, covered with mud, rattled briskly by: the driver bestowing, as he passed, an admonitory lash upon the heavy waggoner who, by keeping on the wrong side of the road, had endangered his arriving at the office, a quarter of a minute after his time. The public-houses, with gas-lights burning inside, were already open. By degrees, other shops began to be unclosed; and a few scattered people were met with. Then, came straggling groups of labourers going to their work; then, men and women with fish-baskets on their heads; donkey-carts laden with vegetables; chaise-carts filled with live-stock or whole carcasses of meat; milkwomen with pails; and an unbroken concourse of people, trudging out with various supplies to the eastern suburbs of the town. As they approached the City, the noise and traffic gradually increased; and when they threaded the streets between Shoreditch and Smithfield, it had swelled into a roar of sound and bustle. It was as light as it was likely to be, till night came on again; and the busy morning of half the London population had begun.

Turning down Sun-street and Crown-street, and crossing Finsbury-square, Mr. Sikes struck, by way of Chiswell-street, into Barbican: thence into Long-lane: and so into Smithfield; from which latter place, arose a tumult of discordant sounds that filled Oliver Twist with surprise and amazement.

It was market-morning. The ground was covered, nearly ankle-deep, with filth and mire; and a thick steam, perpetually rising from the reeking bodies of the cattle, and mingling with the fog, which seemed to rest upon the chimney-tops, hung heavily above. All the pens in the centre of the large area: and as many temporary ones as could be crowded into the vacant space: were filled with sheep; tied up to posts by the gutter side were long lines of beasts and oxen, three or four deep. Countrymen, butchers, drovers, hawkers,[2] boys, thieves, idlers, and vagabonds of every low grade, were mingled together in a dense mass; the whistling of drovers, the barking of dogs, the bellowing and plunging of oxen, the bleating of sheep, the grunting and squeaking of pigs; the cries of hawkers, the shouts, oaths, and quarrelling on all sides; the ringing of bells and roar of voices, that issued from every public-house; the crowding, push-ing, driving, beating, whooping, and yelling; the hideous and discordant din that resounded from every corner of the market; and the unwashed,

1. Oliver and Sikes walk southwest from Bethnal Green into the central London business district, the City, then westward to the cattle market at Smithfield, then through Holborn and Hyde Park Corner to the West End. At Kensington they hitch a ride that takes them through Hammersmith to Isleworth. From there they walk and ride westward to the village of Hampton near Hampton Court and then to the country villages of Sunbury, Upper Halliford, Shepperton, and Chertsey, near the Thames in Surrey, a total distance of about twenty-eight miles from Bethnal Green.
2. Street peddlers. "Drovers": cattle drivers.

unshaven, squalid, and dirty figures constantly running to and fro, and bursting in and out of the throng; rendered it a stunning and bewildering scene, which quite confounded the senses.

Mr. Sikes, dragging Oliver after him, elbowed his way through the thickest of the crowd; and bestowed very little attention on the numerous sights and sounds which so astonished the boy. He nodded, twice or thrice, to a passing friend; and, resisting as many invitations to take a morning dram, pressed steadily onward, until they were clear of the turmoil, and had made their way through Hosier-lane into Holborn.

"Now, young un!" said Sikes, looking up at the clock of St. Andrew's church, "hard upon seven! you must step out. Come, don't lag behind already, Lazy-legs!"

Mr. Sikes accompanied this speech with a jerk at his little companion's wrist; Oliver, quickening his pace into a kind of trot, between a fast walk and a run, kept up with the rapid strides of the house-breaker as well as he could.

They held their course at this rate, until they had passed Hyde Park corner, and were on their way to Kensington: when Sikes relaxed his pace, until an empty cart, which was at some little distance behind, came up. Seeing "Hounslow" written on it, he asked the driver, with as much civility as he could assume, if he would give them a lift as far as Isleworth.

"Jump up," said the man. "Is that your boy?"

"Yes; he's my boy," replied Sikes, looking hard at Oliver, and putting his hand abstractedly into the pocket where the pistol was.

"Your father walks rather too quick for you, don't he, my man?" inquired the driver: seeing that Oliver was out of breath.

"Not a bit of it," replied Sikes, interposing. "He's used to it. Here, take hold of my hand, Ned. In with you!"

Thus addressing Oliver, he helped him into the cart; and the driver, pointing to a heap of sacks, told him to lie down there, and rest himself.

As they passed the different milestones, Oliver wondered, more and more, where his companion meant to take him. Kensington, Hammersmith, Chiswick, Kew Bridge, Brentford, were all passed; and yet they went on as steadily as if they had only just begun their journey. At length, they came to a public-house called the Coach and Horses: a little way beyond which, another road appeared to turn off. And here, the cart stopped.

Sikes dismounted with great precipitation: holding Oliver by the hand all the while; and, lifting him down directly, bestowed a furious look upon him, and rapped the side-pocket with his fist, in a very significant manner.

"Good-bye, boy," said the man.

"He's sulky," replied Sikes, giving him a shake; "he's sulky. A young dog! Don't mind him."

"Not I!" rejoined the other, getting into his cart. "It's a fine day, after all." And he drove away.

Sikes waited until he had fairly gone; and then, telling Oliver he might look about him if he wanted, once again led him forward on his journey.

They turned round to the left, a short way past the public-house; and then, taking a right-hand road, walked on for a long time: passing many large gardens and gentlemen's houses on both sides of the way: and stopping for nothing but a little beer, until they reached a town. Here against the wall of a house, Oliver saw, written up in pretty large letters, "Hampton." They lingered about, in the fields, for some hours. At length, they came back into the town; and turning into an old public-house with a defaced sign-board, ordered some dinner by the kitchen fire.

The kitchen was an old, low-roofed room: with a great beam across the middle of the ceiling: and benches, with high backs to them, by the fire; on which were seated several rough men in smock-frocks,[3] drinking and smoking. They took no notice of Oliver; and very little of Sikes; and, as Sikes took very little notice of them, he and his young comrade sat in a corner by themselves, without being much troubled by their company.

They had some cold meat for dinner; and sat here so long after it, while Mr. Sikes indulged himself with three or four pipes, that Oliver began to feel quite certain they were not going any further. Being much tired with the walk, and getting up so early, he dosed a little at first; and then, quite overpowered by fatigue and the fumes of the tobacco, fell asleep.

It was quite dark when he was awakened by a push from Sikes. Rousing himself sufficiently to sit up and look about him, he found that Worthy in close fellowship and communication with a labouring man, over a pint of ale.

"So, you're going on to Lower Halliford, are you?" inquired Sikes.

"Yes, I am," replied the man, who seemed a little the worse: or better, as the case might be: for drinking; "and not slow about it neither. My horse hasn't got a load behind him going back, as he had coming up in the mornin'; and he won't be long a-doing of it. Here's luck to him! Ecod! he's a good un!"

"Could you give my boy and me a lift as far as there?" demanded Sikes, pushing the ale towards his new friend.

"If you're going directly, I can," replied the man, looking out of the pot. "Are you going to Halliford?"

"Going on to Shepperton," replied Sikes.

"I'm your man as far as I go," replied the other. "Is all paid, Becky?"

---

3. Loose-fitting coarse garments that come down to the knees, usually worn by laborers over or instead of coats.

"Yes, the other gentleman's paid," replied the girl.

"I say!" said the man, with tipsy gravity; "that won't do, you know."

"Why not?" rejoined Sikes. "You're a-going to accommodate us; and wot's to prevent my standing treat for a pint or so, in return?"

The stranger reflected upon this argument, with a very profound face; and having done so, seized Sikes by the hand: and declared he was a real good fellow. To which Mr. Sikes replied, he was joking; as, if he had been sober, there would have been strong reason to suppose he was.

After the exchange of a few more compliments, they bade the company good night, and went out; the girl gathering up the pots and glasses as they did so: and lounging out to the door, with her hands full, to see the party start.

The horse, whose health had been drunk in his absence, was standing outside: ready harnessed to the cart. Oliver and Sikes got in without any further ceremony; and the man to whom he belonged, having lingered for a minute or two "to bear him up," and to defy the hostler[4] and the world to produce his equal, mounted also. Then, the hostler was told to give the horse his head; and, his head being given him, he made a very unpleasant use of it: tossing it into the air with great disdain, and running into the parlour windows over the way; after performing these feats, and supporting himself for a short time on his hind-legs, he started off at great speed, and rattled out of the town right gallantly.

The night was very dark. A damp mist rose from the river, and the marshy ground about; and spread itself over the dreary fields. It was piercing cold, too; all was gloomy and black. Not a word was spoken; for the driver had grown sleepy; and Sikes was in no mood to lead him into conversation. Oliver sat huddled together, in a corner of the cart; bewildered with alarm and apprehension; and figuring strange objects in the gaunt trees, whose branches waved grimly to and fro, as if in some fantastic joy at the desolation of the scene.

As they passed Sunbury church, the clock struck seven. There was a light in the ferry-house window opposite: which streamed across the road: and threw into more sombre shadow a dark yew-tree with graves beneath it. There was a dull sound of falling water not far off; and the leaves of the old tree stirred gently in the night wind. It seemed like quiet music for the repose of the dead.

Sunbury was passed through; and they came again into the lonely road. Two or three miles more; and the cart stopped. Sikes alighted; and, taking Oliver by the hand, they once again walked on.

They turned into no house at Shepperton, as the weary boy had expected; but still kept walking on, in mud and darkness, through gloomy lanes and over cold open wastes, until they came within sight of the lights of a town at no great distance. On looking intently forward, Oliver

4. Stableman.

saw that the water was just below them: and that they were coming to the foot of a bridge.

Sikes kept straight on, until they were close upon the bridge; and then turned suddenly down a bank upon the left.

"The water!" thought Oliver, turning sick with fear. "He has brought me to this lonely place to murder me!"

He was about to throw himself on the ground, and make one struggle for his young life, when he saw that they stood before a solitary house: all ruinous and decayed. There was a window on each side of the dilapidated entrance; and one story above; but no light was visible. It was dark, dismantled: and, to all appearance, uninhabited.

Sikes, with Oliver's hand still in his, softly approached the low porch, and raised the latch. The door yielded to the pressure; and they passed in, together.

Chapter XXII.

THE BURGLARY.

"Hallo!" cried a loud, hoarse voice, directly they had set foot in the passage.

"Don't make such a row," said Sikes, bolting the door. "Shew a glim, Toby."

"Aha! my pal," cried the same voice; "a glim, Barney, a glim! Shew the gentleman in, Barney; and wake up first, if convenient."

The speaker appeared to throw a boot-jack,[1] or some such article, at the person he addressed, to rouse him from his slumbers; for the noise of a wooden body, falling violently, was heard; and then an indistinct muttering, as of a man between asleep and awake.

"Do you hear?" cried the same voice. "There's Bill Sikes in the passage with nobody to do the civil to him; and you sleeping there, as if you took laudanum with your meals, and nothing stronger. Are you any fresher now, or do you want the iron candlestick[2] to wake you thoroughly?"

A pair of slipshod feet shuffled, hastily, across the bare floor of the room, as this interrogatory was put; and there issued, from a door on the right hand: first, a feeble candle: and next, the form of the same individual who has been heretofore described as labouring under the infirmity of speaking through his nose, and officiating as waiter at the public-house on Saffron Hill.

"Bister Sikes!" exclaimed Barney, with real or counterfeit joy; "cub id, sir; cub id."

1. Shoehorn.
2. Probably a pistol. "Laudanum": a widely used mixture of alcohol and opium.

"Here! you get on first," said Sikes, putting Oliver in front of him. "Quicker! or I shall tread upon your heels."

Muttering a curse upon his tardiness, Sikes pushed Oliver before him; and they entered a low dark room with a smoky fire: two or three broken chairs, a table, and a very old couch: on which, with his legs much higher than his head, a man was reposing at full length, smoking a long clay pipe. He was dressed in a smartly-cut snuff-coloured coat, with large brass buttons; an orange neckerchief; a coarse, staring, shawl-pattern waistcoat; and drab breeches. Mr. Crackit (for he it was) had no very great quantity of hair, either upon his head or face; but what he had, was of a reddish dye, and tortured into long corkscrew curls, through which he occasionally thrust some very dirty fingers, ornamented with large common rings. He was a trifle above the middle size, and apparently rather weak in the legs; but this circumstance by no means detracted from his own admiration of his top-boots, which he contemplated, in their elevated situation, with lively satisfaction.

"Bill, my boy!" said this figure, turning his head towards the door, "I'm glad to see you. I was almost afraid you'd given it up: in which case I should have made a personal wentur. Hallo!"

Uttering this exclamation in a tone of great surprise, as his eye rested on Oliver, Mr. Toby Crackit brought himself into a sitting posture, and demanded who that was.

"The boy. Only the boy!" replied Sikes, drawing a chair towards the fire.

"Wud of Bister Fagid's lads," exclaimed Barney, with a grin.

"Fagin's, eh!" exclaimed Toby, looking at Oliver. "Wot an inwalable boy that'll make, for the old ladies' pockets in chapels. His mug is a fortun' to him."

"There—there's enough of that," interposed Sikes, impatiently; and stooping over his recumbent friend, he whispered a few words in his ear: at which Mr. Crackit laughed immensely, and honoured Oliver with a long stare of astonishment.

"Now," said Sikes, as he resumed his seat, "if you'll give us something to eat and drink while we're waiting, you'll put some heart in us; or in me, at all events. Sit down by the fire, younker,[3] and rest yourself; for you'll have to go out with us again to-night, though not very far off."

Oliver looked at Sikes, in mute and timid wonder; and drawing a stool to the fire, sat with his aching head upon his hands: scarcely knowing where he was, or what was passing around him.

"Here," said Toby, as the young Jew placed some fragments of food, and a bottle, upon the table, "Success to the crack!"[4] He rose to honour the toast; and, carefully depositing his empty pipe in a corner, advanced

3. Young man.
4. The burglary.

to the table: filled a glass with spirits: and drank off its contents. Mr. Sikes did the same.

"A drain for the boy," said Toby, half-filling a wine-glass. "Down with it, innocence."

"Indeed," said Oliver, looking piteously up into the man's face; "indeed, I——"

"Down with it!" echoed Toby. "Do you think I don't know what's good for you? Tell him to drink it, Bill."

"He had better!" said Sikes, clapping his hand upon his pocket. "Burn my body, if he isn't more trouble than a whole family of Dodgers. Drink it, you perwerse imp; drink it!"

Frightened by the menacing gestures of the two men, Oliver hastily swallowed the contents of the glass, and immediately fell into a violent fit of coughing: which delighted Toby Crackit and Barney, and even drew a smile from the surly Mr. Sikes.

This done, and Sikes having satisfied his appetite (Oliver could eat nothing but a small crust of bread which they made him swallow), the two men laid themselves down on chairs for a short nap. Oliver retained his stool by the fire; and Barney, wrapped in a blanket, stretched himself on the floor: close outside the fender.[5]

They slept, or appeared to sleep, for some time; nobody stirring but Barney, who rose once or twice to throw coals upon the fire. Oliver fell into a heavy doze: imagining himself straying through the gloomy lanes, or wandering about the dark churchyard, or retracing some one or other of the scenes of the past day: when he was roused by Toby Crackit jumping up and declaring it was half-past one.

In an instant, the other two were on their legs; and all were actively engaged in busy preparation. Sikes and his companion enveloped their necks and chins in large dark shawls, and drew on their great-coats: while Barney, opening a cupboard, brought forth several articles, which he hastily crammed into the pockets.

"Barkers for me, Barney," said Toby Crackit.

"Here they are," replied Barney, producing a pair of pistols. "You loaded them yourself."

"All right!" replied Toby, stowing them away. "The persuaders?"[6]

"I've got 'em," replied Sikes.

"Crape, keys, centre-bit, darkies[7]—nothing forgotten?" inquired Toby: fastening a small crowbar to a loop inside the skirt of his coat.

"All right," rejoined his companion. "Bring them bits of timber, Barney. That's the time of day."

With these words, he took a thick stick from Barney's hands, who,

---

5. A metal frame placed in front of a fireplace to keep coals from falling into the room.
6. Clubs.
7. Shaded lanterns.

having delivered another to Toby, busied himself in fastening on Oliver's cape.

"Now then!" said Sikes, holding out his hand.

Oliver: who was completely stupified by the unwonted exercise, and the air, and the drink that had been forced upon him: put his hand mechanically into that which Sikes extended for the purpose.

"Take his other hand, Toby," said Sikes. "Look out, Barney."

The man went to the door, and returned to announce that all was quiet. The two robbers issued forth with Oliver between them. Barney, having made all fast, rolled himself up as before, and was soon asleep again.

It was now intensely dark. The fog was much heavier than it had been in the early part of the night; and the atmosphere was so damp, that, although no rain fell, Oliver's hair and eyebrows, within a few minutes after leaving the house, had become stiff with the half-frozen moisture that was floating about. They crossed the bridge; and kept on towards the lights which he had seen before. They were at no great distance off; and, as they walked pretty briskly, they soon arrived at Chertsey.

"Slap through[8] the town," whispered Sikes; "there'll be nobody in the way, to-night, to see us."

Toby acquiesced; and they hurried through the main street of the little town, which at that late hour was wholly deserted. A dim light shone at intervals from some bedroom-window; and the hoarse barking of dogs occasionally broke the silence of the night. But there was nobody abroad; and they had cleared the town, as the church bell struck two.

Quickening their pace, they turned up a road upon the left hand. After walking about a quarter of a mile, they stopped before a detached house surrounded by a wall: to the top of which, Toby Crackit, scarcely pausing to take breath, climbed in a twinkling.

"The boy next," said Toby. "Hoist him up; I'll catch hold of him."

Before Oliver had time to look round, Sikes had caught him under the arms; and in three or four seconds he and Toby were lying on the grass on the other side. Sikes followed directly. And they stole cautiously towards the house.

And now, for the first time, Oliver, well nigh mad with grief and terror, saw that housebreaking and robbery, if not murder, were the objects of the expedition. He clasped his hands together, and involuntarily uttered a subdued exclamation of horror. A mist came before his eyes; the cold sweat stood upon his ashy face; his limbs failed him; and he sunk upon his knees.

"Get up!" murmured Sikes, trembling with rage, and drawing the

8. Right through.

pistol from his pocket; "get up, or I'll strew your brains upon the grass."

"Oh! for God's sake let me go!" cried Oliver; "let me run away and die in the fields. I will never come near London; never, never! Oh! pray have mercy on me, and do not make me steal. For the love of all the bright Angels that rest in Heaven, have mercy upon me!"

The man to whom this appeal was made, swore a dreadful oath, and had cocked the pistol, when Toby, striking it from his grasp, placed his hand upon the boy's mouth, and dragged him to the house.

"Hush!" cried the man; "it wont answer here. Say another word, and I'll do your business myself with a crack on the head. That makes no noise; and is quite as certain, and more genteel. Here Bill, wrench the shutter open. He's game enough now, I'll engage. I've seen older hands of his age took the same way, for a minute or two, on a cold night."

Sikes, invoking terrific imprecations upon Fagin's head for sending Oliver on such an errand, plied the crowbar vigorously, but with little noise. After some delay, and some assistance from Toby, the shutter to which he had referred, swung open on its hinges.

It was a little lattice window, about five feet and a half above the ground: at the back of the house: which belonged to a scullery, or small brewing-place, at the end of the passage. The aperture was so small, that the inmates had probably not thought it worth while to defend it more securely; but it was large enough to admit a boy of Oliver's size, nevertheless. A very brief exercise of Mr. Sikes's art, sufficed to overcome the fastening of the lattice; and it soon stood wide open also.

"Now listen, you young limb," whispered Sikes, drawing a dark lantern from his pocket, and throwing the glare full on Oliver's face; "I'm a going to put you through there. Take this light; go softly up the steps straight afore you; and along the little hall to the street-door; unfasten it, and let us in."

"There's a bolt at the top, you won't be able to reach," interposed Toby. "Stand upon one of the hall chairs. There are three there, Bill, with a jolly large blue unicorn and a gold pitchfork on 'em: which is the old lady's arms."

"Keep quiet, can't you?" replied Sikes, with a threatening look. "The room-door is open, is it?"

"Wide," replied Toby, after peeping in to satisfy himself. "The game of that, is, that they always leave it open with a catch, so that the dog, who's got a bed in here, may walk up and down the passage when he feels wakeful. Ha! ha! Barney 'ticed him away to-night. So neat!"

Although Mr. Crackit spoke in a scarcely audible whisper, and laughed without noise, Sikes imperiously commanded him to be silent, and to get to work. Toby complied, by first producing his lantern, and placing it on the ground; and then by planting himself firmly with his head against the wall beneath the window, and his hands upon his knees, so as to make a step of his back. This was no sooner done, than

Sikes, mounting upon him, put Oliver gently through the window with his feet first; and, without leaving hold of his collar, planted him safely on the floor inside.

"Take this lantern," said Sikes, looking into the room. "You see the stairs afore you?"

Oliver, more dead than alive, gasped out, "Yes." Sikes, pointing to the street-door with the pistol-barrel, briefly advised him to take notice that he was within shot all the way; and that if he faltered, he would fall dead that instant.

"It's done in a minute," said Sikes, in the same low whisper. "Directly I leave go of you, do your work. Hark!"

"What's that?" whispered the other man.

They listened intently.

"Nothing," said Sikes, releasing his hold of Oliver. "Now!"

In the short time he had had to collect his senses, the boy had firmly resolved that, whether he died in the attempt or not, he would make one effort to dart up stairs from the hall, and alarm the family. Filled with this idea, he advanced at once, but stealthily.

"Come back!" suddenly cried Sikes aloud. "Back! back!"

Scared by the sudden breaking of the dead stillness of the place, and by a loud cry which followed it, Oliver let his lantern fall, and knew not whether to advance or fly.

The cry was repeated—a light appeared—a vision of two terrified half-dressed men at the top of the stairs swam before his eyes—a flash —a loud noise—a smoke—a crash somewhere, but where he knew not—and he staggered back.

Sikes had disappeared for an instant; but he was up again, and had him by the collar before the smoke had cleared away. He fired his own pistol after the men, who were already retreating; and dragged the boy up.

"Clasp your arm tighter," said Sikes, as he drew him through the window. "Give me a shawl here. They've hit him. Quick! Damnation, how the boy bleeds!"

Then, came the loud ringing of a bell: mingled with the noise of fire-arms, and the shouts of men, and the sensation of being carried over uneven ground at a rapid pace. And then, the noises grew confused in the distance; and a cold deadly feeling crept over the boy's heart; and he saw or heard no more.

Chapter XXIII.

WHICH CONTAINS THE SUBSTANCE OF A PLEASANT CONVERSATION
BETWEEN MR. BUMBLE AND A LADY; AND SHEWS THAT EVEN A BEADLE
MAY BE SUSCEPTIBLE ON SOME POINTS.

The night was bitter cold. The snow lay on the ground, frozen into a hard thick crust; so that only the heaps that had drifted into by-ways and corners were affected by the sharp wind that howled abroad: which, as if expending increased fury on such prey as it found, caught it savagely up in clouds, and, whirling it into a thousand misty eddies, scattered it in air. Bleak, dark, and piercing cold, it was a night for the well-housed and fed to draw round the bright fire and thank God they were at home; and for the homeless starving wretch to lay him down and die. Many hunger-worn outcasts close their eyes in our bare streets, at such times, who, let their crimes have been what they may, can hardly open them in a more bitter world.

Such was the aspect of out-of-door affairs, when Mrs. Corney, the matron of the workhouse to which our readers have been already introduced as the birthplace of Oliver Twist, sat herself down before a cheerful fire in her own little room; and glanced, with no small degree of complacency, at a small round table: on which stood a tray of corresponding size, furnished with all necessary materials for the most grateful meal that matrons enjoy. In fact, Mrs. Corney was about to solace herself with a cup of tea. As she glanced from the table to the fireplace, where the smallest of all possible kettles was singing a small song in a small voice, her inward satisfaction evidently increased,—so much so, indeed, that Mrs. Corney smiled.

"Well!" said the matron, leaning her elbow on the table, and looking reflectively at the fire; "I'm sure we have all on us a great deal to be grateful for! A great deal, if we did but know it. Ah!"

Mrs. Corney shook her head mournfully, as if deploring the mental blindness of those paupers who did *not* know it; and thrusting a silver spoon (private property) into the inmost recesses of a two-ounce tin tea-caddy, proceeded to make the tea.

How slight a thing will disturb the equanimity of our frail minds! The black teapot, being very small and easily filled, ran over while Mrs. Corney was moralising; and the water slightly scalded Mrs. Corney's hand.

"Drat the pot!" said the worthy matron, setting it down very hastily on the hob; "a little stupid thing, that only holds a couple of cups! What use is it of, to anybody! Except," said Mrs. Corney, pausing, "except to a poor desolate creature like me. Oh dear!"

With these words, the matron dropped into her chair; and, once more resting her elbow on the table, thought of her solitary fate. The small teapot, and the single cup, had awakened in her mind sad recollections of Mr. Corney (who had not been dead more than five-and-twenty years); and she was overpowered.

"I shall never get another!" said Mrs. Corney, pettishly; "I shall never get another—like him."

Whether this remark bore reference to the husband, or the teapot, is uncertain. It might have been the latter; for Mrs. Corney looked at it as she spoke: and took it up afterwards. She had just tasted her first cup, when she was disturbed by a soft tap at the room-door.

"Oh, come in with you!" said Mrs. Corney, sharply. "Some of the old women dying, I suppose. They always die when I'm at meals. Don't stand there, letting the cold air in, don't. What's amiss now, eh?"

"Nothing, ma'am, nothing," replied a man's voice.

"Dear me!" exclaimed the matron, in a much sweeter tone, "is that Mr. Bumble?"

"At your service, ma'am," said Mr. Bumble, who had been stopping outside to rub his shoes clean, and to shake the snow off his coat; and who now made his appearance, bearing the cocked hat in one hand and a bundle in the other. "Shall I shut the door, ma'am?"

The lady modestly hesitated to reply, lest there should be any impropriety in holding an interview with Mr. Bumble, with closed doors. Mr. Bumble taking advantage of the hesitation, and being very cold himself, shut it without farther permission.

"Hard weather, Mr. Bumble," said the matron.

"Hard, indeed, ma'am," replied the beadle. "Anti-porochial weather this, ma'am. We have given away, Mr. Corney, we have given away a matter of twenty quartern loaves,[1] and a cheese and a half, this very blessed afternoon; and yet them paupers are not contented."

"Of course not. When would they be, Mr. Bumble?" said the matron, sipping her tea.

"When, indeed, ma'am!" rejoined Mr. Bumble. "Why, here's one man that, in consideration of his wife and large family, has a quartern loaf and a good pound of cheese, full weight. Is he grateful, ma'am, is he grateful? Not a copper farthing's worth of it! What does he do, ma'am, but ask for a few coals; if it's only a pocket handkerchief full, he says! Coals! What would he do with coals? Toast his cheese with 'em, and then come back for more. That's the way with these people, ma'am; give 'em a apron full of coals to-day: and they'll come back for another, the day after to-morrow, as brazen as alabaster."[2]

The matron expressed her entire concurrence in this intelligible simile; and the beadle went on.

"I never," said Mr. Bumble, "see anything like the pitch it's got to.

1. Loaves of bread that measure a quarter of a standard loaf.
2. A hard white stone.

The day afore yesterday, a man—you have been a married woman, ma'am, and I may mention it to you—a man, with hardly a rag upon his back (here Mrs. Corney looked at the floor), goes to our overseer's door when he has got company coming to dinner; and says, he must be relieved, Mrs. Corney. As he wouldn't go away, and shocked the company very much, our overseer sent him out a pound of potatoes and half a pint of oatmeal. 'My heart!' says the ungrateful villain, 'what's the use of *this* to me? You might as well give me a pair of iron spectacles!' 'Very good,' says our overseer, taking 'em away again, 'you won't get anything else here.' 'Then I'll die in the streets!' says the vagrant. 'Oh no, you won't,' says our overseer."

"Ha! ha! That was very good! So like Mr. Grannett, wasn't it?" interposed the matron. "Well, Mr. Bumble?"

"Well, ma'am," rejoined the beadle, "he went away; and he *did* die in the streets. There's a obstinate pauper for you!"

"It beats anything I could have believed," observed the matron emphatically. "But don't you think out-of-door relief[3] a very bad thing, any way, Mr. Bumble? You're a gentleman of experience, and ought to know. Come."

"Mrs. Corney," said the beadle, smiling as men smile who are conscious of superior information, "out-of-door relief, properly managed: properly managed, ma'am: is the porochial safeguard. The great principle of out-of-door relief, is, to give the paupers exactly what they don't want; and then they get tired of coming."

"Dear me!" exclaimed Mrs. Corney. "Well, that is a good one, too!"

"Yes. Betwixt you and me, ma'am," returned Mr. Bumble, "that's the great principle; and that's the reason why, if you look at any cases that get into them owdacious newspapers, you'll always observe that sick families have been relieved with slices of cheese. That's the rule now, Mrs. Corney, all over the country. But, however," said the beadle, stooping to unpack his bundle, "these are official secrets, ma'am; not to be spoken of: except, as I may say, among the porochial officers, such as ourselves. This is the port wine, ma'am, that the board ordered for the infirmary; real, fresh, genuine port wine; only out of the cask this forenoon; clear as a bell; and no sediment!"

Having held the first bottle up to the light, and shaken it well to test its excellence, Mr. Bumble placed them both on the top of a chest of drawers; folded the handkerchief in which they had been wrapped; put it carefully in his pocket; and took up his hat, as if to go.

"You'll have a very cold walk, Mr. Bumble," said the matron.

"It blows, ma'am," replied Mr. Bumble, turning up his coat-collar, "enough to cut one's ears off."

The matron looked, from the little kettle, to the beadle, who was

3. Food for the indigent who do not live in workhouses.

moving towards the door; and as the beadle coughed, preparatory to bidding her good night, bashfully inquired whether—whether he wouldn't take a cup of tea?

Mr. Bumble instantaneously turned back his collar again; laid his hat and stick upon a chair; and drew another chair up to the table. As he slowly seated himself, he looked at the lady. She fixed her eyes upon the little teapot. Mr. Bumble coughed again, and slightly smiled.

Mrs. Corney rose to get another cup and saucer from the closet. As she sat down, her eyes once again encountered those of the gallant beadle; she coloured, and applied herself to the task of making his tea. Again Mr. Bumble coughed,—louder this time than he had coughed yet.

"Sweet? Mr. Bumble," inquired the matron, taking up the sugar-basin.

"Very sweet, indeed, ma'am," replied Mr. Bumble. He fixed his eyes on Mrs. Corney as he said this; and if ever a beadle looked tender, Mr. Bumble was that beadle at that moment.

The tea was made, and handed in silence. Mr. Bumble, having spread a handkerchief over his knees to prevent the crumbs from sullying the splendour of his shorts, began to eat and drink; varying these amusements, occasionally, by fetching a deep sigh; which, however, had no injurious effect upon his appetite, but, on the contrary, rather seemed to facilitate his operations in the tea and toast department.

"You have a cat, ma'am, I see," said Mr. Bumble, glancing at one, who, in the centre of her family, was basking before the fire; "and kittens too, I declare!"

"I am so fond of them, Mr. Bumble, you can't think," replied the matron. "They're so happy, so frolicsome, and so cheerful, that they are quite companions for me."

"Very nice animals, ma'am," replied Mr. Bumble, approvingly; "so very domestic."

"Oh, yes!" rejoined the matron, with enthusiasm; "so fond of their home too, that it's quite a pleasure, I'm sure."

"Mrs. Corney, ma'am," said Mr. Bumble, slowly, and marking the time with his teaspoon, "I mean to say this, ma'am; that any cat, or kitten, that could live with you, ma'am, and not be fond of its home, must be a ass, ma'am."

"Oh, Mr. Bumble!" remonstrated Mrs. Corney.

"It's of no use disguising facts, ma'am," said Mr. Bumble, slowly flourishing the teaspoon with a kind of amorous dignity which made him doubly impressive; "I would drown it myself, with pleasure."

"Then you're a cruel man," said the matron vivaciously, as she held out her hand for the beadle's cup; "and a very hard-hearted man besides."

"Hard-hearted, ma'am," said Mr. Bumble, "hard!" Mr. Bumble resigned his cup without another word; squeezed Mrs. Corney's little finger as she took it; and inflicting two open-handed slaps upon his laced waistcoat, gave a mighty sigh, and hitched his chair a very little morsel farther from the fire.

It was a round table; and as Mrs. Corney and Mr. Bumble had been sitting opposite each other: with no great space between them, and fronting the fire: it will be seen that Mr. Bumble, in receding from the fire, and still keeping at the table, increased the distance between himself and Mrs. Corney; which proceeding, some prudent readers will doubtless be disposed to admire, and to consider an act of great heroism on Mr. Bumble's part: he being in some sort tempted by time, place, and opportunity, to give utterance to certain soft nothings, which, however well they may become the lips of the light and thoughtless, do seem immeasurably beneath the dignity of judges of the land, members of parliament, ministers of state, lord-mayors, and other great public functionaries, but more particularly beneath the stateliness and gravity of a beadle: who (as is well known) should be the sternest and most inflexible among them all.

Whatever were Mr. Bumble's intentions, however: and no doubt they were of the best: it unfortunately happened, as has been twice before remarked, that the table was a round one; consequently Mr. Bumble, moving his chair by little and little, soon began to diminish the distance between himself and the matron; and, continuing to travel round the outer edge of the circle, brought his chair, in time, close to that in which the matron was seated. Indeed, the two chairs touched; and when they did so, Mr. Bumble stopped.

Now, if the matron had moved her chair to the right, she would have been scorched by the fire; and if to the left, she must have fallen into Mr. Bumble's arms; so (being a discreet matron, and no doubt foreseeing these consequences at a glance) she remained where she was, and handed Mr. Bumble another cup of tea.

"Hard-hearted, Mrs. Corney?" said Mr. Bumble, stirring his tea, and looking up into the matron's face; "are *you* hard-hearted, Mrs. Corney?"

"Dear me!" exclaimed the matron, "what a very curious question from a single man. What can you want to know for, Mr. Bumble?"

The beadle drank his tea to the last drop; finished a piece of toast; whisked the crumbs off his knees; wiped his lips; and deliberately kissed the matron.

"Mr. Bumble," cried that discreet lady in a whisper; for the fright was so great, that she had quite lost her voice, "Mr. Bumble, I shall scream!" Mr. Bumble made no reply; but, in a slow and dignified manner, put his arm round the matron's waist.

As the lady had stated her intention of screaming, of course she would have screamed at this additional boldness, but that the exertion was rendered unnecessary by a hasty knocking at the door: which was no sooner heard, than Mr. Bumble darted, with much agility, to the wine-bottles, and began dusting them with great violence: while the matron sharply demanded who was there. It is worthy of remark, as a curious physical instance of the efficacy of a sudden surprise in counteracting the effects of extreme fear, that her voice had quite recovered all its official asperity.

"If you please, mistress," said a withered old female pauper, hideously ugly: putting her head in at the door, "Old Sally is a-going fast."

"Well, what's that to me?" angrily demanded the matron. "I can't keep her alive, can I?"

"No, no, mistress," replied the old woman, "nobody can; she's far beyond the reach of help. I've seen a many people die; little babes and great strong men; and I know when death's a-coming, well enough. But she's troubled in her mind; and when the fits are not on her,—and that's not often, for she is dying very hard,—she says she has got something to tell, which you must hear. She'll never die quiet till you come, mistress."

At this intelligence, the worthy Mrs. Corney muttered a variety of invectives against old women who couldn't even die, without purposely annoying their betters; and, muffling herself in a thick shawl which she hastily caught up, briefly requested Mr. Bumble to stay till she came back, lest anything particular should occur; and, bidding the messenger walk fast, and not be all night hobbling up the stairs, followed her from the room with a very ill grace: scolding all the way.

Mr. Bumble's conduct on being left to himself, was rather inexplicable. He opened the closet, counted the tea-spoons, weighed the sugar-tongs, closely inspected a silver milk-pot to ascertain that it was of the genuine metal; and, having satisfied his curiosity on these points, put on his cocked-hat corner-wise, and danced with much gravity four distinct times round the table. Having gone through this very extraordinary performance, he took off the cocked-hat again; and, spreading himself before the fire with his back towards it, seemed to be mentally engaged in taking an exact inventory of the furniture.

Chapter XXIV.

TREATS OF A VERY POOR SUBJECT. BUT IS A SHORT ONE; AND MAY BE
FOUND OF IMPORTANCE IN THIS HISTORY.

It was no unfit messenger of death, that had disturbed the quiet of the matron's room. Her body was bent by age; her limbs trembled with palsy; and her face, distorted into a mumbling leer, resembled more the grotesque shaping of some wild pencil, than the work of Nature's hand.

Alas! how few of Nature's faces are left to gladden us with their beauty! The cares, and sorrows, and hungerings, of the world, change them as they change hearts; and it is only when those passions sleep, and have lost their hold for ever, that the troubled clouds pass off, and leave Heaven's surface clear. It is a common thing for the countenances of the dead, even in that fixed and rigid state, to subside into the long-forgotten expression of sleeping infancy, and settle into the very look of early life; so calm, so peaceful do they grow again, that those who knew them in their happy childhood, kneel by the coffin's side in awe, and see the Angel even upon earth.

The old crone tottered along the passages, and up the stairs, muttering some indistinct answers to the chidings of her companion; and being at length compelled to pause for breath, gave the light into her hand, and remained behind to follow as she might: while the more nimble superior made her way to the room where the sick woman lay.

It was a bare garret-room, with a dim light burning at the farther end. There was another old woman watching by the bed; and the parish apothecary's[1] apprentice was standing by the fire, making a toothpick out of a quill.

"Cold night, Mrs. Corney," said this young gentleman, as the matron entered.

"Very cold indeed, sir," replied the mistress, in her most civil tones, and dropping a curtsey as she spoke.

"You should get better coals out of your contractors," said the apothecary's deputy, breaking a lump on the top of the fire with the rusty poker; "these are not at all the sort of thing for a cold night."

"They're the board's choosing, sir," returned the matron. "The least they could do, would be to keep us pretty warm: for our places are hard enough."

The conversation was here interrupted by a moan from the sick woman.

"Oh!" said the young man, turning his face towards the bed, as if he had previously quite forgotten the patient, "it's all U. P.[2] there, Mrs. Corney."

"It is, is it, sir?" asked the matron.

"If she lasts a couple of hours, I shall be surprised," said the apothecary's apprentice, intent upon the toothpick's point. "It's a break-up of the system altogether. Is she dozing, old lady?"

The attendant stooped over the bed, to ascertain; and nodded in the affirmative.

"Then perhaps she'll go off in that way, if you don't make a row," said the young man. "Put the light on the floor. She won't see it there."

The attendant did as she was told: shaking her head meanwhile, to intimate that the woman would not die so easily; having done so, she

1. Pharmacist's.
2. All over.

resumed her seat by the side of the other nurse, who had by this time returned. The mistress, with an expression of impatience, wrapped herself in her shawl, and sat at the foot of the bed.

The apothecary's apprentice, having completed the manufacture of the toothpick, planted himself in front of the fire and made good use of it for ten minutes or so: when, apparently growing rather dull, he wished Mrs. Corney joy of her job, and took himself off on tiptoe.

When they had sat in silence for some time, the two old women rose from the bed; and crouching over the fire, held out their withered hands to catch the heat. The flame threw a ghastly light on their shrivelled faces; and made their ugliness appear perfectly terrible, as, in this position, they began to converse in a low voice.

"Did she say any more, Anny dear, while I was gone?" inquired the messenger.

"Not a word," replied the other. "She plucked and tore at her arms for a little time; but I held her hands, and she soon dropped off. She hasn't much strength in her, so I easily kept her quiet. I ain't so weak for an old woman, although I am on parish allowance;—no, no!"

"Did she drink the hot wine the doctor said she was to have?" demanded the first.

"I tried to get it down," rejoined the other. "But her teeth were tight set; and she clenched the mug so hard that it was as much as I could do, to get it back again. So I drank it; and it did me good!"

Looking cautiously round, to ascertain that they were not overheard, the two hags cowered nearer to the fire, and chuckled heartily.

"I mind the time," said the first speaker, "when she would have done the same, and made rare fun of it afterwards."

"Ay, that she would," rejoined the other; "she had a merry heart. A many, many, beautiful corpses she laid out, as nice and neat as waxwork. My old eyes have seen them—ay, and these old hands touched them too; for I have helped her, scores of times."

Stretching forth her trembling fingers as she spoke, the old creature shook them exultingly before her face; and fumbling in her pocket, brought out an old time-discoloured tin snuff-box, from which she shook a few grains into the outstretched palm of her companion, and a few more into her own. While they were thus employed, the matron, who had been impatiently watching until the dying woman should awaken from her stupor, joined them by the fire, and sharply asked how long she was to wait.

"Not long, mistress," replied the second woman, looking up into her face. "We have none of us long to wait for Death. Patience, patience! He'll be here soon enough for us all."

"Hold your tongue, you doting idiot!" said the matron, sternly. "You, Martha, tell me; has she been in this way before?"

"Often," answered the first woman.

"But will never be again," added the second one; "that is, she'll never wake again but once—and mind, mistress, that wont be for long."

"Long or short," said the matron, snappishly, "she wont find me here when she does wake; and take care, both of you, how you worry me again for nothing. It's no part of my duty to see all the old women in the house die, and I won't—that's more. Mind that, you impudent old harridans.[3] If you make a fool of me again, I'll soon cure you, I warrant you!"

She was bouncing away, when a cry from the two women, who had turned towards the bed, caused her to look round. The patient had raised herself upright, and was stretching her arms towards them.

"Who's that?" she cried, in a hollow voice.

"Hush, hush!" said one of the women, stooping over her. "Lie down, lie down!"

"I'll never lie down again alive!" said the woman, struggling. "I *will* tell her! Come here! Nearer! Let me whisper in your ear."

She clutched the matron by the arm; and forcing her into a chair by the bedside, was about to speak, when looking round, she caught sight of the two old women bending forward in the attitude of eager listeners.

"Turn them away," said the woman, drowsily; "make haste! Make haste!"

The two old crones, chiming in together, began pouring out many piteous lamentations that the poor dear was too far gone to know her best friends; and were uttering sundry protestations that they would never leave her, when the superior pushed them from the room, closed the door, and returned to the bedside. On being excluded, the old ladies changed their tone, and cried through the keyhole that old Sally was drunk; which, indeed, was not unlikely; since, in addition to a moderate dose of opium prescribed by the apothecary, she was labouring under the effects of a final taste of gin-and-water which had been privily[4] administered, in the openness of their hearts, by the worthy old ladies themselves.

"Now listen to me," said the dying woman, aloud, as if making a great effort to revive one latent spark of energy. "In this very room—in this very bed—I once nursed a pretty young creetur', that was brought into the house with her feet cut and bruised with walking, and all soiled with dust and blood. She gave birth to a boy, and died. Let me think —what was the year again?"

"Never mind the year," said the impatient auditor; "what about her?"

"Ay," murmured the sick woman, relapsing into her former drowsy state, "what about her?—what about—I know!" she cried, jumping fiercely up: her face flushed, and her eyes starting from her head—"I

3. Haggard and nasty women.
4. Secretly.

robbed her, so I did! She wasn't cold—I tell you she wasn't cold, when I stole it!"

"Stole what, for God's sake?" cried the matron, with a gesture as if she would call for help.

"It!" replied the woman, laying her hand over the other's mouth. "The only thing she had. She wanted clothes to keep her warm, and food to eat; but she had kept it safe, and had it in her bosom. It was gold, I tell you! Rich gold, that might have saved her life!"

"Gold!" echoed the matron, bending eagerly over the woman as she fell back. "Go on, go on—yes—what of it? Who was the mother? When was it?"

"She charged me to keep it safe," replied the woman, with a groan, "and trusted me as the only woman about her. I stole it in my heart when she first shewed it me hanging round her neck; and the child's death, perhaps, is on me besides! They would have treated him better, if they had known it all!"

"Known what?" asked the other. "Speak!"

"The boy grew so like his mother," said the woman, rambling on, and not heeding the question, "that I could never forget it when I saw his face. Poor girl! poor girl! She was so young, too! Such a gentle lamb! Wait; there's more to tell. I have not told you all, have I?"

"No, no," replied the matron, inclining her head to catch the words, as they came more faintly from the dying woman. "Be quick, or it may be too late!"

"The mother," said the woman, making a more violent effort than before; "the mother, when the pains of death first came upon her, whispered in my ear that if her baby was born alive, and thrived, the day might come when it would not feel so much disgraced to hear its poor young mother named. 'And oh, kind Heaven!' she said, folding her thin hands together, 'whether it be boy or girl, raise up some friends for it in this troubled world; and take pity upon a lonely, desolate child, abandoned to its mercy!' "

"The boy's name?" demanded the matron.

"They *called* him Oliver," replied the woman, feebly. "The gold I stole was——"

"Yes, yes—what?" cried the other.

She was bending eagerly over the woman to hear her reply; but drew back, instinctively, as she once again rose, slowly and stiffly, into a sitting posture; then, clutching the coverlet with both hands, muttered some indistinct sounds in her throat, and fell lifeless on the bed.

"Stone dead!" said one of the old women, hurrying in, as soon as the door was opened.

"And nothing to tell, after all," rejoined the matron, walking carelessly away.

The two crones, to all appearance, too busily occupied in the preparations for their dreadful duties to make any reply, were left alone: hovering about the body.

Chapter XXV.

WHEREIN THIS HISTORY REVERTS TO MR. FAGIN AND COMPANY.

While these things were passing in the country workhouse, Mr. Fagin sat in the old den—the same from which Oliver had been removed by the girl—brooding over a dull, smoky fire. He held a pair of bellows upon his knee, with which he had apparently been endeavouring to rouse it into more cheerful action; but he had fallen into deep thought; and with his arms folded on them, and his chin resting on his thumbs, fixed his eyes, abstractedly, on the rusty bars.

At a table behind him, sat the Artful Dodger, Master Charles Bates, and Mr. Chitling: all intent upon a game of whist; the Artful taking dummy[1] against Master Bates and Mr. Chitling. The countenance of the first-named gentleman, peculiarly intelligent at all times, acquired great additional interest from his close observance of the game, and his attentive perusal of Mr. Chitling's hand; upon which, from time to time, as occasion served, he bestowed a variety of earnest glances: wisely regulating his own play, by the result of his observations upon his neighbour's cards. It being a cold night, the Dodger wore his hat, as, indeed, was often his custom within doors. He also sustained a clay pipe between his teeth, which he only removed for a brief space when he deemed it necessary to apply for refreshment to a quart-pot upon the table, which stood ready filled with gin and water for the accommodation of the company.

Master Bates was also attentive to the play; but being of a more excitable nature than his accomplished friend, it was observable that he more frequently applied himself to the gin and water; and moreover indulged in many jests and irrelevant remarks, all highly unbecoming a scientific rubber.[2] Indeed, the Artful, presuming upon their close attachment, more than once took occasion to reason gravely with his companion upon these improprieties: all of which remonstrances, Master Bates received in extremely good part; merely requesting his friend to be "blowed," or to insert his head in a sack, or replying with some other neatly-turned witticism of a similar kind: the happy application of which, excited considerable admiration in the mind of Mr. Chitling. It was remarkable that the latter gentleman and his partner invariably lost; and

1. An imaginary player represented by an open hand that is managed by one of the players. "Whist": a game of cards played by four people in which one suit is trumps and each pair of partners competes to obtain the most rounds (called tricks) of four cards.
2. A set of three or five games in which the third or the fifth game determines the winner.

that the circumstance, so far from angering Master Bates, appeared to afford him the highest amusement, inasmuch as he laughed most uproariously at the end of every deal, and protested that he had never seen such a jolly game in all his born days.

"That's two doubles and the rub," said Mr. Chitling, with a very long face, as he drew half-a-crown from his waistcoat-pocket. "I never see such a feller as you, Jack; you win everything. Even when we've good cards, Charley and I can't make nothing of 'em."

Either the matter or the manner of this remark, which was made very ruefully, delighted Charley Bates so much, that his consequent shout of laughter roused the Jew from his reverie, and induced him to inquire what was the matter.

"Matter, Fagin!" cried Charley. "I wish you had watched the play. Tommy Chitling hasn't won a point; and I went partners with him against the Artful and dum."

"Ay, ay!" said the Jew, with a grin, which sufficiently demonstrated that he was at no loss to understand the reason. "Try 'em again, Tom; try 'em again "

"No more of it for me, thankee, Fagin," replied Mr. Chitling; "I've had enough. That 'ere Dodger has such a run of luck that there's no standing again' him."

"Ha! ha! my dear," replied the Jew, "you must get up very early in the morning, to win against the Dodger."

"Morning!" said Charley Bates; "you must put your boots on overnight; and have a telescope at each eye, and a opera-glass between your shoulders, if you want to come over him."

Mr. Dawkins received these handsome compliments with much philosophy, and offered to cut any gentleman in company, for the first picture-card, at a shilling at a time. Nobody accepting the challenge, and his pipe being by this time smoked out, he proceeded to amuse himself by sketching a ground-plan of Newgate on the table with the piece of chalk which had served him in lieu of counters;[3] whistling, meantime, with peculiar shrillness.

"How precious dull you are, Tommy!" said the Dodger, stopping short when there had been a long silence; and addressing Mr. Chitling. "What do you think he's thinking of, Fagin?"

"How should I know, my dear?" replied the Jew, looking round as he plied the bellows. "About his losses, maybe; or the little retirement in the country that he's just left, eh? Ha! ha! Is that it, my dear?"

"Not a bit of it," replied the Dodger, stopping the subject of discourse as Mr. Chitling was about to reply. "What do *you* say, Charley?"

"*I* should say," replied Master Bates, with a grin, "that he was uncommon sweet upon Betsy. See how he's a-blushing! Oh, my eye! here's

---

3. The small round pieces of metal that were widely used to keep score in card games.

a merry-go-rounder! Tommy Chitling's in love! Oh, Fagin, Fagin! what
a spree!"

Thoroughly overpowered with the notion of Mr. Chitling being the
victim of the tender passion, Master Bates threw himself back in his
chair with such violence, that he lost his balance, and pitched over
upon the floor; where (the accident abating nothing of his merriment)
he lay at full length until his laugh was over, when he resumed his
former position, and began another.

"Never mind him, my dear," said the Jew, winking at Mr. Dawkins,
and giving Master Bates a reproving tap with the nozzle of the bellows.
"Betsy's a fine girl. Stick up to her, Tom. Stick up to her."

"What I mean to say, Fagin," replied Mr. Chitling, very red in the
face, "is, that that isn't anything to anybody here."

"No more it is," replied the Jew; "Charley will talk. Don't mind him,
my dear; don't mind him. Betsy's a fine girl. Do as she bids you, Tom,
and you will make your fortune."

"So I *do* do, as she bids me," replied Mr. Chitling; "I shouldn't have
been milled,[4] if it hadn't been for her advice. But it turned out a good
job for you; didn't it, Fagin! And what's six weeks of it? It must come,
some time or another; and why not in the winter time when you don't
want to go out a-walking so much; eh, Fagin?"

"Ah, to be sure, my dear," replied the Jew.

"You wouldn't mind it again, Tom, would you," asked the Dodger,
winking upon Charley and the Jew, "if Bet was all right?"

"I mean to say that I shouldn't," replied Tom, angrily. "There, now!
Ah! Who'll say as much as that, I should like to know; eh, Fagin?"

"Nobody, my dear," replied the Jew; "not a soul, Tom. I don't know
one of 'em that would do it besides you; not one of 'em, my dear."

"I might have got clear off, if I'd split upon[5] her; mightn't I, Fagin?"
angrily pursued the poor half-witted dupe. "A word from me would have
done it; wouldn't it, Fagin?"

"To be sure it would, my dear," replied the Jew.

"But I didn't blab it; did I, Fagin?" demanded Tom, pouring question
upon question with great volubility.

"No, no, to be sure," replied the Jew; "you were too stout-hearted
for that. A deal too stout, my dear!"

"Perhaps I was," rejoined Tom, looking round; "and if I was, what's
to laugh at, in that; eh, Fagin?"

The Jew, perceiving that Mr. Chitling was considerably roused, hastened to assure him that nobody was laughing; and, to prove the gravity
of the company, appealed to Master Bates, the principal offender. But,
unfortunately, Charley, in opening his mouth to reply that he was never
more serious in his life, was unable to prevent the escape of such a

4. Jailed and worked at the treadmill.
5. Informed against.

violent roar, that the abused Mr. Chitling, without any preliminary ceremonies, rushed across the room, and aimed a blow at the offender, who, being skilful in evading pursuit, ducked to avoid it; and chose his time so well that it lighted on the chest of the merry old gentleman, and caused him to stagger to the wall, where he stood panting for breath, while Mr. Chitling looked on, in intense dismay.

"Hark!" cried the Dodger at this moment, "I heard the tinkler."[6] Catching up the light, he crept softly up stairs.

The bell was rung again, with some impatience, while the party were in darkness. After a short pause, the Dodger reappeared; and whispered Fagin mysteriously.

"What!" cried the Jew, "alone?"

The Dodger nodded in the affirmative; and, shading the flame of the candle with his hand, gave Charley Bates a private intimation, in dumb show, that he had better not be funny just then. Having performed this friendly office, he fixed his eyes on the Jew's face, and awaited his directions.

The old man bit his yellow fingers, and meditated for some seconds; his face working with agitation, the while, as if he dreaded something, and feared to know the worst. At length, he raised his head.

"Where is he?" he asked.

The Dodger pointed to the floor above; and made a gesture, as if to leave the room.

"Yes," said the Jew, answering the mute inquiry; "bring him down. Hush! Quiet, Charley! Gently, Tom! Scarce, scarce!"

This brief direction to Charley Bates, and his recent antagonist, was softly and immediately obeyed. There was no sound of their whereabout, when the Dodger descended the stairs, bearing the light in his hand, and followed by a man in a coarse smock-frock; who, after casting a hurried glance round the room, pulled off a large wrapper which had concealed the lower portion of his face, and disclosed: all haggard, unwashed, and unshorn: the features of flash Toby Crackit.

"How are you, Fagey?" said this worthy, nodding to the Jew. "Pop that shawl away in my castor, Dodger, so that I may know where to find it when I cut; that's the time of day! You'll be a fine young cracksman afore the old file now."[7]

With these words he pulled up the smock frock; and, winding it round his middle, drew a chair to the fire, and placed his feet upon the hob.

"See there, Fagey," he said, pointing disconsolately to his top-boots; "not a drop of Day and Martin[8] since you know when; not a bubble of blacking, by——! But don't look at me in that way, man. All in good time; I can't talk about business till I've eat and drank; so produce the

6. The bell.
7. Better than the old pro himself. "Castor": a hat made of beaver fur. "Cracksman": housebreaker.
8. A brand name of black shoe polish that became a slang term for cheap port wine.

sustainance, and let's have a quiet fill-out[9] for the first time these three days!"

The Jew motioned to the Dodger to place what eatables there were, upon the table; and, seating himself opposite the housebreaker, waited his leisure.

To judge from appearances, Toby was by no means in a hurry to open the conversation. At first, the Jew contented himself with patiently watching his countenance, as if to gain from its expression some clue to the intelligence he brought; but in vain. He looked tired and worn, but there was the same complacent repose upon his features that they always wore; and through dirt, and beard, and whisker, there still shone, unimpaired, the self-satisfied smirk of flash Toby Crackit. Then, the Jew, in an agony of impatience, watched every morsel he put into his mouth; pacing up and down the room, meanwhile, in irrepressible excitement. It was all of no use. Toby continued to eat with the utmost outward indifference, until he could eat no more; then, ordering the Dodger out, he closed the door, mixed a glass of spirits and water, and composed himself for talking.

"First and foremost, Fagey," said Toby.

"Yes, yes!" interposed the Jew, drawing up his chair.

Mr. Crackit stopped to take a draught of spirits and water, and to declare that the gin was excellent; and then, placing his feet against the low mantelpiece, so as to bring his boots to about the level of his eye, quietly resumed,

"First and foremost, Fagey," said the housebreaker, "how's Bill?"

"What!" screamed the Jew, starting from his seat.

"Why, you don't mean to say——" began Toby, turning pale.

"Mean!" cried the Jew, stamping furiously on the ground. "Where are they? Sikes and the boy! Where are they? Where have they been? Where are they hiding? Why have they not been here?"

"The crack failed," said Toby, faintly.

"I know it," replied the Jew, tearing a newspaper from his pocket, and pointing to it. "What more?"

"They fired and hit the boy. We cut over the fields at the back with him between us—straight as the crow flies—through hedge and ditch. They gave chase. D—me! the whole country was awake, and the dogs upon us."

"The boy!" gasped the Jew.

"Bill had him on his back, and scudded like the wind. We stopped to take him between us; his head hung down; and he was cold. They were close upon our heels; every man for himself, and each from the gallows! We parted company, and left the youngster lying in a ditch. Alive or dead, that's all I know about him."

9. Meal.

The Jew stopped to hear no more; but uttering a loud yell, and twining his hands in his hair, rushed from the room, and from the house.

Chapter XXVI.

IN WHICH, A MYSTERIOUS CHARACTER APPEARS UPON THE SCENE; AND MANY THINGS, INSEPARABLE FROM THIS HISTORY, ARE DONE AND PERFORMED.

The old man had gained the street corner, before he began to recover the effect of Toby Crackit's intelligence. He had relaxed nothing of his unusual speed; but was still pressing onward, in the same wild and disordered manner, when the sudden dashing past of a carriage: and a boisterous cry from the foot-passengers, who saw his danger: drove him back upon the pavement. Avoiding, as much as possible, all the main streets; and skulking only through the byways and alleys; he at length emerged on Snow Hill. Here he walked even faster than before; nor did he linger until he had again turned into a court; when, as if conscious that he was now in his proper element, he fell into his usual shuffling pace, and seemed to breathe more freely.

Near to the spot on which Snow Hill and Holborn Hill meet, there opens: upon the right hand as you come out of the city: a narrow and dismal alley leading to Saffron Hill. In its filthy shops are exposed for sale, huge bunches of second-hand silk handkerchiefs, of all sizes and patterns; for here reside the traders who purchase them from pickpockets. Hundreds of these handkerchiefs hang dangling from pegs outside the windows, or flaunting from the door-posts; and the shelves, within, are piled with them. Confined as the limits of Field Lane are, it has its barber, its coffee-shop, its beer-shop, and its fried-fish warehouse. It is a commercial colony of itself: the emporium of petty larceny: visited at early morning, and setting-in of dusk, by silent merchants, who traffic in dark back-parlours; and who go as strangely as they come. Here, the clothesman, the shoe-vamper,[1] and the rag-merchant, display their goods, as sign-boards to the petty thief; here, stores of old iron and bones, and heaps of mildewy fragments of woollen-stuff and linen, rust and rot in the grimy cellars.

It was into this place, that the Jew turned. He was well known to the sallow denizens of the lane; for such of them as were on the look-out to buy or sell, nodded, familiarly, as he passed along. He replied to their salutations in the same way; but bestowed no closer recognition until he reached the further end of the alley; when he stopped, to address a salesman of small stature, who had squeezed as much of his person

---

1. Shoe repairman.

into a child's chair as the chair would hold: and was smoking a pipe at his warehouse door.

"Why, the sight of you, Mr. Fagin, would cure the hoptalmy!"[2] said this respectable trader, in acknowledgment of the Jew's inquiry after his health.

"The neighbourhood was a little too hot, Lively," said Fagin, elevating his eyebrows, and crossing his hands upon his shoulders.

"Well, I've heerd that complaint of it, once or twice before," replied the trader; "but it soon cools down again; don't you find it so?"

Fagin nodded in the affirmative. Pointing in the direction of Saffron Hill, he inquired whether any one was up yonder to-night.

"At the Cripples?" inquired the man.

The Jew nodded.

"Let me see," pursued the merchant, reflecting. "Yes, there's some half-dozen of 'em gone in, that I knows. I don't think your friend's there."

"Sikes is not, I suppose?" inquired the Jew, with a disappointed countenance.

"*Non istwentus*,[3] as the lawyers say," replied the little man, shaking his head, and looking amazingly sly. "Have you got anything in my line to-night?"

"Nothing to-night," said the Jew, turning away.

"Are you going up to the Cripples, Fagin?" cried the little man, calling after him. "Stop! I don't mind if I have a drop there with you!"

But as the Jew, looking back, waved his hand to intimate that he preferred being alone; and, moreover, as the little man could not very easily disengage himself from the chair; the sign of the Cripples was, for a time, bereft of the advantage of Mr. Lively's presence. By the time he had got upon his legs, the Jew had disappeared; so Mr. Lively, after ineffectually standing on tiptoe, in the hope of catching sight of him, again forced himself into the little chair: and, exchanging a shake of the head with a lady in the opposite shop, in which doubt and mistrust were plainly mingled, resumed his pipe with a grave demeanour.

The Three Cripples, or rather the Cripples: which was the sign by which the establishment was familiarly known to its patrons: was the same public-house in which Mr. Sikes and his dog have already figured. Merely making a sign to a man at the bar, Fagin walked straight upstairs; and opening the door of a room, and softly insinuating himself into the chamber, looked anxiously about: shading his eyes with his hand, as if in search of some particular person.

The room was illuminated by two gas-lights; the glare of which, was prevented by the barred shutters, and closely-drawn curtains of faded red, from being visible outside. The ceiling was blackened, to prevent

---

2. An inflammation of the eye; the saying means "You're a sight for sore eyes."
3. Not to be found (Latin).

its colour from being injured by the flaring of the lamps; and the place was so full of dense tobacco-smoke, that at first it was scarcely possible to discern anything more. By degrees, however, as some of it cleared away through the open door, an assemblage of heads, as confused as the noises that greeted the ear, might be made out; and as the eye grew more accustomed to the scene, the spectator gradually became aware of the presence of a numerous company, male and female, crowded round a long table: at the upper end of which, sat a chairman with a hammer of office in his hand; while a professional gentleman, with a blueish nose, and his face tied up for the benefit of a toothache, presided at a jingling piano in a remote corner.

As Fagin stepped softly in, the professional gentleman, running over the keys by way of prelude, occasioned a general cry of order for a song; which, having subsided, a young lady proceeded to entertain the company with a ballad in four verses, between each of which the accompanyist played the melody, all through, as loud as he could. When this was over, the chairman gave a sentiment; after which, the professional gentlemen on the chairman's right and left volunteered a duet: and sang it, with great applause.

It was curious to observe some faces which stood out prominently from among the group. There was the chairman himself, (the landlord of the house,) a coarse, rough, heavy-built fellow, who, while the songs were proceeding, rolled his eyes hither and thither, and, seeming to give himself up to joviality, had an eye for everything that was done, and an ear for everything that was said—and sharp ones, too. Near him, were the singers: receiving, with professional indifference, the compliments of the company: and applying themselves, in turn, to a dozen proffered glasses of spirits and water, tendered by their more boisterous admirers; whose countenances, expressive of almost every vice in almost every grade, irresistibly attracted the attention, by their very repulsiveness. Cunning, ferocity, and drunkenness in all its stages, were there, in their strongest aspects; and women: some with the last lingering tinge of their early freshness, almost fading as you looked: others with every mark and stamp of their sex utterly beaten out, and presenting but one loathsome blank of profligacy and crime: some mere girls, others but young women, and none past the prime of life: formed the darkest and saddest portion of this dreary picture.

Fagin, troubled by no grave emotions, looked eagerly from face to face while these proceedings were in progress; but, apparently, without meeting that of which he was in search. Succeeding, at length, in catching the eye of the man who occupied the chair, he beckoned to him slightly, and left the room, as quietly as he had entered it.

"What can I do for you, Mr. Fagin?" inquired the man, as he followed him out to the landing. "Won't you join us? They'll be delighted, every one of 'em."

The Jew shook his head impatiently, and said in a whisper, "Is *he* here?"

"No," replied the man.

"And no news of Barney?" inquired Fagin.

"None," replied the landlord of the Cripples; for it was he. "He won't stir till it's all safe. Depend on it, they're on the scent down there; and that if he moved, he'd blow upon[4] the thing at once. He's all right enough, Barney is, else I should have heard of him. I'll pound it, that Barney's managing properly. Let him alone for that."

"Will *he* be here to night?" asked the Jew, laying the same emphasis on the pronoun as before.

"Monks, do you mean?" inquired the landlord, hesitating.

"Hush!" said the Jew. "Yes."

"Certain," replied the man, drawing a gold watch from his fob; "I expected him here, before now. If you'll wait ten minutes, he'll be——"

"No, no," said the Jew, hastily; as though, however desirous he might be to see the person in question, he was nevertheless relieved by his absence. "Tell him I came here to see him; and that he must come to me to-night. No, say to-morrow. As he is not here, to-morrow will be time enough."

"Good!" said the man. "Nothing more?"

"Not a word now," said the Jew, descending the stairs.

"I say," said the other, looking over the rails, and speaking in a hoarse whisper; "what a time this would be for a sell![5] I've got Phil Barker here: so drunk, that a boy might take him."

"Aha! But it's not Phil Barker's time," said the Jew, looking up. "Phil has something more to do, before we can afford to part with him; so go back to the company, my dear, and tell them to lead merry lives—*while they last*. Ha! ha! ha!"

The landlord reciprocated the old man's laugh; and returned to his guests. The Jew was no sooner alone, than his countenance resumed its former expression of anxiety and thought. After a brief reflection, he called a hack-cabriolet, and bade the man drive towards Bethnal Green. He dismissed him within some quarter of a mile of Mr. Sikes's residence; and performed the short remainder of the distance, on foot.

"Now," muttered the Jew, as he knocked at the door, "if there is any deep play here, I shall have it out of you, my girl, cunning as you are."

She was in her room, the woman said. Fagin crept softly up stairs, and entered it without any previous ceremony. The girl was alone; lying with her head upon the table, and her hair straggling over it.

"She has been drinking," thought the Jew, coolly, "or perhaps she is only miserable."

4. Give away.
5. The betrayal of an accomplice to the police.

The old man turned to close the door, as he made this reflection; and the noise thus occasioned, roused the girl. She eyed his crafty face narrowly, as she inquired whether there was any news, and listened to his recital of Toby Crackit's story. When it was concluded, she sank into her former attitude, but spoke not a word. She pushed the candle impatiently away; and once or twice, as she feverishly changed her position, shuffled her feet upon the ground; but this was all.

During this silence, the Jew looked restlessly about the room, as if to assure himself that there was no appearances of Sikes having covertly returned. Apparently satisfied with his inspection, he coughed twice or thrice, and made as many efforts to open a conversation; but the girl heeded him no more than if he had been made of stone. At length he made another attempt; and, rubbing his hands together, said, in his most conciliatory tone,

"And where should you think Bill was now, my dear?"

The girl moaned out some half intelligible reply, that she could not tell; and seemed, from the smothered noise that escaped her, to be crying.

"And the boy, too," said the Jew, straining his eyes to catch a glimpse of her face. "Poor leetle child! Left in a ditch, Nance; only think!"

"The child," said the girl, suddenly looking up, "is better where he is, than among us; and if no harm comes to Bill from it, I hope he lies dead in the ditch, and that his young bones may rot there."

"What!" cried the Jew, in amazement.

"Ay, I do," returned the girl, meeting his gaze. "I shall be glad to have him away from my eyes, and to know that the worst is over. I can't bear to have him about me. The sight of him turns me against myself, and all of you."

"Pooh!" said the Jew, scornfully. "You're drunk."

"Am I?" cried the girl, bitterly. "It's no fault of yours, if I am not! you'd never have me anything else, if you had your will, except now; —the humour doesn't suit you, doesn't it?"

"No!" rejoined the Jew, furiously. "It does not."

"Change it, then!" responded the girl, with a laugh.

"Change it!" exclaimed the Jew, exasperated beyond all bounds by his companion's unexpected obstinacy, and the vexation of the night, "I WILL change it! Listen to me, you drab![6] Listen to me, who, with six words, can strangle Sikes as surely as if I had his bull's throat between my fingers now. If he comes back, and leaves that boy behind him,— if he gets off free; and, dead or alive, fails to restore him to me; murder him yourself if you would have him escape Jack Ketch:[7] and do it the moment he sets foot in this room, or, mind me, it will be too late!"

"What is all this?" cried the girl, involuntarily.

6. Slut.
7. A generic term for hangman, from a notorious public hangman active between 1663 and 1686.

"What is it?" pursued Fagin, mad with rage. "When the boy's worth hundreds of pounds to me, am I to lose what chance threw me in the way of getting safely, through the whims of a drunken gang that I could whistle away the lives of! And me bound, too, to a born devil that only wants the will, and has the power to, to——"

Panting for breath, the old man stammered for a word; and in that instant checked the torrent of his wrath, and changed his whole demeanour. A moment before, his clenched hands had grasped the air; his eyes had dilated; and his face grown livid with passion; but now, he shrunk into a chair, and, cowering together, trembled with the apprehension of having himself disclosed some hidden villany. After a short silence, he ventured to look round at his companion. He appeared somewhat reassured, on beholding her in the same listless attitude from which he had first roused her.

"Nancy, dear!" croaked the Jew, in his usual voice. "Did you mind me, dear?"

"Don't worry me, now, Fagin!" replied the girl, raising her head languidly. "If Bill has not done it this time, he will another. He has done many a good job for you, and will do many more when he can; and when he can't, he won't, and so no more about that."

"Regarding this boy, my dear?" said the Jew, rubbing the palms of his hands nervously together.

"The boy must take his chance with the rest," interrupted Nancy, hastily; "and I say again, I hope he is dead, and out of harm's way, and out of yours,—that is, if Bill comes to no harm. And if Toby got clear off, he's pretty sure to be safe; for he's worth two of him any time."

"And about what I was saying, my dear?" observed the Jew, keeping his glistening eye steadily upon her.

"You must say it all over again, if it's any thing you want me to do," rejoined Nancy; "and if it is, you had better wait till to-morrow. You put me up for a minute; but now I'm stupid again."

Fagin put several other questions: all with the same drift of ascertaining whether the girl had profited by his unguarded hints; but she answered them so readily, and was withal so utterly unmoved by his searching looks, that his original impression of her being more than a trifle in liquor, was fully confirmed. Nancy, indeed, was not exempt from a failing which was very common among the Jew's female pupils; and in which, in their tenderer years, they were rather encouraged than checked. Her disordered appearance, and a wholesome perfume of Geneva which pervaded the apartment, afforded strong confirmatory evidence of the justice of the Jew's supposition; and when, after indulging in the temporary display of violence above described, she subsided, first into dulness, and afterwards into a compound of feelings: under the influence of which, she shed tears one minute: and in the next gave

utterance to various exclamations of "Never say die!" and divers calculations as to what might be the amount of the odds so long as a lady
or gentleman was happy: Mr. Fagin, who had had considerable experience of such matters in his time, saw, with great satisfaction, that she
was very far gone indeed.

Having eased his mind by this discovery; and having accomplished
his twofold object of imparting to the girl what he had that night heard,
and of ascertaining, with his own eyes, that Sikes had not returned; Mr.
Fagin again turned his face homeward: leaving his young friend asleep,
with her head upon the table.

It was within an hour of midnight; and the weather being dark and
piercing cold, he had no great temptation to loiter. The sharp wind that
scoured the streets, seemed to have cleared them of passengers, as of
dust and mud, for few people were abroad: and they were to all appearance hastening fast home. It blew from the right quarter for the
Jew, however, and straight before it he went: trembling, and shivering,
as every fresh gust drove him rudely on his way.

He had reached the corner of his own street, and was already fumbling
in his pocket for the door-key, when a dark figure emerged from a
projecting entrance which lay in deep shadow, and, crossing the road,
glided up to him unperceived.

"Fagin!" whispered a voice close to his ear.

"Ah!" said the Jew, turning quickly round, "is that——"

"Yes!" interrupted the stranger, harshly. "I have been lingering here
these two hours. Where the devil have you been?"

"On your business, my dear," replied the Jew, glancing uneasily at
his companion, and slackening his pace as he spoke. "On your business
all night."

"Oh, of course!" said the stranger, with a sneer. "Well; and what's
come of it?"

"Nothing good," said the Jew.

"Nothing bad, I hope?" said the stranger, stopping short, and turning
a startled look on his companion.

The Jew shook his head, and was about to reply, when the stranger,
interrupting him, motioned to the house, before which they had by this
time arrived: remarking, that he had better say what he had got to say,
under cover: for his blood was chilled with standing about so long, and
the wind blew through him.

Fagin looked as if he could have willingly excused himself from taking
home a visitor at that unseasonable hour; and, indeed, muttered something about having no fire; but his companion repeating his request in
a peremptory manner, he unlocked the door, and requested him to close
it softly, while he got a light.

"It's as dark as the grave," said the man, groping forward a few steps.
"Make haste!"

"Shut the door," whispered Fagin from the end of the passage. As he spoke, it closed with a loud noise.

"That wasn't my doing," said the other man, feeling his way. "The wind blew it to, or it shut of its own accord; one or the other. Look sharp with the light, or I shall knock my brains out against something in this confounded hole."

Fagin stealthily descended the kitchen stairs. After a short absence, he returned with a lighted candle, and the intelligence that Toby Crackit was asleep in the back room below, and the boys in the front one. Beckoning the other man to follow him, he led the way up stairs.

"We can say, the few words we've got to say in here, my dear," said the Jew, throwing open a door on the first floor; "and as there are holes in the shutters, and we never shew lights to our neighbours, we'll set the candle on the stairs. There!"

With these words, the Jew, stooping down, placed the candle on an upper flight of stairs, exactly opposite to the room door. This done, he led the way into the apartment; which was destitute of all moveables save a broken arm-chair, and an old couch or sofa without covering, which stood behind the door. Upon this piece of furniture, the stranger flung himself with the air of a weary man; and the Jew, drawing up the armchair opposite, they sat face to face. It was not quite dark; for the door was partially open; and the candle outside, threw a feeble reflection on the opposite wall.

They conversed for some time in whispers. Though nothing of the conversation was distinguishable beyond a few disjointed words here and there, a listener might easily have perceived that Fagin appeared to be defending himself against some remarks of the stranger; and that the latter was in a state of considerable irritation. They might have been talking, thus, for a quarter of an hour or more, when Monks—by which name the Jew had designated the strange man several times in the course of their colloquy—said, raising his voice a little,

"I tell you again, it was badly planned. Why not have kept him here among the rest, and made a sneaking, snivelling pickpocket of him at once?"

"Only hear him!" exclaimed the Jew, shrugging his shoulders.

"Why, do you mean to say you couldn't have done it, if you had chosen?" demanded Monks, sternly. "Haven't you done it, with other boys, scores of times? If you had had patience for a twelvemonth, at most, couldn't you have got him convicted, and sent safely out of the kingdom; perhaps for life?"

"Whose turn would that have served, my dear?" inquired the Jew, humbly.

"Mine," replied Monks.

"But not mine," said the Jew, submissively. "He might have become of use to me. When there are two parties to a bargain, it is only reasonable that the interests of both should be consulted; is it, my good friend?"

"What then?" demanded Monks, sulkily.

"I saw it was not easy to train him to the business," replied the Jew; "he was not like other boys in the same circumstances."

"Curse him, no!" muttered the man, "or he would have been a thief, long ago."

"I had no hold upon him, to make him worse," pursued the Jew, anxiously watching the countenance of his companion. "His hand was not in. I had nothing to frighten him with; which we always must have in the beginning, or we labour in vain. What could I do? Send him out with the Dodger and Charley? We had enough of that, at first, my dear; I trembled for us all."

"*That* was not my doing," observed Monks.

"No, no, my dear!" renewed the Jew. "And I don't quarrel with it now; because, if it had never happened, you might never have clapped eyes upon the boy to notice him, and so led to the discovery that it was him you were looking for. Well; I got him back for you by means of the girl; and then *she* begins to favour him."

"Throttle the girl!" said Monks, impatiently.

"Why, we can't afford to do that just now, my dear," replied the Jew, smiling; "and, besides, that sort of thing is not in our way; or, one of these days, I might be glad to have it done. I know what these girls are, Monks, well. As soon as the boy begins to harden, she'll care no more for him, than for a block of wood. You want him made a thief. If he is alive, I can make him one from this time; and if—if—" said the Jew, drawing nearer to the other,—"it's not likely, mind,—but if the worst comes to the worst, and he is dead——"

"It's no fault of mine if he is!" interposed the other man, with a look of terror, and clasping the Jew's arm with trembling hands. "Mind that, Fagin! I had no hand in it. Anything but his death; I told you from the first. I won't shed blood; it's always found out, and haunts a man besides. If they shot him dead, I was not the cause; do you hear me? Fire this infernal den! What's that?"

"What!" cried the Jew, grasping the coward round the body, with both arms, as he sprung to his feet. "Where?"

"Yonder!" replied the man, glaring at the opposite wall. "The shadow! I saw the shadow of a woman, in a cloak and bonnet, pass along the wainscot like a breath!"

The Jew released his hold; and they rushed tumultuously from the room. The candle, wasted by the draught, was standing where it had been placed. It shewed them, only the empty staircase, and their own white faces. They listened intently; but a profound silence reigned throughout the house.

"It's your fancy," said the Jew, taking up the light, and turning to his companion.

"I'll swear I saw it!" replied Monks, trembling. "It was bending forward, when I saw it first; and when I spoke, it darted away."

The Jew glanced, contemptuously, at the pale face of his associate; and, telling him he could follow, if he pleased, ascended the stairs. They looked into all the rooms; they were cold, bare, and empty. They descended to the passage, and thence into the cellars below. The green damp hung upon the low walls; and the tracks of the snail and slug glistened in the light of the candle; but all was still as death.

"What do you think now?" said the Jew, when they had regained the passage. "Besides ourselves, there's not a creature in the house except Toby and the boys; and they're safe enough. See here!"

As a proof of the fact, the Jew drew forth two keys from his pocket; and explained, that when he first went down stairs, he had locked them in, to prevent any intrusion on the conference.

This accumulated testimony effectually staggered Mr. Monks. His protestations had gradually become less and less vehement as they proceeded in their search without making any discovery; and, now, he gave vent to several very grim laughs, and confessed it could only have been his excited imagination. He declined any renewal of the conversation, however, for that night: suddenly remembering that it was past one o clock; and so the amiable couple parted.

Chapter XXVII.

ATONES FOR THE UNPOLITENESS OF A FORMER CHAPTER; WHICH DESERTED A LADY, MOST UNCEREMONIOUSLY.

As it would be, by no means, seemly in a humble author to keep so mighty a personage as a beadle waiting, with his back to a fire, and the skirts of his coat gathered up under his arms, until such time as it might suit his pleasure to relieve him; and as it would still less become his station, or his gallantry, to involve in the same neglect a lady on whom that beadle had looked with an eye of tenderness and affection, and in whose ear he had whispered sweet words, which, coming from such a quarter, might well thrill the bosom of maid or matron of whatsoever degree; the historian whose pen traces these words: trusting that he knows his place, and that he entertains a becoming reverence for those upon earth to whom high and important authority is delegated: hastens to pay them that respect which their position demands, and to treat them with all that duteous ceremony which their exalted rank, and (by consequence) great virtues, imperatively claim at his hands. Towards this end, indeed, he had purposed to introduce, in this place, a dissertation touching the divine right of beadles, and elucidative of the position, that a beadle can do no wrong; which could not fail to have been both plea-

surable and profitable to the right-minded reader, but which he is unfortunately compelled, by want of time and space, to postpone to some
more convenient and fitting opportunity; on the arrival of which, he
will be prepared to shew, that a beadle properly constituted: that is to
say, a parochial beadle, attached to the parochial workhouse, and attending in his official capacity the parochial church: is, in right and
virtue of his office, possessed of all the excellences and best qualities of
humanity; and that to none of those excellences, can mere companies'
beadles, or court-of-law beadles, or even chapel-of-ease beadles[1] (save
the last, and they in a very lowly and inferior degree), lay the remotest
sustainable claim.

Mr. Bumble had re-counted the tea-spoons, re-weighed the sugar-
tongs, made a closer inspection of the milk-pot, and ascertained to a
nicety the exact condition of the furniture, down to the very horse-hair
seats of the chairs; and had repeated each process full half-a-dozen times;
before he began to think that it was time for Mrs. Corney to return.
Thinking begets thinking; and, as there were no sounds of Mrs. Corney's
approach, it occurred to Mr. Bumble that it would be an innocent and
virtuous way of spending the time, if he were further to allay his curiosity
by a cursory glance at the interior of Mrs. Corney's chest of drawers.

Having listened at the keyhole, to assure himself that nobody was
approaching the chamber, Mr. Bumble, beginning at the bottom, proceeded to make himself acquainted with the contents of the three long
drawers: which, being filled with various garments of good fashion and
texture, carefully preserved between two layers of old newspapers, spec-
kled with dried lavender: seemed to yield him exceeding satisfaction.
Arriving, in course of time, at the right-hand corner drawer (in which
was the key), and beholding therein a small padlocked box, which, being
shaken, gave forth a pleasant sound, as of the chinking of coin, Mr.
Bumble returned with a stately walk to the fireplace; and, resuming his
old attitude, said, with a grave and determined air, "I'll do it!" He
followed up this remarkable declaration, by shaking his head in a waggish
manner for ten minutes, as though he were remonstrating with himself
for being such a pleasant dog; and then, he took a view of his legs in
profile, with much seeming pleasure and interest.

He was still placidly engaged in this latter survey, when Mrs. Corney,
hurrying into the room, threw herself, in a breathless state, on a chair
by the fireside; and covering her eyes with one hand, placed the other
over her heart, and gasped for breath.

"Mrs. Corney," said Mr. Bumble, stooping over the matron, "what
is this, ma'am? has anything happened, ma'am? Pray answer me; I'm
on—on—" Mr. Bumble, in his alarm, could not immediately think of
the word "tenter-hooks," so he said, "broken bottles."

1. See above, p. 21, n. 4. "Chapel-of-ease": a chapel built for the convenience of parishioners
who lived far from the parish church.

"Oh, Mr. Bumble!" cried the lady, "I have been so dreadfully put out!"

"Put out, ma'am!" exclaimed Mr. Bumble; "who has dared to—? I know!" said Mr. Bumble, checking himself, with native majesty, "this is them wicious paupers!"

"It's dreadful to think of!" said the lady, shuddering.

"Then *don't* think of it, ma'am," rejoined Mr. Bumble.

"I can't help it," whimpered the lady.

"Then take something, ma'am," said Mr. Bumble, soothingly. "A little of the wine?"

"Not for the world!" replied Mrs. Corney. "I couldn't,—oh! The top shelf in the right-hand corner—oh!" Uttering these words, the good lady pointed, distractedly, to the cupboard; and underwent a convulsion from internal spasms. Mr. Bumble rushed to the closet; and, snatching a pint green-glass bottle from the shelf thus incoherently indicated, filled a tea-cup with its contents, and held it to the lady's lips.

"I'm better now," said Mrs. Corney, falling back, after drinking half of it.

Mr. Bumble raised his eyes piously to the ceiling in thankfulness; and, bringing them down again to the brim of the cup, lifted it to his nose.

"Peppermint," explained Mrs. Corney, in a faint voice, smiling gently on the beadle as she spoke. "Try it! There's a little; a little something else in it."

Mr. Bumble tasted the medicine with a doubtful look; smacked his lips; took another taste; and put the cup down empty.

"It's very comforting," said Mrs. Corney.

"Very much so indeed, ma'am," said the beadle. As he spoke, he drew a chair beside the matron, and tenderly inquired what had happened to distress her.

"Nothing," replied Mrs. Corney. "I am a foolish, excitable, weak creetur."

"Not weak, ma'am," retorted Mr. Bumble, drawing his chair a little closer. "Are you a weak creetur, Mrs. Corney?"

"We are all weak creeturs," said Mrs. Corney, laying down a general principle.

"So we are," said the beadle.

Nothing was said, on either side, for a minute or two afterwards; by the expiration of that time, Mr. Bumble had illustrated the position by removing his left arm from the back of Mrs. Corney's chair, where it had previously rested: to Mrs. Corney's apron-string, round which it gradually became intwined.

"We are all weak creeturs," said Mr. Bumble.

Mrs. Corney sighed.

"Don't sigh, Mrs. Corney," said Mr. Bumble.

"I can't help it," said Mrs. Corney. And she sighed again.

"This is a very comfortable room, ma'am," said Mr. Bumble, looking round. "Another room and this, ma'am, would be a complete thing."

"It would be too much for one," murmured the lady.

"But not for two, ma'am," rejoined Mr. Bumble, in soft accents. "Eh, Mrs. Corney?"

Mrs. Corney drooped her head, when the beadle said this; the beadle drooped his, to get a view of Mrs. Corney's face. Mrs. Corney, with great propriety, turned her head away, and released her hand to get at her pocket-handkerchief; but insensibly replaced it in that of Mr. Bumble.

"The board allow you coals, don't they, Mrs. Corney?" inquired the beadle, affectionately pressing her hand.

"And candles," replied Mrs. Corney, slightly returning the pressure.

"Coals, candles, and house-rent free," said Mr. Bumble. "Oh, Mrs. Corney, what a Angel you are!"

The lady was not proof against this burst of feeling. She sunk into Mr. Bumble's arms; and that gentleman, in his agitation, imprinted a passionate kiss upon her chaste nose.

"Such porochial perfection!" exclaimed Mr. Bumble, rapturously. "You know that Mr. Slout is worse to-night, my fascinator?"

"Yes," replied Mrs. Corney, bashfully.

"He can't live a week, the doctor says," pursued Mr. Bumble. "He is the master of this establishment; his death will cause a wacancy; that wacancy must be filled up. Oh, Mrs. Corney, what a prospect this opens! What a opportunity for a joining of hearts and housekeepings!"

Mrs. Corney sobbed.

"The little word?" said Mr. Bumble, bending over the bashful beauty. "The one little, little, little word, my blessed Corney?"

"Ye—ye—yes!" sighed out the matron.

"One more," pursued the beadle; "compose your darling feelings for only one more. When is it to come off?"

Mrs. Corney twice essayed to speak; and twice failed. At length, summoning up courage, she threw her arms round Mr. Bumble's neck, and said, it might be as soon as ever he pleased, and that he was "a irresistible duck."

Matters being thus amicably and satisfactorily arranged, the contract was solemnly ratified in another tea-cupful of the peppermint mixture; which was rendered the more necessary, by the flutter and agitation of the lady's spirits. While it was being disposed of, she acquainted Mr. Bumble with the old woman's decease.

"Very good," said that gentleman, sipping his peppermint. "I'll call at Sowerberry's as I go home, and tell him to send to-morrow morning. Was it that as frightened you, love?"

"It wasn't anything particular, dear," said the lady, evasively.

"It must have been something, love," urged Mr. Bumble. "Won't you tell your own B.?"

"Not now," rejoined the lady; "one of these days. After we're married, dear."

"After we're married!" exclaimed Mr. Bumble. "It wasn't any impudence from any of them male paupers as——"

"No, no, love!" interposed the lady, hastily.

"If I thought it was," continued Mr. Bumble; "if I thought as any one of 'em had dared to lift his wulgar eyes to that lovely countenance——"

"They wouldn't have dared to do it, love," responded the lady.

"They had better not!" said Mr. Bumble, clenching his fist. "Let me see any man, porochial, or extra-porochial, as would presume to do it; and I can tell him that he wouldn't do it, a second time!"

Unembellished by any violence of gesticulation, this might have seemed no very high compliment to the lady's charms; but, as Mr. Bumble accompanied the threat with many warlike gestures, she was much touched with this proof of his devotion; and protested, with great admiration, that he was indeed a dove.

The dove then turned up his coat-collar, and put on his cocked-hat; and having exchanged a long and affectionate embrace with his future partner, once again braved the cold wind of the night; merely pausing, for a few minutes, in the male paupers' ward, to abuse them a little; with the view of satisfying himself that he could fill the office of workhouse-master with needful acerbity. Assured of his qualifications, Mr. Bumble left the building with a light heart, and bright visions of his future promotion: which served to occupy his mind until he reached the shop of the undertaker.

Now, Mr. and Mrs. Sowerberry having gone out to tea and supper: and Noah Claypole not being at any time disposed to take upon himself a greater amount of physical exertion than is necessary to a convenient performance of the two functions of eating and drinking: the shop was not closed, although it was past the usual hour of shutting-up. Mr. Bumble tapped with his cane on the counter several times; but, attracting no attention, and beholding a light shining through the glass-window of the little parlour at the back of the shop, he made bold to peep in and see what was going forward; and, when he saw what *was* going forward, he was not a little surprised.

The cloth was laid for supper; and the table was covered with bread and butter, plates, and glasses: a porter-pot, and a wine-bottle. At the upper end of the table, Mr. Noah Claypole lolled negligently in an easy-chair, with his legs thrown over one of the arms: an open clasp-knife in one hand, and a mass of buttered bread in the other; close beside him stood Charlotte, opening oysters from a barrel: which Mr. Claypole condescended to swallow, with remarkable avidity. A more than ordinary redness in the region of the young gentleman's nose, and a kind of fixed wink in his right eye, denoted that he was in a slight degree intoxicated; and these symptoms were confirmed by the intense relish with which he took his oysters, for which nothing but a strong appreciation of their cooling properties, in cases of internal fever, could have sufficiently accounted.

"Here's a delicious fat one, Noah, dear!" said Charlotte; "try him, do; only this one."

"What a delicious thing is a oyster!" remarked Mr. Claypole, after he had swallowed it. "What a pity it is, a number of 'em should ever make you feel uncomfortable; isn't it, Charlotte?"

"It's quite a cruelty," said Charlotte.

"So it is," acquiesced Mr. Claypole. "A'n't yer fond of oysters?"

"Not overmuch," replied Charlotte. "I like to see you eat 'em, Noah dear, better than eating them myself."

"Lor'!" said Noah, reflectively; "how queer!"

"Have another," said Charlotte. "Here's one with such a beautiful, delicate beard!"[2]

"I can't manage any more," said Noah. "I'm very sorry. Come here, Charlotte, and I'll kiss yer."

"What!" said Mr. Bumble, bursting into the room. "Say that again, sir."

Charlotte uttered a scream, and hid her face in her apron; Mr. Claypole, without making any further change in his position than suffering his legs to reach the ground, gazed at the beadle in drunken terror.

"Say it again, you vile, owdacious fellow!" said Mr. Bumble. "How dare you mention such a thing, sir? And how dare you encourage him, you insolent minx? Kiss her!" exclaimed Mr. Bumble, in strong indignation. "Faugh!"

"I didn't mean to do it!" said Noah, blubbering. "She's always a-kissing of me, whether I like it, or not."

"Oh, Noah!" cried Charlotte, reproachfully.

"Yer are; yer know yer are!" retorted Noah. "She's always a-doing of it, Mr. Bumble, sir; she chucks me under the chin, please sir; and makes all manner of love!"

"Silence!" cried Mr. Bumble, sternly. "Take yourself down stairs, ma'am. Noah, you shut up the shop; say another word till your master comes home, at your peril; and, when he does come home, tell him that Mr. Bumble said he was to send a old woman's shell[3] after breakfast to-morrow morning. Do you hear, sir? Kissing!" cried Mr. Bumble,

---

2. The row of gills in bivalves such as oysters; the Victorians believed that oysters acted as an aphrodisiac—hence Charlotte's pleasure at seeing Noah eat them and Noah's sudden amorous overture.
3. Coffin.

holding up his hands. "The sin and wickedness of the lower orders in this porochial district is frightful! If parliament don't take their abominable courses[4] under consideration, this country's ruined, and the character of the peasantry gone for ever!" With these words, the beadle strode, with a lofty and gloomy air, from the undertaker's premises.

And now that we have accompanied him so far on his road home, and have made all necessary preparations for the old woman's funeral, let us set on foot a few inquiries after young Oliver Twist; and ascertain whether he be still lying in the ditch where Toby Crackit left him.

Chapter XXVIII.

LOOKS AFTER OLIVER, AND PROCEEDS WITH HIS ADVENTURES.

"Wolves tear your throats!" muttered Sikes, grinding his teeth. "I wish I was among some of you; you'd howl the hoarser for it."

As Sikes growled forth this imprecation, with the most desperate ferocity that his desperate nature was capable of, he rested the body of the wounded boy across his bended knee; and turned his head, for an instant, to look back at his pursuers.

There was little to be made out, in the mist and darkness; but the loud shouting of men vibrated through the air; and the barking of the neighbouring dogs, roused by the sound of the alarm-bell, resounded in every direction.

"Stop, you white-livered hound!" cried the robber, shouting after Toby Crackit, who, making the best use of his long legs, was already ahead. "Stop!"

The repetition of the word, brought Toby to a dead stand-still. For he was not quite satisfied that he was beyond the range of pistol-shot; and Sikes was in no mood to be played with.

"Bear a hand with the boy," roared Sikes, beckoning furiously to his confederate. "Come back!"

Toby made a show of returning; but ventured, in a low voice, broken for want of breath, to intimate considerable reluctance as he came slowly along.

"Quicker!" cried Sikes, laying the boy in a dry ditch at his feet, and drawing a pistol from his pocket. "Don't play booty with me."

At this moment the noise grew louder. Sikes, again looking round, could discern that the men who had given chase were already climbing the gate of the field in which he stood; and that a couple of dogs were some paces in advance of them.

"It's all up, Bill!" cried Toby; "drop the kid, and show 'em your heels." With this parting advice, Mr. Crackit: preferring the chance of

4. Activities.

being shot by his friend, to the certainty of being taken by his enemies: fairly turned tail, and darted off at full speed. Sikes clenched his teeth; took one look round; threw over the prostrate form of Oliver, the cape in which he had been hurriedly muffled; ran along the front of the hedge, as if to distract the attention of those behind, from the spot where the boy lay; paused, for a second, before another hedge which met it at right angles; and whirling his pistol high into the air, cleared it at a bound, and was gone.

"Ho, ho, there!" cried a tremulous voice in the rear. "Pincher! Neptune! Come here, come here!"

The dogs, who, in common with their masters, seemed to have no particular relish for the sport in which they were engaged, readily answered to the command; and three men, who had by this time advanced some distance into the field, stopped to take counsel together.

"My advice, or, leastways, I should say, my *orders*, is," said the fattest man of the party, "that we 'mediately go home again."

"I am agreeable to anything which is agreeable to Mr. Giles," said a shorter man; who was by no means of a slim figure, and who was very pale in the face, and very polite: as frightened men frequently are.

"I shouldn't wish to appear ill-mannered, gentlemen," said the third, who had called the dogs back, "Mr. Giles ought to know."

"Certainly," replied the shorter man; "and whatever Mr. Giles says, it isn't our place to contradict him. No, no, I know my sitiwation! Thank my stars, I know my sitiwation." To tell the truth, the little man *did* seem to know his situation, and to know perfectly well that it was by no means a desirable one; for his teeth chattered in his head, as he spoke.

"You are afraid, Brittles," said Mr. Giles.

"I a'n't," said Brittles.

"You are," said Giles.

"You're a falsehood, Mr. Giles," said Brittles.

"You're a lie, Brittles," said Mr. Giles.

Now, these four retorts arose from Mr. Giles's taunt; and Mr. Giles's taunt had arisen from his indignation at having the responsibility of going home again, imposed upon himself under cover of a compliment. The third man brought the dispute to a close, most philosophically.

"I'll tell you what it is, gentlemen," said he, "we're all afraid."

"Speak for yourself, sir," said Mr. Giles, who was the palest of the party.

"So I do," replied the man. "It's natural and proper to be afraid, under such circumstances. *I* am."

"So am I," said Brittles; "only there's no call to tell a man he is, so bounceably."

These frank admissions softened Mr. Giles, who at once owned that *he* was afraid; upon which, they all three faced about, and ran back again with the completest unanimity, until Mr. Giles (who had the shortest wind of the party, and was encumbered with a pitchfork) most handsomely insisted on stopping, to make an apology for his hastiness of speech.

"But it's wonderful," said Mr. Giles, when he had explained, "what a man will do, when his blood is up. I should have committed murder: I know I should: if we'd caught one of the rascals."

As the other two were impressed with a similar presentiment; and as their blood, like his, had all gone down again; some speculation ensued upon the cause of this sudden change in their temperament.

"I know what it was," said Mr. Giles; "it was the gate."

"I shouldn't wonder if it was," exclaimed Brittles, catching at the idea.

"You may depend upon it," said Giles, "that that gate stopped the flow of the excitement. I felt all mine suddenly going away, as I was climbing over it."

By a remarkable coincidence, the other two had been visited with the same unpleasant sensation at that precise moment; it was quite obvious, therefore, that it was the gate; especially as there was no doubt regarding the time at which the change had taken place, because all three remembered that they had come in sight of the robbers at the very instant of its occurrence.

This dialogue was held between the two men who had surprised the burglars; and a travelling tinker,[1] who had been sleeping in an outhouse: and who had been roused, together with his two mongrel curs, to join in the pursuit. Mr. Giles acted in the double capacity of butler and steward to the old lady of the mansion; and Brittles was a lad of all-work; who, having entered her service a mere child, was treated as a promising young boy still, though he was something past thirty.

Encouraging each other with such converse as this; but keeping very close together, notwithstanding; and looking apprehensively round, whenever a fresh gust rattled through the boughs; the three men hurried back to a tree, behind which they had left their lantern, lest its light should inform the thieves in what direction to fire. Catching up the light, they made the best of their way home, at a good round trot; and long after their dusky forms had ceased to be discernible, it might have been seen twinkling and dancing in the distance, like some exhalation of the damp and gloomy atmosphere through which it was swiftly borne.

The air grew colder, as day came slowly on; and the mist rolled along the ground like a dense cloud of smoke. The grass was wet; the pathways, and low places, were all mire and water; and the damp breath of an unwholesome wind went languidly by, with a hollow moaning. Still Oliver lay motionless and insensible on the spot where Sikes had left him.

---

1. A repairman of household utensils.

Morning drew on apace. The air became more sharp and piercing, as its first dull hue: the death of night, rather than the birth of day: glimmered faintly in the sky. The objects which had looked dim and terrible in the darkness, grew more and more defined, and gradually resolved into their familiar shapes. The rain came down, thick and fast; and pattered, noisily, among the leafless bushes. But, Oliver felt it not, as it beat against him; for he still lay stretched, helpless and unconscious, on his bed of clay.

At length, a low cry of pain broke the stillness that prevailed; and uttering it, the boy awoke. His left arm, rudely bandaged in a shawl, hung heavy and useless at his side: and the bandage was saturated with blood. He was so weak, that he could scarcely raise himself into a sitting posture; and when he had done so, he looked feebly round for help, and groaned with pain. Trembling in every joint, from cold and exhaustion, he made an effort to stand upright; but, shuddering from head to foot, fell prostrate on the ground.

After a short return of the stupor in which he had been so long plunged, Oliver: urged by a creeping sickness at his heart, which seemed to warn him that if he lay there, he must surely die: got upon his feet, and essayed to walk. His head was dizzy; and he staggered to and fro like a drunken man; but he kept up, nevertheless, and, with his head drooping languidly on his breast, went stumbling onward, he knew not whither.

And now, hosts of bewildering and confused ideas came crowding on his mind. He seemed to be still walking between Sikes and Crackit, who were angrily disputing: for the very words they said, sounded in his ears; and when he caught his own attention, as it were, by making some violent effort to save himself from falling, he found that he was talking to them. Then, he was alone with Sikes, plodding on as they had done the previous day; and as shadowy people passed them, he felt the robber's grasp upon his wrist. Suddenly, he started back at the report of firearms; and there rose into the air, loud cries and shouts; lights gleamed before his eyes; and all was noise and tumult, as some unseen hand bore him hurriedly away. Through all these rapid visions, there ran an undefined, uneasy consciousness of pain, which wearied and tormented him, incessantly.

Thus he staggered on: creeping, almost mechanically, between the bars of gates, or through hedge-gaps as they came in his way: until he reached a road; here the rain began to fall, so heavily, that it roused him.

He looked about; and saw that at no great distance there was a house, which perhaps he could reach. Pitying his condition, they might have compassion on him; and if they did not, it would be better, he thought, to die near human beings, than in the lonely, open fields. He summoned up all his strength for one last trial; and bent his faltering steps towards it.

As he drew nearer to this house, a feeling came over him that he had seen it before. He remembered nothing of its details; but the shape and aspect of the building seemed familiar to him.

That garden-wall! On the grass inside he had fallen on his knees last night, and prayed the two men's mercy. It was the very same house they had attempted to rob.

Oliver felt such fear come over him when he recognised the place, that, for the instant, he forgot the agony of his wound, and thought only of flight. Flight! He could scarcely stand; and if he were in full possession of all the best powers of his slight and youthful frame, whither could he fly? He pushed against the garden-gate; it was unlocked, and swung open on its hinges. He tottered across the lawn; climbed the steps; knocked faintly at the door; and his whole strength failing him, sunk down against one of the pillars of the little portico.

It happened that about this time, Mr. Giles, Brittles, and the tinker, were recruiting[2] themselves, after the fatigues and terrors of the night, with tea and sundries, in the kitchen. Not that it was Mr. Giles's habit to admit to too great familiarity the humbler servants: towards whom it was rather his wont to deport himself with a lofty affability, which, while it gratified, could not fail to remind them of his superior position in society. But, death, fires, and burglary, make all men equals; so Mr. Giles sat with his legs stretched out before the kitchen fender, leaning his left arm on the table, while, with his right, he illustrated a circumstantial and minute account of the robbery, to which his hearers (but especially the cook and housemaid, who were of the party) listened with breathless interest.

"It was about half-past two," said Mr. Giles, "or I wouldn't swear that it mightn't have been a little nearer three, when I woke up, and, turning round in my bed, as it might be so, (here Mr. Giles turned round in his chair, and pulled the corner of the table-cloth over him to imitate bedclothes,) I fancied I heerd a noise."

At this point of the narrative the cook turned pale, and asked the housemaid to shut the door, who asked Brittles, who asked the tinker, who pretended not to hear.

"—Heerd a noise," continued Mr. Giles. "I says, at first, 'This is illusion;' and was composing myself off to sleep, when I heerd the noise again, distinct."

"What sort of a noise?" asked the cook.

"A kind of a busting noise," replied Mr. Giles, looking round him.

"More like the noise of powdering an iron bar on a nutmeg-grater," suggested Brittles.

2. Refreshing.

"It was, when *you* heerd, sir," rejoined Mr. Giles; "but, at this time, it had a busting sound. I turned down the clothes;" continued Giles, rolling back the table-cloth, "sat up in bed; and listened."

The cook and housemaid simultaneously ejaculated "Lor!" and drew their chairs closer together.

"I heerd it now, quite apparent," resumed Mr. Giles. " 'Somebody,' I says, 'is forcing of a door, or window; what's to be done? I'll call up that poor lad, Brittles, and save him from being murdered in his bed; or his throat,' I says, 'may be cut from his right ear to his left, without his ever knowing it.' "

Here, all eyes were turned upon Brittles; who fixed his upon the speaker, and stared at him, with his mouth wide open, and his face expressive of the most unmitigated horror.

"I tossed off the clothes," said Giles, throwing away the table-cloth, and looking very hard at the cook and housemaid, "got softly out of bed; drew on a pair of—"

"Ladies present, Mr. Giles," murmured the tinker.

"—Of *shoes*, sir," said Giles, turning upon him, and laying great emphasis on the word; "seized the loaded pistol that always goes up stairs with the plate-basket;[3] and walked on tiptoes to his room. 'Brittles,' I says, when I had woke him, 'don't be frightened!' "

"So you did," observed Brittles, in a low voice.

" 'We're dead men, I think, Brittles,' I says," continued Giles; " 'but don't be frightened.' "

"*Was* he frightened?" asked the cook.

"Not a bit of it," replied Mr. Giles. "He was as firm—ah! pretty near as firm as I was."

"I should have died at once, I'm sure, if it had been me," observed the housemaid.

"You're a woman," retorted Brittles, plucking up a little.

"Brittles is right," said Mr. Giles, nodding his head, approvingly; "from a woman, nothing else was to be expected. But we, being men, took a dark lantern, that was standing on Brittles's hob; and groped our way down stairs in the pitch dark,—as it might be so."

Mr. Giles had risen from his seat, and taken two steps with his eyes shut, to accompany his description with appropriate action, when he started violently, in common with the rest of the company, and hurried back to his chair. The cook and housemaid screamed.

"It was a knock," said Mr. Giles, assuming perfect serenity. "Open the door, somebody."

Nobody moved.

"It seems a strange sort of thing, a knock coming at such a time in the morning," said Mr. Giles, surveying the pale faces which surrounded

---

3. A cloth-lined basket in which silver spoons and other silver articles are kept.

him, and looking very blank himself; "but the door must be opened. Do you hear, somebody?"

Mr. Giles, as he spoke, looked at Brittles; but that young man, being naturally modest, probably considered himself nobody: and so held that the inquiry could not have any application to him; at all events, he tendered no reply. Mr. Giles directed an appealing glance at the tinker; but he had suddenly fallen asleep. The women were out of the question.

"If Brittles would rather open the door, in the presence of witnesses," said Mr. Giles, after a short silence, "I am ready to make one."

"So am I," said the tinker, waking up, as suddenly as he had fallen asleep.

Brittles capitulated on these terms; and the party being somewhat reassured by the discovery (made on throwing open the shutters) that it was now broad day, took their way up stairs; with the dogs in front; and the two women, who were afraid to stay below, bringing up the rear. By the advice of Mr. Giles, they all talked very loud, to warn any evil-disposed person outside, that they were strong in numbers; and by a master-stroke of policy, originating in the brain of the same ingenious gentleman, the dogs' tails were well pinched, in the hall, to make them bark savagely.

These precautions having been taken, Mr. Giles held on fast by the tinker's arm (to prevent his running away, as he pleasantly said), and gave the word of command to open the door. Brittles obeyed; and the group, peeping timorously over each other's shoulders, beheld no more formidable object than poor little Oliver Twist, speechless and exhausted, who raised his heavy eyes, and mutely solicited their compassion.

"A boy!" exclaimed Mr. Giles, valiantly pushing the tinker into the background. "What's the matter with the—eh?—Why—Brittles—look here—don't you know?"

Brittles, who had got behind the door to open it, no sooner saw Oliver, than he uttered a loud cry. Mr. Giles, seizing the boy by one leg and one arm: fortunately not the broken limb: lugged him straight into the hall, and deposited him at full length on the floor thereof.

"Here he is!" bawled Giles, calling, in a state of great excitement, up the staircase; "here's one of the thieves, ma'am! Here's a thief, miss! Wounded, miss! I shot him, miss; and Brittles held the light."

"In a lantern, miss," cried Brittles, applying one hand to the side of his mouth, so that his voice might travel the better.

The two women-servants ran up stairs to carry the intelligence that Mr. Giles had captured a robber; and the tinker busied himself in endeavouring to restore Oliver, lest he should die before he could be hanged. In the midst of all this noise and commotion, there was heard a sweet female voice, which quelled it, in an instant.

"Giles!" whispered the voice from the stair-head.

"I'm here, miss," replied Mr. Giles. "Don't be frightened, miss; I ain't much injured. He didn't make a very desperate resistance, miss; I was soon too many for him."

"Hush!" replied the young lady; "you frighten my aunt, almost as much as the thieves did. Is the poor creature much hurt?"

"Wounded desperate, miss," replied Giles, with indescribable complacency.

"He looks as if he was a-going, miss," bawled Brittles, in the same manner as before. "Wouldn't you like to come and look at him, miss, in case he should?"

"Hush, pray; there's a good man!" rejoined the young lady. "Wait quietly one instant, while I speak to aunt."

With a footstep as soft and gentle as the voice, the speaker tripped away; and soon returned, with the direction that the wounded person was to be carried, carefully, up stairs to Mr. Giles's room; and that Brittles was to saddle the pony and betake himself instantly to Chertsey: from which place, he was to despatch, with all speed, a constable and doctor.

"But won't you take one look at him, first, miss?" asked Mr. Giles, with as much pride as if Oliver were some bird of rare plumage, that he had skilfully brought down. "Not one little peep, miss?"

"Not now for the world," replied the young lady. "Poor fellow! Oh! treat him kindly, Giles, for my sake!"

The old servant looked up at the speaker, as she turned away; with a glance as proud and admiring as if she had been his own child. Then, bending over Oliver, he helped to carry him up stairs, with the care and solicitude of a woman.

Chapter XXIX.

HAS AN INTRODUCTORY ACCOUNT OF THE INMATES OF THE HOUSE, TO
WHICH OLIVER RESORTED.

In a handsome room: though its furniture had rather the air of old-fashioned comfort, than of modern elegance: there sat two ladies at a well-spread breakfast-table. Mr. Giles, dressed with scrupulous care in a full suit of black, was in attendance upon them. He had taken his station some half-way between the sideboard and the breakfast-table; and with his body drawn up to its full height, his head thrown back, and inclined the merest trifle on one side: his left leg advanced, and his right hand thrust into his waistcoat, while his left hung down by his side, grasping a waiter;[1] looked like one who laboured under a very agreeable sense of his own merits and importance.

Of the two ladies, one was well advanced in years; but the high-backed

1. A tray.

oaken chair in which she sat, was not more upright than she. Dressed with the utmost nicety and precision, in a quaint mixture of by-gone costume: with some slight concessions to the prevailing taste, which rather served to point the old style pleasantly than to impair its effect: she sat, in a stately manner, with her hands folded on the table before her. Her eyes, (and age had dimmed but little of their brightness), were attentively fixed upon her young companion.

The younger lady was in the lovely bloom and spring-time of womanhood; at that age, when, if ever angels be for God's good purposes enthroned in mortal forms, they may be, without impiety, supposed to abide in such as hers.

She was not past seventeen. Cast in so slight and exquisite a mould; so mild and gentle; so pure and beautiful; that earth seemed not her element, nor its rough creatures her fit companions. The very intelligence that shone in her deep blue eye, and was stamped upon her noble head, seemed scarcely of her age or of the world; and yet the changing expression of sweetness and good humour; the thousand lights that played about the face, and left no shadow there; above all, the smile; the cheerful, happy smile; were made for Home; for fireside peace and happiness.

She was busily engaged in the little offices of the table. Chancing to raise her eyes as the elder lady was regarding her, she playfully put back her hair, which was simply braided on her forehead; and threw into one beaming look, such a gush of affection and artless loveliness, that blessed spirits might have smiled to look upon her.

"And Brittles has been gone, upwards of an hour, has he?" asked the old lady, after a pause.

"An hour and twelve minutes, ma'am," replied Mr. Giles, referring to a silver watch, which he drew forth by a black ribbon.

"He is always slow," remarked the old lady.

"Brittles always was a slow boy, ma'am," replied the attendant. And seeing, by-the-by, that Brittles had been a slow boy for upwards of thirty years, there appeared no great probability of his ever being a fast one.

"He gets worse instead of better, I think," said the elder lady.

"It is very inexcusable in him if he stops to play with any other boys," said the young lady, smiling.

Mr. Giles was apparently considering the propriety of indulging in a respectful smile himself, when a gig[2] drove up to the garden-gate: out of which, there jumped a fat gentleman, who ran straight up to the door: and who, getting quickly into the house by some mysterious process, burst into the room, and nearly overturned Mr. Giles and the breakfast-table together.

"I never heard of such a thing!" exclaimed the fat gentleman. "My

2. A light, two-wheeled one-horse carriage.

dear Mrs. Maylie—bless my soul—in the silence of night, too—I *never* heard of such a thing!"

With these expressions of condolence, the fat gentleman shook hands with both ladies; and drawing up a chair, inquired how they found themselves.

"You ought to be dead; positively dead with the fright," said the fat gentleman. "Why didn't you send? Bless me, my man should have come in a minute; and so would I; and my assistant would have been delighted; or anybody, I'm sure, under such circumstances; dear, dear! So unexpected! In the silence of night, too!"

The doctor seemed especially troubled by the fact of the robbery having been unexpected, and attempted in the night-time; as if it were the established custom of gentlemen in the housebreaking way to transact business at noon, and to make an appointment, by the twopenny post,[3] a day or two previous.

"And you, Miss Rose," said the doctor, turning to the young lady, "I——"

"Oh! very much so, indeed," said Rose, interrupting him; "but there is a poor creature up stairs, whom aunt wishes you to see."

"Ah! to be sure," replied the doctor, "so there is. That was your handiwork, Giles, I understand."

Mr. Giles, who had been feverishly putting the tea-cups to rights, blushed very red, and said that he had had that honour.

"Honour, eh?" said the doctor, "well, I don't know; perhaps it's as honourable to hit a thief in a back kitchen, as to hit your man at twelve paces. Fancy that he fired in the air; and you've fought a duel, Giles."

Mr. Giles, who thought this light treatment of the matter, an unjust attempt at diminishing his glory, answered respectfully, that it was not for the like of him to judge about that; but he rather thought it was no joke to the opposite party.

"'Gad that's true!" said the doctor. "Where is he? Shew me the way. I'll look in again, as I come down, Mrs. Maylie. That's the little window that he got in at, eh? Well, I couldn't have believed it!"

Talking all the way, he followed Mr. Giles up stairs; and while he is going up stairs, the reader may be informed, that Mr. Losberne, a surgeon in the neighbourhood, known through a circuit of ten miles round as "the doctor," had grown fat: more from good-humour than from good living: and was as kind and hearty, and withal as eccentric an old bachelor, as will be found in five times that space, by any explorer alive.

The doctor was absent, much longer than either he or the ladies had anticipated. A large flat box was fetched out of the gig; and a bedroom

3. Before the introduction of the countrywide penny post in 1840, any letter mailed within the central area of London to an address in the same area would be delivered for two pence.

bell was rung very often; and the servants ran up and down stairs perpetually; from which tokens it was justly concluded that something
important was going on above. At length he returned; and in reply to
an anxious inquiry after his patient, looked very mysterious, and closed
the door, carefully.

"This is a very extraordinary thing, Mrs. Maylie," said the doctor,
standing with his back to the door, as if to keep it shut.

"He is not in danger, I hope?" said the old lady.

"Why, that would *not* be an extraordinary thing, under the circumstances," replied the doctor; "though I don't think he is. Have you seen
this thief?"

"No," rejoined the old lady.

"Nor heard anything about him?"

"No."

"I beg your pardon, ma'am," interposed Mr. Giles; "but I was going
to tell you about him when Doctor Losberne came in."

The fact was, that Mr. Giles had not, at first, been able to bring his
mind to the avowal, that he had only shot a boy. Such commendations
had been bestowed upon his bravery, that he could not, for the life of
him, help postponing the explanation for a few delicious minutes; during
which he had flourished, in the very zenith of a brief reputation for
undaunted courage.

"Rose wished to see the man," said Mrs. Maylie, "but I wouldn't
hear of it."

"Humph!" rejoined the doctor. "There is nothing very alarming in
his appearance. Have you any objection to see him in my presence?"

"If it be necessary," replied the old lady, "certainly not."

"Then I think it is necessary," said the doctor; "at all events, I am
quite sure that you would deeply regret not having done so, if you
postponed it. He is perfectly quiet and comfortable now. Allow me—
Miss Rose, will you permit me? Not the slightest fear, I pledge you my
honour."

Chapter XXX.

RELATES WHAT OLIVER'S NEW VISITORS THOUGHT OF HIM.

With many loquacious assurances that they would be agreeably surprised in the aspect of the criminal, the doctor drew the young lady's
arm through one of his; and offering his disengaged hand to Mrs. Maylie,
led them, with much ceremony and stateliness, up stairs.

"Now," said the doctor, in a whisper, as he softly turned the handle
of a bedroom-door, "let us hear what you think of him. He has not
been shaved very recently, but he don't look at all ferocious notwith-

standing. Stop, though! Let me first see that he is in visiting order."

Stepping before them, he looked into the room. Motioning them to advance, he closed the door when they had entered; and gently drew back the curtains of the bed. Upon it, in lieu of the dogged, black-visaged ruffian they had expected to behold, there lay a mere child: worn with pain and exhaustion: and sunk into a deep sleep. His wounded arm, bound and splintered up, was crossed upon his breast; his head reclined upon the other arm, which was half hidden by his long hair, as it streamed over the pillow.

The honest gentleman held the curtain in his hand; and looked on, for a minute or so, in silence. Whilst he was watching the patient thus, the younger lady glided softly past; and seating herself in a chair by the bedside, gathered Oliver's hair from his face. As she stooped over him, her tears fell upon his forehead.

The boy stirred, and smiled in his sleep, as though these marks of pity and compassion had awakened some pleasant dream of a love and affection he had never known; as a strain of gentle music, or the rippling of water in a silent place, or the odour of a flower, or even the mention of a familiar word, will sometimes call up sudden dim remembrances of scenes that never were, in this life; which vanish like a breath; and which some brief memory of a happier existence, long gone by, would seem to have awakened, for no voluntary exertion of the mind can ever recall them.

"What can this mean?" exclaimed the elder lady. "This poor child can never have been the pupil of robbers!"

"Vice," sighed the surgeon, replacing the curtain, "takes up her abode in many temples; and who can say that a fair outside shall not enshrine her?"

"But at so early an age!" urged Rose.

"My dear young lady," rejoined the surgeon, mournfully shaking his head; "crime, like death, is not confined to the old and withered alone. The youngest and fairest are too often its chosen victims."

"But, can you—oh, sir! can you really believe that this delicate boy has been the voluntary associate of the worst outcasts of society?" said Rose.

The surgeon shook his head, in a manner which intimated that he feared it was very possible; and observing that they might disturb the patient, led the way into an adjoining apartment.

"But even if he has been wicked," pursued Rose, "think how young he is; think that he may never have known a mother's love, or the comfort of a home; and that ill-usage and blows, or the want of bread, may have driven him to herd with men who have forced him to guilt. Aunt, dear aunt, for mercy's sake, think of this, before you let them drag this sick child to a prison, which in any case must be the grave of all his chances of amendment. Oh! as you love me, and know that I

have never felt the want of parents in your goodness and affection, but
that I might have done so, and might have been equally helpless and
unprotected with this poor child, have pity upon him before it is too
late."

"My dear love!" said the elder lady, as she folded the weeping girl to
her bosom, "do you think I would harm a hair of his head?"

"Oh, no!" replied Rose, eagerly.

"No," said the old lady, with a trembling lip; "my days are drawing
to their close; and may mercy be shewn to me as I shew it to others!
What can I do to save him, sir?"

"Let me think, ma'am," said the doctor; "let me think."

Mr. Losberne thrust his hands into his pockets; and took several turns
up and down the room: often stopping, and balancing himself on his
toes: and frowning frightfully. After various exclamations of "I've got it
now" and "no, I haven't," and as many renewals of the walking and
frowning, he at length made a dead halt, and spoke as follows:

"I think if you give me a full and unlimited commission to bully
Giles, and that little boy, Brittles, I can manage it. He is a faithful fellow
and an old servant, I know; but you can make it up to him in a thousand
ways, and reward him for being such a good shot besides. You don't
object to that?"

"Unless there is some other way of preserving the child," replied Mrs.
Maylie.

"There is no other," said the doctor. "No other, take my word for
it."

"Then my aunt invests you with full power," said Rose, smiling
through her tears; "but pray don't be harder upon the poor fellows than
is indispensably necessary."

"You seem to think," retorted the doctor, "that every body is disposed
to be hard-hearted to-day, except yourself Miss Rose. I only hope, for
the sake of the rising male sex generally, that you may be found in as
vulnerable and soft-hearted a mood by the first eligible young fellow
who appeals to your compassion; and I wish I were a young fellow, that
I might avail myself, on the spot, of such a favourable opportunity for
doing so, as the present."

"You are as great a boy as poor Brittles himself," returned Rose,
blushing.

"Well," said the doctor, laughing heartily, "that is no very difficult
matter. But to return to this boy. The great point of our agreement is
yet to come. He will wake in an hour or so, I dare say; and although I
have told that thick-headed constable-fellow down stairs that he mustn't
be moved or spoken to, on peril of his life, I think we may converse
with him without danger. Now, I make this stipulation—that I shall
examine him in your presence, and that if from what he says, we judge,
and I can show to the satisfaction of your cool reason, that he is a real

and thorough bad one (which is more than possible), he shall be left to his fate, without any further interference on my part, at all events."

"Oh no, aunt!" entreated Rose.

"Oh yes, aunt!" said the doctor. "Is it a bargain?"

"He cannot be hardened in vice," said Rose; "it is impossible."

"Very good," retorted the doctor; "then so much the more reason for acceding to my proposition."

Finally, the treaty was entered into; and the parties thereunto, sat down to wait, with some impatience, until Oliver should awake.

The patience of the two ladies was destined to undergo a longer trial than Mr. Losberne had led them to expect; for hour after hour passed on, and still Oliver slumbered heavily. It was evening, indeed, before the kind-hearted doctor brought them the intelligence, that he was at length sufficiently restored to be spoken to. The boy was very ill, he said, and weak from the loss of blood; but his mind was so troubled with anxiety to disclose something, that he deemed it better to give him the opportunity, than to insist upon his remaining quiet until next morning: which he should otherwise have done.

The conference was a long one; for Oliver told them all his simple history: and was often compelled to stop, by pain and want of strength. It was a solemn thing, to hear, in the darkened room, the feeble voice of the sick child recounting a weary catalogue of evils and calamities which hard men had brought upon him. Oh! if, when we oppress and grind our fellow-creatures, we bestowed but one thought on the dark evidences of human error, which, like dense and heavy clouds, are rising, slowly it is true, but not less surely, to Heaven, to pour their after-vengeance on our heads; if we heard but one instant, in imagination, the deep testimony of dead men's voices, which no power can stifle, and no pride shut out; where would be the injury and injustice: the suffering, misery, cruelty, and wrong: that each day's life brings with it!

Oliver's pillow was smoothed by gentle hands that night; and loveliness and virtue watched him as he slept. He felt calm and happy; and could have died without a murmur.

The momentous interview was no sooner concluded, and Oliver composed to rest again, than the doctor, after wiping his eyes, and condemning them for being weak all at once, betook himself down stairs to open upon Mr. Giles. And finding nobody about the parlours, it occurred to him, that he could perhaps originate the proceedings with better effect in the kitchen; so into the kitchen he went.

There were assembled, in that lower house of the domestic parliament,[1] the women-servants, Mr. Brittles, Mr. Giles, the tinker (who had received a special invitation to regale himself for the remainder of

---

1. Dickens compares the servants gathered in the kitchen downstairs to the members of the British House of Commons, in contrast to the upper house, the House of Lords.

the day, in consideration of his services), and the constable. The latter
gentleman had a large staff, a large head, large features, and large half-
boots; and looked as if he had been taking a proportionate allowance of
ale, as indeed he had.

The adventures of the previous night, were still under discussion; for
Mr. Giles was expatiating upon his presence of mind, when the doctor
entered; and Mr. Brittles, with a mug of ale in his hand, was corrob-
orating everything, before his superior said it.

"Sit still," said the doctor, waving his hand.

"Thank you, sir," said Mr. Giles. "Misses wished some ale to be given
out, sir; and as I felt no ways inclined for my own little room, sir, and
was disposed for company, I am taking mine among 'em here."

Brittles headed a low murmur, by which the ladies and gentlemen
generally, were understood to express the gratification they derived from
Mr. Giles's condescension. Mr. Giles looked round with a patronising
air, as much as to say, that so long as they behaved properly, he would
never desert them.

"How is the patient to-night, sir?" asked Giles.

"So-so;" returned the doctor. "I am afraid you have got yourself into
a scrape there, Mr. Giles."

"I hope you don't mean to say, sir," said Mr. Giles, trembling, "that
he's going to die. If I thought it, I should never be happy again. I
wouldn't cut a boy off: no, not even Brittles here: not for all the plate
in the country, sir."

"That's not the point," said the doctor, mysteriously. "Mr. Giles, are
you a Protestant?"

"Yes, sir, I hope so," faltered Mr. Giles, who had turned very pale.

"And what are you, boy?" said the doctor, turning sharply upon
Brittles.

"Lord bless me, sir!" replied Brittles, starting violently; "I'm the same
as Mr. Giles, sir."

"Then tell me this," said the doctor, "both of you—both of you! Are
you going to take upon yourselves to swear that that boy up stairs is the
boy that was put through the little window last night? Out with it! Come!
We are prepared for you!"

The doctor, who was universally considered one of the best-tempered
creatures on earth, made this demand in such a dreadful tone of anger,
that Giles and Brittles, who were considerably muddled by ale and
excitement, stared at each other in a state of stupefaction.

"Pay attention to the reply, constable, will you?" said the doctor,
shaking his forefinger with great solemnity of manner, and tapping the
bridge of his nose with it, to bespeak the exercise of that worthy's utmost
acuteness. "Something may come of this, before long."

The constable looked as wise as he could, and took up his staff of
office: which had been reclining indolently in the chimney-corner.

"It's a simple question of identity, you will observe," said the doctor.

"That's what it is, sir," replied the constable, coughing with great violence; for he had finished his ale in a hurry, and some of it had gone the wrong way.

"Here's a house broken into," said the doctor, "and a couple of men catch one moment's glimpse of a boy, in the midst of gunpowder-smoke, and in all the distraction of alarm and darkness. Here's a boy comes to that very same house, next morning, and because he happens to have his arm tied up, these men lay violent hands upon him; by doing which, they place his life in great danger, and swear he is the thief. Now, the question is, whether these men are justified by the fact; and if not, in what situation do they place themselves?"

The constable nodded profoundly. He said, if that wasn't law, he would be glad to know what was.

"I ask you again," thundered the doctor, "are you, on your solemn oaths, able to identify that boy?"

Brittles looked doubtfully at Mr. Giles; Mr. Giles looked doubtfully at Brittles; the constable put his hand behind his ear, to catch the reply; the two women and the tinker leant forward to listen; and the doctor glanced keenly round; when a ring was heard at the gate, and at the same moment, the sound of wheels.

"It's the runners!" cried Brittles, to all appearance much relieved.

"The what!" exclaimed the doctor, aghast in his turn.

"The Bow-street officers,[2] sir," replied Brittles, taking up a candle; "me and Mr. Giles sent for 'em this morning."

"What!" cried the doctor.

"Yes," replied Brittles; "I sent a message up by the coachman, and I only wonder they weren't here before, sir."

"You did, did you? Then confound your—slow coaches down here; that's all," said the doctor, walking away.

Chapter XXXI.

INVOLVES A CRITICAL POSITION.

"Who's that?" inquired Brittles, opening the door a little way, with the chain up, and peeping out: shading the candle with his hand.

"Open the door," replied a man outside; "it's the officers from Bow-street, as was sent to, to-day."

Much comforted by this assurance, Brittles opened the door to its full width, and confronted a portly man in a great-coat, who walked in

---

2. An elite corp of detectives called the Bow Street Runners, the predecessors of Scotland Yard's Criminal Investigation Department, was established in 1749 and disbanded in 1839; they were replaced by the Metropolitan Police.

without saying anything more, and wiped his shoes on the mat, as coolly as if he lived there.

"Just send somebody out to relieve my mate, will you, young man?" said the officer; "he's in the gig, minding the prad. Have you got a coach 'us[1] here, that you could put it up in, for five or ten minutes?"

Brittles replying in the affirmative, and pointing out the building, the portly man stepped back to the garden-gate, and helped his companion to put up the gig: while Brittles lighted them, in a state of great admiration. This done, they returned to the house; and, being shewn into a parlour, took off their great-coats and hats, and shewed like what they were.

The man who had knocked at the door, was a stout personage of middle height: aged about fifty: with shiny black hair, cropped pretty close; half-whiskers; a round face; and sharp eyes. The other was a red-headed, bony man, in top-boots: with a rather ill-favoured countenance: and a turned-up, sinister-looking, nose.

"Tell your governor that Blathers and Duff is here, will you?" said the stouter man, smoothing down his hair, and laying a pair of handcuffs on the table. "Oh! Good evening, master. Can I have a word or two with you in private, if you please?"

This was addressed to Mr. Losberne, who now made his appearance; that gentleman, motioning Brittles to retire, brought in the two ladies, and shut the door.

"This is the lady of the house," said Mr. Losberne, motioning towards Mrs. Maylie.

Mr. Blathers made a bow. Being desired to sit down, he put his hat upon the floor, and, taking a chair, motioned Duff to do the same. The latter gentleman, who did not appear quite so much accustomed to good society, or quite so much at his ease in it: one of the two: seated himself, after undergoing several muscular affections of the limbs; and forced the head of his stick into his mouth, with some embarrassment.

"Now, with regard to this here robbery, master," said Blathers. "What are the circumstarnces?"

Mr. Losberne, who appeared desirous of gaining time, recounted them at great length, and with much circumlocution. Messrs. Blathers and Duff looked very knowing meanwhile, and occasionally exchanged a nod.

"I can't say, for certain, till I see the place, of course," said Blathers; "but my opinion at once is,—I don't mind committing myself to that extent,—that this wasn't done by a yokel; eh, Duff?"

"Certainly not," replied Duff.

"And, translating the word yokel for the benefit of the ladies, I ap-

---

1. House. "Prad": horse.

prehend your meaning to be, that this attempt was not made by a countryman?" said Mr. Losberne, with a smile.

"That's it, master," replied Blathers. "This is all about the robbery, is it?"

"All," replied the doctor.

"Now, what is this, about this here boy that the servants are talking on?" said Blathers.

"Nothing at all," replied the doctor. "One of the frightened servants chose to take it into his head, that he had something to do with this attempt to break into the house; but it's nonsense: sheer absurdity."

"Wery easy disproved if it is," remarked Duff.

"What he says is quite correct," observed Blathers, nodding his head in a confirmatory way, and playing carelessly with the handcuffs, as if they were a pair of castanets. "Who is the boy? What account does he give of himself? Where did he come from? He didn't drop out of the clouds, did he, master?"

"Of course not," replied the doctor, with a nervous glance at the two ladies. "I know his whole history; but we can talk about that presently. You would like, first, to see the place where the thieves made their attempt, I suppose?"

"Certainly," rejoined Mr. Blathers. "We had better inspect the premises first, and examine the servants afterwards. That's the usual way of doing business."

Lights were then procured; and Messrs. Blathers and Duff, attended by the native constable, Brittles, Giles, and everybody else in short, went into the little room at the end of the passage and looked out at the window; and afterwards went round by way of the lawn, and looked in at the window; and after that, had a candle handed out to inspect the shutter with; and after that, a lantern to trace the footsteps with; and after that, a pitchfork to poke the bushes with. This done, amidst the breathless interest of all beholders, they came in again; and Mr. Giles and Brittles were put through a melodramatic representation of their share in the previous night's adventures: which they performed some six times over: contradicting each other, in not more than one important respect, the first time, and in not more than a dozen the last. This consummation being arrived at, Blathers and Duff cleared the room, and held a long council together: compared with which, for secrecy and solemnity, a consultation of great doctors on the knottiest point in medicine, would be mere child's play.

Meanwhile, the doctor walked up and down the next room in a very uneasy state; and Mrs. Maylie and Rose looked on, with anxious faces.

"Upon my word," he said, making a halt, after a great number of very rapid turns, "I hardly know what to do."

"Surely," said Rose, "the poor child's story, faithfully repeated to these men, will be sufficient to exonerate him."

"I doubt it, my dear young lady," said the doctor, shaking his head. "I don't think it would exonerate him, either with them, or with legal functionaries of a higher grade. What is he, after all, they would say? A runaway. Judged by mere worldly considerations and probabilities, his story is a very doubtful one."

"You believe it, surely?" interrupted Rose.

"I believe it, strange as it is; and perhaps I may be an old fool for doing so," rejoined the doctor; "but I don't think it is exactly the tale for a practised police-officer, nevertheless."

"Why not?" demanded Rose.

"Because, my pretty cross-examiner," replied the doctor, "because, viewed with their eyes, there are many ugly points about it; he can only prove the parts that look ill: and none of those that look well. Confound the fellows, they *will* have the why and the wherefore, and will take nothing for granted. On his own shewing, you see, he has been the companion of thieves for some time past; he has been carried to a police-office, on a charge of picking a gentleman's pocket; he has been taken away, forcibly, from that gentleman's house, to a place which he cannot describe or point out, and of the situation of which he has not the remotest idea. He is brought down to Chertsey, by men who seem to have taken a violent fancy to him, whether he will or no; and is put through a window to rob a house; and then, just at the very moment when he is going to alarm the inmates, and so do the very thing that would set him all to rights, there rushes into the way, a blundering dog of a half-bred butler, and shoots him; as if on purpose to prevent his doing any good for himself. Don't you see all this?"

"I see it, of course," replied Rose, smiling at the doctor's impetuosity; "but still I do not see anything in it, to criminate the poor child."

"No," replied the doctor; "of course not! Bless the bright eyes of your sex! They never see, whether for good or bad, more than one side of any question; and that is, always, the one which first presents itself to them."

Having given vent to this result of experience, the doctor put his hands into his pockets, and walked up and down the room with even greater rapidity than before.

"The more I think of it," said the doctor, "the more I see that it will occasion endless trouble and difficulty if we put these men in possession of the boy's real story. I am certain it will not be believed; and even if they can do nothing to him in the end, still the dragging it forward, and giving publicity to all the doubts that will be cast upon it, must interfere, materially, with your benevolent plan of rescuing him from misery."

"Oh! what is to be done?" cried Rose. "Dear, dear! why did they send for these people?"

"Why, indeed!" exclaimed Mrs. Maylie. "I would not have had them here, for the world."

"All I know is," said Mr. Losberne at last: sitting down with a kind of desperate calmness, "that we must try and carry it off with a bold face; that's all. The object is a good one, and that must be the excuse. The boy has strong symptoms of fever upon him, and is in no condition to be talked to any more; that's one comfort. We must make the best of it; and if bad be the best, it is no fault of ours. Come in!"

"Well, master," said Blathers, entering the room, followed by his colleague; and making the door fast, before he said any more. "This warn't a put-up thing."

"And what the devil's a put-up thing?" demanded the doctor, impatiently.

"We call it a put-up robbery, ladies," said Blathers, turning to them, as if he pitied their ignorance, but had a contempt for the doctor's, "when the servants is in it."

"Nobody suspected them, in this case," said Mrs. Maylie.

"Wery likely not, ma'am," replied Blathers; "but they might have been in it, for all that."

"More likely on that wery account," said Duff.

"We find it was a town hand," said Blathers, continuing his report; "for the style of work is first-rate."

"Wery pretty indeed it is," remarked Duff, in an under tone.

"There was two of 'em in it," continued Blathers; "and they had a boy with 'em; that's plain from the size of the window. That's all to be said at present. We'll see this lad that you've got up stairs at once, if you please."

"Perhaps they will take something to drink first, Mrs. Maylie?" said the doctor: his face brightening, as if some new thought had occurred to him.

"Oh! to be sure!" exclaimed Rose, eagerly. "You shall have it immediately, if you will."

"Why, thank you, miss!" said Blathers, drawing his coat-sleeve across his mouth; "it's dry work, this sort of duty. Anything that's handy, miss; don't put yourself out of the way, on our accounts."

"What shall it be?" asked the doctor, following the young lady to the sideboard.

"A little drop of spirits, master, if it's all the same," replied Blathers. "It's a cold ride from London, ma'am; and I always find that spirits comes home warmer to the feelings."

This interesting communication was addressed to Mrs. Maylie, who received it very graciously. While it was being conveyed to her, the doctor slipped out of the room.

"Ah!" said Mr. Blathers: not holding his wine-glass by the stem, but grasping the bottom between the thumb and forefinger of his left hand: and placing it in front of his chest; "I have seen a good many pieces of business like this, in my time, ladies."

"That crack down in the back lane at Edmonton,[2] Blathers," said Mr. Duff, assisting his colleague's memory.

"That was something in this way, warn't it?" rejoined Mr. Blathers; "that was done by Conkey Chickweed, that was."

"You always gave that to him," replied Duff. "It was the Family Pet, I tell you. Conkey hadn't any more to do with it than I had."

"Get out!" retorted Mr. Blathers; "I know better. Do you mind that time when Conkey was robbed of his money, though? What a start that was! Better than any novel-book *I* ever see!"

"What was that?" inquired Rose: anxious to encourage any symptoms of good-humour in the unwelcome visiters.

"It was a robbery, miss, that hardly anybody would have been down upon," said Blathers. "This here Conkey Chickweed——"

"Conkey means Nosey, ma'am," interposed Duff.

"Of course the lady knows that, don't she?" demanded Mr. Blathers. "Always interrupting, you are, partner! This here Conkey Chickweed, miss, kept a public-house over Battle-bridge way; and had a cellar, where a good many young lords went to see cockfighting, and badger-drawing,[3] and that; and a wery intellectual manner the sports was conducted in, for I've seen 'em off'en. He warn't one of the family, at that time; and one night he was robbed of three hundred and twenty-seven guineas[4] in a canvass bag: that was stole out of his bedroom in the dead of night, by a tall man with a black patch over his eye, who had concealed himself under the bed, and after committing the robbery, jumped slap out of window: which was only a story high. He was wery quick about it. But Conkey was quick, too; for he was woke by the noise; and darting out of bed, he fired a blunderbuss[5] arter him, and roused the neighbourhood. They set up a hue-and-cry, directly, and when they came to look about 'em, found that Conkey had hit the robber; for there was traces of blood, all the way to some palings a good distance off; and there they lost 'em. However, he had made off with the blunt;[6] and, consequently, the name of Mr. Chickweed, licensed witler, appeared in the Gazette among the other bankrupts; and all manner of benefits and subscriptions, and I don't know what all, was got up for the poor man, who was in a wery low state of mind about his loss, and went up and down the streets, for three or four days, pulling his hair off in such a desperate manner that many people was afraid he might be going to make away with himself. One day he come up to the office, all in a hurry, and had a private

2. The burglary at Edmonton, a village north of central London.
3. The "sport" of using dogs to draw a badger out of its hole.
4. Gold coins.
5. A short gun with a wide bore that fires numbers of balls at the same time, like a shotgun.
6. The cash, money. "Palings": fences.

interview with the magistrate, who, after a deal of talk, rings the bell, and orders Jem Spyers in (Jem was a active officer), and tells him to go and assist Mr. Chickweed in apprehending the man as robbed his house. 'I see him, Spyers,' said Chickweed, 'pass my house yesterday morning.' 'Why didn't you up, and collar him?' says Spyers. 'I was so struck all of a heap, that you might have fractured my skull with a toothpick,' says the poor man; 'but we're sure to have him; for between ten and eleven o'clock at night he passed again.' Spyers no sooner heard this, than he put some clean linen and a comb, in his pocket, in case he should have to stop a day or two; and away he goes, and sets himself down at one of the public-house windows behind the little red curtain: with his hat on: all ready to bolt out, at a moment's notice. He was smoking his pipe here, late at night, when all of a sudden Chickweed roars out 'Here he is! Stop thief! Murder!' Jem Spyers dashes out; and there he sees Chickweed, tearing down the street full-cry. Away goes Spyers; on goes Chickweed; round turns the people; everybody roars out, 'Thieves!'; and Chickweed himself keeps on shouting, all the time, like mad. Spyers loses sight of him a minute as he turns a corner; shoots round; sees a little crowd; dives in; 'Which is the man?' 'D—me!' says Chickweed, 'I've lost him again!' It was a remarkable occurrence, but he warn't to be seen nowhere, so they went back to the public-house; and next morning, Spyers took his old place, and looked out, from behind the curtain, for a tall man with a black patch over his eye, till his own two eyes ached again. At last, he couldn't help shutting 'em, to ease 'em a minute; and the very moment he did so, he hears Chickweed roaring out, 'Here he is!' Off he starts once more, with Chickweed half-way down the street ahead of him; and after twice as long a run as the yesterday's one, the man's lost again! This was done, once or twice more, till one-half the neighbours gave out that Mr. Chickweed had been robbed by the devil, who was playing tricks with him arterwards; and the other half, that poor Mr. Chickweed had gone mad with grief."

"What did Jem Spyers say?" inquired the doctor: who had returned to the room shortly after the commencement of the story.

"Jem Spyers," resumed the officer, "for a long time said nothing at all, and listened to everything without seeming to, which shewed he understood his business. But, one morning, he walked into the bar, and taking out his snuff-box, said, 'Chickweed, I've found out who's done this here robbery.' 'Have you?' said Chickweed. 'Oh, my dear Spyers, only let me have wengeance, and I shall die contented! Oh, my dear Spyers, where is the villain?' 'Come!' said Spyers, offering him a pinch of snuff, 'none of that gammon![7] You did it yourself.' So he had; and a good bit of money he had made by it, too; and nobody would ever have found it out, if he hadn't been so precious anxious to keep up

7. Lying.

appearances; that's more!" said Mr. Blathers, putting down his wine-glass, and clinking the handcuffs together.

"Very curious, indeed," observed the doctor. "Now, if you please, you can walk up stairs."

"If *you* please, sir," returned Mr. Blathers; and closely following Mr. Losberne, the two officers ascended to Oliver's bedroom: Mr. Giles preceding the party, with a lighted candle.

Oliver had been dozing; but looked worse, and was more feverish, than he had appeared yet. Being assisted by the doctor, he managed to sit up in bed for a minute or so; and looked at the strangers without at all understanding what was going forward: in fact, without seeming to recollect where he was, or what had been passing.

"This," said Mr. Losberne, speaking softly, but with great vehemence notwithstanding, "this is the lad, who, being accidentally wounded by a spring-gun[8] in some boyish trespass on Mr. What-d'ye-call-him's grounds, at the back here, comes to the house for assistance this morning, and is immediately laid hold of, and maltreated, by that ingenious gentleman with the candle in his hand: who has placed his life in considerable danger, as I can professionally certify."

Messrs. Blathers and Duff looked at Mr. Giles, as he was thus recommended to their notice; the bewildered butler gazed from them towards Oliver, and from Oliver towards Mr. Losberne, with a most ludicrous mixture of fear and perplexity.

"You don't mean to deny that, I suppose?" said the doctor, laying Oliver gently down again.

"It was all done for the—for the best, sir!" answered Giles. "I am sure I thought it was the boy, or I wouldn't have meddled with him. I am not of an inhuman disposition, sir."

"Thought it was what boy?" inquired the senior officer.

"The housebreaker's boy, sir!" replied Giles. "They—they certainly had a boy."

"Well! Do you think so now?" inquired Blathers.

"Think what, now?" replied Giles, looking vacantly at his questioner.

"Think it's the same boy, Stupid-head?" rejoined Mr. Blathers, impatiently.

"I don't know; I really don't know," said Giles, with a rueful countenance. "I couldn't swear to him."

"What do you think?" asked Mr. Blathers.

"I don't know what to think," replied poor Giles. "I don't think it is the boy; indeed, I'm almost certain that it isn't. You know it can't be."

"Has this man been a-drinking, sir?" inquired Blathers, turning to the doctor.

8. A gun whose trigger can be set off by a wire; frequently used to deter poachers.

"What a precious muddle-headed chap you are!" said Duff: addressing Mr. Giles, with supreme contempt.

Mr. Losberne had been feeling the patient's pulse during this short dialogue; but he now rose from the chair by the bedside, and remarked, that if the officers had any doubts upon the subject, they would perhaps like to step into the next room, and have Brittles before them.

Acting upon this suggestion, they adjourned to a neighbouring apartment, where Mr. Brittles, being called in, involved himself and his respected superior in such a wonderful maze of fresh contradictions and impossibilities, as tended to throw no particular light on any thing, but the fact of his own strong mystification; except, indeed, his declarations that he shouldn't know the real boy, if he were put before him that instant; that he had only taken Oliver to be he, because Mr. Giles had said he was; and that Mr. Giles had, five minutes previously, admitted, in the kitchen, that he began to be very much afraid he had been a little too hasty.

Among other ingenious surmises, the question was then raised, whether Mr. Giles had really hit anybody; and upon examination of the fellow pistol to that which he had fired, it turned out to have no more destructive loading than gunpowder and brown paper: a discovery which made a considerable impression on everybody but the doctor, who had drawn the ball about ten minutes before. Upon no one, however, did it make a greater impression than on Mr. Giles himself; who, after labouring, for some hours, under the fear of having mortally wounded a fellow-creature, eagerly caught at this new idea, and favoured it to the utmost. Finally, the officers, without troubling themselves very much about Oliver, left the Chertsey constable in the house, and took up their rest for that night in the town: promising to return next morning.

With the next morning, there came a rumour, that two men and a boy were in the cage[9] at Kingston, who had been apprehended overnight under suspicious circumstances; and to Kingston Messrs. Blathers and Duff journeyed accordingly. The suspicious circumstances, however, resolving themselves, on investigation, into the one fact, that they had been discovered sleeping under a haystack: which, although a great crime, is only punishable by imprisonment, and is, in the merciful eye of the English law, and its comprehensive love of all the king's subjects, held to be no satisfactory proof, in the absence of all other evidence, that the sleeper, or sleepers, have committed burglary accompanied with violence, and have therefore rendered themselves liable to the punishment of death: Messrs. Blathers and Duff came back again, as wise as they went.

In short, after some more examination, and a great deal more con-

9. A temporary prison for the confinement of suspects.

versation, a neighbouring magistrate was readily induced to take the joint bail of Mrs. Maylie and Mr. Losberne for Oliver's appearance if he should ever be called upon; and Blathers and Duff, being rewarded with a couple of guineas, returned to town with divided opinions on the subject of their expedition: the latter gentleman on a mature consideration of all the circumstances, inclining to the belief that the burglarious attempt had originated with the Family Pet; and the former being equally disposed to concede the full merit of it to the great Mr. Conkey Chickweed.

Meanwhile, Oliver gradually throve and prospered under the united care of Mrs. Maylie, Rose, and the kind-hearted Mr. Losberne. If fervent prayers, gushing from hearts overcharged with gratitude, be heard in heaven—and if they be not, what prayers are!—the blessings which the orphan child called down upon them, sunk into their souls, diffusing peace and happiness.

Chapter XXXII.

OF THE HAPPY LIFE OLIVER BEGAN TO LEAD WITH HIS KIND FRIENDS.

Oliver's ailings were neither slight nor few. In addition to the pain and delay attendant upon a broken limb, his exposure to the wet and cold had brought on fever and ague:[1] which hung about him for many weeks, and reduced him sadly. But, at length, he began, by slow degrees, to get better, and to be able to say sometimes, in a few tearful words, how deeply he felt the goodness of the two sweet ladies, and how ardently he hoped that, when he grew strong and well again, he could do something to shew his gratitude; only something which would let them see the love and duty with which his breast was full; something, however slight, which would prove to them that their gentle kindness had not been cast away; but that the poor boy whom their charity had rescued from misery, or death, was eager to serve them with his whole heart and soul.

"Poor fellow!" said Rose, when Oliver had been one day feebly endeavouring to utter the words of thankfulness that rose to his pale lips: "you shall have many opportunities of serving us, if you will. We are going into the country; and my aunt intends that you shall accompany us. The quiet place, the pure air, and all the pleasures and beauties of spring, will restore you in a few days; and we will employ you, in a hundred ways, when you can bear the trouble."

"The trouble!" cried Oliver. "Oh! dear lady, if I could but work for you; if I could only give you pleasure by watering your flowers, or

---

1. An acute fever with shivering, often malarial.

watching your birds, or running up and down, the whole day long, to make you happy; what would I give to do it!"

"You shall give nothing at all," said Miss Maylie, smiling; "for, as I told you before, we shall employ you in a hundred ways; and if you only take half the trouble to please us, that you promise now, you will make me very happy indeed."

"Happy, ma'am!" cried Oliver; "how kind of you to say so!"

"You will make me happier than I can tell you," replied the young lady. "To think that my dear good aunt should have been the means of rescuing any one from such sad misery as you have described to us, would be an unspeakable pleasure to me; but to know that the object of her goodness and compassion was sincerely grateful and attached, in consequence, would delight me, more than you can well imagine. Do you understand me?" she inquired, watching Oliver's thoughtful face.

"Oh yes, ma'am, yes!" replied Oliver, eagerly; "but I was thinking that I am ungrateful now."

"To whom?" inquired the young lady.

"To the kind gentleman, and the dear old nurse, who took so much care of me before," rejoined Oliver. "If they knew how happy I am, they would be pleased, I am sure."

"I am sure they would," rejoined Oliver's benefactress; "and Mr. Losberne has already been kind enough to promise that, when you are well enough to bear the journey, he will carry you to see them."

"Has he, ma'am?" cried Oliver, his face brightening with pleasure. "I don't know what I shall do for joy when I see their kind faces once again!"

In a short time Oliver was sufficiently recovered to undergo the fatigue of this expedition; and one morning he and Mr. Losberne set out, accordingly, in a little carriage which belonged to Mrs. Maylie. When they came to Chertsey Bridge, Oliver turned very pale, and uttered a loud exclamation.

"What's the matter with the boy?" cried the doctor, as usual, all in a bustle. "Do you see anything—hear anything—feel anything—eh?"

"That, sir," cried Oliver, pointing out of the carriage window. "That house!"

"Yes; well, what of it? Stop, coachman. Pull up here," cried the doctor. "What of the house, my man; eh?"

"The thieves; the house they took me to," whispered Oliver.

"The devil it is!" cried the doctor. "Halloa, there! let me out!"

But before the coachman could dismount from his box, he had tumbled out of the coach, by some means or other; and, running down to the deserted tenement, began kicking at the door like a madman.

"Halloa!" said a little, ugly hump-backed man: opening the door so suddenly, that the doctor, from the very impetus of his last kick, nearly fell forward into the passage. "What's the matter here?"

"Matter!" exclaimed the other, collaring him, without a moment's reflection. "A good deal. Robbery is the matter."

"There'll be murder the matter, too," replied the hump-backed man, coolly, "if you don't take your hands off. Do you hear me?"

"I hear you," said the doctor, giving his captive a hearty shake. "Where's—confound the, fellow, what's his rascally name—Sikes; that's it. Where's Sikes, you thief?"

The hump-backed man stared, as if in excess of amazement and indignation; and twisting himself, dexterously, from the doctor's grasp, growled forth a volley of horrid oaths, and retired into the house. Before he could shut the door, however, the doctor had passed into the parlour, without a word of parley. He looked anxiously round; not an article of furniture; not a vestige of anything, animate or inanimate; not even the position of the cupboards; answered Oliver's description!

"Now," said the hump-backed man, who had watched him keenly, "what do you mean by coming into my house, in this violent way? Do you want to rob me, or to murder me? Which is it?"

"Did you ever know a man come out to do either, in a chariot and pair, you ridiculous old vampire?" said the irritable doctor.

"What do you want, then?" demanded the hunchback, "Will you take yourself off, before I do you a mischief? Curse you!"

"As soon as I think proper," said Mr. Losberne, looking into the other parlour; which, like the first, bore no resemblance whatever to Oliver's account of it. "I shall find you out, some day, my friend."

"Will you?" sneered the ill-favoured cripple. "If you ever want me, I'm here. I haven't lived here mad, and all alone, for five-and-twenty years, to be scared by you. You shall pay for this; you shall pay for this." And so saying, the mis-shapen little demon set up a hideous yell; and danced upon the ground, as if frantic with rage.

"Stupid enough, this," muttered the doctor to himself; "the boy must have made a mistake. Here! Put that in your pocket, and shut yourself up again." With these words he flung the hunchback a piece of money, and returned to the carriage.

The man followed to the chariot door, uttering the wildest imprecations and curses all the way; but as Mr. Losberne turned to speak to the driver, he looked into the carriage, and eyed Oliver for an instant with a glance so sharp and fierce, and at the same time so furious and vindictive, that, waking or sleeping, he could not forget it for months afterwards. He continued to utter the most fearful imprecations, until the driver had resumed his seat; and when they were once more on their way, they could see him some distance behind: beating his feet upon the ground, and tearing his hair, in transports of frenzied rage.

"I am an ass!" said the doctor, after a long silence. "Did you know that before, Oliver?"

"No, sir."

"Then don't forget it another time."

"An ass," said the doctor again, after a further silence of some minutes. "Even if it had been the right place, and the right fellows had been there, what could I have done, single-handed? And if I had had assistance, I see no good that I should have done, except leading to my own exposure, and an unavoidable statement of the manner in which I have hushed up this business. That would have served me right, though. I am always involving myself in some scrape or other, by acting on impulse; and it might have done me good."

Now, the fact was, that the excellent doctor had never acted upon any thing else but impulse all through his life; and it was no bad compliment to the nature of the impulses which governed him, that so far from being involved in any peculiar troubles or misfortunes, he had the warmest respect and esteem of all who knew him. If the truth must be told, he was a little out of temper, for a minute or two, at being disappointed in procuring corroborative evidence of Oliver's story, on the very first occasion on which he had a chance of obtaining any. He soon came round again, however; and finding that Oliver's replies to his questions, were still as straightforward and consistent, and still delivered with as much apparent sincerity and truth, as they had ever been; he made up his mind to attach full credence to them, from that time forth.

As Oliver knew the name of the street in which Mr. Brownlow resided, they were enabled to drive straight thither. When the coach turned into it, his heart beat so violently, that he could scarcely draw his breath.

"Now, my boy, which house is it?" inquired Mr. Losberne.

"That! That!" replied Oliver, pointing eagerly out of the window. "The white house. Oh! make haste! Pray make haste! I feel as if I should die; it makes me tremble so."

"Come, come!" said the good doctor, patting him on the shoulder. "You will see them directly, and they will be overjoyed to find you safe and well."

"Oh! I hope so!" cried Oliver. "They were so good to me; so very very good to me."

The coach rolled on. It stopped. No; that was the wrong house; the next door. It went on a few paces, and stopped again. Oliver looked up at the windows, with tears of happy expectation coursing down his face.

Alas! the white house was empty, and there was a bill in the window. "To Let."

"Knock at the next door," cried Mr. Losberne, taking Oliver's arm in his. "What has become of Mr. Brownlow, who used to live in the adjoining house, do you know?"

The servant did not know; but would go and inquire. She presently returned; and said, that Mr. Brownlow had sold off his goods, and gone to the West Indies, six weeks before. Oliver clasped his hands, and sank feebly backwards.

"Has his housekeeper gone, too?" inquired Mr. Losberne, after a moment's pause.

"Yes, sir;" replied the servant. "The old gentleman, the housekeeper, and a gentleman who was a friend of Mr. Brownlow's, all went together."

"Then, turn towards home again," said Mr. Losberne to the driver; "and don't stop to bait[2] the horses, till you get out of this confounded London!"

"The book-stall keeper, sir?" said Oliver. "I know the way there. See him, pray sir! Do see him!"

"My poor boy, this is disappointment enough for one day," said the doctor. "Quite enough for both of us. If we go to the book-stall keeper's, we shall certainly find that he is dead, or has set his house on fire, or run away. No; home again straight!" And in obedience to the doctor's impulse, home they went.

This bitter disappointment caused Oliver much sorrow and grief, even in the midst of his happiness; for he had pleased himself, many times during his illness, with thinking of all that Mr. Brownlow and Mrs. Bedwin would say to him: and what delight it would be to tell them how many long days and nights he had passed in reflecting on what they had done for him, and in bewailing his cruel separation from them. The hope of eventually clearing himself with them, too, and explaining how he had been forced away, had buoyed him up, and sustained him, under many of his recent trials; and now, the idea that they should have gone so far, and carried with them the belief that he was an impostor and a robber: a belief which might remain uncontradicted to his dying day: was almost more than he could bear.

The circumstance occasioned no alteration, however, in the behaviour of his benefactors. After another fortnight: when the fine warm weather had fairly begun, and every tree and flower was putting forth its young leaves and rich blossoms: they made preparations for quitting the house at Chertsey, for some months. Sending the plate, which had so excited the Jew's cupidity, to the banker's; and leaving Giles and another servant in care of the house; they departed to a cottage at some distance in the country; and took Oliver with them.

Who can describe the pleasure and delight: the peace of mind and soft tranquillity: the sickly boy felt in the balmy air, and among the green hills and rich woods, of an inland village! Who can tell how scenes of peace and quietude sink into the minds of pain-worn dwellers in close and noisy places, and carry their own freshness, deep into their jaded hearts! Men who have lived in crowded, pent-up streets, through lives of toil: and never wished for change; men, to whom custom has indeed been second nature, and who have come almost to love each brick and stone that formed the narrow boundaries of their daily walks: even they,

2. Feed.

with the hand of death upon them, have been known to yearn at last for one short glimpse of Nature's face; and carried, far from the scenes of their old pains and pleasures, have seemed to pass at once into a new state of being; and crawling forth, from day to day, to some green sunny spot, have had such memories wakened up within them by the mere sight of sky, and hill, and plain, and glistening water, that a foretaste of heaven itself has soothed their quick decline, and they have sunk into their tombs as peacefully as the sun: whose setting they watched from their lonely chamber window but a few hours before: faded from their dim and feeble sight! The memories which peaceful country scenes call up, are not of this world, nor its thoughts and hopes. Their gentle influence may teach us how to weave fresh garlands for the graves of those we loved: may purify our thoughts, and bear down before it old enmity and hatred; but beneath all this, there lingers, in the least re-flective mind, a vague and half-formed consciousness of having held such feelings long before, in some remote and distant time; which calls up solemn thoughts of distant times to come, and bends down pride and worldliness beneath it.

It was a lovely spot to which they repaired. Oliver, whose days had been spent among squalid crowds, and in the midst of noise and brawl-ing, seemed to enter on a new existence there. The rose and honeysuckle clung to the cottage walls; the ivy crept round the trunks of the trees; and the garden-flowers perfumed the air with delicious odours. Hard by, was a little churchyard; not crowded with tall unsightly gravestones, but full of humble mounds, covered with fresh turf and moss: beneath which, the old people of the village lay at rest. Oliver often wandered here; and thinking of the wretched grave in which his mother lay, would sometimes sit him down and sob unseen; but, when he raised his eyes to the deep sky overhead, he would cease to think of her as lying in the ground, and would weep for her, sadly, but without pain.

It was a happy time. The days were peaceful and serene; the nights brought with them neither fear nor care; no languishing in a wretched prison, or associating with wretched men; nothing but pleasant and happy thoughts. Every morning he went to a white-headed old gentleman, who lived near the little church: who taught him to read better, and to write: and spoke so kindly, and took such pains, that Oliver could never try enough to please him. Then, he would walk with Mrs. Maylie and Rose; and hear them talk of books; or perhaps sit near them, in some shady place, and listen whilst the young lady read: which he could have done, until it grew too dark to see the letters. Then he had his own lesson for the next day to prepare; and at this, he would work hard, in a little room which looked into the garden, till evening came slowly on, when the ladies would walk out again, and he with them: listening with such pleasure to all they said: and so happy if they wanted a flower that he could climb to reach, or had forgotten anything he could run to fetch: that he could never be quick enough about it. When it became quite dark, and they returned home, the young lady would sit down to the piano, and play some pleasant air, or sing, in a low and gentle voice, some old song which it pleased her aunt to hear. There would be no candles lighted at such times as these; and Oliver would sit by one of the windows, listening to the sweet music, in a perfect rapture.

And when Sunday came, how differently the day was spent, from any way in which he had ever spent it yet! and how happily too; like all the other days in that most happy time! There was the little church, in the morning, with the green leaves fluttering at the windows: the birds singing without: and the sweet-smelling air stealing in at the low porch, and filling the homely building with its fragrance. The poor people were so neat and clean, and knelt so reverently in prayer, that it seemed a pleasure, not a tedious duty, their assembling there together; and though the singing might be rude, it was real, and sounded more musical (to Oliver's ears at least) than any he had ever heard in church before. Then, there were the walks as usual, and many calls at the clean houses of the labouring men; and at night, Oliver read a chapter or two from the Bible: which he had been studying all the week, and in the performance of which duty he felt more proud and pleased, than if he had been the clergyman himself.

In the morning, Oliver would be a-foot by six o'clock, roaming the fields, and plundering the hedges, far and wide, for nosegays of wild flowers, with which he would return laden, home; and which it took great care and consideration to arrange, to the best advantage, for the embellishment of the breakfast-table. There was fresh groundsel,[3] too, for Miss Maylie's birds, with which Oliver: who had been studying the subject under the able tuition of the village clerk: would decorate the cages, in the most approved taste. When the birds were made all spruce and smart for the day, there was usually some little commission of charity to execute in the village; or failing that, there was rare cricket-playing, sometimes, on the green; or failing that, there was always something to do in the garden, or about the plants, to which Oliver: who had studied this science also, under the same master, who was a gardener by trade: applied himself with hearty goodwill, until Miss Rose made her appearance; when there were a thousand commendations to be bestowed on all he had done.

So three months glided away; three months which, in the life of the most blessed and favoured of mortals, might have been unmingled happiness; and which, in Oliver's, were true felicity indeed. With the purest and most amiable generosity on one side; and the truest, warmest, soulfelt gratitude on the other; it is no wonder that, by the end of that short time, Oliver Twist had become completely domesticated with the old

---

3. A common weed often used for bird feed.

lady and her niece: and that the fervent attachment of his young and sensitive heart, was repaid by their pride in, and attachment to, himself.

Chapter XXXIII.

WHEREIN THE HAPPINESS OF OLIVER AND HIS FRIENDS, EXPERIENCES A SUDDEN CHECK.

Spring flew swiftly by, and summer came; and if the village had been beautiful at first, it was now in the full glow and luxuriance of its richness. The great trees, which had looked shrunken and bare in the earlier months, had now burst into strong life and health; and stretching forth their green arms over the thirsty ground, converted open and naked spots into choice nooks, where was a deep and pleasant shade from which to look upon the wide prospect, steeped in sunshine, which lay stretched out beyond. The earth had donned her mantle of brightest green; and shed her richest perfumes abroad. It was the prime and vigour of the year; all things were glad and flourishing.

Still the same quiet life went on at the little cottage, and the same cheerful serenity prevailed among its inmates. Oliver had long since grown stout and healthy; but health or sickness made no difference in his warm feelings to those about him, though they do in the feelings of a great many people. He was still the same gentle, attached, affectionate creature that he had been when pain and suffering had wasted his strength; and when he was dependent for every slight attention and comfort on those who tended him.

One beautiful night, they had taken a longer walk than was customary with them; for the day had been unusually warm, and there was a brilliant moon; and a light wind had sprung up, which was unusually refreshing. Rose had been in high spirits, too, and they had walked on, in merry conversation, until they had far exceeded their ordinary bounds. Mrs. Maylie being fatigued, they returned more slowly home. The young lady, merely throwing off her simple bonnet, sat down to the piano, as usual; after running abstractedly over the keys for a few minutes, she fell into a low and very solemn air; and as she played it, they heard her sob, as if she were weeping.

"Rose, my dear!" said the elder lady.

Rose made no reply, but played a little quicker, as though the words had roused her from some painful thoughts.

"Rose, my love!" cried Mrs. Maylie, rising hastily, and bending over her. "What is this? In tears! My dear child, what distresses you?"

"Nothing, aunt; nothing," replied the young lady. "I don't know what it is; I can't describe it; but I feel——"

"Not ill my love?" interposed Mrs. Maylie.

"No, no! Oh, not ill!" replied Rose: shuddering, as though some deadly chillness were passing over her, while she spoke; "I shall be better presently. Close the window, pray."

Oliver hastened to comply with her request. The young lady, making an effort to recover her cheerfulness, strove to play some livelier tune; but her fingers dropped powerless on the keys: and covering her face with her hands, she sank upon a sofa, and gave vent to the tears which she was now unable to repress.

"My child!" said the elder lady, folding her arms about her, "I never saw you thus before."

"I would not alarm you if I could avoid it," rejoined Rose; "but indeed I have tried very hard, and cannot help this. I fear I *am* ill, aunt."

She was, indeed; for, when candles were brought, they saw that in the very short time which had elapsed since their return home, the hue of her countenance had changed to a marble whiteness. Its expression had lost nothing of its beauty; but it was changed; and there was an anxious, haggard look about the gentle face, which it had never worn before. Another minute, and it was suffused with a crimson flush: and a heavy wildness came over the soft blue eye; again this disappeared, like the shadow thrown by a passing cloud: and she was once more deadly pale.

Oliver, who watched the old lady anxiously, observed that she was alarmed by these appearances; and so, in truth, was he; but seeing that she affected to make light of them, he endeavoured to do the same; and they so far succeeded, that when Rose was persuaded by her aunt to retire for the night, she was in better spirits, and appeared even in better health: assuring them that she felt certain she should rise in the morning, quite well.

"I hope," said Oliver, when Mrs. Maylie returned, "that nothing is the matter? She don't look well to-night, but——"

The old lady motioned to him not to speak; and sitting herself down in a dark corner of the room, remained silent for some time. At length, she said, in a trembling voice:

"I hope not, Oliver. I have been very happy with her for some years: too happy, perhaps. It may be time that I should meet with some misfortune; but I hope it is not this."

"What?" inquired Oliver.

"The heavy blow," said the old lady, "of losing the dear girl who has so long been my comfort and happiness."

"Oh! God forbid!" exclaimed Oliver, hastily.

"Amen to that, my child!" said the old lady, wringing her hands.

"Surely there is no danger of anything so dreadful?" said Oliver. "Two hours ago, she was quite well."

"She is very ill now," rejoined Mrs. Maylie; "and will be worse, I am sure. My dear, dear Rose! Oh, what should I do without her!"

She gave way to such great grief, that Oliver, suppressing his own emotion, ventured to remonstrate with her; and to beg, earnestly, that, for the sake of the dear young lady herself, she would be more calm.

"And consider, ma'am," said Oliver, as the tears forced themselves into his eyes, despite his efforts to the contrary. "Oh! consider how young and good she is, and what pleasure and comfort she gives to all about her. I am sure—certain—quite certain—that, for your sake, who are so good yourself; and for her own; and for the sake of all she makes so happy; she will not die. Heaven will never let her die so young."

"Hush!" said Mrs. Maylie, laying her hand on Oliver's head. "You think like a child, poor boy. But you teach me my duty, notwithstanding. I had forgotten it for a moment, Oliver, but I hope I may be pardoned, for I am old, and have seen enough of illness and death to know the agony of separation from the objects of our love. I have seen enough, too, to know that it is not always the youngest and best who are spared to those that love them; but this should give us comfort in our sorrow; for Heaven is just; and such things teach us, impressively, that there is a brighter world than this; and that the passage to it is speedy. God's will be done! I love her; and He knows how well!"

Oliver was surprised to see that as Mrs. Maylie said these words, she checked her lamentations as though by one struggle; and drawing herself up as she spoke, became composed and firm. He was still more astonished to find that this firmness lasted; and that, under all the care and watching which ensued, Mrs. Maylie was ever ready and collected: performing all the duties which devolved upon her, steadily, and, to all external appearance, even cheerfully. But he was young, and did not know what strong minds are capable of, under trying circumstances. How should he, when their possessors so seldom know themselves?

An anxious night ensued. When morning came, Mrs. Maylie's predictions were but too well verified. Rose was in the first stage of a high and dangerous fever.

"We must be active, Oliver, and not give way to useless grief," said Mrs. Maylie, laying her finger on her lip, as she looked steadily into his face; "this letter must be sent, with all possible expedition, to Mr. Losberne. It must be carried to the market-town, which is not more than four miles off, by the footpath across the fields; and thence dispatched, by an express on horseback, straight to Chertsey. The people at the inn will undertake to do this; and I can trust to you to see it done, I know."

Oliver could make no reply, but looked his anxiety to be gone at once.

"Here is another letter," said Mrs. Maylie, pausing to reflect; "but whether to send it now, or wait until I see how Rose goes on, I scarcely know. I would not forward it, unless I feared the worst."

"Is it for Chertsey, too, ma'am?" inquired Oliver: impatient to execute his commission, and holding out his trembling hand for the letter.

"No," replied the old lady, giving it to him mechanically. Oliver glanced at it, and saw that it was directed to Harry Maylie, Esquire, at some great lord's house in the country; where, he could not make out.

"Shall it go, ma'am?" asked Oliver, looking up, impatiently.

"I think not," replied Mrs. Maylie, taking it back. "I will wait until to-morrow."

With these words, she gave Oliver her purse, and he started off, without more delay, at the greatest speed he could muster.

Swiftly he ran across the fields, and down the little lanes which sometimes divided them: now almost hidden by the high corn on either side, and now emerging in an open field, where the mowers and hay-makers were busy at their work; nor did he stop once, save now and then, for a few seconds, to recover breath, until he came, in a great heat, and covered with dust, on the little market-place of the market-town.

Here he paused, and looked about for the inn. There was a white bank, and a red brewery, and a yellow town-hall; and in one corner there was a large house, with all the wood about it painted green: before which was the sign of "The George." To this he hastened, as soon as it caught his eye.

He spoke to a postboy who was dozing under the gateway; and who, after hearing what he wanted, referred him to the hostler; who after hearing all he had to say again, referred him to the landlord; who was a tall gentleman in a blue neckcloth, a white hat, drab breeches, and boots with tops to match: leaning against a pump by the stable-door, picking his teeth with a silver toothpick.

This gentleman walked with much deliberation into the bar to make out the bill: which took a long time making out: and after it was ready, and paid, a horse had to be saddled, and a man to be dressed, which took up ten good minutes more; meanwhile Oliver was in such a desperate state of impatience and anxiety, that he felt as if he could have jumped upon the horse himself, and galloped away, full tear, to the next stage. At length, all was ready; and the little parcel having been handed up, with many injunctions and intreaties for its speedy delivery, the man set spurs to his horse, and rattling over the uneven paving of the market-place, was out of the town, and galloping along the turnpike-road, in a couple of minutes.

It was something to feel certain that assistance was sent for; and that no time had been lost. Oliver hurried up the inn-yard, with a somewhat lighter heart: and was turning out of the gateway when he accidentally stumbled against a tall man, wrapped in a cloak: who was at that moment coming out of the inn-door.

"Hah!" cried the man, fixing his eyes on Oliver, and suddenly re-coiling. "What the devil's this?"

"I beg your pardon, sir," said Oliver; "I was in a great hurry to get home, and didn't see you were coming."

"Death!" muttered the man to himself, glaring at the boy with his large dark eyes. "Who would have thought of it! Grind him to ashes! He'd start up from a marble coffin, to come in my way!"

"I am sorry," stammered Oliver, confused by the strange man's wild look. "I hope I have not hurt you!"

"Rot his bones!" murmured the man, in a horrible passion: between his clenched teeth; "if I had only had the courage to say the word, I might have been free of him in a night. Curses on your head, and black death on your heart, you imp! What are you doing here?"

The man shook his fist, and gnashed his teeth, as he uttered these words incoherently. He advanced towards Oliver, as if with the intention of aiming a blow at him, but fell violently on the ground: writhing and foaming, in a fit.[1]

Oliver gazed, for a moment, at the struggles of the madman (for such he supposed him to be); and then darted into the house for help. Having seen him safely carried into the hotel, he turned his face homewards: running as fast as he could, to make up for lost time: and recalling, with a great deal of astonishment and some fear, the extraordinary behaviour of the person from whom he had just parted.

The circumstance did not dwell in his recollection long, however; for when he reached the cottage, there was enough to occupy his mind, and to drive all considerations of self completely from his memory.

Rose Maylie had rapidly grown worse; and before midnight was de-lirious. A medical practitioner, who resided on the spot, was in constant attendance upon her; and after first seeing the patient, he had taken Mrs. Maylie aside, and pronounced her disorder to be one of a most alarming nature. "In fact," he said, "it would be little short of a miracle, if she recovered."

How often did Oliver start from his bed that night, and stealing out, with noiseless footstep, to the staircase, listen for the slightest sound from the sick chamber! How often did a tremble shake his frame, and cold drops of terror start upon his brow, when a sudden trampling of feet caused him to fear that something too dreadful to think of, had even then occurred! And what had been the fervency of all the prayers he had ever uttered, compared with those he poured forth, now, in the agony and passion of his supplication for the life and health of the gentle creature, who was tottering on the deep grave's verge!

The suspense: the fearful, acute suspense: of standing idly by while

---

1. Monks is an epileptic.

the life of one we dearly love, is trembling in the balance; the racking thoughts that crowd upon the mind, and make the heart beat violently, and the breath come thick, by the force of the images they conjure up before it; the desperate anxiety *to be doing something* to relieve the pain, or lessen the danger, which we have no power to alleviate; the sinking of soul and spirit, which the sad remembrance of our helplessness produces; what tortures can equal these; what reflections or endeavours can, in the full tide and fever of the time, allay them!

Morning came; and the little cottage was lonely and still. People spoke in whispers; anxious faces appeared at the gate, from time to time; and women and children went away in tears. All the livelong day, and for hours after it had grown dark, Oliver paced softly up and down the garden: raising his eyes every instant to the sick chamber, and shuddering to see the darkened window, looking as if death lay stretched inside. Late at night, Mr. Losberne arrived. "It is hard," said the good doctor, turning away as he spoke; "so young: so much beloved: but there is very little hope."

Another morning. The sun shone brightly: as brightly as if it looked upon no misery or care; and, with every leaf and flower in full bloom about her: with life, and health, and sounds and sights of joy, surrounding her on every side: the fair young creature lay, wasting fast. Oliver crept away to the old churchyard: and sitting down on one of the green mounds, wept for her, in silence.

There was such peace and beauty in the scene; so much of brightness and mirth in the sunny landscape; such blithesome music in the songs of the summer birds; such freedom in the rapid flight of the rook, careering overhead; so much of life and joyousness in all; that when the boy raised his aching eyes, and looked about, the thought instinctively occurred to him, that this was not a time for death; that Rose could surely never die when humbler things were all so glad and gay; that graves were for cold and cheerless winter: not for sunlight and fragrance. He almost thought that shrouds were for the old and shrunken; and that they never wrapped the young and graceful form within their ghastly folds.

A knell from the church bell broke harshly on these youthful thoughts. Another! Again! It was tolling for the funeral service. A group of humble mourners entered the gate: wearing white favours; for the corpse was young. They stood uncovered by a grave; and there was a mother: a mother once: among the weeping train. But the sun shone brightly, and the birds sang on.

Oliver turned homewards; thinking on the many kindnesses he had received from the young lady; and wishing that the time could come over again, that he might never cease showing her how grateful and attached he was. He had no cause for self-reproach on the score of neglect, or want of thought, for he had been devoted to her service; and yet a hundred little occasions rose up before him on which he fancied he might have been more zealous, and more earnest, and wished he had been. We need be careful how we deal with those about us; when every death carries to some small circle of survivors, thoughts of so much omitted, and so little done; of so many things forgotten, and so many more which might have been repaired. There is no remorse so deep, as that which is unavailing; if we would be spared its tortures, let us remember this, in time.

When he reached home, Mrs. Maylie was sitting in the little parlour. Oliver's heart sank at sight of her; for she had never left the bedside of her niece; and he trembled to think what change could have driven her away. He learnt that she had fallen into a deep sleep, from which she would waken, either to recovery and life, or to bid them farewell, and die.

They sat, listening, and afraid to speak, for hours. The untasted meal was removed; and with looks which showed that their thoughts were elsewhere, they watched the sun as he sank lower and lower, and, at length, cast over sky and earth those brilliant hues which herald his departure. Their quick ears caught the sound of an approaching footstep; and they both involuntarily darted to the door, as Mr. Losberne entered.

"What of Rose?" cried the old lady. "Tell me at once! I can bear it; anything but suspense! Oh, tell me! in the name of Heaven!"

"You must compose yourself," said the doctor, supporting her. "Be calm, my dear ma'am, pray."

"Let me go, in God's name! My dear child! She is dead! She is dying!"

"No!" cried the doctor, passionately. "As He is good and merciful, she will live to bless us all, for years to come."

The lady fell upon her knees, and tried to fold her hands together; but the energy which had supported her so long, fled up to Heaven with her first thanksgiving; and she sank into the friendly arms which were extended to receive her.

Chapter XXXIV.

CONTAINS SOME INTRODUCTORY PARTICULARS RELATIVE TO A YOUNG
GENTLEMAN WHO NOW ARRIVES UPON THE SCENE; AND A NEW
ADVENTURE WHICH HAPPENED TO OLIVER.

It was almost too much happiness to bear. Oliver felt stunned and stupified by the unexpected intelligence; he could not weep, or speak, or rest. He had scarcely the power of understanding anything that had passed, until, after a long ramble in the quiet evening air, a burst of tears came to his relief; and he seemed to awaken, all at once, to a full sense of the joyful change that had occurred, and the almost insupportable load of anguish which had been taken from his breast.

The night was fast closing in, when he returned homewards: laden with flowers which he had culled, with peculiar care, for the adornment of the sick chamber. As he walked briskly along the road, he heard behind him the noise of some vehicle, approaching at a furious pace. Looking round, he saw that it was a post-chaise,[1] driven at great speed; and as the horses were galloping, and the road was narrow, he stood leaning against a gate until it should have passed him.

As it dashed on, Oliver caught a glimpse of a man in a white nightcap, whose face seemed familiar to him, although his view was so brief that he could not identify the person. In another second or two, the nightcap was thrust out of the chaise-window; and a stentorian voice bellowed to the driver to stop: which he did as soon as he could pull up his horses. Then, the nightcap once again appeared; and the same voice called Oliver by his name.

"Here!" cried the voice. "Master Oliver, what's the news? Miss Rose! Master O-li-ver!"

"Is it you, Giles?" cried Oliver, running up to the chaise-door.

Giles popped out his nightcap again, preparatory to making some reply, when he was suddenly pulled back by a young gentleman who occupied the other corner of the chaise, and who eagerly demanded what was the news.

"In a word," cried the gentleman, "better or worse?"

"Better—much better!" replied Oliver, hastily.

"Thank Heaven!" exclaimed the gentleman. "You are sure?"

"Quite, sir," replied Oliver. "The change took place only a few hours ago; and Mr. Losberne says, that all danger is at an end."

The gentleman said not another word, but, opening the chaise-door, leaped out, and taking Oliver hurriedly by the arm, led him aside.

"You are quite certain? There is no possibility of any mistake on your part, my boy, is there?" demanded the gentleman, in a tremulous voice. "Pray do not deceive me, by awakening any hopes that are not to be fulfilled."

"I would not for the world, sir," replied Oliver. "Indeed you may believe me. Mr. Losberne's words were, that she would live to bless us all for many years to come. I heard him say so."

The tears stood in Oliver's eyes as he recalled the scene which was the beginning of so much happiness; and the gentleman turned his face away, and remained silent, for some minutes. Oliver thought he heard him sob, more than once; but he feared to interrupt him by any further

---

1. An enclosed carriage, carrying from two to four people, hired for travel from stagecoach house to stagecoach house; the driver rides one of the horses.

remark—for he could well guess what his feelings were—and so stood apart, feigning to be occupied with his nosegay.

All this time, Mr. Giles, with the white nightcap on, had been sitting upon the steps of the chaise, supporting an elbow on each knee, and wiping his eyes with a blue cotton pocket-handkerchief dotted with white spots. That the honest fellow had not been feigning emotion, was abundantly demonstrated by the very red eyes with which he regarded the young gentleman, when he turned round and addressed him.

"I think you had better go on to my mother's in the chaise, Giles," said he. "I would rather walk slowly on, so as to gain a little time before I see her. You can say I am coming."

"I beg your pardon, Mr. Harry," said Giles: giving a final polish to his ruffled countenance with the handkerchief; "but if you would leave the postboy to say that, I should be very much obliged to you. It wouldn't be proper for the maids to see me in this state, sir; I should never have any more authority with them if they did."

"Well," rejoined Harry Maylie, smiling, "you can do as you like. Let him go on with the luggage, if you wish it, and do you follow with us. Only first exchange that nightcap for some more appropriate covering, or we shall be taken for madmen."

Mr. Giles, reminded of his unbecoming costume, snatched off and pocketed his nightcap; and substituted a hat, of grave and sober shape, which he took out of the chaise. This done, the postboy drove off; and Giles, Mr. Maylie, and Oliver, followed at their leisure.

As they walked along, Oliver glanced from time to time with much interest and curiosity at the new-comer. He seemed about five-and-twenty years of age, and was of the middle height; his countenance was frank and handsome; and his demeanour singularly easy and prepossessing. Notwithstanding the difference between youth and age, he bore so strong a likeness to the old lady, that Oliver would have had no great difficulty in imagining their relationship, even if he had not already spoken of her as his mother.

Mrs. Maylie was anxiously waiting to receive her son when he reached the cottage; and the meeting did not take place without great emotion on both sides.

"Mother!" whispered the young man; "why did you not write before?"

"I did," replied Mrs. Maylie; "but, on reflection, I determined to keep back the letter until I had heard Mr. Losberne's opinion."

"But why," said the young man, "why run the chance of that occurring which so nearly happened? If Rose had—I cannot utter that word now—if this illness had terminated differently, how could you ever have forgiven yourself! How could I ever have known happiness again!"

"If that *had* been the case, Harry," said Mrs. Maylie, "I fear your happiness would have been effectually blighted; and that your arrival here a day sooner or a day later, would have been of very, very little import."

"And who can wonder if it be so, mother?" rejoined the young man; "or why should I say, *if?*—It is—it is—you know it, mother—you must know it!"

"I know that she deserves the best and purest love the heart of man can offer," said Mrs. Maylie; "I know that the devotion and affection of her nature require no ordinary return, but one that shall be deep and lasting. If I did not feel this, and know, besides, that a changed behaviour in one she loved would break her heart, I should not feel my task so difficult of performance, or have to encounter so many struggles in my own bosom, when I take what seems to me to be the strict line of duty."

"This is unkind, mother," said Harry. "Do you still suppose that I am a boy ignorant of my own mind, and mistaking the impulses of my own soul?"

"I think, my dear son," returned Mrs. Maylie, laying her hand upon his shoulder, "that youth has many generous impulses which do not last; and that among them are some, which, being gratified, become only the more fleeting. Above all, I think," said the lady, fixing her eyes on her son's face, "that if an enthusiastic, ardent, and ambitious man marry a wife on whose name there is a stain, which, though it originate in no fault of hers, may be visited by cold and sordid people upon her, and upon his children also: and, in exact proportion to his success in the world, be cast in his teeth, and made the subject of sneers against him: he may—no matter how generous and good his nature—one day repent of the connexion he formed in early life; and she may have the pain and torture of knowing that he does so."

"Mother," said the young man, impatiently, "he would be a selfish brute, unworthy alike of the name of man and of the woman you describe, who acted thus."

"You think so now, Harry," replied his mother.

"And ever will!" said the young man. "The mental agony I have suffered, during the last two days, wrings from me the undisguised avowal to you of a passion which, as you well know, is not one of yesterday, nor one I have lightly formed. On Rose, sweet, gentle girl! my heart is set, as firmly as ever heart of man was set on woman. I have no thought, no view, no hope, in life beyond her; and if you oppose me in this great stake, you take my peace and happiness in your hands, and cast them to the wind. Mother, think better of this, and of me, and do not disregard the warm feelings of which you seem to think so little."

"Harry," said Mrs. Maylie, "it is because I think so much of warm and sensitive hearts, that I would spare them from being wounded. But we have said enough, and more than enough, on this matter just now."

"Let it rest with Rose, then," interposed Harry. "You will not press these overstrained opinions of yours, so far as to throw any obstacle in my way?"

"I will not," rejoined Mrs. Maylie; "but I would have you consider——"

"I *have* considered!" was the impatient reply; "Mother, I have considered, years and years. I have considered ever since I have been capable of serious reflection. My feelings remain unchanged, as they ever will; and why should I suffer the pain of a delay in giving them vent, which can be productive of no earthly good? No! Before I leave this place, Rose shall hear me."

"She shall," said Mrs. Maylie.

"There is something in your manner, which would almost imply that she will hear me coldly, mother," said the young man.

"Not coldly," rejoined the old lady; "far from it."

"How then?" urged the young man. "She has formed no other attachment?"

"No, indeed," replied his mother; "you have, or I mistake, too strong a hold on her affections already." "What I would say," resumed the old lady, stopping her son as he was about to speak, "is this. Before you stake your all on this chance; before you suffer yourself to be carried to the highest point of hope; reflect for a few moments, my dear child, on Rose's history, and consider what effect the knowledge of her doubtful birth may have on her decision: devoted as she is to us, with all the intensity of her noble mind, and with that perfect sacrifice of self which, in all matters, great or trifling, has always been her characteristic."

"What do you mean?"

"That I leave you to discover," replied Mrs. Maylie. "I must go back to her. God bless you!"

"I shall see you again to-night?" said the young man, eagerly.

"By and by," replied the lady; "when I leave Rose."

"You will tell her I am here?" said Harry.

"Of course," replied Mrs. Maylie.

"And say how anxious I have been, and how much I have suffered, and how I long to see her. You will not refuse to do this, mother?"

"No," said the old lady; "I will tell her all." And pressing her son's hand, affectionately, she hastened from the room.

Mr. Losberne and Oliver had remained at another end of the apartment while this hurried conversation was proceeding. The former now held out his hand to Harry Maylie; and hearty salutations were exchanged between them. The doctor then communicated, in reply to multifarious questions from his young friend, a precise account of his patient's situation; which was quite as consolatory and full of promise, as Oliver's statement had encouraged him to hope; and to the whole of which, Mr. Giles, who affected to be busy about the luggage, listened with greedy ears.

"Have you shot anything particular, lately, Giles?" inquired the doctor, when he had concluded.

"Nothing particular, sir," replied Mr. Giles, colouring up to the eyes.

"Nor catching any thieves, nor identifying any housebreakers?" said the doctor.

"None at all, sir," replied Mr. Giles, with much gravity.

"Well," said the doctor, "I am sorry to hear it, because you do that sort of thing so admirably. Pray, how is Brittles?"

"The boy is very well, sir," said Mr. Giles, recovering his usual tone of patronage; "and sends his respectful duty, sir."

"That's well," said the doctor. "Seeing you here, reminds me, Mr. Giles, that on the day before that on which I was called away so hurriedly, I executed, at the request of your good mistress, a small commission in your favour. Just step into this corner a moment, will you?"

Mr. Giles walked into the corner with much importance, and some wonder: and was honoured with a short whispering conference with the doctor; on the termination of which, he made a great many bows, and retired with steps of unusual stateliness. The subject matter of this conference was not disclosed in the parlour, but the kitchen was speedily enlightened concerning it; for Mr. Giles walked straight thither, and having called for a mug of ale, announced, with an air of majestic mystery, which was highly effective, that it had pleased his mistress, in consideration of his gallant behaviour on the occasion of that attempted robbery, to deposit, in the local savings-bank, the sum of five and twenty pounds, for his sole use and benefit. At this, the two women-servants lifted up their hands and eyes: and supposed that Mr. Giles would begin to be quite proud now; whereunto Mr. Giles, pulling out his shirt-frill, replied, "No, no;" and that if they observed that he was at all haughty to his inferiors, he would thank them to tell him so. And then he made a great many other remarks: no less illustrative of his humility: which were received with equal favour and applause; and were, withal, as original, and as much to the purpose, as the remarks of great men commonly are.

Above stairs, the remainder of the evening passed cheerfully away; for the doctor was in high spirits; and however fatigued or thoughtful Harry Maylie might have been, at first, he was not proof against the worthy gentleman's good humour: which displayed itself in a great variety of sallies and professional recollections, and an abundance of small jokes, which struck Oliver as being the drollest things he had ever heard, and caused him to laugh proportionately: to the evident satisfaction of the doctor, who laughed immoderately at himself, and made Harry laugh almost as heartily, by the very force of sympathy. So they were as pleasant a party as, under the circumstances, they could well have been; and it was late before they retired, with light and thankful hearts, to take that rest of which, after the doubt and suspense they had recently undergone, they stood so much in need.

Oliver rose next morning, in better heart; and went about his usual early occupations, with more hope and pleasure than he had known for many days. The birds were once more hung out, to sing, in their old places; and the sweetest wild flowers that could be found, were once more gathered to gladden Rose with their beauty and fragrance. The melancholy which had seemed to the sad eyes of the anxious boy to hang, for days past, over every object: beautiful as all were: was dispelled by magic. The dew seemed to sparkle more brightly on the green leaves; the air to rustle among them with a sweeter music; and the sky itself to look more blue and bright. Such is the influence which the condition of our own thoughts, exercises, even over the appearance of external objects. Men who look on nature, and their fellow-men, and cry that all is dark and gloomy, are in the right; but the sombre colours are reflections from their own jaundiced eyes and hearts. The real hues are delicate, and need a clearer vision.

It is worthy of remark, and Oliver did not fail to note it at the time, that his morning expeditions were no longer made alone. Harry Maylie, after the very first morning when he met Oliver coming laden home, was seized with such a passion for flowers, and displayed such a taste in their arrangement, as left his young companion far behind. If Oliver were behindhand in these respects, however, he knew where the best were to be found; and morning after morning they scoured the country together, and brought home the fairest that blossomed. The window of the young lady's chamber was opened now; for she loved to feel the rich summer air stream in, and revive her with its freshness; but there always stood in water, just inside the lattice, one particular little bunch, which was made up with great care, every morning. Oliver could not help noticing that the withered flowers were never thrown away, although the little vase was regularly replenished; nor could he help observing, that whenever the doctor came into the garden, he invariably cast his eyes up to that particular corner, and nodded his head most expressively, as he set forth on his morning's walk. Pending these observations, the days were flying by; and Rose was rapidly recovering.

Nor did Oliver's time hang heavy on his hands; although the young lady had not yet left her chamber; and there were no evening walks: save now and then, for a short distance, with Mrs. Maylie. He applied himself, with redoubled assiduity, to the instructions of the white-headed old gentleman: and laboured so hard that his quick progress surprised even himself. It was while he was engaged in this pursuit, that he was greatly startled and distressed by a most unexpected occurrence.

The little room in which he was accustomed to sit, when busy at his books, was on the ground-floor, at the back of the house. It was quite a cottage-room, with a lattice-window: around which were clusters of jessamine and honeysuckle, that crept over the casement, and filled the place with their delicious perfume. It looked into a garden, whence a wicket-gate opened into a small paddock; all beyond was fine meadowland and wood. There was no other dwelling near, in that direction; and the prospect it commanded was very extensive.

One beautiful evening, when the first shades of twilight were beginning to settle upon the earth, Oliver sat at this window, intent upon his books. He had been poring over them for some time; and as the day had been uncommonly sultry, and he had exerted himself a great deal; it is no disparagement to the authors: whoever they may have been: to say, that gradually and by slow degrees, he fell asleep.

There is a kind of sleep that steals upon us sometimes, which, while it holds the body prisoner, does not free the mind from a sense of things about it, and enable it to ramble at its pleasure. So far as an overpowering heaviness, a prostration of strength, and an utter inability to control our thoughts or power of motion, can be called sleep, this is it; and yet we have a consciousness of all that is going on about us; and if we dream at such a time, words which are really spoken, or sounds which really exist at the moment, accommodate themselves with surprising readiness to our visions, until reality and imagination become so strangely blended that it is afterwards almost a matter of impossibility to separate the two. Nor is this, the most striking phenomenon incidental to such a state. It is an undoubted fact, that although our senses of touch and sight be for the time dead, yet our sleeping thoughts, and the visionary scenes that pass before us, will be influenced, and materially influenced, by the *mere silent presence* of some external object: which may not have been near us when we closed our eyes: and of whose vicinity we have had no waking consciousness.[2]

Oliver knew, perfectly well, that he was in his own little room; that his books were lying on the table before him; and that the sweet air was stirring among the creeping plants outside. And yet he was asleep. Suddenly, the scene changed; the air became close and confined; and he thought, with a glow of terror, that he was in the Jew's house again. There sat the hideous old man, in his accustomed corner: pointing at him: and whispering to another man, with his face averted, who sat beside him.

"Hush, my dear!" he thought he heard the Jew say; "it is he, sure enough. Come away."

"He!" the other man seemed to answer; "could I mistake him, think you? If a crowd of devils were to put themselves into his exact shape, and he stood amongst them, there is something that would tell me how

---

2. Oliver is described as in a hypnagogic trance, the hypnotic-like state that precedes actual sleep.

to point him out. If you buried him fifty feet deep, and took me across his grave, I should know, if there wasn't a mark above it, that he lay buried there. I should!"

The man seemed to say this, with such dreadful hatred, that Oliver awoke with the fear, and started up.

Good Heaven! what was that, which sent the blood tingling to his heart, and deprived him of his voice, and of power to move! There—there—at the window; close before him; so close, that he could have almost touched him before he started back: with his eyes peering into the room, and meeting his: there stood the Jew! And beside him, white with rage, or fear, or both, were the scowling features of the very man who had accosted him at the inn-yard.

It was but an instant, a glance, a flash, before his eyes; and they were gone. But they had recognised him, and he them; and their look was as firmly impressed upon his memory, as if it had been deeply carved in stone, and set before him from his birth. He stood transfixed for a moment; and then, leaping from the window into the garden, called loudly for help.

Chapter XXXV.

CONTAINING THE UNSATISFACTORY RESULT OF OLIVER'S ADVENTURE, AND A CONVERSATION OF SOME IMPORTANCE BETWEEN HARRY MAYLIE AND ROSE.

When the inmates of the house, attracted by Oliver's cries, hurried to the spot from which they proceeded, they found him, pale and agitated, pointing in the direction of the meadows behind the house, and scarcely able to articulate the words, "The Jew! the Jew!"

Mr. Giles was at a loss to comprehend what this outcry meant; but Harry Maylie, whose perceptions were something quicker, and who had heard Oliver's history from his mother, understood it at once.

"What direction did he take?" he asked, catching up a heavy stick which was standing in a corner.

"That," replied Oliver, pointing out the course the men had taken; "I missed them, in an instant."

"Then, they are in the ditch!" said Harry. "Follow! And keep as near me, as you can." So saying, he sprang over the hedge, and darted off with a speed which rendered it matter of exceeding difficulty for the others to keep near him.

Giles followed as well as he could; and Oliver followed too; and in the course of a minute or two, Mr. Losberne, who had been out walking, and just then returned, tumbled over the hedge after them, and picking himself up with more agility than he could have been supposed to possess, struck into the same course at no contemptible speed: shouting all the while, most prodigiously, to know what was the matter.

On they all went; nor stopped they once to breathe, until the leader, striking off into an angle of the field indicated by Oliver, began to search, narrowly, the ditch and hedge adjoining; which afforded time for the remainder of the party to come up: and for Oliver to communicate to Mr. Losberne the circumstances that had led to so vigorous a pursuit.

The search was all in vain. There were not even the traces of recent footsteps, to be seen. They stood, now, on the summit of a little hill, commanding the open fields in every direction for three or four miles. There was the village in the hollow on the left; but, in order to gain that, after pursuing the track Oliver had pointed out, the men must have made a circuit of open ground, which it was impossible they could have accomplished in so short a time. A thick wood skirted the meadow-land in another direction; but they could not have gained that covert for the same reason.

"It must have been a dream, Oliver," said Harry Maylie.

"Oh no, indeed, sir," replied Oliver, shuddering at the very recollection of the old wretch's countenance; "I saw him too plainly for that. I saw them both, as plainly as I see you now."

"Who was the other?" inquired Harry and Mr. Losberne, together.

"The very same man I told you of, who came so suddenly upon me at the inn," said Oliver. "We had our eyes fixed full upon each other; and I could swear to him."

"They took this way?" demanded Harry; "are you sure?"

"As I am that the men were at the window," replied Oliver, pointing down, as he spoke, to the hedge which divided the cottage-garden from the meadow. "The tall man leaped over, just there; and the Jew, running a few paces to the right, crept through that gap."

The two gentlemen watched Oliver's earnest face, as he spoke; and looking from him to each other, seemed to feel satisfied of the accuracy of what he said. Still, in no direction were there any appearances of the trampling of men in hurried flight. The grass was long; but it was trodden down nowhere, save where their own feet had crushed it. The sides and brinks of the ditches, were of damp clay; but in no one place could they discern the print of men's shoes, or the slightest mark which would indicate that any feet had pressed the ground for hours before.

"This is strange!" said Harry.

"Strange!" echoed the doctor. "Blathers and Duff, themselves, could make nothing of it."

Notwithstanding the evidently useless nature of their search, they did not desist until the coming on of night rendered its further prosecution hopeless; and, even then, they gave it up with reluctance. Giles was dispatched to the different alehouses in the village: furnished with the best description Oliver could give of the appearance and dress of the strangers. Of these the Jew was, at all events, sufficiently remarkable to be remembered, supposing he had been seen drinking, or loitering about; but he returned without any intelligence, calculated to dispel or lessen the mystery.

On the next day, further search was made, and the inquiries renewed; but with no better success. On the day following, Oliver and Mr. Maylie repaired to the market-town, in the hope of seeing or hearing something of the men there; but this effort was equally fruitless; and after a few days, the affair began to be forgotten, as most affairs are, when wonder, having no fresh food to support it, dies away of itself.

Meanwhile, Rose was rapidly recovering. She had left her room; was able to go out; and mixing once more with the family, carried joy into the hearts of all.

But although this happy change had a visible effect on the little circle; and although cheerful voices and merry laughter were once more heard in the cottage; there was, at times, an unwonted restraint upon some there: even upon Rose herself: which Oliver could not fail to remark. Mrs. Maylie and her son were often closeted together for a long time; and more than once Rose appeared with traces of tears upon her face. After Mr. Losberne had fixed a day for his departure to Chertsey, these symptoms increased; and it became evident that something was in progress which affected the peace of the young lady, and of somebody else besides.

At length, one morning, when Rose was alone in the breakfast-parlour, Harry Maylie entered; and, with some hesitation, begged permission to speak with her for a few moments.

"A few: a very few: will suffice, Rose," said the young man, drawing his chair towards her. "What I shall have to say, has already presented itself to your mind; the most cherished hopes of my heart are not unknown to you, though from my lips you have not yet heard them stated."

Rose had been very pale from the moment of his entrance; but that might have been the effect of her recent illness. She merely bowed; and bending over some plants that stood near, waited in silence for him to proceed.

"I—I—ought to have left here, before," said Harry.

"You should, indeed," replied Rose. "Forgive me for saying so, but I wish you had."

"I was brought here, by the most dreadful and agonising of all apprehensions," said the young man; "the fear of losing the one dear being on whom my every wish and hope are fixed. You had been dying: trembling between earth and heaven. We know that when the young, the beautiful, and good, are visited with sickness, their pure spirits insensibly turn towards their bright home of lasting rest; we know, Heaven help us! that the best and fairest of our kind, too often fade in blooming."

There were tears in the eye of the gentle girl, as these words were spoken; and when one fell upon the flower over which she bent, and glistened brightly in its cup, making it more beautiful, it seemed as though the outpouring of her fresh young heart, claimed kindred with the loveliest things in nature.

"An angel," continued the young man, passionately; "a creature as fair and innocent of guile as one of God's own angels, fluttered between life and death. Oh! who could hope, when the distant world to which she was akin, half opened to her view, that she would return to the sorrow and calamity of this! Rose, Rose, to know that you were passing away like some soft shadow, which a light from above, casts upon the earth; to have no hope that you would be spared to those who linger here; to know no reason why you should be; to feel that you belonged to that bright sphere whither so many of the fairest and the best have winged their early flight; and yet to pray, amid all these consolations, that you might be restored to those who loved you—these were distractions almost too great to bear. They were mine, by day and night; and with them, came such a rushing torrent of fears, and apprehensions, and selfish regrets, lest you should die, and never know how devotedly I loved you, as almost bore down sense and reason in its course. You recovered; day by day, and almost hour by hour, some drop of health came back, and mingling with the spent and feeble stream of life which circulated languidly within you, swelled it again to a high and rushing tide. I have watched you change almost from death to life: with eyes that moistened with their eagerness and deep affection. Do not tell me that you wish I had lost this; for it has softened my heart to all mankind."

"I did not mean that," said Rose, weeping; "I only wish you had left here, that you might have turned to high and noble pursuits again; to pursuits well worthy of you."

"There is no pursuit more worthy of me: more worthy of the highest nature that exists: than the struggle to win such a heart as yours," said the young man, taking her hand. "Rose, my own dear Rose; for years; for years; I have loved you: hoping to win my way to fame, and then come proudly home and tell you it had been pursued only for you to share; thinking, in my day-dreams, how I would remind you, in that happy moment, of the many silent tokens I had given of a boy's attachment: and claim your hand, as in redemption of some old mute contract that had been sealed between us. That time has not arrived; but here, with no fame won, and no young vision realised, I give to you the heart so long your own, and stake my all upon the words with which you greet the offer."

"Your behaviour has ever been kind and noble," said Rose, mastering the emotions by which she was agitated. "As you believe that I am not insensible or ungrateful, so hear my answer."

"It is, that I may endeavour to deserve you; it is, dear Rose?"

"It is," replied Rose, "that you must endeavour to forget me; not as your old and dearly-attached companion, for that would wound me deeply: but, as the object of your love. Look into the world; think how many hearts you would be proud to gain, are there. Confide some other passion to me, if you will; and I will be the truest, warmest, and most faithful friend you have."

There was a pause, during which, Rose, who had covered her face with one hand, gave free vent to her tears. Harry still retained the other.

"And your reasons, Rose," he said, at length, in a low voice; "your reasons for this decision?"

"You have a right to know them," rejoined Rose. "You can say nothing to alter my resolution. It is a duty that I must perform. I owe it, alike to others, and to myself."

"To yourself?"

"Yes, Harry; I owe it to myself, that I, a friendless, portionless girl, with a blight upon my name, should not give your friends reason to suspect that I had sordidly yielded to your first passion, and fastened myself, a clog, on all your hopes and projects. I owe it to you and yours, to prevent you from opposing, in the warmth of your generous nature, this great obstacle to your progress in the world."

"If your inclinations chime with your sense of duty——" Harry began.

"They do not," replied Rose, colouring deeply.

"Then you return my love?" said Harry. "Say but that, dear Rose; say but that; and soften the bitterness of this hard disappointment!"

"If I could have done so, without doing heavy wrong to him I loved," rejoined Rose, "I could have——"

"Have received this declaration very differently?" said Harry. "Do not conceal that from me, at least, Rose."

"I could," said Rose. "Stay," she added, disengaging her hand, "why should we prolong this painful interview? Most painful to me, and yet productive of lasting happiness notwithstanding; for it will be happiness to know that I once held the high place in your regard which I now occupy; and every triumph you achieve in life will animate me with new fortitude and firmness. Farewell, Harry! As we have met to-day, we meet no more; but in other relations than those in which this conversation would have placed us, may we be long and happily entwined; and may every blessing that the prayers of a true and earnest heart can call down from the source of all truth and sincerity, cheer and prosper you!"

"Another word, Rose," said Harry. "Your reason in your own words. From your own lips, let me hear it."

"The prospect before you," answered Rose, firmly, "is a brilliant one;

all the honours to which great talents and powerful connexions can help men in public life, are in store for you. But, those connexions are proud; and I will neither mingle with such as hold in scorn the mother who gave me life; nor bring disgrace or failure on the son of her who has so well supplied that mother's place. In a word," said the young lady, turning away, as her temporary firmness forsook her, "there is a stain upon my name,[1] which the world visits on innocent heads. I will carry it into no blood but my own; and the reproach shall rest alone on me."

"One word more, Rose. Dearest Rose! one more!" cried Harry, throwing himself before her. "If I had been less—less fortunate, the world would call it; if some obscure and peaceful life had been my destiny; if I had been poor, sick, helpless; would you have turned from me then? Or has my probable advancement to riches and honour, given this scruple birth?"

"Do not press me to reply," answered Rose. "The question does not arise, and never will. It is unfair, unkind, to urge it."

"If your answer be what I almost dare to hope it is," retorted Harry, "it will shed a gleam of happiness upon my lonely way, and light the dreary path before me. It is not an idle thing to do so much, by the utterance of a few brief words, for one who loves you beyond all else. Oh, Rose! in the name of my ardent and enduring attachment; in the name of all I have suffered for you, and all you doom me to undergo; answer me this one question!"

"Then, if your lot had been differently cast," rejoined Rose; "if you had been even a little, but not so far, above me; if I could have been a help and comfort to you in some humble scene of peace and retirement, and not a blot and drawback in ambitious and distinguished crowds; I should have been spared this trial. I have every reason to be happy, very happy, now; but then, Harry, I own I should have been happier."

Busy recollections of old hopes: cherished as a girl, long ago: crowded into the mind of Rose, while making this avowal; but they brought tears with them, as old hopes will when they come back withered; and they relieved her.

"I cannot help this weakness, and it makes my purpose stronger," said Rose, extending her hand. "I must leave you now, indeed."

"I ask one promise," said Harry. "Once, and only once more,—say within a year, but it may be much sooner,—let me speak to you again on this subject, for the last time."

"Not to press me to alter my right determination," replied Rose, with a melancholy smile; "it will be useless."

"No," said Harry; "to hear you repeat it, if you will; finally repeat it. I will lay at your feet, whatever of station or fortune I may possess; and

1. Rose is here referring to the mystery surrounding her birth and family.

if you still adhere to your present resolution, will not seek, by word or act, to change it."

"Then let it be so," rejoined Rose; "it is but one pang the more, and by that time I may be enabled to bear it better."

She extended her hand again. But the young man caught her to his bosom; and imprinting one kiss on her beautiful forehead, hurried from the room.

Chapter XXXVI.

IS A VERY SHORT ONE, AND MAY APPEAR OF NO GREAT IMPORTANCE IN ITS PLACE. BUT IT SHOULD BE READ NOTWITHSTANDING, AS A SEQUEL TO THE LAST, AND A KEY TO ONE THAT WILL FOLLOW WHEN ITS TIME ARRIVES.

"And so you are resolved to be my travelling-companion this morning; eh?" said the doctor, as Harry Maylie joined him and Oliver at the breakfast table. "Why, you are not in the same mind or intention two half-hours together."

"You will tell me a different tale one of these days," said Harry, colouring without any perceptible reason.

"I hope I may have good cause to do so," replied Mr. Losberne; "though I confess I don't think I shall. But yesterday morning you had made up your mind, in a great hurry, to stay here, and to accompany your mother, like a dutiful son, to the sea-side. Before noon, you announce that you are going to do me the honour of accompanying me as far as I go on your road to London. And at night, you urge me, with great mystery, to start before the ladies are stirring; the consequence of which is, that young Oliver here is pinned down to his breakfast when he ought to be ranging the meadows after botanical phenomena of all kinds. Too bad, isn't it, Oliver?"

"I should have been very sorry not to have been at home when you and Mr. Maylie went away, sir," rejoined Oliver.

"That's a fine fellow," said the doctor; "you shall come and see me when you return. But, to speak seriously, Harry; has any communication from the great nobs,[1] produced this sudden anxiety on your part to be gone?"

"The great nobs," replied Harry: "under which designation, I presume, you include my most stately uncle: have not communicated with me at all, since I have been here; nor, at this time of the year, is it likely that anything would occur to render necessary my immediate attendance among them."

---

1. Harry's wealthy, fashionable friends and relatives who have promised to help him rise in the world.

"Well," said the doctor, "you are a queer fellow. But of course they will get you into parliament at the election before Christmas, and these sudden shiftings and changes are no bad preparation for political life. There's something in that; good training is always desirable, whether the race be for place, cup, or sweepstakes."

Harry Maylie looked as if he could have followed up this short dialogue by one or two remarks that would have staggered the doctor not a little; but he contented himself with saying, "We shall see," and pursued the subject no farther. The post-chaise drove up to the door shortly afterwards; and Giles coming in for the luggage, the good doctor bustled out, to see it packed.

"Oliver," said Harry Maylie, in a low voice, "let me speak a word with you."

Oliver walked into the window-recess to which Mr. Maylie beckoned him; much surprised at the mixture of sadness and boisterous spirits, which his whole behaviour displayed.

"You can write well now?" said Harry, laying his hand upon his arm.

"I hope so, sir," replied Oliver.

"I shall not be at home again, perhaps for some time; I wish you would write to me—say once a fortnight: every alternate Monday: to the General Post Office in London. Will you?"

"Oh! certainly, sir; I shall be proud to do it," exclaimed Oliver, greatly delighted with the commission.

"I should like to know how—how my mother and Miss Maylie are," said the young man; "and you can fill up a sheet by telling me what walks you take, and what you talk about, and whether she—they, I mean, seem happy and quite well. You understand me?"

"Oh! quite, sir, quite," replied Oliver.

"I would rather you did not mention it to them," said Harry, hurrying over his words; "because it might make my mother anxious to write to me oftener, and it is a trouble and worry to her. Let it be a secret between you and me; and mind you tell me every thing; I depend upon you."

Oliver, quite elated and honoured by a sense of his importance, faithfully promised to be secret and explicit in his communications; and Mr. Maylie took leave of him, with many warm assurances of his regard and protection.

The doctor was in the chaise; Giles (who, it had been arranged, should be left behind) held the door open in his hand; and the women-servants were in the garden, looking on. Harry cast one slight glance at the latticed window, and jumped into the carriage.

"Drive on!" he cried, "hard, fast, full gallop. Nothing short of flying will keep pace with me, to-day."

"Halloa!" cried the doctor, letting down the front glass in a great hurry, and shouting to the postilion; "something very far short of flying will keep pace with me. Do you hear?"

Jingling and clattering, till distance rendered its noise inaudible, and its rapid progress only perceptible to the eye, the vehicle wound its way along the road, almost hidden in a cloud of dust: now wholly disappearing, and now becoming visible again: as intervening objects, or the intricacies of the way, permitted. It was not until even the dusty cloud was no longer to be seen, that the gazers dispersed.

And there was one looker-on, who remained with eyes fixed upon the spot where the carriage had disappeared, long after it was many miles away; for behind the white curtain which had shrouded her from view when Harry raised his eyes towards the window, sat Rose herself.

"He seems in high spirits and happy," she said, at length. "I feared for a time he might be otherwise. I was mistaken. I am very, very glad."

Tears are signs of gladness as well as grief; but those which coursed down Rose's face, as she sat pensively at the window, still gazing in the same direction, seemed to tell more of sorrow than of joy.

Chapter XXXVII.

IN WHICH THE READER MAY PERCEIVE A CONTRAST, NOT UNCOMMON IN
MATRIMONIAL CASES.

Mr. Bumble sat in the workhouse parlour, with his eyes moodily fixed on the cheerless grate, whence, as it was summer time, no brighter gleam proceeded, than the reflection of certain sickly rays of the sun, which were sent back from its cold and shining surface. A paper flycage dangled from the ceiling, to which he occasionally raised his eyes in gloomy thought; and, as the heedless insects hovered round the gaudy network, Mr. Bumble would heave a deep sigh, while a more gloomy shadow overspread his countenance. Mr. Bumble was meditating; and it might be that the insects brought to mind, some painful passage in his own past life.

Nor was Mr. Bumble's gloom the only thing calculated to awaken a pleasing melancholy in the bosom of a spectator. There were not wanting other appearances, and those closely connected with his own person, which announced that a great change had taken place in the position of his affairs. The laced coat, and the cocked hat; where were they? He still wore knee-breeches, and dark cotton stockings on his nether limbs; but they were not *the* breeches. The coat was wide-skirted; and in that respect like *the* coat, but, oh, how different! The mighty cocked-hat was replaced by a modest round one. Mr. Bumble was no longer a beadle.

There are some promotions in life, which, independent of the more substantial rewards they offer, acquire peculiar value and dignity from the coats and waistcoats connected with them. A field-marshal has his uniform; a bishop his silk apron; a counsellor his silk gown; a beadle his cocked-hat. Strip the bishop of his apron, or the beadle of his hat and lace; what are they? Men. Mere men. Dignity, and even holiness too, sometimes, are more questions of coat and waistcoat than some people imagine.

Mr. Bumble had married Mrs. Corney, and was master of the workhouse. Another beadle had come into power; and on him the cocked-hat, gold-laced coat, and staff, had all three descended.

"And to-morrow two months it was done!" said Mr. Bumble, with a sigh. "It seems a age."

Mr. Bumble might have meant that he had concentrated a whole existence of happiness into the short space of eight weeks; but the sigh —there was a vast deal of meaning in the sigh.

"I sold myself," said Mr. Bumble, pursuing the same train of reflection, "for six teaspoons, a pair of sugar-tongs, and a milk-pot; with a small quantity of second-hand furniture, and twenty pound in money. I went very reasonable. Cheap, dirt cheap!"

"Cheap!" cried a shrill voice in Mr. Bumble's ear: "You would have been dear at any price; and dear enough I paid for you, Lord above knows that!"

Mr. Bumble turned, and encountered the face of his interesting consort, who, imperfectly comprehending the few words she had overheard of his complaint, had hazarded the foregoing remark at a venture.

"Mrs. Bumble, ma'am!" said Mr. Bumble, with sentimental sternness.

"Well?" cried the lady.

"Have the goodness to look at me," said Mr. Bumble, fixing his eyes upon her.

"If she stands such a eye as that," said Mr. Bumble to himself, "she can stand anything. It is a eye I never knew to fail with paupers; and if it fails with her, my power is gone."

Whether an exceedingly small expansion of eye be sufficient to quell paupers, who, being lightly fed, are in no very high condition; or whether the late Mrs. Corney was particularly proof against eagle glances; are matters of opinion. The matter of fact, is, that the matron was in no way overpowered by Mr. Bumble's scowl, but on the contrary, treated it with great disdain, and even raised a laugh thereat, which sounded as though it were genuine.

On hearing this most unexpected sound, Mr. Bumble looked first incredulous, and afterwards, amazed. He then relapsed into his former state; nor did he rouse himself until his attention was again awakened by the voice of his partner.

"Are you going to sit snoring there, all day?" inquired Mrs. Bumble.

"I am going to sit here, as long as I think proper, ma'am," rejoined Mr. Bumble; "and although I was *not* snoring, I shall snore, gape, sneeze, laugh, or cry, as the humour strikes me; such being my prerogative."

"Your prerogative!" sneered Mrs. Bumble, with ineffable contempt.

"I said the word, ma'am," observed Mr. Bumble. "The prerogative of a man is to command."

"And what's the prerogative of a woman, in the name of Goodness?" cried the relict of Mr. Corney, deceased.

"To obey, ma'am," thundered Mr. Bumble. "Your late unfort'nate husband should have taught it you; and then, perhaps, he might have been alive now. I wish he was, poor man!"

Mrs. Bumble, seeing at a glance, that the decisive moment had now arrived: and that a blow struck for the mastership on one side or other, must necessarily be final and conclusive: no sooner heard this allusion to the dead and gone, than she dropped into a chair; and with a loud scream that Mr. Bumble was a hard-hearted brute, fell into a paroxysm of tears.

But, tears were not the things to find their way to Mr. Bumble's soul; his heart was waterproof. Like washable beaver hats that improve with rain, his nerves were rendered stouter and more vigorous by showers of tears, which, being tokens of weakness, and so far tacit admissions of his own power, pleased and exalted him. He eyed his good lady with looks of great satisfaction; and begged, in an encouraging manner, that she should cry her hardest: the exercise being looked upon, by the faculty, as strongly conducive to health.

"It opens the lungs, washes the countenance, exercises the eyes, and softens down the temper," said Mr. Bumble. "So, cry away."

As he discharged himself of this pleasantry, Mr. Bumble took his hat from a peg; and putting it on, rather rakishly, on one side, as a man might, who felt he had asserted his superiority in a becoming manner, thrust his hands into his pockets, and sauntered towards the door with much ease and waggishness depicted in his whole appearance.

Now, Mrs. Corney that was, had tried the tears, because they were less troublesome than a manual assault; but she was quite prepared to make trial of the latter mode of proceeding, as Mr. Bumble was not long in discovering.

The first proof he experienced of the fact, was conveyed in a hollow sound, immediately succeeded by the sudden flying off of his hat to the opposite end of the room. This preliminary proceeding laying bare his head, the expert lady, clasping him tight round the throat with one hand, inflicted a shower of blows (dealt with singular vigour and dexterity) upon it with the other. This done, she created a little variety by scratching his face, and tearing his hair off; and having, by this time, inflicted as much punishment as she deemed necessary for the offence, she pushed him over a chair, which was luckily well situated for the purpose: and defied him to talk about his prerogative again, if he dared.

"Get up!" said Mrs. Bumble, in a voice of command. "And take yourself away from here, unless you want me to do something desperate."

Mr. Bumble rose with a very rueful countenance: wondering much what something desperate might be; and, picking up his hat, looked towards the door.

"Are you going?" demanded Mrs. Bumble.

"Certainly, my dear, certainly," rejoined Mr. Bumble, making a quicker motion towards the door. "I didn't intend to—I'm going, my dear! You are so very violent, that really I—"

At this instant, Mrs. Bumble stepped hastily forward to replace the carpet, which had been kicked up in the scuffle. Mr. Bumble immediately darted out of the room, without bestowing another thought on his unfinished sentence: leaving the late Mrs. Corney in full possession of the field.

Mr. Bumble was fairly taken by surprise, and fairly beaten. He had a decided propensity for bullying; derived no inconsiderable pleasure from the exercise of petty cruelty; and, consequently, was (it is needless to say) a coward. This is by no means a disparagement to his character; for many official personages, who are held in high respect and admiration, are the victims of similar infirmities. The remark is made, indeed, rather in his favour than otherwise, and with a view of impressing the reader with a just sense of his qualifications for office.

But, the measure of his degradation was not yet full. After making a tour of the house, and thinking, for the first time, that the poor-laws really were too hard on people; and that men who ran away from their wives, leaving them chargeable to the parish, ought, in justice, to be visited with no punishment at all, but rather rewarded as meritorious individuals who had suffered much; Mr. Bumble came to a room where some of the female paupers were usually employed in washing the parish linen: and whence the sound of voices in conversation, now proceeded.

"Hem!" said Mr. Bumble, summoning up all his native dignity. "These women at least shall continue to respect the prerogative. Hallo! hallo there! What do you mean by this noise, you hussies?"

With these words, Mr. Bumble opened the door, and walked in with a very fierce and angry manner: which was at once exchanged for a most humiliated and cowering air, as his eyes unexpectedly rested on the form of his lady wife.

"My dear," said Mr. Bumble, "I didn't know you were here."

"Didn't know I was here!" repeated Mrs. Bumble. "What do *you* do here?"

"I thought they were talking rather too much to be doing their work properly, my dear," replied Mr. Bumble: glancing distractedly at a couple of old women at the wash-tub, who were comparing notes of admiration at the workhouse-master's humility.

"*You* thought they were talking too much?" said Mrs. Bumble. "What business is it of yours?"

"Why, my dear—" urged Mr. Bumble, submissively.

"What business is it of yours?" demanded Mrs. Bumble, again.

"It's very true, you're matron here, my dear," submitted Mr. Bumble; "but I thought you mightn't be in the way just then."

"I'll tell you what, Mr. Bumble," returned his lady. "We don't want any of your interference. You're a great deal too fond of poking your nose into things that don't concern you: making everybody in the house, laugh, the moment your back is turned: and making yourself look like a fool every hour in the day. Be off; come!"

Mr. Bumble, seeing with excruciating feelings, the delight of the two old paupers, who were tittering together most rapturously, hesitated for an instant. Mrs. Bumble, whose patience brooked no delay, caught up a bowl of soap-suds, and motioning him towards the door, ordered him instantly to depart, on pain of receiving the contents upon his portly person.

What could Mr. Bumble do? He looked dejectedly round, and slunk away; and, as he reached the door, the titterings of the paupers broke into a shrill chuckle of irrepressible delight. It wanted but this. He was degraded in their eyes; he had lost caste and station before the very paupers; he had fallen from all the height and pomp of beadleship, to the lowest depth of the most snubbed hen-peckery.

"All in two months!" said Mr. Bumble, filled with dismal thoughts. "Two months! No more than two months ago, I was not only my own master, but everybody else's, so far as the porochial workhouse was concerned, and now!——"

It was too much. Mr. Bumble boxed the ears of the boy who opened the gate for him (for he had reached the portal in his reverie); and walked, distractedly, into the street.

He walked up one street, and down another, until exercise had abated the first passion of his grief; and then the revulsion of feeling made him thirsty. He passed a great many public-houses; and at length paused before one in a by-way, whose parlour, as he gathered from a hasty peep over the blinds, was deserted, save by one solitary customer. It began to rain, heavily, at the moment. This determined him. Mr. Bumble stepped in; and ordering something to drink, as he passed the bar, entered the apartment into which he had looked from the street.

The man who was seated there, was tall and dark: and wore a large cloak. He had the air of a stranger; and seemed, by a certain haggardness in his look, as well as by the dusty soils on his dress, to have travelled some distance. He eyed Bumble askance, as he entered, but scarcely deigned to nod his head in acknowledgment of his salutation.

Mr. Bumble had quite dignity enough for two: supposing even that the stranger had been more familiar: so he drank his gin-and-water in silence, and read the paper with great show of pomp and circumstance.[1]

It so happened, however: as it will happen very often, when men fall into company under such circumstances: that Mr. Bumble felt, every now and then, a powerful inducement, which he could not resist, to steal a look at the stranger; and that whenever he did so, he withdrew his eyes, in some confusion, to find that the stranger was at that moment stealing a look at him. Mr. Bumble's awkwardness was enhanced by the very remarkable expression of the stranger's eye, which was keen and bright, but shadowed by a scowl of distrust and suspicion, unlike anything he had ever observed before, and most repulsive to behold.

When they had encountered each other's glance several times in this way, the stranger, in a harsh, deep voice, broke silence.

"Were you looking for me," he said, "when you peered in at the window?"

"Not that I am aware of, unless you're Mr.——" Here Mr. Bumble stopped short; for he was curious to know the stranger's name, and thought, in his impatience, he might supply the blank.

"I see you were not," said the stranger; an expression of quiet sarcasm playing about his mouth; "or you would have known my name. You don't know it. I would recommend you not to inquire."

"I meant no harm, young man," observed Mr. Bumble, majestically.

"And have done none," said the stranger.

Another silence succeeded this short dialogue: which was again broken by the stranger.

"I have seen you before, I think," said he. "You were differently dressed at that time, and I only passed you in the street, but I should know you again. You were beadle here, once; were you not?"

"I was," said Mr. Bumble, in some surprise; "porochial beadle."

"Just so," rejoined the other, nodding his head. "It was in that character I saw you. What are you now?"

"Master of the workhouse," rejoined Mr. Bumble, slowly and impressively, to check any undue familiarity the stranger might otherwise assume. "Master of the workhouse, young man!"

"You have the same eye to your own interest, that you always had, I doubt not?" resumed the stranger, looking keenly into Mr. Bumble's eyes, as he raised them in astonishment at the question. "Don't scruple to answer freely, man. I know you pretty well, you see."

"I suppose, a married man," replied Mr. Bumble, shading his eyes with his hand, and surveying the stranger, from head to foot, in evident perplexity, "is not more averse to turning an honest penny when he can, than a single one. Porochial officers are not so well paid that they can afford to refuse any little extra fee, when it comes to them in a civil and proper manner."

1. From Shakespeare, *Othello* 3.3.351.

The stranger smiled, and nodded his head again: as much as to say, he had not mistaken his man; then rang the bell.

"Fill this glass again," he said, handing Mr. Bumble's empty tumbler to the landlord. "Let it be strong and hot. You like it so, I suppose?"

"Not too strong," replied Mr. Bumble, with a delicate cough.

"You understand what that means, landlord!" said the stranger, drily.

The host smiled, disappeared, and shortly afterwards returned with a steaming jorum:[2] of which, the first gulp brought the water into Mr. Bumble's eyes.

"Now listen to me," said the stranger, after closing the door and window. "I came down to this place, to-day, to find you out; and, by one of those chances which the devil throws in the way of his friends sometimes, you walked into the very room I was sitting in, while you were uppermost in my mind. I want some information from you. I don't ask you to give it for nothing, slight as it is. Put up that, to begin with."

As he spoke, he pushed a couple of sovereigns across the table to his companion; carefully, as though unwilling that the chinking of money should be heard without. When Mr. Bumble had scrupulously examined the coins, to see that they were genuine: and had put them up, with much satisfaction, in his waistcoat-pocket: he went on;

"Carry your memory back—let me see—twelve years, last winter."

"It's a long time," said Mr. Bumble. "Very good. I've done it."

"The scene, the workhouse."

"Good!"

"And the time, night."

"Yes."

"And the place, the crazy hole, wherever it was, in which miserable drabs brought forth the life and health so often denied to themselves; gave birth to puling children for the parish to rear; and hid their shame, rot 'em, in the grave!"

"The lying-in room, I suppose?" said Mr. Bumble, not quite following the stranger's excited description.

"Yes," said the stranger. "A boy was born there."

"A many boys," observed Mr. Bumble, shaking his head, despondingly.

"A murrain[3] on the young devils!" cried the stranger; "I speak of one; a meek-looking, pale-faced hound, who was apprenticed down here, to a coffin-maker: I wish he had made his coffin, and screwed his body in it: and who afterwards ran away to London, as it was supposed."

"Why, you mean Oliver! Young Twist!" said Mr. Bumble; "I remember him, of course. There was n't a obstinater young rascal——"

"It's not of him I want to hear; I've heard enough of him," said the stranger, stopping Mr. Bumble in the very outset of a tirade on the

2. A large drinking bowl.
3. Pestilence.

subject of poor Oliver's vices. "It's of a woman; the hag that nursed his mother. Where is she?"

"Where is she?" said Mr. Bumble, whom the gin-and-water had rendered facetious. "It would be hard to tell. There's no midwifery there, whichever place she's gone to; so I suppose she's out of employment any way."

"What do you mean?" demanded the stranger, sternly.

"That she died last winter," rejoined Mr. Bumble.

The man looked fixedly at him when he had given this information, and although he did not withdraw his eyes for some time afterwards, his gaze gradually became vacant and abstracted, and he seemed lost in thought. For some time, he appeared doubtful whether he ought to be relieved or disappointed by the intelligence; but at length he breathed more freely: and withdrawing his eyes, observed that it was no great matter. With that, he rose, as if to depart.

Mr. Bumble was cunning enough; and he at once saw that an opportunity was opened, for the lucrative disposal of some secret in the possession of his better half. He well remembered the night of old Sally's death, which the occurrences of that day had given him good reason to recollect, as the occasion on which he had proposed to Mrs. Corney; and although that lady had never confided to him the disclosure of which she had been the solitary witness, he had heard enough to know that it related to something that had occurred in the old woman's attendance, as workhouse nurse, upon the young mother of Oliver Twist. Hastily calling this circumstance to mind, he informed the stranger, with an air of mystery, that one woman had been closeted with the old harridan shortly before she died; and that she could, as he had reason to believe, throw some light on the subject of his inquiry.

"How can I find her?" said the stranger, thrown off his guard; and plainly shewing that all his fears (whatever they were) were aroused afresh by the intelligence.

"Only through me," rejoined Mr. Bumble.

"When?" cried the stranger, hastily.

"To-morrow," rejoined Bumble.

"At nine in the evening," said the stranger, producing a scrap of paper, and writing down upon it, an obscure address by the water-side, in characters that betrayed his agitation; "at nine in the evening, bring her to me there. I needn't tell you to be secret. It's your interest."

With these words, he led the way to the door: after stopping to pay for the liquor that had been drunk; and shortly remarking that their roads were different, departed, without more ceremony than an emphatic repetition of the hour of appointment for the following night.

On glancing at the address, the parochial functionary observed that it contained no name. The stranger had not gone far, so he made after him to ask it.

"Who's that?" cried the man, turning quickly round, as Bumble touched him on the arm. "Following me!"

"Only to ask a question," said the other, pointing to the scrap of paper. "What name am I to ask for?"

"Monks!" rejoined the man; and strode, hastily, away.

Chapter XXXVIII.

CONTAINING AN ACCOUNT OF WHAT PASSED BETWEEN MR. AND MRS.
BUMBLE, AND MONKS, AT THEIR NOCTURNAL INTERVIEW.

It was a dull, close, overcast summer evening: and the clouds, which had been threatening all day, spread out in a dense and sluggish mass of vapour, already yielded large drops of rain, and seemed to presage a violent thunder-storm: when Mr. and Mrs. Bumble, turning out of the main street of the town, directed their course towards a scattered little colony of ruinous houses, distant from it some mile and a-half, or thereabouts, and erected on a low unwholesome swamp, bordering upon the river.

They were both wrapped in old and shabby outer garments, which might, perhaps, serve the double purpose of protecting their persons from the rain, and sheltering them from observation. The husband carried a lantern, from which, however, no light yet shone; and trudged on, a few paces in front, as though—the way being dirty—to give his wife the benefit of treading in his heavy foot-prints. They went on, in profound silence; every now and then, Mr. Bumble relaxed his pace, and turned his head as if to make sure that his helpmate was following; then, discovering that she was close at his heels, he mended his rate of walking, and proceeded, at a considerable increase of speed, towards their place of destination.

This was far from being a place of doubtful character; for it had long been known as the residence of none but low and desperate ruffians, who, under various pretences of living by their labour, subsisted chiefly on plunder and crime. It was a collection of mere hovels: some hastily built with loose bricks: others of old worm-eaten ship timber: jumbled together without any attempt at order or arrangement, and planted, for the most part, within a few feet of the river's bank. A few leaky boats drawn up on the mud, and made fast to the dwarf wall which skirted it: and here and there an oar or coil of rope: appeared, at first, to indicate that the inhabitants of these miserable cottages pursued some avocation on the river; but a glance at the shattered and useless condition of the articles thus displayed, would have led a passer-by, without much difficulty, to the conjecture that they were disposed there, rather for the preservation of appearances than with any view to their being actually employed.

In the heart of this cluster of huts; and skirting the river, which its upper stories overhung; stood a large building, formerly used as a manufactory of some kind: and which had, in its day, probably furnished employment to the inhabitants of the surrounding tenements. But it had long since gone to ruin. The rat, the worm, and the action of the damp, had weakened and rotted the piles on which it stood; and a considerable portion of the building had already sunk down into the water beneath; while the remainder, tottering and bending over the dark stream, seemed to wait a favourable opportunity of following its old companion, and involving itself in the same fate.

It was before this ruinous building that the worthy couple paused, as the first peal of distant thunder reverberated in the air, and the rain commenced pouring violently down.

"The place should be somewhere here," said Bumble, consulting a scrap of paper he held in his hand.

"Halloa there!" cried a voice from above.

Following the sound, Mr. Bumble raised his head; and descried a man looking out of a door, breast-high, on the second story.

"Stand still, a minute," cried the voice; "I'll be with you directly." With which the head disappeared, and the door closed.

"Is that the man?" asked Mr. Bumble's good lady.

Mr. Bumble nodded in the affirmative.

"Then, mind what I told you," said the matron; "and be careful to say as little as you can, or you'll betray us at once."

Mr. Bumble, who had eyed the building with very rueful looks, was apparently about to express some doubts relative to the advisability of proceeding any farther with the enterprise just then, when he was prevented by the appearance of Monks: who opened a small door, near which they stood, and beckoned them inwards.

"Come!" he cried impatiently, stamping his foot upon the ground. "Don't keep me here!"

The woman, who had hesitated at first, walked boldly in, without any further invitation. Mr. Bumble, who was ashamed or afraid to lag behind, followed: obviously very ill at his ease, and with scarcely any of that remarkable dignity which was usually his chief characteristic.

"What the devil made you stand lingering there, in the wet?" said Monks, turning round, and addressing Bumble, after he had bolted the door behind them.

"We—we were only cooling ourselves," stammered Bumble, looking apprehensively about him.

"Cooling yourselves!" retorted Monks. "Not all the rain that ever fell, or ever will fall, will put as much of hell's fire out, as a man can carry about with him. You won't cool yourself so easily; don't think it!"

With this agreeable speech, Monks turned short upon the matron, and bent his fierce gaze upon her, till even she, who was not easily cowed, was fain to withdraw her eyes, and turn them towards the ground.

"This is the woman, is it?" demanded Monks.

"Hem! That is the woman," replied Mr. Bumble, mindful of his wife's caution.

"You think women never can keep secrets, I suppose?" said the matron, interposing, and returning, as she spoke, the searching look of Monks.

"I know they will always keep *one* till it's found out," said Monks contemptuously.

"And what may that be?" asked the matron in the same tone.

"The loss of their own good name," replied Monks. "So, by the same rule, if a woman's a party to a secret that might hang or transport her, I'm not afraid of her telling it to anybody; not I. Do you understand me?"

"No," rejoined the matron, slightly colouring as she spoke.

"Of course you don't!" said Monks. "How should you?"

Bestowing something half-way between a smile and a scowl upon his two companions, and again beckoning them to follow him, the man hastened across the apartment, which was of considerable extent, but low in the roof. He was preparing to ascend a steep staircase, or rather ladder, leading to another floor of warehouses above: when a bright flash of lightning streamed down the aperture, and a peal of thunder followed, which shook the crazy building to its centre.

"Hear it!" he cried, shrinking back. "Hear it! Rolling and crashing on as if it echoed through a thousand caverns where the devils were hiding from it. I hate the sound!"

He remained silent for a few moments; and then, removing his hands suddenly from his face, showed, to the unspeakable discomposure of Mr. Bumble, that it was much distorted, and discoloured.

"These fits come over me, now and then," said Monks, observing his alarm; "and thunder sometimes brings them on. Don't mind me now; it's all over for this once."

Thus speaking, he led the way up the ladder; and hastily closing the window-shutter of the room into which it led, lowered a lantern which hung at the end of a rope and pulley passed through one of the heavy beams in the ceiling: and which cast a dim light upon an old table and three chairs that were placed beneath it.

"Now," said Monks, when they had all three seated themselves, "the sooner we come to our business, the better for all. The woman knows what it is; does she?"

The question was addressed to Bumble; but his wife anticipated the reply, by intimating that she was perfectly acquainted with it.

"He is right in saying that you were with this hag the night she died; and that she told you something—"

"About the mother of the boy you named," replied the matron interrupting him. "Yes."

"The first question is, of what nature was her communication?" said Monks.

"That's the second," observed the woman with much deliberation. "The first is, what may the communication be worth?"

"Who the devil can tell that, without knowing of what kind it is?" asked Monks.

"Nobody better than you, I am persuaded," answered Mrs. Bumble: who did not want for spirit, as her yokefellow could abundantly testify.

"Humph!" said Monks significantly, and with a look of eager inquiry; "there may be money's worth to get, eh?"

"Perhaps there may," was the composed reply.

"Something that was taken from her," said Monks. "Something that she wore. Something that—"

"You had better bid," interrupted Mrs. Bumble. "I have heard enough, already, to assure me that you are the man I ought to talk to."

Mr. Bumble, who had not yet been admitted by his better half into any greater share of the secret than he had originally possessed, listened to this dialogue with outstretched neck and distended eyes: which he directed towards his wife and Monks, by turns, in undisguised astonishment; increased, if possible, when the latter sternly demanded what sum was required for the disclosure.

"What's it worth to you?" asked the woman, as collectedly as before.

"It may be nothing; it may be twenty pounds," replied Monks. "Speak out, and let me know which."

"Add five pounds to the sum you have named; give me five-and-twenty pounds in gold," said the woman; "and I'll tell you all I know. Not before."

"Five-and-twenty pounds!" exclaimed Monks, drawing back.

"I spoke as plainly as I could," replied Mrs. Bumble. "It's not a large sum, either."

"Not a large sum for a paltry secret, that may be nothing when it's told!" cried Monks impatiently; "and which has been lying dead for twelve years past, or more!"

"Such matters keep well, and, like good wine, often double their value in course of time," answered the matron, still preserving the resolute indifference she had assumed. "As to lying dead, there are those who will lie dead for twelve thousand years to come, or twelve million, for anything you or I know, who will tell strange tales at last!"

"What if I pay it for nothing?" asked Monks, hesitating.

"You can easily take it away again," replied the matron. "I am but a woman; alone here; and unprotected."

"Not alone, my dear, nor unprotected neither," submitted Mr. Bumble, in a voice tremulous with fear; "*I* am here, my dear. And besides," said Mr. Bumble, his teeth chattering as he spoke, "Mr. Monks is too much of a gentleman to attempt any violence on parochial persons. Mr. Monks is aware that I am not a young man, my dear, and also that I am a little run to seed, as I may say; but he has heerd: I say I have no doubt Mr. Monks has heerd, my dear: that I am a very determined officer, with very uncommon strength, if I'm once roused. I only want a little rousing; that's all."

As Mr. Bumble spoke, he made a melancholy feint of grasping his lantern with fierce determination; and plainly showed, by the alarmed expression of every feature, that he *did* want a little rousing, and not a little, prior to making any very warlike demonstration: unless, indeed, against paupers, or other person or persons trained down for the purpose.

"You are a fool," said Mrs. Bumble, in reply; "and had better hold your tongue."

"He had better have cut it out, before he came, if he can't speak in a lower tone," said Monks, grimly. "So! He's your husband, eh?"

"He my husband!" tittered the matron, parrying the question.

"I thought as much, when you came in," rejoined Monks, marking the angry glance which the lady darted at her spouse as she spoke. "So much the better; I have less hesitation in dealing with two people, when I find that there's only one will between them. I'm in earnest. See here!"

He thrust his hand into a side-pocket; and producing a canvas bag, told out twenty-five sovereigns on the table, and pushed them over to the woman.

"Now," he said, "gather them up; and when this cursed peal of thunder, which I feel is coming up to break over the house-top, is gone, let's hear your story."

The thunder: which seemed in fact much nearer, and to shiver and break almost over their heads: having subsided, Monks, raising his face from the table, bent forward to listen to what the woman should say. The faces of the three nearly touched, as the two men leant over the small table in their eagerness to hear, and the woman also leant forward to render her whisper audible. The sickly rays of the suspended lantern falling directly upon them, aggravated the paleness and anxiety of their countenances: which, encircled by the deepest gloom and darkness, looked ghastly in the extreme.

"When this woman, that we called old Sally, died," the matron began, "she and I were alone."

"Was there no one bye!" asked Monks, in the same hollow whisper; "no sick wretch or idiot in some other bed? No one who could hear, and might, by possibility, understand?"

"Not a soul," replied the woman; "we were alone. *I* stood alone beside the body when death came over it."

"Good," said Monks, regarding her attentively. "Go on."

"She spoke of a young creature," resumed the matron, "who had brought a child into the world some years before; not merely in the same room; but in the same bed in which she then lay dying."

"Ay?" said Monks, with quivering lip, and glancing over his shoulder. "Blood! How things come about!"

"The child was the one you named to him last night," said the matron, nodding carelessly towards her husband; "the mother this nurse had robbed."

"In life?" asked Monks.

"In death," replied the woman, with something like a shudder. "She stole from the corpse, when it had hardly turned to one, that which the dead mother had prayed her, with her last breath, to keep for the infant's sake."

"She sold it?" cried Monks, with desperate eagerness; "did she sell it? Where? When? To whom? How long before?"

"As she told me, with great difficulty, that she had done this," said the matron; "she fell back and died."

"Without saying more?" cried Monks, in a voice which, from its very suppression, seemed only the more furious. "It's a lie! I'll not be played with. She said more. I'll tear the life out of you both, but I'll know what it was."

"She didn't utter another word," said the woman, to all appearance unmoved (as Mr. Bumble was very far from being) by the strange man's violence; "but she clutched my gown, violently, with one hand, which was partly closed; and when I saw that she was dead, and so removed the hand by force, I found it clasped a scrap of dirty paper."

"Which contained—" interposed Monks, stretching forward.

"Nothing," replied the woman; "it was a pawnbroker's duplicate."[1]

"For what?" demanded Monks.

"In good time I'll tell you," said the woman. "I judge that she had kept the trinket, for some time, in the hope of turning it to better account; and then, had pawned it; and had saved or scraped together, money to pay the pawnbroker's interest year by year, and prevent its running out; so that if anything came of it, it could still be redeemed. Nothing had come of it; and, as I tell you, she died with the scrap of paper, all worn and tattered, in her hand. The time was out in two days; I thought something might one day come of it too; and so redeemed the pledge."

"Where is it now?" asked Monks quickly.

"*There*," replied the woman. And, as if glad to be relieved of it, she hastily threw upon the table, a small kid[2] bag scarcely large enough for

1. Receipt.
2. Leather made from the skin of a young goat.

a French watch, which Monks pouncing upon, tore open with trembling hands. It contained a little gold locket: in which were two locks of hair, and a plain gold wedding-ring.

"It has the word 'Agnes' engraved on the inside," said the woman. "There is a blank left for the surname; and then follows the date, which is within a year before the child was born. I found out that."

"And this is all?" said Monks, after a close and eager scrutiny of the contents of the little packet.

"All," replied the woman.

Mr. Bumble drew a long breath, as if he were glad to find that the story was over, and no mention made of taking the five-and-twenty pounds back again; and now, he took courage to wipe off the perspiration, which had been tickling over his nose, unchecked, during the whole of the previous dialogue.

"I know nothing of the story, beyond what I can guess at," said his wife, addressing Monks, after a short silence; "and I want to know nothing; for it's safer not. But I may ask you two questions, may I?"

"You may ask," said Monks, with some show of surprise; "but whether I answer or not is another question."

"—Which makes three," observed Mr. Bumble, essaying a stroke of facetiousness.

"Is that what you expected to get from me?" demanded the matron.

"It is," replied Monks. "The other question?"

"What you propose to do with it? Can it be used against me?"

"Never," rejoined Monks; "nor against me either. See here! But don't move a step forward, or your life's not worth a bulrush!"[3]

With these words, he suddenly wheeled the table aside, and pulling an iron ring in the boarding, threw back a large trap-door, which opened close at Mr. Bumble's feet, and caused that gentleman to retire several paces backward, with great precipitation.

"Look down," said Monks, lowering the lantern into the gulf. "Don't fear me. I could have let you down, quietly enough, when you were seated over it, if that had been my game."

Thus encouraged, the matron drew near to the brink; and even Mr. Bumble himself, impelled by curiosity, ventured to do the same. The turbid water, swollen by the heavy rain, was rushing rapidly on below; and all other sounds were lost in the noise of its plashing and eddying, against the green and slimy piles. There had once been a water mill beneath; and the tide, foaming and chafing round the few rotten stakes, and fragments of machinery that yet remained, seemed to dart onward, with a new impulse, when freed from the obstacles which had unavailingly attempted to stem its headlong course.

3. A fragile reed.

"If you flung a man's body down there, where would it be to-morrow morning?" said Monks, swinging the lantern to and fro in the dark well.

"Twelve miles down the river, and cut to pieces besides," replied Bumble, recoiling at the very thought.

Monks drew the little packet from his breast, where he had hurriedly thrust it; and tying it to a leaden weight, which had formed a part of some pulley, and was lying on the floor, dropped it into the stream. It fell straight, and true as a die; clove the water with a scarcely audible splash; and was gone.

The three looking into each other's faces, seemed to breathe more freely.

"There!" said Monks, closing the trap-door, which fell heavily back into its former position. "If the sea ever gives up its dead, as books say it will, it will keep its gold and silver to itself, and that trash among it. We have nothing more to say, and may break up our pleasant party."

"By all means," observed Mr. Bumble, with great alacrity.

"You'll keep a quiet tongue in your head; will you?" said Monks, with a threatening look. "I am not afraid of your wife."

"You may depend upon me, young man," answered Mr. Bumble, bowing himself gradually towards the ladder, with excessive politeness. "On every body's account, young man; on my own, you know, Mr. Monks."

"I am glad, for your sake, to hear it," remarked Monks. "Light your lantern! And get away from here, as fast as you can."

It was fortunate that the conversation terminated at this point, or Mr. Bumble, who had bowed himself to within six inches of the ladder, would infallibly have pitched headlong into the room below. He lighted his lantern from that which Monks had detached from the rope, and now carried in his hand; and, making no effort to prolong the discourse, descended in silence: followed by his wife. Monks brought up the rear, after pausing on the steps to satisfy himself that there were no other sounds to be heard, than the beating of the rain without, and the rushing of the water.

They traversed the lower room, slowly, and with caution; for Monks started at every shadow; and Mr. Bumble, holding his lantern a foot above the ground, walked not only with remarkable care, but with a marvellously light step for a gentleman of his figure: looking nervously about him for hidden trap-doors. The gate at which they had entered, was softly unfastened and opened by Monks; and, merely exchanging a nod with their mysterious acquaintance, the married couple emerged into the wet and darkness outside.

They were no sooner gone, than Monks, who appeared to entertain an invincible repugnance to being left alone, called to a boy who had been hidden somewhere below; and bidding him go first, and bear the light, returned to the chamber he had just quitted.

Chapter XXXIX.

INTRODUCES SOME RESPECTABLE CHARACTERS WITH WHOM THE READER
IS ALREADY ACQUAINTED, AND SHOWS HOW MONKS AND THE JEW LAID
THEIR WORTHY HEADS TOGETHER.

On the evening following that upon which the three worthies mentioned in the last chapter, disposed of their little matter of business as
therein narrated, Mr. William Sikes, awakening from a nap, drowsily
growled forth an inquiry what time of night it was.

The room in which Mr. Sikes propounded this question, was not one
of those he had tenanted, previous to the Chertsey expedition, although
it was in the same quarter of the town, and was situated at no great
distance from his former lodgings. It was not, in appearance, so desirable
a habitation as his old quarters: being a mean and badly-furnished apartment, of very limited size: lighted only by one small window in the
shelving roof, and abutting on a close and dirty lane. Nor were there
wanting other indications of the good gentleman's having gone down in
the world of late; for a great scarcity of furniture, and total absence of
comfort, together with the disappearance of all such small moveables
as spare clothes and linen, bespoke a state of extreme poverty; while the
meagre and attenuated condition of Mr. Sikes himself would have fully
confirmed these symptoms, if they had stood in any need of corrob-
oration.

The housebreaker was lying on the bed, wrapped in his white great-
coat, by way of dressing-gown, and displaying a set of features in no
degree improved by the cadaverous hue of illness, and the addition of
a soiled nightcap, and a stiff, black beard of a week's growth. The dog
sat at the bedside: now eyeing his master with a wistful look, and now
pricking his ears, and uttering a low growl as some noise in the street,
or in the lower part of the house, attracted his attention. Seated by the
window, busily engaged in patching an old waistcoat which formed a
portion of the robber's ordinary dress, was a female: so pale and reduced
with watching and privation, that there would have been considerable
difficulty in recognising her as the same Nancy who has already figured
in this tale, but for the voice in which she replied to Mr. Sikes's question.

"Not long gone seven," said the girl. "How do you feel to-night, Bill?"

"As weak as water," replied Mr. Sikes, with an imprecation on his
eyes and limbs. "Here; lend us a hand; and let me get off this thundering
bed, anyhow."

Illness had not improved Mr. Sikes's temper; for, as the girl raised
him up, and led him to a chair, he muttered various curses on her
awkwardness: and struck her.

"Whining, are you?" said Sikes. "Come! Don't stand snivelling there.

If you can't do anything better than that, cut off altogether. D' ye hear me?"

"I hear you," replied the girl, turning her face aside, and forcing a laugh. "What fancy have you got in your head now?"

"Oh! you've thought better of it, have you?" growled Sikes, marking the tear which trembled in her eye. "All the better for you, you have."

"Why, you don't mean to say, you'd be hard upon me to-night, Bill," said the girl, laying her hand upon his shoulder.

"No!" cried Mr. Sikes. "Why not?"

"Such a number of nights," said the girl, with a touch of woman's tenderness, which communicated something like sweetness of tone, even to her voice; "such a number of nights as I've been patient with you, nursing and caring for you, as if you had been a child: and this the first that I've seen you like yourself; you wouldn't have served me as you did just now, if you'd thought of that, would you? Come, come; say you wouldn't."

"Well, then," rejoined Mr. Sikes. "I wouldn't. Why, damme, now, the girl's whining again!"

"It's nothing," said the girl, throwing herself into a chair. "Don't you seem to mind me. It'll soon be over."

"What'll be over?" demanded Mr. Sikes in a savage voice. "What foolery are you up to, now, again? Get up, and bustle about, and don't come over me with your woman's nonsense."

At any other time, this remonstrance, and the tone in which it was delivered, would have had the desired effect; but the girl being really weak and exhausted, dropped her head over the back of the chair, and fainted, before Mr. Sikes could get out a few of the appropriate oaths with which, on similar occasions, he was accustomed to garnish his threats. Not knowing, very well, what to do, in this uncommon emergency; for Miss Nancy's hysterics were usually of that violent kind which the patient fights and struggles out of, without much assistance; Mr. Sikes tried a little blasphemy: and finding that mode of treatment wholly ineffectual, called for assistance.

"What's the matter here, my dear?" said the Jew, looking in.

"Lend a hand to the girl, can't you?" replied Sikes impatiently. "Don't stand chattering and grinning at me!"

With an exclamation of surprise, Fagin hastened to the girl's assistance, while Mr. John Dawkins (otherwise the Artful Dodger), who had followed his venerable friend into the room, hastily deposited on the floor a bundle with which he was laden; and snatching a bottle from the grasp of Master Charles Bates who came close at his heels, uncorked it in a twinkling with his teeth, and poured a portion of its contents down the patient's throat: previously taking a taste, himself, to prevent mistakes.

"Give her a whiff of fresh air with the bellows, Charley," said Mr.

Dawkins; "and you slap her hands, Fagin, while Bill undoes the petticuts."

These united restoratives, administered with great energy: especially that department consigned to Master Bates, who appeared to consider his share in the proceedings, a piece of unexampled pleasantry: were not long in producing the desired effect. The girl gradually recovered her senses; and, staggering to a chair by the bedside, hid her face upon the pillow: leaving Mr. Sikes to confront the new-comers, in some astonishment at their unlooked-for appearance.

"Why, what evil wind has blowed you here?" he asked of Fagin.

"No evil wind at all, my dear," replied the Jew; "for evil winds blow nobody any good; and I've brought something good with me, that you'll be glad to see. Dodger, my dear, open the bundle; and give Bill the little trifles that we spent all our money on, this morning."

In compliance with Mr. Fagin's request, the Artful untied his bundle, which was of large size, and formed of an old tablecloth; and handed the articles it contained, one by one, to Charley Bates: who placed them on the table, with various encomiums on their rarity and excellence.

"Sitch a rabbit pie, Bill," exclaimed that young gentleman, disclosing to view a huge pasty; "sitch delicate creeturs, with sitch tender limbs, Bill, that the wery bones melt in your mouth, and there's no occasion to pick 'em; half a pound of seven and sixpenny green,[1] so precious strong that if you mix it with biling water, it'll go nigh to blow the lid of the tea-pot off; a pound and a half of moist sugar that the niggers didn't work at all, at, afore they got it up, to sitch a pitch of goodness —oh no! Two half-quartern brans; pound of best fresh; piece of double Glo'ster; and, to wind up all, some of the rightest sort[2] you ever lushed!"

Uttering this last panegyric, Master Bates produced, from one of his extensive pockets, a full-sized wine-bottle, carefully corked; while Mr. Dawkins, at the same instant, poured out a wine-glassful of raw spirits from the bottle he carried: which the invalid tossed down his throat without a moment's hesitation.

"Ah!" said the Jew, rubbing his hands with great satisfaction. "You'll do, Bill; you'll do now."

"Do!" exclaimed Mr. Sikes; "I might have been done for, twenty times over, afore you'd have done anything to help me. What do you mean by leaving a man in this state, three weeks and more, you false-hearted wagabond?"

"Only hear him, boys!" said the Jew, shrugging his shoulders. "And us come to bring him all these beau-ti-ful things."

"The things is well enough in their way," observed Mr. Sikes: a little soothed as he glanced over the table; "but what have you got to say for

1. Tea leaves.
2. Liquor. "Two half-quartern brans": small loaves of coarse bread. "Fresh": butter. "Double Glo'ster": cheese.

yourself, why you should leave me here, down in the mouth, health, blunt,[3] and everything else; and take no more notice of me, all this mortal time, than if I was that 'ere dog.—Drive him down, Charley!"

"I never see such a jolly dog as that," cried Master Bates, doing as he was desired. "Smelling the grub like a old lady a going to market! He'd make his fortun on the stage that dog would, and rewive the drayma[4] besides."

"Hold your din," cried Sikes, as the dog retreated under the bed: still growling angrily. "What have you got to say for yourself, you withered old fence,[5] eh?"

"I was away from London, a week and more, my dear, on a plant,"[6] replied the Jew.

"And what about the other fortnight?" demanded Sikes. "What about the other fortnight that you've left me lying here, like a sick rat in his hole?"

"I couldn't help it, Bill," replied the Jew. "I can't go into a long explanation before company; but I couldn't help it, upon my honour."

"Upon your what?" growled Sikes, with excessive disgust. "Here! Cut me off a piece of that pie, one of you boys, to take the taste of that out of my mouth, or it'll choke me dead."

"Don't be out of temper, my dear," urged the Jew submissively. "I have never forgot you, Bill; never once."

"No! I'll pound it that you han't," replied Sikes, with a bitter grin. "You've been scheming and plotting away, every hour that I've laid shivering and burning here; and Bill was to do this; and Bill was to do that; and Bill was to do it all, dirt cheap, as soon as he got well: and was quite poor enough for your work! If it hadn't been for the girl, I might have died."

"There now, Bill," remonstrated the Jew, eagerly catching at the word. "If it hadn't been for the girl! Who but poor ould Fagin was the means of your having such a handy girl about you?"

"He says true enough there!" said Nancy, coming hastily forward. "Let him be; let him be."

Nancy's appearance gave a new turn to the conversation; for the boys, receiving a sly wink from the wary old Jew, began to ply her with liquor: of which, however, she partook very sparingly; while Fagin, assuming an unusual flow of spirits, gradually brought Mr. Sikes into a better temper, by affecting to regard his threats as a little pleasant banter; and, moreover, by laughing very heartily at one or two rough jokes, which, after repeated applications to the spirit-bottle, he condescended to make.

3. Money.
4. Revive the drama.
5. Dealer in stolen goods.
6. A criminal scheme.

"It's all very well," said Mr. Sikes; "but I must have some blunt from you to-night."

"I haven't a piece of coin about me," replied the Jew.

"Then you've got lots at home," retorted Sikes; "and I must have some from there."

"Lots!" cried the Jew, holding up his hands. "I haven't so much as would——"

"I don't know how much you've got, and I dare say you hardly know yourself, as it would take a pretty long time to count it," said Sikes; "but I must have some to-night; and that's flat."

"Well, well!" said the Jew, with a sigh, "I'll send the Artful round presently."

"You won't do nothing of the kind," rejoined Mr. Sikes. "The Artful's a deal too artful, and would forget to come, or lose his way, or get dodged by traps and so be perwented, or anything for an excuse, if you put him up to it. Nancy shall go to the ken and fetch it, to make all sure; and I'll lie down and have a snoose while she's gone."

After a great deal of haggling and squabbling, the Jew beat down the amount of the required advance from five pounds to three pounds four and sixpence: protesting with many solemn asseverations that that would only leave him eighteenpence to keep house with; Mr. Sikes sullenly remarking that if he couldn't get any more he must be content with that, Nancy prepared to accompany him home; while the Dodger and Master Bates put the eatables in the cupboard. The Jew then, taking leave of his affectionate friend, returned homewards, attended by Nancy and the boys: Mr. Sikes, meanwhile, flinging himself on the bed, and composing himself to sleep away the time until the young lady's return.

In due course, they arrived at the Jew's abode, where they found Toby Crackit and Mr. Chitling intent upon their fifteenth game at cribbage, which it is scarcely necessary to say the latter gentleman lost; and with it, his fifteenth and last sixpence: much to the amusement of his young friends. Mr. Crackit, apparently somewhat ashamed at being found relaxing himself with a gentleman so much his inferior in station and mental endowments, yawned, and inquiring after Sikes, took up his hat to go.

"Has nobody been, Toby?" asked the Jew.

"Not a living leg," answered Mr. Crackit, pulling up his collar; "it's been as dull as swipes.[7] You ought to stand something handsome, Fagin, to recompense me for keeping house so long. Damme, I'm as flat as a juryman; and should have gone to sleep, as fast as Newgate, if I hadn't had the good natur' to amuse this youngster. Horrid dull, I'm blessed if I an't!"

7. Flat beer.

With these, and other ejaculations of the same kind, Mr. Toby Crackit swept up his winnings, and crammed them into his waistcoat pocket with a haughty air, as though such small pieces of silver were wholly beneath the consideration of a man of his figure; this done, he swaggered out of the room, with so much elegance and gentility, that Mr. Chitling, bestowing numerous admiring glances on his legs and boots till they were out of sight, assured the company that he considered his acquaintance cheap at fifteen sixpences an interview, and that he didn't value his losses the snap of his little finger.

"Wot a rum chap you are, Tom!" said Master Bates, highly amused by this declaration.

"Not a bit of it," replied Mr. Chitling. "Am I Fagin?"

"A very clever fellow, my dear," said the Jew, patting him on the shoulder, and winking to his other pupils.

"And Mr. Crackit *is* a heavy swell;[8] an't he Fagin?" asked Tom.

"No doubt at all of that, my dear," replied the Jew.

"And it *is* a creditable thing to have his acquaintance; an't it Fagin?" pursued Tom.

"Very much so, indeed, my dear," replied the Jew. "They're only jealous, Tom, because he won't give it to them."

"Ah!" cried Tom, triumphantly, "that's where it is! He has cleaned me out. But I can go and earn some more, when I like; can't I Fagin?"

"To be sure you can," replied the Jew; "and the sooner you go, the better, Tom; so make up your loss at once, and don't lose any more time. Dodger! Charley! It's time you were on the lay.[9] Come! It's near ten, and nothing done yet."

In obedience to this hint, the boys, nodding to Nancy, took up their hats, and left the room; the Dodger and his vivacious friend indulging, as they went, in many witticisms at the expense of Mr. Chitling; in whose conduct, it is but justice to say, there was nothing very conspicuous or peculiar: inasmuch as there are a great number of spirited young bloods upon town, who pay a much higher price than Mr. Chitling for being seen in good society: and a great number of fine gentlemen (composing the good society aforesaid) who establish their reputation upon very much the same footing as flash Toby Crackit.

"Now," said the Jew, when they had left the room, "I'll go and get you that cash, Nancy. This is only the key of a little cupboard where I keep a few odd things the boys get, my dear. I never lock up my money, for I've got none to lock up, my dear—ha! ha! ha!—none to lock up. It's a poor trade, Nancy, and no thanks; but I'm fond of seeing the young people about me; and I bear it all; I bear it all. Hush!" he said, hastily concealing the key in his breast; "who's that? Listen!"

8. A dressy show-off.
9. On the job.

The girl, who was sitting at the table with her arms folded, appeared in no way interested in the arrival: or to care whether the person, whoever he was, came or went: until the murmur of a man's voice reached her ears. The instant she caught the sound, she tore off her bonnet and shawl, with the rapidity of lightning, and thrust them under the table. The Jew, turning round immediately afterwards, she muttered a complaint of the heat: in a tone of languor that contrasted, very remarkably, with the extreme haste and violence of this action: which, however, had been unobserved by Fagin, who had his back towards her at the time.

"Bah!" whispered the Jew, as though nettled by the interruption; "it's the man I expected before; he's coming down stairs. Not a word about the money while he's here, Nance. He won't stop long. Not ten minutes, my dear."

Laying his skinny forefinger upon his lip, the Jew carried a candle to the door, as a man's step was heard upon the stairs without. He reached it, at the same moment as the visiter, who, coming hastily into the room, was close upon the girl before he observed her.

It was Monks.

"Only one of my young people," said the Jew, observing that Monks drew back, on beholding a stranger. "Don't move, Nancy."

The girl drew closer to the table, and glancing at Monks with an air of careless levity, withdrew her eyes; but as he turned his towards the Jew, she stole another look: so keen and searching, and full of purpose, that if there had been any bystander to observe the change, he could hardly have believed the two looks to have proceeded from the same person.

"Any news?" inquired the Jew.

"Great."

"And—and—good?" asked the Jew, hesitating as though he feared to vex the other man by being too sanguine.

"Not bad, any way," replied Monks with a smile. "I have been prompt enough this time. Let me have a word with you."

The girl drew closer to the table, and made no offer to leave the room, although she could see that Monks was pointing to her. The Jew: perhaps fearing that she might say something aloud about the money, if he endeavoured to get rid of her: pointed upwards, and took Monks out of the room.

"Not that infernal hole we were in before," she could hear the man say as they went upstairs. The Jew laughed; and making some reply which did not reach her, seemed, by the creaking of the boards, to lead his companion to the second story.

Before the sound of their footsteps had ceased to echo through the house, the girl had slipped off her shoes; and drawing her gown loosely over her head, and muffling her arms in it, stood at the door, listening with breathless interest. The moment the noise ceased, she glided from the room; ascended the stairs with incredible softness and silence; and was lost in the gloom above.

The room remained deserted for a quarter of an hour or more; the girl glided back with the same unearthly tread; and, immediately afterwards, the two men were heard descending, Monks went at once into the street; and the Jew crawled up stairs again for the money. When he returned, the girl was adjusting her shawl and bonnet, as if preparing to be gone.

"Why, Nance," exclaimed the Jew, starting back as he put down the candle, "how pale you are!"

"Pale!" echoed the girl, shading her eyes with her hand, as if to look steadily at him.

"Quite horrible," said the Jew. "What have you been doing to yourself?"

"Nothing that I know of, except sitting in this close place for I don't know how long and all," replied the girl carelessly. "Come! Let me get back; that's a dear."

With a sigh for every piece of money, Fagin told the amount into her hand. They parted without more conversation, merely interchanging a "good night."

When the girl got into the open street, she sat down upon a doorstep; and seemed, for a few moments, wholly bewildered and unable to pursue her way. Suddenly, she arose; and hurrying on, in a direction quite opposite to that in which Sikes was awaiting her return, quickened her pace, until it gradually resolved into a violent run. After completely exhausting herself, she stopped to take breath; and, as if suddenly recollecting herself, and deploring her inability to do something she was bent upon, wrung her hands, and burst into tears.

It might be that her tears relieved her, or that she felt the full hopelessness of her condition; but she turned back; and hurrying with nearly as great rapidity in the contrary direction: partly to recover lost time, and partly to keep pace with the violent current of her own thoughts: soon reached the dwelling where she had left the housebreaker.

If she betrayed any agitation, when she presented herself to Mr. Sikes, he did not observe it; for merely inquiring if she had brought the money, and receiving a reply in the affirmative, he uttered a growl of satisfaction, and replacing his head upon the pillow, resumed the slumbers which her arrival had interrupted.

It was fortunate for her that the possession of money occasioned him so much employment next day in the way of eating and drinking; and withal had so beneficial an effect in smoothing down the asperities of his temper; that he had neither time nor inclination to be very critical upon her behaviour and deportment. That she had all the abstracted and nervous manner of one who is on the eve of some bold and hazardous step, which it has required no common struggle to resolve upon, would have been obvious to the lynx-eyed Jew, who would most probably have taken the alarm at once; but Mr. Sikes lacking the niceties of discrimination, and being troubled with no more subtle misgivings than those which resolve themselves into a dogged roughness of behaviour towards everybody; and being, furthermore, in an unusually amiable condition, as has been already observed; saw nothing unusual in her demeanour, and indeed, troubled himself so little about her, that, had her agitation been far more perceptible than it was, it would have been very unlikely to have awakened his suspicions.

As that day closed in, the girl's excitement increased; and, when night came on, and she sat by, watching until the housebreaker should drink himself asleep, there was an unusual paleness in her cheek, and a fire in her eye, that even Sikes observed with astonishment.

Mr. Sikes, being weak from the fever, was lying in bed, taking hot water with his gin to render it less inflammatory; and had pushed his glass towards Nancy to be replenished for the third or fourth time, when these symptoms first struck him.

"Why, burn my body!" said the man, raising himself on his hands as he stared the girl in the face. "You look like a corpse come to life again. What's the matter?"

"Matter!" replied the girl. "Nothing. What do you look at me so hard for?"

"What foolery is this?" demanded Sikes, grasping her by the arm, and shaking her roughly. "What is it? What do you mean? What are you thinking of?"

"Of many things, Bill," replied the girl, shivering, and as she did so, pressing her hands upon her eyes. "But, Lord! what odds in that?"[1]

The tone of forced gaiety in which the last words were spoken, seemed to produce a deeper impression on Sikes than the wild and rigid look which had preceded them.

"I tell you wot it is," said Sikes; "if you haven't caught the fever, and got it comin' on, now, there's something more than usual in the wind, and something dangerous, too. You're not a-going to—— No, damme! you wouldn't do that!"

"Do what?" asked the girl.

"There ain't," said Sikes, fixing his eyes upon her, and muttering the words to himself; "there ain't a stauncher-hearted gal going, or I'd have cut her throat three months ago. She's got the fever coming on; that's it."

Fortifying himself with this assurance, Sikes drained the glass to the bottom, and then, with many grumbling oaths, called for his physic.[2] The girl jumped up, with great alacrity; poured it quickly out, but with

1. What's the good of that?
2. Medicine.

her back towards him; and held the vessel to his lips, while he drank off the contents.

"Now," said the robber, "come and sit aside of me, and put on your own face; or I'll alter it so, that you won't know it again when you *do* want it."

The girl obeyed. Sikes, locking her hand in his, fell back upon the pillow: turning his eyes upon her face. They closed; opened again; closed once more; again opened. He shifted his position restlessly; and, after dozing again, and again, for two or three minutes, and as often springing up with a look of terror, and gazing vacantly about him, was suddenly stricken, as it were, while in the very attitude of rising, into a deep and heavy sleep. The grasp of his hand relaxed; the upraised arm fell languidly by his side; and he lay like one in a profound trance.

"The laudanum has taken effect at last," murmured the girl, as she rose from the bedside. "I may be too late, even now."

She hastily dressed herself in her bonnet and shawl: looking fearfully round, from time to time, as if, despite the sleeping draught, she expected every moment to feel the pressure of Sikes's heavy hand upon her shoulder; then, stooping softly over the bed, she kissed the robber's lips; and then, opening and closing the room-door with noiseless touch, hurried from the house.

A watchman was crying half-past nine, down a dark passage through which she had to pass, in gaining the main thoroughfare.

"Has it long gone the half-hour?" asked the girl.

"It'll strike the hour in another quarter," said the man: raising his lantern to her face.

"And I cannot get there, in less than an hour or more," muttered Nancy: brushing swiftly past him, and gliding rapidly down the street.

Many of the shops were already closing in the back lanes and avenues through which she tracked her way, in making from Spitalfields towards the West-End of London. The clock struck ten, increasing her impatience. She tore along the narrow pavement: elbowing the passengers from side to side; and darting almost under the horses' heads, crossed crowded streets, where clusters of persons were eagerly watching their opportunity to do the like.

"The woman is mad!" said the people, turning to look after her as she rushed away.

When she reached the more wealthy quarter of the town, the streets were comparatively deserted; and here her headlong progress excited a still greater curiosity in the stragglers whom she hurried past. Some quickened their pace behind, as though to see whither she was hastening at such an unusual rate; and a few made head upon her, and looked back: surprised at her undiminished speed; but they fell off one by one; and when she neared her place of destination, she was alone.

It was a family hotel in a quiet but handsome street near Hyde Park.

As the brilliant light of the lamp which burnt before its door, guided her to the spot, the clock struck eleven. She had loitered for a few paces as though irresolute, and making up her mind to advance; but the sound determined her, and she stepped into the hall. The porter's seat was vacant. She looked round with an air of incertitude, and advanced towards the stairs.

"Now, young woman!" said a smartly-dressed female, looking out from a door behind her, "who do you want here?"

"A lady who is stopping in this house," answered the girl.

"A lady!" was the reply, accompanied with a scornful look. "What lady?"

"Miss Maylie," said Nancy.

The young woman, who had, by this time, noted her appearance, replied only by a look of virtuous disdain; and summoned a man to answer her. To him, Nancy repeated her request.

"What name am I to say?" asked the waiter.

"It's of no use saying any," replied Nancy.

"Nor business?" said the man.

"No, nor that neither," rejoined the girl. "I must see the lady."

"Come!" said the man, pushing her towards the door. "None of this! Take yourself off."

"I shall be carried out, if I go!" said the girl violently; "and I can make that a job that two of you won't like to do. Isn't there any body here," she said, looking round, "that will see a simple message carried for a poor wretch like me?"

This appeal produced an effect on a good-tempered-faced man-cook, who with some other of the servants was looking on, and who stepped forward to interfere.

"Take it up for her, Joe; can't you?" said this person.

"What's the good?" replied the man. "You don't suppose the young lady will see such as her; do you?"

This allusion to Nancy's doubtful character, raised a vast quantity of chaste wrath in the bosoms of four housemaids, who remarked, with great fervour, that the creature was a disgrace to her sex; and strongly advocated her being thrown, ruthlessly, into the kennel.

"Do what you like with me," said the girl, turning to the men again; "but do what I ask you first, and I ask you to give this message for God Almighty's sake."

The soft-hearted cook added his intercession, and the result was that the man, who had first appeared, undertook its delivery.

"What's it to be," said the man, with one foot on the stairs.

"That a young woman earnestly asks to speak to Miss Maylie alone," said Nancy; "and that if the lady will only hear the first word she has to say, she will know whether to hear her business, or to have her turned out of doors as an impostor."

"I say," said the man, "you're coming it strong!"

"You give the message," said the girl firmly; "and let me hear the answer."

The man ran up stairs. Nancy remained, pale and almost breathless, listening with quivering lip to the very audible expressions of scorn, of which the chaste housemaids were very prolific; and of which they became still more so, when the man returned, and said the young woman was to walk up stairs.

"It's no good being proper in this world," said the first housemaid.

"Brass can do better than the gold what has stood the fire," said the second.

The third contented herself with wondering "what ladies was made of;" and the fourth took the first in a quartette of "Shameful!" with which the Dianas[3] concluded.

Regardless of all this: for she had weightier matters at heart: Nancy followed the man with trembling limbs, to a small antechamber, lighted by a lamp from the ceiling. Here he left her, and retired.

Chapter XL.

A STRANGE INTERVIEW, WHICH IS A SEQUEL TO THE LAST CHAPTER.

The girl's life had been squandered in the streets, and among the most noisome of the stews[1] and dens of London, but there was something of the woman's original nature[2] left in her still; and when she heard a light step approaching the door opposite to that by which she had entered, and thought of the wide contrast which the small room would in another moment contain, she felt burdened with the sense of her own deep shame: and shrunk as though she could scarcely bear the presence of her with whom she had sought this interview.

But struggling with these better feelings was pride,—the vice of the lowest and most debased creatures no less than of the high and self-assured. The miserable companion of thieves and ruffians, the fallen outcast of low haunts, the associate of the scourings of the jails and hulks,[3] living within the shadow of the gallows itself,—even this degraded being felt too proud to betray a feeble gleam of the womanly feeling which she thought a weakness, but which alone connected her with that humanity, of which her wasting life had obliterated so many, many traces when a very child.

3. Chaste women, after the virginal Roman goddess Diana.
1. Houses of prostitution.
2. Dickens believed in the doctrine of the moral sentiments: that human beings are born with moral inclinations and that women especially have a natural inborn propensity toward goodness.
3. Decommissioned ships used as prisons.

She raised her eyes sufficiently to observe that the figure which presented itself was that of a slight and beautiful girl; and then, bending them on the ground, tossed her head with affected carelessness as she said:

"It's a hard matter to get to see you, lady. If I had taken offence, and gone away, as many would have done, you'd have been sorry for it one day, and not without reason, either.

"I am very sorry if any one has behaved harshly to you," replied Rose. "Do not think of that. Tell me why you wished to see me. I am the person you inquired for."

The kind tone of this answer, the sweet voice, the gentle manner, the absence of any accent of haughtiness or displeasure, took the girl completely by surprise, and she burst into tears.

"Oh, lady, lady!" she said, clasping her hands passionately before her face, "if there was more like you, there would be fewer like me,—there would—there would!"

"Sit down," said Rose earnestly; "you distress me. If you are in poverty or affliction I shall be truly glad to relieve you if I can,—I shall indeed. Sit down."

"Let me stand, lady," said the girl, still weeping, "and do not speak to me so kindly till you know me better. It is growing late. Is—is—that door shut?"

"Yes," said Rose, recoiling a few steps, as if to be nearer assistance in case she should require it. "Why?"

"Because," said the girl, "I am about to put my life, and the lives of others, in your hands. I am the girl that dragged little Oliver back to old Fagin's, the Jew's, on the night he went out from the house in Pentonville."

"You!" said Rose Maylie.

"I, lady!" replied the girl. "I am the infamous creature you have heard of, that lives among the thieves, and that never from the first moment I can recollect my eyes and senses opening on London streets have known any better life, or kinder words than they have given me, so help me God! Do not mind shrinking openly from me, lady. I am younger than you would think, to look at me, but I am well used to it. The poorest women fall back, as I make my way along the crowded pavement."

"What dreadful things are these!" said Rose, involuntarily falling from her strange companion.

"Thank Heaven upon your knees, dear lady," cried the girl, "that you had friends to care for and keep you in your childhood, and that you were never in the midst of cold and hunger, and riot and drunkenness, and—and something worse than all—as I have been from my cradle; I may use the word, for the alley and the gutter were mine, as they will be my deathbed."

"I pity you!" said Rose in a broken voice. "It wrings my heart to hear you!"

"Heaven bless you for your goodness!" rejoined the girl. "If you knew what I, am sometimes, you would pity me, indeed. But I have stolen away from those who would surely murder me, if they knew I had been here, to tell you what I have overheard. Do you know a man named Monks?"

"No," said Rose.

"He knows you," replied the girl; "and knew you were here, for it was by hearing him tell the place that I found you out."

"I never heard the name," said Rose.

"Then he goes by some other amongst us," rejoined the girl, "which I more than thought before. Sometime ago, and soon after Oliver was put into your house on the night of the robbery, I—suspecting this man—listened to a conversation held between him and Fagin in the dark. I found out, from what I heard, that Monks—the man I asked you about, you know—"

"Yes," said Rose, "I understand."

"—That Monks," pursued the girl, "had seen him accidentally with two of our boys on the day we first lost him, and had known him directly to be the same child that he was watching for, though I couldn't make out why. A bargain was struck with Fagin, that if Oliver was got back he should have a certain sum; and he was to have more for making him a thief, which this Monks wanted for some purpose of his own."

"For what purpose?" asked Rose.

"He caught sight of my shadow on the wall as I listened, in the hope of finding out," said the girl; "and there are not many people besides me that could have got out of their way in time to escape discovery. But I did; and I saw him no more till last night."

"And what occurred then?"

"I'll tell you, lady. Last night he came again. Again they went up stairs, and I, wrapping myself up so that my shadow should not betray me, again listened at the door. The first words I heard Monks say were these: 'So the only proofs of the boy's identity lie at the bottom of the river, and the old hag that received them from the mother is rotting in her coffin.' They laughed, and talked of his success in doing this; and Monks, talking on about the boy, and getting very wild, said, that though he had got the young devil's money safely now, he'd rather have had it the other way; for, what a game it would have been to have brought down the boast of the father's will, by driving him through every jail in town, and then hawling him up for some capital felony, which Fagin could easily manage, after having made a good profit of him besides."

"What is all this!" said Rose.

"The truth, lady, though it comes from my lips," replied the girl. "Then, he said, with oaths common enough in my ears, but strange to yours, that if he could gratify his hatred by taking the boy's life without bringing his own neck in danger, he would; but, as he couldn't, he'd be upon the watch to meet him at every turn in life; and if he took advantage of his birth and history, he might harm him yet. 'In short Fagin,' he says, 'Jew as you are, you never laid such snares as I'll contrive for my young brother, Oliver.' "

"His brother!" exclaimed Rose.

"Those were his words," said Nancy, glancing uneasily round, as she had scarcely ceased to do, since she began to speak, for a vision of Sikes haunted her perpetually. "And more. When he spoke of you and the other lady, and said it seemed contrived by Heaven, or the devil, against him, that Oliver should come into your hands, he laughed, and said there was some comfort in that too, for how many thousands and hundreds of thousands of pounds would you not give, if you had them, to know who your two-legged spaniel was."

"You do not mean," said Rose, turning very pale, "to tell me that this was said in earnest?"

"He spoke in hard and angry earnest, if a man ever did," replied the girl, shaking her head. "He is an earnest man when his hatred is up. I know many who do worse things; but I'd rather listen to them all a dozen times, than to that Monks once. It is growing late, and I have to reach home without suspicion of having been on such an errand as this. I must get back quickly."

"But what can I do?" said Rose. "To what use can I turn this communication without you? Back! Why do you wish to return to companions you paint in such terrible colours? If you repeat this information to a gentleman whom I can summon in an instant from the next room, you can be consigned to some place of safety without half an hour's delay."

"I wish to go back," said the girl. "I must go back, because—how can I tell such things to an innocent lady like you?—because among the men I have told you of, there is one: the most desperate among them all: that I can't leave; no, not even to be saved from the life I am leading now."

"Your having interfered in this dear boy's behalf before," said Rose; "your coming here, at so great a risk, to tell me what you have heard; your manner, which convinces me of the truth of what you say; your evident contrition, and sense of shame; all lead me to believe that you might be yet reclaimed. Oh!" said the earnest girl, folding her hands as the tears coursed down her face, "do not turn a deaf ear to the entreaties of one of your own sex; the first—the first, I do believe, who ever appealed to you in the voice of pity and compassion. Do hear my words, and let me save you yet, for better things."

"Lady," cried the girl, sinking on her knees, "dear, sweet, angel lady, you *are* the first that ever blessed me with such words as these, and if I had heard them years ago, they might have turned me from a life of sin and sorrow; but it is too late—it is too late!"

"It is never too late," said Rose, "for penitence and atonement."

"It is," cried the girl, writhing in the agony of her mind; "I cannot leave him now! I could not be his death."

"Why should you be?" asked Rose.

"Nothing could save him," cried the girl. "If I told others what I have told you, and led to their being taken, he would be sure to die. He is the boldest, and has been so cruel!"

"Is it possible," cried Rose, "that for such a man as this, you can resign every future hope, and the certainty of immediate rescue? It is madness."

"I don't know what it is," answered the girl; "I only know that it is so, and not with me alone, but with hundreds of others as bad and wretched as myself. I must go back. Whether it is God's wrath for the wrong I have done, I do not know; but I am drawn back to him through every suffering and ill usage: and should be, I believe, if I knew that I was to die by his hand at last."

"What am I to do?" said Rose. "I should not let you depart from me thus."

"You should, lady, and I know you will," rejoined the girl, rising. "You will not stop my going because I have trusted in your goodness, and forced no promise from you, as I might have done."

"Of what use, then, is the communication you have made?" said Rose. "This mystery must be investigated, or how will its disclosure to me, benefit Oliver, whom you are anxious to serve?"

"You must have some kind gentleman about you that will hear it as a secret, and advise you what to do," rejoined the girl.

"But where can I find you again when it is necessary?" asked Rose. "I do not seek to know where these dreadful people live, but where will you be walking or passing at any settled period from this time?"

"Will you promise me that you will have my secret strictly kept, and come alone, or with the only other person that knows it; and that I shall not be watched or followed?" asked the girl.

"I promise you solemnly," answered Rose.

"Every Sunday night, from eleven until the clock strikes twelve," said the girl without hesitation, "I will walk on London Bridge if I am alive."

"Stay another moment," interposed Rose, as the girl moved hurriedly towards the door. "Think once again on your own condition, and the opportunity you have of escaping from it. You have a claim on me: not only as the voluntary bearer of this intelligence, but as a woman lost almost beyond redemption. Will you return to this gang of robbers, and to this man, when a word can save you? What fascination is it that can take you back, and make you cling to wickedness and misery? Oh! is there no chord in your heart that I can touch! Is there nothing left, to which I can appeal against this terrible infatuation!"

"When ladies as young, and good, and beautiful as you are," replied the girl steadily, "give away your hearts, love will carry you all lengths—even such as you, who have home, friends, other admirers, every thing to fill them. When such as I, who have no certain roof but the coffin-lid, and no friend in sickness or death but the hospital nurse, set our rotten hearts on any man, and let him fill the place that has been a blank through all our wretched lives, who can hope to cure us? Pity us, lady—pity us for having only one feeling of the woman left, and for having that turned, by a heavy judgment, from a comfort and a pride, into a new means of violence and suffering."

"You will," said Rose, after a pause, "take some money from me, which may enable you to live without dishonesty—at all events until we meet again?"

"Not a penny," replied the girl, waving her hand.

"Do not close your heart against all my efforts to help you," said Rose, stepping gently forward. "I wish to serve you indeed."

"You would serve me best, lady," replied the girl, wringing her hands, "if you could take my life at once; for I have felt more grief to think of what I am, to-night, than I ever did before, and it would be something not to die in the same hell in which I have lived. God bless you, sweet lady, and send as much happiness on your head as I have brought shame on mine!"

Thus speaking, and sobbing aloud, the unhappy creature turned away; while Rose Maylie, overpowered by this extraordinary interview, which had more the semblance of a rapid dream than an actual occurrence, sank into a chair, and endeavoured to collect her wandering thoughts.

Chapter XLI.

CONTAINING FRESH DISCOVERIES, AND SHOWING THAT SURPRISES, LIKE MISFORTUNES, SELDOM COME ALONE.

Her situation was, indeed, one of no common trial and difficulty. While she felt the most eager and burning desire to penetrate the mystery in which Oliver's history was enveloped, she could not but hold sacred the confidence which the miserable woman with whom she had just conversed, had reposed in her, as a young and guileless girl. Her words and manner had touched Rose Maylie's heart; and, mingled with her love for her young charge, and scarcely less intense in its truth and fervour, was her fond wish to win the outcast back to repentance and hope.

They only proposed remaining in London three days, prior to departing for some weeks to a distant part of the coast. It was now midnight of the first day. What course of action could she determine upon, which could be adopted in eight-and-forty hours? Or how could she postpone the journey without exciting suspicion?

Mr. Losberne was with them, and would be for the next two days; but Rose was too well acquainted with the excellent gentleman's impetuosity, and foresaw too clearly the wrath with which, in the first explosion of his indignation, he would regard the instrument of Oliver's re-capture, to trust him with the secret, when her representations in the girl's behalf could be seconded by no experienced person. These were all reasons for the greatest caution and most circumspect behaviour in communicating it to Mrs. Maylie, whose first impulse would infallibly be to hold a conference with the worthy doctor on the subject. As to resorting to any legal adviser, even if she had known how to do so, it was scarcely to be thought of, for the same reasons. Once the thought occurred to her of seeking assistance from Harry; but this awakened the recollection of their last parting, and it seemed unworthy of her to call him back, when—the tears rose to her eyes as she pursued this train of reflection—he might have by this time learnt to forget her, and to be happier away.

Disturbed by these different reflections; inclining, now to one course and then to another, and again recoiling from all, as each successive consideration presented itself to her mind; Rose passed a sleepless and anxious night. After more communing with herself next day, she arrived at the desperate conclusion of consulting Harry.

"If it be painful to him," she thought, "to come back here, how painful will it be to me! But perhaps he will not come; he may write, or he may come himself, and studiously abstain from meeting me—he did when he went away. I hardly thought he would; but it was better for us both." And here, Rose dropped the pen, and turned away, as though the very paper which was to be her messenger should not see her weep.

She had taken up the same pen, and laid it down again fifty times, and had considered and reconsidered the first line of her letter without writing the first word, when Oliver, who had been walking in the streets, with Mr. Giles for a body-guard, entered the room in such breathless haste and violent agitation, as seemed to betoken some new cause of alarm.

"What makes you look so flurried?" asked Rose, advancing to meet him.

"I hardly know how; I feel as if I should be choked," replied the boy. "Oh dear! to think that I should see him at last, and you should be able to know that I have told you all the truth!"

"I never thought you had told us anything but the truth," said Rose, soothing him. "But what is this?—of whom do you speak?"

"I have seen the gentleman," replied Oliver, scarcely able to articulate, "the gentleman who was so good to me—Mr. Brownlow, that we have so often talked about."

"Where?" asked Rose.

"Getting out of a coach," replied Oliver, shedding tears of delight, "and going into a house. I didn't speak to him—I couldn't speak to him, for he didn't see me, and I trembled so, that I was not able to go up to him. But Giles asked, for me, whether he lived there, and they said he did. Look here," said Oliver, opening a scrap of paper, "here it is; here's where he lives—I'm going there directly! Oh, dear me, dear me! what shall I do when I come to see him and hear him speak again!"

With her attention not a little distracted by these, and a great many other incoherent exclamations of joy, Rose read the address, which was Craven-street, in the Strand,[1] and very soon determined upon turning the discovery to account.

"Quick!" she said, "tell them to fetch a hackney-coach,[2] and be ready to go with me. I will take you there directly, without a minute's loss of time. I will only tell my aunt that we are going out for an hour, and be ready as soon as you are."

Oliver needed no prompting to despatch, and in little more than five minutes they were on their way to Craven-street. When they arrived there, Rose left Oliver in the coach, under pretence of preparing the old gentleman to receive him; and sending up her card by the servant, requested to see Mr. Brownlow on very pressing business. The servant soon returned, to beg that she would walk up stairs; and, following him into an upper room, Miss Maylie was presented to an elderly gentleman of benevolent appearance, in a bottle-green coat. At no great distance from whom, was seated another old gentleman, in nankeen breeches and gaiters: who did not look particularly benevolent, and who was sitting with his hands clasped on the top of a thick stick, and his chin propped thereupon.

"Dear me," said the gentleman, in the bottle-green coat, hastily rising with great politeness, "I beg your pardon, young lady—I imagined it was some importunate person who—I beg you will excuse me. Be seated, pray."

"Mr. Brownlow, I believe, sir?" said Rose, glancing from the other gentleman to the one who had spoken.

"That is my name," said the old gentleman. "This is my friend, Mr. Grimwig. Grimwig, will you leave us for a few minutes?"

"I believe," interposed Miss Maylie, "that at this period of our inter-

---

1. The main street in central London connecting the City with the borough of Westminster.
2. A four-wheeled coach for public hire, seating six, pulled by two horses.

view, I need not give that gentleman the trouble of going away. If I am correctly informed, he is cognizant of the business on which I wish to speak to you."

Mr. Brownlow inclined his head. Mr. Grimwig, who had made one very stiff bow, and risen from his chair, made another very stiff bow, and dropped into it again.

"I shall surprise you very much, I have no doubt," said Rose, naturally embarrassed; "but you once showed great benevolence and goodness to a very dear young friend of mine, and I am sure you will take an interest in hearing of him again."

"Indeed!" said Mr. Brownlow.

"Oliver Twist you knew him as," replied Rose.

The words no sooner escaped her lips, than Mr. Grimwig, who had been affecting to dip into a large book that lay on the table, upset it with a great crash, and falling back in his chair, discharged from his features every expression but one of the most unmitigated wonder, and indulged in a prolonged and vacant stare; then, as if ashamed of having betrayed so much emotion, he jerked himself, as it were, by a convulsion into his former attitude, and looking out straight before him emitted a long, deep whistle, which seemed, at last, not to be discharged on empty air, but to die away in the innermost recesses of his stomach.

Mr. Brownlow was no less surprised, although his astonishment was not expressed in the same eccentric manner. He drew his chair nearer to Miss Maylie's, and said,

"Do me the favour, my dear young lady, to leave entirely out of the question that goodness and benevolence of which you speak, and of which nobody else knows anything; and if you have it in your power to produce any evidence which will alter the unfavourable opinion I was once induced to entertain of that poor child, in Heaven's name put me in possession of it."

"A bad one! I'll eat my head if he is not a bad one," growled Mr. Grimwig, speaking by some ventriloquial power,[3] without moving a muscle of his face.

"He is a child of a noble nature and a warm heart," said Rose, colouring; "and that Power which has thought fit to try him beyond his years, has planted in his breast affections and feelings which would do honour to many who have numbered his days six times over."

"I'm only sixty-one," said Mr. Grimwig, with the same rigid face. "And, as the devil's in it if this Oliver is not twelve years old at least, I don't see the application of that remark."

"Do not heed my friend, Miss Maylie," said Mr. Brownlow; "he does not mean what he says."

"Yes, he does," growled Mr. Grimwig.

---

3. The power of a ventriloquist.

"No, he does not," said Mr. Brownlow, obviously rising in wrath as he spoke.

"He'll eat his head, if he doesn't," growled Mr. Grimwig.

"He would deserve to have it knocked off, if he does," said Mr. Brownlow.

"And he'd uncommonly like to see any man offer to do it," responded Mr. Grimwig, knocking his stick upon the floor.

Having gone thus far, the two old gentlemen severally took snuff, and afterwards shook hands, according to their invariable custom.

"Now, Miss Maylie," said Mr. Brownlow, "to return to the subject in which your humanity is so much interested. Will you let me know what intelligence you have of this poor child: allowing me to premise that I exhausted every means in my power of discovering him, and that since I have been absent from this country, my first impression that he had imposed upon me, and had been persuaded by his former associates to rob me, has been considerably shaken."

Rose, who had had time to collect her thoughts, at once related, in a few natural words, all that had befallen Oliver since he left Mr. Brownlow's house; reserving Nancy's information for that gentleman's private ear, and concluding with the assurance that his only sorrow, for some months past, had been the not being able to meet with his former benefactor and friend.

"Thank God!" said the old gentleman. "This is great happiness to me; great happiness. But you have not told me where he is now, Miss Maylie. You must pardon my finding fault with you,—but why not have brought him?"

"He is waiting in a coach at the door," replied Rose.

"At this door!" cried the old gentleman. With which he hurried out of the room, down the stairs, up the coach-steps, and into the coach, without another word.

When the room-door closed behind him, Mr. Grimwig lifted up his head, and converting one of the hind legs of his chair into a pivot, described three distinct circles with the assistance of his stick and the table: sitting in it all the time. After performing this evolution, he rose and limped as fast as he could up and down the room at least a dozen times, and then stopping suddenly before Rose, kissed her without the slightest preface.

"Hush!" he said, as the young lady rose in some alarm at this unusual proceeding. "Don't be afraid. I'm old enough to be your grandfather. You're a sweet girl. I like you. Here they are!"

In fact, as he threw himself at one dexterous dive into his former seat, Mr. Brownlow returned accompanied by Oliver, whom Mr. Grimwig received very graciously; and if the gratification of that moment had been the only reward for all her anxiety and care in Oliver's behalf, Rose Maylie would have been well repaid.

"There is somebody else who should not be forgotten, by the by," said Mr. Brownlow, ringing the bell. "Send Mrs. Bedwin here, if you please."

The old housekeeper answered the summons with all despatch; and dropping a curtsey at the door, waited for orders.

"Why, you get blinder every day, Bedwin," said Mr. Brownlow, rather testily.

"Well, that I do, sir," replied the old lady. "People's eyes, at my time of life, don't improve with age, sir."

"I could have told you that," rejoined Mr. Brownlow; "but put on your glasses, and see if you can't find out what you were wanted for, will you?"

The old lady began to rummage in her pocket for her spectacles. But Oliver's patience was not proof against this new trial; and yielding to his first impulse, he sprung into her arms.

"God be good to me!" cried the old lady, embracing him; "it is my innocent boy!"

"My dear old nurse!" cried Oliver.

"He would come back—I knew he would," said the old lady, holding him in her arms. "How well he looks, and how like a gentleman's son he is dressed again! Where have you been, this long, long while? Ah! the same sweet face, but not so pale; the same soft eye, but not so sad. I have never forgotten them or his quiet smile, but have seen them every day, side by side with those of my own dear children, dead and gone since I was a lightsome young creature." Running on thus, and now holding Oliver from her to mark how he had grown, now clasping him to her and passing her fingers fondly through his hair, the good soul laughed and wept upon his neck by turns.

Leaving her and Oliver to compare notes at leisure, Mr. Brownlow led the way into another room; and there, heard from Rose a full narration of her interview with Nancy, which occasioned him no little surprise and perplexity. Rose also explained her reasons for not making a confident of her friend Mr. Losberne in the first instance; the old gentleman considered that she had acted prudently, and readily undertook to hold solemn conference with the worthy doctor himself. To afford him an early opportunity for the execution of this design, it was arranged that he should call at the hotel at eight o'clock that evening, and that in the mean time Mrs. Maylie should be cautiously informed of all that had occurred. These preliminaries adjusted, Rose and Oliver returned home.

Rose had by no means overrated the measure of the good doctor's wrath. Nancy's history was no sooner unfolded to him, than he poured forth a shower of mingled threats and execrations; threatened to make her the first victim of the combined ingenuity of Messrs. Blathers and Duff; and actually put on his hat preparatory to sallying forth immediately to obtain the assistance of those worthies. And, doubtless, he would, in this first outbreak, have carried the intention into effect without a moment's consideration of the consequences, if he had not been restrained, in part, by corresponding violence on the side of Mr. Brownlow, who was himself of an irascible temperament, and partly by such arguments and representations as seemed best calculated to dissuade him from his hotbrained purpose.

"Then what the devil is to be done?" said the impetuous doctor, when they had rejoined the two ladies. "Are we to pass a vote of thanks to all these vagabonds, male and female, and beg them to accept a hundred pounds, or so, apiece, as a trifling mark of our esteem, and some slight acknowledgment of their kindness to Oliver?"

"Not exactly that," rejoined Mr. Brownlow laughing; "but we must proceed gently and with great care."

"Gentleness and care!" exclaimed the doctor. "I'd send them one and all to——"

"Never mind where," interposed Mr. Brownlow. "But reflect whether sending them any where is likely to attain the object we have in view."

"What object?" asked the doctor.

"Simply, the discovery of Oliver's parentage, and regaining for him the inheritance of which, if this story be true, he has been fraudulently deprived."

"Ah!" said Mr. Losberne, cooling himself with his pocket-handkerchief; "I almost forgot that."

"You see," pursued Mr. Brownlow; "placing this poor girl entirely out of the question, and supposing it were possible to bring these scoundrels to justice without compromising her safety, what good should we bring about?"

"Hanging a few of them at least, in all probability," suggested the doctor, "and transporting the rest."

"Very good," replied Mr. Brownlow smiling; "but no doubt they will bring that about for themselves in the fulness of time, and if we step in to forestal them, it seems to me that we shall be performing a very Quixotic[4] act, in direct opposition to our own interest—or at least to Oliver's, which is the same thing."

"How?" inquired the doctor.

"Thus. It is quite clear that we shall have extreme difficulty in getting to the bottom of this mystery, unless we can bring this man, Monks, upon his knees. That can only be done by stratagem, and by catching him when he is not surrounded by these people. For, suppose he were apprehended, we have no proof against him. He is not even (so far as we know, or as the facts appear to us) concerned with the gang in any of their robberies. If he were not discharged, it is very unlikely that he

---

4. Idealistic and impractical.

could receive any further punishment than being committed to prison as a rogue and vagabond; and of course ever afterwards his mouth is so obstinately closed that he might as well, for our purposes, be deaf, dumb, blind, and an idiot."

"Then," said the doctor impetuously, "I put it to you again, whether you think it reasonable that this promise to the girl should be considered binding; a promise made with the best and kindest intentions, but really—"

"Do not discuss the point, my dear young lady, pray," said Mr. Brownlow, interrupting Rose as she was about to speak. "The promise shall be kept. I don't think it will, in the slightest degree, interfere with our proceedings. But, before we can resolve upon any precise course of action, it will be necessary to see the girl; to ascertain from her whether she will point out this Monks, on the understanding that he is to be dealt with by us, and not by the law; or, if she will not, or cannot do that, to procure from her such an account of his haunts and description of his person, as will enable us to identify him. She cannot be seen until next Sunday night; this is Tuesday. I would suggest that, in the mean time, we remain perfectly quiet, and keep these matters secret, even from Oliver himself."

Although Mr. Losberne received with many wry faces a proposal involving a delay of five whole days, he was fain to admit that no better course occurred to him just then; and as both Rose and Mrs. Maylie sided very strongly with Mr. Brownlow, that gentleman's proposition was carried unanimously.

"I should like," he said, "to call in the aid of my friend Grimwig. He is a strange creature, but a shrewd one, and might prove of material assistance to us; I should say that he was bred a lawyer, and quitted the bar in disgust because he had only one brief and a motion of course[5] in twenty years, though whether that is a recommendation or not, you must determine for yourselves."

"I have no objection to your calling in your friend if I may call in mine," said the doctor.

"We must put it to the vote," replied Mr. Brownlow, "who may he be?"

"That lady's son, and this young lady's—very old friend," said the doctor, motioning towards Mrs. Maylie, and concluding with an expressive glance at her niece.

Rose blushed deeply, but she did not make any audible objection to this motion (possibly she felt in a hopeless minority); and Harry Maylie and Mr. Grimwig were accordingly added to the committee.

"We stay in town, of course," said Mrs. Maylie, "while there remains the slightest prospect of prosecuting this inquiry with a chance of success.

---

5. He had only one written legal argument and one application for a court ruling to speed the progress of a legal action; in other words, he had no business.

I will spare neither trouble nor expense in behalf of the object in which we are all so deeply interested, and I am content to remain here, if it be for twelve months, so long as you assure me that any hope remains."

"Good!" rejoined Mr. Brownlow. "And as I see on the faces about me, a disposition to inquire how it happened that I was not in the way to corroborate Oliver's tale, and had so suddenly left the kingdom, let me stipulate that I shall be asked no questions until such time as I may deem it expedient to forestal them by telling my own story. Believe me, I make this request with good reason, for I might otherwise excite hopes destined never to be realised, and only increase difficulties and disappointments already quite numerous enough. Come! Supper has been announced, and young Oliver, who is all alone in the next room, will have begun to think, by this time, that we have wearied of his company, and entered into some dark conspiracy to thrust him forth upon the world."

With these words, the old gentleman gave his hand to Mrs. Maylie, and escorted her into the supper-room. Mr. Losberne followed, leading Rose; and the council was, for the present, effectually broken up.

Chapter XLII.

AN OLD ACQUAINTANCE OF OLIVER'S, EXHIBITING DECIDED MARKS OF GENIUS, BECOMES A PUBLIC CHARACTER IN THE METROPOLIS.

Upon the very same night when Nancy, having lulled Mr. Sikes to sleep, hurried on her self-imposed mission to Rose Maylie, there advanced towards London, by the Great North Road,[1] two persons, upon whom it is expedient that this history should bestow some attention.

They were a man and woman; or perhaps they would be better described as a male and female; for the former was one of those long-limbed, knock-kneed, shambling, bony people, to whom it is difficult to assign any precise age,—looking as they do, when they are yet boys, like undergrown men, and when they are almost men, like overgrown boys. The woman was young, but of a robust and hardy make, as she need have been to bear the weight of the heavy bundle which was strapped to her back. Her companion was not encumbered with much luggage, as there merely dangled from a stick, which he carried over his shoulder, a small parcel wrapped in a common handkerchief, and apparently light enough. This circumstance, added to the length of his legs, which were of unusual extent, enabled him with much ease to keep some half-dozen paces in advance of his companion, to whom he occasionally turned with an impatient jerk of the head: as if reproaching her tardiness, and urging her to greater exertion.

1. The main highway from the north into London.

Thus, they toiled along the dusty road, taking little heed of any object within sight, save when they stepped aside to allow a wider passage for the mail-coaches which were whirling out of town, until they passed through Highgate archway,[2] when the foremost traveller stopped, and called impatiently to his companion,

"Come on, can't yer? What a lazybones yer are, Charlotte."

"It's a heavy load, I can tell you," said the female, coming up, almost breathless with fatigue.

"Heavy! What are yer talking about? What are yer made for?" rejoined the male traveller, changing his own little bundle as he spoke, to the other shoulder. "Oh, there yer are, resting again! Well, if yer ain't enough to tire any body's patience out, I don't know what is!"

"Is it much farther?" asked the woman, resting herself against a bank, and looking up with the perspiration streaming from her face.

"Much farther! Yer as good as there," said the long-legged tramper pointing out before him. "Look there! Those are the lights of London."

"They're a good two mile off, at least," said the woman despondingly.

"Never mind whether they're two mile off, or twenty," said Noah Claypole; for he it was; "but get up and come on, or I'll kick yer, and so I give yer notice."

As Noah's red nose grew redder with anger, and as he crossed the road while speaking, as if fully prepared to put his threat into execution, the woman rose without any further remark, and trudged onward by his side.

"Where do you mean to stop for the night, Noah?" she asked, after they had walked a few hundred yards.

"How should I know?" replied Noah, whose temper had been considerably impaired by walking.

"Near, I hope," said Charlotte.

"No, not near," replied Mr. Claypole. "There! Not near; so don't think it."

"Why not?"

"When I tell yer that I don't mean to do a thing, that's enough, without any why, or because either," replied Mr. Claypole with dignity.

"Well, you needn't be so cross," said his companion.

"A pretty thing it would be, wouldn't it, to go and stop at the very first public-house outside the town, so that Sowerberry, if he come up after us, might poke in his old nose, and have us taken back in a cart with handcuffs on," said Mr. Claypole in a jeering tone. "No! I shall go and lose myself among the narrowest streets I can find, and not stop till we come to the very out-of-the-wayest house I can set eyes on. 'Cod, yer may thank yer stars I've got a head; for if we hadn't gone, at first, the wrong road a purpose, and come back across country, yer'd have

2. A viaduct across the Great North Road, indicating entrance into the village of Highgate, just north of central London.

been locked up hard and fast a week ago, my lady. And serve yer right for being a fool."

"I know I ain't as cunning as you are," replied Charlotte; "but don't put all the blame on me, and say *I* should have been locked up. You would have been if I had been, any way."

"Yer took the money from the till, yer know yer did," said Mr. Claypole.

"I took it for you, Noah, dear," rejoined Charlotte.

"Did I keep it?" asked Mr. Claypole.

"No, you trusted in me, and let me carry it like a dear, and so you are," said the lady, chucking him under the chin, and drawing her arm through his.

This was indeed the case; but as it was not Mr. Claypole's habit to repose a blind and foolish confidence in any body, it should be observed, in justice to that gentleman, that he had trusted Charlotte to this extent, in order that, if they were pursued, the money might be found on her: which would leave him an opportunity of asserting his utter innocence of any theft, and would greatly facilitate his chances of escape. Of course, he entered at this juncture, into no explanation of his motives, and they walked on very lovingly together.

In pursuance of this cautious plan, Mr. Claypole went on, without halting, until he arrived at the Angel at Islington,[3] where he wisely judged, from the crowd of passengers and number of vehicles, that London began in earnest. Just pausing to observe which appeared the most crowded streets, and consequently the most to be avoided, he crossed into Saint John's Road, and was soon deep in the obscurity of the intricate and dirty ways which, lying between Gray's Inn Lane and Smithfield, render that part of the town one of the lowest and worst that improvement has left in the midst of London.

Through these streets, Noah Claypole walked, dragging Charlotte after him; now stepping into the kennel to embrace at a glance the whole external character of some small public-house; and now jogging on again, as some fancied appearance induced him to believe it too public for his purpose. At length, he stopped in front of one, more humble in appearance and more dirty than any he had yet seen; and, having crossed over and surveyed it from the opposite pavement, graciously announced his intention of putting up there, for the night.

"So give us the bundle," said Noah, unstrapping it from the woman's shoulders, and slinging it over his own; "and don't yer speak, except when yer spoke to. What's the name of the house—t-h-r—three what?"

"Cripples," said Charlotte.

"Three Cripples," repeated Noah, "and a very good sign too. Now, then! Keep close at my heels, and come along." With these injunctions,

---

3. The London terminus of the Great North Road and of stagecoaches to London from the north.

he pushed the rattling door with his shoulder, and entered the house, followed by his companion.

There was nobody in the bar but a young Jew, who, with his two elbows on the counter, was reading a dirty newspaper. He stared very hard at Noah, and Noah stared very hard at him.

If Noah had been attired in his charity-boy's dress, there might have been some reason for the Jew opening his eyes so wide; but as he had discarded the coat and badge, and wore a short smock-frock over his leathers, there seemed no particular reason for his appearance exciting so much attention in a public-house.

"Is this the Three Cripples?" asked Noah.

"That is the dabe of this ouse," replied the Jew.

"A gentleman we met on the road, coming up from the country, recommended us here," said Noah, nudging Charlotte, perhaps to call her attention to this most ingenious device for attracting respect, and perhaps to warn her to betray no surprise. "We want to sleep here to-night."

"I'b dot certaid you cad," said Barney, who was the attendant sprite; "but I'll idquire."

"Show us the tap, and give us a bit of cold meat and a drop of beer while yer inquiring, will yer?" said Noah.

Barney complied by ushering them into a small back-room, and setting the required viands before them; having done which, he informed the travellers that they could be lodged that night, and left the amiable couple to their refreshment.

Now, this back-room was immediately behind the bar, and some steps lower, so that any person connected with the house, undrawing a small curtain which concealed a single pane of glass fixed in the wall of the last-named apartment, about five feet from its flooring, could not only look down upon any guests in the back-room without any great hazard of being observed (the glass being in a dark angle of the wall, between which and a large upright beam the observer had to thrust himself), but could, by applying his ear to the partition, ascertain with tolerable distinctness, their subject of conversation. The landlord of the house had not withdrawn his eye from this place of espial[4] for five minutes, and Barney had only just returned from making the communication above related, when Fagin, in the course of his evening's business, came into the bar to inquire after some of his young pupils.

"Hush!" said Barney: "stradegers id the next roob."

"Strangers!" repeated the old man in a whisper.

"Ah! Ad rub uds too," added Barney. "Frob the cuttry, but subthig in your way, or I'b bistaked."

4. Observation point.

Fagin appeared to receive this communication with great interest. Mounting on a stool, he cautiously applied his eye to the pane of glass, from which secret post he could see Mr. Claypole taking cold beef from the dish, and porter from the pot, and administering homœopathic doses[5] of both to Charlotte, who sat patiently by, eating and drinking at his pleasure.

"Aha!" whispered the Jew, looking round to Barney, "I like that fellow's looks. He'd be of use to us; he knows how to train the girl already. Don't make as much noise as a mouse, my dear, and let me hear 'em talk—let me hear 'em."

The Jew again applied his eye to the glass, and turning his ear to the partition, listened attentively: with a subtle and eager look upon his face, that might have appertained to some old goblin.

"So I mean to be a gentleman," said Mr. Claypole, kicking out his legs, and continuing a conversation, the commencement of which Fagin had arrived too late to hear. "No more jolly old coffins, Charlotte, but a gentleman's life for me; and, if yer like yer shall be a lady."

"I should like that well enough, dear," replied Charlotte; "but tills ain't to be emptied every day, and people to get clear off after it."

"Tills be blowed!" said Mr. Claypole; "there's more things besides tills to be emptied."

"What do you mean?" asked his companion.

"Pockets, women's ridicules,[6] houses, mail-coaches, banks!" said Mr. Claypole, rising with the porter.

"But you can't do all that, dear," said Charlotte.

"I shall look out to get into company with them as can," replied Noah. "They'll be able to make us useful some way or another. Why, you yourself are worth fifty women; I never see such a precious sly and deceitful creetur as yer can be when I let yer."

"Lor, how nice it is to hear you say so!" exclaimed Charlotte, imprinting a kiss upon his ugly face.

"There, that'll do: don't yer be too affectionate, in case I'm cross with yer," said Noah, disengaging himself with great gravity. "I should like to be the captain of some band, and have the whopping of 'em, and follering 'em about, unbeknown to themselves. That would suit me, if there was good profit; and if we could only get in with some gentlemen of this sort, I say it would be cheap at that twenty-pound note you've got,—especially as we don't very well know how to get rid of it ourselves."

After expressing this opinion, Mr. Claypole looked into the porter-pot with an aspect of deep wisdom; and having well shaken its contents, nodded condescendingly to Charlotte, and took a draught, wherewith

5. Doses of a medicine of which massive doses would in a healthy person produce the same symptoms as those of the disease being treated.
6. Small pocketbooks (a variant spelling of "reticules").

he appeared greatly refreshed. He was meditating another, when the sudden opening of the door, and the appearance of a stranger, interrupted him.

The stranger was Mr. Fagin. And very amiable he looked, and a very low bow he made, as he advanced, and, setting himself down at the nearest table, ordered something to drink of the grinning Barney.

"A pleasant night, sir, but cool for the time of year," said Fagin, rubbing his hands. "From the country, I see, sir?"

"How do yer see that?" asked Noah Claypole.

"We have not so much dust as that in London," replied the Jew, pointing from Noah's shoes to those of his companion, and from them to the two bundles.

"Yer a sharp feller," said Noah. "Ha! ha! only hear that, Charlotte!"

"Why, one need be sharp in this town, my dear," replied the Jew, sinking his voice to a confidential whisper; "and that's the truth."

The Jew followed up this remark by striking the side of his nose with his right forefinger,—a gesture which Noah attempted to imitate, though not with complete success, in consequence of his own nose not being large enough for the purpose. However, Mr. Fagin seemed to interpret the endeavour as expressing a perfect coincidence with his opinion, and put about the liquor which Barney reappeared with, in a very friendly manner.

"Good stuff that," observed Mr. Claypole, smacking his lips.

"Dear!" said Fagin. "A man need be always emptying a till, or a pocket, or a woman's reticule, or a house, or a mail-coach, or a bank, if he drinks it regularly."

Mr. Claypole no sooner heard this extract from his own remarks than he fell back in his chair, and looked from the Jew to Charlotte with a countenance of ashy paleness and excessive terror.

"Don't mind me, my dear," said Fagin, drawing his chair closer. "Ha! ha! it was lucky it was only me that heard you by chance. It was very lucky it was only me."

"I didn't take it," stammered Noah, no longer stretching out his legs like an independent gentleman, but coiling them up as well as he could under his chair; "it was all her doing: yer've got it now, Charlotte, yer know yer have."

"No matter who's got it, or who did it, my dear!" replied Fagin, glancing, nevertheless, with a hawk's eye at the girl and the two bundles. "I'm in that way myself, and I like you for it."

"In what way?" asked Mr. Claypole, a little recovering.

"In that way of business," rejoined Fagin; "and so are the people of the house. You've hit the right nail upon the head, and are as safe here as you could be. There is not a safer place in all this town than is the Cripples; that is, when I like to make it so, and I've taken a fancy to

you and the young woman; so I've said the word, and you may make
your minds easy."

Noah Claypole's mind might have been at ease after this assurance,
but his body certainly was not; for he shuffled and writhed about, into
various uncouth positions: eyeing his new friend meanwhile with mingled fear and suspicion.

"I'll tell you more," said the Jew, after he had reassured the girl, by
dint of friendly nods and muttered encouragements. "I have got a friend
that I think can gratify your darling wish, and put you in the right way,
where you can take whatever department of the business you think will
suit you best at first, and be taught all the others."

"Yer speak as if yer were in earnest," replied Noah.

"What advantage would it be to me to be anything else?" inquired
the Jew, shrugging his shoulders. "Here! Let me have a word with you
outside."

"There's no occasion to trouble ourselves to move," said Noah, getting
his legs by gradual degrees abroad again. "She'll take the luggage up
stairs the while. Charlotte, see to them bundles!"

This mandate, which had been delivered with great majesty, was
obeyed without the slightest demur; and Charlotte made the best of her
way off with the packages while Noah held the door open, and watched
her out.

"She's kept tolerably well under, ain't she?" he asked as he resumed
his seat: in the tone of a keeper who has tamed some wild animal.

"Quite perfect," rejoined Fagin, clapping him on the shoulder.
"You're a genius, my dear."

"Why, I suppose if I wasn't, I shouldn't be here," replied Noah. "But,
I say, she'll be back if yer lose time."

"Now, what do you think?" said the Jew. "If you was to like my friend,
could you do better than join him?"

"Is he in a good way of business; that's where it is?" responded Noah,
winking one of his little eyes.

"The top of the tree," said the Jew; "employs a power of hands; and
has the very best society in the profession."

"Regular town-maders?" asked Mr. Claypole.

"Not a countryman among 'em; and I don't think he'd take you, even
on my recommendation, if he didn't run rather short of assistants just
now," replied the Jew.

"Should I have to hand over?" said Noah, slapping his breeches-
pocket.

"It couldn't possibly be done without," replied Fagin, in a most decided manner.

"Twenty pound, though,—it's a lot of money!"

"Not when it's in a note you can't get rid of," retorted Fagin. "Number and date taken, I suppose? Payment stopped at the Bank? Ah! It's not worth much to him. It'll have to go abroad, and he couldn't sell it for a great deal in the market."

"When could I see him?" asked Noah doubtfully.

"To-morrow morning," replied the Jew.

"Where?"

"Here."

"Um!" said Noah. "What's the wages?"

"Live like a gentleman—board and lodging, pipes and spirits, free— half of all you earn, and half of all the young woman earns," replied Mr. Fagin.

Whether Noah Claypole, whose rapacity was none of the least comprehensive,[7] would have acceded even to these glowing terms, had he been a perfectly free agent, is very doubtful; but as he recollected that, in the event of his refusal it was in the power of his new acquaintance to give him up to justice immediately (and more unlikely things had come to pass), he gradually relented, and said he thought that would suit him.

"But, yer see," observed Noah, "as she will be able to do a good deal, I should like to take something very light."

"A little fancy work?"[8] suggested Fagin.

"Ah! something of that sort," replied Noah. "What do you think would suit me now? Something not too trying for the strength, and not very dangerous, you know. That's the sort of thing!"

"I heard you talk of something in the spy way upon the others, my dear," said the Jew. "My friend wants somebody who would do that well, very much."

"Why, I did mention that, and I shouldn't mind turning my hand to it sometimes," rejoined Mr. Claypole slowly; "but it wouldn't pay by itself, you know."

"That's true!" observed the Jew, ruminating or pretending to ruminate. "No, it might not."

"What do you think, then?" asked Noah, anxiously regarding him. "Something in the sneaking way, where it was pretty sure work, and not much more risk than being at home."

"What do you think of the old ladies?" asked the Jew. "There's a good deal of money made in snatching their bags and parcels, and running round the corner."

"Don't they holler out a good deal, and scratch sometimes?" asked Noah, shaking his head. "I don't think that would answer my purpose. Ain't there any other line open?"

"Stop!" said the Jew, laying his hand on Noah's knee. "The kinchin lay."

7. Whose greed had no limits.
8. Pimping.

"What's that?" demanded Mr. Claypole.

"The kinchins, my dear," said the Jew, "is the young children that's sent on errands by their mothers, with sixpences and shillings; and the lay is just to take their money away—they've always got it ready in their hands,—and then knock 'em into the kennel, and walk off very slow, as if there was nothing else the matter but a child fallen down and hurt itself. Ha! ha! ha!"

"Ha! ha!" roared Mr. Claypole, kicking up his legs in an ecstasy. "Lord, that's the very thing!"

"To be sure it is," replied Fagin; "and you can have a few good beats chalked out in Camden-town, and Battle-bridge,[9] and neighbourhoods like that, where they're always going errands; and you can upset as many kinchins as you want, any hour in the day. Ha! ha! ha!"

With this, Fagin poked Mr. Claypole in the side, and they joined in a burst of laughter both long and loud.

"Well, that's all right!" said Noah, when he had recovered himself, and Charlotte had returned. "What time to-morrow shall we say?"

"Will ten do?" asked the Jew, adding, as Mr. Claypole nodded assent, "What name shall I tell my good friend?"

"Mr. Bolter," replied Noah, who had prepared himself, for such an emergency. "Mr. Morris Bolter. This is Mrs. Bolter."

"Mrs. Bolter's humble servant," said Fagin, bowing with grotesque politeness. "I hope I shall know her better very shortly."

"Do you hear the gentleman, Char-lotte?" thundered Mr. Claypole.

"Yes, Noah, dear!" replied Mrs. Bolter, extending her hand.

"She calls me Noah, as a sort of fond way of talking," said Mr. Morris Bolter, late Claypole, turning to the Jew. "You understand?"

"Oh yes, I understand—perfectly," replied Fagin, telling the truth for once. "Good night! Good night!"

With many adieus and good wishes, Mr. Fagin went his way. Noah Claypole, bespeaking his good lady's attention, proceeded to enlighten her relative to the arrangement he had made, with all that haughtiness and air of superiority, becoming, not only a member of the sterner sex, but a gentleman who appreciated the dignity of a special appointment on the kinchin lay, in London and its vicinity.

Chapter XLIII.

WHEREIN IS SHOWN HOW THE ARTFUL DODGER GOT INTO TROUBLE.

"And so it was you that was your own friend, was it?" asked Mr. Claypole, otherwise Bolter, when, by virtue of the compact entered into

---

9. A residential area, now part of Greater London, just north of Clerkenwell and Bloomsbury.

between them, he had removed next day to the Jew's house. "'Cod, I thought as much last night!"

"Every man's his own friend, my dear," replied Fagin, with his most insinuating grin. "He hasn't as good a one as himself anywhere."

"Except sometimes," replied Morris Bolter, assuming the air of a man of the world. "Some people are nobody's enemies but their own, yer know."

"Don't believe that!" said the Jew. "When a man's his own enemy, it's only because he's too much his own friend; not because he's careful for everybody but himself. Pooh! pooh! There ain't such a thing in nature."

"There oughtn't to be, if there is," replied Mr. Bolter.

"That stands to reason," said the Jew. "Some conjurers say that number three is the magic number, and some say number seven. It's neither, my friend, neither. It's number one."

"Ha! ha!" cried Mr. Bolter. "Number one for ever."

"In a little community like ours, my dear," said the Jew, who felt it necessary to qualify this position, "we have a general number one; that is, you can't consider yourself as number one, without considering me too as the same, and all the other young people."

"Oh, the devil!" exclaimed Mr. Bolter.

"You see," pursued the Jew, affecting to disregard this interruption, "we are so mixed up together, and identified in our interests, that it must be so. For instance, it's your object to take care of number one—meaning yourself."

"Certainly," replied Mr. Bolter. "Yer about right there."

"Well! You can't take care of yourself, number one, without taking care of me, number one."

"Number two, you mean," said Mr. Bolter, who was largely endowed with the quality of selfishness.

"No, I don't!" retorted the Jew. "I'm of the same importance to you, as you are to yourself."

"I say," interrupted Mr. Bolter, "yer a very nice man, and I'm very fond of yer; but we ain't quite so thick together, as all that comes to."

"Only think," said the Jew, shrugging his shoulders, and stretching out his hands; "only consider. You've done what's a very pretty thing, and what I love you for doing; but what at the same time would put the cravat round your throat, that's so very easily tied and so very difficult to unloose—in plain English, the halter!"

Mr. Bolter put his hand to his neckerchief, as if he felt it inconveniently tight; and murmured an assent, qualified in tone but not in substance.

"The gallows," continued Fagin, "the gallows, my dear, is an ugly finger-post,[1] which points out a very short and sharp turning that has stopped many a bold fellow's career on the broad highway. To keep in the easy road, and keep it at a distance, is object number one with you."

"Of course it is," replied Mr. Bolter. "What do yer talk about such things for?"

"Only to show you my meaning clearly," said the Jew, raising his eyebrows. "To be able to do that, you depend upon me. To keep my little business all snug, I depend upon you. The first is your number one, the second my number one. The more you value your number one, the more careful you must be of mine; so we come at last to what I told you at first—that a regard for number one holds us all together, and must do so, unless we would all go to pieces in company."

"That's true," rejoined Mr. Bolter, thoughtfully. "Oh! yer a' cunning old codger!"

Mr. Fagin saw, with delight, that this tribute to his powers was no mere compliment, but that he had really impressed his recruit with a sense of his wily genius, which it was most important that he should entertain in the outset of their acquaintance. To strengthen an impression so desirable and useful, he followed up the blow by acquainting him, in some detail, with the magnitude and extent of his operations; blending truth and fiction together, as best served his purpose; and bringing both to bear, with so much art, that Mr. Bolter's respect visibly increased, and became tempered, at the same time, with a degree of wholesome fear, which it was highly desirable to awaken.

"It's this mutual trust we have in each other, that consoles me under heavy losses," said the Jew. "My best hand was taken from me, yesterday morning."

"Yer don't mean to say he died?" cried Mr. Bolter.

"No, no," replied Fagin, "not so bad as that. Not quite so bad."

"What, I suppose he was——"

"Wanted," interposed the Jew. "Yes, he was wanted."

"Very particular?" inquired Mr. Bolter.

"No," replied the Jew, "not very. He was charged with attempting to pick a pocket, and they found a silver snuff-box on him,—his own, my dear, his own, for he took snuff himself, and was very fond of it. They remanded him till to-day, for they thought they knew the owner. Ah! he was worth fifty boxes, and I'd give the price of as many to have him back. You should have known the Dodger, my dear; you should have known the Dodger."

"Well, but I shall know him, I hope; don't yer think so?" said Mr. Bolter.

---

1. A directional sign at the crossing of two roads.

"I'm doubtful about it," replied the Jew, with a sigh. "If they don't get any fresh evidence, it'll only be a summary conviction, and we shall have him back again after six weeks or so; but, if they do, it's a case of lagging.[2] They know what a clever lad he is; he'll be a lifer. They'll make the Artful nothing less than a lifer."

"What do yer mean by lagging and a lifer?" demanded Mr. Bolter. "What's the good of talking in that way to me; why don't yer speak so as I can understand yer?"

Fagin was about to translate these mysterious expressions into the vulgar tongue; and, being interpreted, Mr. Bolter would have been informed that they represented that combination of words, "transportation for life," when the dialogue was cut short by the entry of Master Bates, with his hands in his breeches' pockets, and his face twisted into a look of semi-comical woe.

"It's all up, Fagin," said Charley, when he and his new companion had been made known to each other.

"What do you mean?" asked the Jew with trembling lips.

"They've found the gentleman as owns the box; two or three more's a coming to 'dentify him; and the Artful's booked for a passage out," replied Master Bates. "I must have a full suit of mourning, Fagin, and a hatband, to wisit him in, afore he sets out upon his travels. To think of Jack Dawkins—lummy[3] Jack—the Dodger—the Artful Dodger—going abroad for a common twopenny-halfpenny sneeze-box! I never thought he'd ha' done it under a gold watch, chain, and seals, at the lowest. Oh, why didn't he rob some rich old gentleman of all his walables, and go out *as* a gentleman, and not like a common prig, without no honour nor glory!"

With this expression of feeling for his unfortunate friend, Master Bates sat himself on the nearest chair with an aspect of chagrin and despondency.

"What do you talk about his having neither honour nor glory for!" exclaimed Fagin, darting an angry look at his pupil. "Wasn't he always top-sawyer[4] among you all! Is there one of you that could touch him or come near him on any scent! Eh?"

"Not one," replied Master Bates, in a voice rendered husky by regret; "not one."

"Then what do you talk of?" replied the Jew angrily; "what are you blubbering for?"

"'Cause it isn't on the rec-ord, is it?" said Charley, chafed into perfect defiance of his venerable friend by the current of his regrets; "'cause it can't come out in the 'dictment; cause nobody will never know half of

2. Exile to Australia.
3. First-rate.
4. The best man.

what he was. How will he stand in the Newgate Calendar?[5] P'raps not be there at all. Oh, my eye, my eye, wot a blow it is!"

"Ha! ha!" cried the Jew extending his right hand, and turning to Mr. Bolter in a fit of chuckling which shook him as though he had the palsy; "see what a pride they take in their profession, my dear. Ain't it beautiful?"

Mr. Bolter nodded assent; and the Jew, after contemplating the grief of Charley Bates for some seconds with evident satisfaction, stepped up to that young gentleman and patted him on the shoulder.

"Never mind, Charley," said Fagin soothingly; "it'll come out, it'll be sure to come out. They'll all know what a clever fellow he was; he'll show it himself, and not disgrace his old pals and teachers. Think how young he is too! What a distinction, Charley, to be lagged at his time of life!"

"Well, it is a honour that is!" said Charley, a little consoled.

"He shall have all he wants," continued the Jew. "He shall be kept in the Stone Jug,[6] Charley, like a gentleman. Like a gentleman! With his beer every day, and money in his pocket to pitch and toss with, if he can't spend it."

"No, shall he though?" cried Charley Bates.

"Ay, that he shall," replied the Jew, "and we'll have a big-wig, Charley: one that's got the greatest gift of the gab: to carry on his defence; and he shall make a speech for himself too, if he likes; and we'll read it all in the papers—'Artful Dodger—shrieks of laughter—here the court was convulsed'—eh, Charley, eh?"

"Ha! ha!" laughed Master Bates, "what a lark that would be, wouldn't it, Fagin? I say, how the Artful would bother 'em, wouldn't he?"

"Would!" cried the Jew. "He shall—he will!"

"Ah, to be sure, so he will," repeated Charley, rubbing his hands.

"I think I see him now," cried the Jew, bending his eyes upon his pupil.

"So do I," cried Charley Bates. "Ha! ha! ha! so do I. I see it all afore me, upon my soul I do, Fagin. What a game! What a regular game! All the big-wigs trying to look solemn, and Jack Dawkins addressing of 'em as intimate and comfortable as if he was the judge's own son making a speech arter dinner—ha! ha! ha!"

In fact, the Jew had so well humoured his young friend's eccentric disposition, that Master Bates, who had at first been disposed to consider the imprisoned Dodger rather in the light of a victim, now looked upon him as the chief actor in a scene of most uncommon and exquisite humour, and felt quite impatient for the arrival of the time when his

5. An ongoing, intermittent series of books containing biographies of the most notorious criminals confined in Newgate.
6. Jail.

old companion should have so favourable an opportunity of displaying his abilities.

"We must know how he gets on to-day, by some handy means or other," said Fagin. "Let me think."

"Shall I go?" asked Charley.

"Not for the world," replied the Jew. "Are you mad, my dear; stark mad, that you'd walk into the very place where—No, Charley, no. One is enough to lose at a time."

"You don't mean to go yourself, I suppose?" said Charley with a humorous leer.

"That wouldn't quite fit," replied Fagin shaking his head.

"Then why don't you send this new cove?" asked Master Bates, laying his hand on Noah's arm. "Nobody knows him."

"Why, if he didn't mind—" observed the Jew.

"Mind!" interposed Charley. "What should *he* have to mind?"

"Really nothing, my dear," said Fagin, turning to Mr. Bolter, "really nothing."

"Oh, I dare say about that, yer know," observed Noah, backing towards the door, and shaking his head with a kind of sober alarm. "No, no— none of that. It's not in my department, that ain't."

"Wot department has he got, Fagin?" inquired Master Bates, surveying Noah's lanky form with much disgust. "The cutting away when there's anything wrong, and the eating all the wittles when there's everything right; is that his branch?"

"Never mind," retorted Mr. Bolter; "and don't yer take liberties with yer superiors, little boy, or yer'll find yerself in the wrong shop."

Master Bates laughed so vehemently at this magnificent threat, that it was some time before Fagin could interpose, and represent to Mr. Bolter that he incurred no possible danger in visiting the police-office; that, inasmuch as no account of the little affair in which he had been engaged, nor any description of his person, had yet been forwarded to the metropolis, it was very probable that he was not even suspected of having resorted to it for shelter; and that, if he were properly disguised, it would be as safe a spot for him to visit as any in London, inasmuch as it would be, of all places, the very last, to which he could be supposed likely to resort of his own free will.

Persuaded, in part, by these representations but overborne in a much greater degree by his fear of the Jew, Mr. Bolter at length consented, with a very bad grace, to undertake the expedition. By Fagin's directions, he immediately substituted for his own attire, a waggoner's frock, velveteen breeches, and leather leggings: all of which articles the Jew had at hand. He was likewise furnished with a felt hat well garnished with turnpike tickets; and a carter's[7] whip. Thus equipped, he was to saunter

---

7. A wagon driver's.

into the office, as some country fellow from Covent Garden market might be supposed to do for the gratification of his curiosity; and as he was as awkward, ungainly, and raw-boned a fellow as need be, Mr. Fagin had no fear but that he would look the part to perfection.

These arrangements completed, he was informed of the necessary signs and tokens by which to recognise the artful Dodger, and was conveyed by Master Bates through dark and winding ways to within a very short distance of Bow-street.[8] Having described the precise situation of the office, and accompanied it with copious directions how he was to walk straight up the passage, and when he got into the yard take the door up the steps on the right-hand side, and pull off his hat as he went into the room, Charley Bates bade him hurry on alone, and promised to bide his return on the spot of their parting.

Noah Claypole, or Morris Bolter as the reader pleases, punctually followed the directions he had received, which—Master Bates being pretty well acquainted with the locality—were so exact that he was enabled to gain the magisterial presence without asking any question, or meeting with any interruption, by the way. He found himself jostled among a crowd of people, chiefly women, who were huddled together in a dirty frowsy room, at the upper end of which was a raised platform railed off from the rest, with a dock for the prisoners on the left hand against the wall, a box for the witnesses in the middle, and a desk for the magistrates on the right; the awful locality last named, being screened off by a partition which concealed the bench from the common gaze, and left the vulgar to imagine (if they could) the full majesty of justice.

There were only a couple of women in the dock, who were nodding to their admiring friends, while the clerk read some depositions to a couple of policemen and a man in plain clothes who leant over the table. A jailer stood reclining against the dock-rail, tapping his nose listlessly with a large key, except when he repressed an undue tendency to conversation among the idlers, by proclaiming silence; or looked sternly up to bid some woman "Take that baby out," when the gravity of justice was disturbed by feeble cries, half-smothered in the mother's shawl, from some meagre infant. The room smelt close and unwholesome; the walls were dirt-discoloured; and the ceiling blackened. There was an old smoky bust over the mantel-shelf, and a dusty clock above the dock—the only thing present, that seemed to go on as it ought; for depravity, or poverty, or an habitual acquaintance with both, had left a taint on all the animate matter, hardly less unpleasant than the thick greasy scum on every inanimate object that frowned upon it.

Noah looked eagerly about him for the Dodger; but although there were several women who would have done very well for that distinguished character's mother or sister, and more than one man who might

8. A street in Covent Garden best known for its police station.

be supposed to bear a strong resemblance to his father, nobody at all answering the description given him of Mr. Dawkins was to be seen. He waited in a state of much suspense and uncertainty until the women, being committed for trial, went flaunting out; and then was quickly relieved by the appearance of another prisoner whom he felt at once could be no other than the object of his visit.

It was indeed Mr. Dawkins, who, shuffling into the office with the big coat sleeves tucked up as usual, his left hand in his pocket, and his hat in his right hand, preceded the jailer, with a rolling gait altogether indescribable, and, taking his place in the dock, requested in an audible voice to know what he was placed in that 'ere disgraceful situation for.

"Hold your tongue, will you?" said the jailer.

"I'm an Englishman, an't I?" rejoined the Dodger. "Where are my priwileges?"

"You'll get your privileges soon enough," retorted the jailer, "and pepper with 'em."[9]

"We'll see wot the Secretary of State for the Home Affairs has got to say to the beaks, if I don't," replied Mr. Dawkins. "Now then! Wot is this here business? I shall thank the madg'strates to dispose of this here little affair, and not to keep me while they read the paper, for I've got an appointment with a genelman in the city, and as I'm a man of my word and wery punctual in business matters, he'll go away if I ain't there to my time, and then pr'aps there won't be an action for damage against them as kept me away. Oh no, certainly not!"

At this point, the Dodger, with a show of being very particular with a view to proceedings to be had thereafter, desired the jailer to communicate "the names of them two files[1] as was on the bench," which so tickled the spectators, that they laughed almost as heartily as Master Bates could have done if he had heard the request.

"Silence there!" cried the jailer.

"What is this?" inquired one of the magistrates.

"A pick-pocketing case, your worship."

"Has the boy ever been here before?"

"He ought to have been, a many times," replied the jailer. "He has been pretty well everywhere else. *I* know him well, your worship."

"Oh! you know me, do you?" cried the Artful making a note of the statement. "Wery good. That's a case of deformation[2] of character any way."

Here there was another laugh, and another cry of silence.

"Now then, where are the witnesses?" said the clerk.

"Ah! that's right," added the Dodger. "Where are they? I should like to see 'em."

---

9. You'll be in more trouble than you think.
1. Fellows (disrespectful slang).
2. Defamation.

This wish was immediately gratified, for a policeman stepped forward who had seen the prisoner attempt the pocket of an unknown gentleman in a crowd, and indeed take a handkerchief therefrom, which, being a very old one, he deliberately put back again, after trying it on his own countenance. For this reason, he took the Dodger into custody as soon as he could get near him, and the said Dodger, being searched, had upon his person a silver snuff-box, with the owner's name engraved upon the lid. This gentleman had been discovered on reference to the Court Guide,[3] and being then and there present, swore that the snuff-box was his, and that he had missed it on the previous day, the moment he had disengaged himself from the crowd before referred to. He had also remarked a young gentleman in the throng, particularly active in making his way about, and that young gentleman was the prisoner before him.

"Have you anything to ask this witness boy?" said the magistrate.

"I wouldn't abase myself by descending to hold no conversation with him," replied the Dodger.

"Have you anything to say at all?"

"Do you hear his worship ask if you've anything to say?" inquired the jailer, nudging the silent Dodger with his elbow.

"I beg your pardon," said the Dodger, looking up with an air of abstraction. "Did you redress[4] yourself to me, my man?"

"I never see such an out-and-out young wagabond, your worship," observed the officer with a grin. "Do you mean to say anything, you young shaver?"

"No," replied the Dodger, "not here, for this ain't the shop for justice; besides which, my attorney is a-breakfasting this morning with the Wice President of the House of Commons; but I shall have something to say elsewhere, and so will he, and so will a wery numerous and 'spectable circle of acquaintance as'll make them beaks wish they'd never been born, or that they'd got their footmen to hang 'em up to their own hat-pegs, 'afore they let 'em come out this morning to try it on upon me. I'll——"

"There! He's fully committed!" interposed the clerk. "Take him away."

"Come on," said the jailer.

"Oh ah! I'll come on," replied the Dodger, brushing his hat with the palm of his hand. "Ah! (to the Bench) it's no use your looking frightened; I won't show you no mercy, not a ha'porth of it. You'll pay for this, my fine fellers. I wouldn't be you for something! I wouldn't go free, now, if you was to fall down on your knees and ask me. Here, carry me off to prison! Take me away!"

3. A list kept by the court of people who have reported stolen goods or made statements to the police and the court in regard to crimes having been committed against them.
4. Address.

With these last words, the Dodger suffered himself to be led off by the collar; threatening, till he got into the yard, to make a parliamentary business of it; and then grinning in the officer's face, with great glee and self-approval.

Having seen him locked up by himself in a little cell, Noah made the best of his way back to where he had left Master Bates. After waiting here some time, he was joined by that young gentleman, who had prudently abstained from showing himself until he had looked carefully abroad from a snug retreat, and ascertained that his new friend had not been followed by any impertinent person.

The two hastened back together, to bear to Mr. Fagin the animating news that the Dodger was doing full justice to his bringing-up, and establishing for himself a glorious reputation.

Chapter XLIV.

THE TIME ARRIVES, FOR NANCY TO REDEEM HER PLEDGE TO ROSE MAYLIE. SHE FAILS.

Adept as she was, in all the arts of cunning and dissimulation, the girl Nancy could not wholly conceal the effect which the knowledge of the step she had taken, worked upon her mind. She remembered that both the crafty Jew and the brutal Sikes had confided to her, schemes, which had been hidden from all others: in the full confidence that she was trustworthy and beyond the reach of their suspicion. Vile as those schemes were, desperate as were their originators, and bitter as were her feelings towards the Jew, who had led her, step by step, deeper and deeper down into an abyss of crime and misery, whence was no escape; still, there were times when, even towards him, she felt some relenting, lest her disclosure should bring him within the iron grasp he had so long eluded, and he should fall at last—richly as he merited such a fate—by her hand.

But, these were the mere wanderings of a mind unable wholly to detach itself from old companions and associations, though enabled to fix itself steadily on one object, and resolved not to be turned aside by any consideration. Her fears for Sikes would have been more powerful inducements to recoil while there was yet time; but she had stipulated that her secret should be rigidly kept, she had dropped no clue which could lead to his discovery, she had refused, even for his sake, a refuge from all the guilt and wretchedness that encompassed her—and what more could she do! She was resolved.

Though all her mental struggles terminated in this conclusion, they forced themselves upon her, again and again, and left their traces too. She grew pale and thin, even within a few days. At times, she took no heed of what was passing before her, or no part in conversations where once, she would have been the loudest. At other times, she laughed without merriment, and was noisy without cause or meaning. At others—often within a moment afterwards—she sat silent and dejected, brooding with her head upon her hands, while the very effort by which she roused herself, told, more forcibly than even these indications, that she was ill at ease, and that her thoughts were occupied with matters very different and distant from those in course of discussion by her companions.

It was Sunday night, and the bell of the nearest church struck the hour. Sikes and the Jew were talking, but they paused to listen. The girl looked up from the low seat on which she crouched, and listened too. Eleven.

"An hour this side of midnight," said Sikes, raising the blind to look out and returning to his seat. "Dark and heavy it is too. A good night for business this."

"Ah!" replied the Jew. "What a pity, Bill, my dear, that there's none quite ready to be done."

"You're right for once," replied Sikes gruffly. "It is a pity, for I'm in the humour too."

The Jew sighed, and shook his head despondingly.

"We must make up for lost time when we've got things into a good train. That's all I know," said Sikes.

"That's the way to talk, my dear," replied the Jew, venturing to pat him on the shoulder. "It does me good to hear you."

"Does you good does it!" cried Sikes. "Well, so be it."

"Ha! ha! ha!" laughed the Jew, as if he were relieved by even this concession. "You're like yourself to-night, Bill! Quite like yourself."

"I don't feel like myself when you lay that withered old claw on my shoulder, so take it away," said Sikes casting off the Jew's hand.

"It makes you nervous, Bill,—reminds you of being nabbed, does it?" said the Jew, determined not to be offended.

"Reminds me of being nabbed by the devil," returned Sikes. "There never was another man with such a face as yours, unless it was your father, and I suppose *he* is singeing his grizzled red beard by this time, unless you came straight from the old 'un[1] without any father at all betwixt you; which I shouldn't wonder at, a bit."

Fagin offered no reply to this compliment; but, pulling Sikes by the sleeve, pointed his finger towards Nancy, who had taken advantage of the foregoing conversation to put on her bonnet, and was now leaving the room.

"Hallo!" cried Sikes. "Nance. Where's the gal going to at this time of night?"

---

1. The devil.

"Not far."

"What answer's that?" returned Sikes. "Where are you going?"

"I say, not far."

"And I say where?" retorted Sikes. "Do you hear me?"

"I don't know where," replied the girl.

"Then I do," said Sikes, more in the spirit of obstinacy than because he had any real objection to the girl going where she listed. "Nowhere. Sit down."

"I'm not well. I told you that before," rejoined the girl. "I want a breath of air."

"Put your head out of the winder," replied Sikes.

"There's not enough there," said the girl. "I want it in the street."

"Then you won't have it," replied Sikes. With which assurance he rose, locked the door, took the key out, and pulling her bonnet from her head, flung it up to the top of an old press.[2] "There," said the robber. "Now stop quietly where you are, will you."

"It's not such a matter as a bonnet would keep me," said the girl turning very pale. "What do you mean, Bill? Do you know what you're doing?"

"Know what I'm——Oh!" cried Sikes turning to Fagin, "she's out of her senses, you know, or she daren't talk to me in that way."

"You'll drive me on to something desperate," muttered the girl placing both hands upon her breast, as though to keep down by force some violent outbreak. "Let me go, will you,—this minute—this instant—"

"No!" said Sikes.

"Tell him to let me go, Fagin. He had better. It'll be better for him. Do you hear me?" cried Nancy stamping her foot upon the ground.

"Hear you!" repeated Sikes turning round in his chair to confront her. "Ay! And if I hear you for half a minute longer, the dog shall have such a grip on your throat as'll tear some of that screaming voice out. Wot has come over you, you jade![3] Wot is it?"

"Let me go," said the girl with great earnestness; then sitting herself down on the floor, before the door, she said, "Bill, let me go; you don't know what you're doing. You don't, indeed. For only one hour—do—do."

"Cut my limbs off one by one!" cried Sikes, seizing her roughly by the arm, "if I dont think the gal's stark raving mad. Get up."

"Not till you let me go—not till you let me go—Never—never!" screamed the girl. Sikes looked on, for a minute, watching his opportunity, and suddenly pinioning her hands dragged her, struggling and wrestling with him by the way, into a small room adjoining, where he sat himself on a bench, and thrusting her into a chair, held her down

2. A large cupboard.
3. Hussy.

by force. She struggled and implored by turns until twelve o'clock had struck, and then, wearied and exhausted, ceased to contest the point any further. With a caution, backed by many oaths, to make no more efforts to go out that night, Sikes left her to recover at leisure and rejoined the Jew.

"Whew!" said the housebreaker wiping the perspiration from his face. "Wot a precious strange gal that is!"

"You may say that, Bill," replied the Jew thoughtfully. "You may say that."

"Wot did she take it into her head to go out to-night for, do you think?" asked Sikes. "Come; you should know her better than me. Wot does it mean?"

"Obstinacy; woman's obstinacy, I suppose, my dear," replied the Jew shrugging his shoulders.

"Well, I suppose it is," growled Sikes. "I thought I had tamed her, but she's as bad as ever."

"Worse," said the Jew thoughtfully. "I never knew her like this, for such a little cause."

"Nor I," said Sikes. "I think she's got a touch of that fever in her blood yet, and it won't come out—eh?"

"Like enough," replied the Jew.

"I'll let her a little blood, without troubling the doctor, if she's took that way again," said Sikes.

The Jew nodded an expressive approval of this mode of treatment.

"She was hanging about me all day, and night too, when I was stretched on my back; and you, like a black-hearted wolf as you are, kept yourself aloof," said Sikes. "We was very poor too all the time, and I think, one way or other, it's worried and fretted her; and that being shut up here so long has made her restless—eh?"

"That's it, my dear," replied the Jew in a whisper. "Hush!"

As he uttered these words, the girl herself appeared and resumed her former seat. Her eyes were swollen and red; she rocked herself to and fro; tossed her head; and after a little time, burst out laughing.

"Why, now she's on the other tack!" exclaimed Sikes, turning a look of excessive surprise on his companion.

The Jew nodded to him to take no further notice just then; and, in a few minutes, the girl subsided into her accustomed demeanour. Whispering Sikes that there was no fear of her relapsing, Fagin took up his hat and bade him good-night. He paused when he reached the room-door, and looking round, asked if somebody would light him down the dark stairs.

"Light him down," said Sikes, who was filling his pipe. "It's a pity he should break his neck himself, and disappoint the sight-seers. Show him a light."

Nancy followed the old man down stairs, with a candle. When they reached the passage, he laid his finger on his lip, and drawing close to the girl, said, in a whisper,

"What is it, Nancy, dear?"

"What do you mean?" replied the girl in the same tone.

"The reason of all this," replied Fagin. "If *he*"—he pointed with his skinny fore-finger up the stairs—"is so hard with you, (he's a brute, Nance, a brute-beast) why don't you——"

"Well!" said the girl, as Fagin paused, with his mouth almost touching her ear, and his eyes looking into hers.

"No matter just now," said the Jew. "We'll talk of this again. You have a friend in me, Nance; a staunch friend. I have the means at hand, quiet and close. If you want revenge on those that treat you like a dog —like a dog! worse than his dog, for he humours him sometimes— come to me. I say, come to me. He is the mere hound of a day, but you know me, of old, Nance."

"I know you well," replied the girl, without manifesting the least emotion. "Good night."

She shrunk back, as Fagin offered to lay his hand on hers, but said good night again, in a steady voice, and, answering his parting look with a nod of intelligence, closed the door between them.

Fagin walked towards his own home, intent upon the thoughts that were working within his brain. He had conceived the idea—not from what had just passed, though that had tended to confirm him, but slowly and by degrees—that Nancy, wearied of the housebreaker's brutality, had conceived an attachment for some new friend. Her altered manner, her repeated absences from home alone, her comparative indifference to the interests of the gang for which she had once been so zealous, and, added to these, her desperate impatience to leave home that night at a particular hour, all favoured the supposition, and rendered it, to him at least, almost matter of certainty. The object of this new liking was not among his myrmidons.[4] He would be a valuable acquisition with such an assistant as Nancy, and must (thus Fagin argued) be secured without delay.

There was another, and a darker object, to be gained. Sikes knew too much, and his ruffian taunts had not galled the Jew the less, because the wounds were hidden. The girl must know, well, that if she shook him off, she could never be safe from his fury, and that it would be surely wreaked—to the maiming of limbs, or perhaps the loss of life— on the object of her more recent fancy. "With a little persuasion," thought Fagin, "what more likely than that she would consent to poison him! Women have done such things, and worse, to secure the same object before now. There would be the dangerous villain: the man I

4. Faithful followers, after Achilles' soldiers in the Trojan War.

hate: gone; another secured in his place; and my influence over the girl, with a knowledge of this crime to back it, unlimited."

These things passed through the mind of Fagin, during the short time he sat alone, in the housebreaker's room; and with them uppermost in his thoughts, he had taken the opportunity afterwards afforded him, of sounding the girl in the broken hints he threw out at parting. There was no expression of surprise, no assumption of an inability to understand his meaning. The girl clearly comprehended it. Her glance at parting showed *that*.

But perhaps she would recoil from a plot to take the life of Sikes, and that was one of the chief ends to be attained. "How," thought the Jew, as he crept homewards, "can I increase my influence with her? what new power can I acquire?"

Such brains are fertile in expedients. If, without extracting a confession from herself, he laid a watch, discovered the object of her altered regard, and threatened to reveal the whole history to Sikes (of whom she stood in no common fear) unless she entered into his designs, could he not secure her compliance?

"I can," said Fagin almost aloud. "She durst not refuse me then. Not for her life, not for her life! I have it all. The means are ready, and shall be set to work. I shall have you yet!"

He cast back a dark look, and a threatening motion of the hand, towards the spot where he had left the bolder villain; and went on his way: busying his bony hands in the folds of his tattered garment, which he wrenched tightly in his grasp, as though there were a hated enemy crushed with every motion of his fingers.

Chapter XLV.

NOAH CLAYPOLE IS EMPLOYED BY FAGIN ON A SECRET MISSION.

The old man was up, betimes, next morning, and waited impatiently for the appearance of his new associate, who, after a delay which seemed interminable, at length presented himself, and commenced a voracious assault on the breakfast.

"Bolter," said the Jew, drawing up a chair and seating himself opposite. "Morris Bolter."

"Well, here I am," returned Noah. "What's the matter? Don't yer ask me to do anything till I have done eating. That's a great fault in this place. Yer never get time enough over yer meals."

"You can talk as you eat, can't you?" said Fagin, cursing his dear young friend's greediness from the very bottom of his heart.

"Oh yes, I can talk. I get on better when I talk," said Noah, cutting a monstrous slice of bread. "Where's Charlotte?"

"Out," said Fagin. "I sent her out this morning with the other young woman, because I wanted us to be alone."

"Oh!" said Noah. "I wish yer'd ordered her to make some buttered toast first. Well. Talk away. Yer won't interrupt me."

There seemed, indeed, no great fear of anything interrupting him, as he had evidently sat down with a determination to do a great deal of business.

"You did well yesterday, my dear," said the Jew. "Beautiful! Six shillings and ninepence halfpenny on the very first day! The kinchin lay will be a fortune to you."

"Don't yer forget to add three pint-pots and a milk-can," said Mr. Bolter.

"No, no, my dear," replied the Jew. "The pint-pots were great strokes of genius; but the milk-can was a perfect masterpiece."

"Pretty well, I think, for a beginner," remarked Mr. Bolter, complacently. "The pots I took off airy railings, and the milk-can was standing by itself outside a public-house. I thought it might get rusty with the rain, or catch cold, yer know. Eh? Ha! ha! ha!"

The Jew affected to laugh very heartily; and Mr. Bolter, having had his laugh out, took a series of large bites, which finished his first hunk of bread and butter, and assisted himself to a second.

"I want you, Bolter," said Fagin, leaning over the table, "to do a piece of work for me, my dear, that needs great care and caution."

"I say," rejoined Bolter, "don't yer go shoving me into danger, or sending me to any more o' yer police-offices. That don't suit me, that don't; and so I tell yer."

"There's not the smallest danger in it—not the very smallest," said the Jew; "it's only to dodge a woman."

"An old woman?" demanded Mr. Bolter.

"A young one," replied Fagin.

"I can do that pretty well, I know," said Bolter. "I was a regular cunning sneak when I was at school. What am I to dodge her for? Not to—"

"Not to do anything," interrupted the Jew, "but to tell me where she goes, who she sees, and, if possible, what she says; to remember the street, if it is a street, or the house, if it is a house; and to bring me back all the information you can."

"What'll yer give me?" asked Noah, setting down his cup, and looking his employer, eagerly, in the face.

"If you do it well, a pound, my dear. One pound," said Fagin, wishing to interest him in the scent as much as possible. "And that's what I never gave yet, for any job of work where there wasn't valuable consideration to be gained."

"Who is she?" inquired Noah.

"One of us."

"Oh Lor!" cried Noah, curling up his nose. "Yer doubtful of her, are yer?"

"She has found out some new friends, my dear, and I must know who they are," replied the Jew.

"I see," said Noah. "Just to have the pleasure of knowing them, if they're respectable people, eh? Ha! ha! ha! I'm your man."

"I knew you would be," cried Fagin, elated by the success of his proposal.

"Of course, of course," replied Noah. "Where is she? Where am I to wait for her? When am I to go?"

"All that, my dear, you shall hear from me. I'll point her out at the proper time," said Fagin. "You keep ready, and leave the rest to me."

That night, and the next, and the next again, the spy sat booted and equipped in his carter's dress: ready to turn out at a word from Fagin. Six nights passed—six long weary nights—and on each, Fagin came home with a disappointed face, and briefly intimated that it was not yet time. On the seventh, he returned earlier, and with an exultation he could not conceal. It was Sunday.

"She goes abroad to-night," said Fagin, "and on the right errand, I'm sure; for she has been alone all day, and the man she is afraid of, will not be back much before daybreak. Come with me. Quick!"

Noah started up without saying a word; for the Jew was in a state of such intense excitement that it infected him. They left the house stealthily, and, hurrying through a labyrinth of streets, arrived at length before a public-house, which Noah recognised as the same in which he had slept, on the night of his arrival in London.

It was past eleven o'clock, and the door was closed. It opened softly on its hinges as the Jew gave a low whistle. They entered, without noise; and the door was closed behind them.

Scarcely venturing to whisper, but substituting dumb show for words, Fagin, and the young Jew who had admitted them, pointed out the pane of glass to Noah, and signed to him to climb up and observe the person in the adjoining room.

"Is that the woman?" he asked, scarcely above his breath.

The Jew nodded yes.

"I can't see her face well," whispered Noah. "She is looking down, and the candle is behind her."

"Stay there," whispered Fagin. He signed to Barney, who withdrew. In an instant, the lad entered the room adjoining, and, under pretence of snuffing the candle, moved it into the required position, and, speaking to the girl, caused her to raise her face.

"I see her now," cried the spy.

"Plainly?" asked the Jew.

"I should know her among a thousand."

He hastily descended, as the room-door opened, and the girl came out. Fagin drew him behind a small partition which was curtained off, and they held their breaths as she passed within a few feet of their place of concealment, and emerged by the door at which they had entered.

"Hist!" cried the lad who held the door. "Dow."[5]

Noah exchanged a look with Fagin, and darted out.

"To the left," whispered the lad; "take the left had, and keep od the other side."

He did so; and, by the light of the lamps, saw the girl's retreating figure, already at some distance before him. He advanced as near as he considered prudent, and kept on the opposite side of the street, the better to observe her motions. She looked nervously round, twice or thrice, and once stopped to let two men who were following close behind her, pass on. She seemed to gather courage as she advanced, and to walk with a steadier and firmer step. The spy preserved the same relative distance between them, and followed: with his eye upon her.

Chapter XLVI.

THE APPOINTMENT KEPT.

The church clocks chimed three quarters past eleven, as two figures emerged on London Bridge. One, which advanced with a swift and rapid step, was that of a woman, who looked eagerly about her as though in quest of some expected object; the other figure was that of a man, who slunk along in the deepest shadow he could find, and, at some distance, accommodated his pace to hers: stopping when she stopped: and, as she moved again, creeping stealthily on: but never allowing himself, in the ardour of his pursuit, to gain upon her footsteps. Thus, they crossed the bridge, from the Middlesex to the Surrey shore:[1] when the woman, apparently disappointed in her anxious scrutiny of the foot-passengers, turned back. The movement was sudden; but he who watched her, was not thrown off his guard by it; for, shrinking into one of the recesses which surmount the piers of the bridge, and leaning over the parapet the better to conceal his figure, he suffered her to pass by, on the opposite pavement. When she was about the same distance in advance as she had been before, he slipped quietly down, and followed her again. At nearly the centre of the bridge, she stopped. The man stopped too.

It was a very dark night. The day had been unfavourable, and at that hour and place there were few people stirring. Such as there were, hurried quickly past: very possibly without seeing, but certainly without noticing, either the woman, or the man who kept her in view. Their

5. Down.
1. London Bridge connects the oldest part of London, in Middlesex County, on the north shore of the river Thames, to the suburbs on the south shore, in the county of Surrey; both areas are now part of Greater London.

appearance was not calculated to attract the importunate regards of such of London's destitute population, as chanced to take their way over the bridge that night in search of some cold arch or doorless hovel wherein to lay their heads; they stood there in silence: neither speaking nor spoken to, by any one who passed.

A mist hung over the river, deepening the red glare of the fires that burnt upon the small craft moored off the different wharfs, and rendering darker and more indistinct the mirky buildings on the banks. The old smoke-stained storehouses on either side, rose heavy and dull from the dense mass of roofs and gables, and frowned sternly upon water too black to reflect even their lumbering shapes. The tower of old Saint Saviour's church,[2] and the spire of Saint Magnus, so long the giant-warders of the ancient bridge, were visible in the gloom; but the forest of shipping below bridge, and the thickly scattered spires of churches above, were nearly all hidden from the sight.

The girl had taken a few restless turns to and fro—closely watched meanwhile by her hidden observer—when the heavy bell of St. Paul's tolled for the death of another day. Midnight had come upon the crowded city. The palace, the night-cellar, the jail, the madhouse: the chambers of birth and death, of health and sickness: the rigid face of the corpse and the calm sleep of the child: midnight was upon them all.

The hour had not struck two minutes, when a young lady, accompanied by a grey-haired gentleman, alighted from a hackney-carriage within a short distance of the bridge, and, having dismissed the vehicle, walked straight towards it. They had scarcely set foot upon its pavement, when the girl started, and immediately made towards them.

They walked onward, looking about them with the air of persons who entertained some very slight expectation which had little chance of being realised, when they were suddenly joined by this new associate. They halted with an exclamation of surprise, but suppressed it immediately; for a man in the garments of a countryman came close up—brushed against them, indeed—at that precise moment.

"Not here," said Nancy hurriedly. "I am afraid to speak to you here. Come away—out of the public road—down the steps yonder!"

As she uttered these words, and indicated, with her hand, the direction in which she wished them to proceed, the countryman looked round, and roughly asking what they took up the whole pavement for, passed on.

The steps to which the girl had pointed, were those which, on the Surrey bank, and on the same side of the bridge as Saint Saviour's church, form a landing-stairs from the river. To this spot, the man bearing the appearance of a countryman, hastened unobserved; and after a moment's survey of the place, he began to descend.

2. Now Southwark Cathedral.

These stairs are a part of the bridge; they consist of three flights. Just below the end of the second, going down, the stone wall on the left terminates in an ornamental pier or pedestal facing towards the Thames. At this point, the lower steps widen: so that a person turning that angle of the wall, is necessarily unseen by any others on the stairs who chance to be above him, if only a step. The countryman looked hastily round, when he reached this point; and as there seemed no better place of concealment, and, the tide being out, there was plenty of room, he slipped aside, with his back to the pier, and there waited: pretty certain that they would come no lower, and that even if he could not hear what was said, he could follow them again, with safety.

So tardily stole the time in this lonely place, and so eager was the spy to penetrate the motives of an interview so different from what he had been led to expect, that he more than once gave the matter up for lost, and persuaded himself, either that they had stopped far above, or had resorted to some entirely different spot to hold their mysterious conversation. He was on the very point of emerging from his hiding-place, and regaining the road above, when he heard the sound of footsteps, and directly afterwards of voices almost close at his ear.

He drew himself straight upright against the wall, and, scarcely breathing, listened attentively.

"This is far enough," said a voice, which was evidently that of the gentleman. "I will not suffer the young lady to go any farther. Many people would have distrusted you too much to have come even so far, but you see I am willing to humour you."

"To humour me!" cried the voice of the girl whom he had followed. "You're considerate, indeed, sir. To humour me! Well, well, it's no matter."

"Why, for what," said the gentleman in a kinder tone, "for what purpose can you have brought us to this strange place? Why not have let me speak to you, above there, where it is light, and there is something stirring, instead of bringing us to this dark and dismal hole?"

"I told you before," replied Nancy, "that I was afraid to speak to you there. I don't know why it is," said the girl, shuddering, "but I have such a fear and dread upon me to-night that I can hardly stand."

"A fear of what?" asked the gentleman, who seemed to pity her.

"I scarcely know of what," replied the girl. "I wish I did. Horrible thoughts of death, and shrouds with blood upon them, and a fear that has made me burn as if I was on fire, have been upon me all day. I was reading a book to-night, to wile the time away, and the same things came into the print."

"Imagination," said the gentleman, soothing her.

"No imagination," replied the girl in a hoarse voice. "I'll swear I saw 'coffin' written in every page of the book in large black letters,—aye, and they carried one close to me, in the streets to-night."

"There is nothing unusual in that," said the gentleman. "They have passed me often."

"*Real ones,*" rejoined the girl. "This was not."

There was something so uncommon in her manner, that the flesh of the concealed listener crept as he heard the girl utter these words, and the blood chilled within him. He had never experienced a greater relief than in hearing the sweet voice of the young lady as she begged her to be calm, and not allow herself to become the prey of such fearful fancies.

"Speak to her kindly," said the young lady to her companion. "Poor creature! She seems to need it."

"Your haughty religious people would have held their heads up to see me as I am to-night, and preached of flames and vengeance," cried the girl. "Oh, dear lady, why ar'n't those who claim to be God's own folks as gentle and as kind to us poor wretches as you, who, having youth, and beauty, and all that they have lost, might be a little proud instead of so much humbler?"

"Ah!" said the gentleman. "A Turk turns his face, after washing it well, to the East, when he says his prayers; these good people, after giving their faces such a rub against the World as to take the smiles off, turn, with no less regularity, to the darkest side of Heaven. Between the Mussulman and the Pharisee,[3] commend me to the first!"

These words appeared to be addressed to the young lady, and were perhaps uttered with the view of affording Nancy time to recover herself. The gentleman, shortly afterwards, addressed himself to her.

"You were not here last Sunday night," he said.

"I couldn't come," replied Nancy; "I was kept by force."

"By whom?"

"Him that I told the young lady of before."

"You were not suspected of holding any communication with anybody on the subject which has brought us here to-night, I hope?" asked the old gentleman.

"No," replied the girl, shaking her head. "It's not very easy for me to leave him unless he knows why; I couldn't have seen the lady when I did, but that I gave him a drink of laudanum before I came away."

"Did he awake before you returned?" inquired the gentleman.

"No; and neither he nor any of them suspect me."

"Good," said the gentleman. "Now listen to me."

"I am ready," replied the girl, as he paused for a moment.

"This young lady," the gentleman began, "has communicated to me, and to some other friends who can be safely trusted, what you told her nearly a fortnight since. I confess to you that I had doubts, at first, whether you were to be implicitly relied upon, but now I firmly believe you are."

3. A hypocritically self-righteous Christian. "Mussulman": Moslem.

"I am," said the girl earnestly.

"I repeat that I firmly believe it. To prove to you that I am disposed to trust you, I tell you without reserve, that we propose to extort the secret, whatever it may be, from the fears of this man Monks. But if—if—" said the gentleman, "he cannot be secured, or, if secured, cannot be acted upon as we wish, you must deliver up the Jew."

"Fagin," cried the girl, recoiling.

"That man must be delivered up by you," said the gentleman.

"I will not do it! I will never do it!" replied the girl. "Devil that he is, and worse than devil as he has been to me, I will never do that."

"You will not?" said the gentleman, who seemed fully prepared for this answer.

"Never!" returned the girl.

"Tell me why?"

"For one reason," rejoined the girl firmly, "for one reason, that the lady knows and will stand by me in, I know she will, for I have her promise; and for this other reason, besides, that, bad life as he has led, I have led a bad life too; there are many of us who have kept the same courses together, and I'll not turn upon them, who might—any of them—have turned upon me, but didn't, bad as they are."

"Then," said the gentleman, quickly, as if this had been the point he had been aiming to attain; "put Monks into my hands, and leave him to me to deal with."

"What if he turns against the others?"

"I promise you that in that case, if the truth is forced from him, there the matter will rest; there must be circumstances in Oliver's little history which it would be painful to drag before the public eye, and if the truth is once elicited, they shall go scot free."

"And if it is not?" suggested the girl.

"Then," pursued the gentleman, "this Jew shall not be brought to justice without your consent. In such a case I could show you reasons, I think, which would induce you to yield it."

"Have I the lady's promise for that?" asked the girl.

"You have," replied Rose. "My true and faithful pledge."

"Monks would never learn how you knew what you do?" said the girl, after a short pause.

"Never," replied the gentleman. "The intelligence should be so brought to bear upon him, that he could never even guess."

"I have been a liar, and among liars from a little child," said the girl after another interval of silence, "but I will take your words."

After receiving an assurance from both, that she might safely do so, she proceeded in a voice so low that it was often difficult for the listener to discover even the purport of what she said, to describe, by name and situation, the public-house whence she had been followed that night. From the manner in which she occasionally paused, it appeared as if the gentleman were making some hasty notes of the information she communicated. When she had thoroughly explained the localities of the place, the best position from which to watch it without exciting observation, and the night and hour on which Monks was most in the habit of frequenting it, she seemed to consider for a few moments, for the purpose of recalling his features and appearance more forcibly to her recollection.

"He is tall," said the girl, "and a strongly made man, but not stout; he has a lurking walk; and as he walks, constantly looks over his shoulder, first on one side, and then on the other. Don't forget that, for his eyes are sunk in his head so much deeper than any other man's, that you might almost tell him by that alone. His face is dark, like his hair and eyes; and, although he can't be more than six or eight and twenty, withered and haggard. His lips are often discoloured and disfigured with the marks of teeth; for he has desperate fits, and sometimes even bites his hands and covers them with wounds—why did you start?" said the girl, stopping suddenly.

The gentleman replied, in a hurried manner, that he was not conscious of having done so, and begged her to proceed.

"Part of this," said the girl, "I've drawn out from other people at the house I tell you of, for I have only seen him twice, and both times he was covered up in a large cloak. I think that's all I can give you to know him by. Stay though," she added. "Upon his throat: so high that you can see a part of it below his neckerchief when he turns his face: there is—"

"A broad red mark, like a burn or scald," cried the gentleman.

"How's this!" said the girl. "You know him!"

The young lady uttered a cry of surprise, and for a few moments they were so still that the listener could distinctly hear them breathe.

"I think I do," said the gentleman, breaking silence. "I should by your description. We shall see. Many people are singularly like each other. It may not be the same."

As he expressed himself to this effect, with assumed carelessness, he took a step or two nearer the concealed spy, as the latter could tell from the distinctness with which he heard him mutter, "It must be he!"

"Now," he said, returning: so it seemed by the sound: to the spot where he had stood before, "you have given us most valuable assistance, young woman, and I wish you to be the better for it. What can I do to serve you?"

"Nothing," replied Nancy.

"You will not persist in saying that," rejoined the gentleman with a voice and emphasis of kindness that might have touched a much harder and more obdurate heart. "Think now. Tell me."

"Nothing, sir," rejoined the girl, weeping. "You can do nothing to help me. I am past all hope, indeed."

"You put yourself beyond its pale," said the gentleman. "The past has been a dreary waste with you, of youthful energies mis-spent, and such priceless treasures lavished, as the Creator bestows but once and never grants again, but, for the future, you may hope. I do not say that it is in our power to offer you peace of heart and mind, for that must come as you seek it; but a quiet asylum, either in England, or, if you fear to remain here, in some foreign country, it is not only within the compass of our ability but our most anxious wish to secure to you. Before the dawn of morning, before this river wakes to the first glimpse of daylight, you shall be placed as entirely beyond the reach of your former associates, and leave as utter an absence of all trace behind you, as if you were to disappear from the earth this moment. Come! I would not have you go back to exchange one word with any old companion, or take one look at any old haunt, or breathe the very air which is pestilence and death to you. Quit them all, while there is time and opportunity!"

"She will be persuaded now," cried the young lady. "She hesitates, I am sure."

"I fear not, my dear," said the gentleman.

"No sir, I do not," replied the girl after a short struggle. "I am chained to my old life. I loathe and hate it now, but I cannot leave it. I must have gone too far to turn back,—and yet I don't know, for if you had spoken to me so, some time ago, I should have laughed it off. But," she said, looking hastily round, "this fear comes over me again. I must go home."

"Home!" repeated the young lady, with great stress upon the word.

"Home, lady," rejoined the girl. "To such a home as I have raised for myself with the work of my whole life. Let us part. I shall be watched or seen. Go! Go! If I have done you any service, all I ask is, that you leave me, and let me go my way alone."

"It is useless," said the gentleman with a sigh. "We compromise her safety, perhaps, by staying here. We may have detained her longer than she expected already."

"Yes, yes," urged the girl. "You have."

"What," cried the young lady, "can be the end of this poor creature's life!"

"What!" repeated the girl. "Look before you, lady. Look at that dark water. How many times do you read of such as I who spring into the tide, and leave no living thing, to care for, or bewail them. It may be years hence, or it may be only months, but I shall come to that at last."

"Do not speak thus, pray," returned the young lady sobbing.

"It will never reach your ears, dear lady, and God forbid such horrors should!" replied the girl. "Good night, good night!"

The gentleman turned away.

"This purse," cried the young lady. "Take it for my sake, that you may have some resource in an hour of need and trouble."

"No!" replied the girl. "I have not done this for money. Let me have that to think of. And yet—give me something that you have worn: I should like to have something—no, no, not a ring—your gloves or handkerchief—anything that I can keep, as having belonged to you, sweet lady. There. Bless you! God bless you. Good night, good night!"

The violent agitation of the girl, and the apprehension of some discovery which would subject her to ill-usage and violence, seemed to determine the gentleman to leave her, as she requested. The sound of retreating footsteps was audible, and the voices ceased.

The two figures of the young lady and her companion soon afterwards appeared upon the bridge. They stopped at the summit of the stairs.

"Hark!" cried the young lady, listening. "Did she call! I thought I heard her voice."

"No, my love," replied Mr. Brownlow, looking sadly back. "She has not moved, and will not till we are gone."

Rose Maylie lingered, but the old gentleman drew her arm through his, and led her, with gentle force, away. As they disappeared, the girl sunk down nearly at her full length upon one of the stone stairs, and vented the anguish of her heart in bitter tears.

After a time she arose, and with feeble and tottering steps ascended to the street. The astonished listener remained motionless on his post for some minutes afterwards, and having ascertained, with many cautious glances round him, that he was again alone, crept slowly from his hiding-place, and returned, stealthily and in the shade of the wall, in the same manner as he had descended.

Peeping out, more than once, when he reached the top, to make sure that he was unobserved, Noah Claypole darted away at his utmost speed, and made for the Jew's house as fast as his legs would carry him.

Chapter XLVII.

FATAL CONSEQUENCES.

It was nearly two hours before daybreak; that time, which, in the autumn of the year, may be truly called the dead of night; when the streets are silent and deserted; when even sound appears to slumber, and profligacy and riot have staggered home to dream; it was at this still and silent hour, that the Jew sat watching in his old lair, with face so distorted and pale, and eyes so red and bloodshot, that he looked less like a man, than like some hideous phantom: moist from the grave, and worried by an evil spirit.

He sat crouching over a cold hearth, wrapped in an old torn coverlet, with his face turned towards a wasting candle that stood upon a table by his side. His right hand was raised to his lips, and as, absorbed in thought, he bit his long black nails, he disclosed among his toothless gums a few such fangs as should have been a dog's or rat's.

Stretched upon a mattress on the floor, lay Noah Claypole, fast asleep. Towards him the old man sometimes directed his eyes for an instant, and then brought them back again to the candle: which, with long-burnt wick drooping almost double, and hot grease falling down in clots upon the table, plainly showed that his thoughts were busy elsewhere.

Indeed they were. Mortification at the overthrow of his notable scheme; hatred of the girl who had dared to palter[1] with strangers; an utter distrust of the sincerity of her refusal to yield him up; bitter disappointment at the loss of his revenge on Sikes; the fear of detection, and ruin, and death; and a fierce and deadly rage kindled by all; these were the passionate considerations which, following close upon each other with rapid and ceaseless whirl, shot through the brain of Fagin, as every evil thought and blackest purpose lay working at his heart.

He sat without changing his attitude in the least, or appearing to take the smallest heed of time, until his quick ear seemed to be attracted by a footstep in the street.

"At last," muttered the Jew, wiping his dry and fevered mouth. "At last!"

The bell rang gently, as he spoke. He crept up stairs to the door, and presently returned accompanied by a man muffled to the chin, who carried a bundle under one arm. Sitting down, and throwing back his outer coat, the man displayed the burly frame of Sikes.

"There!" he said, laying the bundle on the table. "Take care of that, and do the most you can with it. It's been trouble enough to get; I thought I should have been here, three hours ago."

Fagin laid his hand upon the bundle, and locking it in the cupboard, sat down again without speaking. But he did not take his eyes off the robber, for an instant, during this action; and now that they sat over against each other, face to face, he looked fixedly at him, with his lips quivering so violently, and his face so altered by the emotions which had mastered him, that the housebreaker involuntarily drew back his chair, and surveyed him with a look of real affright.

"Wot now?" cried Sikes. "Wot do you look at a man so for?"

The Jew raised his right hand, and shook his trembling forefinger in the air; but his passion was so great, that the power of speech was for the moment gone.

"Damme!" said Sikes, feeling in his breast with a look of alarm. "He's gone mad. I must look to myself here."

1. To talk in a low voice and bargain.

"No, no," rejoined Fagin, finding his voice. "It's not—you're not the person, Bill. I've no—no fault to find with you."

"Oh, you haven't, haven't you?" said Sikes, looking sternly at him, and ostentatiously passing a pistol into a more convenient pocket. "That's lucky—for one of us. Which one that is, don't matter."

"I've got that to tell you, Bill," said the Jew, drawing his chair nearer, "will make you worse than me."

"Aye?" returned the robber with an incredulous air. "Tell away! Look sharp, or Nance will think I'm lost."

"Lost!" cried Fagin. "She has pretty well settled that, in her own mind, already."

Sikes looked with an aspect of great perplexity into the Jew's face, and reading no satisfactory explanation of the riddle there, clenched his coat collar in his huge hand and shook him soundly.

"Speak, will you!" he said; "or if you don't, it shall be for want of breath. Open your mouth and say wot you've got to say in plain words. Out with it, you thundering old cur, out with it!"

"Suppose that lad that's lying there——" Fagin began.

Sikes turned round to where Noah was sleeping, as if he had not previously observed him. "Well!" he said, resuming his former position.

"Suppose that lad," pursued the Jew, "was to peach—blow upon us all—first seeking out the right folks for the purpose, and then having a meeting with 'em in the street to paint our likenesses, describe every mark that they might know us by, and the crib where we might be most easily taken. Suppose he was to do all this, and besides to blow upon a plant we've all been in, more or less—of his own fancy; not grabbed, trapped, tried, earwigged[2] by the parson and brought to it on bread and water,—but of his own fancy; to please his own taste; stealing out at nights to find those most interested against us, and peaching to them. Do you hear me?" cried the Jew, his eyes flashing with rage. "Suppose he did all this, what then?"

"What then!" replied Sikes with a tremendous oath. "If he was left alive till I came, I'd grind his skull under the iron heel of my boot into as many grains as there are hairs upon his head."

"What if I did it!" cried the Jew almost in a yell. "I, that know so much, and could hang so many besides myself!"

"I don't know," replied Sikes, clenching his teeth and turning white at the mere suggestion. "I'd do something in the jail that 'ud get me put in irons; and if I was tried along with you, I'd fall upon you with them in the open court, and beat your brains out afore the people. I should have such strength," muttered the robber, poising his brawny arm, "that I could smash your head as if a loaded wagon had gone over it."

2. Intimidated.

"You would?"

"Would I!" said the housebreaker. "Try me."

"If it was Charley, or the Dodger, or Bet, or——"

"I don't care who," replied Sikes impatiently. "Whoever it was, I'd serve them the same."

Fagin again looked hard at the robber; and, motioning him to be silent, stooped over the bed upon the floor, and shook the sleeper to rouse him. Sikes leant forward in his chair: looking on with his hands upon his knees, as if wondering much what all this questioning and preparation was to end in.

"Bolter, Bolter! Poor lad!" said Fagin, looking up with an expression of devilish anticipation, and speaking slowly and with marked emphasis. "He's tired—tired with watching for *her* so long,—watching for *her*, Bill."

"Wot d'ye mean?" asked Sikes, drawing back.

The Jew made no answer, but bending over the sleeper again, hauled him into a sitting posture. When his assumed name had been repeated several times, Noah rubbed his eyes, and, giving a heavy yawn, looked sleepily about him.

"Tell me that again—once again, just for him to hear," said the Jew, pointing to Sikes as he spoke.

"Tell yer what?" asked the sleepy Noah, shaking himself pettishly.

"That about—Nancy," said the Jew, clutching Sikes by the wrist, as if to prevent his leaving the house before he had heard enough. "You followed her?"

"Yes."

"To London Bridge?"

"Yes."

"Where she met two people?"

"So she did."

"A gentleman, and a lady that she had gone to of her own accord before, who asked her to give up all her pals, and Monks first, which she did—and to describe him, which she did—and to tell her what house it was that we meet at, and go to, which she did—and where it could be best watched from, which she did—and what time the people went there, which she did. She did all this. She told it all every word without a threat, without a murmur—she did—did she not?" cried the Jew, half mad with fury.

"All right," replied Noah, scratching his head. "That's just what it was!"

What did they say, about last Sunday?" demanded the Jew.

"About last Sunday!" replied Noah, considering. "Why, I told yer that before."

"Again. Tell it again!" cried Fagin, tightening his grasp on Sikes, and brandishing his other hand aloft, as the foam flew from his lips.

"They asked her," said Noah, who, as he grew more wakeful, seemed to have a dawning perception who Sikes was, "they asked her why she didn't come, last Sunday, as she promised. She said she couldn't."

"Why—why?" interrupted the Jew triumphantly. "Tell him that."

"Because she was forcibly kept at home by Bill, the man she had told them of before," replied Noah.

"What more of him?" cried the Jew. "What more of the man she had told them of before? Tell him that, tell him that."

"Why, that she couldn't very easily get out of doors unless he knew where she was going to," said Noah; "and so the first time she went to see the lady, she—ha! ha! ha! it made me laugh when she said it, that it did—she gave him a drink of laudanum."

"Hell's fire!" cried Sikes, breaking fiercely from the Jew. "Let me go!"

Flinging the old man from him, he rushed from the room, and darted, wildly and furiously, up the stairs.

"Bill, Bill!" cried the Jew, following him hastily. "A word. Only a word."

The word would not have been exchanged, but that the housebreaker was unable to open the door: on which he was expending fruitless oaths and violence, when the Jew came panting up.

"Let me out," said Sikes. "Don't speak to me; it's not safe. Let me out, I say."

"Hear me speak a word," rejoined the Jew, laying his hand upon the lock. "You won't be——"

"Well," replied the other.

"You won't be—too—violent, Bill?" whined the Jew.

The day was breaking, and there was light enough for the men to see each other's faces. They exchanged one brief glance; there was a fire in the eyes of both, which could not be mistaken.

"I mean," said Fagin, showing that he felt all disguise was now useless, "not too violent for safety. Be crafty, Bill, and not too bold."

Sikes made no reply; but, pulling open the door, of which the Jew had turned the lock, dashed into the silent streets.

Without one pause, or moment's consideration; without once turning his head to the right, or left, or raising his eyes to the sky, or lowering them to the ground, but looking straight before him with savage resolution: his teeth so tightly compressed that the strained jaw seemed starting through his skin; the robber held on his headlong course, nor muttered a word, nor relaxed a muscle, until he reached his own door. He opened it, softly, with a key; strode lightly up the stairs; and entering his own room, double-locked the door, and lifting a heavy table against it, drew back the curtain of the bed.

The girl was lying, half-dressed, upon it. He had roused her from her sleep, for she raised herself with a hurried and startled look.

"Get up!" said the man.

"It *is* you, Bill!" said the girl, with an expression of pleasure at his return.

"It is," was the reply. "Get up."

There was a candle burning, but the man hastily drew it from the candlestick, and hurled it under the grate. Seeing the faint light of early day, without, the girl rose to undraw the curtain.

"Let it be," said Sikes, thrusting his hand before her. "There's light enough for wot I've got to do."

"Bill," said the girl, in the low voice of alarm, "why do you look like that at me!"

The robber sat regarding her, for a few seconds, with dilated nostrils and heaving breast; and then, grasping her by the head and throat, dragged her into the middle of the room, and looking once towards the door, placed his heavy hand upon her mouth.

"Bill, Bill!" gasped the girl, wrestling with the strength of mortal fear,—"I—I won't scream or cry—not once—hear me—speak to me —tell me what I have done!"

"You know, you she devil!" returned the robber, suppressing his breath. "You were watched to-night; every word you said was heard."

"Then spare my life for the love of Heaven, as I spared yours," rejoined the girl, clinging to him. "Bill, dear Bill, you cannot have the heart to kill me. Oh! think of all I have given up, only this one night, for you. You *shall* have time to think, and save yourself this crime; I will not loose my hold, you cannot throw me off. Bill, Bill, for dear God's sake, for your own, for mine, stop before you spill my blood! I have been true to you, upon my guilty soul I have!"

The man struggled, violently, to release his arms; but those of the girl were clasped round his, and tear her as he would, he could not tear them away.

"Bill," cried the girl, striving to lay her head upon his breast, "the gentleman, and that dear lady, told me to-night of a home in some foreign country where I could end my days in solitude and peace. Let me see them again, and beg them, on my knees, to show the same mercy and goodness to you; and let us both leave this dreadful place, and far apart lead better lives, and forget how we have lived, except in prayers, and never see each other more. It is never too late to repent. They told me so—I feel it now—but we must have time—a little, little time!"

The house-breaker freed one arm, and grasped his pistol. The certainty of immediate detection if he fired, flashed across his mind even in the midst of his fury; and he beat it twice with all the force he could summon, upon the upturned face that almost touched his own.

She staggered and fell: nearly blinded with the blood that rained down from a deep gash in her forehead; but raising herself, with difficulty, on her knees, drew from her bosom a white handkerchief—Rose Maylie's own—and holding it up, in her folded hands, as high towards Heaven as her feeble strength would allow, breathed one prayer for mercy to her Maker.

It was a ghastly figure to look upon. The murderer staggering backward to the wall, and shutting out the sight with his hand, seized a heavy club and struck her down.

Chapter XLVIII.

THE FLIGHT OF SIKES.

Of all bad deeds that, under cover of the darkness, had been committed within wide London's bounds since night hung over it, that was the worst. Of all the horrors that rose with an ill scent upon the morning air, that was the foulest and most cruel.

The sun,—the bright sun, that brings back, not light alone, but new life, and hope, and freshness to man—burst upon the crowded city in clear and radiant glory. Through costly-coloured glass and paper-mended window, through cathedral dome and rotten crevice, it shed its equal ray. It lighted up the room where the murdered woman lay. It did. He tried to shut it out, but it would stream in. If the sight had been a ghastly one in the dull morning, what was it, now, in all that brilliant light!

He had not moved; he had been afraid to stir. There had been a moan and motion of the hand; and, with terror added to hate, he had struck and struck again. Once he threw a rug over it; but it was worse to fancy the eyes, and imagine them moving towards him, than to see them glaring upward, as if watching the reflection of the pool of gore that quivered and danced in the sunlight on the ceiling. He had plucked it off again. And there was the body—mere flesh and blood, no more—but such flesh, and so much blood!

He struck a light, kindled a fire, and thrust the club into it. There was hair upon the end, which blazed and shrunk into a light cinder, and, caught by the air, whirled up the chimney. Even that frightened him, sturdy as he was; but he held the weapon till it broke, and then piled it on the coals to burn away, and smoulder into ashes. He washed himself, and rubbed his clothes; there were spots that would not be removed, but he cut the pieces out, and burnt them. How those stains were dispersed about the room! The very feet of the dog were bloody.

All this time he had, never once, turned his back upon the corpse; no, not for a moment. Such preparations completed, he moved, backward, towards the door: dragging the dog with him, lest he should soil his feet anew and carry out new evidences of the crime into the streets. He shut the door softly, locked it, took the key, and left the house.

He crossed over, and glanced up at the window, to be sure that nothing was visible from the outside. There was the curtain still drawn, which she would have opened to admit the light she never saw again. It lay nearly under there. *He* knew that. God, how the sun poured down upon the very spot!

The glance was instantaneous. It was a relief to have got free of the room. He whistled on the dog, and walked rapidly away.

He went through Islington; strode up the hill at Highgate on which stands the stone in honour of Whittington;[1] turned down to Highgate Hill, unsteady of purpose, and uncertain where to go; struck off to the right again, almost as soon as he began to descend it; and taking the foot path across the fields, skirted Caen Wood, and so came out on Hampstead Heath.[2] Traversing the hollow by the Vale of Health, he mounted the opposite bank, and crossing the road which joins the villages of Hampstead and Highgate, made along the remaining portion of the heath to the fields at North End, in one of which he laid himself down under a hedge, and slept.

Soon he was up again, and away,—not far into the country, but back towards London by the high-road—then back again—then over another part of the same ground as he had already traversed—then wandering up and down in fields, and lying on ditches' brinks to rest, and starting up to make for some other spot, and do the same, and ramble on again.

Were could he go, that was near and not too public, to get some meat and drink? Hendon.[3] That was a good place, not far off, and out of most people's way. Thither he directed his steps,—running sometimes, and sometimes, with a strange perversity, loitering at a snail's pace, or stopping altogether and idly breaking the hedges with his stick. But when he got there, all the people he met—the very children at the doors—seemed to view him with suspicion. Back he turned again, without the courage to purchase bit or drop, though he had tasted no food for many hours; and once more he lingered on the Heath, uncertain where to go.

He wandered over miles and miles of ground, and still came back to the old place. Morning and noon had passed, and the day was on the wane, and still he rambled to and fro, and up and down, and round and round, and still lingered about the same spot. At last he got away, and shaped his course for Hatfield.[4]

It was nine o'clock at night, when the man, quite tired out, and the dog, limping and lame from the unaccustomed exercise, turned down the hill by the church of the quiet village, and plodding along the little

1. A monument in honor of Richard (Dick) Whittington, lord mayor of London, 1397–98. When young and impoverished, Whittington, so the legend recounts, paused to rest at Highgate as he was leaving London and heard the bells of London calling to him, "Turn again, Whittington, Lord Mayor of London."
2. A large wooded park that separates the villages of Hampstead and Highgate, now part of Greater London.
3. A town about two miles northwest of Highgate.
4. A town in Hertfordshire about fifteen miles northwest of central London.

street, crept into a small public-house, whose scanty light had guided them to the spot. There was a fire in the tap-room and some country-labourers were drinking before it. They made room for the stranger, but he sat down in the furthest corner, and ate and drank alone, or rather with his dog: to whom he cast a morsel of food from time to time.

The conversation of the men assembled here, turned upon the neighbouring land, and farmers; and when those topics were exhausted, upon the age of some old man who had been buried on the previous Sunday: the young men present considering him very old, and the old men present declaring him to have been quite young—not older, one white-haired grandfather said, than he was—with ten or fifteen year of life in him at least—if he had taken care; if he had taken care.

There was nothing to attract attention, or excite alarm, in this. The robber, after paying his reckoning, sat silent and unnoticed in his corner, and had almost dropped asleep, when he was half wakened by the noisy entrance of a new-comer.

This was an antic fellow, half pedlar and half mountebank, who travelled about the country on foot, to vend hones, strops, razors, wash-balls, harness-paste,[5] medicine for dogs and horses, cheap perfumery, cosmetics, and such-like wares, which he carried in a case slung to his back. His entrance was the signal for various homely jokes with the countrymen, which slackened not until he had made his supper, and opened his box of treasures, when he ingeniously contrived to unite business with amusement.

"And what be that stoof?[6] Good to eat, Harry?" asked a grinning countryman, pointing to some composition-cakes in one corner.

"This," said the fellow, producing one, "this is the infallible and invaluable composition for removing all sorts of stain, rust, dirt, mildew, spick, speck, spot, or spatter, from silk, satin, linen, cambric, cloth, crape, stuff, carpet, merino, muslin, bombazeen,[7] or woollen stuff. Wine-stains, fruit-stains, beer-stains, water-stains, paint-stains, pitch-stains, any stains, all come out at one rub with the infallible and invaluable composition. If a lady stains her honour, she has only need to swallow one cake and she's cured at once—for it's poison. If a gentleman wants to prove his, he has only need to bolt one little square, and he has put it beyond question—for it's quite as satisfactory as a pistol-bullet, and a great deal nastier in the flavour, consequently the more credit in taking it. One penny a square. With all these virtues, one penny a square!"

5. A paste to be rubbed into harness leather to soften and polish it. "Mountebank": a traveling salesman who entertains his customers as part of his sales pitch. "Hones": stones on which to sharpen knives. "Strops": leather straps on which to sharpen razors.
6. Stuff.
7. A cotton fabric sometimes combined with silk; the material favored for black mourning clothes. "Cambric": fine white linen. "Merino": a soft fine wool.

There were two buyers directly, and more of the listeners plainly hesitated. The vendor observing this, increased in loquacity.

"It's all bought up as fast as it can be made," said the fellow. "There are fourteen water-mills, six steam-engines, and a galvanic battery,[8] always a-working upon it, and they can't make it fast enough, though the men work so hard that they die off, and the widows is pensioned directly, with twenty pound a-year for each of the children, and a premium of fifty for twins. One penny a square! Two halfpence is all the same, and four farthings is received with joy. One penny a-square! Wine-stains, fruit-stains, beer-stains, water-stains, paint-stains, pitch-stains, mud-stains, blood-stains! Here is a stain upon the hat of a gentleman in company, that I'll take clean out, before he can order me a pint of ale."

"Hah!" cried Sikes starting up. "Give that back."

"I'll take it clean out, sir," replied the man, winking to the company, "before you can come across the room to get it. Gentlemen all, observe the dark stain upon this gentleman's hat, no wider than a shilling, but thicker than a half-crown. Whether it is a wine-stain, fruit-stain, beer-stain, water-stain, paint-stain, pitch-stain, mud-stain, or blood-stain—"

The man got no further, for Sikes with a hideous imprecation overthrew the table, and tearing the hat from him, burst out of the house.

With the same perversity of feeling and irresolution that had fastened upon him, despite himself, all day, the murderer, finding that he was not followed, and that they most probably considered him some drunken sullen fellow, turned back up the town, and getting out of the glare of the lamps of a stage-coach that was standing in the street, was walking past, when he recognised the mail from London, and saw that it was standing at the little post-office. He almost knew what was to come; but he crossed over, and listened.

The guard was standing at the door, waiting for the letter-bag. A man, dressed like a gamekeeper, came up at the moment, and he handed him a basket which lay ready on the pavement.

"That's for your people," said the guard. "Now, look alive in there, will you. Damn that'ere bag, it warn't ready night afore last; this won't do, you know!"

"Anything new up in town, Ben?" asked the gamekeeper, drawing back to the window-shutters, the better to admire the horses.

"No, nothing that I knows on," replied the man, pulling on his gloves. "Corn's up a little.[9] I heerd talk of a murder, too, down Spitalfields way, but I don't reckon much upon it."

---

8. A battery that produces energy by chemical action.
9. The price of wheat has risen a little on the grain market; "corn" in England refers to wheat and other grains.

"Oh, that's quite true," said a gentleman inside, who was looking out of the window. "And a dreadful murder it was."

"Was it sir?" rejoined the guard, touching his hat. "Man or woman, pray, sir?"

"A woman," replied the gentleman. "It is supposed——"

"Now, Ben," cried the coachman impatiently.

"Damn that 'ere bag," said the guard; "are you gone to sleep in there?"

"Coming!" cried the office keeper, running out.

"Coming," growled the guard. "Ah, and so's the young 'ooman of property that's going to take a fancy to me, but I don't know when. Here, give hold. All ri—ight!"

The horn sounded a few cheerful notes, and the coach was gone.

Sikes remained standing in the street, apparently unmoved by what he had just heard, and agitated by no stronger feeling than a doubt where to go. At length he went back again, and took the road which leads from Hatfield to St. Albans.[1]

He went on doggedly; but as he left the town behind him, and plunged into the solitude and darkness of the road, he felt a dread and awe creeping upon him which shook him to the core. Every object before him, substance or shadow, still or moving, took the semblance of some fearful thing; but these fears were nothing compared to the sense that haunted him of that morning's ghastly figure following at his heels. He could trace its shadow in the gloom, supply the smallest item of the outline, and note how stiff and solemn it seemed to stalk along. He could hear its garments rustling in the leaves; and every breath of wind came laden with that last low cry. If he stopped it did the same. If he ran, it followed—not running too: that would have been a relief: but like a corpse endowed with the mere machinery of life, and borne on one slow melancholy wind that never rose or fell.

At times, he turned, with desperate determination, resolved to beat this phantom off, though it should look him dead; but the hair rose on his head, and his blood stood still: for it had turned with him and was behind him then. He had kept it before him that morning, but it was behind him now—always. He leaned his back against a bank, and felt that it stood above him, visibly out against the cold night-sky. He threw himself upon the road—on his back upon the road. At his head it stood, silent, erect, and still—a living grave-stone, with its epitaph in blood.

Let no man talk of murderers escaping justice, and hint that Providence must sleep. There were twenty score of violent deaths in one long minute of that agony of fear.

There was a shed in a field he passed, that offered shelter for the night. Before the door, were three tall poplar trees, which made it very

1. Another town in Hertfordshire, about two miles from Hatfield.

dark within; and the wind moaned through them with a dismal wail. He *could not* walk on, till daylight came again; and here he stretched himself close to the wall—to undergo new torture.

For now, a vision came before him, as constant and more terrible than that from which he had escaped. Those widely staring eyes, so lustreless and so glassy, that he had better borne to see them than think upon them, appeared in the midst of the darkness: light in themselves, but giving light to nothing. There were but two, but they were every-where. If he shut out the sight, there came the room with every well-known object—some, indeed, that he would have forgotten, if he had gone over its contents from memory—each in its accustomed place. The body was in *its* place, and its eyes were as he saw them when he stole away. He got up, and rushed into the field without. The figure was behind him. He re-entered the shed, and shrunk down once more. The eyes were there, before he had lain himself along.

And here he remained, in such terror as none but he can know, trembling in every limb, and the cold sweat starting from every pore, when suddenly there arose upon the night-wind the noise of distant shouting, and the roar of voices mingled in alarm and wonder. Any sound of men in that lonely place, even though it conveyed a real cause of alarm, was something to him. He regained his strength and energy at the prospect of personal danger; and, springing to his feet, rushed into the open air.

The broad sky seemed on fire. Rising into the air with showers of sparks, and rolling one above the other, were sheets of flame, lighting the atmosphere for miles round, and driving clouds of smoke in the direction where he stood. The shouts grew louder as new voices swelled the roar, and he could hear the cry of Fire! mingled with the ringing of an alarm-bell, the fall of heavy bodies, and the crackling of flames as they twined round some new obstacle, and shot aloft as though refreshed by food. The noise increased as he looked. There were people there—men and women—light, bustle. It was like new life to him. He darted onward—straight, headlong—dashing through brier and brake, and leaping gate and fence as madly as the dog, who careered with loud and sounding bark before him.

He came upon the spot. There were half-dressed figures tearing to and fro, some endeavouring to drag the frightened horses from the stables, others driving the cattle from the yard and out-houses, and others coming laden from the burning pile, amidst a shower of falling sparks, and the tumbling down of red-hot beams. The apertures, where doors and windows stood an hour ago, disclosed a mass of raging fire; walls rocked and crumbled into the burning well; the molten lead and iron poured down, white hot, upon the ground. Women and children shrieked, and men encouraged each other with noisy shouts and cheers. The clanking of the engine-pumps, and the spiriting and hissing of the water as it fell upon the blazing wood, added to the tremendous roar. He shouted, too, till he was hoarse; and, flying from memory and himself, plunged into the thickest of the throng.

Hither and thither he dived that night: now working at the pumps, and now hurrying through the smoke and flame, but never ceasing to engage himself wherever noise and men were thickest. Up and down the ladders, upon the roofs of buildings, over floors that quaked and trembled with his weight, under the lee of falling bricks and stones, in every part of that great fire was he; but he bore a charmed life, and had neither scratch nor bruise, nor weariness nor thought, till morning dawned again, and only smoke and blackened ruins remained.

This mad excitement over, there returned, with tenfold force, the dreadful consciousness of his crime. He looked suspiciously about him, for the men were conversing in groups, and he feared to be the subject of their talk. The dog obeyed the significant beck of his finger, and they drew off, stealthily, together. He passed near an engine where some men were seated, and they called to him to share in their refreshment. He took some bread and meat; and as he drank a draught of beer, heard the firemen, who were from London, talking about the murder. "He has gone to Birmingham, they say," said one: "but they'll have him yet, for the scouts are out, and by to-morrow night there'll be a cry all through the country."

He hurried off, and walked till he almost dropped upon the ground; then lay down in a lane, and had a long, but broken and uneasy, sleep. He wandered on again, irresolute and undecided, and oppressed with the fear of another solitary night.

Suddenly, he took the desperate resolution of going back to London.

"There's somebody to speak to there, at all events," he thought. "A good hiding-place, too. They'll never expect to nab me there, after this country scent. Why can't I lay by for a week or so, and, forcing blunt from Fagin, get abroad to France! Damme, I'll risk it."

He acted upon this impulse without delay, and choosing the least frequented roads began his journey back, resolved to lie concealed within a short distance of the metropolis, and, entering it at dusk by a circuitous route, to proceed straight to that part of it which he had fixed on for his destination.

The dog, though,—if any descriptions of him were out, it would not be forgotten that the dog was missing, and had probably gone with him. This might lead to his apprehension as he passed along the streets. He resolved to drown him, and walked on, looking about for a pond: picking up a heavy stone and tying it to his handkerchief as he went.

The animal looked up into his master's face while these preparations were making; and, whether his instinct apprehended something of their purpose, or the robber's sidelong look at him was sterner than ordinary, skulked a little farther in the rear than usual, and cowered as he came more slowly along. When his master halted at the brink of a pool, and looked round to call him, he stopped outright.

"Do you hear me call? Come here!" cried Sikes.

The animal came up from the very force of habit; but as Sikes stooped to attach the handkerchief to his throat, he uttered a low growl and started back.

"Come back!" said the robber, stamping on the ground.

The dog wagged his tail, but moved not. Sikes made a running noose and called him again.

The dog advanced, retreated, paused an instant, turned, and scoured away at his hardest speed.

The man whistled again and again, and sat down and waited in the expectation that he would return. But no dog appeared, and at length he resumed his journey.

Chapter XLIX.

MONKS AND MR. BROWNLOW AT LENGTH MEET. THEIR CONVERSATION, AND THE INTELLIGENCE THAT INTERRUPTS IT.

The twilight was beginning to close in, when Mr. Brownlow alighted from a hackney-coach at his own door, and knocked softly. The door being opened, a sturdy man got out of the coach and stationed himself on one side of the steps, while another man, who had been seated on the box, dismounted too, and stood upon the other side. At a sign from Mr. Brownlow, they helped out a third man, and taking him between them, hurried him into the house. This man was Monks.

They walked in the same manner up the stairs without speaking, and Mr. Brownlow, preceding them, led the way into a back-room. At the door of this apartment, Monks, who had ascended with evident reluctance, stopped. The two men looked to the old gentleman as if for instructions.

"He knows the alternative," said Mr. Brownlow. "If he hesitates or moves a finger but as you bid him, drag him into the street, call for the aid of the police, and impeach him as a felon in my name.

"How dare you say this of me?" asked Monks.

"How dare you urge me to it, young man?" replied Mr. Brownlow, confronting him with a steady look. "Are you mad enough to leave this house? Unhand him. There, sir. You are free to go, and we to follow. But I warn you, by all I hold most solemn and most sacred, that the instant you set foot in the street, that instant will I have you apprehended on a charge of fraud and robbery. I am resolute and immoveable. If you are determined to be the same, your blood be upon your own head!"

"By what authority am I kidnapped in the street and brought here by these dogs?" asked Monks, looking from one to the other of the men who stood beside him.

"By mine," replied Mr. Brownlow. "Those persons are indemnified by me. If you complain of being deprived of your liberty—you had power and opportunity to retrieve it as you came along, but you deemed it advisable to remain quiet—I say again, throw yourself for protection on the law. I will appeal to the law too; but when you have gone too far to recede, do not sue to me for leniency, when the power will have passed into other hands; and do not say I plunged you down the gulf into which you rushed yourself."

Monks was plainly disconcerted, and alarmed besides. He hesitated.

"You will decide quickly," said Mr. Brownlow, with perfect firmness and composure. "If you wish me to prefer my charges publicly, and consign you to a punishment the extent of which, although I can, with a shudder, foresee, I cannot control, once more, I say, you know the way. If not, and you appeal to my forbearance, and the mercy of those you have deeply injured, seat yourself, without a word, in that chair. It has waited for you two whole days."

Monks muttered some unintelligible words, but wavered still.

"You will be prompt," said Mr. Brownlow. "A word from me, and the alternative has gone for ever."

Still the man hesitated.

"I have not the inclination to parley," said Mr. Brownlow, "and, as I advocate the dearest interests of others, I have not the right."

"Is there—" demanded Monks with a faltering tongue,—"is there—no middle course?"

"None."

Monks looked at the old gentleman, with an anxious eye, but, reading in his countenance nothing but severity and determination, walked into the room, and, shrugging his shoulders, sat down.

"Lock the door on the outside," said Mr. Brownlow to the attendants, "and come when I ring."

The men obeyed, and the two were left alone together.

"This is pretty treatment, sir," said Monks, throwing down his hat and cloak, "from my father's oldest friend."

"It is because I was your father's oldest friend, young man," returned Mr. Brownlow; "it is because the hopes and wishes of young and happy years were bound up with him, and that fair creature of his blood and kindred who rejoined her God in youth, and left me here a solitary, lonely man; it is because he knelt with me beside his only sister's death-bed when he was yet a boy, on the morning that would—but Heaven willed otherwise—have made her my young wife; it is because my seared heart clung to him, from that time forth, through all his trials and errors, till he died; it is because old recollections and associations fill my heart, and even the sight of you brings with it old thoughts of him; it is because of all these things that I am moved to treat you gently now—yes, Edward Leeford, even now—and blush for your unworthiness who bear the name."

"What has the name to do with it?" asked the other, after contemplating, half in silence, and half in dogged wonder, the agitation of his companion. "What is the name to me?"

"Nothing," replied Mr. Brownlow, "nothing to you. But it was *hers*, and even at this distance of time brings back to me, an old man, the glow and thrill which I once felt, only to hear it repeated by a stranger. I am very glad you have changed it—very—very."

"This is all mighty fine," said Monks (to retain his assumed designation) after a long silence, during which he had jerked himself in sullen defiance to and fro, and Mr. Brownlow had sat, shading his face with his hand. "But what do you want with me?"

"You have a brother," said Mr. Brownlow, rousing himself: "a brother, the whisper of whose name in your ear when I came behind you in the street, was, in itself, almost enough to make you accompany me hither, in wonder and alarm."

"I have no brother," replied Monks. "You know I was an only child. Why do you talk to me of brothers? You know that, as well as I."

"Attend to what I do know, and you may not," said Mr. Brownlow. "I shall interest you by and by. I know that of the wretched marriage, into which family pride, and the most sordid and narrowest of all ambition, forced your unhappy father when a mere boy, you were the sole and most unnatural issue."

"I don't care for hard names," interrupted Monks with a jeering laugh. "You know the fact, and that's enough for me."

"But I also know," pursued the old gentleman, "the misery, the slow torture, the protracted anguish of that ill-assorted union. I know how listlessly and wearily each of that wretched pair dragged on their heavy chain through a world that was poisoned to them both. I know how cold formalities were succeeded by open taunts; how indifference gave place to dislike, dislike to hate, and hate to loathing, until at last they wrenched the clanking bond asunder, and retiring a wide space apart, carried each a galling fragment, of which nothing but death could break the rivets, to hide it in new society beneath the gayest looks they could assume. Your mother succeeded: she forgot it soon. But it rusted and cankered at your father's heart for years."

"Well, they were separated," said Monks, "and what of that?"

"When they had been separated for some time," returned Mr. Brownlow, "and your mother, wholly given up to continental frivolities, had utterly forgotten the young husband ten good years her junior, who, with prospects blighted, lingered on at home, he fell among new friends. *This* circumstance, at least, you know already."

"Not I," said Monks, turning away his eyes and beating his foot upon the ground, as a man who is determined to deny everything. "Not I."

"Your manner, no less than your actions, assures me that you have never forgotten it, or ceased to think of it with bitterness," returned Mr. Brownlow. "I speak of fifteen years ago, when you were not more than eleven years old, and your father but one-and-thirty—for he was, I repeat, a boy, when *his* father ordered him to marry. Must I go back to events which cast a shade upon the memory of your parent, or will you spare it, and disclose to me the truth?"

"I have nothing to disclose," rejoined Monks. "You must talk on if you will."

"These new friends, then," said Mr. Brownlow, "were a naval officer retired from active service, whose wife had died some half-a-year before, and left him with two children—there had been more, but, of all their family, happily but two survived. They were both daughters; one a beautiful creature of nineteen, and the other a mere child of two or three years old."

"What's this to me?" asked Monks.

"They resided," said Mr. Brownlow, without seeming to hear the interruption, "in a part of the country to which your father in his wanderings had repaired, and where he had taken up his abode. Acquaintance, intimacy, friendship, fast followed on each other. Your father was gifted as few men are. He had his sister's soul and person. As the old officer knew him more and more, he grew to love him. I would that it had ended there. His daughter did the same."

The old gentleman paused; Monks was biting his lips, with his eyes fixed upon the floor; seeing this, he immediately resumed:

"The end of a year found him contracted, solemnly contracted, to that daughter; the object of the first, true, ardent, only passion of a guileless, untried girl."

"Your tale is of the longest," observed Monks, moving restlessly in his chair.

"It is a true tale of grief and trial, and sorrow, young man," returned Mr. Brownlow, "and such tales usually are; if it were one of unmixed joy and happiness, it would be very brief. At length one of those rich relations to strengthen whose interest and importance your father had been sacrificed, as others are often—it is no uncommon case—died, and to repair the misery he had been instrumental in occasioning, left him *his* panacea for all griefs—Money. It was necessary that he should immediately repair to Rome, whither this man had sped for health, and where he had died, leaving his affairs in great confusion. He went; was seized with mortal illness there; was followed, the moment the intelligence reached Paris, by your mother who carried you with her; he died the day after her arrival, leaving no will—*no will*—so that the whole property fell to her and you."

At this part of the recital Monks held his breath, and listened with a face of intense eagerness, though his eyes were not directed towards the speaker. As Mr. Brownlow paused, he changed his position with the air of one who has experienced a sudden relief, and wiped his hot face and hands.

"Before he went abroad, and as he passed through London on his way," said Mr. Brownlow slowly, and fixing his eyes upon the other's face, "he came to me."

"I never heard of that," interrupted Monks in a tone intended to appear incredulous, but savouring more of disagreeable surprise.

"He came to me, and left with me, among some other things, a picture—a portrait painted by himself—a likeness of this poor girl—which he did not wish to leave behind, and could not carry forward on his hasty journey. He was worn by anxiety and remorse almost to a shadow; talked in a wild, distracted way, of ruin and dishonour worked by him; confided to me his intention to convert his whole property, at any loss, into money, and, having settled on his wife and you a portion of his recent acquisition, to fly the country—I guessed too well he would not fly alone—and never see it more. Even from me, his old and early friend, whose strong attachment had taken root in the earth that covered one most dear to both—even from me he withheld any more particular confession, promising to write and tell me all, and after that to see me once again, for the last time on earth. Alas! *That* was the last time. I had no letter, and I never saw him more.

"I went," said Mr. Brownlow, after a short pause, "I went, when all was over, to the scene of his—I will use the term the world would freely use, for worldly harshness or favour are now alike to him—of his guilty love: resolved that if my fears were realized that erring child should find one heart and home to shelter and compassionate her. The family had left that part a week before; they had called in such trifling debts as were outstanding, discharged them, and left the place by night. Why, or whither, none can tell."

Monks drew his breath yet more freely, and looked round with a smile of triumph.

"When your brother," said Mr. Brownlow, drawing nearer to the other's chair, "When your brother: a feeble, ragged, neglected child: was cast in my way by a stronger hand than chance, and rescued by me from a life of vice and infamy"—

"What!" cried Monks.

"By me," said Mr. Brownlow. "I told you I should interest you before long. I say by me—I see that your cunning associate suppressed my name, although, for aught he knew, it would be quite strange to your ears. When he was rescued by me, then, and lay recovering from sickness in my house, his strong resemblance to this picture I have spoken of, struck me with astonishment. Even when I first saw him in all his dirt and misery, there was a lingering expression in his face that came upon me like a glimpse of some old friend flashing on one in a vivid dream. I need not tell you he was snared away before I knew his history—"

"Why not?" asked Monks hastily.

"Because you know it well."

"I!"

"Denial to me is vain," replied Mr. Brownlow. "I shall show you that I know more than that."

"You—you—can't prove anything against me," stammered Monks. "I defy you to do it!"

"We shall see," returned the old gentleman with a searching glance. "I lost the boy, and no efforts of mine could recover him. Your mother being dead, I knew that you alone could solve the mystery if anybody could, and as when I had last heard of you you were on your own estate in the West Indies—whither, as you well know, you retired upon your mother's death to escape the consequences of vicious courses here—I made the voyage. You had left it, months before, and were supposed to be in London, but no one could tell where. I returned. Your agents had no clue to your residence. You came and went, they said, as strangely as you had ever done: sometimes for days together and sometimes not for months: keeping to all appearance the same low haunts and mingling with the same infamous herd who had been your associates when a fierce ungovernable boy. I wearied them with new applications. I paced the streets by night and day, but until two hours ago all my efforts were fruitless, and I never saw you for an instant."

"And now you do see me," said Monks, rising boldly, "what then? Fraud and robbery are high-sounding words—justified, you think, by a fancied resemblance in some young imp to an idle daub[1] of a dead man's. Brother! You don't even know that a child was born of this maudlin pair; you don't even know that."

"I *did not*," replied Mr. Brownlow, rising too; "but within the last fortnight I have learnt it all. You have a brother; you know it, and him. There was a will, which your mother destroyed, leaving the secret and the gain to you at her own death. It contained a reference to some child likely to be the result of this sad connection, which child was born, and accidentally encountered by you, when your suspicions were first awakened by his resemblance to his father. You repaired to the place of his birth. There existed proofs—proofs long suppressed—of his birth and parentage. Those proofs were destroyed by you, and now, in your own words to your accomplice the Jew, '*the only proofs of the boy's identity lie at the bottom of the river, and the old hag that received them from the mother is rotting in her coffin.*' Unworthy son, coward, liar,—you, who hold your councils with thieves and murderers in dark rooms at night,—you, whose plots and wiles have brought a violent death upon

---

1. A crude amateurish painting.

the head of one worth millions such as you,—you, who from your cradle were gall and bitterness to your own father's heart, and in whom all evil passions, vice, and profligacy, festered, till they found a vent in a hideous disease[2] which has made your face an index even to your mind—you, Edward Leeford, do you still brave me!"

"No, no, no!" returned the coward, overwhelmed by these accumulated charges.

"Every word!" cried the old gentleman, "every word that has passed between you and this detested villain, is known to me. Shadows on the wall have caught your whispers, and brought them to my ear; the sight of the persecuted child has turned vice itself, and given it the courage and almost the attributes of virtue. Murder has been done, to which you were morally if not really a party."

"No, no," interposed Monks. "I—I—know nothing of that; I was going to inquire the truth of the story when you overtook me. I didn't know the cause. I thought it was a common quarrel."

"It was the partial disclosure of your secrets," replied Mr. Brownlow. "Will you disclose the whole?"

"Yes, I will."

"Set your hand to a statement of truth and facts, and repeat it before witnesses?"

"That I promise too."

"Remain quietly here, until such a document is drawn up, and proceed with me to such a place as I may deem most advisable, for the purpose of attesting it?"

"If you insist upon that, I'll do that also," replied Monks.

"You must do more than that," said Mr. Brownlow. "Make restitution to an innocent and unoffending child, for such he is, although the offspring of a guilty and most miserable love. You have not forgotten the provisions of the will. Carry them into execution so far as your brother is concerned, and then go where you please. In this world you need meet no more."

While Monks was pacing up and down, meditating with dark and evil looks on this proposal and the possibilities of evading it: torn by his fears on the one hand and his hatred on the other: the door was hurriedly unlocked, and a gentleman (Mr. Losberne) entered the room in violent agitation.

"The man will be taken," he cried. "He will be taken to-night!"

"The murderer?" asked Mr. Brownlow.

"Yes, yes," replied the other. "His dog has been seen lurking about some old haunt, and there seems little doubt that his master either is, or will be, there, under cover of the darkness. Spies are hovering about in every direction. I have spoken to the men who are charged with his

2. Probably syphilis, which sometimes produces disfiguring sores on the face.

capture, and they tell me he can never escape. A reward of a hundred pounds is proclaimed by Government to-night."

"I will give fifty more," said Mr. Brownlow, "and proclaim it with my own lips upon the spot, if I can reach it. Where is Mr. Maylie?"

"Harry? As soon as he had seen your friend here, safe in a coach with you, he hurried off to where he heard this," replied the doctor, "and mounting his horse sallied forth to join the first party at some place in the outskirts agreed upon between them."

"The Jew," said Mr. Brownlow; "what of him?"

"When I last heard, he had not been taken, but he will be, or is, by this time. They're sure of him."

"Have you made up your mind?" asked Mr. Brownlow, in a low voice, of Monks.

"Yes," he replied. "You—you—will be secret with me?"

"I will. Remain here till I return. It is your only hope of safety."

They left the room, and the door was again locked.

"What have you done?" asked the doctor in a whisper.

"All that I could hope to do, and even more. Coupling the poor girl's intelligence with my previous knowledge, and the result of our good friend's inquiries on the spot, I left him no loophole of escape, and laid bare the whole villany which by these lights became plain as day. Write and appoint the evening after to-morrow, at seven, for the meeting. We shall be down there, a few hours before, but shall require rest: especially the young lady, who *may* have greater need of firmness than either you or I can quite foresee just now. But my blood boils to avenge this poor murdered creature. Which way have they taken?"

"Drive straight to the office and you will be in time," replied Mr. Losberne. "I will remain here."

The two gentlemen hastily separated; each in a fever of excitement wholly uncontrollable.

Chapter L.

THE PURSUIT AND ESCAPE.

Near to that part of the Thames on which the church at Rotherhithe abuts, where the buildings on the banks are dirtiest and the vessels on the river blackest with the dust of colliers[1] and the smoke of close-built low-roofed houses, there exists, at the present day, the filthiest, the strangest, the most extraordinary of the many localities that are hidden in London, wholly unknown, even by name, to the great mass of its inhabitants.

To reach this place, the visitor has to penetrate through a maze of

---

1. Coal ships. "Rotherhithe": a rough area of warehouses and docks south of the river Thames.

close, narrow, and muddy streets, thronged by the roughest and poorest
of water-side people, and devoted to the traffic they may be supposed
to occasion. The cheapest and least delicate provisions are heaped in
the shops; the coarsest and commonest articles of wearing apparel dangle
at the salesman's door, and stream from the house-parapet and windows.
Jostling with unemployed labourers of the lowest class, ballast-heavers,
coal-whippers, brazen women, ragged children, and the very raff and
refuse[2] of the river, he makes his way with difficulty along, assailed by
offensive sights and smells from the narrow alleys which branch off on
the right and left, and deafened by the clash of ponderous waggons that
bear great piles of merchandise from the stacks of warehouses that rise
from every corner. Arriving, at length, in streets remoter and less-
frequented than those through which he has passed, he walks beneath
tottering house-fronts projecting over the pavement, dismantled walls
that seem to totter as he passes, chimneys half crushed half hesitating
to fall, windows guarded by rusty iron bars that time and dirt have almost
eaten away, and every imaginable sign of desolation and neglect.

In such a neighbourhood, beyond Dockhead in the Borough of South-
work, stands Jacob's Island, surrounded by a muddy ditch, six or eight
feet deep and fifteen or twenty wide when the tide is in, once called
Mill Pond, but known in these days as Folly Ditch. It is a creek or inlet
from the Thames, and can always be filled at high water by opening
the sluices[3] at the Lead Mills from which it took its old name. At such
times, a stranger, looking from one of the wooden bridges thrown across
it at Mill-lane, will see the inhabitants of the houses on either side
lowering from their back doors and windows, buckets, pails, domestic
utensils of all kinds, in which to haul the water up; and when his eye
is turned from these operations to the houses themselves, his utmost
astonishment will be excited by the scene before him. Crazy wooden
galleries common to the backs of half-a-dozen houses, with holes from
which to look upon the slime beneath; windows, broken and patched:
with poles thrust out, on which to dry the linen that is never there;
rooms so small, so filthy, so confined, that the air would seem too
tainted even for the dirt and squalor which they shelter; wooden chambers thrusting themselves out above the mud, and threatening to fall
into it—as some have done; dirt-besmeared walls and decaying foundations; every repulsive lineament of poverty, every loathsome indication
of filth, rot, and garbage; all these ornament the banks of Folly Ditch.

In Jacob's Island, the warehouses are roofless and empty; the walls
are crumbling down; the windows are windows no more; the doors are
falling into the streets; the chimneys are blackened, but they yield no

2. Low-class people. "Ballast-heavers": men who load and unload gravel, stones, and other
   materials used as ballast on ships. "Coal-whippers": men who pull coal out of a ship's hold
   by means of a pulley.
3. Artificial channels with gates for regulating the flow of water. "Folly Ditch": a small inlet of
   the Thames near Bermondsey in southeast London.

smoke. Thirty or forty years ago, before losses and chancery suits came upon it, it was a thriving place; but now it is a desolate island indeed. The houses have no owners; they are broken open, and entered upon by those who have the courage; and there they live, and there they die. They must have powerful motives for a secret residence, or be reduced to a destitute condition indeed, who seek a refuge in Jacob's Island.

In an upper room of one of these houses—a detached house of fair size, ruinous in other respects, but strongly defended at door and window: of which house the back commanded the ditch in manner already described—there were assembled three men, who, regarding each other every now and then with looks expressive of perplexity and expectation, sat for some time in profound and gloomy silence. One of these was Toby Crackit, another Mr. Chitling, and the third a robber of fifty years, whose nose had been almost beaten in, in some old scuffle, and whose face bore a frightful scar which might probably be traced to the same occasion. This man was a returned transport, and his name was Kags.

"I wish," said Toby turning to Mr. Chitling, "that you had picked out some other crib when the two old ones got too warm, and had not come here my fine feller."

"Why didn't you blunder-head?" said Kags.

"Well, I thought you'd have been a little more glad to see me than this," replied Mr. Chitling, with a melancholy air.

"Why look'e, young gentleman," said Toby, "when a man keeps himself so very ex-clusive as I have done, and by that means has a snug house over his head with nobody prying and smelling about it, it's rather a startling thing to have the honour of a wisit from a young gentleman (however respectable and pleasant a person he may be to play cards with at conweniency) circumstanced as you are."

"Especially, when the exclusive young man has got a friend stopping with him, that's arrived sooner than was expected from foreign parts, and is too modest to want to be presented to the Judges on his return," added Mr. Kags.

There was a short silence, after which Toby Crackit, seeming to abandon as hopeless any further effort to maintain his usual devil-may-care swagger, turned to Chitling and said,

"When was Fagin took then?"

"Just at dinner-time—two o'clock this afternoon. Charley and I made our lucky up the wash'us chimney, and Bolter got into the empty water-butt,[4] head downwards; but his legs were so precious long that they stuck out at the top, and so they took him too."

"And Bet?"

"Poor Bet! She went to see the body, to speak to who it was," replied Chitling, his countenance falling more and more, "and went off mad,

---

4. A large barrel set on end to catch rainwater from a roof. "Lucky": escape.

screaming and raving, and beating her head against the boards; so they put a strait weskut[5] on her and took her to the hospital—and there she is."

"Wot's come of young Bates?" demanded Kags.

"He hung about, not to come over here afore dark, but he'll be here soon," replied Chitling. "There's nowhere else to go to now, for the people at the Cripples are all in custody, and the bar of the ken—I went up there and see it with my own eyes—is filled with traps."

"This is a smash," observed Toby biting his lips. "There's more than one will go with this."

"The sessions are on," said Kags: "if they get the inquest over, and Bolter turns King's evidence: as of course he will, from what he's said already: they can prove Fagin an accessory before the fact, and get the trial on on Friday, and he'll swing in six days from this, by G——!"

"You should have heard the people groan," said Chitling; "the officers fought like devils or they'd have torn him away. He was down once, but they made a ring round him, and fought their way along. You should have seen how he looked about him, all muddy and bleeding, and clung to them as if they were his dearest friends. I can see 'em now, not able to stand upright with the pressing of the mob, and dragging him along amongst 'em; I can see the people jumping up, one behind another, and snarling with their teeth and making at him like wild beasts; I can see the blood upon his hair and beard, and hear the cries with which the women worked themselves into the centre of the crowd at the street corner, and swore they'd tear his heart out!"

The horror-stricken witness of this scene pressed his hands upon his ears, and with his eyes closed got up and paced violently to and fro, like one distracted.

Whilst he was thus engaged, and the two men sat by in silence with their eyes fixed upon the floor, a pattering noise was heard upon the stairs, and Sikes's dog bounded into the room. They ran to the window, down stairs, and into the street. The dog had jumped in at an open window; he made no attempt to follow them, nor was his master to be seen.

"What's the meaning of this!" said Toby, when they had returned. "He can't be coming here. I—I—hope not."

"If he was coming here, he'd have come with the dog," said Kags, stooping down to examine the animal, who lay panting on the floor. "Here! Give us some water for him; he has run himself faint."

"He's drunk it all up, every drop," said Chitling, after watching the dog some time in silence. "Covered with mud—lame—half-blind—he must have come a long way."

"Where can he have come from!" exclaimed Toby. "He's been to

5. A straitjacket.

the other kens of course, and finding them filled with strangers come on here, where he's been many a time and often. But where can he have come from first, and how comes he here alone, without the other!"

"He" (none of them called the murderer by his old name) "He can't have made away with himself. What do you think?" said Chitling.

Toby shook his head.

"If he had," said Kags, "the dog 'ud want to lead us away to where he did it. No. I think he's got out of the country, and left the dog behind. He must have given him the slip somehow, or he wouldn't be so easy."

This solution, appearing the most probable one, was adopted as the right; and the dog creeping under a chair, coiled himself up to sleep, without more notice from anybody.

It being now dark, the shutter was closed, and a candle lighted and placed upon the table. The terrible events of the last two days had made a deep impression on all three, increased by the danger and uncertainty of their own position. They drew their chairs closer together, starting at every sound. They spoke little, and that in whispers, and were as silent and awe-stricken as if the remains of the murdered woman lay in the next room.

They had sat thus, some time, when suddenly was heard a hurried knocking at the door below.

"Young Bates," said Kags, looking angrily round to check the fear he felt himself.

The knocking came again. No, it wasn't he. He never knocked like that.

Crackit went to the window, and, shaking all over, drew in his head. There was no need to tell them who it was; his pale face was enough. The dog too was on the alert in an instant, and ran whining to the door.

"We must let him in," he said, taking up the candle.

"Isn't there any help for it?" asked the other man in a hoarse voice.

"None. He *must* come in."

"Don't leave us in the dark," said Kags, taking down a candle from the chimney-piece, and lighting it, with such a trembling hand that the knocking was twice repeated before he had finished.

Crackit went down to the door, and returned followed by a man with the lower part of his face buried in a handkerchief, and another tied over his head under his hat. He drew them slowly off. Blanched face, sunken eyes, hollow cheeks, beard of three days' growth, wasted flesh, short thick breath; it was the very ghost of Sikes.

He laid his hand upon a chair which stood in the middle of the room, but shuddering as he was about to drop into it, and seeming to glance over his shoulder, dragged it back close to the wall—as close as it would go—ground it against it—and sat down.

Not a word had been exchanged. He looked from one to another in silence. If an eye were furtively raised and met his, it was instantly averted. When his hollow voice broke silence, they all three started. They seemed never to have heard its tones before.

"How came that dog here?" he asked.

"Alone. Three hours ago."

"To-night's paper says that Fagin's taken. Is it true, or a lie?"

"True."

They were silent again.

"Damn you all," said Sikes, passing his hand across his forehead. "Have you nothing to say to me?"

There was an uneasy movement among them, but nobody spoke.

"You that keep this house," said Sikes, turning his face to Crackit, "do you mean to sell me, or to let me lie here till this hunt is over?"

"You must stop here, if you think it safe," returned the person addressed, after some hesitation.

Sikes carried his eyes slowly up the wall behind him: rather trying to turn his head than actually doing it: and said, "Is—it—the body—is it buried?"

They shook their heads.

"Why isn't it!" he retorted with the same glance behind him. "Wot do they keep such ugly things above the ground for?—Who's that knocking?"

Crackit intimated, by a motion of his hand as he left the room, that there was nothing to fear; and directly came back with Charley Bates behind him. Sikes sat opposite the door, so that the moment the boy entered the room he encountered his figure.

"Toby," said the boy falling back, as Sikes turned his eyes towards him, "why didn't you tell me this, down stairs?"

There had been something so tremendous in the shrinking off of the three, that the wretched man was willing to propitiate even this lad. Accordingly he nodded, and made as though he would shake hands with him.

"Let me go into some other room," said the boy, retreating still farther.

"Why, Charley!" said Sikes, stepping forward, "don't you—don't you know me?"

"Don't come nearer me," answered the boy, still retreating, and looking, with horror in his eyes, upon the murderer's face. "You monster!"

The man stopped half-way, and they looked at each other; but Sikes's eyes sunk gradually to the ground.

"Witness you three," cried the boy shaking his clenched fist, and becoming more and more excited as he spoke. "Witness you three— I'm not afraid of him—if they come here after him, I'll give him up; I will. I tell you out at once. He may kill me for it if he likes, or if he dares, but if I'm here I'll give him up. I'd give him up if he was to be boiled alive. Murder! Help! If there's the pluck of a man among you three, you'll help me. Murder! Help! Down with him!"

Pouring out these cries, and accompanying them with violent gesticulation, the boy actually threw himself, single-handed, upon the strong man, and in the intensity of his energy, and the suddenness of his surprise, brought him heavily to the ground.

The three spectators seemed quite stupified. They offered no interference, and the boy and man rolled on the ground together; the former, heedless of the blows that showered upon him, wrenching his hands tighter and tighter in the garments about the murderer's breast, and never ceasing to call for help with all his might.

The contest, however, was too unequal to last long. Sikes had him down, and his knee was on his throat, when Crackit pulled him back with a look of alarm, and pointed to the window. There were lights gleaming below, voices in loud and earnest conversation, the tramp of hurried footsteps—endless they seemed in number—crossing the nearest wooden bridge. One man on horseback seemed to be among the crowd; for there was the noise of hoofs rattling on the uneven pavement. The gleam of lights increased; the footsteps came more thickly and noisily on. Then, came a loud knocking at the door, and then a hoarse murmur from such a multitude of angry voices as would have made the boldest quail.

"Help!" shrieked the boy in a voice that rent the air. "He's here! Break down the door!"

"In the King's name," cried voices without; and the hoarse cry arose again, but louder.

"Break down the door!" screamed the boy. "I tell you they'll never open it. Run straight to the room where the light is. Break down the door!"

Strokes, thick and heavy, rattled upon the door and lower window-shutters as he ceased to speak, and a loud huzzah burst from the crowd; giving the listener, for the first time, some adequate idea of its immense extent.

"Open the door of some place where I can lock this screeching Hell-babe," cried Sikes fiercely; running to and fro, and dragging the boy, now, as easily as if he were an empty sack. "That door. Quick!" He flung him in, bolted it, and turned the key. "Is the down-stairs door fast?"

"Double-locked and chained," replied Crackit, who, with the other two men, still remained quite helpless and bewildered.

"The panels—are they strong?"

"Lined with sheet-iron."

"And the windows too?"

"Yes, and the windows."

"Damn you!" cried the desperate ruffian, throwing up the sash and menacing the crowd. "Do your worst! I'll cheat you yet!"

Of all the terrific yells that ever fell on mortal ears, none could exceed the cry of the infuriated throng. Some shouted to those who were nearest, to set the house on fire; others roared to the officers to shoot him dead. Among them all, none showed such fury as the man on horseback, who, throwing himself out of the saddle, and bursting through the crowd as if he were parting water, cried, beneath the window, in a voice that rose above all others, "Twenty guineas to the man who brings a ladder!"

The nearest voices took up the cry, and hundreds echoed it. Some called for ladders, some for sledge-hammers; some ran with torches to and fro as if to seek them, and still came back and roared again; some spent their breath in impotent curses and execrations; some pressed forward with the ecstasy of madmen, and thus impeded the progress of those below; some among the boldest attempted to climb up by the water-spout and crevices in the wall; and all waved to and fro, in the darkness beneath, like a field of corn[6] moved by an angry wind: and joined from time to time in one loud furious roar.

"The tide," cried the murderer, as he staggered back into the room, and shut the faces out, "the tide was in as I came up. Give me a rope, a long rope. They're all in front. I may drop into the Folly Ditch, and clear off that way. Give me a rope, or I shall do three more murders and kill myself at last."

The panic-stricken men pointed to where such articles were kept; the murderer, hastily selecting the longest and strongest cord, hurried up to the house-top.

All the windows in the rear of the house had been long ago bricked up, except one small trap in the room where the boy was locked, and that was too small even for the passage of his body. But, from this aperture, he had never ceased to call on those without, to guard the back; and thus, when the murderer emerged at last on the house-top by the door in the roof, a loud shout proclaimed the fact to those in front, who immediately began to pour round, pressing upon each other in one unbroken stream.

He planted a board, which he had carried up with him for the purpose, so firmly against the door that it must be matter of great difficulty to open it from the inside; and creeping over the tiles, looked over the low parapet.

The water was out, and the ditch a bed of mud.

The crowd had been hushed during these few moments, watching his motions and doubtful of his purpose, but the instant they perceived it and knew it was defeated, they raised a cry of triumphant execration to which all their previous shouting had been whispers. Again and again

6. See above, p. 320, n. 9.

it rose. Those who were at too great a distance to know its meaning, took up the sound; it echoed and re-echoed; it seemed as though the whole city had poured its population out to curse him.

On pressed the people from the front—on, on, on, in a strong struggling current of angry faces, with here and there a glaring torch to light them up, and show them out in all their wrath and passion. The houses on the opposite side of the ditch had been entered by the mob; sashes were thrown up, or torn bodily out; there were tiers and tiers of faces in every window; and cluster upon cluster of people clinging to every house-top. Each little bridge (and there were three in sight) bent beneath the weight of the crowd upon it. Still the current poured on, to find some nook or hole from which to vent their shouts, and only for an instant see the wretch.

"They have him now," cried a man on the nearest bridge. "Hurrah!"

The crowd grew light with uncovered heads; and again the shout uprose.

"I promise fifty pounds," cried an old gentleman from the same quarter, "fifty pounds to the man who takes him alive. I will remain here, till he comes to ask me for it."

There was another roar. At this moment the word was passed among the crowd that the door was forced at last, and that he who had first called for the ladder had mounted into the room. The stream abruptly turned, as this intelligence ran from mouth to mouth; and the people at the windows, seeing those upon the bridges pouring back, quitted their stations, and, running into the street, joined the concourse that now thronged pell-mell to the spot they had left: each man crushing and striving with his neighbour, and all panting with impatience to get near the door, and look upon the criminal as the officers brought him out. The cries and shrieks of those who were pressed almost to suffocation, or trampled down and trodden under foot in the confusion, were dreadful; the narrow ways were completely blocked up; and at this time, between the rush of some to regain the space in front of the house, and the unavailing struggles of others to extricate themselves from the mass, the immediate attention was distracted from the murderer, although the universal eagerness for his capture was, if possible, increased.

The man had shrunk down, thoroughly quelled by the ferocity of the crowd, and the impossibility of escape; but, seeing this sudden change with no less rapidity than it had occurred, he sprung upon his feet, determined to make one last effort for his life by dropping into the ditch, and, at the risk of being stifled, endeavouring to creep away in the darkness and confusion.

Roused into new strength and energy, and stimulated by the noise within the house which announced that an entrance had really been effected, he set his foot against the stack of chimneys, fastened one end of the rope tightly and firmly round it, and with the other made a strong running noose by the aid of his hands and teeth almost in a second. He could let himself down by the cord to within a less distance of the ground than his own height, and had his knife ready in his hand to cut it then and drop.

At the very instant when he brought the loop over his head previous to slipping it beneath his arm-pits, and when the old gentleman before-mentioned (who had clung so tight to the railing of the bridge as to resist the force of the crowd, and retain his position) earnestly warned those about him that the man was about to lower himself down—at that very instant the murderer, looking behind him on the roof, threw his arms above his head, and uttered a yell of terror.

"The eyes again!" he cried, in an unearthly screech.

Staggering as if struck by lightning, he lost his balance and tumbled over the parapet. The noose was at his neck. It ran up with his weight, tight as a bow-string, and swift as the arrow it speeds. He fell for five-and-thirty feet. There was a sudden jerk, a terrific convulsion of the limbs; and there he hung, with the open knife clenched in his stiffening hand.

The old chimney quivered with the shock, but stood it bravely. The murderer swung lifeless against the wall; and the boy, thrusting aside the dangling body which obscured his view, called to the people to come and take him out, for God's sake.

A dog, which had lain concealed till now, ran backwards and forwards on the parapet with a dismal howl, and, collecting himself for a spring, jumped for the dead man's shoulders. Missing his aim, he fell into the ditch, turning completely over as he went; and striking his head against a stone, dashed out his brains.

Chapter LI.

AFFORDING AN EXPLANATION OF MORE MYSTERIES THAN ONE, AND COMPREHENDING A PROPOSAL OF MARRIAGE WITH NO WORD OF SETTLEMENT OR PIN-MONEY.

The events narrated in the last chapter were yet but two days old, when Oliver found himself, at three o'clock in the afternoon, in a travelling-carriage rolling fast towards his native town. Mrs. Maylie, and Rose, and Mrs. Bedwin, and the good doctor, were with him; and Mr. Brownlow followed in a post-chaise, accompanied by one other person whose name had not been mentioned.

They had not talked much upon the way; for Oliver was in a flutter of agitation and uncertainty which deprived him of the power of collecting his thoughts, and almost of speech, and appeared to have scarcely less effect on his companions, who shared it, in at least an equal degree.

He and the two ladies had been very carefully made acquainted by Mr. Brownlow with the nature of the admissions which had been forced from Monks; and although they knew that the object of their present journey was to complete the work which had been so well begun, still the whole matter was enveloped in enough of doubt and mystery to leave them in endurance of the most intense suspense.

The same kind friend had, with Mr. Losberne's assistance, cautiously stopped all channels of communication through which they could receive intelligence of the dreadful occurrences that had so recently taken place. "It was quite true," he said, "that they must know them before long, but it might be at a better time than the present, and it could not be at a worse." So, they travelled on in silence: each busied with reflections on the object which had brought them together: and no one disposed to give utterance to the thoughts which crowded upon all.

But if Oliver, under these influences, had remained silent while they journeyed towards his birth-place by a road he had never seen, how the whole current of his recollections ran back to old times, and what a crowd of emotions were wakened up in his breast, when they turned into that which he had traversed on foot: a poor houseless wandering boy, without a friend to help him, or a roof to shelter his head.

"See there, there!" cried Oliver, eagerly clasping the hand of Rose, and pointing out at the carriage window; "that's the stile I came over; there are the hedges I crept behind for fear any one should overtake me and force me back! Yonder is the path across the fields, leading to the old house where I was a little child! Oh Dick, Dick, my dear old friend, if I could only see you now!"

"You will see him soon," replied Rose, gently taking his folded hands between her own. "You shall tell him how happy you are, and how rich you have grown, and that in all your happiness you have none so great as the coming back to make him happy too."

"Yes, yes," said Oliver, "and we'll—we'll take him away from here, and have him clothed and taught, and send him to some quiet country place where he may grow strong and well,—shall we?"

Rose nodded "yes," for the boy was smiling through such happy tears that she could not speak.

"You will be kind and good to him, for you are to every one," said Oliver. "It will make you cry, I know, to hear what he can tell; but never mind, never mind, it will be all over, and you will smile again —I know that too—to think how changed he is; you did the same with me. He said 'God bless you' to me when I ran away," cried the boy with a burst of affectionate emotion; "and I will say 'God bless you' now, and show him how I love him for it!"

As they approached the town, and at length drove through its narrow streets, it became matter of no small difficulty to restrain the boy within reasonable bounds. There was Sowerberry's the undertaker's, just as it

used to be, only smaller and less imposing in appearance than he remembered it—there were all the well-known shops and houses, with
almost every one of which he had some slight incident connected—
there was Gamfield's cart, the very cart he used to have, standing at the
old public-house door—there was the workhouse, the dreary prison of
his youthful days, with its dismal windows frowning on the street—there
was the same lean porter standing at the gate, at sight of whom Oliver
involuntarily shrunk back, and then laughed at himself for being so
foolish, then cried, then laughed again—there were scores of faces at
the doors and windows that he knew quite well—there was nearly everything as if he had left it but yesterday, and all his recent life had been
but a happy dream.

But it was pure, earnest, joyful reality. They drove straight to the door
of the chief hotel (which Oliver used to stare up at, with awe, and think
a mighty palace, but which had somehow fallen off in grandeur and
size); and here was Mr. Grimwig all ready to receive them, kissing the
young lady, and the old one too, when they got out of the coach, as if
he were the grandfather of the whole party, all smiles and kindness, and
not offering to eat his head—no, not once; not even when he contra-
dicted a very old postboy about the nearest road to London, and maintained he knew it best, though he had only come that way once, and
that time fast asleep. There was dinner prepared, and there were bed-
rooms ready, and everything was arranged as if by magic.

Notwithstanding all this, when the hurry of the first half hour was
over, the same silence and constraint prevailed that had marked their
journey down. Mr. Brownlow did not join them at dinner, but remained
in a separate room. The two other gentlemen hurried in and out with
anxious faces, and, during the short intervals when they were present,
conversed apart. Once, Mrs. Maylie was called away, and after being
absent for nearly an hour, returned with eyes swollen with weeping. All
these things made Rose and Oliver, who were not in any new secrets,
nervous and uncomfortable. They sat wondering, in silence; or, if they
exchanged a few words, spoke in whispers, as if they were afraid to hear
the sound of their own voices.

At length, when nine o'clock had come, and they began to think
they were to hear no more that night, Mr. Losberne and Mr. Grimwig
entered the room, followed by Mr. Brownlow and a man whom Oliver
almost shrieked with surprise to see; for they told him it was his
brother, and it was the same man he had met at the market-town, and
seen looking in with Fagin at the window of his little room. Monks
cast a look of hate, which, even then, he could not dissemble, at the
astonished boy, and sat down near the door. Mr. Brownlow, who had
papers in his hand, walked to a table near which Rose and Oliver were
seated.

"This is a painful task," said he, "but these declarations, which have been signed in London before many gentlemen, must be in substance repeated here. I would have spared you the degradation, but we must hear them from your own lips before we part, and you know why."

"Go on," said the person addressed, turning away his face. "Quick. I have almost done enough, I think. Don't keep me here."

"This child," said Mr. Brownlow, drawing Oliver to him, and laying his hand upon his head, "is your half-brother; the illegitimate son of your father, my dear friend Edwin Leeford, by poor young Agnes Fleming, who died in giving him birth."

"Yes," said Monks, scowling at the trembling boy: the beating of whose heart he might have heard. "That is their bastard child."

"The term you use," said Mr. Brownlow, sternly, "is a reproach to those who long since passed beyond the feeble censure of the world. It reflects disgrace on no one living, except you who use it. Let that pass. He was born in this town?"

"In the workhouse of this town," was the sullen reply. "You have the story there." He pointed impatiently to the papers as he spoke.

"I must have it here too," said Mr. Brownlow, looking round upon the listeners.

"Listen then! You!" returned Monks. "His father being taken ill at Rome, was joined by his wife, my mother, from whom he had been long separated, who went from Paris and took me with her—to look after his property, for what I know, for she had no great affection for him, nor he for her. He knew nothing of us, for his senses were gone, and he slumbered on till next day, when he died. Among the papers in his desk were two, dated on the night his illness first came on, directed to yourself;" he addressed himself to Mr. Brownlow; "and enclosed in a few short lines to you, with an intimation on the cover of the package that it was not to be forwarded till after he was dead. One of these papers was a letter to this girl Agnes; the other, a will."

"What of the letter?" asked Mr. Brownlow.

"The letter?—A sheet of paper crossed and crossed again, with a penitent confession, and prayers to God to help her. He had palmed a tale on the girl that some secret mystery—to be explained one day—prevented his marrying her just then; and so she had gone on, trusting patiently to him, until she trusted too far, and lost what none could ever give her back. She was, at that time, within a few months of her confinement. He told her all he had meant to do, to hide her shame, if he had lived, and prayed her, if he died, not to curse his memory, or think the consequences of their sin would be visited on her or their young child; for all the guilt was his. He reminded her of the day he had given her the little locket and the ring with her christian name engraved upon it, and a blank left for that which he hoped one day to have bestowed upon her—prayed her yet to keep it, and wear it next her heart, as she had done before—and then ran on, wildly, in the same words, over and over again, as if he had gone distracted. I believe he had."

"The will," said Mr. Brownlow, as Oliver's tears fell fast.

Monks was silent.

"The will," said Mr. Brownlow, speaking for him, "was in the same spirit as the letter. He talked of miseries which his wife had brought upon him; of the rebellious disposition, vice, malice, and premature bad passions of you, his only son, who had been trained to hate him; and left you, and your mother, each an annuity of eight hundred pounds. The bulk of his property he divided into two equal portions—one for Agnes Fleming, and the other for their child, if it should be born alive and ever come of age. If it were a girl, it was to inherit the money unconditionally; but if a boy, only on the stipulation that in his minority he should never have stained his name with any public act of dishonour, meanness, cowardice, or wrong. He did this, he said, to mark his confidence in the mother, and his conviction—only strengthened by approaching death—that the child would share her gentle heart, and noble nature. If he were disappointed in this expectation, then the money was to come to you; for then, and not till then, when both children were equal, would he recognise your prior claim upon his purse, who had none upon his heart, but had, from an infant, repulsed him with coldness and aversion."

"My mother," said Monks, in a louder tone, "did what a woman should have done—she burnt this will. The letter never reached its destination; but that, and other proofs, she kept, in case they ever tried to lie away the blot. The girl's father had the truth from her with every aggravation that her violent hate—I love her for it now—could add. Goaded by shame and dishonour, he fled with his children into a remote corner of Wales, changing his very name that his friends might never know of his retreat; and here, no great while afterwards, he was found dead in his bed. The girl had left her home, in secret, some weeks before; he had searched for her, on foot, in every town and village near; and it was on the night when he returned home, assured that she had destroyed herself, to hide her shame and his, that his old heart broke."

There was a short silence here, until Mr. Brownlow took up the thread of the narrative.

"Years after this," he said, "this man's—Edward Leeford's—mother came to me. He had left her, when only eighteen; robbed her of jewels and money; gambled, squandered, forged, and fled to London: where for two years he had associated with the lowest outcasts. She was sinking under a painful and incurable disease, and wished to recover him before she died. Inquiries were set on foot, and strict searches made. They were unavailing for a long time, but ultimately successful; and he went back with her to France."

"There she died," said Monks, "after a lingering illness; and, on her death-bed, she bequeathed these secrets to me, together with her un-quenchable and deadly hatred of all whom they involved—though she need not have left me that, for I had inherited it long before. She would not believe that the girl had destroyed herself and the child too, but was filled with the impression that a male child had been born, and was alive. I swore to her, if ever it crossed my path, to hunt it down; never to let it rest; to pursue it with the bitterest and most unrelenting animosity; to vent upon it the hatred that I deeply felt, and to spit upon the empty vaunt of that insulting will by dragging it, if I could, to the very gallows-foot. She was right. He came in my way at last. I began well; and, but for babbling drabs, I would have finished as I began!"

As the villain folded his arms tight together, and muttered curses on himself in the impotence of baffled malice, Mr. Brownlow turned to the terrified group beside him, and explained that the Jew, who had been his old accomplice and confident, had a large reward for keeping Oliver ensnared: of which some part was to be given up, in the event of his being rescued: and that a dispute on this head had led to their visit to the country house for the purpose of identifying him.

"The locket and ring?" said Mr. Brownlow, turning to Monks.

"I bought them from the man and woman I told you of, who stole them from the nurse, who stole them from the corpse," answered Monks without raising his eyes. "You know what became of them."

Mr. Brownlow merely nodded to Mr. Grimwig, who, disappearing with great alacrity, shortly returned, pushing in Mrs. Bumble, and drag-ging her unwilling consort after him.

"Do my hi's deceive me!" cried Mr. Bumble with ill-feigned enthu-siasm, "or is that little Oliver? Oh O-li-ver, if you know'd how I've been a-grieving for you—!"

"Hold your tongue, fool," murmured Mrs. Bumble.

"Isn't natur, natur, Mrs. Bumble!" remonstrated the workhouse mas-ter. "Can't I be supposed to feel—I as brought him up porochially—when I see him a-setting here, among ladies and gentlemen of the very affablest description! I always loved that boy as if he'd been my—my—my own grandfather," said Mr. Bumble, halting for an appropriate comparison. "Master Oliver, my dear, you remember the blessed gentle-man in the white waistcoat? Ah! he went to heaven last week, in a oak coffin with plated handles, Oliver."

"Come, sir," said Mr. Grimwig, tartly; "suppress your feelings."

"I will do my endeavours, sir," replied Mr. Bumble. "How do you do, sir? I hope you are very well."

This salutation was addressed to Mr. Brownlow, who had stepped up to within a short distance of the respectable couple. He inquired, as he pointed to Monks,

"Do you know that person?"

"No," replied Mrs. Bumble flatly.

"Perhaps *you* don't?" said Mr. Brownlow, addressing her spouse.

"I never saw him in all my life," said Mr. Bumble.

"Nor sold him anything, perhaps?"

"No," replied Mrs. Bumble.

"You never had, perhaps, a certain gold locket and ring?" said Mr. Brownlow.

"Certainly not," replied the matron. "Why are we brought here, to answer to such nonsense as this?"

Again Mr. Brownlow nodded to Mr. Grimwig; and again that gentleman limped away, with extraordinary readiness. But not again did he return with a stout man and wife; for, this time, he led in two palsied women, who shook and tottered as they walked.

"You shut the door the night old Sally died," said the foremost one, raising her shrivelled hand, "but you couldn't shut out the sound, nor stop the chinks."

"No, no," said the other, looking round her and wagging her toothless jaws. "No, no, no."

"We heard her try to tell you what she'd done, and saw you take a paper from her hand, and watched you too, next day, to the pawn-broker's shop," said the first.

"Yes," added the second, "and it was a 'locket and gold ring.' We found out that, and saw it given you. We were bye. Oh! we were bye."

"And we know more than that," resumed the first, "for she told us often, long ago, that the young mother had told her that, feeling she should never get over it, she was on her way, at the time that she was taken ill, to die near the grave of the father of the child."

"Would you like to see the pawnbroker himself?" asked Mr. Grimwig with a motion towards the door.

"No," replied the woman; "if he"—she pointed to Monks—"has been coward enough to confess, as I see he has, and you have sounded all these hags till you found the right ones, I have nothing more to say. I *did* sell them, and they're where you'll never get them. What then?"

"Nothing," replied Mr. Brownlow, "except that it remains for us to take care that you are neither of you employed in a situation of trust again. You may leave the room."

"I hope," said Mr. Bumble, looking about him with great ruefulness, as Mr. Grimwig disappeared with the two old women, "I hope that this unfortunate little circumstance will not deprive me of my porochial office?"

"Indeed it will," replied Mr. Brownlow. "You may make up your mind to that, and think yourself well off besides."

"It was all Mrs. Bumble. She *would* do it," urged Mr. Bumble; first looking round, to ascertain that his partner had left the room.

"That is no excuse," returned Mr. Brownlow. "You were present on the occasion of the destruction of these trinkets, and, indeed, are the more guilty of the two, in the eye of the law; for the law supposes that your wife acts under your direction."

"If the law supposes that," said Mr. Bumble, squeezing his hat emphatically in both hands, "thé law is a ass—a idiot. If that's the eye of the law, the law's a bachelor; and the worst I wish the law is, that his eye may be opened by experience—by experience."

Laying great stress on the repetition of these two words, Mr. Bumble fixed his hat on very tight, and, putting his hands in his pockets, followed his helpmate down stairs.

"Young lady," said Mr. Brownlow, turning to Rose, "give me your hand. Do not tremble. You need not fear to hear the few remaining words we have to say."

"If they have—I do not know how they can, but if they have—any reference to me," said Rose, "pray let me hear them at some other time. I have not strength or spirits now."

"Nay," returned the old gentleman, drawing her arm through his; "you have more fortitude than this, I am sure. Do you know this young lady, sir?"

"Yes," replied Monks.

"I never saw you before," said Rose faintly.

"I have seen you often," returned Monks.

"The father of the unhappy Agnes had *two* daughters," said Mr. Brownlow. "What was the fate of the other—the child?"

"The child," replied Monks, "when her father died in a strange place, in a strange name, without a letter, book, or scrap of paper that yielded the faintest clue by which his friends or relatives could be traced—the child was taken by some wretched cottagers, who reared it as their own."

"Go on," said Mr. Brownlow, signing to Mrs. Maylie to approach. "Go on!"

"You couldn't find the spot to which these people had repaired," said Monks, "but where friendship fails, hatred will often force a way. My mother found it, after a year of cunning search—ay, and found the child."

"She took it, did she?"

"No. The people were poor, and began to sicken—at least the man did—of their fine humanity; so she left it with them, giving them a small present of money which would not last long, and promising more, which she never meant to send. She didn't quite rely, however, on their discontent and poverty for the child's unhappiness, but told the history of the sister's shame, with such alterations as suited her; bade them take good heed of the child, for she came of bad blood; and told them she was illegitimate, and sure to go wrong at one time or other. The circumstances countenanced all this; the people believed it; and there the child dragged on an existence, miserable enough even to satisfy us, until a widow lady, residing, then, at Chester, saw the girl by chance, pitied her, and took her home. There was some cursed spell, I think, against us; for in spite of all our efforts she remained there and was happy. I lost sight of her, two or three years ago, and saw her no more until a few months back."

"Do you see her now?"

"Yes. Leaning on your arm."

"But not the less my niece," cried Mrs. Maylie, folding the fainting girl in her arms; "not the less my dearest child. I would not lose her now, for all the treasures of the world. My sweet companion, my own dear girl!"

"The only friend I ever had," cried Rose, clinging to her. "The kindest, best of friends. My heart will burst. I cannot—cannot—bear all this."

"You have borne more, and have been, through all, the best and gentlest creature that ever shed happiness on every one she knew," said Mrs. Maylie, embracing her tenderly. "Come, come, my love, remember who this is who waits to clasp you in his arms, poor child! See here—look, look, my dear!"

"Not aunt," cried Oliver, throwing his arms about her neck: "I'll never call her aunt—sister, my own dear sister, that something taught my heart to love so dearly from the first! Rose, dear, darling Rose!"

Let the tears which fell, and the broken words which were exchanged in the long close embrace between the orphans, be sacred. A father, sister, and mother, were gained, and lost, in that one moment. Joy and grief were mingled in the cup; but there were no bitter tears: for even grief itself arose so softened, and clothed in such sweet and tender recollections, that it became a solemn pleasure, and lost all character of pain.

They were a long, long time alone. A soft tap at the door, at length announced that some one was without. Oliver opened it, glided away, and gave place to Harry Maylie.

"I know it all," he said, taking a seat beside the lovely girl. "Dear Rose, I know it all."

"I am not here by accident," he added after a lengthened silence; "nor have I heard all this to-night, for I knew it yesterday—only yesterday. Do you guess that I have come to remind you of a promise?"

"Stay," said Rose. "You *do* know all?"

"All. You gave me leave, at any time within a year, to renew the subject of our last discourse."

"I did."

"Not to press you to alter your determination," pursued the young man, "but to hear you repeat it, if you would. I was to lay whatever of station or fortune I might possess at your feet, and if you still adhered to your former determination, I pledged myself, by no word or act, to seek to change it."

"The same reasons which influenced me then, will influence me now," said Rose firmly. "If I ever owed a strict and rigid duty to her, whose goodness saved me from a life of indigence and suffering, when should I ever feel it, as I should to-night? It is a struggle," said Rose, "but one I am proud to make; it is a pang, but one my heart shall bear."

"The disclosure of to-night, —" Harry began.

"The disclosure of to-night," replied Rose softly, "leaves me in the same position, with reference to you, as that in which I stood before."

"You harden your heart against me, Rose," urged her lover.

"Oh, Harry, Harry," said the young lady, bursting into tears; "I wish I could, and spare myself this pain."

"Then why inflict it on yourself?" said Harry, taking her hand. "Think, dear Rose, think what you have heard to-night."

"And what have I heard! What have I heard!" cried Rose. "That a sense of his deep disgrace so worked upon my own father that he shunned all—there, we have said enough, Harry, we have said enough."

"Not yet, not yet," said the young man, detaining her as she rose. "My hopes, my wishes, prospects, feelings: every thought in life except my love for you: have undergone a change. I offer you, now, no distinction among a bustling crowd; no mingling with a world of malice and detraction, where the blood is called into honest cheeks by aught but real disgrace and shame; but a home—a heart and home—yes, dearest Rose, and those, and those alone, are all I have to offer."

"What do you mean!" she faltered.

"I mean but this—that when I left you last, I left you with a firm determination to level all fancied barriers between yourself and me; resolved that if my world could not be yours, I would make yours mine; that no pride of birth should curl the lip at you, for I would turn from it. This I have done. Those who have shrunk from me because of this, have shrunk from you, and proved you so far right. Such power and patronage: such relatives of influence and rank: as smiled upon me then, look coldly now; but there are smiling fields and waving trees in England's richest county; and by one village church—mine, Rose, my own—there stands a rustic dwelling which you can make me prouder of, than all the hopes I have renounced, a thousandfold. This is *my* rank and station now, and her I lay it down!"[1]

"It's a trying thing waiting supper for lovers," said Mr. Grimwig, waking up, and pulling his pocket handkerchief from over his head.

Truth to tell, the supper had been waiting a most unreasonable time. Neither Mrs. Maylie, nor Harry, nor Rose (who all came in together), could offer a word in extenuation.

---

1. Harry Maylie has given up his hopes for worldly advancement and has become the clergyman of a rural Anglican church; his university degree qualifies him for the position.

"I had serious thoughts of eating my head to-night," said Mr. Grim-wig, "for I began to think I should get nothing else. I'll take the liberty, if you'll allow me, of saluting the bride that is to be."

Mr. Grimwig lost no time in carrying this notice into effect upon the blushing girl; and the example, being contagious, was followed both by the doctor and Mr. Brownlow. Some people affirm that Harry Maylie had been observed to set it, originally, in a dark room adjoining; but the best authorities consider this downright scandal: he being young and a clergyman.

"Oliver, my child," said Mrs. Maylie, "where have you been, and why do you look so sad? There are tears stealing down your face at this moment. What is the matter?"

It is a world of disappointment: often to the hopes we most cherish, and hopes that do our nature the greatest honour.

Poor Dick was dead!

Chapter LII.

THE JEW'S LAST NIGHT ALIVE.

The court was paved, from floor to roof, with human faces. Inquisitive and eager eyes peered from every inch of space. From the rail before the dock, away into the sharpest angle of the smallest corner in the galleries, all looks were fixed upon one man—the Jew. Before him and behind: above, below, on the right and on the left: he seemed to stand surrounded by a firmament, all bright with gleaming eyes.

He stood there, in all this glare of living light, with one hand resting on the wooden slab before him, the other held to his ear, and his head thrust forward to enable him to catch with greater distinctness every word that fell from the presiding judge, who was delivering his charge to the jury. At times, he turned his eyes sharply upon them to observe the effect of the slightest featherweight in his favour; and when the points against him were stated with terrible distinctness, looked towards his counsel, in mute appeal that he would, even then, urge something in his behalf. Beyond these manifestations of anxiety, he stirred not hand or foot. He had scarcely moved since the trial began; and now that the judge ceased to speak, he still remained in the same strained attitude of close attention, with his gaze bent on him, as though he listened still.

A slight bustle in the court, recalled him to himself. Looking round, he saw that the jurymen had turned together, to consider of their verdict. As his eyes wandered to the gallery, he could see the people rising above each other to see his face: some hastily applying their glasses to their eyes: and others whispering their neighbours with looks expressive of abhorrence. A few there were, who seemed unmindful of him, and looked only to the jury, in impatient wonder how they could delay. But in no one face—not even among the women, of whom there were many there—could he read the faintest sympathy with himself, or any feeling but one of all absorbing interest that he should be condemned.

As he saw all this in one bewildered glance, the death-like stillness came again, and looking back, he saw that the jurymen had turned towards the judge. Hush!

They only sought permission to retire.

He looked, wistfully, into their faces, one by one, when they passed out, as though to see which way the greater number leant; but that was fruitless. The jailer touched him on the shoulder. He followed mechanically to the end of the dock, and sat down on a chair. The man pointed it out, or he would not have seen it.

He looked up into the gallery again. Some of the people were eating, and some fanning themselves with handkerchiefs; for the crowded place was very hot. There was one young man sketching his face in a little note-book. He wondered whether it was like, and looked on when the artist broke his pencil-point, and made another with his knife, as any idle spectator might have done.

In the same way, when he turned his eyes towards the judge, his mind began to busy itself with the fashion of his dress, and what it cost, and how he put it on. There was an old fat gentleman on the bench, too, who had gone out, some half an hour before, and now come back. He wondered within himself whether this man had been to get his dinner, what he had had, and where he had had it; and pursued this train of careless thought until some new object caught his eye and roused another.

Not that, all this time, his mind was, for an instant, free from one oppressive overwhelming sense of the grave that opened at his feet; it was ever present to him, but in a vague and general way, and he could not fix his thoughts upon it. Thus, even while he trembled, and turned burning hot at the idea of speedy death, he fell to counting the iron spikes before him, and wondering how the head of one had been broken off, and whether they would mend it, or leave it as it was. Then, he thought of all the horrors of the gallows and the scaffold—and stopped to watch a man sprinkling the floor to cool it—and then went on to think again.

At length there was a cry of silence, and a breathless look from all towards the door. The jury returned, and passed him close. He could glean nothing from their faces; they might as well have been of stone. Perfect stillness ensued—not a rustle—not a breath—Guilty.

The building rang with a tremendous shout, and another, and another, and then it echoed deep loud groans that gathered strength as they swelled out, like angry thunder. It was a peal of joy from the populace outside, greeting the news that he would die on Monday.

The noise subsided, and he was asked if he had anything to say why sentence of death should not be passed upon him. He had resumed his listening attitude, and looked intently at his questioner while the demand was made; but it was twice repeated before he seemed to hear it, and then he only muttered that he was an old man—an old man—an old man—and so, dropping into a whisper, was silent again.

The judge assumed the black cap,[1] and the prisoner still stood with the same air and gesture. A woman in the gallery uttered some exclamation, called forth by this dread solemnity; he looked hastily up as if angry at the interruption, and bent forward yet more attentively. The address was solemn and impressive; the sentence fearful to hear. But he stood, like a marble figure, without the motion of a nerve. His haggard face was still thrust forward, his under-jaw hanging down, and his eyes staring out before him, when the jailer put his hand upon his arm, and beckoned him away. He gazed stupidly about him for an instant, and obeyed.

They led him through a paved room under the court, where some prisoners were waiting till their turns came, and others were talking to their friends, who crowded round a grate which looked into the open yard. There was nobody there, to speak to *him*; but, as he passed, the prisoners fell back to render him more visible to the people who were clinging to the bars: and they assailed him with opprobrious names, and screeched and hissed. He shook his fist, and would have spat upon them; but his conductors hurried him on, through a gloomy passage lighted by a few dim lamps, into the interior of the prison.

Here, he was searched, that he might not have about him the means of anticipating the law; this ceremony performed, they led him to one of the condemned cells, and left him there—alone.

He sat down on a stone bench opposite the door, which served for seat and bedstead; and casting his blood-shot eyes upon the ground, tried to collect his thoughts. After a while, he began to remember a few disjointed fragments of what the judge had said: though it had seemed to him, at the time, that he could not hear a word. These gradually fell into their proper places, and by degrees suggested more: so that in a little time he had the whole, almost as it was delivered. To be hanged by the neck, till he was dead—that was the end. To be hanged by the neck till he was dead.

As it came on very dark, he began to think of all the men he had known who had died upon the scaffold; some of them through his means. They rose up, in such quick succession, that he could hardly count them. He had seen some of them die,—and had joked too, because they died with prayers upon their lips. With what a rattling noise the

---

1. The cap an English judge placed on his head when about to pronounce a death sentence.

drop went down; and how suddenly they changed, from strong and vigorous men to dangling heaps of clothes!

Some of them might have inhabited that very cell—sat upon that very spot. It was very dark; why didn't they bring a light? The cell had been built for many years. Scores of men must have passed their last hours there. It was like sitting in a vault strewn with dead bodies—the cap, the noose, the pinioned arms, the faces that he knew, even beneath that hideous veil—Light, light!

At length, when his hands were raw with beating against the heavy door and walls, two men appeared: one bearing a candle, which he thrust into an iron candlestick fixed against the wall: the other dragging in a mattress on which to pass the night; for the prisoner was to be left alone no more.

Then came night—dark, dismal, silent night. Other watchers are glad to hear the church-clocks strike, for they tell of life and coming day. To the Jew, they brought despair. The boom of every iron bell came laden with the one, deep, hollow sound—Death. What availed the noise and bustle of cheerful morning, which penetrated even there, to him? It was another form of knell, with mockery added to the warning.

The day passed off—day! There was no day; it was gone as soon as come—and night came on again; night so long, and yet so short; long in its dreadful silence, and short in its fleeting hours. At one time he raved and blasphemed; and at another howled and tore his hair. Venerable men of his own persuasion had come to pray beside him, but he had driven them away with curses. They renewed their charitable efforts, and he beat them off.

Saturday night. He had only one night more to live. And as he thought of this, the day broke—Sunday.

It was not until the night of this last awful day, that a withering sense of his helpless, desperate state came in its full intensity upon his blighted soul; not that he had ever held any defined or positive hope of mercy, but that he had never been able to consider more than the dim probability of dying so soon. He had spoken little to either of the two men, who relieved each other in their attendance upon him; and they, for their parts, made no effort to rouse his attention. He had sat there, awake, but dreaming. Now, he started up, every minute, and with gasping mouth and burning skin, hurried to and fro, in such a paroxysm of fear and wrath that even they—used to such sights—recoiled from him with horror. He grew so terrible, at last, in all the tortures of his evil conscience, that one man could not bear to sit there, eyeing him alone; and so the two kept watch together.

He cowered down upon his stone bed, and thought of the past. He had been wounded with some missiles from the crowd on the day of his capture, and his head was bandaged with a linen cloth. His red hair hung down upon his bloodless face; his beard was torn, and twisted into knots; his eyes shone with a terrible light; his unwashed flesh, crackled with the fever that burnt him up. Eight—nine—ten. If it was not a trick to frighten him, and those were the real hours treading on each other's heels, where would he be, when they came round again! Eleven! Another struck, before the voice of the previous hour had ceased to vibrate. At eight, he would be the only mourner in his own funeral train; at eleven————

Those dreadful walls of Newgate, which have hidden so much misery and such unspeakable anguish, not only from the eyes, but, too often and too long, from the thoughts, of men, never held so dread a spectacle as that. The few who lingered as they passed, and wondered what the man was doing who was to be hung to-morrow, would have slept but ill that night, if they could have seen him.

From early in the evening until nearly midnight, little groups of two and three presented themselves at the lodge-gate, and inquired, with anxious faces, whether any reprieve had been received. These being answered in the negative, communicated the welcome intelligence to clusters in the street, who pointed out to one another the door from which he must come out, and showed where the scaffold would be built, and, walking with unwilling steps away, turned back to conjure up the scene. By degrees they fell off, one by one; and, for an hour, in the dead of night, the street was left to solitude and darkness.

The space before the prison was cleared, and a few strong barriers, painted black, had been already thrown across the road to break the pressure of the expected crowd,[2] when Mr. Brownlow and Oliver appeared at the wicket, and presented an order of admission to the prisoner, signed by one of the sheriffs. They were immediately admitted into the lodge.

"Is the young gentleman to come too, sir?" said the man whose duty it was to conduct them. "It's not a sight for children, sir."

"It is not indeed, my friend," rejoined Mr. Brownlow; "but my business with this man is intimately connected with him; and as this child has seen him in the full career of his success and villany, I think it well—even at the cost of some pain and fear—that he should see him now."

These few words had been said apart, so as to be inaudible to Oliver. The man touched his hat; and glancing at Oliver with some curiosity, opened another gate, opposite to that by which they had entered, and led them on, through dark and winding ways, towards the cells.

"This," said the man, stopping in a gloomy passage where a couple of workmen were making some preparations in profound silence,—"this

2. See above, p. 69, n. 5.

is the place he passes through. If you step this way, you can see the door he goes out at."

He led them into a stone kitchen, fitted with coppers for dressing[3] the prison food, and pointed to a door. There was an open grating above it, through which came the sound of men's voices, mingled with the noise of hammering, and the throwing down of boards. They were putting up the scaffold.

From this place, they passed through several strong gates, opened by other turnkeys from the inner side; and, having entered an open yard, ascended a flight of narrow steps, and came into a passage with a row of strong doors on the left hand. Motioning them to remain where they were, the turnkey knocked at one of these with his bunch of keys. The two attendants, after a little whispering, came out into the passage, stretching themselves as if glad of the temporary relief, and motioned the visitors to follow the jailer into the cell. They did so.

The condemned criminal was seated on his bed, rocking himself from side to side, with a countenance more like that of a snared beast than the face of a man. His mind was evidently wandering to his old life, for he continued to mutter, without appearing conscious of their presence otherwise than as a part of his vision.

"Good boy, Charley—well done—" he mumbled. "Oliver too, ha! ha! ha! Oliver too—quite the gentleman now—quite the—take that boy away to bed!"

The jailer took the disengaged hand of Oliver; and, whispering him not to be alarmed, looked on without speaking.

"Take him away to bed!" cried the Jew. "Do you hear me, some of you? He has been the—the—somehow the cause of all this. It's worth the money to bring him up to it—Bolter's throat, Bill; never mind the girl—Bolter's throat as deep as you can cut. Saw his head off!"

"Fagin," said the jailer.

"That's me!" cried the Jew, falling, instantly, into the attitude of listening he had assumed upon his trial. "An old man, my Lord; a very old, old man!"

"Here," said the turnkey, laying his hand upon his breast to keep him down. "Here's somebody wants to see you, to ask you some questions, I suppose. Fagin, Fagin! Are you a man?"

"I shan't be one long," replied the Jew, looking up with a face retaining no human expression but rage and terror. "Strike them all dead! What right have they to butcher me?"

As he spoke, he caught sight of Oliver and Mr. Brownlow. Shrinking to the furthest corner of the seat, he demanded to know what they wanted there.

3. Cooking.

"Steady," said the turnkey, still holding him down. "Now, sir, tell him what you want—quick, if you please, for he grows worse as the time gets on."

"You have some papers," said Mr. Brownlow advancing, "which were placed in your hands, for better security, by a man called Monks."

"It's all a lie together," replied the Jew. "I haven't one—not one."

"For the love of God," said Mr. Brownlow solemnly, "do not say that now, upon the very verge of death; but tell me where they are. You know that Sikes is dead; that Monks has confessed; that there is no hope of any further gain. Where are those papers?"

"Oliver," cried the Jew, beckoning to him. "Here, here! Let me whisper to you."

"I am not afraid," said Oliver in a low voice, as he relinquished Mr. Brownlow's hand.

"The papers," said the Jew, drawing him towards him, "are in a canvass bag, in a hole a little way up the chimney in the top front-room. I want to talk to you, my dear. I want to talk to you."

"Yes, yes," returned Oliver. "Let me say a prayer. Do! Let me say one prayer. Say only one, upon your knees, with me, and we will talk till morning."

"Outside, outside," replied the Jew, pushing the boy before him to-wards the door, and looking vacantly over his head. "Say I've gone to sleep—they'll believe *you*. You can get me out, if you take me so. Now then, now then!"

"Oh! God forgive this wretched man!" cried the boy with a burst of tears.

"That's right, that's right," said the Jew. "That'll help us on. This door first. If I shake and tremble, as we pass the gallows, don't you mind, but hurry on. Now, now, now!"

"Have you nothing else to ask him, sir?" inquired the turnkey.

"No other question," replied Mr. Brownlow. "If I hoped we could recall him to a sense of his position—"

"Nothing will do that, sir," replied the man, shaking his head. "You had better leave him."

The door of the cell opened, and the attendants returned.

"Press on, press on," cried the Jew. "Softly, but not so slow. Faster, faster!"

The men laid hands upon him, and disengaging Oliver from his grasp, held him back. He struggled with the power of desperation, for an instant; and, then sent up cry upon cry that penetrated even those massive walls, and rang in their ears until they reached the open yard.

It was some time before they left the prison. Oliver nearly swooned after this frightful scene, and was so weak that for an hour or more, he had not the strength to walk.

Day was dawning when they again emerged. A great multitude had already assembled; the windows were filled with people, smoking and playing cards to beguile the time; the crowd were pushing, quarrelling, and joking. Everything told of life and animation, but one dark cluster of objects in the very centre of all—the black stage, the cross-beam, the rope, and all the hideous apparatus of death.

Chapter LIII.

AND LAST.

The fortunes of those who have figured in this tale, are nearly closed. The little that remains to their historian to relate, is told in few and simple words.

Before three months had passed, Rose Fleming and Harry Maylie were married, in the village church which was henceforth to be the scene of the young clergyman's labours; on the same day they entered into possession of their new and happy home.

Mrs. Maylie took up her abode with her son and daughter-in-law, to enjoy, during the tranquil remainder of her days, the greatest felicity that age and worth can know—the contemplation of the happiness of those on whom the warmest affections and tenderest cares of a well-spent life, have been unceasingly bestowed.

It appeared, on full and careful investigation, that if the wreck of property remaining in the custody of Monks (which had never prospered either in his hands or in those of his mother) were equally divided between himself and Oliver, it would yield, to each, little more than three thousand pounds. By the provisions of his father's will, Oliver would have been entitled to the whole; but Mr. Brownlow, unwilling to deprive the elder son of the opportunity of retrieving his former vices and pursuing an honest career, proposed this mode of distribution, to which his young charge joyfully acceded.

Monks, still bearing that assumed name, retired, with his portion, to a distant part of the New World: where, having quickly squandered it, he once more fell into his old courses, and, after undergoing a long confinement for some fresh act of fraud and knavery, at length sunk under an attack of his old disorder, and died in prison. As far from home, died the chief remaining members of his friend Fagin's gang.

Mr. Brownlow adopted Oliver as his own son. Removing with him and the old housekeeper to within a mile of the parsonage-house, where his dear friends resided, he gratified the only remaining wish of Oliver's warm and earnest heart, and thus linked together a little society, whose condition approached as nearly to one of perfect happiness as can ever be known in this changing world.

Soon after the marriage of the young people, the worthy doctor returned to Chertsey, where, bereft of the presence of his old friends, he would have been discontented if his temperament had admitted of such a feeling; and would have turned quite peevish if he had known how. For two or three months, he contented himself with hinting that he feared the air began to disagree with him; then, finding that the place really was, to him, no longer what it had been before, he settled his business on his assistant, took a bachelor's cottage just outside the village of which his young friend was pastor, and instantaneously recovered. Here, he took to gardening, planting, fishing, carpentering, and various other pursuits of a similar kind: all undertaken with his characteristic impetuosity; and in each and all, he has since become famous throughout the neighbourhood, as a most profound authority.

Before his removal, he had managed to contract a strong friendship for Mr. Grimwig, which that eccentric gentleman cordially reciprocated. He is accordingly visited by him a great many times in the course of the year. On all such occasions, Mr. Grimwig plants, fishes, and carpenters with great ardour; doing everything in a very singular and unprecedented manner, but always maintaining, with his favourite asseveration,[1] that his mode is the right one. On Sundays, he never fails to criticise the sermon to the young clergyman's face: always informing Mr. Losberne, in strict confidence afterwards, that he considers it an excellent performance, but deems it as well not to say so. It is a standing and very favourite joke for Mr. Brownlow to rally him on his old prophecy concerning Oliver, and to remind him of the night on which they sat, with the watch between them, waiting his return; but Mr. Grimwig contends that he was right in the main, and, in proof thereof, remarks that Oliver *did not come back*, after all: which always calls forth a laugh on his side, and increases his good-humour.

Mr. Noah Claypole: receiving a free pardon from the Crown in consequence of being admitted approver[2] against the Jew: and considering his profession not altogether as safe a one as he could wish: was, for some little time, at a loss for the means of a livelihood, not burthened with too much work. After some consideration, he went into business as an Informer, in which calling he realises a genteel subsistence. His plan is, to walk out once a week during church time, attended by Charlotte in respectable attire. The lady faints away at the doors of charitable publicans, and the gentleman being accommodated with threepennyworth of brandy to restore her, lays an information next day, and pockets half the penalty.[3] Sometimes Mr. Claypole faints himself, but the result is the same.

Mr. and Mrs. Bumble, deprived of their situations, were gradually

---

1. Positive declaration.
2. Testifier.
3. Makes a complaint the next day that the tavernkeeper has violated the Sunday laws, and gets to keep half the fine. "Publicans": proprietors of taverns.

reduced to great indigence and misery, and finally became paupers in that very same workhouse in which they had once lorded it over others. Mr. Bumble has been heard to say, that in this reverse and degradation, he has not even spirits to be thankful for being separated from his wife.

As to Mr. Giles and Brittles, they still remain in their old posts, although the former is bald, and the last-named boy quite grey. They sleep at the parsonage, but divide their attentions so equally among its inmates, and Oliver, and Mr. Brownlow, and Mr. Losberne, that to this day the villagers have never been able to discover to which establishment they properly belong.

Master Charles Bates, appalled by Sikes's crime, fell into a train of reflection whether an honest life was not, after all, the best. Arriving at the conclusion that it certainly was, he turned his back upon the scenes of the past, resolved to amend it in some new sphere of action. He struggled hard, and suffered much, for some time; but having a contented disposition, and a good purpose, succeeded in the end; and, from being a farmer's drudge, and a carrier's lad, is now the merriest young grazier in all Northamptonshire.[4]

And now, the hand that traces these words, falters, as it approaches the conclusion of its task: and would weave, for a little longer space, the thread of these adventures.

I would fain linger yet with a few of those among whom I have so long moved, and share their happiness by endeavouring to depict it. I would show Rose Maylie in all the bloom and grace of early womanhood, shedding on her secluded path in life, such soft and gentle light, as fell on all who trod it with her, and shone into their hearts. I would paint her the life and joy of the fire-side circle and the lively summer group; I would follow her through the sultry fields at noon, and hear the low tones of her sweet voice in the moonlit evening walk; I would watch her in all her goodness and charity abroad, and the smiling untiring discharge of domestic duties at home; I would paint her and her dead sister's child happy in their mutual love, and passing whole hours together in picturing the friends whom they had so sadly lost; I would summon before me, once again, those joyous little faces that clustered round her knee, and listen to their merry prattle; I would recall the tones of that clear laugh, and conjure up the sympathising tear that glistened in the soft blue eye. These, and a thousand looks and smiles, and turns of thought and speech—I would fain recall them every one.

How Mr. Brownlow went on, from day to day, filling the mind of his adopted child with stores of knowledge, and becoming attached to him, more and more, as his nature developed itself, and showed the thriving seeds of all he wished him to become—how he traced in him new traits of his early friend, that awakened in his own bosom old

---

4. A region seventy-five miles northwest of London.

remembrances, melancholy and yet sweet and soothing—how the two orphans, tried by adversity, remembered its lessons in mercy to others, and mutual love, and fervent thanks to Him who had protected and preserved them—these are all matters which need not to be told. I have said that they were truly happy; and without strong affection, and humanity of heart, and gratitude to that Being whose code is Mercy, and whose great attribute is Benevolence to all things that breathe, true happiness can never be attained.

Within the altar of the old village church, there stands a white marble tablet, which bears as yet but one word,—"Agnes!" There is no coffin in that tomb; and may it be many, many years, before another name is placed above it! But, if the spirits of the Dead ever come back to earth, to visit spots hallowed by the love—the love beyond the grave—of those whom they knew in life, I believe that the shade of Agnes sometimes hovers round that solemn nook. I believe it none the less, because that nook is in a Church, and she was weak and erring.

BACKGROUNDS
AND SOURCES

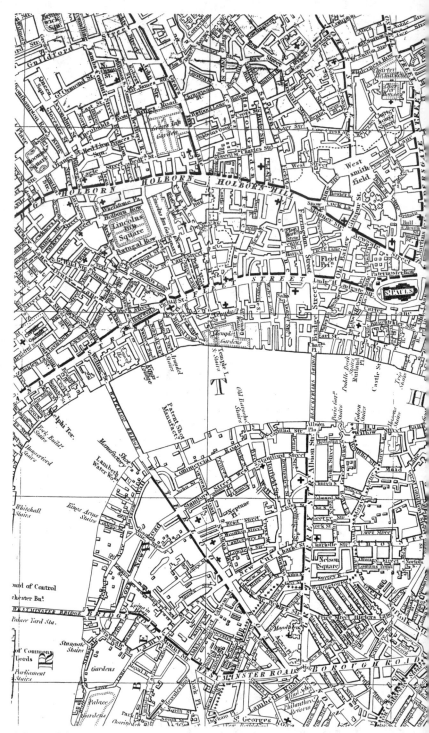

A Map of the London of *Oliver Twist* (1828). Courtesy of the Huntington Library.

[The Poor Law Debate]†

As in former sessions, the attention of parliament was repeatedly called by petitions to the depressed state of the agricultural interest. Government admitted that these complaints were not altogether unfounded, but found it more difficult to devise expedients by which they might be removed. * * * To diminish this pressure was one professed object of a bill for altering and amending the poor-laws,¹ one of the few important measures that were carried through during the session. Soon after their accession to office, the present ministry had appointed a commission of inquiry into the state and operation of the poor-laws, as more useful for collecting facts than any parliamentary committee. The inquiries of the commissioners were to be directed towards ascertaining what was the cause why, in some parts of the country, the poor-laws were considered a benefit by parishes, while in others their operation had been ruinous and destructive; and why in some agricultural districts certain parishes existed in which the poor-laws appeared to do no harm at all. It was expected that the information thus obtained would enable parishes, where injurious effects had arisen, to profit by the example of other parishes where different arrangements had led to different consequences. The commissioners had made their report, and an abstract of the evidence which they had taken had been printed in the course of the preceding session. That report impressed government so strongly with a conviction of the evils produced by the system in many districts of the country, that they resolved to propose a remedy to parliament. Lord Althorp accordingly, on the 17th April, moved for leave to bring in a bill to alter and amend the laws relating to the Poor.

The necessity of interference was maintained upon the ground that the present administration of these laws tended directly to the destruction of all property in the country, and that even to the labouring classes, whom they had been intended to benefit, nothing could be more fatal than to allow the present course to be continued. It was the abuse of the system, not the system itself that was to blame. The abuses were scarcely older than the beginning of the present century, and had originated in measures intended for the benefit of that class of the community to whose interests and welfare they were now most destructively opposed. * * * The 36th of George III, laid down the principle, that the relief

---

† From *The Annual Register*, 1834 (London, 1835) 222–24, 227, 232–35, 238, 241, 243–44, 247, 249, 252–55, 256.
1. The controversial Poor Law Amendment Act, also known as the New Poor Law, became law in 1835. As this selection from the parliamentary debate preceding its passage makes clear, the New Poor Law's key provision forced the nonworking and the working poor who needed public assistance into special institutions called workhouses, where they could be supported more cheaply than outside (see above, p. 17, n. 1); it also reorganized public assistance into larger, more efficient administrative units and placed the financial responsibility for illegitimate children entirely on their mothers.

to paupers ought to be given in such a manner as to place them in a situation of comfort. Now, however desirable it might be to place all our countrymen in a situation of comfort, yet to give such relief as was described in this statute was the duty of private charity, and should not be provided for by a compulsory rate. The effect of this law had been to give the magistrates the power of ordering relief to be given to the poor in their own dwellings; and the same principle being followed up by the magistrates, it led from bad to worse, till all feelings of independence on the part of the labourers had been almost entirely extinguished in many parts of the country, and instead of the paupers being placed in a state of comfort, all the labouring population, in many districts of the country, had been brought into a state of deplorable misery and distress.

The dangers to be incurred by leaving matters as they stood, were so great and so urgent, that although the length of time, during which this system had been going on, rendered it necessary to legislate with caution, it was absolutely necessary to meet the difficulties of the case, adopt sounder principles, and carry them unflinchingly into execution. * * *

It was on the nature of this growing mischief, and the necessity of effectually checking it, that lord Althorp defended the first part of the government plan, which consisted in intrusting the poor-laws to a board of commissioners.

*   *   *

The great principles of the proposed plan, then, went to this, to stop the allowance system—to deprive the magistracy of the power of ordering out-door relief—to alter in certain cases the constitution of parochial vestries[2]—to give large discretionary powers to the central commissioners—to simplify the law of settlement and removal—to render the mother of an illegitimate child liable to support it, and save from imprisonment for its aliment[3] the putative father, to whom she might swear it.

The bill, by which these principles were to be carried into effect, having been brought in, the second reading was opposed by colonel Evans, one of the members for Westminster. While he admitted, that many things in the administration of the poor-laws required amendment, and that, in particular, some alteration was necessary to cure the mischievous tendency of out-door relief,—he thought that the whole bill was corrupted by the abolition of the powers of local vestries, and by the creation of the central board of commissioners; an expedient which was not necessary, had nothing in accordance with our general principles of legislation, and which could be effective for nothing but giving to the crown a vast increase of patronage.

2. Local community or parish governing boards.
3. Support.

*   *   *

In the committee, a good deal of discussion took place as regarded the effect of the bill in establishing workhouses, a system which many members viewed with great distaste, and the extension of which they much dreaded, from the power given to the commissioners to assess parishes for the purpose of erecting workhouses. They were apprehensive that this mode of assistance would be universally adopted, to the exclusion of all out-of-door relief.

*   *   *

By the proposed clause, if a labouring man fell sick, or was deprived by other causes of his ability to support his family, and required a little temporary relief, he would be driven, with perhaps a large family, into the workhouse, from which it would be impossible to say when he would return. This would be a very great hardship, and would be attended with the most injurious consequences. The same observation applied to widows, to orphans, illegitimate children, and others, who, from want of a little temporary relief, which could be administered at the discretion of persons on the spot, might be confined to the workhouse for the rest of their days. The clause was bad, too, in point of economy, for by forcing a whole family to seek protection in the workhouse, expenses to a much greater extent must be necessarily incurred to the parish, than if they were relieved at their own home. In many instances the aged poor were content to receive half-a-crown a-week from the parish funds in aid of their maintenance out of the workhouse; whereas, if they were compelled to reside within the workhouse, a much larger sum of money must be expended in their support. The temporary relief required would be small; but, by being confined to the workhouse, they would be prevented from obtaining employment, and consequently would remain for a much longer period a burthen upon the parish. Besides, in many instances the members of the same family might be separated and placed in different workhouses, by which means the amount would be greatly augmented. In large manufacturing towns, where it was impossible to find employment for the poor, the operation of this clause would be peculiarly injurious. Before the men went to the workhouse, they would be compelled to sell all their furniture, hand-looms, &c.; and having disposed of every thing they possessed and gone to the workhouse, they had no prospect of ever returning to their work, as the most they would be allowed was a penny a-day from the workhouse. * * * All this evil might be averted by a temporary relief out of the workhouse.

*   *   *

The clauses which relieved the fathers of illegitimate children from all legal obligation to maintain them, and laid that burden on the mother as if she had been a widow, occasioned a good deal of discussion.— Mr. Robinson, member for Worcester, moved that these clauses should be omitted, by no means on the ground that he held the existing law, as to bastardy, to be faultless, but because he thought it clear that this was not the sort of amendment which it required. The proposed clauses removed the liability of the putative father. He did not object to so much of them as repealed certain acts affecting the mother; but he did decidedly object to the part which removed the liability from the father. He objected to the 70th clause, which had an *ex post facto* operation,[4] as it relieved all putative fathers who were now under recognizances or in custody for not giving security for the support of any child already sworn to them, but not yet born, from all such recognizances,[5] and directed their discharge on application to a visiting magistrate. In the 71st clause he found, to his astonishment as a man and a Christian, that the liability, which was removed from the father, was placed on the mother of an illegitimate child, and that she was bound to support it. In the 72nd clause the same principle was adopted, but carried much farther. It proposed, that in case the woman should be unable to support her bastard child, the liability should rest on her father, or if he were not alive, or being alive, was not able to support it, then the liability was to fall on the grandfather or grandmother. Could the house seriously entertain propositions of this nature, or consent to pass enactments so contrary to every principle of justice and humanity? If the fathers of bastard children were to be relieved from the burthen of contributing to the support of their children, on whom was that burthen to fall? On the mother, said the supporters of the bill. But in nineteen out of twenty cases, in which a female gave birth for the first time to a bastard child, it would be found that she was not able to maintain herself and child. It had been said, that if you threw upon the woman the burthen of maintaining her bastard child, you would lessen her disposition to indulge in licentious passion. That man, however, knew little of human character, who fancied that this would render deviations from chastity less frequent. Prudential considerations might paralyze, but they never could annihilate the natural desires of woman; nor would it stop the career of licentious men to inform them that they might commit seduction with perfect impunity, and that they might gratify their wicked inclinations at the sole expense of their victims. He was anxious to learn from the supporters of the bill, on what principle they proposed to relieve the man, who was the most guilty party, from the consequences of his misconduct, and to charge them all upon the unfortunate woman. He much feared that these clauses would lead to the concealment of the birth of children, and to infanticide after their birth—offences which were already too rife among us. If the restraint, which this clause contemplated, should be found to fail in practice, and if females should still listen and yield to the solicitations of vicious men, it was impossible to conceive that, with all the shame which they must undergo, and with all the struggles which they

4. A law applied retroactively to previously existing situations.
5. Legal obligations.

must encounter to support their children, they would not often be driven to destroy their offspring. It was a great mistake to represent our poor-laws as the cause of licentiousness; for the number of illegitimate children born in countries where there were no poor-laws, was much greater than here.

Lord Althorp protested against these provisions being discussed as matters of feeling; they must be looked at as they affected, not one portion of society, but the whole of it; and looking at the question in this point of view, he was prepared to support this part of the bill, "as a boon to the female population." The experience of every man taught him that one of the effects of the bastardy laws was to inflict great mischief on the female population. Another was, that it diminished the inducements of every female to retain her chastity. A third effect of these laws was, that, under the operation of the existing enactments, females attempted by the number of their bastards, to obtain a settlement in marriage, and the tendency of the existing law counteracted in a great degree that moral feeling, on which success in this question mainly depended. A fourth was, that if the allowance charged for the child upon the father was large, it was given to the mother, whether she wanted it or not. He was afraid that perjury was often committed by the mothers to obtain a large allowance from men who had never had the slightest connexion with them; at any rate there was a strong inducement for a woman to filiate her child[6] upon a man who had not begotten it, provided that he was rich and could make a large allowance. Another effect of this system was, that women with two or three bastard children were often in a better situation than those women who had none. Such were the most prominent evils arising from the existence of our present code of bastardy laws. They took from the woman every feeling which was calculated to nourish modesty of thought and delicacy of conduct. They placed a check upon the man, and held out to the woman an inducement to violate the laws of chastity. The check was applied in the quarter where it was calculated to be the weakest, whilst the inducement was held out to the other sex, as if for the purpose of counteracting that great moral check which arises out of the principles of human nature. He was satisfied that, for many years past, the existing law had been most detrimental in its consequences upon the lower orders.

* * *

His lordship, [the lord chancellor] after giving a historical account of the progress of the poor-laws, pointed out the manner in which they had become the sources of so much evil. * * * The law of nature ordained that a parent should support his child, and a child his parents; but the poor-laws stepped in, and told them to do no such thing, for it

6. To assign paternity to her illegitimate child.

would take that duty upon itself. Such a law denaturalized men, and made them act in a way of which they otherwise would never have dreamed; it made them say, as they had been known to say, "I will expose my children in the streets, unless you relieve them. I will turn my bed-rid mother out of the house, and lay her down at the overseer's door, unless you order me relief for her." These evils, ruinous in themselves, were all aggravated by the tendency of the system, which produced them, to increase the number of individuals subjected to their influence; for the wit of man could not have devised a more direct encouragement to improvident marriages than was afforded by the present system of the poor-laws, of which this was, in fact, the corner-stone. The language which the law held to the poor was this:—"Contract marriages if you please, and your children shall be supported at the expense of the parish;" thus tempting the poor man into an imprudent marriage—too probable an event in itself, to require any legislative incentive—instead of inducing him to postpone marriage, till he had the means of supporting a family.

The consequences of all this on the property of the country were as melancholy as any other effects resulting from the poor-laws. He would not say that many farms were deserted, and many parishes given up to waste (though he knew of one or two farms, and of one parish, which were in that condition); but the system was tending to that point, and the fact of one parish being thrown out of cultivation inevitably tended to throw three or four others into waste. Nor was it only our fields that suffered; the character of the people which cultivated them was degraded. Such a system took away all sense of shame; it deprived men of all feelings of personal dignity, self-respect, and independence, and prevented them from seeking, in the honest paths of industry, support for themselves and their families. Formerly it was considered a disgrace, nay, almost something criminal, to be dependent on the poor-rates; but now the peasantry demanded the parish allowance with an erect port and a manly air. * * *

The change which the bill proposed to make in the law of bastardy, was, he admitted, a bold measure, but; it was, at the same time, a good one.

* * *

Lord Wynford moved that the bill should be read[7] a second time that day six months, not however on the ground that there was not much in the administration of the poor-laws which required to be corrected, but because he conceived that the remedies proposed by the bill were partly unnecessary, and partly inefficient, while some of them were tyrannical; and because, at all events, there was not sufficient time

7. Submitted for formal discussion and debate.

remaining during the session for discussing so many questions of such deep and complicated importance.

* * *

The earl of Winchilsea, the duke of Richmond, and duke of Wellington supported the motion for the second reading, though they did not approve of all the various provisions in the bill. The duke of Wellington was satisfied that, if it was proper to pass the bill, there was ample time during the present session to carry it regularly through all its stages, and it was the duty of their lordships, without any further delay, to proceed with a measure which, if necessary at all, was necessary now. * * * The bill before the house was unquestionably the best which had ever been devised. * * *

He [the bishop of Exeter] could not help thinking that the report bore traces of an *animus* not favourable to its weight. In the report, the fathers of bastard children were spoken of as "unfortunate" persons. "He was an unfortunate young man" who was brought before the justices for this offence; but whenever the mother was spoken of, allusion was certain to be made to her "vice." You did not meet with this form of expression in a solitary instance only; on the contrary, it pervaded the whole report. The language of the report was, "The female is the most to blame."— "continued illicit intercourse originated with the female." * * * Now, he * * * would carry it one step further. He would say, that the father and mother of an illegitimate child, when ascertained, should both be required to support it. This was its right from the instant it drew breath; and it was impossible to imagine any process of sound thinking by which it could be made, that the duty of providing for the infant was less incumbent on the father than on the mother, or that it could even be reconciled with justice, that the former should escape, while all the burden was thrown upon the latter.

* * *

The earl of Falmouth was against the clause, and deprecated the idea of laying the charge upon the female; for he was satisfied that in nine cases out of ten the seducer was the real offender. The bill, it was true, provided, that where the mother could not support the child, recourse might be had to the putative father; but in the rural districts the provisions of the bill would defeat its object: for the father, being an agricultural labourer, would contrive to reach another district, far out of the reach of the parish authorities, long before the birth; and the security to the parish was entirely lost by the repeal of the power to summon the putative father during the pregnancy of the woman.

* * *

The Lord Chancellor begged the house to bear in mind, that the question before them was strictly one of expediency. It was not the object of this bill to do honour to female virtue; it was not its object, as had been assumed, to make women chaste and men continent; its primary intent was directed to other objects.

*   *   *

In replying, the bishop of Exeter reminded the house of what the effect of this clause upon the mother would truly be. Being unable to support her child, she would immediately be consigned to the poorhouse. What was to become of her then? To marry was out of the question; for few men would be found to marry a woman, with the knowledge, that the burthen of supporting her illegitimate offspring would be thrown on him. In such a case, then, the workhouse was like the *inferno* of Dante, and might very properly have inscribed over it the words—"Whoever enters here leaves hope behind." When once an unfortunate woman entered the workhouse, there she would be obliged to remain.

*   *   *   The bill passed on the 8th of August, the third reading having been carried by forty-five to fifteen.

[The Poor Law Riots]†

Poor Law Riots—*Bedford*—John Burgoyne, William Setting, Richard Warner, and John Boxford, were capitally indicted for feloniously remaining in a state of riot for the space of one hour after proclamation made and the reading of the Riot Act.[1]

This was one of the riots which had prevailed in various parts of Bedfordshire, in consequence of putting in force the recent statute for the amendment of the poor laws. It appeared in evidence, that, by virtue of the 26th section of that act a union had been formed of several parishes in this county for the better administration of the poor laws, and that guardians had been appointed for the various parishes included in such union. On Thursday, the 14th of May last, the guardians assembled at the workhouse in the central parish of Ampthill, for the purpose of hearing the complaints of the paupers residing within the union, and transacting the general business of the confederation. A very large assembly of the guardians took place, and whilst they were in deliberation in the workhouse, a crowd of from 200 to 300 people collected in the workhouse garden, which surrounded that building. The conduct of the assembled mob was very riotous; they made use of several threats of a serious nature against the guardians who were assembled inside. Many of the mob were armed with bludgeons, and a great quantity of pebble paving-

---

† From *The Annual Register, 1835* (London, 1836) 110–11.

1. The statement to an unlawful assembly of people that they are acting criminally according to the law determining the proper conduct of public acitivity. For arrests to be made, the appropriate authority had indeed to read publicly the provisions of the law to the people about to be charged and to request that they disperse—hence the modern idiom "to read the riot act."

stones was torn from the pavement of the garden-walk, and laid ready for use if occasion should offer. Several of the guardians came out into the garden and addressed the people, assuring them that if they had any statement to make, or any complaint to prefer, or if they wished for information respecting the power and intentions of the assembled guardians, they should be patiently listened to, if they would but conduct themselves in an orderly and peaceable manner. These addresses were answered by cries of "Blood and bread," "No bread," "Break their heads," "One and all," and others of a like kind. The cries of "No bread" were uttered in consequence of its being understood that the union were inclined to act upon that portion of the new statute, which authorizes the giving of relief in clothing and food, and not in money, under certain circumstances. Seeing the violent conduct of the mob, the guardians returned from the garden into the consulting room at the workhouse, but they had no sooner taken their seats at the table than some stones were throw from the garden into the room, which caused the greatest perplexity and consternation. This state of things continued for a considerable time, during which nearly all the windows of the workhouse were demolished. There were plenty of constables in the crowd, who took various persons into custody, but the prisoners were rescued from their power. Thus matters continued from ten o'clock till half-past one, when it was suggested in the guardians' room that there was a necessity for reading the Riot Act, and it was unanimously agreed that that should be done. H. Musgrave, Esq., a magistrate of the county, who was also one of the board of guardians, accordingly read the Riot Act. After this a notice was published in the Market-place, stating that the "Riot Act had been read, and that any one remaining in a state of riot or tumult for one hour would be guilty of a capital felony."[2] This warning was also written in large legible characters, and affixed to the four corners of the market-house, but the mob tore the notices down instantly. The assembly still continued, the civil force was overpowered, and the rioting, throwing of stones, and tumultuous cries of "No bread," "All money," &c., were renewed and kept up for a long time. Several of the neighbouring magistrates had in the mean time arrived at the spot, and adjourned to the White Hart Inn, for the purpose of being at hand in case of emergency. The guardians also adjourned to that inn, and having made their way through the crowd as well as they could, they succeeded in joining the justices. The mob followed them and continued their disturbance in front of the inn. This state of things continued for three or four hours after the reading of the Riot Act, and it was proved that three of the prisoners were very active in encouraging the mob to acts of violence during the affray, and that they remained in a state of insubordination and riot for more than an hour after proclamation had

2. A crime punishable by death.

been made, and the Riot Act read. No serious injury, however, appeared to have occurred during this disturbance, but one or two of the guardians were slightly wounded by the stones that were thrown.—The prisoners, in their defence, declared that "they had no malice in their hearts," and that all that they wanted was to provide for their families; and they declared that they had not the least notion that they had incurred the capital pains and penalties of the statute of the 1st George I., by reason of remaining on the ground for the space of an hour after the reading of the Riot Act.—The jury found Burgoyne, Setting, and Boxford *Guilty*, and acquited Warner.

CHARLES DICKENS

Letters About *Oliver Twist* (1837–64)†

To Richard Bentley,¹ January 24, 1837

Furnivals Inn. | Tuesday Morning

My Dear Sir.

Oliver Twist making nearly eleven pages, I have only five more to write for the next Miscellany—and those five I am compelled—*really* compelled;—in such matters, it is not a word that I easily admit into my vocabulary—to defer until some future opportunity, and to make up, as I am carried on by my subject. Mrs. Dickens has been for some days past, in a very low and alarming state;² and although she is a little better this morning, I am obliged to be constantly with her, being the only person who can prevail upon her to take ordinary nourishment. I have been labouring for two days past, under a violent attack of God knows what, in the head; and in addition to all my other worry, am experiencing the debility, sickness, and all the other comfortable symptoms consequent upon about as much medicine as would be given to an ordinary-sized horse. Although I have perhaps the best subject I ever thought of, I really *cannot* write under these combined disadvantages.

If I thought it would injure the next Number, I should find no relief in sitting idle, but it will not, I am certain. I have thrown my whole heart and soul into Oliver Twist, and most confidently believe he will make a feature in the work, and be very popular.   *   *   * We shall have

---

† From the Pilgrim Edition, *The Letters of Charles Dickens*, vol. 1, ed. Madeline House and Graham Storey. Copyright © 1965. Reprinted by permission of Oxford University Press. Pp. 237, 257–58, 259–60, 267, 319, 343–44, 439, 441. Letters to Eliza Davis, on p. 378, are from the Nonesuch Edition of *The Letters of Charles Dickens*, vol. 3, ed. Walter Dexter. Copyright © 1938. Pp. 356–57, 405.

1. The founder of a major Victorian publishing house and the publisher of *Bentley's Miscellany*, Richard Bentley (1794–1871) contracted with Dickens to edit his new weekly magazine and to write *Oliver Twist* for publication in the *Miscellany* in weekly installments.

2. Earlier in the month Catherine Dickens had given birth to the Dickenses' first child, "a son and heir."

a very strong number, and I am sure you cannot doubt my anxiety and interest in our joint behalf.

Believe me
My Dear Sir
Faithfully Yours
CHARLES DICKENS

To Richard Bentley, May 8, 1837

48 Doughty Street. | Monday morning [On mourning paper] My Dear Sir.

I am most sorry to inform you that Mrs. Dickens' sister whom you saw here, after accompanying us to the Theatre on Saturday Evening in the best health and spirits, was taken suddenly ill, and died in my arms yesterday afternoon[3]—since which time her mother has been also lying here in a state of insensibility. She was our constant friend and companion, and the loss independent of its fearful suddenness, is severely felt by us. I have given the Printer matter to go on with, and tomorrow or at furthest next day, will send him more. I must entreat you to spare me in the meanwhile.

Dear Sir
Faithfully Yours
CHARLES DICKENS

To Thomas Beard,[4] May 17, 1837

Collins's Farm. North End | Hampstead | Wednesday Evening My Dear Beard.

I received your kind letter in due course. I should have written to you myself, to communicate the dreadful occurrence, but I had so many distressing appeals to my attention and exertions, that I was compelled to postpone doing so for a time.

I presume you heard from my father, that on the Saturday Night we had been to the Theatre—that we returned home as usual—that poor Mary was in the same health and spirits in which you have so often seen her—that almost immediately after she went up stairs to bed she was taken ill—and that next day she died. Thank God she died in my arms, and the very last words she whispered were of me.

Of our sufferings at the time, and all through the dreary week that ensued, I will say nothing—no one can imagine what they were. You have seen a good deal of her, and can feel for us, and imagine what a

---

3. The sudden death of Mary Hogarth (1819–37) at the age of seventeen had a powerful impact on Dickens. She is partly memorialized in the depiction of Rose Maylie in *Oliver Twist*. "Mourning paper": It was the Victorian custom to use stationery with a wide black border on all sides for a period of time after the death of a family member.
4. A journalist who had worked closely with him on the *Morning Chronicle*, Beard (1807–91) was an intimate friend of Dickens'.

blank she has left behind. The first burst of my grief has passed, and I can think and speak of her, calmly and dispassionately. I solemnly believe that so perfect a creature never breathed. I knew her inmost heart, and her real worth and value. She had not a fault.

* * *

I have been so shaken and unnerved by the loss of one whom I so dearly loved that I have been compelled to lay aside all thoughts of my usual monthly work, for once; and we have come here for quiet and change.

To Thomas Haines,[5] June 3, 1837

48 Doughty St.—Mecklenburgh Square |
Saturday June 3rd. 1837.

My Dear Sir.

* * *

In my next number of Oliver Twist, I must have a magistrate; and casting about for a magistrate whose harshness and insolence would render him a fit subject to be "shewn up" I have, as a necessary consequence, stumbled upon Mr. Laing of Hatton Garden celebrity.[6] I know the man's character perfectly well, but as it would be necessary to describe his appearance also, I ought to have seen him, which (fortunately or unfortunately as the case may be) I have never done.

In this dilemma it occurred to me that perhaps I might under your auspices be smuggled into the Hatton Garden office for a few moments some morning. If you can further my object, I shall be really very greatly obliged to you.

* * *

To George Cruikshank,[7] October 13, 1837

Doughty Street | Friday Night

My Dear Cruikshank

I inclose you the first eleven slips of Oliver which I will send for on Monday Morning early. I think you will find a very good subject at page 10, which we will call "Oliver's reception by Fagin and the boys".

In haste

Faithfully Yours

CHARLES DICKENS

5. A highly respected reporter specializing in police activities.
6. See above, p. 77, n.3.
7. The illustrator of Oliver Twist, Cruikshank (1792–1878) was already a famous artist when Bentley engaged him in 1836 to illustrate Dickens' Sketches by Boz. A prolific illustrator and artist, Cruikshank did not again collaborate with Dickens after Oliver, though they continued friends. After Dickens' death, Cruikshank claimed without warrant that he had originated the idea for Oliver Twist.

To John Forster,[8] Mid-December 1837

Thursday

My Dear Forster.

Come on and give *me* a call, and let us have "a bit o' talk." My missis is going out to dinner (I *ought* to go, but I have got a bad cold). Come and sit here and read, or work, or do something, while I write the *last* chapter of Oliver which will be arter a lamb chop. Excuse a wafer and believe me ever yours—CD.

To Richard Bentley, October 3, 1838

Doughty Street | Wednesday Morning

My Dear Sir

I have such work in point of quantity and time with Oliver, and am applying it with such hearty energy, that I have given out at my door that I am out of town for a fortnight. Pray favor the notion with all Miscellany ladies and gentlemen that may happen to come under your notice.

I think you will be struck with the last volume. It is difficult to manage, but I am doing it with greater care, and I think with greater power than I have been able to bring to bear on anything yet. I saw the Edinburgh Review notice last night, and it praises Oliver to the skies.

*   *   *

Faithfully Yours
CHARLES DICKENS

To John Forster, October 6 or 13, 1838

Saturday Morning

My Dear Forster,

I dreamt last night—strange to say—of the books you have sent home. I don't ride till tomorrow, not having yet disposed of the Jew[9] who is such an out and outer that I don't know what to make of him.

Always

C.D.

---

8. Dickens' closest friend, Forster (1812–76) acted as his personal and business advisor as well as his editor and literary agent. A distinguished man of letters himself, Forster excelled as a reviewer, literary critic, and biographer. After Dickens' death, Forster published the first biography of Dickens.
9. Fagin

To Eliza Davis,[1] July 10, 1863

Gad's Hill Place, Higham by Rochester, Kent
Friday, July Tenth, 1863

DEAR MADAM,—I hope you will excuse this tardy reply to your letter. It is often impossible for me, by any means, to keep pace with my correspondents. I must take leave to say, that if there be any general feeling on the part of the intelligent Jewish people, that I have done them what you describe as "a great wrong," they are a far less sensible, a far less just, and a far less good-tempered people than I have always supposed them to be. Fagin, in Oliver Twist, is a Jew, because it unfortunately was true of the time to which that story refers, that that class of criminal almost invariably was a Jew. But surely no sensible man or woman of your persuasion can fail to observe—firstly, that all the rest of the wicked *dramatis personæ* are Christians; and secondly, that he is called a "Jew," not because of his religion, but because of his race. If I were to write a story, in which I described a Frenchman or a Spaniard as "the Roman Catholic," I should do a very indecent and unjustifiable thing; but I make mention of Fagin as the Jew, because he is one of the Jewish people, and because it conveys that kind of idea of him which I should give my readers of a Chinaman, by calling him a Chinese.

The enclosed is quite a nominal subscription towards the good object in which you are interested;[2] but I hope it may serve to show you that I have no feeling towards the Jewish people but a friendly one. I always speak well of them, whether in public or in private, and bear my testimony (as I ought to do) to their perfect good faith in such transactions as I have ever had with them; and in my Child's History of England, I have lost no opportunity of setting forth their cruel persecution in old times.—Dear Madam—faithfully yours.

To Eliza Davis, November 16, 1864

Gad's Hill Place, Higham by Rochester, Kent
Wednesday, November Sixteenth, 1864

DEAR MADAM,—I have received your letter with great pleasure, and hope to be (as I've always been in my heart) the best of friends with the Jewish people. The error you point out to me had occurred to me—as most errors do to most people—when it was too late to correct it.[3] But it will

1. Eliza Davis was the wife of a businessman to whom Dickens in 1860 had sold the lease of his home at Tavistock Place before moving to Gad's Hill. The transaction was amicable, and Dickens liked and admired the Davises. He was surprised and defensive when Mrs. Davis, herself Jewish, called his attention to the antisemitic implications of his depiction of Fagin. He was soon to write a novel, *Our Mutual Friend* (1864–65), in which one of the important characters is a "good" Jew.
2. Dickens, who later accepted from Mrs. Davis the gift of a Hebrew-English Bible, here contributed money to a Jewish charity.
3. The error at issue has not been identified but most likely has to do with the depiction of Riah, the Jewish character in *Our Mutual Friend*.

do no harm. The peculiarities of dress and manners are fixed together for the sake of picturesqueness.—Dear Madam,—Yours.

Table of Installments
and Chapter-Division
in Different Editions of *Oliver Twist*†

Bentley's Miscellany		1838–41		1846	
Feb. 1837	10½ pp.				
[Bk. I]	i	Vol. I	i	Jan.	i
	ii		ii		ii
Mar. 1837	12½ pp.				
	iii		iii		iii
	iv		iv		iv
Apr. 1837	12½ pp.				
	v		v		v
	vi		vi		vi
May 1837	12 pp.				
	vii		vii	Feb.	vii
	viii		viii		viii
No June instalment					
July 1837	14¼ pp.				
	ix		ix		ix
	x		x		x
	xi		xi		xi
Aug. 1837	13¾ pp.				
	xii		xii		xii
	xiii		xiii	Mar.	xiii
Sept. 1837	14 pp.				
	xiv		xiv		xiv
	xv		xv		xv
No October instalment					
Nov. 1837	15 pp.				
	xvi		xvi		xvi
	xvii		xvii		xvii

†Reprinted by permission from the Clarendon edition of *Oliver Twist*, ed. Kathleen Tillotson. Copyright © 1966 by the Oxford University Press. Pp. 369–71.

Bentley's Miscellany		1838–41		1846	
Dec. 1837	14 pp.				
	xviii		xviii	Apr.	xviii
	xix		xix		xix
Jan. 1838	16 pp.				
	xx	Vol. II	xx		xx
	xxi		xxi		xxi
	xxii		xxii		xxii
Feb. 1838	15½ pp.				
Bk. II	i		xxiii		xxiii
	ii		xxiv	May	xxiv
	iii		xxv		xxv
Mar. 1838	15½ pp.				
	iv		xxvi		xxvi
	v		xxvii		xxvii
Apr. 1838	15½ pp.				
	vi		xxviii		xxviii
	vii		xxix		xxix
				June	xxx
May 1838	15½ pp.				
	viii		xxx		xxxi
	ix		xxxi		xxxii
June 1838	14¾ pp.				
	x		xxxii		xxxiii
	xi		xxxiii		xxxiv
July 1838	16 pp.				
	xii		xxxiv	July	xxxv
	xiii		xxxv		xxxvi
	xiv		xxxvi		xxxvii
Aug. 1838	16 pp.				
Bk. III	i	Vol. III	xxxvii		xxxviii
	ii		xxxviii		xxxix (pt.)
No September instalment					
Oct. 1838	16½ pp.				
	iii		xxxix		xxxix (pt.)
				Aug.	xl
	iv		xl		xli

Bentley's Miscellany	1838–41	1846
Nov. 1838 16 pp.		
v	xli	xlii
vi	xlii	xliii
Dec. 1838 16 pp.		
vii	xliii	xliv
		Sept. xlv
viii	xliv	xlvi
Jan. 1839 16 pp.		
ix	xlv	xlvii
x	xlvi	xlviii
xi	xlvii	xlix
Feb. 1839 16 pp.		
xii	xlviii	Oct. l
xiii (pt.)		(instalment begins mid-chapter)
Mar. 1839 7½ pp.		
xiii (pt.)	xlix	li
Apr. 1839 10 pp.		
xiv	l	lii
xv	li	liii

CHARLES DICKENS

[An Appeal to Fallen Women]†

28 Oct. 1847

You will see, on beginning to read this letter, that it is not addressed to you by name. But I address it to a woman—a very young woman still—who was born to be happy, and has lived miserably; who has no

† From the Pilgrim Edition, *The Letters of Charles Dickens*, vol. 5, ed. Madeline House and Graham Storey. Copyright © 1965. Reprinted by permission of Oxford University Press. Appendix D. Angela Burdett Coutts (1814–1906) inherited from her banker father a huge fortune, some of which she devoted to philanthropic activities. Dickens, who met her in the late 1830s, became her close friend, confidential advisor, and managerial partner in her philanthropic work. In May 1847, under Dickens' supervision and with Coutts's money, a suitable house in the London suburb of Shepherd's Bush was rented and renovated to serve as a home and rehabilitation center for prostitutes. To bring the home to the attention of London prostitutes, Dickens wrote a brief "letter" that was printed and distributed selectively to possible applicants. Dickens, who acted as executive manager of Urania Cottage, hoped that retraining in manners and morals would eventually make the reformed prostitutes suitable for emigration to Australia and South Africa and for marriage.

prospect before her but sorrow, or behind her but a wasted youth; who, if she has ever been a mother, has felt shame, instead of pride, in her own unhappy child.

You are such a person, or this letter would not be put into your hands. If you have ever wished (I know you must have done so, sometimes) for a chance of rising out of your sad life, and having friends, a quiet home, means of being useful to yourself and others, peace of mind, self-respect, everything you have lost, pray read it attentively, and reflect upon it afterwards. I am going to offer you, not the chance but the certainty of all these blessings, if you will exert yourself to deserve them. And do not think that I write to you as if I felt myself very much above you, or wished to hurt your feelings by reminding you of the situation in which you are placed. GOD forbid! I mean nothing but kindness to you, and I write as if you were my sister.

Think, for a moment, what your present situation is. Think how impossible it is that it ever can be better if you continue to live as you have lived, and how certain it is that it must be worse. You know what the streets are; you know how cruel the companions that you find there, are; you know the vices practised there, and to what wretched conse-quences they bring you, even while you are young. Shunned by decent people, marked out from all other kinds of women as you walk along, avoided by the very children, hunted by the police, imprisoned, and only set free to be imprisoned over and over again—reading this very letter in a common jail—you have, already, dismal experience of the truth. But, to grow old in such a way of life, and among such com-pany—to escape an early death from terrible disease, or your own maddened hand, and arrive at old age in such a course—will be an aggra-vation of every misery that you know now, which words cannot describe. Imagine for yourself the bed on which you, then an object terrible to look at, will lie down to die. Imagine all the long, long years of shame, want, crime, and ruin, that will rise before you. And by that dreadful day, and by the Judgment that will follow it, and by the recollection you are certain to have then, when it is too late, of the offer that is made to you now, when it is NOT too late, I implore you to think of it, and weigh it well!

There is a lady in this town,[1] who, from the windows of her house, has seen such as you going past at night, and has felt her heart bleed at the sight. She is what is called a great lady; but she has looked after you with compassion, as being of her own sex and nature; and the thought of such fallen women has troubled her in her bed. She has resolved to open, at her own expense, a place of refuge very near London, for a small number of females, who, without such help, are lost for ever: and to make it A HOME for them. In this Home they will be taught all household work that would be useful to them in a home of their

1. That is, Coutts.

own, and enable them to make it comfortable and happy. In this Home, which stands in a pleasant country lane, and where each may have her little flower-garden, if she pleases, they will be treated with the greatest kindness; will lead an active, cheerful, healthy life; will learn many things it is profitable and good to know; and, being entirely removed from all who have any knowledge of their past career, will begin life afresh, and be able to win a good name and character. And because it is not the lady's wish that these young women should be shut out from the world, after they have repented and have learned how to do their duty there, and because it *is* her wish and object that they may be restored to society—a comfort to themselves and it—they will be supplied with every means, when some time shall have elapsed, and their conduct shall have fully proved their earnestness and reformation, to go abroad, where, in a distant country, they may become the faithful wives of honest men, and live and die in peace.

I have been told that those who see you daily in this place, believe that there are virtuous inclinations lingering within you, and that you may be reclaimed. I offer the Home I have described in these few words, to you.

But, consider well before you accept it. As you are to pass from the gate of this Prison to a perfectly new life, where all the means of happiness from which you are now shut out, are opened brightly to you, so remember, on the other hand, that you must have the strength to leave behind you, all old habits. You must resolve to set a watch upon yourself, and to be firm in your control over yourself, and to restrain yourself; to be patient, gentle, persevering, and good-tempered. Above all things, to be truthful in every word you speak. Do this, and all the rest is easy. But you must solemnly remember that if you enter this Home without such constant resolutions, you will occupy, unworthily and uselessly, the place of some other unhappy girl, now wandering and lost; and that her ruin, no less than your own, will be upon your head, before Almighty God, who knows the secrets of our breasts, and Christ, who died upon the Cross, to save us.

In case there should be anything you wish to know, or any question you would like to ask, about this Home, you have only to say so, and every information shall be given to you. Whether you accept it or reject it, think of it. If you awake in the silence and solitude of night, think of it then. If any remembrance ever comes into your mind of any time when you were innocent and very different, think of it then. If you should be softened by a moment's recollection of any tenderness or affection you have ever felt, or that has ever been shown to you, or of any kind word that has ever been spoken to you, think of it then. If ever your poor heart is moved to feel, truly, what you might have been, and what you are, oh think of it then, and consider what you may be yet!

Believe me that I am, indeed,

YOUR FRIEND.

CHARLES DICKENS

Sikes and Nancy†

CHAPTER I

Fagin the receiver of stolen goods was up, betimes, one morning, and waited impatiently for the appearance of his new associate, Noah Claypole, otherwise Morris Bolter; who at length presented himself, and, cutting a monstrous slice of bread, commenced a voracious assault on the breakfast.

'Bolter, *Bolter.*'[1]

'Well, here I am. What's the matter? Don't yer ask me to do anything till I have done eating. That's a great fault in this place. Yer never get time enough over yer meals.'

'You can talk as you eat, can't you?'

'Oh yes, I can talk. I get on better when I talk. *Talk away.* Yer won't interrupt me.'

There seemed, indeed, no great fear of anything interrupting him, as he had evidently sat down with a determination to do a deal of business.

'I want you, Bolter,' *leaning over the table,* 'to do a piece of work for me, my dear, that needs great care and caution.'

'I say, don't yer go a-shoving me into danger, yer know. That don't suit me, that don't; and so I tell yer.'

'There's not the smallest danger in it—not the very smallest; it's only to *dodge a woman.*'

'An old woman?'

'A young one.'

'I can do that pretty well. I was a regular sneak when I was at school. What am I to dodge her for? Not to——'

'Not to do anything, but tell me where she goes, who she sees, and, if possible, what she says; to remember the street, if it is a street, or the house, if it is a house; and to bring me back all the information you can.'

'What'll yer give me?'

'If you do it well, a pound, my dear. One pound. And that's what I never gave yet, for any job of work where there wasn't valuable consideration to be got.'

'Who is she?'

---

† This text of the reading Dickens composed and performed frequently to large audiences is taken from *Charles Dickens, The Public Readings,* ed. Philip Collins. Copyright © 1975. Reprinted by permission of Oxford University Press. Pp. 472–86.
1. Throughout this piece, italics indicate Dickens' underlining in his printed prompt copy to remind himself to read these words with special emphasis.

'One of us.'

'Oh Lor! Yer doubtful of her, are yer?'

'She has found out some new friends, my dear, and I must know who they are.'

'I see. Ha! ha! ha! I'm your man. Where is she? Where am I to wait for her? Where am I to go?'

'All that, my dear, you shall hear from me. I'll point her out at the proper time. You keep ready, in the clothes I have got here for you, and leave the rest to me.'

That night, and the next, and the next again, the spy sat booted and equipped in the disguise of a carter: ready to turn out at a word from Fagin. Six nights passed, and on each, Fagin came home with a disappointed face, and briefly intimated that it was not yet time. On the seventh he returned exultant. It was Sunday Night.

'She goes abroad to-night,' said Fagin, 'and on the right errand, I'm sure; for she has been alone all day, and the man she is afraid of will not be back much before daybreak. Come with me! Quick!'

They left the house, and, stealing through a labyrinth of streets, arrived at length before a public-house. It was past eleven o'clock, and the door was closed; but it opened softly as Fagin gave a low whistle. They entered, without noise.

Scarcely venturing to whisper, but substituting dumb show for words, Fagin pointed out a pane of glass high in the wall to Noah, and signed to him to climb up, on a piece of furniture below it, and observe the person in the adjoining room.

'Is that the woman?'

Fagin nodded 'yes'.

'I can't see her face well. She is looking down, and the candle is behind her.'

'Stay there.' He signed to the lad, who had opened the house-door to them; who withdrew—entered the room adjoining, and, under pretence of snuffing the candle, moved it in the required position; then he spoke to the girl, causing her to raise her face.

'I see her now!'

'Plainly?'

'I should know her among a thousand.'

The spy descended, the room-door opened, and the girl came out. Fagin drew him behind a small partition, and they held their breath as she passed within a few feet of their place of concealment, and emerged by the door at which they had entered.

'*After her!!* To the *left*. Take the left hand, and keep on the other side. *After her!!*'

The spy darted off; and, by the light of the street lamps, saw the girl's retreating figure, already at some distance before him. He advanced as near as he considered prudent, and kept on the opposite side of the street. *She looked nervously round.* She seemed to gather courage as she advanced, and to walk with a steadier and firmer step. The spy preserved the same relative distance between them, and followed.

CHAPTER II

The churches chimed three quarters past eleven, as the two figures emerged on London Bridge. The young woman advanced with a swift and rapid step, and looked about her as though in quest of some expected object; the young man, who slunk along in the deepest shadow he could find, and, at some distance, accommodated his pace to hers: stopping when she stopped: and as she moved again, creeping stealthily on: but never allowing himself, in the ardour of his pursuit, to gain upon her. Thus, they crossed the bridge, from the Middlesex to the Surrey shore, when the woman, disappointed in her anxious scrutiny of the foot-passengers, turned back. The movement was sudden; but the man was not thrown off his guard by it; for, shrinking into one of the recesses which surmount the piers of the bridge, and leaning over the parapet the better to conceal his figure, he suffered her to pass. When she was about the same distance in advance as she had been before, he slipped quietly down, and followed her again. At nearly the centre of the bridge she stopped. He stopped.

It was a very dark night. The day had been unfavourable, and at that hour and place there were few people stirring. Such as there were, hurried past: possibly without seeing, certainly without noticing, either the woman, or the man. Their appearance was not attractive of such of London's destitute population, as chanced to take their way over the bridge that night; and they stood there in silence: neither speaking nor spoken to.

The girl had taken a few turns to and fro—closely watched by her hidden observer—*when the heavy bell of St. Paul's tolled for the death of another day. Midnight had come upon the crowded city. Upon the palace, the night-cellar, the jail, the madhouse: the chambers of birth and death, of health and sickness, upon the rigid face of the corpse and the calm sleep of the child.*

A young lady, accompanied by a grey-haired gentleman, alighted from a hackney-carriage. They had scarcely set foot upon the pavement of the bridge, when the girl started, and joined them.

'Not here!! I am afraid to speak to you here. Come away—out of the public road—down the steps yonder!'

The steps to which she pointed, were those which, on the Surrey bank, and on the same side of the bridge as Saint Saviour's Church, form a landing-stairs from the river. To this spot the spy hastened unobserved; and after a moment's survey of the place, he began to descend.

These stairs are a part of the bridge; they consist of three flights. Just below the end of the second, going down, the stone wall on the left terminates in an ornamental pilaster facing towards the Thames. At this point the lower steps widen: so that a person turning that angle of the wall, is necessarily unseen by any others on the stairs who chance to be above, if only a step. The spy looked hastily round, when he reached this point; and as there seemed no better place of concealment, and as the tide being out there was plenty of room, he slipped aside, with his back to the pilaster, and there waited: pretty certain that they would come no lower down.

So tardily went the time in this lonely place, and so eager was the spy, that he was on the point of emerging from his hiding-place, and regaining the road above, when he heard the sound of footsteps, and directly afterwards of voices almost close at his ear.

He drew himself straight upright against the wall, and listened attentively.

'This is far enough,' *said a voice, which was evidently that of the gentleman.* 'I will not suffer the young lady to go any further. Many people would have distrusted you too much to have come even so far, but you see I am willing to humour you.'

'To humour me!' *cried the voice of the girl* whom he had followed. 'You're considerate, indeed, sir. To humour me! Well, well, it's no matter.'

'Why, for what purpose can you have brought us to this strange place? Why not have let me speak to you, above there, where it is light, and there is something stirring, instead of bringing us to this dark and dismal hole?'

'I told you before, that I was afraid to speak to you there. I don't know why it is,' *said the girl shuddering,* 'but I have such a fear and dread upon me to-night that I can hardly stand.'

'A fear of what?'

'I scarcely know of what—I wish I did. Horrible thoughts of *death*— and *shrouds* with *blood* upon them—and a fear that has made me burn as if I was on fire—have been upon me all day. I was reading a book to-night, to while the time away, and the same things came into the print.'

'Imagination!'

'No imagination. I swear I saw "*coffin*" written in every page of the book in large black letters,—aye, and they carried one close to me, in the streets to-night.'

'There is nothing unusual in that. They have passed me often.'

'*Real ones*. This was not.'

'Pray speak to her kindly,' said the young lady to the grey-haired gentleman. 'Poor creature! She seems to need it.'

'Bless you, miss, for that! Your haughty religious people would have

held their heads up to see me as I am to-night, and would have preached
of flames and vengeance. Oh, dear lady, why ar'n't those who claim to
be God's own folks, as gentle and as kind to us poor wretches as you!'

—'You were not here last Sunday night, girl, as you appointed.'

'I couldn't come. I was kept by force.'

'By whom?'

'Bill——Sikes—him that I told the young lady of before.'

'You were not suspected of holding any communication with anybody
on the subject which has brought us here to-night, I hope?'

'No,' replied the girl, shaking her head. 'It's not very easy for me to
leave him unless he knows why; I couldn't have seen the lady when I
did, but that I gave him a drink of *laudanum* before I came away.'

'Did he awake before you returned?'

'No; and neither he nor any of them suspect me.'

'Good. Now listen to me. I am Mr. Brownlow, this young lady's
friend. I wish you, in this young lady's interest, and for her sake, to
deliver up Fagin.'

'Fagin! I will not do it! I will never do it! Devil that he is, and worse
than devil as he has been to me, as my Teacher in all Devilry, I will
never do it.'

'Why?'

'For the reason that, bad life as he has led, I have led a bad life too;
for the reason that there are many of us who have kept the same courses
together, and I'll not turn upon them, who might—any of them—have
turned upon me, but didn't, bad as they are. Last, for the reason—(*how
can I say it with the young lady here!*)—that, among them, there is
one—*this Bill*—*this Sikes*—the most desperate of all—*that I can't leave.*
Whether it is God's wrath for the wrong I have done, I don't know, but
I am drawn back to him through everything, and I should be, I believe,
if I knew that I was to *die* by his hand!'

'But, put one man—not him—not one of the gang—the one man
Monks into my hands, and leave him to me to deal with.'

'What if he turns against the others?'

'I promise you that, in that case, there the matter shall rest; they shall
go scot free.'

'Have I the lady's promise for that?'

'You have,' replied Rose Maylie, the young lady.

'I have been a liar, and among liars from a little child, but I will take
your words.'

After receiving an assurance from both, that she might safely do so,
she proceeded in a voice so low that it was often difficult for the listener
to discover even the purport of what she said, to describe the means by
which this one man Monks might be found and taken. But nothing
would have induced her to compromise one of her own companions;
little reason though she had, poor wretch! to spare them.

'Now,' said the gentleman, when she had finished, 'you have given us most valuable assistance, young woman, and I wish you to be the better for it. What can I do to serve you?'

'Nothing.'

'You will not persist in saying that; think now; take time. Tell me.'

'Nothing, sir. You can do nothing to help me. I am past all hope.'

'You put yourself beyond the pale of hope. The past has been a dreary waste with you, of youthful energies mis-spent, and such treasures lavished, as the Creator bestows but once and never grants again, but, *for the future, you may hope!* [I do not say that it is in our power to offer you peace of heart and mind, for that must come as you seek it; but a quiet asylum, either in England, or, if you fear to remain here, in some foreign country, it is not only within the compass of our ability but our most anxious wish to secure you. Before the dawn of morning, before this river wakes to the first glimpse of daylight, you shall be placed as entirely beyond the reach of your former associates, and leave as complete an absence of all trace behind you, as if you were to disappear from the earth this moment.] Come! I would not have you go back to exchange one word with any old companion, or take one look at any old haunt. Quit them all, while there is time and opportunity!'

'She will be persuaded now,' cried the young lady

'I fear not, my dear.'

'*No, sir—no miss.* I am chained to my old life. I *loathe* and *hate* it, but I cannot *leave* it.—When ladies as young and good, as happy and beautiful as you, miss, give away your hearts, love will carry even you all lengths. When such as I, who have no certain roof but the coffin-lid, and no friend in sickness or death but the hospital-nurse, set our rotten hearts on any man, who can hope to cure us!—This fear comes over me again. I must go home. Let us part. I shall be watched or seen. Go! Go! If I have done you any service, all I ask is, leave me, and let me go my way alone.'

'Take this purse,' cried the young lady. 'Take it for my sake, that you may have some resource in an hour of need and trouble.'

'No! I have not done this for *money. Let me have that to think of.* And yet——give me something that you have worn—I should like to have something—*no, no,* not a *ring*, they'd rob me of that—your *gloves* or *handkerchief*—anything that I can keep, as having belonged to you. There. *Bless you! God bless you!! Good-night, good-night!*'

The agitation of the girl, and the apprehension of some discovery which would subject her to violence, seemed to determine the gentleman to leave her. The sound of retreating footsteps followed, and the voices ceased.

After a time Nancy ascended to the street. The spy remained on his post for some minutes, and then, *after peeping out,* to make sure that he was unobserved, darted away, and made for Fagin's house as fast as his legs would carry him.

CHAPTER III

It was nearly two hours before daybreak; that time which in the autumn of the year, may be truly called the dead of night; when the streets are silent and deserted; when even sound appears to slumber, and profligacy and riot have staggered home to dream; it was at this still and silent hour, that Fagin sat in his old lair. Stretched upon a mattress on the floor, lay Noah Claypole, otherwise *Morris Bolter*, fast asleep. Towards him the old man sometimes directed his eyes for an instant, and then brought them back again to the wasting candle.

He sat without changing his attitude, or appearing to take the smallest heed of time, until the door-bell rang. He crept up-stairs, and presently returned accompanied by a man muffled to the chin, who carried a bundle under one arm. Throwing back his outer coat, the man displayed the *burly frame of Sikes, the housebreaker*.

'There!' laying the bundle on the table. 'Take care of that, and do the most you can with it. It's been trouble enough to get. I thought I should have been here three hours ago.'

Fagin laid his hand upon the bundle, and locked it in the cupboard. But he did not take *his eyes off the robber, for an instant*.

'Wot now?' cried Sikes. 'Wot do you look at a man, like that, for?'

Fagin raised his right hand, and shook his trembling forefinger in the air.

'Hallo!' *feeling in his breast*. 'He's gone mad. I must look to myself here.'

'No, no, it's not—you're not the person, Bill. I've no—no fault to find with you.'

'Oh! you haven't, haven't you?' *passing a pistol into a more convenient pocket*. 'That's lucky—for one of us. Which one that is, don't matter.'

'I've got that to tell you, Bill, will make you worse than me.'

'Aye? Tell away! Look sharp, or Nance will think I'm lost.'

'*Lost!* She has pretty well settled that, in her own mind, already.'

He looked, perplexed, into the old man's face, and reading no satisfactory explanation of the riddle there, clenched his coat collar in his huge hand and shook him soundly.

'Speak, will you? Or if you don't, it shall be for want of breath. Open your mouth and say wot you've got to say. Out with it, you *thundering, blundering, wondering* old *cur*, out with it!'

'Suppose that lad that's lying there——' Fagin began.

Sikes turned round to where Noah was sleeping, as if he had not previously observed him. 'Well?'

'Suppose that lad was to peach—to blow upon us all. Suppose that

lad was to do it, of his own fancy—not grabbed, tried, earwigged by the
parson and brought to it on bread and water,—but of his own fancy; to
please his own taste; stealing out at nights to do it. Do you hear me?
Suppose he did all this, what then?'

'What then? If he was left alive till I came, I'd grind his skull under
the iron heel of my boot into as many grains as there are hairs upon
his head.'

'What if *I* did it! *I*, that know so much, and could hang so many
besides myself!'

'I don't know. I'd do something in the jail that 'ud get me put in
irons; and, if I was tried along with you, I'd fall upon you with them
in the open court, and beat your brains out afore the people. I'd smash
your head as if a loaded waggon had gone over it.'

Fagin looked hard at the robber; and, motioning him to be silent,
stooped over the bed upon the floor, and shook the sleeper to rouse
him.

'Bolter! Bolter! *Poor lad!*' said Fagin, looking up with an expression
of devilish anticipation, and speaking slowly and with marked emphasis.
'*He's tired*—tired with watching for *her* so long—watching for *her*, Bill.'

'Wot d'ye mean?'

Fagin made no answer, but bending over the sleeper again, hauled
him into a sitting posture. When his assumed name had been repeated
several times, Noah rubbed his eyes, and, giving a heavy yawn, looked
sleepily about him.

'Tell me that again—once again, just for him to hear,' said the Jew,
pointing to Sikes as he spoke.

'Tell yer what?' *asked the sleepy Noah, shaking himself pettishly.*

'That about——NANCY!! You followed her?'

'Yes.'

'To London Bridge?'

'Yes.'

'Where she met two people?'

'So she did.'

'A gentleman and a lady that she had gone to of her own accord
before, who asked her to give up all her pals, and Monks first, which
she did—and to describe him, which *she did*—and to tell her what house
it was that we meet at, and go to, which *she did*—and where it could
be best watched from, which *she did*—and what time the people went
there, which *she did. She did all this.* She told it *all*, every word, without
a threat, without a murmur—*she did*—*did she not?*'

'All right,' *replied Noah, scratching his head.* 'That's just what it was!'

'What did they say about last Sunday?'

'About last Sunday! Why, I told yer that before.'

'Again. *Tell it again!*'

'They asked her,' *as he grew more wakeful, and seemed to have a* dawning perception who Sikes was, 'they asked her why she didn't come, last Sunday, as she promised. She said she couldn't.'

'Why? Tell *him* that.'

'Because she was forcibly kept at home by Bill—Sikes——the man that she had told them of before.'

'What more of him? What more of Bill—Sikes—the man she had told them of before? Tell him that, *tell him that.*'

'Why, that she couldn't very easily get out of doors unless he knew where she was going to, and so the first time she went to see the lady, she—ha! ha! ha! it made me *laugh* when she said it, *that* did—she gave him, a drink *of laudanum!!* ha! ha! ha!'

Sikes rushed from the room, and darted up the stairs.

'Bill, *Bill!*' cried Fagin, following him, hastily. 'A word. Only a word.'

'Let me out. Don't *speak* to me! it's not *safe. Let me out.*'

'Hear me speak a word,' rejoined Fagin, *laying his hand upon the lock.* 'You won't be——you won't be——too—*violent*, Bill?'

The day was breaking, and there was light enough for the men to see each other's faces. They exchanged a brief glance; there was the same fire in the eyes of both.

'I mean, not too——*violent*——for——for——*safety.* Be *crafty*, Bill, and not too *bold.*'

The robber dashed into the silent streets.

Without one pause, or moment's consideration; without once turning his head to the right or left; without once raising his eyes to the sky, or lowering them to the ground, but looking straight before him with savage resolution: he muttered not a word, nor relaxed a muscle, until he reached his own house-door.——He opened it, *softly*, with a key; strode lightly up the stairs; and entering his own room, *double-locked the door, and drew back the curtain of the bed.*

The girl was lying, half-dressed, upon the bed. He had roused her from her sleep, for she raised herself with a hurried and startled look.

'Get up!'

'It *is* you, Bill!'

'Get up!!!'

There was a candle burning, but he drew it from the candlestick, and hurled it under the grate. Seeing the faint light of early day without, the girl rose to undraw the curtain.

'Let it be. There's light enough for wot I've got to do.'——

'Bill, *why do you look like that at me?*'

The robber regarded her, for a few seconds, with dilated nostrils and heaving breast; then, grasping her by the head and throat, dragged her into the middle of the room, and placed his heavy hand upon her mouth.

'You were watched to-night, *you she-devil; every word you said was heard.*'

'Then if every word I said was heard, it was heard that I spared you.

Bill, *dear Bill,* you cannot have the heart to kill me. Oh! think of all I
have given up, only this one night, for *you.* Bill, *Bill!* For dear God's
sake, for your own, for mine, stop before you *spill my blood!!!* I have
been *true* to you, *upon my guilty soul I have!!!* The gentleman and that
dear lady told me to-night of a home in some foreign country where I
could end my days in solitude and peace. Let me see them again, and
beg them, on my knees, to show the same mercy to you; and let us both
leave this dreadful place, and far apart lead better lives, and forget how
we have lived, except in prayers, and never see each other more. It is
never too late to repent. They told me so—I feel it now. But we must
have *time*—we must have a *little, little time!*'

*The housebreaker freed one arm, and grasped his pistol. The certainty
of immediate detection if he fired, flashed across his mind; and he beat
it twice upon the upturned face that almost touched his own.*

She staggered and fell, but raising herself on her knees, *she drew from
her bosom a white handkerchief—Rose Maylie's—and holding it up
towards Heaven, breathed one prayer, for mercy to her Maker.*

*It was a ghastly figure to look upon. The murderer staggering backward
to the wall, and shutting out the sight with his hand, seized a heavy
club, and struck her* down!!

The bright sun burst upon the crowded city in clear and radiant glory.
*Through costly-coloured glass and paper mended window, through ca-
thedral dome and rotten crevice, it shed its equal ray* It lighted up the
room where *the murdered woman* lay. It did. He tried to shut it out, but
it would stream in. If the sight had been a *ghastly* one in the *dull
morning,* what was it, *now,* in all that *brilliant light!!!*

He had not moved; he had been afraid to stir. There had been a moan
and motion of the hand; and, with terror added to rage, he had struck
and struck again. Once he threw a rug over it; but it was worse to *fancy*
the *eyes,* and imagine them moving towards him, than to see them
glaring upward, as if *watching the reflection of the pool of gore that
quivered and danced in the sunlight on the ceiling.* He had plucked it
off again. And there was the body—mere flesh and blood, no more—
but *such flesh, and so much blood!!!*

He struck a light, kindled a fire, and thrust the club into it. There
was hair upon the end, which shrunk into a light cinder, and whirled
up the chimney. Even that frightened him; but he held the weapon till
it broke, and then piled it on the coals to burn away, and smoulder into
ashes. He washed himself, and rubbed his clothes; there were spots upon
them that would not be removed, but he cut the pieces out, and burnt
them. *How those stains were dispersed about the room! The very feet of
his dog were bloody!!!!*

All this time he had, *never once,* turned his *back* upon the *corpse.*
He now moved, *backward,* towards the door: dragging the dog with him,
shut the door softly, locked it, took the key, and left the house.

As he gradually left the town behind him all that day, and plunged that night into the solitude and darkness of the country, he was *haunted by that ghastly figure following at his heels.* He could hear its garments rustle in the leaves; and every breath of wind came laden with that last low cry. If *he* stopped, *it* stopped. If *he ran, it followed*; not running too—that would have been a relief—but borne on one slow melancholy air that never rose or fell.

At times, he turned to beat this phantom off, though it should look him dead; but the hair rose on his head, and his blood stood still, for it had turned with him, and was behind him then. He leaned his back against a bank, and felt that it stood above him, visibly out against the cold night sky. He threw himself on his back upon the road. *At his head it stood, silent, erect, and still: a human gravestone with its epitaph in Blood!!*

Suddenly, towards daybreak, he took the desperate resolution of going back to London. 'There's somebody to speak to there, at all events. A hiding-place, too, in our gang's old house in Jacob's Island.—I'll risk it.'

Choosing the least frequented roads for his journey back, he resolved to lie concealed within a short distance of the city until it was dark night again, and then proceed to his destination. He did this, and limped in among three affrighted fellow-thieves, the ghost of himself—blanched face, sunken eyes, hollow cheeks—*his dog at his heels covered with mud, lame, half blind, crawling as if those stains had poisoned him!!*

All three men shrank away. Not one of them spake.

'You that keep this house.—Do you mean to sell me, or to let me lie here 'till the hunt is over?'

'You may stop if you think it safe. But what man ever escaped the men who are after you!'

Hark!!!! A great sound coming on like a rushing fire! What? *Tracked so soon?* The hunt was up already? Lights gleaming below, voices in loud and earnest talk, hurried tramp of footsteps on the wooden bridges over Folly Ditch, a beating on the heavy door and window-shutters of the house, a waving crowd in the outer darkness like a field of corn moved by an angry storm!

'The tide was in, as I come up. Give me a rope. I may drop from the top of the house, at the back into the Folly Ditch, and clear off that way, or be stifled. *Give me a rope!*'

No one stirred. They pointed to where they kept such things, and the murderer hurried with a strong cord to the housetop. *Of all the terrific yells* that ever fell on *mortal ears, none could exceed* the furious cry when *he was seen.* Some shouted to those who were nearest, to set the house on fire; others adjured the officers to shoot him dead; others, with ex-ecrations, clutched and tore at him in the empty air; some called for ladders, some for sledge-hammers; some ran with torches to and fro, to seek them. '*I promise Fifty Pounds*,' cried Mr. *Brownlow* from the nearest bridge, 'to *the man who takes that murderer alive!*'

He set his foot against the stack of chimneys, fastened one end of the rope firmly round it, and with the other made a strong running noose by the aid of his hands and teeth. With the cord round his back, he could let himself down to within a less distance of the ground than his own height, and had his knife ready in his hand to cut the cord, and drop.

At the instant that he brought the loop over his head before slipping it beneath his arm-pits, *looking behind him* on the *roof* he *threw up his arms, and yelled, 'The eyes again!'* Staggering as if struck by lightning, he lost his balance and tumbled over the parapet. The noose was at his neck; it ran up with his weight; tight as a bowstring, and swift as the arrow it speeds. He fell five-and-thirty feet, and hung with his open *knife clenched in his stiffening hand!!!*

The *dog* which had lain concealed 'till now, ran backwards and forwards on the parapet with a dismal howl, and, collecting himself for a spring, jumped for the *dead man's shoulders*. Missing his aim, he fell into the ditch, turning over as he went, and striking against a stone, *dashed out his brains!!*

THE END OF THE READING

EARLY REVIEWS

[JOHN FORSTER]

From *The Examiner*, September 10, 1837†

The story of *Oliver Twist*, so far as it has yet proceeded,[1] is its author's masterpiece, and mean as the subject appears to be—the account of the Progress of a Parish Boy—promises to take its place among the higher prose fictions of the language. Appearing in detached portions in a monthly magazine, and written, we presume, as the occasion arises monthly—the variety and vigour of character thrown into each separate part is indeed surprising. The art of copying from nature as it really exists in the common walks of life has not been carried to greater perfection, or to finer results in the way of combination, by the most eminent writers. We have heard it objected to the *Pickwick Papers* that they are now and then extravagant, and certainly, in spite of the reality of their wit and humour, the sort of extravaganza of adventure they are founded on warrants the objection. But to *Oliver Twist* no such censure in any way applies. The *Pickwick* may be lively caricaturing, but this is exact painting. The scrupulous reader may make what deduction he pleases for the "lowness" of the subject—the absolute truth and precision of its delineation are not to be disputed. And truly, where the object of a writer is exact description, the characteristics of humanity, whether treated of in a history of kings or of parish boys, are pretty much the same. Indeed we wish that all history were written in the spirit of Oliver Twist's history. When the great Fielding[2] proposed to vindicate the use and dignity of his style of writing against the loftier pretensions of professed historians, he merely observed that in their productions nothing was true but names and dates, whereas in his everything was true but names and dates. Here, unquestionably, the advantage was on Fielding's side, and we think Mr. Dickens entitled to the advantages of the comparison also. He has risen to sudden eminence and unprecedented popularity by simply pursuing an *original* course. Unlike Washington Irving,[3] who, with many graces and felicities of style, has never got beyond revivals of the *Spectators* and *Tatlers* and such mere anachronisms of literature (as though society had made no movement for the last century)—Mr. Dickens, seeing all the allowances to be made for change

---

† Published anonymously. Reprinted from *The Dickensian* 34 (1937–38): 29–32.
1. Almost one-fourth had been published at the time of this review.
2. Henry Fielding (1707–54), author of *The Adventures of Joseph Andrews* (1742) and *The History of Tom Jones* (1749), makes the following observation in the "Preface" to *Joseph Andrews* and in the discussions of the art of fiction that form the first chapters of each of the eighteen books of *Tom Jones*.
3. American novelist (1783–1859); *The Spectator* and *The Tatler* were British magazines, originating in the eighteenth century, famous for the wit and quality of their essays.

of manners and scene, struck at once at the variety and distinctness
of character now actually existing among ourselves, and in that
achieved his popularity. In his writing we find *reality*. A Parson
Adams or a Sir Roger de Coverley are not raised from the dead by
the galvanic process[4] we have alluded to in Washington Irving's
case, but yet simplicity and generosity of character, or selfishness
and cunning, exist there in like proportions as of old. For we have
not got rid of the vices and absurdities that were the novelists' material some century since, we have only in a certain sort compounded for them. We refine upon them, disguise them, equivocate
with them more, but still they are obvious enough, and of course most
obvious in those classes of society that can least afford refinement or
disguise.

Oliver Twist is the history of a child born in a workhouse and brought
up by the parish overseers. The account of his mother's death is a
masterly piece of the tragedy of common life—full of deep pathos, and
with fine touches of the grotesque. * * *

No one can read this without feeling a strong and sudden interest in
Oliver, and the interest never after ceases. We think it necessary to
observe, at the same time, that in the first two or three chapters of his
history, an unwarrantable and unworthy use is made of certain bugbears
of popular prejudice and vulgar cant connected with the new poor law,
which we are surprised to see such a writer as Mr. Dickens resorting to.
The attempt to elevate the pauper in our sympathies at the cost of the
struggling labourer—to leave rate-payers[5] lean with their work and hunger, so that the pauper may be stuffed to the proper extent of comfort
—which all these allusions in Oliver's case would seem to tend to—is
a system of curious philanthropy which we confess we cannot understand. But leaving this, which, as we have said, only colours the first
three chapters of Oliver's history, we must admit the force and distinctness with which the various parish authorities are gradually brought
upon the scene. In the second chapter Bumble, the parish beadle, and
Mrs. Mann, the out-nurse of the branch workhouse, poor little Oliver
himself, the "gentleman in the white waistcoat," and the parish board,
carry with them as strongly the conviction of identity as if we had seen
the faces;—in the next three chapters Mr. Gamfield the chimney-sweep,
and Sowerberry the undertaker, with Oliver's mistress, Mrs. Sowerberry,
and Oliver's mistress's servant, Charlotte, and Noah Claypole, Oliver's
fellow apprentice, leave equally distinct impressions of themselves:—
and better than all is the exquisite delicacy of natural sentiment, which,
in spite of every disadvantage, clings to Oliver himself, and, jostled as

4. A chemical process for producing electricity. "Parson Adams": a comic character in Fielding's
   Joseph Andrews. "Sir Roger de Coverley": a fictional character prominent in a number of the
   essays written by Joseph Addison and Richard Steele and published in *The Spectator*.
5. Taxpayers.

he is in this miserable crowd, preserves him from the vice of its pollution. This is beautifully imagined, and is executed in a few of those masterly touches which hit the very springs of nature. We see it where Bumble brings him away from the branch workhouse, when an agony of childish grief breaks from him on leaving the wretched home where he had met with no kind word or look, but which still contains his little companions in misery; we follow it through many very tender passages; and we have it in all its truth and strength in the following scene: Noah Claypole is a hulking, cowardly "charity boy," who has borne silently all sorts of ignominious taunts from the shop-boys of the neighbourhood, but now revenges them with interest on the nameless workhouse orphan.

* * *

Oliver is enjoying for the first time, comfort and happiness. The progress of his slow recovery from an illness watched over with kindly solicitude, is beautifully told, and some slight but happy occasional touches serve to connect him more nearly than by common sympathies with his good-hearted benefactor. This old gentleman, Mr. Brownlow, and his crabbed selfish old friend, Mr. Grimwig, add themselves to the other group of distinct and visible characters in this veritable history, solidly made out, and well contrasted. * * *

We leave Oliver Twist, at a trying point of his story, once more in the haunt of the thieves. We leave him most reluctantly, and so will every reader who has any capacity to see and feel whatsoever is most loveable, hateful, or laughable, in the character of the everyday life about him. We feel as deep an interest in little Oliver's own fate, as in that of a friend we have long known and loved. And yet little Oliver, and all his vicissitudes, and all his motley associates, so far as they have yet gone, are shut up in something less than a hundred pages of *Bentley's Miscellany*. It is a wonderful power which these really fine writers have!

ANONYMOUS

From *The Spectator*, November 24, 1838†

* * *

That this author exhibits genius in embodying London character, and very remarkable skill in making use of peculiarities of expression, even to the current phrase of the day, is undoubtedly true; but he has higher merits, and other elements of success. His powers of pathos, sadly touching rather than tearful, are great; he has a hearty sympathy with humanity, however degraded by vice or disguised by circumstances, and

† Pp. 1114–16.

a quick perception to detect the existence of the good, however overlaid; his truth and nature in dialogue are conspicuous to all; he has the great art of bringing his actors and incidents before the reader by a few effective strokes; though deficient in *narrative*, his *description* is sometimes nicely true, and often powerful; and his command of language considerable, without his style ever appearing forced. In addition to these qualities, he has a manly self-reliance—above all pretence, and all conventional servilities of classes and coteries; nor does he ever, with a sickly vanity, obtrude *himself* upon the reader's attention. Above all, he has genius to vivify his observation.

*　*　*

ANONYMOUS

From *The Literary Gazette, and Journal of the Belles Lettres*, November 24, 1838†

We were early in the field to hail the rising star of Mr. Dickens's genius; and much have we rejoiced to witness its brilliant ascent above the horizon, till it became fixed in the literary firmament as a luminary of the first magnitude, and shed its pleasant light over the admiring world. In noticing the publication of *Oliver Twist* in an entire form, after it has graced and given interest to "Bentley's Miscellany" for so many months * * * we will neither enter upon a review, nor attempt to illustrate this particular work by quotations. * * * We cannot, however, pass over this production so very briefly; and we would advert to one quality which Mr. Dickens has displayed to an extent altogether unequalled, if we except, perhaps, the mighty names of Shakespeare and Scott. We allude to the creation of individual character: to the raising up and embodying of a number of original human beings in so substantial a form, and endowed with such living feelings and passions, and acting in so real and natural a manner, that they immediately become visibly, personally, and intimately known to us; and we no more doubt of their existence than if we had seen them in the flesh, conversed with them, and observed their conduct. * * * What felicity and acuteness of observation does this single feature in his literary course proclaim! And it is, after all, but a single feature. He has dug deep into the human mind; and he has nobly directed his energies to the exposure of evils— the workhouse, the starving school, the factory system, and many other things, at which blessed nature shudders and recoils. As a moralist and reformer of cruel abuses, we have the warmer thanks of the community

† P. 741.

to offer him. Long may he live to increase our debt of gratitude, while
he charms us with many more creations, and another and another still
succeeds!

ANONYMOUS

From *Monthly Review*, January 1839†

Although the greater portion of [*Oliver Twist*] has appeared in the periodical numbers of *Bentley's Miscellany*, and may therefore be considered to lie out of our way, yet there are special reasons why we should
devote a few pages to the work, now that it is in its finished state. In
the first place, about half of the third volume is entirely new to the
public; in the second place, we have reason to presume that the majority
of our country readers are unacquainted with the production, extremely
popular though it be among certain classes and in the metropolis; and
thirdly, at the risk of being called heretics, insensible, or undiscerning,
we feel bound to speak in a strain of the work much more moderate in
regard to its merits than has lately and hitherto been the language of
the majority of our contemporary journalists. After the slightest possible
glance at the outline of the story, we shall quote two or three passages
of considerable length from the latter portion of it, these passages being
amongst the most admired and eulogised parts, if we are to judge from
the frequency from which they have been cited in the newspapers and
periodicals that have recently been loudest in their praises; and then
offer such observations upon the production as a whole, as well as upon
the features of our extracts, as appear to us just and necessary.

The story of Oliver Twist consists rather of a succession of sketches
of character, scenes, and events as these are supposed, with much seeming of truth, to exist among London paupers, pauper officers, the relatives
and friends of paupers, receivers of stolen goods, thieves, etc., than of
a cunningly conceived plot, or a progressively arresting tale, when each
chapter enchains the attention, not only with a sustained, but increasing
power. We are in the "Parish Boy's Progress" introduced to a foundling,
who runs away from his master, gets among thieves, innocently enough,
and innocent continuing. Magistrates, benevolent persons, thieves and
their accomplices or associates, are hence brought under the reader's
eye,—a ruffian housebreaker, Sikes, Nancy, his girl, who is not thoroughly depraved, and a reprobate, unmatched villain Jew, Fagin by
name, being leading characters on the one side of Twist, while a family
of Maylies, etc., range and act on brighter principles. In the course of

---

† Reprinted from *The Dickensian* 1 (1905): 35–40.

the work there are many comic pieces and hits; but towards its close,
where the worthless and bad have to meet with the novelist's retribution,
and the good have to be rewarded, grave and serious passages predomi-
nate.

*   *   *

As to construction, the story does not by any means come up to
Fielding's or Smollett's fictions.[1] It is, as before hinted, a mere string
of sketches that might be carried to any length, or if cut short at any
part, a chapter might wind up the indefinite thread. The author's closeness and accuracy of observation are so remarkable that there need be
no stop to his truths. But the highest aim of a novelist should be to
enchain the reader's mind upon one central group of life and scenery,
so as to produce an abiding lesson of a tangible and definite character,
and so as to place, as it were, the spectator upon a summit, whence he
might survey regions far and wide around to the enlargement and refinement of his sensibilities.

As to the moral qualities of *Oliver Twist* * * * there is with Boz[2] too
much of muscular agony, so that his most laboured pictures have fully
more of the horrible in them than of the awful and grand.

Again in the present tale or string of stories, it looks as if he revelled,
while painting low or degraded nature, among objects which, unless
merely subservient to finer and higher elements equally well drawn and
finished, never can awaken our nobler sympathies, nor prune and in-
vigorate the wings of these awakened sensibilities. On this account, we
cannot place our author among those novelists who are models in regard
to the inculcation of moral sentiments and the lessons that refine while
they delight.

Not that Mr. Dickens is an immoral writer. It is not in his nature to
be such; it is the furthest possible thing from his intention, evidently,
to write for the mere sake of gain, of entertainment, or of merely harmless
fiction. He has high and pure aims; nor can he have failed of doing
good, morally speaking. See how he identifies himself uniformly with
the oppressed; how with his sly yet effective humour he has exposed
systematic and institutional abuses; and what is more, how forcibly he
shows that the vilest in the population is far more an object of commiseration than of anger. Still we must recur to the opinion already
given, that neither his subjects nor his manner of treating them, especially in *Oliver Twist*, can ever entitle him to the highest rank of our
moral fictionists. He is a Crabbe rather than a Richardson, or a Gold-

1. See above, p. 399, n. 2. Tobias Smollett (1721–71), author of *The Adventures of Roderick
   Random* (1748) and *The Expedition of Humphry Clinker* (1771).
2. Dickens used the pseudonym Boz for the serial publication and for the first edition of *Oliver
   Twist.*

smith; but then he is twenty times superior to Sterne,[3] or rather has not one particle of that sentimentality which intoxicates and vitiates while it seems merely to etherealise.

Yet were it not the purity of his nature and the excellence of his purpose, joined to admirable tact and delicate taste, it would be impossible for Boz to preserve the moral influence which he undoubtedly possesses, or to avoid offending against feelings which none can safely touch. On this account, tenderly and warily though he has borne himself, it would be dangerous for a less skilful and considerate performer to adventure after him; and therefore we advise everyone to eschew him as a model. Who but he, that would attempt such an experiment, could have represented the character of Nancy in full, who had descended far from the ways of virtue and leagued herself with desperadoes and robbers, and yet not only have preserved her a true woman in various respects, but never to have trenched upon delicacy or written a word that can send a blush to the face of innocence? In this single instance alone there is a fine mastery; and for this as well as many other excellences we admire Mr. Dickens; but who shall follow him and be so faultless?

[RICHARD FORD]

From *Quarterly Review*, 1839†

* * *

His works are a sign of the times; their periodical return excites more interest than that of Halley's comet. They, like good sermons, contribute to our moral health, for mirth, cakes, ale, and ginger hot in the mouth do us good, Mr. Froude's negation of negus[1] to the contrary notwithstanding. The works of Boz come out in numbers, suited to this age of division of labour, cheap and not too long—double merits: there is just enough to make us rise from the feast, as all doctors of divinity and medicine do from dinner, with an appetite for more: in fact, Boz is the only *work* which the superficial acres of type called newspapers leave the human race time to peruse. His popularity is unbounded—not that that of itself is a test of either honesty or talent. * * * Though dealing

---

3. Laurence Sterne (1713–68), author of *Tristram Shandy* (1759–67). George Crabbe (1754–1832), the English poet and author of *The Village*, had the reputation of being a grim realist interested in accurate description rather than in moral lessons or inspiration; Samuel Richardson (1689–1761) and Oliver Goldsmith (1728–74) were well known as moralists.

† Published anonymously in the *Quarterly Review* 64 (1839): 83–102.

1. A mixture of wine (usually port or sherry) and hot water, sweetened with sugar and nutmeg. Apparently Richard Hurrell Froude (1803–36), an Anglican minister, had preached against its consumption.

with the dregs of society, he is never indelicate, indecent, nor irreligious; he never approves nor countenances the gross, the immoral, or offensive: he but holds these vices up in a pillory,[2] as a warning of the disgrace of criminal excess. Boz, like the bee, buzzes amid honey without clogging his wings; he handles pitch charmingly; the tips of the thumb and fore-finger of the cigaresque señoras[3] of Paraguay are infinitely more discoloured. He tells a tale of real crushing misery in plain, and therefore most effective, language; he never *then* indulges in false sentimentality, or mawkish, far-fetched verbiage. Fagin, Sikes, and the dog especially, are always in their proper and natural places, always speaking, barking, and acting exactly as they ought to have done, and, as far as we are able to judge, with every appearance of truth. Boz sketches localities, particularly in London, with marvellous effect; he concentrates with the power of a camera lucida. Born with an organic bump[4] for distinct observation of men and things, he sees with the eye, and writes with the pen of an artist—we mean with artistical skill, and not as artists write. He translates nature and life.

* * *

Boz fails whenever he attempts to write for effect; his descriptions of rural felicity and country scenery, of which he clearly knows much less than of London, where he is quite at home and wide awake, are, except when comical, over-laboured and out of nature. His 'gentle and genteel folks' are unendurable; they are devoid of the grace, repose, and ease of good society; a something between Cheltenham[5] and New York. * * * Boz is, nevertheless, never vulgar when treating on subjects which are avowedly vulgar. He deals truly with human nature, which never can degrade; he takes up everything, good, bad, or indifferent, which he works up into a rich alluvial[6] deposit. He is natural, and that never can be ridiculous.

* * *

* * * This is the great objection which we feel towards Oliver Twist. It deals with the outcasts of humanity, who do their dirty work in work, pot, and watch houses, to finish on the Newgate drop. Alas! for the Horatian precept, 'Virginibus puerisque canto.'[7] The happy ignorance of innocence is disregarded. Our youth should not even suspect the possibility of such hidden depths of guilt, for their tender memories are wax to receive and marble to retain. These infamies feed the innate evil

2. A wooden frame with holes for the head and hands in which offenders were locked for public display and scorn.
3. Cigar-smoking women.
4. The pseudoscience of phrenology claimed that bumps on the cranium reveal the personality and qualities of the individual. "Camera lucida": an optical device, particularly handy for sketching, that projects an exact image of an object onto a plain surface.
5. A small city in west-central England noted in the eighteenth and nineteenth centuries as a genteel retirement haven for military officers and other professionals.
6. Containing sediment deposited by flowing water.
7. "I sing for the innocent maidens and boys" (from the Roman poet Horace [65–8 B.C.], Odes 1.1). "Newgate drop": the gallows.

principle, which luxuriates in the supernatural and horrid, the dread
and delight of our childhood, which is never shaken off, for no man
entirely outlives the nursery. We object to the familiarising our ingen-
uous youth with 'slang;' it is based in travestie of better things. * * *
The jests and jeers of the 'slangers' leave a sting behind them. They
corrupt pure taste and pervert morality, for vice loses shame when treated
as a fool-born joke, and those who are not ashamed to talk of a thing
will not be long ashamed to put it into practice.

⁂ * *

Oliver Twist, again, is directed against the poor-law and workhouse
system, and in our opinion with much unfairness. The abuses which
he ridicules are not only exaggerated, but in nineteen cases out of twenty
do not at all exist. Boz so rarely mixes up politics, or panders to vulgar
prejudices about serious things, that we regret to see him joining in an
outcry which is partly factious, partly sentimental, partly interested.

* * *

The whole tale rivals in improbabilities those stories in which the
hero at his birth is cursed by a wicked fairy and protected by a good
one; but Oliver himself, to whom all these improbabilities happen, is
the most improbable of all. He is represented to be a pattern of modern
excellence, guileless himself, and measuring others by his own innocence; delicate and high-minded, affectionate, noble, brave, generous,
with the manners of a son of a most distinguished gentleman, not only
uncorrupted but incorruptible: less absurd would it be to expect to gather
grapes on thorns, to find pearls in dunghills, violets in Drury Lane,[1] or
make silk purses of sows' ears.

* * *

While the romantic approve, and metaphysicians speculate on the
abstract possibility of this union of virtue and vice, we all sympathise
with Nancy's melancholy fate: her death is drawn with a force which
quite appals. This devotedness to her unworthy companion, to whom,
notwithstanding her early history, she is clearly constant, forms her
redeeming point. * * * Nancy is described as aware of her degraded
situation: she felt the awe of the undefiledness of virtue, at which vice
stands abashed; yet, when Miss Maylie, who, seeing only the horror and
guilt, calmly reasons, and attempts to save her from Sikes, Nancy, who
loves, is faithful and unmoved. We may indeed *speculate* whether such
metal, had it been cast in a better mould, would not have run true and
clear. We can only *reason* on what of necessity must have been the
result of the influences to which she had been exposed from her birth
downwards. Notwithstanding that the greater tendency in woman towards the gentler affections renders a Nancy somewhat less improbable
than an Oliver, we fear that both characters must be considered contrary

---

1. A street and theater in London frequented by prostitutes.

to the laws of human nature and experience everywhere, and particularly in England. Here, a woman once lost descends instantaneously, as through a trap-door, into unknown depths, to be heard of no more. There is no climbing up again, none to forgive, none to say 'sin no more;' all throw the first stone, all press on the bruised reed,—and her own sex the heaviest: not only those who are themselves unscathed, merely because they have never known want, misery, or temptation; but even the wise, the thoughtful, the experienced, the truly and intrinsically pure,—even they can pardon every crime and cover every shame save that of an erring sister.

* * *

It is hardly fair to conclude an article, however brief and desultory, upon Oliver Twist, without making some allusion to the obligations under which author and reader are laid by the graphic running commentary of Mr. Cruikshank's etchings. This, we suspect, may be as great an artist in his own way as Boz himself—and it is difficult to say, on laying down the book, how much of the powerful impression we are conscious of may be due, not to the pen, but to the pencil. * * *

* * * [Cruikshank's] *Bumble's Courtship*—his *Fagin's Crib*, &c., might have been anticipated—his *Sikes attempting to Murder the Dog*, and his *Jew in the Condemned Cell*,[2] have amply justified the novelist's shrewd prognostication, and proved a range of power perhaps unrivalled since Hogarth.[3]

WILLIAM MAKEPEACE THACKERAY

[On *Oliver Twist*][†]

* * * No one has read that remarkable tale of *Oliver Twist* without being interested in poor Nancy and her murderer; and especially amused and tickled by the gambols of the Artful Dodger and his companions. The power of the writer is so amazing, that the reader at once becomes his captive, and must follow him whithersoever he leads; and to what are we led? Breathless to watch all the crimes of Fagin, tenderly to deplore the errors of Nancy, to have for Bill Sikes a kind of pity and admiration, and an absolute love for the society of the Dodger. All these heroes stepped from the novel on to the stage; and the whole London

---

2. George Cruikshank created twenty-four illustrations for *Oliver Twist*. See above, p. 376, n. 7.
3. British painter and engraver (1697–1764), noted for his expressive power and brilliance as a pictorial storyteller.
† From *Catherine: A Story, Fraser's Magazine* (May 1839–Feb. 1840); reprinted from *The Oxford Thackeray*, ed. George Saintsbury, n.d. One of the best-known Victorian novelists and a friend of Dickens, Thackeray (1811–63) is best known for his novel *Vanity Fair* (1847–48).

public, from peers to chimney-sweeps, were interested about a set of ruffians whose occupations are thievery, murder, and prostitution. A most agreeable set of rascals, indeed, who have their virtues, too, but not good company for any man. We had better pass them by in decent silence; for, as no writer can or dare tell the *whole* truth concerning them, and faithfully explain their vices, there is no need to give *ex-parte*[1] statements of their virtues.

And what came of *Oliver Twist?* The public wanted something more extravagant still, more sympathy for thieves, and so *Jack Sheppard*[2] makes his appearance. Jack and his two wives, and his faithful Blueskin, and his gin-drinking mother, that sweet Magdalen!—with what a wonderful gravity are all their adventures related, with what an honest simplicity and vigour does Jack's biographer record his actions and virtues! We are taught to hate Wild, to be sure; but then it is because he betrays thieves, the rogue! And yet bad, ludicrous, monstrous as the idea of this book is, we read, and read, and are interested, too. The author has a wondrous faith, and a most respectable notion, of the vastness of his subject. There is not one particle of banter in his composition; good and bad ideas, he hatches all with the same great gravity; and is just as earnest in his fine description of the storm on the Thames, and his admirable account of the escape from Newgate; as in the scenes in Whitefriars,[3] and the conversation at Wild's, than which nothing was ever written more curiously unnatural. We are not, however, here criticizing the novels, but simply have to speak of the Newgate part of them, which gives birth to something a great deal worse than bad taste, and familiarizes the public with notions of crime. In the dreadful satire of *Jonathan Wild*, no reader is so dull as to make the mistake of admiring, and can overlook the grand and hearty contempt of the author for the character he has described; the bitter wit of the *Beggars' Opera*,[4] too, hits the great, by showing their similarity with the wretches that figure in the play; and though the latter piece is so brilliant in its mask of gaiety and wit, that a very dull person may not see the dismal reality thus disguised, moral, at least, there is in the satire, for those who will take the trouble to find it. But in the sorrows of Nancy and the exploits of Sheppard, there is no such lurking moral, as far as we have been able to discover; we are asked for downright sympathy in the one case, and are called on in the second to admire the gallantry of a thief. The street-walker may be a very virtuous person, and the robber as brave as Wellington:[5] but it is better to leave them alone, and their qualities, good and bad. The pathos

1. Partisan.
2. A popular novel (1839) by Dickens' friend Harrison Ainsworth (1805–82), which glorified the life of a highwayman.
3. A network of London slums near Fleet Street.
4. See above, p. 4, n. 5. "*Jonathan Wild*": Henry Fielding's novel *The Life and Death of Jonathan Wilde the Great* (1743).
5. Arthur Wellesley (1769–1852), duke of Wellington, the British military leader in the Napoleonic Wars.

of the workhouse scenes in *Oliver Twist*, of the Fleet Prison descriptions in *Pickwick*, *is* genuine and pure—as much of this as you please; as tender a hand to the poor, as kindly a word to the unhappy, as you will; but, in the name of common-sense, let us not expend our sympathies on cut-throats, and other such prodigies of evil!

ANONYMOUS

Charles Dickens and His Works†

Few writers have risen so rapidly into extensive popularity as Dickens, and that by no mean or unjustifiable panderings to public favour, or the use of low arts of tricking, puffery, or pretence. Four years ago his name was almost unknown, except in some narrow newspaper circles; and his compositions had not extended beyond ephemeral sketches and essays, which, though shrewd, clever, and amusing, would never have been collected as they now are into volumes, but for the speedily acquired and far-diffused fame of *Pickwick*. Before we pass from these sketches, we must say that they contain germs of almost every character Boz has since depicted, as well as of his incidents and stories, and that they display the quaint peculiarities of his style. Some of them, indeed, are, we think, better than any thing which he has written in his more celebrated performances.

*   *   *

We might easily go over the leading characters in the great novelists, not only of our own literature, but of all others * * * but we have said quite enough already to shew that the objection which Mr. Dickens so strangely imagines to have been made against those eminent writers, of drawing characters that come and go like the men and women whom we encounter in the world—an objection, in truth, involving the highest praise—is not the objection which a careful reader of his collected works would make against him. There are no such characters in the world as Pickwick, Snodgrass, or Winkle [characters in Dickens' first novel, *Pickwick Papers*, 1837]. The transformations effected by the magic wand of Harlequin[1] are nothing to the transformations which these personages undergo, in their progress from the beginning to the end of the volume in which they appear. The conversion, for instance, of the Clown or Pantaloon into a pair of romantic lovers could not be more extraordinary than that which transforms Mr. Winkle from being such a fellow as

† From *Fraser's Magazine* 21 (April 1840): 381–400.
1. The archetypal magician, usually mute and acrobatic, in the popular genre of pantomime, elaborate Christmas comedies performed annually in London.

"could not possibly have been mistaken for any thing but a sportsman, if he had not borne an equal resemblance to a twopenny postman," into the favoured suitor of the elegant Arabella Allan.

In *Oliver Twist*, Mr. Dickens has just the same defect,—one which certainly cannot be urged against the great novelists. * * * This dreamy and stupid old man [Mr. Brownlow] displays not merely great goodness of heart, which certainly is not inconsistent with carelessness and abstraction, but what *is* inconsistent with these characteristics, unwearied zeal in tracing out the intricacies of a complicated plot, and determined activity in pursuing a murderer to his last haunt of refuge. If we look over any of the pictures in which he figures, and compare them with the text, we will find it impossible to believe that such features as those bestowed upon him by the artist could have been kindled into energetic emotion of any kind, except, perhaps, of petulance or impatience. Or, again, is the Nance of the first volume the same Nance that we find in the third?—

* * *

Now, without asking where Nancy got her fine sentiments, may we not ask where she got her fine English? She talks the common slang of London, in its ordinary dialect, in the beginning of the novel; at the end no heroine that ever went mad in white satin talked more picked and perfumed sentences of sentimentality. When Sir Walter Scott[2] sends Jeannie Deans to plead before Queen Caroline for the life of her sister Effie, he puts a speech in her mouth, which her majesty pronounces to be eloquence, and its readers will agree with the queen, but he does not commit the mistake of translating it into any other dialect than the Auld Reekie Scotch[3] which Jeannie has spoken throughout. Nor does Mr. Dickens commit the mistake, when he produces Sam Weller as doing an act of generous devotion to his imprisoned master, of making him abandon the genuine Cockney in which that eloquent gentleman on all other occasions communicates his ideas.

* * *

In *Oliver Twist* it is, no doubt, very satisfactory to the lovers of poetical justice that Fagin should be hanged, but the Old Bailey justice that consigned him to the gallows is somewhat peculiar. For the benefit and the instruction of our legal readers, we shall give the case as far as we find it reported in 3 Twist and Dickens, 243, 185, 191:—

 " 'When was Fagin took then?'
 " 'Just at dinner-time—two o'clock this afternoon,' was the reply. 'Charley and I made our lucky up the wash'us chimney, and Bolter

---

2. Scott (1771–1832), the most esteemed and successful English novelist before Dickens, published *The Heart of Midlothian* in 1818; Jeannie and Effie Deans are two of the principal characters.
3. The dialect of Scottish associated with Edinburgh.

got into the empty water-butt, head downwards, but his legs was
so precious long that they stuck out at the top, and so they took
him too.'

" 'And Bet?'

" 'Poor Bet! She went to see the body, to speak to who it was,'
replied Chitling, his countenance falling more and more, 'and went
off mad, screaming and raving, and beating her head against the
boards, so they put a strait weskut on her and took her to the
hospital—and there she is.'

" 'Wot's come of young Bates?' demanded Kags.

" 'He hung about, not to come over here afore dark, but he'll
be here soon,' replied Chitling. 'There's nowhere else to go to now,
for the people at the Cripples are all in custody, and the bar of the
ken—I went up there and saw it with my own eyes—is filled with
traps.'

" 'This is a smash,' observed Toby, biting his lip. 'There's more
than one will go with this.'

" 'The sessions are on,' said Kags: 'if they get the inquest over;
if Bolter turns king's evidence, as of course he will, from what he's
said already; they can prove Fagin an accessory before the fact,
and get the trial on on Friday; he'll swing in six days from this,
by G—!' "

They can prove Fagin as accessory before the fact, and how? The facts
are these. Nance, the murdered woman, had been overheard making
communications to Mr. Brownlow, which, in the opinion of Fagin,
compromised the safety of the gang, and he determined to excite the
anger of Bill Sikes against her. The robber is already in a bad humour,
and when the ruffianly old Jew has contrived to excite at once his wrath
and his curiosity, he thus proceeds: [The reviewer quotes the passage
that appears in this volume on pp. 313–15, from "Suppose that lad that's
lying . . ." to ". . . a drink of laudanum."]

Now, in all this, Fagin has done nothing more than report what
Morris Bolter, *alias* Noah Claypole, had told him; and if Bill Sikes flies
into a fury, that is only because such is the gentleman's natural temperament; and, besides, he had a very fair *primá facie*[4] case of suspecting
that his lady-love had committed the most atrocious of all crimes against
the society of which he and she were component members, viz. that
known in their own language by the name of splitting. Sikes bursts away
from Fagin, and will not listen to any thing further.

*   *   *

Here all the crime of Fagin, so far as words go, consists in his rec-
ommending Mr. Sikes not to be too violent—to be crafty, and not too
bold; advice which in itself is highly praiseworthy. If Fagin had a proper
counsel, the learned gentleman might have expatiated upon the ad-

4. At first sight, self-evident.

mirable temper and prudence of the old man in giving such advice at such a moment. It clearly means, Do not hurt a hair of the girl's head—no violence of any kind. Use prudence and wisdom in averting the dangers impending over you, in consequence of the treachery or imprudence of the lady—but harm her not. Be crafty, but not violent. What could be better? * * * But then the look? Was not *that* murderous? Perhaps; but it would be very hard to make a villanous look matter of legal proof against a man. If it could be so made,

> " 'Twould thin the land, such numbers would swing
> Upon Tyburn tree."

> *   *   *

However, admit the doctrine that a man's looking murder, while advising moderation, is enough to make him an accessory before the fact, and that a clerk of the crown would be found ingenious enough to frame a count in the indictment upon it, and we allow that, if the popular and liberal branch of the legislature proceeds as it has been doing for some time, and the attorney-general continues to display so much dexterity in drawing up warrants, there is no saying what we may come to at last,—admit all this, yet still who was to prove it? Nobody was present when this look murderous was given but Sikes and Fagin,—the former of whom was dead, and the latter on his trial. To the House of Commons alone, of all judicial or sham judicial bodies, does the power belong of examining prisoners for the purpose of eliciting evidence against themselves. * * * Fagin was not present at the murder, aiding, abetting, or advising. Bill Sikes was like Coriolanus[5] among the Volscians—"Alone he did it." The Jew had what Mr. Weller the elder would have called a clear case of "a alleybi;" and if that eminent jarvey and jurisconsult,[6] according to Mr. Dickens the younger, was wrong in thinking that all the courts of the realm were to be regulated by the practice of the Old Bailey, it is equally clear that Mr. Dickens himself does not know what that practice really is.

The judge, however, before whom Mr. Dickens brings the cause, and the jury to whom he sends it for trial, are determined to hang Fagin, to oblige the tender-hearted students of the circulating library.

> *   *   *

Poor Fagin, then, after having been charged *upon* by the judge—for decidedly the attack must have been far more in the style military than the style legal—was sentenced upon Friday to be hanged on Monday, —the crime being, "that he exchanged one brief glance with the said William, commonly called Bill, Sikes, there being at the time aforesaid a fire in the eyes of each—that is to say, in the eyes of the said William,

---

5. The hero of Shakespeare's tragedy *Coriolanus* (1608), a proud Roman general who is destroyed by collaborating with the Volscians, Rome's enemies, after he has been banished from Rome.
6. Carriage driver and expert in the law.

commonly called Bill, Sikes, and the said Emmanuel, otherwise Monney, Fagin." A short shrift! * * * After this notable sentence, we do not wonder that Fagin should be sent to the gallows raving mad, or that people are permitted to visit him in the condemned cell after the midnight preceding the morning of his execution, in order to play upon his fears, to extort from him some document required in a legal investigation. * * * But for this, and many other slips in his stories and style, Boz has offered the adequate excuse, viz. the nature of his publication, in which every thing was to be postponed to the necessity of periodical appearance. We can hardly believe him implicitly when he tells us that the artists designed *after* his hints. In fact, many of his sketches are little more than catalogues of what we find in the pictures, done with the minuteness of an appraiser. The picture, in fact, sold the number, and the writing was a matter of secondary consideration, so far as sale was concerned. Every one, even the dull reviewer in the *Quarterly*, is struck with the intense folly of displaying Oliver Twist as a model of virtue, elegance, and refinement, after an education under Mr. Bumble the beadle, Mr. Sowerberry the undertaker, and Mr. Fagin the fence; but the artist wanted the attractive subject of a boy growing up from the meagre poverty of workhouse childhood to the graceful beauty of happy youth, and the letterpress was written "to match, as per order." So of Nicholas Nickleby. The son of so idiotic a mother, flung into such scenes, reduced to such extremities, and furnished with such trifling means of mental or bodily cultivation, could not have cut the figure, and done all the fine things which he is made to get through; but the painter wanted "a nice young man" for his sketches, and he had him accordingly. And again, the necessity of filling a certain quantity of pages per month imposed upon the writer a great temptation to amplify trifling incidents, and to swell sentence after sentence with any sort of words that would occupy space. The very spirit of a penny-a-liner, for instance, breaks out in the prolix descriptions of the various walks through the streets of London, every turn in which is enumerated with the accuracy of a cabman. *Oliver Twist* and *Nicholas Nickleby* are stuffed with "passages that lead to nothing," merely to fill the necessary room. Now, in the separate monthly essays this was no harm,—on the contrary, it was of positive good to the main object, viz. the sale; but when we find them collected, they do not improve the sequence of the story, or advance the fame of the writer. In short, the habits of the reporter break out—the copy is to be given in—and what shall we write of but what we know? How fill the paper, but by reports of debates, meetings, societies, police-offices, courts of justice, vestry-rooms, and so forth, spun out as amusingly and as lengthily as possible, all with a view to the foreman's bill at the end?

But this is the only fault of Boz—if fault it can be called, to make hay while the sun shines. We wish him well; but talking of literature in any other light than that of a hack trade, we do not like this novel-writing by scraps against time. He can never do himself or his readers justice. * * * He has one great merit, independent of his undoubted powers of drollery, observation, and caricature—he has not lent his pen to any thing that can give countenance to vice or degradation; and he has always espoused the cause of the humble, the persecuted, and the oppressed. This of itself would cover far more literary sins than Boz has to answer for; and, indeed, we do not remember any of importance enough to require covering at all. * * *

ANONYMOUS

Literary Recipes†

A STARTLING ROMANCE

Take a small boy, charity, factory, carpenter's apprentice, or otherwise, as occasion may serve—stew him well down in vice—garnish largely with oaths and flash songs—boil him in a cauldron of crime and improbabilities. Season equally with good and bad qualities—infuse petty larceny, affection, benevolence, and burglary, honour and housebreaking, amiability and arson—boil all gently. Stew down a mud mother—a gang of robbers—several pistols—a bloody knife. Serve up with a couple of murders—and season with a hanging-match.

N.B.[1] Alter the ingredients to a beadle and a workhouse—the scenes may be the same, but the whole flavour of vice will be lost, and the boy will turn out a perfect pattern.—Strongly recommended for weak stomachs.

---

† From *Punch* (Aug. 7, 1841): 39.
1. *Nota bene:* pay special attention to (Latin).

CRITICISM

HENRY JAMES

[On *Oliver Twist* and Cruikshank]†

* * *

The whole question dwells for me in a single small reminiscence, though there are others still: that of my having been sent to bed one evening, in Fourteenth Street, as a very small boy, at an hour when, in the library and under the lamp, one of the elder cousins from Albany, the youngest of an orphaned brood of four, of my grandmother's most extravagant adoption, had begun to read aloud to my mother the new, which must have been the first, installment of David Copperfield. I had feigned to withdraw, but had only retreated to cover close at hand, the friendly shade of some screen or drooping table-cloth, folded up behind which and glued to the carpet, I held my breath and listened. I listened long and drank deep while the wondrous picture grew, but the tense cord at last snapped under the strain of the Murdstones and I broke into the sobs of sympathy that disclosed my subterfuge. I was this time effectively banished, but the ply then taken was ineffaceable. I remember indeed just afterwards finding the sequel, in especial the vast extrusion of the Micawbers, beyond my actual capacity; which took a few years to grow adequate—years in which the general contagious consciousness, and our own household response not least, breathed heavily through Hard Times, Bleak House and Little Dorrit; the seeds of acquaintance with Chuzzlewit and Dombey and Son, these coming thickly on, I had found already sown. I was to feel that I had been born, born to a rich awareness, under the very meridian; there sprouted in those years no such other crop of ready references as the golden harvest of Copperfield. Yet if I was to wait to achieve the happier of these recognitions I had already pored over Oliver Twist—albeit now uncertain of the relation borne by that experience to the incident just recalled. When Oliver was new to me, at any rate, he was already old to my betters; whose view of his particular adventures and exposures must have been concerned, I think, moreover, in the fact of my public and lively wonder about them. It was an exhibition deprecated—to infant innocence I judge; unless indeed my remembrance of enjoying it only on the terms of fitful snatches in another, though a kindred, house is due mainly to the existence there of George Cruikshank's splendid form of the work, of which our own foreground was clear. It perhaps even seemed to me more Cruikshank's than Dickens's; it was a thing of such vividly terrible images, and all marked with that peculiarity of Cruikshank that the

† From *A Small Boy and Others* (New York, 1913) 118–20, 309–10.

419

offered flowers or goodnesses, the scenes and figures intended to comfort
and cheer, present themselves under his hand as but more subtly sinister,
or more suggestively queer, than the frank badnesses and horrors. The
nice people and the happy moments, in the plates, frightened me almost
as much as the low and the awkward; which didn't however make the
volumes a source of attraction the less toward that high and square old
back-parlour just westward of Sixth Avenue (as we in the same street
were related to it) that formed, romantically, half our alternative domestic
field and offered to our small inquiring steps a larger range and privilege.
If the Dickens of those years was, as I have just called him, the great
actuality of the current imagination, so I at once meet him in force as
a feature even of conditions in which he was but indirectly involved.

                              * * *

   * * * The London people had for themselves, at the same time, an
exuberance of type; we found it in particular a world of costume, often
of very odd costume—the most intimate notes of which were the post-
men in their frock-coats of military red and their black beaver hats; the
milkwomen, in hats that often emulated these, in little shawls and strange
short, full frocks, revealing enormous boots, with their pails swung from
their shoulders on wooden yokes; the inveterate footmen hooked behind
the coaches of the rich, frequently in pairs and carrying staves, together
with the mounted and belted grooms without the attendance of whom
riders, of whichever sex—and riders then were much more numerous
—almost never went forth. The range of character, on the other hand,
reached rather dreadfully down; there were embodied and exemplified
"horrors" in the streets beside which any present exhibition is pale, and
I well remember the almost terrified sense of their salience produced in
me a couple of years later, on the occasion of a flying return from the
Continent with my father, by a long, an interminable drive westward
from the London Bridge railway-station. It was a soft June evening, with
a lingering light and swarming crowds, as they then seemed to me, of
figures reminding me of George Cruikshank's Artful Dodger and his Bill
Sikes and his Nancy, only with the bigger brutality of life, which pressed
upon the cab, the early-Victorian fourwheeler, as we jogged over the
Bridge, and cropped up in more and more gas-lit patches for all our
course, culminating, somewhere far to the west, in the vivid picture,
framed by the cab-window, of a woman reeling backward as a man felled
her to the ground with a blow in the face.

                              * * *

GEORGE GISSING

Oliver Twist†

It was a proof of Dickens's force and originality that, whilst still engaged upon *Pickwick*, with the laughter of a multitude flattering his joyous and eager temper, he chose for his new book such a subject as that of *Oliver Twist*. The profound seriousness of his genius, already suggesting itself in the course of Mr. Pickwick's adventures, was fully declared in "The Parish Boy's Progress." Doubts might well have been entertained as to the reception by the public of this squalid chronicle, this story of the workhouse, the thieves' den, and the condemned cell; as a matter of fact, voices were soon raised in protest, and many of *Pickwick's* admirers turned away in disgust. When the complete novel appeared, a *Quarterly* reviewer attacked it vigorously, declaring the picture injurious to public morals, and the author's satire upon public institutions mere splenetic extravagance. For all this Dickens was prepared. Consciously, deliberately, he had begun the great work of his life, and he had strength to carry with him the vast majority of English readers. His mistakes were those of a generous purpose. When criticism had said its say, the world did homage to a genial moralist, a keen satirist, and a leader in literature.

* * *

Oliver Twist had a twofold moral purpose: to exhibit the evil working of the Poor Law Act, and to give a faithful picture of the life of thieves in London. The motives hung well together, for in Dickens's view the pauper system was directly responsible for a great deal of crime. It must be remembered that, by the new Act of 1834, outdoor sustenance was as much as possible done away with, paupers being henceforth relieved only on condition of their entering a workhouse, while the workhouse life was made thoroughly uninviting, among other things by the separation of husbands and wives, and parents and children. Against this seemingly harsh treatment of a helpless class Dickens is very bitter; he regards such legislation as the outcome of cold-blooded theory, evolved by well-to-do persons of the privileged caste, who neither perceive nor care about the result of their system in individual suffering. "I wish some well-fed philosopher, whose meat and drink turn to gall within him; whose blood is ice, whose heart is iron, could have seen Oliver Twist clutching at the dainty viands that the dog had neglected. . . . There is only one thing I should like better, and that would be to see the philosopher making the same sort of meal himself, with the same relish." (Chapter IV.) By "philosopher" Dickens meant a political-

† From *The Immortal Dickens* (London, 1925) 63–87.

economist; he uses the word frequently in this book, and always in the spirit which moved Carlyle when speaking of "the dismal science." He is the thorough-going advocate of the poor, the uncompromising Radical. Speaking with irony of the vices nourished in Noah Claypole by vicious training, he bids us note "how impartially the same amiable qualities are developed in the finest lord and the dirtiest charity boy." This partisanship lay in his genius; it was one of the sources of his strength; its entire sincerity enabled him to carry out the great task set before him, that of sweetening in some measure the Augean stable of English social life in the early half of our century.

That he was in error on the point immediately at issue mattered little. The horrible condition of the poor which so exasperated him resulted (in so far as it was due to any particular legislation) from the old Poor Law, which, by its system of granting relief in aid of insufficient wages had gone far towards pauperizing the whole of agricultural England. Not in a year or two could this evil be remedied. Dickens, seeing only the hardship of the inevitable reform, visited upon the authors of that reform indignation merited by the sluggishness and selfishness which had made it necessary. In good time the new Act justified itself; it helped to bring about increase of wages and to awaken self-respect, so far as self-respect is possible in the toilers perforce living from hand to mouth. But Dickens's quarrel with the "guardians of the poor" lay far too deep to be affected by such small changes; his demand was for justice and for mercy, in the largest sense, for a new spirit in social life. Now that his work is done, with that of Carlyle and Ruskin to aid its purpose, a later generation applauds him for throwing scorn upon mechanical "philosophy." Constitutional persons, such as Macaulay, might declare his views on social government beneath contempt; but those views have largely prevailed, and we see their influence ever extending. Readers of *Oliver Twist*, nowadays, do not concern themselves with the technical question; Oliver "asks for more," and has all our sympathies; be the law old or new, we are made to perceive that, more often than not, "the law is an ass," and its proceedings invalid in the court of conscience.

In a preface to *Oliver* (written in 1841)[1] Dickens spoke at length of its second purpose, and defended himself against critics who had objected to his dealing with the lives of pickpockets and burglars. His aim, he tells us, was to discredit a school of fiction then popular, which glorified the thief in the guise of a gallant highwayman; the real thief, he declared, he had nowhere found portrayed, save in Hogarth, and his own intention was to show the real creature, vile and miserable, "for ever skulking uneasily through the dirtiest paths of life." From the category of evil examples in fiction of the day, he excepts "Sir Edward Bulwer's admi-

1. See above, pp. 3–7 [*Editor*].

rable and powerful novel of Paul Clifford," having for that author a singular weakness not easily explained. His own scenes lie in "the cold, wet, shelterless midnight streets of London," in "foul and frowsy dens," in "haunts of hunger and disease"; and "where"—he asks—"are the attractions of these things?"

*   *   *

It was undoubtedly Dickens's conviction that, within limits imposed by decency, he had told the truth, and nothing but the truth, about his sordid and criminal characters. Imagine his preface to have been written fifty years later, and it would be all but appropriate to some representative of a daring school of "naturalism," asserting his right to deal with the most painful facts of life. "I will not abate one hole in the Dodger's coat, or one scrap of curl-paper in the girl's dishevelled hair." True, he feels obliged so to manipulate the speech of these persons that it shall not "offend the ear," but that seemed to him a matter of course. He appeals to the example of the eighteenth-century novelists, who were unembarrassed in their choice of subjects. He will stand or fall by his claim to have made a true picture. The little hero of the book is as real to him as Bill Sikes. "I wished to show, in little Oliver, the principle of good surviving through every adverse circumstance, and triumphing at last." Think what we may of his perfectly sincere claim, the important thing, in our retrospect, is the spirit in which he made it. After a long interval during which English fiction was represented by the tawdry unreal or the high imaginative (I do not forget the homely side of Scott, but herein Scott stood alone), a new writer demands attention for stories of obscure lives, and tells his tale so attractively that high and low give ear. It is a step in social and political history; it declares the democratic tendency of the new age. Here is the significance of Dickens's early success, and we do not at all understand his place in English literature if we lose sight of this historic point of view.

By comparison with the book which preceded it, *Oliver Twist* seems immature. Putting aside the first chapter or two, *Pickwick* is an astonishingly ripe production, marvellous as the work of a man of five and twenty, who had previously published only a few haphazard sketches of contemporary life. *Oliver*, on the other hand, might well pass for a first effort. Attempting a continued story, the author shows at once his weakest side, the defect which he will never outgrow. There is no coherency in the structure of the thing; the plotting is utterly without ingenuity, the mysteries are so artificial as to be altogether uninteresting. Again, we must remember the time at which Dickens was writing. Our modern laws of fiction did not exist; a story was a story, not to be judged by the standard of actual experience. Moreover, it had always to be borne in mind how greatly Dickens was under the influence of the stage, which at one time he had seriously studied with a view to becoming an actor; all through his books the theatrical tendency is manifest, not a little to their detriment. Obviously he saw a good deal of *Oliver Twist* as if from before the footlights, and even in the language of his characters the traditional note of melodrama is occasionally sounded. When, long years after, he horrified a public audience by his "reading" of the murder of Nancy, it was a singular realization of hopes cherished in his early manhood. Not content with his fame as an author, he delighted in giving proof that he possessed in a high degree the actor's talent. In our own day the popularity of the stage is again exerting an influence on the methods of fiction; such intermingling of two very different arts must always be detrimental to both.

Put aside the two blemishes of the book—on the one hand, Monks with his insufferable (often ludicrous) rant, and his absurd machinations; on the other, the feeble idyllicism of the Maylie group—and there remains a very impressive picture of the wretched and the horrible. Oliver's childish miseries show well against a background of hopeless pauperdom; having regard to his origin, we grant the "gentle, attached, affectionate creature," who is so unlike a typical workhouse child, and are made to feel his sufferings among people who may be called inhuman, but who in truth are human enough, the circumstances considered. Be it noted that, whereas even Mr. Bumble is at moments touched by natural sympathy, and Mr. Sowerberry would be not unkind if he had his way, the women of this world—Mrs. Corney, Mrs. Sowerberry, and the workhouse hags—are fiercely cruel; in them, as in many future instances, Dickens draws strictly from his observation, giving us the very truth in despite of sentiment. Passing from the shadow of the workhouse to that of criminal London, we submit to the effect which Dickens alone can produce; London as a place of squalid mystery and terror, of the grimly grotesque, of labyrinthine obscurity and lurid fascination, is Dickens's own; he taught people a certain way of regarding the huge city, and to this day how common it is to see London with Dickens's eyes. The vile streets, accurately described and named; the bare, filthy rooms inhabited by Fagin and Sikes and the rest of them; the hideous public-house to which thieves resort are before us with a haunting reality. Innumerable scarcely noticed touches heighten the impression; we know, for instance, exactly what these people eat and drink, and can smell the dish of sheep's head, flanked with porter, which Nancy sets before her brutal companion. Fagin is as visible as Shylock; we hear the very voices of the Artful Dodger and of Charley Bates, whose characters are so admirably unlike in similarity; Nancy herself becomes credible by force of her surroundings and in certain scenes (for instance, that of her hysterical fury in Chapter XVI) is life itself. The culminating horrors have a wild picturesqueness unlike anything achieved by other novelists; one never forgets Sikes's wanderings after the murder (with that scene in the inn with the pedlar), nor his death in Jacob's Island, nor Fagin in the condemned cell. These things could not be more vividly presented. The novelist's first duty is to make us see what he has seen himself, whether with the actual eye or with that of imagination, and no one ever did this more successfully than Dickens in his best moments.

His allusion (in the Preface) to Hogarth suggests a comparison of these two great artists, each of whom did such noteworthy work in the same field. On the whole, one observes more of contrast than of likeness in the impressions they severally leave upon us; the men differed widely in their ways of regarding life and were subjected to very different influences. But the life of the English poor as seen by Dickens in his youth had undergone little outward change from that which was familiar to Hogarth, and it is *Oliver Twist* especially that reminds us of the other's stern moralities in black-and-white. Not improbably they influenced the young writer's treatment of his subject. He never again deals in such unsoftened horrors as those death-scenes in the workhouse, or draws a figure so peculiarly base as that of Noah Claypole; his humour at moments is grim, harsh, unlike the ordinary Dickens note, and sometimes seems resolved to show human nature at its worst, as in the passage when Oliver runs after the coach, induced by promise of a half penny, only to be scoffed at when he falls back in weariness and pain (Chapter VIII). Dickens is, as a rule, on better terms with his rascals and villains; they generally furnish matter for a laugh; but half-a-dozen faces in *Oliver* have the very Hogarth stamp, the lines of bestial ugliness which disgust and repel.

One is often inclined to marvel that, with such a world to draw upon for his material, the world of the lower classes in the England of sixty years ago, he was able to tone his work with so genial a humanity. The features of that time, as they impress our imagination, are for the most part either ignoble or hideous, and a Hogarth in literature would seem a more natural outcome of such conditions than the author of *Pickwick* and the *Christmas Carol*. Dickens's service to civilization by the liberality of his thought cannot be too much insisted upon. The atmosphere of that age was a stifling Puritanism. "I have been very happy for some years," says Mrs. Maylie; "too happy, perhaps. It may be time that I should meet with some misfortune." (Chapter XXXIII.) Against the state of mind declared in this amazing utterance, Dickens instinctively rebelled; he believed in happiness, in its moral effect, and in the right of all to have their share in it. Forced into contemplation of the gloomiest aspects of human existence, his buoyant spirit would not be held in darkness; as his art progressed, it dealt more gently with oppressive themes. Take, for instance, the mortuary topic, which has so large a place in the life of the poor, and compare Mr. Sowerberry's business, squalid and ghastly, with that of Mr. Mould in *Chuzzlewit*, where humour prevails over the repulsive, and that again with the picture of Messrs. Omer and Joram in *Copperfield*, which touches mortality with the homeliest kindness. The circumstances, to be sure, are very different, but their choice indicates the movement of the author's mind. It was by virtue of his ever-hopeful outlook that Dickens became such a force for good.

Disposing of those of his characters who remain alive at the end, he assures us, as in a fairy tale, that the good people lived happily ever after, and we are quite ready to believe it. Among the evildoers he distinguishes, Mr. Bumble falls to his appropriate doom; Noah Claypole disappears in the grime which is his native element—severity, in his case unmitigated by the reflection that he, too, was a parish-boy and a creature of circumstances. Charley Bates it is impossible to condemn; his jollity is after Dickens's own heart, and, as there is always hope for the boy who can laugh, one feels it natural enough that he is last heard of as "the merriest young grazier in all Northamptonshire." But what of his companion, Mr. Dawkins, the Dodger? Voices pleaded for him; the author was besought to give him a chance; but of the Dodger we have no word. His last appearance is in Chapter XLIII, perhaps the best in the book. We know how Dickens must have enjoyed the writing of that chapter; Mr. Dawkins before the Bench is a triumph of his most characteristic humour. What more is to be told of the Dodger after that?

We take philosophic leave of him, assured that he is "doing full justice to his bringing-up, and establishing for himself a glorious reputation."

GRAHAM GREENE

The Young Dickens†

A critic must try to avoid being a prisoner of his time, and if we are to appreciate *Oliver Twist* at its full value we must forget that long shelf-load of books, all the stifling importance of a great author, the scandals and the controversies of the private life; it would be well too if we could forget the Phiz and the Cruikshank illustrations that have frozen the excited, excitable world of Dickens into a hall of waxworks, where Mr Mantalini's whiskers have always the same trim, where Mr Pickwick perpetually turns up the tails of his coat, and in the Chamber of Horrors Fagin crouches over an undying fire. His illustrators, brilliant craftsmen though they were, did Dickens a disservice, for no character any more will walk for the first time into our memory as we ourselves imagine him and *our* imagination after all has just as much claim to truth as Cruikshank's.

Nevertheless the effort to go back is well worth while. The journey

---

† "The Young Dickens," copyright 1951, renewed © 1979 by Graham Greene from *The Lost Childhood and Other Essays*. Pp. 101–10. Used by permission of Viking Penguin, a division of Penguin Books USA Inc.

is only a little more than a hundred years long, and at the other end of the road is a young author whose sole claim to renown in 1836 had been the publication of some journalistic sketches and a number of comic operettas: *The Strange Gentleman, The Village Coquette, Is She His Wife?* I doubt whether any literary Cortez at that date would have yet stood them upon his shelves. Then suddenly with *The Pickwick Papers* came popularity and fame. Fame falls like a dead hand on an author's shoulder, and it is well for him when it falls only in later life. How many in Dickens's place would have withstood what James called 'the great corrupting contact of the public', the popularity founded, as it almost always is, on the weakness and not the strength of an author?

The young Dickens, at the age of twenty-five, had hit on a mine that paid him a tremendous dividend. Fielding and Smollett, tidied and refined for the new industrial bourgeoisie, had both salted it; Goldsmith had contributed sentimentality and Monk Lewis horror. The book was enormous, shapeless, familiar (that important recipe for popularity). What Henry James wrote of a long-forgotten French critic applies well to the young Dickens: 'He is homely, familiar and colloquial; he leans his elbows on his desk and does up his weekly budget into a parcel the reverse of compact. You can fancy him a grocer retailing tapioca and hominy full weight for the price; his style seems a sort of integument of brown paper.'

This is, of course, unfair to *The Pickwick Papers* The driest critic could not have quite blinkered his eyes to those sudden wide illuminations of comic genius that flap across the waste of words like sheet lightning, but could he have foreseen the second novel, not a repetition of this great loose popular holdall, but a short melodrama, tight in construction, almost entirely lacking in broad comedy, and possessing only the sad twisted humour of the orphan's asylum?

> ' "You'll make your fortune, Mr Sowerberry," said the beadle, as he thrust his thumb and forefinger into the proffered snuff-box of the undertaker: which was an ingenious little model of a patent coffin.'

Such a development was as inconceivable as the gradual transformation of that thick boggy prose into the delicate and exact poetic cadences, the music of memory, that so influenced Proust.

We are too inclined to take Dickens as a whole and to treat his juvenilia with the same kindness or harshness as his later work. *Oliver Twist* is still juvenilia—magnificent juvenilia: it is the first step on the road that led from *Pickwick* to *Great Expectations*, and we condone the faults of taste in the early book the more readily if we recognize the distance Dickens had to travel. These two typical didactic passages can act as the first two milestones at the opening of the journey, the first from *Pickwick*, the second from *Oliver Twist*.

'And numerous indeed are the hearts to which Christmas brings a brief season of happiness and enjoyment. How many families, whose members have been dispersed and scattered far and wide, in the restless struggles of life, are then reunited, and meet once again in that happy state of companionship and mutual goodwill, which is a source of such pure and unalloyed delight, and one so incompatible with the cares and sorrows of the world, that the religious belief of the most civilized nations, and the rude traditions of the roughest savages, alike number it among the first joys of a future condition of existence, provided for the blest and happy.'

'The boy stirred and smiled in his sleep, as though these marks of pity and compassion had awakened some pleasant dream of a love and affection he had never known. Thus, a strain of gentle music, or the rippling of water in a silent place, or the odour of a flower, or the mention of a familiar word, will sometimes call up sudden dim remembrances of scenes that never were, in this life; which vanish like a breath; which some brief memory of a happier existence, long gone by, would seem to have awakened; which no voluntary exertion of the mind can ever recall.'

The first is certainly brown paper: what it wraps has been chosen by the grocer to suit his clients' tastes, but cannot we detect already in the second passage the tone of Dickens's secret prose, that sense of a mind speaking to itself with no one there to listen, as we find it in *Great Expectations*?

'It was fine summer weather again, and, as I walked along, the times when I was a little helpless creature, and my sister did not spare me, vividly returned. But they returned with a gentle tone upon them that softened even the edge of Tickler. For now, the very breath of the beans and clover whispered to my heart that the day must come when it would be well for my memory that others walking in the sunshine should be softened as they thought of me.'

It is a mistake to think of *Oliver Twist* as a realistic story: only late in his career did Dickens learn to write realistically of human beings; at the beginning he invented life and we no more believe in the temporal existence of Fagin or Bill Sikes than we believe in the existence of that Giant whom Jack slew as he bellowed his Fee Fi Fo Fum. There were real Fagins and Bill Sikes and real Bumbles in the England of his day, but he had not drawn them, as he was later to draw the convict Magwitch; these characters in *Oliver Twist* are simply parts of one huge invented scene, what Dickens in his own preface called 'the cold wet shelterless midnight streets of London.' How the phrase goes echoing on through the books of Dickens until we meet it again so many years later in 'the weary western streets of London on a cold dusty spring night' which were so melancholy to Pip. But Pip was to be as real as the weary streets, while Oliver was as unrealistic as the cold wet midnight of which he formed a part.

This is not to criticize the book so much as to describe it. For what an imagination this youth of twenty-six had that he could invent so monstrous and complete a legend! We are not lost with Oliver Twist round Saffron Hill: we are lost in the interstices of one young, angry, gloomy brain, and the oppressive images stand out along the track like the lit figures in a Ghost Train tunnel.

'Against the wall were ranged, in regular array, a long row of elm boards cut into the same shape, looking in the dim light, like high shouldered ghosts with their hands in their breeches pockets.'

We have most of us seen those nineteenth-century prints where the bodies of naked women form the face of a character, the Diplomat, the Miser, and the like. So the crouching figure of Fagin seems to form the mouth, Sikes with his bludgeon the jutting features, and the sad lost Oliver the eyes of one man, as lost as Oliver.

Chesterton, in a fine imaginative passage, has described the mystery behind Dickens's plots, the sense that even the author was unaware of what was really going on, so that when the explanations come and we reach, huddled into the last pages of *Oliver Twist*, a naked complex narrative of illegitimacy and burnt wills and destroyed evidence, we simply do not believe. 'The secrecy is sensational; the secret is tame. The surface of the thing seems more awful than the core of it. It seems almost as if these grisly figures, Mrs Chadband and Mrs Clennam, Miss Havisham and Miss Flite, Nemo and Sally Brass, were keeping something back from the author as well as from the reader. When the book closes we do not know their real secret. They soothed the optimistic Dickens with something less terrible than the truth.'

What strikes the attention most in this closed Fagin universe are the different levels of unreality. If, as one is inclined to believe, the creative writer perceives his world once and for all in childhood and adolescence, and his whole career is an effort to illustrate his private world in terms of the great public world we all share, we can understand why Fagin and Sikes in their most extreme exaggerations move us more than the benevolence of Mr Brownlow or the sweetness of Mrs Maylie—they touch with fear as others never really touch with love. It was not that the unhappy child, with his hurt pride and his sense of hopeless insecurity, had not encountered human goodness—he had simply failed to recognize it in those streets between Gadshill and Hungerford Market which had been as narrowly enclosed as Oliver Twist's. When Dickens at this early period tried to describe goodness he seems to have remembered the small stationers' shops on the way to the blacking factory with their coloured paper scraps of angels and virgins, or perhaps the face of some old gentleman who had spoken kindly to him outside Warren's factory. He had swum up towards goodness from the deepest world of his experience, and on this shallow level the conscious brain has taken a hand, trying to construct characters to represent virtue and, because his age demanded it, triumphant virtue, but all he can produce are powdered wigs and gleaming spectacles and a lot of bustle with bowls of broth and a pale angelic face. Compare the way in which we first meet evil with his introduction of goodness.

> 'The walls and ceiling of the room were perfectly black with age and dirt. There was a deal table before the fire: upon which were a candle, stuck in a ginger-beer bottle, two or three pewter pots, a loaf and butter, and a plate. In a frying pan, which was on the fire, and which was secured to the mantel-shelf by a string, some sausages were cooking; and standing over them, with a toasting-fork in his hand, was a very old shrivelled Jew, whose villainous-looking and repulsive face was obscured by a quantity of matted red hair. He was dressed in a greasy flannel gown, with his throat bare . . . "This is him, Fagin," said Jack Dawkins: "my friend Oliver Twist." The Jew grinned; and, making a low obeisance to Oliver, took him by the hand, and hoped he should have the honour of his intimate acquaintance.'

Fagin has always about him this quality of darkness and nightmare. He never appears on the daylight streets. Even when we see him last in the condemned cell, it is in the hours before the dawn. In the Fagin darkness Dickens's hand seldom fumbles. Hear him turning the screw of horror when Nancy speaks of the thoughts of death that have haunted her:

> ' "Imagination," said the gentleman, soothing her.
> "No imagination," replied the girl in a hoarse voice. "I'll swear I saw 'coffin' written in every page of the book in large black letters,—aye, and they carried one close to me, in the streets tonight."
> "There is nothing unusual in that," said the gentleman. "They have passed me often."
> "Real ones," rejoined the girl. "This was not." '

Now turn to the daylight world and our first sight of Rose:

> 'The younger lady was in the lovely bloom and springtime of womanhood; at that age, when, if ever angels be for God's good purposes enthroned in mortal forms, they may be, without impiety, supposed to abide in such as hers. She was not past seventeen. Cast in so slight and exquisite a mould; so mild and gentle; so pure and beautiful; that earth seemed not her element, nor its rough creatures her fit companions.'

Or Mr Brownlow as he first appeared to Oliver:

> 'Now, the old gentleman came in as brisk as need be; but he
> had no sooner raised his spectacles on his forehead, and thrust his
> hands behind the skirts of his dressing-gown to take a good long
> look at Oliver, than his countenance underwent a very great variety
> of odd contortions . . . The fact is, if the truth must be told, that
> Mr Brownlow's heart, being large enough for any six ordinary old
> gentlemen of humane disposition, forced a supply of tears into his
> eyes by some hydraulic process which we are not sufficiently phil-
> osophical to be in a condition to explain.'

How can we really believe that these inadequate ghosts of goodness
can triumph over Fagin, Monks, and Sikes? And the answer, of course,
is that they never could have triumphed without the elaborate machinery
of the plot disclosed in the last pages. This world of Dickens is a world
without God; and as a substitute for the power and the glory of the
omnipotent and omniscient are a few sentimental references to heaven,
angels, the sweet faces of the dead, and Oliver saying, 'Heaven is a long
way off, and they are too happy there to come down to the bedside of
a poor boy.' In this Manichaean world we can believe in evil-doing,
but goodness wilts into philanthropy, kindness, and those strange vague
sicknesses into which Dickens's young women so frequently fall and
which seem in his eyes a kind of badge of virtue, as though there were
a merit in death.

But how instinctively Dickens's genius recognized the flaw and made
a virtue out of it. We cannot believe in the power of Mr Brownlow, but
nor did Dickens, and from his inability to believe in his own good
character springs the real tension of his novel. The boy Oliver may not
lodge in our brain like David Copperfield, and though many of Mr
Bumble's phrases have become and deserve to have become familiar
quotations we can feel he was manufactured: he never breathes like Mr
Dorrit; yet Oliver's predicament, the nightmare fight between the darkness, where the demons walk, and the sunlight, where ineffective goodness makes its last stand in a condemned world, will remain part of our
imaginations forever. We read of the defeat of Monks, and of Fagin
screaming in the condemned cell, and of Sikes dangling from his self-
made noose, but we don't believe. We have witnessed Oliver's temporary
escapes too often and his inevitable recapture: *there* is the truth and the
creative experience. We know that when Oliver leaves Mr Brownlow's
house to walk a few hundred yards to the bookseller, his friends will
wait in vain for his return. All London outside the quiet shady street in
Pentonville belongs to his pursuers; and when he escapes again into the
house of Mrs Maylie in the fields beyond Shepperton, we know his
security is false. The seasons may pass, but safety depends not on time

but on daylight. As children we all knew that: how all day we could
forget the dark and the journey to bed. It is with a sense of relief that
at last in twilight we see the faces of the Jew and Monks peer into the
cottage window between the sprays of jessamine. At that moment we
realize how the whole world, and not London only, belongs to these
two after dark. Dickens, dealing out his happy endings and his unreal
retributions, can never ruin the validity and dignity of that moment.
'They had recognized him, and he them; and their look was as firmly
impressed upon his memory, as if it had been deeply carved in stone,
and set before him from his birth.'

'From his birth'—Dickens may have intended that phrase to refer to
the complicated imbroglios of the plot that lie outside the novel, 'something less terrible than the truth'. As for the truth, is it too fantastic to
imagine that in this novel, as in many of his later books, creeps in,
unrecognized by the author, the eternal and alluring taint of the Manichee, with its simple and terrible explanation of our plight, how the
world was made by Satan and not by God, lulling us with the music of
despair?

J. HILLIS MILLER

Oliver Twist†

Oliver's story begins and the moment of his becoming potentially
human occurs when he becomes aware of his solitude and in the same
moment becomes instinctively aware that it is intolerable to him. Oliver's
experience of solitude is not posited upon a prior experience of its opposite. He has never known any other condition: "The boy had no
friends to care for, or to care for him. The regret of no recent separation
was fresh in his mind; the absence of no loved and well-remembered
face sank heavily into his heart. But his heart *was* heavy, notwithstanding" (5). It is only because Oliver's heart *is* heavy notwithstanding, only
because he has an awareness of his state which does not depend on
anything outside himself, that he can turn now to the outside world and
demand from it some form of that love which he feels to be his natural
right as a human being.

But when he turns to the world he finds something very different
from the first undifferentiated gloom. He finds that the world does not
simply leave the outcast in the open to die. It aggressively addresses itself
to the destruction of the helpless being to which it gives no place. Once
the decision is made that the outcast has no reason for existing, the

† From *Charles Dickens, The World of His Novels* (Cambridge, 1958) 36–84. Reprinted by
permission of Harvard University Press.

world sets about deliberately to fill up the vacuum it has created by a legislative fiat. For even the space he takes up is needed. The world rushes violently in to bury him away out of sight, to take back the volume he occupied, and even to consume the very substance of his body. The characters of *Oliver Twist* find themselves in a world in which they are from the first moment and at every moment in extreme danger. Not how to "succeed," how to "rise in the world," but how to live in this world at all, is their problem. Neither the social world nor the world of nature is willing to give them the means of life. The thieves would have starved to death either in or out of a workhouse if they had not turned to crime, and Oliver's most pressing need is not the status and comfort of a recognized place in society, but simply breathing room and food.

The outcast is likely to be starved or smothered or crushed to death by mere accident, for the world goes on as though he were not in it. * * * The characters in *Oliver Twist* are obsessed with a fear of being hanged, a fear which is expressed with hallucinatory intensity in the description of Fagin's "last night alive" and is fulfilled in the death of Sikes (52, 50). In the narration of both of these deaths the motif of hanging is merged with the image of a dark suffocating interior. Hanging is a frightening mixture of two fears which operate throughout *Oliver Twist*—the fear of falling and the fear of being crushed or suffocated. A man is hanged out in the open, in full view of the crowd, and the executioner drops him into the air. But beneath his black hood the victim is as completely alone, enclosed in the dark, as if he were in the depths of a dungeon. And what more proper symbol of the crushing, suffocating violence of the hostile world than the instantaneous tightening of the noose? Fagin and Sikes merely act out the death which has threatened Oliver from the beginning, and has, in his case too, been connected with the image of close imprisonment in a dark room. When Oliver is locked in the "dark and solitary room" after he has asked for "more," Dickens comments: "It appears, at first sight, not unreasonable to suppose, that, if he had entertained a becoming feeling of respect for the prediction of the gentleman in the white waistcoat, he would have established that sage individual's prophetic character, once and for ever, by tying one end of his pocket-handkerchief to a hook in the wall, and attaching himself to the other" (3).

* * *

Apparently there is no escape. One demands life from this world only to be met by even more determined hostility. Against this calculated effort to destroy him, Oliver has for defense only what Bumble calls his "artificial soul and spirit" (7). Only the "good sturdy spirit" "implanted" "in Oliver's breast" by "nature or inheritance" (2) will keep him alive. It is both nature *and* inheritance, both the self that Oliver has inherited from his unknown parents, and his "natural goodness." Both are necessary to keep Oliver alive at all.

But at the heart of the novel is the fear that this "good sturdy spirit" will seize by violence what belongs to it by right—status and the goods of this world—and thus transform its innocence into a guilt which no longer deserves approval and status. He is saved by the fact that he is naturally "grateful and attached" (32), as Rose Maylie calls him, and, far from planning to seize by force the goods and status he lacks, is simply looking for someone to whom he can be related as a child to the parents who seem to him the source of all value and the absolute judges of right and wrong.

There is little active volition in Oliver, no will to do something definite, to carve out for himself a place in the solid and hostile world, to choose a course oriented toward the future and follow it out without regard to the sacrifices necessary. No, all Oliver's volition is the volition of passive resistance. Oliver wills to live, and therefore resists violently all the attempts of the world to crush him or bury him or make him into a thief. But at the center of this fierce will there is passivity, the passivity of waiting, of expectation, of "great expectations." Oliver will not seize for himself a place in the world, nor will he join in the attempts of the thieves to create a society in the depths of the slums. But neither will he allow the world of honest men to destroy him. He resists the crushing walls of his prison because he expects that somehow they will turn into a soft protecting enclosure, into a cradle, a comfortable nook where he will be securely cared for.

But before this can happen Oliver must endure a long trial, a sequence of experiences which is essentially the detailed exploration of the world as it is for the outcast. And without any external evidence at all that he is other than he seems to be, gallows' bait, Oliver must act as if he were what he wants to be, a good boy, the son of a gentleman.

Apparently there is no escape. No novel could be more completely dominated by an imaginative complex of claustrophobia. No other novel by Dickens returns so frequently to images of dark dirty rooms with no apparent exit. At various times Oliver is imprisoned in "the coal-cellar" (2), in a "dark and solitary room" (3), in a "little room by himself" (3), in a "cell" "in shape and size something like an area cellar, only not so light. It was most intolerably dirty" (11). He is almost apprenticed as a chimney sweep, and is finally taken on by an undertaker who begins by pushing him "down a steep flight of stairs into a stone cell, damp and dark: forming the ante-room to the coal-cellar" (4). He sleeps in the workshop among the coffins: "The shop was close and hot. The atmosphere seemed tainted with the smell of coffins. The recess beneath the counter in which his flock mattress was thrust, looked like a grave" (5).

*   *   *

This world is wholly incomprehensible to Oliver. The exterior confusion of sights and sounds is matched by an interior bewilderment.

Oliver's state of mind as prisoner of the thieves in these underground interiors is usually that of semi-conscious anxiety. He has little awareness or understanding of his plight. He has merely a vague knowledge that he is living in a kind of earthly hell, not the least unpleasant part of which is the fact that he does not comprehend most of what is going on around him. This failure to understand actually protects Oliver from the complicity of too much knowledge of the thieves' world. But this is another of the things he does not know, and he remains aware only of the confusion itself and of his failure to understand it:

> Oliver tried to reply, but his tongue failed him. He was deadly pale; and the whole place seemed turning round and round. (11)

> Oliver looked at Sikes, in mute and timid wonder; and drawing a stool to the fire, sat with his aching head upon his hands, scarcely knowing where he was, or what was passing around him. (22)

Over and over again we see Oliver simply falling asleep in these "foul and frowsy dens, where vice is closely packed and lacks the room to turn" (Preface to the third edition, *OT*, p. ix). Cut off altogether from the past and the future, enclosed in a narrow shadowy present which does not make sense, he loses consciousness altogether, so exhausted is he by anxiety and by his failure to comprehend what is happening to him. More precisely, he is reduced to the simplest and most undifferentiated form of consciousness, sleep.

✻ ✻ ✻

Fagin's gang is an authentic society and provides the security and sense of belonging to a community which Oliver has never before known, but these goods are not won without a price. The price is the permanent loss of the kind of life among honest men of which Oliver instinctively dreams: ". . . the wily old Jew had the boy in his toils. Having prepared his mind, by solitude and gloom, to prefer any society to the companionship of his own sad thoughts in such a dreary place, he was now slowly instilling into his soul the poison which he hoped would blacken it, and change its hue for ever" (18). Oliver among the thieves is, in fact, totally excluded from the life of protected security he desires. He is as truly outcast as if he were starving in the open, however warm and comfortable and even cheerful the interior of Fagin's den may be. Oliver's situation in the world is to be at once "hedged round and round" (20) and abandoned in the open. His relation to the thieves leads him inevitably to the moment when, left behind by Sikes after the failure of a robbery, he lies unconscious in a ditch in the rain (28).

But it is in Dickens' treatment of the lives of the thieves themselves rather than in his treatment of Oliver that we can see most clearly why he rejects the attempt by the outcasts to create an autonomous society of their own.

In the first place, the thieves' society is unstable. It is built on the principle of internal treason, and it is constantly threatened by destruction from the outside. If the least chink in the walls lets the beams of the hidden candle out into the night, the society of the "upper world" will rush in and destroy the hidden society of outcasts. The two qualities of disloyalty and danger from without are causally related. It is because the thieves live through raids on the world of honest men that they are, ultimately, disloyal to one another. They are inevitably disloyal because only by caring more for their own individual safety than for their common safety can they survive. It is Fagin who lives most deliberately by a philosophy of "every man for himself," and it is Fagin, consequently, who lives longest.

Fagin's apparent philosophy of one for all hides an actual philosophy which sacrifices all for one. He lives only by condemning others to death. If he does not do this, they will turn *him* in. Just as he moves from den to den, so he must constantly replace the members of his gang. A society defining itself as evil, that is, as the denial of all social laws, can only live by perpetual metamorphosis. Fagin is accordingly a shape-changer, a master of disguise, but his best disguise is the constantly changing membership of his gang. He can only survive by being nothing and by doing nothing himself, that is, by committing his crimes only by proxy and remaining himself the empty center of all this crime, the void of evil itself. For positive evil in this world is inevitably punished; the man who sets himself up against society always comes to be hanged. The periphery around Fagin, all the boys and adult thieves who work for him, are one by one plucked away and hanged or transported. It is only by maintaining this solid wall of active evil committed by others between himself and the world of good that Fagin can continue to live at the center of his dark hollow den.

The true relation of the thieves to one another is given not by the image of a mutually loyal group crouching around their single candle in an underground room, but by the recurrent motif of spying. Fagin himself spies on Oliver and on other members of his gang; Nancy finds out the secrets of Oliver's birth by spying on Fagin and Monks; Nancy herself is spied on by Fagin's representative. Her betrayal of the thieves is thus discovered and her death brought about. And Oliver is spied on by Fagin and Monks as he dwells in what he assumes to be the total security of Mrs. Maylie's country home. All the thieves are in constant fear not only that someone in the outside world will observe and identify them but that they will be observed and betrayed by one of their own number. Oliver's share in this general fear of the unseen look that steals one's secret is a measure of the degree of his participation, in spite of himself, in the thieves' psychology. For the world of honest men the thieves' world is invisible. When Oliver takes Dr. Losberne to the house where he has been with the thieves, everything is changed. They are met by "a little ugly hump-backed man" whom Oliver has never seen before, and when they enter the house "not an article of furniture; not a vestige of anything, animate or inanimate; not even the position of the cupbords: [answers] Oliver's description" (32). Only Oliver, with his unwilling complicity in the underworld, sees the dwarf's "glance so sharp and fierce and at the same time so furious and vindictive, that, waking or sleeping, he could not forget it for months afterwards" (32).

The thieves, then, are constantly threatened, within and without, by the possibility that their secret will be revealed. * * * But if the attempt to escape from isolation through a relationship to the world of good men is a failure, so equally is the attempt to establish relationships inside the underworld. The tragic end of the Sikes-Nancy liaison is final judgment on the futility of the attempt to keep love alive within a society which is excluded from the daylight of law and convention. Within such a society all voluntary relationships are evil. They are evil because there is nothing outside of themselves which justifies them. They cannot be other than illicit. Sikes and Nancy are inevitably destroyed by their guilty love, a love that is guilty because it is outside social sanctions. The only alternatives for them are death or separation and reintegration into the honest world: "Bill," pleads Nancy a moment before Sikes murders her, "the gentleman and that dear lady, told me to-night of a home in some foreign country where I could end my days in solitude and peace. Let me see them again, and beg them, on my knees, to show the same mercy and goodness to you; and let us both leave this dreadful place, and far apart lead better lives, and forget how we have lived, except in prayers, and never see each other more" (47).

Dickens, at this stage of his career, is willing to sacrifice all, even faithfulness in love, to the need to escape from social ostracism. For the outcast, it seems, is in an impossible dilemma. He is now nothing, because society has chosen to reject him utterly. But if he tries to take a place he will be even more certainly defined as an outlaw and all the more surely destroyed. Oliver's only hope is somehow to escape from the underground society altogether. But this seems impossible.

* * *

More than once Oliver does escape and is able to explore the external world, to make an active search for its meaning. Does this world have the same hostility that the walls of the dark interior world possessed? The windowless room corresponded to Oliver's interior darkness, to the semiconscious stupor which was his initial condition. Perhaps the exterior world may be controlled by understanding it. Perhaps it may be held at arm's length, may be comprehended, may even be forced to correspond exactly to his inner state and thus to offer an escape from the total separation between inner and outer worlds imaged in Oliver's melancholy gaze out the back garret-window at the "confused and crowded mass of house-tops, blackened chimneys, and gable-ends."

*   *   *

This new state of isolation is in a way more desperate than the first. The walls of Oliver's prison were at least close to him and were a kind of comfort in themselves. And the outcast can no longer be consoled by the idea that everything will be all right if only he can escape from his prison. The outside world is revealed as simply the opposite extreme from the inside world. Instead of being close and suffocating it is absolutely open. And what can be seen at a distance in the clear light forms a kind of solid barrier just as hostile as the damp walls within which Oliver has been immured. It is now a hostility of withdrawal and silence rather than of active violence against Oliver. The world constitutes itself still as a solid wall, but it is now a wall of indifference rather than of hate. In the distance between himself and the closed shutters or the cold stars Oliver can see for the first time his total isolation. It is an isolation which is both material and social. He is cut off from the community behind the closed shutters as much as from the stars or the trees.

*   *   *

The urban labyrinth turns out to be nothing more than an endless daedal prison. As in a dream, Oliver wanders through intricate streets which are different but which do not seem to lead anywhere. And the darkness, narrowness, muddiness, crookedness of this maze make it difficult to distinguish it from the underground prison in which the hero first found himself. The hero and his avatars are as much lost and as much enclosed outside as they were inside, and there is repeated over and over the sequence of a rapid walk, sometimes a flight, through streets which get narrower and narrower and dirtier and dirtier and more and more intricate and finally lead to the doors of one of the subterranean interiors. *   *   *

At the deepest imaginative level the London of *Oliver Twist* is no longer a realistic description of the unsanitary London of the thirties but is the dream or poetic symbol of an infernal labyrinth, inhabited by the devil himself: "The mud lay thick upon the stones, and a black mist hung over the streets; the rain fell sluggishly down, and everything felt cold and clammy to the touch. It seemed just the night when it befitted such a being as the Jew to be abroad. As he glided stealthily along, creeping beneath the shelter of the walls and doorways, the hideous old man seemed like some loathsome reptile, engendered in the slime and darkness through which he moved: crawling forth, by night, in search of some rich offal for a meal" (19). Fagin is as much dream as reality. He is often called the devil (19, 44), or shown in a pose that recalls the devil: crouching over a fire with a toasting fork (8), or other implement (20, 25), or gloating over his hidden treasure (9). Dickens had been reading Defoe's *History of the Devil* with great interest while he was writing *Oliver Twist*, but his reading, it seems evident, only reinforced the image of the archetype of evil which was already present in his imagination. Fagin is imagined too vividly in his combination of supernatural and animal qualities to be the mere copy of traditional and literary representations of the devil: ". . . Fagin sat watching in his old lair, with face so distorted and pale, and eyes so red and bloodshot, that he looked less like a man, than like some hideous phantom, moist from the grave, and worried by an evil spirit. . . . and as, absorbed in thought, he bit his long black nails, he disclosed among his toothless gums a few such fangs as should have been a dog's or rat's" (47).

At the center of the labyrinth, then, is Fagin, the personified principle of the world cut off altogether from the light and the good. There he crouches, greedy to possess Oliver altogether by making him a thief, but hiding, perhaps, the secret that will make possible Oliver's permanent escape from the labyrinth. The only escape from the prison, it may be, is to descend into its very heart and to wrest from the darkness its secret. Oliver does not know this, of course. He only knows that there is a centripetal force which seems to pull him toward the center of the labyrinth, however hard he tries to escape. When Oliver flees from his living grave at Sowerberry's it is not outward through the maze to freedom, but into the intricacy of London, toward the dark center of the labyrinth—Fagin's den. And when Oliver's rescuer sends Oliver out on an errand he has only to turn down a bystreet by accident (15) to be plunged back into the labyrinth and recaptured by Fagin.

The true meaning of the labyrinth image is perhaps revealed in a phrase Dickens uses about Nancy: "Fagin . . . had led her, step by step, deeper and deeper down into an abyss of crime and misery, whence was no escape" (44). Movement in the Dickensian labyrinth is always inward and downward toward the center, and never outward toward freedom. The labyrinth is really an abyss, a bottomless pit of mud and darkness in which one can be lost forever, forever separated from the world of light and freedom. And the labyrinth is also a moral abyss. It is the world into which Oliver will be permanently plunged if the thieves succeed in hardening him and making him into one of themselves.

*   *   *

Until the very end of the novel all the characters are living in the midst of experiences which have the total opacity of the present and cannot yet be seen in retrospect as having the logical structure of a destiny. The mystery, the unintelligibility, of the present is perfectly expressed by these scenes of multiplicity in a state of rapid, aimless agitation. The exterior scene is exactly matched by the state of mind of the inhabitants of this world of bewildering uncertainty and unpredictable change. Rose Maylie's interview with Nancy "had more the semblance of a rapid dream than an actual occurrence." She sinks into a chair and endeavors "to collect her wandering thoughts" (40). Fagin's violent thoughts when he learns he has been betrayed follow "close upon each other with rapid and ceaseless whirl" (47). At a crisis in the story Mr. Losberne and Mr. Brownlow hastily separate "each in a fever of excitement wholly uncontrollable" (49), and we see Oliver "in a flutter of agitation and uncertainty, which [deprives] him of the power of collecting his thoughts" (51).

But there is one case in *Oliver Twist* in which a character seeks out such a scene, and succeeds in losing his self-consciousness by identifying himself with the violent agitation of the world. When Sikes, after the murder of Nancy, has wandered through the countryside attempting to lose himself and his past, but lingering obsessively "about the same spot," he succeeds for a few hours in forgetting himself and his crime at the scene of a great fire (48). Sikes can forget himself momentarily because he has found an external scene which corresponds exactly to his inner state and can be intermingled with it. The objective fire is matched by Sikes' internal fever, and at the height of his "ecstacy" he is as much inside the fire as the fire is inside him: "in every part of that great fire was he" (48). Only if a person is in a state of self-destructive disintegration, consuming himself with some inner conflict, will the multitudinousness of the world be an appropriate projection of the self. Only then will self-forgetfulness be possible. And even this transcendence of the subject-object cleavage is only momentary: "This mad excitement over, there returned, with tenfold force, the dreadful consciousness of his crime" (48). The external fire is burned to "smoke and blackened ruins," but Sikes' inner fire burns on, and would be satisfied not by any mere chaotic swirling of the world such as bewildered Oliver at Smithfield, but by a gigantic holocaust which would consume the whole world in consuming him.

*   *   *

The search through the labyrinth, then, has come face to face with the absolute impasse of a world which, hovering at a distance, regards one with an implacable stare. It is a universe which has become all eyes, eyes which see into every corner of one's soul, and do not leave any recess which is free or secret. But worse is to follow. Three times in the novel for three different characters the direction of the labyrinth changes, the seeker becomes the sought, he who had rushed frantically through endless crooked streets seeking some escape now flees even more frantically from the active enmity of the mob. The labyrinth is turned into a hostile crowd which, no longer remaining at a distance, turns on the protagonist and hunts him down:

> "Stop thief! Stop thief!" The cry is taken up by a hundred voices, and the crowd accumulate at every turning. Away they fly, splashing through the mud, and rattling along the pavements: up go the

windows, out run the people, onward bear the mob, a whole audience desert Punch in the very thickest of the plot, and, joining
the rushing throng, swell the shout, and lend fresh vigour to the
cry, "Stop thief! Stop thief!"

"Stop thief! Stop thief!" There is a passion *for hunting something*
deeply implanted in the human breast. One wretched breathless
child, panting with exhaustion; terror in his looks; agony in his
eyes; large drops of perspiration streaming down his face; strains
every nerve to make head upon his pursuers; and as they follow on
his track, and gain upon him every instant, they hail his decreasing
strength with still louder shouts, and whoop and scream with joy.
(10)

Here the entire world seems to have turned animate and to be chasing
Oliver down the endless dreamlike corridors of the London labyrinth.
And the aim of the mob is not simply to catch him, but to "crowd"
him to death. The crowd "jostles" and "struggles" centripetally toward
Oliver, and will suffocate him or crush him if it can: " 'Give him a
little air!' 'Nonsense he don't deserve it' " (10). In the same way the
crowd tries to tear Fagin to pieces like a pack of wild animals when once
he is dragged out of his den into the light of day (50), and another
crowd, beside itself with rage and hatred, presses like a "strong struggling
current of angry faces" around the house where Sikes is at bay, "to curse
him" and kill him if they can (50).

The similarity of these three passages impresses upon us forcibly the
kinship between Oliver and the thieves. Fagin dies "for" Oliver the death
he would have died. The embodiment of all the evil in the novel, he
is the scapegoat whose death, even more than Sikes', destroys all that
evil, and makes it possible for Oliver to "live happily ever after." The
description of his "last night alive" and of Oliver's visit to the condemned
man forms the penultimate chapter of the novel, coming just before the
account of Oliver's subsequent happiness and preparing for it. In this
scene, Fagin says, quite correctly, that Oliver has betrayed him and
caused his death: "He has been the—the—somehow the cause of all
this" (52). In the delirium of his fear Fagin claims a secret friendship
and even kinship with Oliver, tells him where the papers containing the
clue to the mystery of his life are hidden, and tries to get Oliver to
smuggle him out of the prison. The few steps toward the gallows Oliver
and Fagin take together testify to their profound consubstantiality.
Oliver, by accepting the identity among honest men imposed upon him
by the discovery of the secrets of his origin, has betrayed the identity as
a pariah which was apparently his from birth. It is Oliver himself who
is the real spy in the novel. Fagin dies the death Oliver would have
died, but in choosing Mr. Brownlow's "little society" Oliver must betray
and destroy the underground society which Fagin has created for protection against a world in which he and the other thieves are useless

and despised, "the very scum and refuse of the land" (Preface to the third edition. *OT*, p. x).[1]

* * *

Indeed there is a good deal of covert sympathy even for Fagin, especially in the description of his capture and death. Fagin in jail is as much a figure to be pitied as hated (52), and it is clear that Dickens strongly identified himself with Fagin, and in writing of his death lived with intensity the death of the outcast, utterly cut off from society, hated by all the world, and implacably destroyed by it. It was, one feels, because he could imagine so vividly the life of the outcast that he strove so desperately in novel after novel to prove that the outcast was not really outcast, that there was a hidden identity waiting for him among the honest men who enjoy with complacency a secure status and the comforting sense that, like Dr. Losberne, they can act upon impulse and yet do no wrong because they are naturally and incorruptibly good (32).

Oliver, then, is in the same situation as Sikes or Fagin. For all three the human or material world is not simply unintelligible multiplicity in agitated motion. It is a great solid force which rushes in toward the isolated one at the center. There is escape neither underground nor out in the open for the outcasts. Both inside and out they are threatened by the remorselessly hostile wall of a world which converges on the central figure. ". . . the great, black, ghastly gallows clos[es] up their prospects, turn them where they may" (Preface to the third edition, *OT*, p. viii). They seek in vain for a tiny aperture through which they may escape.

The main axis of the nuclear structure of *Oliver Twist* is a fear of exclusion which alternates with a fear of enclosure. Between these two poles the novel oscillates. On the one hand there is the fear that one will be completely cut off from the world and from other men. Thrust into an empty world from which everything has receded to an unattainable distance, one is left only with a need, a lack, the need to be related to the world, to find a ground to stand on and a roof over one's head. On the other hand, there is the fear that the world will approach too near, that one will be buried alive, squeezed to death, or suffocated, that freedom and even life itself will be crushed out. At a level beneath the superficial coherence of narrated events, at a level where all the characters reduce themselves into isomorphic representations of a few basic possibilities, *Oliver Twist* is the search for a way of life which will escape from these two extremes. For the extremes of enclosure and exclusion come in the end to the same thing, from the point of view of individual existence. They are the failure to *be* someone, and to have that identity recognized by the outside world, to be someone in security and without guilt. The extreme of exclusion images that failure in a

---

1. See above, p. 5 [*Editor*].

total evaporation of the self into a murky world where nothing can be distinguished clearly or where everything has retreated to an unattainable distance. The extreme of enclosure images the loss of identity in a narrowing down of the limits of selfhood until finally one ceases altogether to exist—like a snuffed candle flame. Oliver requires some firm ground to stand on and a warm protective covering, material or human, around him and above him. In a world in which there is nothing but himself and a dark unsubstantial mist he is nothing, and he would rather be related to the world as a slave among slaves than not be related at all. But on the other hand the world must not approach too close. It must be a protective and approving gaze, not a suffocating coercion, a secure foundation, not the solid enclosure of the prison, or the grave: "Mother! dear, dear mother, bury me in the open fields—anywhere but in these dreadful streets. I should like to be where you can see my grave, but not in these close crowded streets; they have killed me." The passage is from the *Sketches by Boz,* but there, as in *Oliver Twist,* the city is the place where one is crushed to death by the walls and the crowds or suffocated by the "closeness."

Oliver's search, then, is for a physical and social world which will offer support but not coercion, protection but not imprisonment, which will be tangibly *there,* but there at a certain safe distance. It is a world of which he has had no knowledge except in his dreams.

Suddenly Oliver is extricated. He wakes to find himself in a kind of world he has never known. Both times when Oliver is transported into the good world there is an interval of unconsciousness between, followed by a period of serious illness. When he sinks into unconsciousness from the strain of his intolerable life there seems no possible escape. When he comes to his senses again he is in a transformed world. There is an absolute discontinuity between the two worlds. The movement from the bad world to the good one is as mysterious and as unpredictable as his initial incarceration in the dark world or as his redescent into the inferno when Fagin recaptures him. He simply finds everything suddenly changed. At first he does not know where he is, and the absolute transmutation of scene makes possible an absolute transmutation of self: "What room is this? Where have I been brought to? . . . This is not the place I went to sleep in." He has collapsed in the police office of the horrible Mr. Fang. He awakens to see "a motherly old lady, very neatly and precisely dressed" (12), sitting at needlework in an armchair by his curtained bed. All his past life seems a nightmare from which he has finally awakened to a life anterior to anything he has known in his actual life: "Weak, and thin, and pallid, he awoke at last from what seemed to have been a long and troubled dream" (12).

What are the characteristics of the new world in which Oliver so suddenly finds himself? Is it simply the opposite of the dark world of his

initial interment? Is it freedom, openness, light, intelligible order rather
than darkness, enclosedness, and incoherence?

*   *   *

Indeed, it soon becomes apparent that the country world is rather the
reverse of the subterranean city world than its opposite. The country
world combines the freedom Oliver had when he lay dying in the open
with the enclosedness of the claustral interiors to produce a protected
enclosure which is yet open to the outside and in direct contact with it.
It is a paradise not of complete freedom but of a cosy security which
looks out upon openness and enjoys it from the inside: "The little room
in which he was accustomed to sit, when busy at his books, was on the
ground-floor, at the back of the house. It was quite a cottage-room, with
a lattice-window: around which were clusters of jessamine and honeysuckle, that crept over the casement, and filled the place with their
delicious perfume. It looked into a garden, whence a wicket-gate opened
into a small paddock; all beyond, was fine meadow-land and wood.
There was no other dwelling near, in that direction; and the prospect it
commanded was very extensive" (34, and see 14). The ideal situation
in *Oliver Twist*, then, is to be securely enclosed in a refuge which is
yet open to the outside, in direct contact with the outside air and commanding an *extensive* view into the distance. Here Oliver possesses the
entire surrounding world, *commands* it, by being able to see it, and yet
he is secluded from view himself. He possesses intimacy, security, and
expansion, openness, breadth of view: "The great trees . . . converted
open and naked spots into choice nooks, where was a deep and pleasant
shade from which to look upon the wide prospect, steeped in sunshine,
which lay stretched beyond" (33).

*   *   *

Oliver knows now what he wants—a present which will be a protected
repose combining freedom and enclosure. But he does not know how
to possess this paradise on earth in permanent security. It seems to be
in perpetual danger of being at any moment overrun and replaced by
the dark past. The present, then, is altogether intolerable for Oliver,
whether he is in the midst of a dark enclosed world which is accelerating
toward his destruction, or whether he is in a calm protected world which
may at any time be invaded and destroyed by the other world. The
present in *Oliver Twist* is characterized by a failure to know who one
is or to attain any acceptable identity. It is also characterized by a failure
to understand the outside world. Oliver can only submit passively to a
succession of present moments which do not relate coherently to one
another. The world imposes a random rhythm of escape and capture.
Oliver has only his "sturdy spirit" to defend himself, and because of the
taboo against taking matters into his own hands he can use that spirit
only to keep himself alive by passive resistance. Time in this unrelieved

present either "steals tardily," slows down, coagulates, and freezes into an endless present of suffering, bewilderment, and interior emptiness, or, like a broken clock, it accelerates madly under the impulsion of fear toward the death that seems rushing out of the imminent future: "The day passed off. Day? There was no day: it was gone as soon as come— and night came on again; night so long, and yet so short; long in its dreadful silence, and short in its fleeting hours. . . . Eight—nine—ten. If it was not a trick to frighten him, and those were the real hours treading on each other's heels, where would he be, when they came round again! Eleven! Another struck, before the voice of the previous hour had ceased to vibrate. At eight, he would be the only mourner in his own funeral train; at eleven—" (52). The future then is a blank wall—an inevitable death by hanging. Only one dim hope appears. The present is able to be, through the phenomenon of affective memory, the reliving, the recapturing, of a past time.

* * *

Three distinct forms of repetition through memory of a past time may be distinguished in *Oliver Twist*.

First, there is the experience already described which links a present with a past moment in Oliver's own life. There is no escape here. Oliver is merely plunged back into the procession of enclosed and threatened moments which began with his birth and is carrying him implacably onward, even when he seems to have escaped, toward an outcast's death

But there is another form of memory, a form which seems to connect the present with a supernatural paradise, a paradise which is anterior to all Oliver's present life, but which the present seems somehow to reveal. And it is revealed as a promise, the promise of an eventual escape out of this world of pain and suffering.

* * *

But this is not what Oliver wants. All the intimations of a supernatural state of bliss which Oliver receives from the earthly world only serve to accentuate the shortcomings of the latter. What Oliver wants is to possess his heaven on earth. The "memories" of a prior state of bliss called forth by "peaceful country scenes" only separate more radically the present real earthly world and the distant unattainable paradise. ". . . heaven is," as Oliver says, "a long way off; and they are too happy there, to come down to the bedside of a poor boy" (12). Graham Greene has spoken of the "Manicheanism" of the world of *Oliver Twist*,[2] and indeed there does seem to be initially an absolute breach between heaven and the intolerable earthly world—which is a kind of hell. But the problem of the novel is precisely how to join these two apparently irreconcilable worlds, how to bring heaven to earth. It seems, though, that the only

2. See above, p. 131 [*Editor*].

way to reach heaven is through death. Again and again any state of calm
happiness, any beautiful landscape, and even any state of complete moral
goodness is equated with death.

                              *   *   *

But still Dickens can be caught up in the vision of a natural innocence
which is brought into this world at birth from a prenatal heaven and
which is regained at death after passing through a world which is predominantly evil: "Alas! How few of Nature's faces are left alone to
gladden us with their beauty! The cares, and sorrows, and hungerings,
of the world, change them as they change hearts; and it is only when
those passions sleep, and have lost their hold for ever, that the troubled
clouds pass off, and leave Heaven's surface clear. It is a common thing
for the countenances of the dead, even in that fixed and rigid state, to
subside into the long-forgotten expression of sleeping infancy, and settle
into the very look of early life . . ." (24). Heaven, then, is the place
where all that has been lost in this fallen world is regained, and it is a
place of which one may have glimpses momentarily athwart the almost
totally unrelieved gloom of this world.

There seems no escape from this world but by death.

However, one final form remains of the repetition through memory
of a past state: one may find signs in the present of a secret past life
which existed *on this earth* before one was born. When those signs are
understood, their revelations may be accepted as a definition of what
one really is. Then it will be possible to live ever afterward in a kind of
paradise on earth, a paradise regained which is the present lightened
and spiritualized because it is a repetition of one's prenatal earthly past.
If *Oliver Twist* is in one sense Oliver's procession through a sequence
of opaque and meaningless present moments, it is in another sense the
slow discovery, in the midst of that confusion, of a secret which will
make all seem orderly and significant. As in all of Dickens' novels, there
is a mystery at the center of apparently unrelated events which will make
them turn out in retrospect to be orderly and intelligible. Here the
mystery is the secret of Oliver's birth. When it is solved he can live
happily ever after because now he knows who he *is*. He discovers his
essence, his intrinsic nature, and with it acquires a place in society.

But the total dramatic pattern of *Oliver Twist* suggests that Oliver can
have happiness so completely in the end only because he has lost it so
completely at the beginning. If there had not been an absolute break in
the chain of time which determines each person's present identity by
an ineluctable series of causes and effects, and if there had not been an
absolute break in the chain of community relationships by which parents
and adults own, control, and judge, as well as protect, their children,
would the secure life Oliver covets have been so desirable after all? Does
not Dickens secretly enjoy the situation of the outcast, with an enjoyment
nonetheless intense for being hidden far beneath the surface? If the

outcast is, in one sense, entirely coerced, in another sense he is entirely free, entirely untrammeled by any direct ties to any other human being. Even if Oliver secretly and almost unconsciously believes that he is something other than the "bad 'un," destined for the gallows, which everyone names him, that belief has no evident source in the external world. It depends only on Oliver himself for its existence. And Oliver can claim his inheritance only after he has proved that he really is who he is in a world which does not give him any reflection or recognition of that identity. Oliver can only become himself by forming a relation between what he is initially, a wholly independent self, depending on and sustained by nothing external, and the self he discovers himself already to be. The distance between these two selves is absolutely necessary. Hence the extreme importance of the clause of Oliver's father's will providing that he shall inherit the money "only on the stipulation that in his minority he should never have stained his name with any public act of dishonour, meanness, cowardice, or wrong" (51).

Dickens, then, in a manner contrives to have both his contradictory needs simultaneously. Oliver is self-determining in that, without any knowledge of who he really is, he has had to defend his essence from the world that tries to make him a thief. But in the end he is entirely the protégé of the outside world, and submits without quarrel to a life under the approving eyes of Mr. Brownlow and the Maylies. Finally, when all the secrets are out, having been wrested by force from the heart of the dark world, Mr. Brownlow adopts Oliver "as his son," and Oliver has what he wants at last as a member of "a little society, whose condition approached as nearly to one of perfect happiness as can ever be known in this changing world" (53). He has the landscape of reconciled enclosure and freedom, now personified in Rose Maylie, literally his aunt, but in a way mother and sister to him too, and described in language which identifies her with the ideal scene of the novel: "I would show Rose Maylie in all the bloom and grace of early womanhood, shedding on her secluded path in life soft and gentle light, that fell on all who trod it with her, and shone into their hearts" (53). And he has the selfhood he has sought, a selfhood which he has not chosen or created, but which has been given to him from the outside: "Mr. Brownlow went on, from day to day, filling the mind of his adopted child with stores of knowledge, and becoming attached to him, more and more, as his nature developed itself, and showed the thriving seeds of all he wished him to become— . . . he traced in him new traits of his early friend, that awakened in his own bosom old remembrances, melancholy and yet sweet and soothing . . ." (53).

Oliver has at last what he wants. He has reconciled freedom and the desire for self-determination with the desire not to choose what he is to be, to have the choice made for him, and then to be protected and accepted by society. Mr. Brownlow *fills* the empty spirit of Oliver with

those "stores of knowledge" which will make him an authentic member
of the middle class, but this education only reveals that Oliver has been
all along potentially what Mr. Brownlow wants to make him in actuality.
His selfhood is both made for him by Mr. Brownlow and yet prior to
Mr. Brownlow's education of him. And this reconciliation of contradictory needs is possible because Oliver is willing to exist as the image
of his father, willing to take as the definition of his essential selfhood
those traits which are the repetition of his father's nature. He is willing
to accept an identification of himself which does not derive, ultimately,
from anything he has done, but only from what his parents were. In
order to escape from the harsh world into which he has been born, a
world in which the extreme of enclosedness combines with the extreme
of isolation, Oliver is willing to live out his life facing backward into
the past, spending with Rose Maylie "whole hours . . . in picturing the
friends whom they had so sadly lost" (53). He escapes from an intolerable
present and a frightening future by making the present a reduplication
of a past safely over and done with, and by turning his back altogether
on the future and on autonomous action. He lives happily ever after,
but only by living in a perpetual childhood of submission to protection
and direction from without.

The ending of *Oliver Twist* is a resolution of Dickens' single great
theme, the search of the outcast for status and authentic identity, but
it is a resolution which is essentially based on self-deception and on an
unwillingness to face fully his apprehension of the world. It is a resolution
which will not satisfy him for long.

HARRY STONE

Dickens and the Jews†

"I know," wrote Dickens in 1854, "of no reason the Jews can have
for regarding me as 'inimical' to them." It may seem curious that Dickens
could find no reason for such feelings, for even today, with his later
atonement on record, most well-read persons thinking of Dickens and
Jews can remember only the repulsive Fagin. Fagin's name, like Shylock's, has become a synonym for meanness and depravity, and Dickens'
and Shakespeare's villainous Jews are the best-known Jewish characters
in English literature. And yet, one can understand Dickens' protesting
his bewilderment at charges of anti-Semitism, for his attitude toward
Jews changed greatly between *Oliver Twist* (1837–39) and *Our Mutual
Friend* (1864–65).

† From *Victorian Studies* 2.3 (1959): 223–53. Reprinted by permission of the Trustees of Indiana
University.

What his attitude was originally, and what it grew to be, though often the subject of general remarks, has not received the detailed attention it deserves. Most writers on the subject have been content to expatiate on Fagin, mention Riah, and judge Dickens. Few have dealt with the abundant materials which lie outside *Oliver Twist* and *Our Mutual Friend,* and no one has used one of the most revealing sources for understanding Dickens' attitude toward Jews—the periodicals he edited from 1837 to 1839 and from 1850 until his death in 1870. The result has been an incomplete picture, or a picture drawn from a point of view which is so selective that it falsifies the major image while focusing a minor detail. That major image is important. For Dickens' drift from careless prejudice to at least an intellectual understanding is both a significant personal achievement and a revealing symptom of the evolving patterns of Victorian culture.

* * *

Oliver Twist grew out of an era and a literary tradition which was predominantly anti-Semitic. Laws, parliamentary debates, newspapers, magazines, songs, and plays, as well as novels, reflect the latent anti-Semitism which was a part of the early Victorian heritage. In 1830 a Jew could not open a shop within the city of London, be called to the Bar, receive a university degree, or sit in Parliament. Sir Robert Peel, who a few years later championed the Jewish cause, was still in 1830 opposing Jewish emancipation on the strange grounds that the restricted Jew was not like his free compatriots. "The Jew," said Sir Robert, speaking against the removal of Jewish disabilities, "is not a degraded subject of the state; he is rather regarded in the light of an alien—he is excluded because he will not amalgamate with us in any of his usages or habits —he is regarded as a foreigner. In the history of the Jews . . . we find enough to account for the prejudice which exists against them." That prejudice was accentuated by the occupations Jews were compelled to enter by English law and custom. In 1830 the majority of England's twenty to thirty thousand Jews earned their living through buying and selling old clothes, peddling, and moneylending. Portraits in fiction of Jewish clothesdealers staggering under huge bags of rags, bearded peddlers haggling with country housewives, and miserly usurers gloating over their secret treasures were given reality not only by a long literary tradition but by the intermittent evidence of the London streets. And the exotic evil which the average Londoner of that day felt sure lay hidden in bag or beard or countinghouse was occasionally confirmed by sensational newspaper reports. In the summer of 1830 the respectable citizenry of London were being diverted by the trial of one Isaac (Ikey) Solomons, a Jewish fence who, like Fagin, dealt in stolen jewelry, clothing, and fabrics. Ikey Solomons, although acquitted on all charges of burglary and theft, was finally convicted of possessing stolen goods and sentenced to seven years' transportation. His case was so notorious that a play of the period entitled *Van Diemen's Land* was rechristened *Ikey Solomons*, and one of its minor characters, Barney Fence, a stereotyped stage-Jew, was transformed into Ikey himself.

Such a transformation reflected the ubiquitous anti-Semitism of the period. The early Victorian Londoner, for instance, could have his suspicions about Jews intensified by the humorous *Punch* as well as the sober *Times*. *Punch*, when founded in 1841, was a liberal journal which usually espoused humanitarian reforms. Yet it was anti-Jewish during most of the period. It opposed Jewish emancipation, drew cartoons of bloated and bejeweled Jews, made jokes at the expense of Disraeli's Jewish origins, and poked fun at Jewish occupations. Leech, in a representative cartoon, drew a picture of the House of Commons populated by a grossly caricatured array of pudgy, thick-lipped, dusky-chinned Jews (XII [1847], 149). *Punch's* attitude was predictable, for in spite of its radical leanings, many members of its staff—G. A. à Beckett, Leech, Thackeray, Jerrold, and Brooks (all friends of Dickens)—had exhibited in varying degrees the pandemic anti-Semitism of the period.

It was difficult to escape anti-Jewish prejudice. Victorian street literature reflected that prejudice as faithfully as Parliament and *Punch*. Songs about Jews were popular in early nineteenth-century England, and the typical contemporary "Jew's Song" was loaded with slander. * * * The typical Jew (on the stage, for example) had changed little since Marlowe's Barabas and Shakespeare's Shylock. He was a rapacious moneylender, or perhaps later, a thieving peddler or old-clothes dealer. By the late eighteenth century he usually shuffled about the stage in black gabardine and a broadbrimmed hat, poked his red hair, red whiskers, and hooked nose into the faces of those with whom he haggled, and spoke in thick outlandish accents. The best-known dramatists of the preceding age—Cibber, Foote, Fielding, Garrick, and Sheridan—whose plays still dominated the boards in Dickens' youth, had all created Jews who were mean or wicked. And later nondramatic writers—Lamb, Cobbett, and Hewlett, for example—continued the tradition.

In his early writings, Dickens reflects the dominant anti-Semitism of his time. Although (with the exception of *Oliver Twist*) there are no extended Jewish portraits in his early works, his writings contain many revealing allusions, comments, and descriptions. The Jew who emerges from these references engages in standard "Jewish" occupations, possesses the stage-Jew's physical characteristics, and exhibits supposedly "Jewish" mannerisms. The Jews in *Sketches by Boz* (1833–37) are old-clothes dealers, costume suppliers, sheriff's officers, sponging-house proprietors, and the like. One meets in *Sketches by Boz* "red-headed and red-whiskered Jews who forcibly haul you into their squalid houses, and thrust you into a suit of clothes, whether you will or not," and Dickens adds he detests such Jews. Mr. Nathan, a costume supplier in *Sketches*

by Boz, is another "red-headed and red-whiskered Jew." And the sponging house described in *Sketches* (the description based upon Dickens'
trip to Sloman's sponging house in 1834 to rescue his father) is run by
a Mr. Solomon Jacobs and entourage. The Jews in *Pickwick* (1836–38)
are also costume brokers, sheriff's officers, peddlers, and old-clothes
dealers.

Dickens' Jews are unpleasant and conventionalized; and through these
Jews he transmits his temper and that of the age. "He's richer than any
Jew," says Quilp in the *Old Curiosity Shop* (1840–41); and in *Barnaby
Rudge* (1841), when Gashford thinks of Jews, he thinks of money and
beards. Dickens' image of the Jews frequently emerges by implication
rather than direct statement. In *Dombey and Son* (1846–48), after in-
troducing a Jew of "Mosaic Arabian cast of countenance," who is vulgar
and insolent and who inquires with materialistic effrontery "what the
figure of them crimson and gold hangings might have been, when new
bought," Dickens goes on to label an incoming swarm of secondhand
dealers "Jew and Christian," perhaps in an attempt to sound unpreju-
diced, but the effect of the phrase is to call attention to the Jews and
associate them once more with repellent traits: "Herds of shabby vam-
pires, Jew and Christian, overrun the house, sounding the plate-glass
mirrors with their knuckles, striking discordant octaves on the grand
piano, drawing wet forefingers over the pictures, breathing on the blades
of the best dinner-knives, punching the squabs of chairs and sofas with
their dirty fists, touzling the featherbeds, opening and shutting all the
drawers, balancing the silver spoons and forks, looking into the very
threads of the drapery and linen, and disparaging everything."

Dickens does not like these men, and he despises their occupation
and methods. He usually takes a similar attitude toward any Jewish
entrepreneur. He scorns the aggressive Jewish secondhand clothes sales-
men, and he condescends to the Jewish costume brokers. His feelings
never flare into active hatred; they smolder fitfully in a vague hostility.
"Bills," says Mr. Micawber (*David Copperfield*, 1849–50), are "a convenience to the mercantile world, for which, I believe, we are originally
indebted to the Jews." And then Micawber adds that Jews "appear to
me to have had a devilish deal too much to do with them ever since."

* * *

Oliver Twist, then, was the work of an author who accepted and
reflected the anti-Semitism of his milieu. And yet *Oliver Twist* is not
as anti-Semitic as one might expect; Fagin is less a premeditated attack
upon the Jews than a convenient villain drawn to an ancient pattern.
He exhibits, for instance, a number of stereotyped stage-Jew characteristics: red hair and whiskers, hooked nose, shuffling gait, and long gabardine coat and broadbrimmed hat. Furthermore, he is a dealer in
secondhand clothes and trinkets, the Jewish occupation par excellence.
And Dickens makes him, in accordance with the traditional recipe,

frightening and repellent. When the reader first meets him he is described as "a very old shrivelled Jew, whose villainous-looking and repulsive face was obscured by a quantity of matted red hair"; and his actions in the book and his miserable end fulfill his menacing introduction. But Fagin is strangely lacking in other traits of the literary Jew. He has no lisp, dialect, or nasal intonation (although Barney, a minor confederate of Fagin, described as "another Jew: younger than Fagin, but nearly as vile and repulsive in appearance," talks with a perpetual cold in his head, saying, "Dot a shoul" for "Not a soul," and so forth. And Fagin goes through no act, ritual, or pattern which identifies him as a Jew. Actually, aside from his conventionalized physical traits and old-clothes dealings, his main claim to Jewishness is the fact that Dickens constantly labels him "the Jew." It seems fair to assume that Fagin was a Jew because for Dickens and his readers he made a picturesque and believable villain.

But that Dickens could create Fagin is a reflection of his indifference to the implications of his portrait. And this is true even though he attempted here and there to underline the distinction between Fagin the individual and Fagin the Jew. In Fagin's first appearance he is portrayed toasting a sausage—an act which immediately brands him a renegade Jew. And in the condemned cell, in one of the reader's final glimpses of him, Dickens again contrasts him with the Jews as a whole. "Venerable men of his own persuasion," he writes, "had come to pray beside him, but he had driven them away with curses. They renewed their charitable efforts, and he beat them off." It seems strange that Dickens could believe these touches would offset the implications of the remainder of his portrait, but his attitude toward the Jews was negligent at best, and he probably gave little thought to Fagin's anti-Semitic ramifications.

Yet the times were changing and Dickens was changing with them. The years 1830 to 1860 witnessed a steady rise in the status of English Jewry. Legal barriers were swept away, commercial restrictions removed, and social antagonisms lessened. Jews held offices in local and national government, became connected through marriage with prominent families, took part increasingly in the social and artistic affairs of the country, and grew in power and numbers. The most dramatic token of their rising status occurred on 26 July 1858 when, after years of struggle, Baron Lionel Rothschild was allowed to use a modified oath and take his seat in Parliament. This symbolic event correctly mirrored the mood of the nation, for although anti-Semitism was still common and even fashionable, it was confined more and more to emotional and personal channels; the Jew's right to exercise the prerogatives of a British subject was increasingly admitted.

*   *   *

* * * In 1867–68, a few years before his death, a new edition of his works, "The Charles Dickens Edition," was being issued by Chapman and Hall. Dickens revised the volumes in this edition for copyright purposes, supplying new or modified prefaces, cutting phrases here or there, canceling occasional passages, adding minor touches, and making other corrections. The text of this edition has been followed in almost all subsequent reprintings of his books.

In *Oliver Twist* he made hundreds of emendations, but the most important and most numerous by far concern Fagin and the Jews. Beginning with Chapter XXXIX, he went through *Oliver Twist* and eliminated the bulk of the references to Fagin as "the Jew," canceling that term entirely, or replacing it with "he," or with "Fagin." For example, in Chapter XXXIX, he struck out twenty-three references to Fagin as "the Jew"; in Chapters XLIV and XLV (a single chapter in the original version), he eliminated thirty-one of thirty-seven references to "the Jew"; and in Chapter LII, in which the very title is changed from "The Jew's Last Night Alive" to "Fagin's Last Night Alive," he canceled eleven allusions to Fagin as "the Jew," leaving a single reference to "the Jew" in the entire chapter.

The effect of these changes is to eliminate, for the most part, the one important link connecting Fagin with the Jews. In the last third of the revised version, page after page which had formerly emphasized that a Jew was doing this or that bit of villainy, now merely reported that Fagin was doing it; and whole segments of the novel contained scarcely the mention of "Jew."

These final revisions are doubly significant. For Dickens' journey had been the journey of his times. When the period opened Mordecai was "clinking his shining chink," *Punch* was reveling in gross caricatures of Jews, and Thackeray was writing parody crime-fiction under the libelous pseudonym of "Ikey Solomons, Jr." Sixty years later, when the period drew to a close, the Jews had largely achieved their present status in English society. But in 1864 the battle was still hot; Jews were still struggling for recognition and understanding. At this juncture Dickens chose to help the Jews, and this in spite of his own lingering prejudices and misconceptions. There was no hypocrisy in this. He had moved with the changing times, he had undergone an undoubted intellectual conversion, but he was not always able to expunge the emotions and associations of his formative years, of the more prejudiced age which had set its imprint upon him. Yet in terms of his intentions, in terms of his attempts to influence the public, he had, in his artistic lifetime, come full circle: not merely because he created a good Jew to blot out a bad one, but because he enforced in many ways—in his letters, books, magazines, and emendations—the doctrine he had enunciated through Riah's lips, a doctrine he had been approaching slowly, but had only recently accepted. His silent excisions in *Oliver Twist* were one more way station in his journey; his voluntary emendations demonstrate again that intellectually at least he had come to understand and regret a prej-

udice more typical of an earlier day. In his new understanding he was
mirroring the new times, just as in his earlier anti-Semitism he had
reflected the old. And yet by 1864 and *Our Mutual Friend* he was not
merely mirroring; despite his occasional confusions and ambivalences,
he was urging forward the Victorian advance toward toleration. For in
his relationship with the Jews, as in other areas of his life and art, Dickens
was a maker as well as a creature of his times.

PHILIP COLLINS

[Dickens and Murder]†

'I used, when I was at school,' wrote Dickens, 'to take in the *Terrific
Register*, making myself unspeakably miserable, and frightening my very
wits out of my head, for the small charge of a penny weekly; which
considering that there was an illustration to every number, in which
there was always a pool of blood, and at least one body, was cheap.' As
a young man, he still had a 'passion for sensational novels', which he
would 'carry away by the pile' from his circulating library. Boys and
men of all periods have shared these tastes, for which popular literature
and drama has catered in various fashions. Often the sensational stories
have been set in the past, or in a foreign country where evil notoriously
flourishes, or in both. Italy was a favourite for Elizabethan dramatists,
as for Gothic romancers: the 'Westerns' of today, and Mr Graham
Greene's sultry settings, are variants on the old methods of escape into
violence and vice. Early in his career, Dickens began exploiting this,
along with his other strong suits—humour, pathos, and social reformism. *Sketches by Boz* contained two short stories of melodramatic type,
'The Black Veil' and 'The Drunkard's Death'; he was proud of these,
and Edgar Allan Poe highly praised the former, but they are wretched
efforts—as are the stories of violence interpolated into *Pickwick Papers*,
the significance of which has been discussed in a famous passage by Mr
Edmund Wilson. But before *Pickwick* was begun, Dickens had already
formed the idea for two novels which were to present evil and violence
more fully and successfully—*Barnaby Rudge* and (as Professor Kathleen
Tillotson has recently argued) *Oliver Twist*.[1]

As everyone has noted, *Barnaby Rudge* might have been given the
sub-title of *Waverley—'Tis Sixty Years Since*—and Scott is certainly an
important impulse behind this novel. Scott was much the most popular

---

† From "Murder: From Bill Sikes to Bradley Headstone," in *Dickens and Crime* (London, 1962)
256–63. Reprinted by permission of The Macmillan Press Ltd.
1. Kathleen Tillotson, "Oliver Twist," *Essays and Studies* (1959): 87–91; Edmund Wilson, *The
Wound and the Bow* (N.Y., 1941) 16–17.

novelist of any repute before Dickens; his influence was omnipresent, and had been felt in the sensation-novel as well as elsewhere. Ainsworth's Preface to *Rookwood* (1834) does not mention Scott, but Scott provides half the formula: 'I resolved to attempt a story in the bygone style of Mrs Radcliffe (which had always inexpressible charms for me), substituting an old English squire, an old English manorial residence, and an old English highwayman, for the Italian marchese, the castle, and the brigand of the great mistress of Romance.' Romance, he thought, was 'destined shortly to undergo an important change', as the structure inherited from Horace Walpole, Monk Lewis, Mrs Radcliffe and Maturin was modified by the influence of the recent German and French writers, Hoffman, Tieck, Hugo, Dumas, Balzac and Lacroix. *Rookwood*, set in the mid-eighteenth century, and centred on Dick Turpin, was vastly popular, and a few years later Ainsworth repeated the formula, with even greater success, in *Jack Sheppard* (1839), the hero of which is a housebreaker instead of highwayman, the period being now Jonathan Wild's London. With this novel, Ainsworth became 'the literary lion of the day', a contemporary recalled. 'For a time Dickens's star paled.' Ainsworth was not alone in this field, of course. Lytton's *Paul Clifford* (1830) had a highwayman-hero, and his *Pelham* (1828), *Eugene Aram* (1832), *Ernest Maltravers* (1837) and *Alice* (1838) also had crime-themes, while in 1834 Charles Whitehead published his *Autobiography of Jack Ketch* and *Lives of the Highwaymen*.

Reviewers began talking of a 'Newgate School of Novelists', and they included *Oliver Twist* among its products. At the end of the 1830s, Thackeray serialised in *Fraser's Magazine* (1839–40) his anti-Newgate School novel *Catherine*, and there Dickens stands accused beside Bulwer Lytton and Ainsworth. A couple of years later, an early number of *Punch* contained among its 'Literary Recipes' some advice about how to cook up 'A Startling Romance'—

> Take a small boy, charity, factory, carpenter's apprentice, or otherwise, as occasion may serve—stew him well down in vice—garnish largely with oaths and flash songs—boil him in a cauldron of crime and improbabilities. Season equally with good and bad qualities—infuse petty larceny, affection, benevolence, and burglary, honour and housebreaking, amiability and arson—boil all gently. Stew down a mad mother—a gang of robbers—several pistols—a bloody knife. Serve up with a couple of murders—and season with a hanging-match.
>
> N.B. Alter the ingredients to a beadle and a work-house—the scenes may be the same, but the whole flavour of vice will be lost, and the boy will turn out a perfect pattern.—Strongly recommended for weak stomachs.

Again, Dickens—though more suitable for 'weak stomachs'—finds himself indicted with Ainsworth, Lytton, Mrs Trollope and others here glanced at: and much the same was being said by other reviewers, preachers, and social workers. A Police Commissioner reported several young delinquents as testifying to the popularity of *Oliver Twist*. 'On Sundays,' said one of them, describing his fellow youngsters at Common Lodging Houses, 'they play cards, dominoes, and pitch-halfpenny, read *Jack Sheppard*, *Oliver Twist*, *Martha Willis*, and publications of the kind, and plan robberies.'

Dickens was very annoyed to be put in this category. He admired *Pelham* and *Paul Clifford* ('admirable and most powerful'), and he was personally friendly with Lytton and Whitehead. In 1838 he and Ainsworth and Forster formed a 'Trio Club'—they were inseparable companions at this period. He had inserted a footnote in *Sketches by Boz* praising *Rookwood*, but in the 1839 edition he deleted it, having changed his mind on the subject, doubtless because, having been attacked in the reviews along with Ainsworth, he realised how little, in fact, their fictional aims coincided, and wanted to dissociate himself from Ainsworth as far as was decent. It was difficult to do so explicitly, not only because Ainsworth was a close friend, but also because *Jack Sheppard* had begun appearing in *Bentley's Miscellany* shortly before Dickens handed over to him the editorship of this journal. The further fact, that Cruikshank illustrated both *Oliver Twist* and *Jack Sheppard*, doubtless encouraged the public and the reviewers to exaggerate the resemblance between the two novels. Dickens wrote privately to a friend in 1839: 'I am by some jolter-headed enemies most unjustly and untruly charged with having written a book after Mr Ainsworth's fashion. Unto these jolter-heads and their intensely concentrated humbug I shall take an early opportunity of temperately replying.' He wanted to 'disavow any sympathy with that school', and he had no sympathy at all for 'the late lamented John Sheppard', but he had to wait for a suitable opportunity to do so and to shield himself without seeming 'ungenerous and unmanly'.

The preface to the 1841 edition of *Oliver Twist* provided an occasion for 'saying a few words in explanation of my aim and object'.[2] Fortified by an epigraph from *Tom Jones*, and invoking 'examples and precedents . . . in the noblest range of English literature' (Fielding, Defoe, Goldsmith, Smollett, Richardson, and Mackenzie), he defends his choice of characters 'from the most criminal and degraded of London's population' and his method of presenting them.

> I had read of thieves by scores—seductive fellows (amiable for the most part), faultless in dress, plump in pocket, choice in horseflesh, bold in bearing, fortunate in gallantry, great at a song, a bottle, pack of cards or dice-box, and fit companions for the bravest. But

2. See above, pp. 3–7 [*Editor*].

I had never met (except in Hogarth) with the miserable reality. It appeared to me that to draw a knot of such associates in crime as really do exist; to paint them in all their deformity, in all their wretchedness, in all the squalid poverty of their lives; to show them as they really are, for ever skulking uneasily through the dirtiest paths of life, with the great, black, ghastly gallows closing up their prospect, turn them where they may; it appeared to me that to do this, would be to attempt a something which was greatly needed, and which would be a service to society.

He excludes *Paul Clifford* from his imputations (though in fact its moral casuistry is decidedly vulnerable, rather in the way of Mr Graham Greene, the Bulwer Lytton *de nos jours*), and it is clearly *Rookwood* and *Jack Sheppard* that he has most in mind, though he mentions no names. He also attacks the Italianised Gothic romances and dramas—or, at least, those people who are enchanted by 'a Massaroni in green velvet' but find 'a Sikes in fustian . . . insupportable'. 'I will not, for these readers, abate one hole in the Dodger's coat, or one scrap of curl-paper in the girl's dishevelled hair,' he proclaims, though he assures the reader that, while telling 'the stern and plain truth, . . . unattractive and repulsive', he will 'banish from the lips of the lowest character . . . any expression that could by possibility offend; and rather lead to the unavoidable inference that its existence was of the most debased and vicious kind, than to prove it elaborately by words and deeds'. In later editions, indeed, as Professor Tillotson has shown, he progressively bowdlerised the mild vocabulary that resulted from this policy, though in its original edition even the nineteen-year-old maiden Queen Victoria was able to read it without scandal. She found it 'excessively interesting'.

Dickens certainly was justified in distinguishing his purposes from Ainsworth's. 'Turpin was the hero of my boyhood,' Ainsworth had acknowledged in the Preface to *Rookwood*; and, referring to the famous 'ride to York' passage, he wrote, 'So thoroughly did I identify myself with the flying highwayman that, once started, I found it impossible to halt.' (He wrote the whole hundred pages, indeed, at one sitting of twenty-four hours.) He made no pretence of a moral purpose: 'I fear I have but imperfectly fulfilled the office imposed upon me; having, as I will freely confess, had, throughout, an eye rather on the reader's amusement than his edification.' And at the end of the novel he offered a final salute to his hero: 'Turpin (why disguise it?) was hanged at York in 1739. His firmness deserted him not at the last. . . . Oh rare Dick Turpin! . . . Perhaps, we may have placed him in too favourable a point of view; and yet we know not. . . .' Jack Sheppard's exploits were recounted with a similar frank sensationalism, uncontrolled by any moral curiosity.

Dickens never indulges his criminals like this: nor does he attempt the more ambitious 'metaphysical speculation and analysis' that Bulwer Lytton had claimed as his sanction for presenting his criminals so sympathetically. Eugene Aram, according to Lytton, was 'a person who, till the detection of the crime for which he was sentenced [murder], had appeared of the mildest character and the most unexceptionable morals . . . so benevolent that he would rob his own to administer to the necessities of another, so humane that he would turn aside from the worm in his path. . . .' Dickens had no interest in such alleged complexities of character (for him, as we have seen, murderers were always men of vicious temperament), nor did he in *Oliver Twist* or elsewhere, make a central issue of what Lytton claimed as his two-fold object in *Paul Clifford*:

> First, to draw attention to two errors in our penal institutions— viz., a vicious Prison-discipline, and a sanguinary Criminal Code—the habit of corrupting the boy by the very punishment that ought to redeem him, and then hanging the man, at the first occasion, as the easiest way of getting rid of our own blunders. . . . A second and lighter object . . . was to show that there is nothing essentially different between vulgar vice and fashionable vice—and that the slang of the one circle is but an easy paraphrase of the cant of the other.

Dickens was willing to use such arguments on behalf of minor offenders, such as Nancy, or of characters whose crimes (generally unspecified) were committed long ago, like Magwitch: but he never condones or invites a sympathetic understanding for his major and active criminals.

Nevertheless, despite his differences from the 'Newgate School', he belonged to it. *Oliver Twist*, it should be remembered, was the first novel he had written off his own bat. The idea of *Pickwick* had not been his, but its huge popularity was an invitation to him to repeat its success with a further comic novel. He surprised and to some extent disappointed his public by writing *Oliver Twist* instead. *Oliver* belongs very much to the late 1830s, and could not have been written at any other time. 'Un Roman au Gout du Jour', is Professor Monod's appropriate title for his useful chapter on this novel in *Dickens romancier*.[3] Though protesting explicitly and implicitly against some of the moral obliquities of the 'Newgate Novel', Dickens was drawn to the subject of *Oliver Twist*— as to the earlier 'Visit to Newgate'—more by the desire to exploit this exciting material than by any high-minded cathartic intention. Even Thackeray, whose *Catherine* was much more explicitly and insistently an anti-Newgate novel, found himself developing a moral wobble as he became involved in his subject.[4] It was 'a mistake all through', he decided soon afterwards—'it was not made disgusting enough that is the fact,

3. Sylvère Monod, *Dickens the Novelist* (Norman: U of Oklahoma P, 1968).
4. See above, pp. 408–10 [*Editor*].

and the triumph of it would have been to make readers so horribly
horrified as to cause them to give up or rather throw up the book and
all of it's kind, whereas you see the author had a sneaking kindness for
his heroine, and did not like to make her utterly worthless.' Thackeray
was, rightly, less severe upon *Oliver Twist* than upon Lytton's 'juggling
and thimblerigging with virtue and vice' and Ainsworth's amorality, and
he chiefly attacked *Oliver Twist* at its weakest point (in this respect)—
the virtues imputed to Nancy. Anyway, he argues, such novels 'fami-
liarise the public with notions of crime. . . . In the name of common-
sense, let us not expend our sympathies on cut-throats, and other such
prodigies of evil!'

Few would now wish to attack or defend Nancy on moral grounds,
her unreality as a literary creation removing her from the area of discussion: it is an index of changing taste and outlook that she could, at
that time, arouse such denunciations, or, indeed, high praise from many
critics who had misgivings about the moral tendency, or the literary
quality, of other aspects of the book. It is not Nancy, but Bill Sikes,
who still excites our interest, and raises critical and moral problems,
and we of course have a further interest in this character, which was
denied to the original readers and reviewers. I refer to the Public Reading,
Sikes and Nancy, which Dickens delivered in the last years of his life
—a performance greatly admired, and deplored, at the time, and said
by some of his friends to have caused, or hastened, his death. As he
claimed in his Preface to *Oliver Twist*, Dickens had stripped crime of
the charms and allurements which it bore in many contemporary novels
and plays. 'The cold, wet, shelterless midnight streets of London; the
foul and frowsy dens, where vice is closely packed and lacks the room
to turn; the haunts of hunger and disease, the shabby rags that scarcely
hold together: where are the attractions of these things?' Nancy's behaviour, he said, was based on what he had often seen and read of 'in
actual life around me', and he had, 'for years, tracked it through many
profligate and noisome ways.' He did not merely rely on the common
repute of the Saffron Hill area where Fagin lives, its thieves' dens, 'flash-
houses,' and stolen-handkerchief trade; he knew the area well. Many
independent reports of it provide striking parallels, and several readers
familiar with the facts acknowledge the accuracy of *Oliver Twist* as a
guide to Metropolitan criminal life of this period. Fagin was, as everyone
saw, based on the famous Jewish fence, Ikey Solomon, and his methods
of employing and training boy pick-pockets were the standard practice,
and remained so for several decades. Even Sikes, it has been said, was
based on an actual criminal. A friend of Cruikshank's recorded that a
burglar named Bill was among the visitors to Cruikshank's parlour, and
so were a girl and a boy on whom Nancy and Oliver were based. ' "Jaw
away, Bill," Dickens would say, and Dickens took shorthand notes while
Cruikshank did the sketching.' But this story is clearly as apocryphal as

Cruikshank's fantastic claim that it was he, not Dickens, that devised
Oliver Twist.

Within his self-imposed limits of a decent reticence, Dickens creates
a convincing and accurate picture of the London underworld, rather
over-emphasising the squalor and misery, and suppressing its feckless
jollity. Beyond its documentary value—which is considerable—the
novel remains of course a powerful symbol of moral evil and darkness.
Fagin, Dickens told Forster when writing the concluding chapters, 'is
such an out and outer that I don't know what to make of him;' Sikes,
he wrote in the Preface, was one of those 'insensible and callous natures
that do become, at last, utterly and irredeemably bad'. Sikes had been
bad enough, at the beginning of the book. He is first introduced, shouting
oaths and kicking his already much-injured dog across the room:

> The man who growled out these words, was a stoutly-built fellow
> about five-and-thirty, in a black velveteen coat, very soiled drab
> breeches, lace-up half-boots, and gray cotton stockings, which in-
> closed a bulky pair of legs, with large, swelling calves—the kind
> of legs, which, in such costume, always look in an unfinished and
> incomplete state without a set of fetters to garnish them. He had a
> brown hat on his head, and a dirty belcher handkerchief round his
> neck; with the long, frayed ends of which he smeared the beer from
> his face as he spoke. He disclosed, when he had done so, a broad,
> heavy countenance with a beard of three day's growth, and two
> scowling eyes; one of which displayed various parti-coloured symp-
> toms of having been recently damaged by a blow.

His coarse brutality is insisted upon at every subsequent entrance: so are
the squalor and uncertainty of his criminal life. The hideout in Spitalfields to which he retreats after the Chertsey housebreaking is described
as 'a mean and badly-furnished apartment, of very limited size; lighted
only by one small window in the shelving roof, and abutting on a close
and dirty lane. . . . A great scarcity of furniture, and total absence of
comfort, together with the disappearance of all such small movables as
spare clothes and linen, bespoke a state of extreme poverty'. He bullies,
indeed terrifies, the pathetic boy-hero Oliver; then he brutally murders
his mistress Nancy, when she, having been touched by Oliver's sufferings, has tried to help him to escape from the clutches of the gang. It
is, however, at this point that Sikes becomes, in a sense, a sympathetic
character.

*   *   *

JOHN BAYLEY

Oliver Twist: "Things as they really are"†

Oliver Twist is a modern novel. It has the perennially modern pretension of rejecting the unreality of a previous mode, of setting out to show us 'things as they really are'. But its modernity is more radical and more unsettling than this pretension implies; it can still touch us—as few novels out of the past can—on a raw nerve; it can still upset and discountenance us. *Pickwick* is not modern. It is a brilliant and successful recreation of the English novel's atmospheres and personalities; but Dickens, like Kipling, had a bargain with his daemon not to repeat a success. It was not *Pickwick* that made Thackeray ruefully praise Dickens's perpetual modernity, or Chesterton announce that Dickens had remained modern while Thackeray had become a classic.

Oliver Twist lacks only one attribute of the modern novel—complete self-consciousness. No novelist has profited more richly than Dickens from not examining what went on in his own mind. His genius avoids itself like a sleep-walker avoiding an open window. Chesterton says what a good thing it is we are not shown Pecksniff's thoughts—they would be too horrible—but the point about Pecksniff is that he has no thoughts. he is as much of a sleep-walker as Dickens: he is the perfect hypocrite because he does not know what he is like. Dickens recoiled from what he called 'dissective' art, and if he had been able and willing to analyse the relation between our inner and outer selves he could never have created the rhetoric that so marvellously ignores the distinction between them. Unlike us, he had no diagrammatic view of mind, no constricting terminology for the psyche. The being of Bumble, Pecksniff, Mrs. Gamp is not compartmented: their inner being *is* their outer self. When Mrs. Gamp says: 'We never know what's hidden in each other's hearts; and if we had glass windows there, we'd need to keep the shutters up, some of us, I do assure you'—she is saying something that will be true of John Jasper and Bradley Headstone, but the great early characters are in fact windowed and shutterless. Noah Claypole carousing with Charlotte over the oysters, a *mass* of bread and butter in his hand; Bumble announcing the cause of Oliver's rebellion to Mrs. Sowerberry—' "It's not madness, Ma'am, it's meat", said the beadle after a few moments of deep meditation'—their monstrosity luxuriates without depth or concealment. When Proust sets out to 'overgo' the Dickensian monster with his Charlus and Françoise, the ebullience and energy are seen to proceed

† From *Dickens and the Twentieth Century*, ed. John Gross and Gabriel Pearron (London, 1962) 49–64. Reprinted by permission.

from a creative centre which is meticulous, reflective, and the reverse of energetic: the peculiar Victorian harmony of created and creating energy is lost.

Their wholeness and harmony have a curious effect on the evil of Dickens's monsters: it sterilizes it in performance but increases it in idea. The energy of Fagin or Quilp seems neutral; there is not enough gap between calculation and action for it to proceed to convincingly evil works. By contrast, Iago and Verhovensky are monsters because they know what they are doing; their actions let us loathe them and recoil from them into freedom, but we cannot recoil from Dickens's villains: they are the more frightening and haunting because we cannot expel them for what they do; they have the unexpungable nature of our own nightmares and our own consciousness.

We cannot recoil—that is the point. For in spite of the apparent openness of its energy and indignation *Oliver Twist* is in fact the kind of novel in which we are continually oppressed by the disingenuousness of our own impulses and fantasies, the kind of novel in which the heroine, say, is immured in a brothel, and in which we, like her, both shrink from the fate and desire it.

*   *   *

Oliver Twist is not a satisfying novel—it does not liberate us. In achieving what might be called the honesty of the dream world it has to stay in prison. The sense of complete reality in fiction can perhaps only be achieved by the author's possessing, and persuading his reader to share, a sense of different worlds, different and indeed almost incompatible modes of feeling and being. The awareness of difference is the awareness of freedom, and it is, moreover, the knowledge of reality we normally experience in life. But in *Oliver Twist* there are no such contrasts, no such different worlds. Even the apparent contrast between Fagin's world and that of Rose Maylie and Mr. Brownlow is not a real one, and this is not because the happy Brownlow world is rendered sentimentally and unconvincingly by Dickens, but because the two do in fact co-exist in consciousness: they are twin sides of the same coin of fantasy, not two real places that exist separately in life. And there is no true activity in the two worlds, only the guilty or desperately innocent daydreams of our double nature.

*   *   *

As we shall see, Dickens frequently defends himself against the charge of using literary devices and conventions by pointing out their similarity to real life, and he seems to imply that he is using the dream atmosphere as a kind of convention in this spirit. He gives two accounts of the nature of waking dreams, the first at Fagin's, and the second when just after the flower episode Oliver sees Fagin and Monks at the window of the Maylie's parlour and their eyes meet. 'There is a kind of sleep that steals upon us sometimes which, while it holds the body prisoner, does not free the mind from a sense of things about it, and enable it to ramble at its pleasure.' (Ch. 34.) So similar are the two accounts of this state that it seems likely Dickens repeated himself accidentally in the hurry of composition (for the second half of the novel was written under great pressure), but the effect is none the less potent for that. It is a dream from which Oliver awakes to find it true, even though no footprints of the pair can be found. It recalls the earlier waking dream, when he lay watching Fagin sorting his stolen goods, and we realize it is not physical distance that keeps him from Fagin's house, a house which had once belonged to respectable people like the Maylies, and in which the mirrors of the unused rooms where Fagin and Monks confer now only reflect the dusty floor and the slimy track of the snail.

That the two worlds are one in the mind appears even in Cruickshank's drawings, where Oliver often has a distinct look of Fagin. Henry James remarked that as a child the pictures of the good places and people frightened him more than the bad![1] It is often said, and with some justice, that Dickens muddles the message of his novel by making Oliver immune to an environment which is denounced as necessarily corrupting. But Oliver is not psychologically immune, nor is Dickens, nor are we. It is true that Dickens cheerfully adopts a vaguely Rousseauesque notion of the innocent warped and made evil by institutions—('what human nature may be made to be') and also seems to adopt with equal readiness the tory doctrine that birth and breeding will win through in the end. But however muddled as propaganda—indeed perhaps because they are muddled—these contradictions are entirely resolved in the imaginative certainty of the novel. Dickens might well proclaim, as he did to critics who found Nancy's love for Sikes implausible—that IT IS TRUE! His imagination makes nonsense, just as life does, of theories of how human beings will or will not behave in a given environment. Notwithstanding the claustrophobic nature of the book, and its heavy dream atmosphere, Dickens's triumph is to have made Oliver—and Charley Bates and Nancy too—free of all human possibility, free in spirit and impulse against all physical and factual likelihood. The world of the novel may be a prison but they are not finally enclosed in it. And he has made this ultimate freedom seem true.

Still, Fagin's wish to incriminate Oliver, and hence confine him for ever in the evil world, is an objective and social terror as well as a psychological one. There remains the plain and sickening fact that Fagin's school and all it stands for extinguishes the hope and chance of better things, though not necessarily the capacity for them: of his pupils, Oliver escapes by the needs of the plot, Charley Bates by the death of Sikes and Fagin, and Nancy not at all. Dickens himself had been at

1. See above, pp. 419–20 [Editor].

Fagin's school—the blacking factory—and the boy who chiefly be-
friended him there was actually called Fagin. No wonder Fagin the
criminal is such an ambivalent figure when the real Fagin's kindness
had, so to speak, threatened to inure Dickens to the hopeless routine of
the wage-slave. So passionate was the young Dickens's desire for the
station in life to which he felt entitled, and so terrifying his sense that
it was being denied him, that he must have hated the real Fagin for the
virtue which he could not bear to accept or recognize in that nightmare
world, because it might help to subdue him into it. The real Fagin's
kindness becomes the criminal Fagin's villainy.

*   *   *

The power of *Oliver Twist* depends more than any other of Dickens's
novels on his personality and background—that is why one has to insist
on them so much. Everything in the novel means something else; it is
shot through and through with involuntary symbolism, with that peculiar
egocentric modernity which Edmund Wilson tells us to be fiction's
discovery of its true self. Except possibly for Giles the butler, nobody
and nothing exists merely in itself. Even the famous 'household' passages,
like Oliver asking for more, do not have the legendary authority of an
epic moment but make a piercing appeal to something private and
vulnerable in the memory of the reader. 'Things as they really are' turn
out to be things as the fantasy fears, and feared in childhood, that they
may be. In *David Copperfield* childhood fantasy is also dominant, but
in the objective setting of true existences, David's mother, Peggotty,
Betsy Trotwood, and Barkis—there is the breadth and solidity of epic.
In *Oliver Twist* the child is *right*: there is no suggestion that his vision
of monsters is illusory or incomplete, and the social shock to us is that
the child here is right to see things thus—the system is monstrous because
he finds it to be so. His vision is the lens to focus Dickens's *saeva
indignatio* [savage indignation]. The grotesque conversation between
Noah, Bumble, and the gentleman in the white waistcoat, about what
is to be done with Oliver, is true because it is just how Oliver would
imagine it. But in *Copperfield* the child may be wrong; he only partially
apprehends the existences around him, and Murdstone, for instance, is
more arresting and intriguing than anyone in *Oliver Twist* because there
is no assumption that David really knows what he is like.

*   *   *

In seeking to disarm criticism by drawing his readers into a hypnotic
unity with the tale and the author, Dickens relies heavily on convention
to increase both the shared hypnosis and the emotion of truth. As Forster
tells us, he delighted in coincidence and in pointing out how common
it was in life. And in *Oliver Twist* he positively takes refuge in melodramatic ceremonial: it would be a disaster if the taste of the age had
allowed him to describe what must have been the continual and brutish
sexual activity in Fagin's hole—(*Jonathan Wild*, and *The Beggar's Op-*

era, which Dickens protests is unrealistic, are much franker about this)—or to have rendered the actual oaths of Sikes instead of giving him grotesquely and perhaps deliberately exaggerated euphemisms like 'Wolves tear your throats!' . . . Though he may not have been conscious of it, Dickens knew that such disguises and prevarications are indeed the truth of the fantasy. And he enhances their effect by putting them beside facts of a neutral and professional kind, like his catalogue of the districts—Exmouth Street, Hockley in the Hole, Little Saffron Hill, etc.—through which Oliver is led by the Artful Dodger, and through which Sikes wanders after the murder. * * * Dickens was the first to protest against the new French 'realism', because he felt it might discredit his mystery. He has often been blamed for giving the happy ending to *Great Expectations*, in deference to Bulwer Lytton, but he has there a sure sense, as in *Oliver Twist*, not of what the *donnée* demanded, but of upholding the kinds of agreement he had made with the reader. The artistic rigour of a Flaubert alienates, and Dickens is faithful only to what he and his audience can make of the thing together.

Yet in his last novels he is beginning to hold the reader off. It is extremely illuminating to compare *Oliver Twist* with *Edwin Drood*, because we are not required to participate in the exquisitely murderous atmosphere of the last novel. We can stand back, and watch the familiar two worlds—the world of goodness and innocence and the world of murder and hallucination—conjured into a real and objective existence. Canon Crisparkle and his mother, the Virginia creeper, and the home-made wines and jellies, are solid and reassuring presences: they have strength as well as gentleness. Rosa Budd and Helena Landless, 'a beautiful barbaric captive brought from some wild tropical dominion', are as meticulously alive as Jasper, raising his high voice in the shadowy choir and hating the rôle he has made for himself. Dickens has adopted the principle of depth; hypocrisy is real at last. Instead of the divided nature being flat and two-dimensional as a Rorschach ink-blot, spreading over the whole of life, it now exists in and perceives an upper and lower world. At the cost of transforming his social earnestness into an earnestness of craftsmanship Dickens keeps his imagination working at full pressure, but in a new sphere of complication and plurality. His vision proves to be as fecund as Shakespeare's, and to have the same power of continued transformation. It was transforming itself afresh when he died.

So far I have stressed the waking nightmare which is the imaginative principle of *Oliver Twist*, and the way it dispels any true distinction between the world of darkness which Oliver is in, and the world of light which he longs for. None the less the impressive power of the novel does depend upon a most effective distinction, of quite another kind, and of the force of which Dickens seems equally unaware. It is the distinction between crime and murder.

We are apt to forget how early-Victorian society, the society of laissez-faire, took for granted individual conditions of privacy and isolation. It was a society where each unit, each family and household, led their secret lives with an almost neurotic antipathy to external interference. It was the age of the private gentleman who wanted nothing but to be left alone. He could ignore politics, the Press, the beggar who happened to be dying of hunger in the coachhouse; he need feel no pressure of social or national existence. Noah Claypole provides an ironic gloss when he says about Oliver: 'let him alone! Why, everyone lets him pretty much alone!' And the poor had the same instincts as their betters. At the time of the Crimea, when a suggestion of conscription was raised, labourers and miners said they would take to the woods or go underground rather than be caught for it. There has probably never been a time when England was—in the sociological phrase—less integrated.

Dickens has a most disturbing feeling for this. Like most Victorians his sense of other things, other places and people, was founded on fear and distrust. The Boz of the Sketches seems to hate and fear almost everything, even though it fascinates him. For unlike other people he had no home to go to, no hole in which he could feel secure. Normal living and the life of crime are almost indistinguishable in *Oliver Twist*, for both are based on the burrow. Both Jacob's Island and the town where Oliver is born consist largely of derelict houses which are not owned or occupied in the normal way but taken possession of as burrows, or 'kens', with an 'aperture made into them wide enough for the passage of a human body'. Fagin, who when out of doors is compared to a reptile 'looking for a meal of some rich offal', has his den on Saffron Hill; when he first enters the district Oliver sees that from several of these holes 'great ill-looking fellows were cautiously emerging, bound, to all appearance, on no very well-disposed or harmless errands'. The stiltedness of the writing here somehow emphasizes the effect of evening beasts coming out on their normal business. Mr. Brownlow (whose name oddly suggests a fox) and Mr. Grimwig are holed up in Clerkenwell; Mrs. Corney has her snug corner in the workhouse; the Maylies live behind the walls of their Chertsey house as if it were in the Congo. The house to which Oliver is taken before the abortive 'crack', and which he afterwards identifies, is found then to have some quite different tenant, an evil creature who is hastily left to his own devices. A man on the run makes the round of the kens and finds them already full, as if they were shells tenanted by crabs.

All these people have the same outlook and the same philosophy of life, a philosophy which that private gentleman, Fagin, sums up as 'looking after No. 1'. As one would expect, Dickens can see nothing in the idea of 'private vices, public virtues' except a degradingly mutual kind of blackmail. In presenting his characters as animals, purposeful, amoral, and solitary in their separate colonies, with no true gregarious-ness or power of cohesion, he draws a terrifying imaginative indictment of what private life may be like in an open society, in his age or in our own.

Murder transforms all this. Like a magic wand it changes the animals back into men again: what we think of as 'human nature' returns with a rush. And it is an extraordinary and sinister irony that makes murder the only imaginative vindication in the book of human stature and human meaningfulness. Though Dickens may not have bargained for the effect it is the crowning stroke in the satirical violence of his novel. Just as murder, in the Victorian literary mythology, was cleaner than sex, so in Dickens's vision is it more human than crime and the in-humanity of social institutions, for crime is the most characteristic aspect of the social order. Bumble, Fagin and the rest are evil beings because they are not human beings; they are doing the best they can for them-selves in their business, and Sikes was similarly an animal in the business—'the mere hound of a day' as Fagin says—until murder turns him into a kind of man. Thereupon, too, society develops the cohesion and point that it had lacked before—indeed this, like so much else in the book, is grotesquely though effectively overdone. Nancy's murder assumes the proportions of a national crisis, 'Spies', we hear, 'are hov-ering about in every direction'. Significantly, until the murder no one seems to take notice of Fagin—he is engrossed in his repellent business like any other citizen—but after it he is nearly lynched. Crime is like animal or mechanical society, cold, separated, and professional, but murder is like the warmth and conviviality which Dickens always praises—a great uniter.

Undoubtedly Dickens is saying something here about society which has lost none of its potency. With a shudder we realize what we are still like. Of course, Dickens had a perfectly 'healthy' interest in murder and hanging, just as he took a normal English pleasure in illness, funerals, and ballads like 'the blood-drinker's burial'; but murder in *Oliver Twist* has a more metaphysical status, is less literary and less purely morbid and professional, than any other in Dickens.

* * *

Dostoevsky, a great admirer of *Oliver Twist*, also makes murder a kind of social revelation. Writers who learn from Dickens usually develop explicitly an effect which is implicit in their source, and Dostoevsky makes Roskolnikov a rebel who murders the old money-lender out of frustration, as a kind of thwarted substitute for idealist terrorism. We know from his diary that Dostoevsky was bothered by Roskolnikov's lack of an obvious motive—he realized that the significance with which the author endowed the crime was showing too clearly through the story. But Sikes's motive is brutally simple and straightforward. Nancy must be got rid of because she has betrayed the gang: the whole burrow principle of looking after No. 1 demands her instant elimination. * * *

* * *

Oliver is not in a position to despair of the middle class, or anything else, and the humility of this is communicated in some way to the author and moves us more than all his later stridency. Oliver is a true everyman: he does not, like David Copperfield or D. H. Lawrence, shriek at us incredulously—'They did this to *me!*' It is logical that he has no character, because he has no physical individuality—he is the child element in a nightmare which is otherwise peopled by animals, and precariously by men. Child, beast, and man indeed merge and change places phantasmagorically throughout the book. Oliver is sometimes adult, almost middle-aged, and sometimes like an animal himself, as when his eyes glisten at the sight of the scraps of meat in Mrs. Sowerberry's kitchen —one of the few really physical intimations of him we have. After the murder the lesser criminals are as lost and bewildered as children, and the hardened Kags begs for a candle, saying 'Don't leave me in the dark'. Sikes and Nancy, as hero and heroine, have their transformation from beast to man: only Fagin remains a reptile throughout and to the end, losing at last even his human powers of speech and intellect and crouching in the dock like something snared, his glittering eyes 'looking on when an artist broke his pencil point and made another with his knife, as any idle spectator might have done.' He has the animal victim's unnerving air of detachment from his own predicament, and the butchery of one kind of beast by another is the final horror of his execution. 'Are you a man, Fagin?' asks the gaoler.

> 'I shan't be one long,' he replied, looking up with a face containing no human expression but rage and terror. 'Strike them all dead! What right have they to butcher me?'

It is a horribly penetrating appeal, when we think of society as *Oliver Twist* presents it. And in contrast to the almost heroic death of Sikes, Fagin will lose even his animal identity at the very end, and revert to a dreadful human simulacrum, 'a dangling heap of clothes'.

'To be thoroughly earnest is everything, and to be anything short of it is nothing.' Dickens's credo about novel-writing is certainly true of *Oliver Twist*, but whereas in the later novels this seriousness extends to the technique which fashions symbols and symbolic atmospheres—the famous fogs, prison, dust, etc.—he does not insist on, or even seem aware of, the animal symbolism here: it hits the reader like a sleepwalker's blow, involuntarily administered. It seems a natural product of the imagination, like that of Shakespeare and Hardy; though Dickens's later

symbolic technique is closer to Lawrence's, purposeful and claustrophobic, the meaning too unified to expand into an ordinary human
range of possibility. Character remains imprisoned. * * * The nonsense
talked by Bumble, Pecksniff, or Squeers, their total lack of the responsibilities of intercourse, mark Dickens's most contemptuous, though
most inspired, refusal to recognize an inner self in such persons. But
Sikes and Nancy have an eloquence, a brutal and urgent power of
communication, that shows how seriously Dickens takes them, and how
seriously they are compelled to take themselves. The dimension of these
two is the triumph of the novel, and it closely corresponds to the main
feat—surely unique in the history of the novel—which Dickens has
achieved in combining the genre of Gothic nightmare with that of social
denunciation, so that each enhances the other.

KEITH HOLLINGSWORTH

The Newgate Novel and the Moral Argument, 1837–40†

The "Real" World of Oliver Twist

Although Dickens' interest in crime and criminals was lifelong, it was
the early novel, *Oliver Twist*, which for a time placed him among the
Newgate novelists. Its "low" material was disliked by a few readers even
to the beginning of the twentieth century. * * * *Oliver Twist* was attached to the contemporary scene in a fashion not equalled in the other
Newgate novels. It reflected the prevalence of juvenile crime; the recent
development of the trade in stolen goods, which seemed in the twenties
almost to be keeping pace with legitimate commerce; and the general
attention to crime and punishment.

The story originally appeared in the new *Bentley's Miscellany*, of
which Dickens was undertaking the editorship and for which he was to
furnish original fiction. The first issue of the magazine came out in
January 1837; the first of twenty installments of the novel appeared in
the February number. On three occasions it was omitted: June 1837
(after the death of Mrs. Dickens' sister, Mary Hogarth), October 1837,
and September 1838. During the early months of *Oliver Twist*, when
Dickens was also finishing the *Pickwick Papers*, he was less than a week
ahead of the printer with each. In the spring of 1838, though he then
had *Nicholas Nickleby* under way also, he was apparently getting far
ahead of monthly deadlines; he finished the writing of *Oliver Twist* early

† From *The Newgate Novel, 1830–1847* (Detroit, 1963) 111–65.

in September 1838. The completed book was published two months later; the serial ran on in *Bentley's* through April 1839.

*   *   *

Besides observing the streets of London, Dickens must have read what came to hand about youthful criminals, and he probably sought out more. The newspapers of any year of the period show the kind of notice given to young thieves: when they were brought before a magistrate there was little opportunity for discrimination between the novice and the professional criminal. Judges had certain discretionary powers, but the jury, deciding between guilty and not guilty, knew that the penalty of imprisonment or transportation or indeed death was as applicable to the boy of ten or twelve as to the man of thirty. The attitude of the judge did of course make a great difference in the handling of an individual case. Real innocence might receive pity, but the system and the minds which carried it on were not constituted to deal with boys who were still at the beginning of a criminal career.

The newspapers had made Dickens' readers equally well prepared to accept Fagin. Isaac or Ikey Solomon, whose name (with *s* added) Thackeray was to take as a burlesque pseudonym for *Catherine*, had become known as the most successful and elusive of London fences, and his activities had been extensively reported. Dickens' receiver is not shown to have so large a business as Solomon's nor does his character parallel Solomon's in detail, but the notoriety of the actual person was such that every adult reader must have thought of him. The case had been closed, so far as the English courts were concerned, when Solomon was transported to Australia in 1831, but references to him were frequent for years thereafter. Born in 1785, he was first a peddler, a passer of bad coins, and a pickpocket. He learned to deal in stolen goods and made enormous profits. For many years the police knew of his operations, but the requirements of the law for identifying stolen goods were so stringent that a conviction was hard to obtain. No great ingenuity seems to have been matched against Solomon's, but the accounts do not suggest that he paid for immunity. In making the traffic of a fence into a well-organized business, Solomon was extremely careful to see that identifying marks on all objects were removed before the goods came to rest in his house. It was a precaution which no one had applied so consistently before. (Dickens' Fagin sets Oliver Twist at removing the marks from handkerchiefs.) One writer has it that as Solomon advanced in his career he dealt only in big lots; he advised the thieves who supplied him not to take continual risks on small jobs but to live better by carrying off one or two well-planned large operations in a year.

*   *   *

Oliver Twist reflects also the parliamentary attention given to revision of the criminal law, an attention nearly constant between 1833 and 1837. For observing the social and political legislation of a great period of change, Dickens had experience unparalleled by that of other novelists, for he began a four-year period of parliamentary reporting in the reform year, 1832. He was twenty years old when he first entered the reporters' gallery of the House of Commons. After or concurrently with work on another paper, he was employed by the *Mirror of Parliament*, a journal which emulated the completeness of *Hansard*; he was with the *Mirror* for two sessions. By August 1834, he had achieved a coveted position with the *Morning Chronicle*, which he resigned two years later, at the close of the session in August 1836. His work for the *Chronicle* kept him chiefly in the Commons, but on numerous occasions he was sent to cover important parliamentary elections in the towns. Such absences were of short duration, a few days at a time. He must surely have been aware of every important measure which the House of Commons dealt with between March 1832 and August 1836.

Although Dickens was no longer a reporter in this conclusive year, 1837, there is every reason to suppose that he followed the course of the pending legislation. Bills proposed by the Royal Commission were introduced in the Commons in March and passed without difficulty; they were delayed in the Lords, where the second reading did not occur until July 4, after which they had to return to the Commons in their amended form. The completed acts, which received the royal assent at the close of the session on July 17, were certainly among the principal achievements of that parliament.

The dates are interesting. It cannot have been by accident that Dickens inserted an argument against capital punishment into *Oliver Twist* while the long-awaited measures were at the obstacle of the House of Lords. Fagin, the vicious exploiter of other men's theft, looks over his treasures and mutters to himself:

> What a fine thing capital punishment is! Dead men never repent; dead men never bring awkward stories to light. Ah, it's a fine thing for the trade! Five of 'em strung up in a row, and none left to play booty, or turn white-livered!

Nothing could have been more topical and current at the beginning of July 1837, when this came to the readers of *Bentley's Miscellany*.

* * *

Other contemporary influences involved close personal relationships. It would be surprising if Dickens, ambitious as he was, had not paid attention to the most popular books of the early thirties; and his association with their authors, Ainsworth and Bulwer, forms part of the background of Newgate novel controversy. The relations of the three, or four when we include Forster, may be followed in Dickens' letters and in the several biographies. At some time in 1834, Dickens met Ainsworth; he was one of Ainsworth's numerous guests in 1834 and 1835. Ainsworth then was a literary lion, Dickens still a reporter.

Through Ainsworth he met in 1836 John Forster, literary editor of the *Examiner*, who was to be his life-long friend and his biographer; probably through Ainsworth he met Bulwer. After he met Forster, the relation between the two grew faster than the friendship of either with Ainsworth; but both were, for the next two years and more, increasingly associated with Ainsworth. They rode together, dined together, and called themselves the Trio. Ainsworth and Dickens talked of collaborating on a book. During January and February 1839, Dickens was effecting his separation from his publisher, Bentley. He was not sorry to have Ainsworth replace him as editor of *Bentley's Miscellany*, though Ainsworth may have been hoping for that outcome. A breach came, however, when Dickens was led to suspect that Ainsworth had misrepresented Forster's part in the negotiations. After Dickens' letter of protest, March 26, 1839, the familiar letters and the trio dinners ceased. Forster's attitude will be spoken of in connection with *Jack Sheppard*. The friendship of Dickens and Ainsworth, despite some later exchanges of dinners, was not on its old footing, and by 1845 even their meetings were rare accidents. A small residue of the association with Ainsworth remains in the name of Sikes, in *Oliver Twist*; a James Sykes figures in the historical accounts of Jack Sheppard. Perhaps there is another in Fagin's giving Oliver a *Newgate Calendar* to read.

*   *   *

Oliver Twist has great vitality and a large measure of realism in its Newgate furnishings. There is force in the workhouse scenes; there is psychological conviction in the crisis of the murderer and the condemned man. "Fagin's Last Night Alive" employs essentially the method that was to be rediscovered later and named internal monologue or stream of consciousness. To enjoy the story, however, one must set no limit on coincidence, and be ready to accept a birth-mystery for the hero, with another added for good measure. This staple of fiction, unknown parentage—the use of which weakens the logic of the humanitarian sermon—was quite in harmony with Dickens' predilections; as a child he had noticed a handsome little chimney sweep and had been sure the boy was the lost heir of some illustrious man. The sweep "believed he'd been born in the Vurkis, but he'd never know'd his father." Oliver, unfortunately, has no substance as a character.

Dickens makes an effort to have his several classes of characters speak appropriately, though Oliver has the improbable language and deportment of a little gentleman. There is a limited amount of underworld slang, introduced so carefully that the genteel reader need never be at a loss for the meaning. One gets the impression that Dickens had indeed heard the thieves' language in idiomatic context—but that his acquaintance with it was not extended or familiar. If it had been, he would not have been able, even in censoring them, to let his low characters relapse into the stately literary rhythms they sometimes use. George Gissing,

quoting Sikes's exclamation, "Wolves tear your throats!" pointed out
that the influence of contemporary melodrama reached beyond Dickens'
plot to his very language.[1] The words of Toby Crackit, telling Fagin
about the unsuccessful robbery, illustrate the author's divergencies. "The
crack failed," Toby says in words of one syllable; but a little later, with
an original nautical phrase, he says that Bill Sikes "scudded like the
wind."

Both language and action are cleansed for presentation to the family
circle. In the preface to the third edition Nancy is called a prostitute;
she is never so named in the story, and her occupation is most delicately
suggested, chiefly through her protestations of guilt. Dickens wishes to
show repulsive truth, but—

> No less consulting my own taste, than the manners of the age, I
> endeavoured, while I painted it in all its fallen and degraded aspects,
> to banish from the lips of the lowest character I introduced, any
> expression that could by possibility offend; and rather to lead to the
> unavoidable inference that its existence was of the most debased
> and vicious kind, than to prove it elaborately by words and deeds.
> In the case of the girl, in particular, I kept this intention constantly
> in view.[2]

Much of Dickens' writing is affected by this practice of leading to "unavoidable inference"; he is thoroughly conscious of the method, but its
application seems almost automatic. Humphry House comments that
the atmosphere Oliver was plunged into in London would have been
"drenched in sex."[3] Dickens could, it is true, have made Nancy more
realistic if he had been willing to do so, but he would have had to heap
disgust upon her, and he was sensitive to popular taste. His reticence,
though, does not seem merely calculated. The whole conception of
Nancy is sympathetic: one feels it to have been quite as important that
Charles Dickens should be fond of her as that readers should not protest.
For this, she had, while remaining a prostitute, to take on, in Mr.
Brownlow's words, "the courage and almost the attributes of virtue."

Nancy's original, as we have seen, was the girl in the hospital. The
development of the character, however, has another involvement, Nancy's association with Rose Maylie. Rose is the first of the several girl
characters in the novels drawn, one feels sure, from Mary Hogarth, the
young sister-in-law who lived with Dickens and his wife. Seventeen
years old, Mary died of a sudden illness in May 1837, when Dickens
had been married a little more than a year. His diary and his letters at
the time show a sorrow patterned by convention but as deep and as
devastating as any tragedy of young love and death in romantic literature.

1. See above, pp. 421–26 [Editor].
2. See above, p. 6 [Editor].
3. Humphry House, The Dickens World (London, 1941) 217.

The heightened quality of his feeling for her is hard to explain. He wrote in *Bentley's* (to account for the omission of the installment of *Oliver Twist* which he had been unable to work on) that the editor was mourning "the death of a very dear young relative . . . whose society has been for a long time the chief solace of his labours." Almost five years later he wrote to Forster, at the time of another death in the Hogarth family:

> The desire to be buried next her is as strong upon me now, as it was five years ago; and I *know* (for I don't think there ever was love like that I bear her) that it will never diminish. . . . I cannot bear the thought of being excluded from her dust. . . . I shall drive over there, please God, on Thursday morning, before they get there; and look at her coffin.

The fictional Rose Maylie is, to take the words of Dickens' epitaph for Mary Hogarth, "young, beautiful, and good." Near to the first anniversary of Mary's death, in the June 1838 installment of *Oliver Twist*, he gave Rose a severe illness, though he stopped short of making it a fatal one.

Nancy, who was to be so much criticized, is the counterpart, among the low characters, of Rose Maylie. Rose is "not past seventeen"; neither is Nancy, although her original, the hospital patient, was five or six years older. Both girls are kind to the boy hero, with whose unhappy life Dickens had reason to feel a close identification. A penitent sinner, Nancy arouses pity for her ruined youth when she is brought face to face with the girl of sheltered virtue. If Rose and other innocent young girls in Dickens are astral bodies emanating from Mary Hogarth, surely Nancy may be regarded as another, whose creation likewise afforded him satisfaction. The sentiment he lavished upon her thus becomes understandable, as well as his later warmth in her defense.

Dickens wrote no death scene for Rose Maylie—he allowed her to recover. In effect, Nancy dies in her place. When the time comes for the murder of Nancy, the event is given special fury and pathos. A degree of identification of the two girls' characters has been achieved. Nancy's good impulses have made her appealing, and she has become pure in heart through her contact with Oliver and Rose; her final supplication to Sikes is that he go away with her so that they may "far apart lead better lives, and forget how we have lived, except in prayers, and never see each other more." Unmoved, Sikes brutally kills her. In a sense, then, Dickens wrote the death scene after all. In emotional terms, he created and defended Nancy as the unadmitted sexual aspect of Mary Hogarth—and then expiated his sin with Nancy's death.

Oliver Twist was the more Newgate novel because of the author's fascination with crimes of violence, although his treatment of them brought him considerable praise and almost no specific blame. When Dickens was to do a murder he set himself to wring the most from it.

In the famous scene of the killing of Nancy he unfortunately tries for a stagey pathos before she dies, and so falsifies his conception, but the occasion has impressive moments. A little after her death, the morning sun lights the room; Sikes, in a daze, makes pointless efforts to remove, not the body, but the blood and the weapon, in a kind of unreasoned ritual:

> He struck a light, kindled a fire, and thrust the club into it. There was hair upon the end, which blazed and shrunk into a light cinder, and, caught by air, whirled up the chimney. Even that frightened him, sturdy as he was; but he held the weapon till it broke, and then piled it on the coals to burn away, and smoulder into ashes. He washed himself, and rubbed his clothes; there were spots that would not be removed, but he cut the pieces out, and burnt them. How those stains were dispersed about the room! The very feet of the dog were bloody.

In following the behavior of Sikes after the murder, Dickens maintains urgency and tension to a high degree; and in the few minutes which Sikes spends with the boys of the gang in their last hiding-place, he makes both boys and man conscious of the murderer's isolation from mankind. Such parts of the story are impressive.

The murder is by no means a necessity of the plot. Indeed, it is forced. Nancy has been portrayed as deeply attached and Sikes as violent by nature, but there has been nothing to show that his feeling for her could be attended by murderous passion at a supposed betrayal. Evil-tempered as he is, he might be expected to clout her on the head and then to leave London till the trouble should blow over. Or, since he has had a hanging look from the beginning, he might have gone to the gallows; but Dickens found himself writing his way toward a murder, and Sikes must do it.

Whatever the Newgate novel owes, then, to social circumstances or literary fashion, it owes something more to the arrival, in the eighteen-thirties, of a writer who had a deep personal interest in crime. Edmund Wilson, in "Dickens: the Two Scrooges," points out the rebellion which compelled Dickens to an identification with murderers. He finds its origin in the psychic trauma of Dickens' childhood despair:

> He identified himself readily with the thief and even more readily with the murderer. The man of powerful will who finds himself opposed to society must, if he cannot upset it or if his impulse to do so is blocked, feel a compulsion to commit what society regards as one of the capital crimes against itself. With the antisocial heroes of Dostoevsky, this crime is usually murder or rape; with Dickens it is usually murder. . . . In Dickens' novels, this theme recurs with a probing of the psychology of the murderer, which becomes ever more convincing and intimate.

The obsession with murderers can also be traced, outside the novels, in the interests which Dickens frequently displayed to the end of his life. The death of Nancy was the most exciting of the dramatic readings in his last platform appearances; no one can fail to be impressed by his determination, against all advice, to include it and by his extraordinary satisfaction in the performance. "In deciding to add the murder of Nancy to his repertory," says Edgar Johnson, "he was sentencing himself to death." He would not give up, and the murder scene was in the renewed series of readings that began six months before he died.

＊ ＊ ＊

One can imagine Dickens' objections, on several grounds, to being classified as a writer of the Newgate school, though he did not express them publicly for more than two years. His attitude is to be seen in a letter to R. H. Horne, written near the end of 1839, when Thackeray's *Catherine* and Ainsworth's *Sheppard* were still running their courses:

> I am by some jolter-headed enemies most unjustly and untruly charged with having written a book after Mr. Ainsworth's fashion. Unto these jolter-heads and their intensely concentrated humbug I shall take an early opportunity of temperately replying. If this opportunity had presented itself and I had made this vindication, I could have no objection to set my hand to what I know to be true concerning the late lamented John Sheppard, but I feel a great repugnance to do so now, lest it should seem an ungenerous and unmanly way of disavowing any sympathy with that school, and a means of shielding myself.

Dickens' delicacy does him credit, especially since this was during the time of his definite estrangement from Ainsworth. There would have been a certain embarrassment, too, in joining with Thackeray against Ainsworth, when Thackeray had already tarred Dickens and Bulwer with the same brush.

The temperate reply which Dickens planned was written in April 1841, as a preface to the third edition of *Oliver Twist*, and most of it has been retained in later ones. Dickens withdrew nothing and defended himself with vigor.

> It is, it seems, a very coarse and shocking circumstance, that some of the characters in these pages are chosen from the most criminal and degraded of London's population; that Sikes is a thief, and Fagin a receiver of stolen goods; that the boys are pickpockets, and the girl is a prostitute.
>
> I confess I have yet to learn that a lesson of the purest good may not be drawn from the vilest evil.[4]

4. See above, p. 3 [*Editor*].

He is answering, with the conviction of an evangelist, the satire of Thackeray, the chidings of reviewers, and most recently, the jesting of Bon Gaultier, in *Tait's Magazine*. He dissociates himself from the merely entertaining Newgate writers—even little Oliver represents "the principle of Good"—and asserts his reforming aim. He has read of scores of gallant seductive thieves, "great at a song" (*Rookwood* was full of songs): "But I had never met (except in Hogarth) with the miserable reality. It appeared to me that to draw a knot of such associates in crime as really do exist . . . would be a service to society." Dickens points out that his book offers no enticement "for the most jolter-headed of juveniles." Since he specifically exempts from censure *The Beggar's Opera* and *Paul Clifford*, this preface includes a pointed refusal to sanction Ainsworth publicly. It must have been interpreted so by Dickens' former friend, who in 1836 had praised Dickens in the preface to a new edition of *Rookwood*. The two prefaces, five years apart, compose an irony of time and change. The forceful effort which Dickens makes to separate himself from Ainsworth and assert his own purposes shows how strongly he felt the criticism. Thackeray's article, in particular, roused him to a vehement reply. The preface closes with a defiant word against hypocritical refinement ("It is wonderful how Virtue turns from dirty stockings") and an eloquent defense of the truth of Nancy:

> It is useless to discuss whether the conduct and character of the girl seems natural or unnatural, probable or improbable, right or wrong. It is true. Every man who has watched these melancholy shades of life knows it to be so. Suggested to my mind long ago— long before I dealt in fiction—by what I often saw and read of, in actual life around me, I have, for years, tracked it through many profligate and noisome ways, and found it still the same. From the first introduction of that poor wretch, to her laying her bloody head upon the robber's breast, there is not one word exaggerated or overwrought. It is emphatically God's truth. . . . It involves the best and worst shades of our common nature . . . it is a contradiction, an anomaly, an apparent impossibility, but it is a truth.

This last paragraph must surely have been written for Thackeray.

In 1844, R. H. Horne published his *New Spirit of the Age*, which contains echoes of the controversy. Although the author assumes a wide public appreciation of Dickens, he defends Dickens as a moralist, and the first book he undertakes to praise is not *Pickwick* but *Oliver Twist*. Though it is "the work which is most open to animadversion," it has a beneficial moral tendency. Of Dickens' defence in the 1841 preface, he says, "It is unanswerable, but ought not to have been needed."

STEVEN MARCUS

Who Is Fagin?†

Fagin is back in the news. The English musical play, *Oliver!* has stirred up the same kind of protest from various Jewish groups that the film of *Oliver Twist* did a decade ago. Alec Guinness's lisping, asthmatic, and vaguely homosexual Fagin of the film has in the newest version been displaced by an out-and-out East End type. In so far as protest against such representations is directed against the implicit equation they set up between certain conventional Jewish characteristics and moral malignity, it is of course justified. Yet we should note that the dramatic interpretations of Fagin have always, in some degree, been radical departures from the Fagin of the novel. While Dickens was still writing *Oliver Twist*, a theatrical pirate made an adaptation of it which Dickens went to see. It was so offensively bad that in the middle of the first scene the young novelist laid himself down on the floor of his box and never rose until the curtain dropped.

Nevertheless, there is some reason behind all this confusion about how to interpret Fagin on the stage, for he is one of Dickens's most puzzling characters. Much has been written about him, though very little light has been cast. Indeed, one of the most recent and most intelligent discussions of the subject—in Edgar Rosenberg's excellent book, *From Shylock to Svengali*—ends with the writer throwing up his hands in frustration. "But how *can* one account for Fagin?" Mr Rosenberg asks, making reference to how, given what we know of Dickens's experience, Fagin should have come about. In order to track down these "curious processes," he believes, "one should have to command some ultimate psychology." Mr Rosenberg may be right, but I do think that something at least can be done even without the help of such "ultimate" assurances.

It has often been remarked that although Fagin—with his "villainous-looking and repulsive face . . . obscured by a quantity of matted red hair," and his "greasy flannel gown"—is got up in the traditional habit of the stage Jew, Judas and devil, there is otherwise nothing particularly Jewish about him. This formulation may not be entirely exact, and it has been alternatively suggested that Fagin is a renegade Jew. In any event, when we first see him, he is cooking sausages for his boys, and it is clear throughout that such matters as the dietary laws and the customs of the Jewish community mean nothing to him. In fact, on the eve of

† Excerpt from *Dickens: From Pickwick to Dombey* by Steven Marcus. Pp. 358–78. Copyright © 1965 by Steven Marcus. Reprinted by permission of HarperCollins Publishers.

his execution, "Venerable men of his own persuasion had come to pray beside him, but he had driven them away with curses. They renewed their charitable efforts, and he beat them off." Furthermore, he does not even speak with an accent or in any particular dialect—unless it be the thieves' cant into which he, like his non-Jewish associates, often drops. This is all the more pointed because the one other Jew in *Oliver Twist*, Barney, the boy-of-all-work at The Cripples, speaks with the pronounced nasality which was apparently characteristic of London Jews during the eighteenth and nineteenth centuries. So far as speech is concerned, Fagin resembles no one so much as his opposite and counterpart, Oliver Twist, whose own speech—the most improbable and pure-bred English—is also symbolic of his alienation from the world in which he finds himself. And indeed, from the point of view of that "respectable" society which had recently created the New Poor Law of 1834, Oliver Twist—a bastard, an orphan and a workhouse child—and Fagin a vicious criminal—were alike if not identical. Under the new Malthusian dispensation, the English poor were to be treated so harshly and punitively that they were to have been willing to do almost anything rather than throw themselves on the tender mercies of the state. Poverty was at last tantamount to crime, and the new "unions" or workhouses soon came to be universally known as Bastilles. At this stage in the development of modern industrial society, the pauper and the criminal were regarded equally as outcasts. Both existed on the periphery of society; at the same time both existed within the shadow of that central and indispensable social institution, the prison—one of the many implications of this being that, in modern society at least, what seems to be marginal and alien can in fact prove to be central and essential, as the history of modern art and literature repeatedly indicates. Both paupers and criminals also existed within their own society or class, and one of the chief imaginative devices in *Oliver Twist* consists in Dickens's representation of the values, habits, and structure of ordinary "respectable" society as analogous to those which inform the world of the thieves and the paupers. Oliver and Fagin are at the focus of this remarkable vision. They are symbiotic characters, like Mr Pickwick and Sam Weller, or Don Quixote and Sancho Panza, or Stephen Dedalus and Leopold Bloom—that is to say, we cannot understand them apart from each other.

But we know something else about Fagin, something anterior to his function in this novel. We know how he got his name. Dickens took it from the name of a boy who played a part in the chief episode of his childhood. Our present purpose requires that we read this immortal story anew.

I

Charles Dickens spent most of his childhood in the vicinity of Rochester, where his father, John Dickens, was employed as a clerk in the Navy Pay Office. John Dickens was a vivacious, energetic, garrulous, ambitious, but somehow incompetent man. He aspired particularly to genteel speech and manners, and clearly thought of himself as a rising young man. And with reason, for his parents had been domestic servants. It is also evident that Charles, his second child and oldest son, was his father's favorite and special object of his pride. Although Charles had been, in John Forster's words, "a very little and a very sickly boy" who suffered from "attacks of violent spasm which disabled him for any active exertion," he was a precocious child and gave early evidence of a talent for imaginative play, for reciting and acting and singing little comic songs. His father delighted in his son's small exertions of talent, and often found occasion to show them off before friends and guests. It was at this time too that John Dickens bought a set of cheap reprints of the classic novels, which his son chanced upon, read, re-read and re-read again, living in them and impersonating his favorite characters with what was already characteristic intensity. "When I think of it," he wrote years later, "the picture always arises in my mind of a summer evening, the boys at play in the churchyard, and I sitting on my bed, reading as if for life." We will return to this memory.

Meanwhile things were not improving for his father. The family kept growing, in that inexorable nineteenth century way; and John Dickens, kindly yet improvident, well-meaning but, like Mr Micawber (who is a partial portrait of him), unable to meet the unyielding demands of the world of money and domestic responsibilities, began to descend the slippery slope of respectability which he had until then been confidently climbing. At the bottom of that decline, of course, gaped the abyss of that special middle-class hell, poverty. Sometime in the latter part of 1822, he was transferred to London, where the family was installed in a little four-room house in Camden Town. And things kept getting worse.

Charles had been attending school in Chatham and apparently expected that his parents would continue his education when they were settled in London, but they did not. It was a cause of undying bitterness to him. As he would write years later:

> I know my father to be as kindhearted and generous a man as ever lived in the world. But, in the ease of his temper, and the straitness of his means, he appeared to have utterly lost at this time the idea of educating me at all; and to have utterly put from him the notion that I had any claim upon him, in that regard, whatever. So I degenerated into cleaning his boots of a morning, and my own; and making myself useful in the work of the little house; and looking

after my younger brothers and sisters (we were now six in all); and going on such poor errands as arose out of our poor way of living.

Matters continued so for upwards of a year: the family's fortunes steadily worsened, possessions were sold off (including, at the very outset, the books), schemes for salvation came to nothing, arrest for debt constantly threatened. As for Charles, forgotten amid the general hopelessness and distraction, he was afflicted by the recurrence of his early malady—spasms in the side often accompanied by fever—which had for a time subsided.

The crisis was reached in February 1824, the month of Charles's twelfth birthday. Within two weeks, he was sent to work and his father was imprisoned for debt. Through the influence of a friendly relation, Charles was employed at a blacking warehouse, at 30 Hungerford Stairs, Strand: his wages were six or seven shillings a week, his hours 8 A.M. to 8 P.M. Edgar Johnson in his biography of Dickens properly reminds us that none of these circumstances were unusual for that time: boys were often sent to work at an earlier age, and the average period of schooling then and even later was something short of two years. What was unusual was that these things were happening to the person who was to become Charles Dickens, though his parents could hardly have been expected to know it. The boy himself, and the man after him, felt utterly violated. When he came to write about the incident twenty-five years later, his bitterness had not staled:

> It is wonderful to me how I could have been so easily cast away at such an age. It is wonderful to me, that, even after my descent into the poor little drudge I had been since we came to London, no one had compassion enough on me—a child of singular abilities, quick, eager, delicate, and soon hurt, bodily or mentally—to suggest that something might have been spared, as certainly it might have been, to place me at any common school. . . . No one made any sign. My father and mother were quite satisfied. They could hardly have been more so, if I had been twenty years of age, distinguished at a grammar-school, and going to Cambridge.

Coupled with the emotions of betrayal and desertion were those of social disgrace and humiliation—the young prince suddenly discovers that he may be the swineherd's son, and not the other way around.

Eleven days after Charles began to work at Warren's Blacking, his father was arrested; his last words addressed to his sobbing son as he entered the gates of the Marshalsea was that the sun had set upon him forever. As he heard this the boy felt that his heart was really breaking. Soon after John Dickens entered prison, Mrs Dickens and her four younger children moved in with him. (Bankrupt as they were, they retained a little servant girl whom they had gotten from the Chatham workhouse: they were not, one must recall, paupers. These monstrous and pathetic distinctions are treated with incomparable mastery in *Little Dorrit*.) Charles was left to live alone on the outside, an outcast of freedom, a "small Cain" as he called himself. He was able to visit his parents and family on Sundays, but for some time he had to live without any "assistance whatever . . . from Monday morning until Saturday night. No advice, no counsel, no encouragement, no consolation, no support, from any one that I can call to mind, so help me God." Left to shift for himself, his sense of abandonment and humiliation often seemed to border upon despair; he later thought it a miracle that he had been spared to survive. "I know that I worked from morning to night, with common men and boys, a shabby child. . . . I know that I lounged about the streets, insufficiently and unsatisfactorily fed. I know that, but for the mercy of God, I might easily have been, for any care that was taken of me, a little robber or a little vagabond." If the impossible could happen, and Oliver Twist grow up into a man, this is what he would say—provided, of course, that were to retain his virtue of telling the truth.

After John Dickens had been in prison for three months, his mother, the former domestic servant, died and left her son a legacy large enough to secure his release. The family was reunited, but nothing was done about Charles. "I had the same wanderings about the streets as I used to have, and was just as solitary and self-dependent as before; but I had not the same difficulty in merely living. I never however heard a word of being taken away, or of being otherwise than quite provided for." In the event, only a chance quarrel between his father and the relation who had gotten the work for Charles brought his drudgery to an end. The conditions of this quarrel we shall recur to, but we may note here that it was [at] his father's insistence that Charles left the warehouse.

Dickens could never forget the entire episode, but neither could he in certain senses confront it. For years he literally avoided the spot on which the warehouse stood. Moreover, this period of his childhood remained an absolute secret to everyone except his close friend Forster, whom Dickens allowed to read the autobiographical fragment, written sometime in the late 1840s, from which I have been quoting. Although this remarkable document speaks for itself—and in its human impressiveness tends to make most comment seem trifling—if we recall that it was written by the greatest *comic* genius who ever lived, our sense of the nature and origins of comedy may be enlarged. Perhaps Plato was right when, at the end of *The Symposium*, he asserted through Socrates that the genius of comedy is the same as that of tragedy.

But the document we have been discussing was also written by a man who had become the most famous, successful, and adulated novelist of his time, who wrote it at the height of his fame and in the fullness of his powers. "My whole nature was so penetrated with the grief and humiliation of such considerations," he nevertheless stated, "that even now, famous and caressed and happy, I often forget in my dreams that I have a dear wife and children; even that I am a man; and wander desolately back to that time of my life." Though he might keep that time a dark secret even from his family—and his reasons for doing so were complex—it was never far from his mind. Indeed, it figures in some central way in every novel he wrote; and we cannot understand the creative thrust of his life without taking into account his developing attitudes toward this episode, as we find them successively transmuted in novel after novel. I am not suggesting this as, so to speak, a "key" to Dickens. There is no such thing for an artist, especially a great one, just as there is no single way of regarding or understanding a work of art. Nevertheless, this episode, and Dickens's extreme ambivalence toward it—he was at once virtually unable to speak about it and obsessively drawn to it—became one of the foci or gathering places of his creative impulses. It provides us, furthermore, with an unsurpassable instance of how in a great genius the "impersonal" achievement of art is inseparable from an engagement on the artist's part with the deepest, most personal stresses of his experience.

II

And now to Fagin. When Charles first went to work at the warehouse, he was installed in a small recess in the counting-house, a privilege of class and relation. His work was "to cover the pots of paste-blacking" with two kinds of paper, then tie them round with a string, clip the paper close and neat, and paste a printed label on each pot. "Two or three boys were kept at similar duty downstairs on similar wages. One of them came up, in a ragged apron and a paper cap, on the first Monday morning, to show me the trick of using the string and tying the knot. His name was Bob Fagin; and I took the liberty of using his name, long afterwards, in *Oliver Twist*." So casual and off-hand a revelation of what must by nature be a highly charged fact is itself evidence of the high charge. It hardly requires the command of an "ultimate psychology" to see that there is no great distance between Bob Fagin's induction of Charles on his first day of work into the secrets of wrapping and tying, and the wonderful scene in which Fagin teaches class in elementary and advanced pocketpicking. His methods are admirably progressive: strictly learning by doing. The boys are rewarded for proficiency, and even Oliver, pure, innocent, and until that moment perfectly isolated in misery, is so charmed by the "game," and by Fagin's superb imitation of the victim that for the first time in the novel, he laughs, and is happy, and feels at home. Immediately thereafter, he has his own first lesson, and does quite well at it, another tribute to Fagin's intuitive skills as an educator. Never try to instruct a child who seems unhappy: neither

Freud nor John Dewey can be held accountable for communicating this diabolic wisdom to our age. The Devil himself has been at it all along.

When Charles started work it was proposed that his relative, who was employed in the counting-house, would teach him something—something more "academic," that is, than fancy wrapping and tying—during the dinner-hour. But this sad little idea, along with Charles's privileged segregation in the counting-house recess, soon proved incompatible with the conduct of business, and "it was not long, before Bob Fagin and I, and another boy [called Poll Green], . . . worked generally, side by side. Bob Fagin was an orphan, and lived with his brother-in-law, a waterman." Poll Green's father worked at Drury-Lane theater, and Poll's little sister, "did imps in the pantomimes." All innocent and pleasant enough in tone, and so it must have seemed to those who worked with or observed the small twelve-year-old briskly performing among the pots and paste.

But it did not seem that way from the inside, and Dickens's very next sentence reveals in stark dialectical terms the other side of the reality he was experiencing.

> No words can express the secret agony of my soul as I sunk into this companionship; compared these everyday associates with those of my happier childhood; and felt my early hopes of growing up to be a learned and distinguished man, crushed in my breast. The deep remembrance of the sense I had of being utterly neglected and hopeless; of the shame I felt in my position; of the misery it was to my young heart to believe that, day by day, what I had learned, and thought, and delighted in, and raised my fancy and my emulation up by, was passing away from me, never to be brought back any more; cannot be written.

These are certainly the emotions of Oliver Twist, but, the reader is entitled to ask, what "happier childhood" did the workhouse orphan, unlike his creator, have to look back to? We will, I think, be able presently to account for this discrepancy.

Nevertheless, Charles held a special "station" at the warehouse and was treated "as one upon a different footing from the rest." At the same time, he

> never said, to man or boy, how it was that I came to be there, or gave the least indication of being sorry that I was there. That I suffered in secret, and that I suffered exquisitely, no one ever knew but I. . . . But I kept my own counsel, and I did my work. I knew from the first, that if I could not do my work as well as any of the rest, I could not hold myself above slight and contempt. I soon became at least as expeditious and as skillful with my hands, as either of the other boys. Though perfectly familiar with them, my conduct and manners were different enough from theirs to place

a space between us. They, and the men, always spoke of me as "the young gentleman."

Two of the older men occasionally called him Charles, but "it was mostly when we were very confidential, and when I had made some efforts to entertain them over our work with the results of some of the old readings, which were fast perishing out of my mind. Poll Green uprose once, and rebelled against the 'young gentleman' usage; but Bob Fagin settled him speedily."

Amidst the pathos and ambiguity of emotion in such passages, the myriad analogies between this experience and *Oliver Twist* are unmistakable. The differences are equally informing: in *Oliver Twist* it is Fagin and the Dodger who do the entertaining, who provide the gaiety amid the novel's darkness; in real life it was the deserted, neglected, suffering child—that is to say the latent novelist, the person who created Fagin and had Fagin within him—who did the entertaining. Oliver Twist suffers exquisitely and in public, and would have become the world's most incompetent pickpocket had he ever permitted himself really to learn; in life, the suffering was concealed, the dexterity was open and pronounced (in later years Dickens was a brilliant amateur magician) and aggressive. Oliver tells us what Dickens suffered passively; but Dickens also had Jack Hawkins, the Artful Dodger, master pickpocket and comic genius hidden within him.

But there is that line about Bob Fagin cutting short Poll Green's rebellion against the status of "the young gentleman." In the novel Fagin's role is to be tempter and corruptor; his intention is to make Oliver into a thief and so deprive him of his birthright, for he is in fact the son of a gentleman and will inherit his father's estate "only on the stipulation that in his minority he should never have stained his name with any public act of dishonour, meanness, cowardice, or wrong." That Oliver knows nothing of this until the very end is characteristic of the novel's miraculous and parabolic machinery, and also serves to remind us that in writing it Dickens had more things in mind than an imaginative recreation of his autobiography. Yet Fagin's method—his style of tempting and corrupting Oliver—is, at first, to use friendliness, warmth and protectiveness; the escaped workhouse orphan, "a poor houseless, wandering boy, without a friend to help him, or a roof to shelter his head," isolated and alienated in an alienating world, finds his first shelter and affection in the person of "the merry old gentleman." This very affection, the thing Oliver most wants and needs, is at the same time the greatest threat to his moral existence. To trust in it and to return it would be to betray his unknown father and his unknown birthright. And so young Charles must have felt about Bob Fagin's benevolent and protective interferences on his behalf; the paradox, of course, was that Bob was acting to preserve "the young gentleman's" status, while Fagin's amicable devices have the opposite purpose. Furthermore, friendship with Bob Fagin, the brother-in-law of a waterman, would in Charles's condition have been equivalent to an admission that his lostness and desolation were not merely real but somehow permanent.

This acute and profound ambivalence received fuller expression in the course of Charles's experience at the warehouse. Cheerful, skillful, and resourceful as he was and strove to be, his inner sufferings could not be wholly denied, and he was seized repeatedly with his "old disorder." On the occasion of a particularly bad attack, he says,

> Bob Fagin was very good to me. . . . I suffered such excruciating pain at that time, that they made a temporary bed of straw . . . and I rolled on the floor, and Bob filled empty blacking-bottles with hot water, and applied relays of them to my side, half the day.

Toward evening he began to feel better.

> But Bob (who was much bigger and older than I) did not like the idea of my going home alone, and took me under his protection. I was too proud to let him know about the prison; and after making several efforts to get rid of him, to all of which Bob Fagin in his goodness was deaf, shook hands with him on the steps of a house near Southwark-bridge on the Surrey side, making believe that I lived there. As a finishing piece of reality in case of his looking back, I knocked at the door, I recollect, and asked, when the woman opened it, if that was Mr Robert Fagin's house.

Oliver Twist, the workhouse boy, is the son of a gentleman; and it is Fagin's task to prevent him from discovering that secret and entering upon that salvation. In life, young Charles Dickens was the son of a gentleman who was at the time inhabiting comfortable but close apartments in the Marshalsea prison; and it is *he* who keeps the secret from Fagin. The shame of admitting this secret is, in part, transformed in the novel into Oliver's incorruptibility and innocence, his instinctive repugnance for lying or stealing: so strangely are some of our virtues derived. In both instances, however, the danger is connected with a companionship or affection which is at once needed and intolerable; Bob Fagin's protectiveness is transformed into Fagin's treacherous maternal care.

This episode reverberates in many other ways in *Oliver Twist*—the knocking at the door, for example, turns up properly transformed. Fagin's final grand plot to destroy Oliver is to send him into the country as Bill Sikes's assistant in a breaking-and-entering job. Terrorized, Oliver goes along, though inwardly resolved to alarm the family. However, he is immediately discovered, is shot in the dark, and hauled back out. The robbers flee carrying the wounded boy but are forced to leave him in a ditch. Oliver lies there insensible till dawn; then he rouses himself and begins to "stumble onward, he knew not whither." He staggers on, sees a house; it happens to be the one broken into the night before; terrified, he has neither strength to fly nor a place to fly to. He makes it to the door, knocks and collapses; he has committed himself to fate. Who lives in this house? The Maylies—who turn out to be his own true family. So, an innocent lie, told to protect a poor boy's pride and shame from the meddling of a kindly and curious Bob Fagin, and sealed by a knock on some stranger's door, turns out in the novel to be the poor boy's deliverance: the innocent lie becomes Oliver's coercion into the burglary; the knock on the door which permitted him to keep his father's imprisonment a secret becomes the knock on the door which leads him to his family, his father and his identity. Oliver Twist endures his trial, discovers who his father is, and is confirmed in his identity by the discovery—the "parish Boy's progress" ends in the knowledge that he is the son of a gentleman, something few readers by that point would dare to doubt. Charles Dickens, "the young gentleman," kept his father's disgrace a secret from Bob Fagin, and was confirmed in the concealment; that refusal to betray his father—and his father in himself—even as he, young Charles, felt betrayed and abandoned by him, is one of his chief sources of strength as a novelist. And the conflict from which this strength emerges—his relation to his father—supplies what I believe to be the master theme of Dickens's novels.

Yet if we return to this incident from Dickens's young life, we are struck by what he called the "finishing piece of reality," his knocking at the door and asking "if that was Mr Robert Fagin's house." It is a fine piece of audacity and presence of mind: certainly it is something we cannot imagine Oliver Twist ever doing. But we can imagine the Artful Dodger or Fagin—if he could get away with it—doing it; in fact, it is precisely the kind of thing that Fagin puts Nancy up to in order to recapture Oliver. The ruse that Charles invented to escape from Bob Fagin's friendly clutches is transformed in *Oliver Twist* into one of the devices that Fagin commands against the orphan boy.

We see, then, that Dickens's recreation in the novel of his boyhood experience has a tolerable inner coherence. In particular, his mixed attitudes toward Bob Fagin and Fagin seem up to a point remarkably congruent. When as a small boy, Dickens told Forster, he was taken for a walk through a criminal district of London, he felt "a profound attraction of repulsion." This phrase fairly suggests something of Dickens's attitude toward Fagin, and toward Bob Fagin too, although it might be more precise to say that toward Bob he felt the reverse, a profound repulsion of attraction. Yet if we could do no more than demonstrate that Dickens had transposed what he felt about Bob Fagin on to the figure of Fagin, we would not have advanced very far in our understanding of the fictional Fagin. We might of course go through *Oliver*

Twist in tedious detail, exhibiting how in literally scores of places Dickens was imaginatively alluding to events from his boyhood. But this would in itself bring us no nearer to a solution of the problem. Bob Fagin, after all, was a boy, however much bigger, older, and tougher than Charles he might have seemed. Fagin is a terrible old man, Jew, devil, demon and master-criminal. The difference remains large.

III

Bob Fagin is mentioned once more, toward the end of the autobiographical fragment. Sometime during Charles's period of employment, but after his father had been released from prison, Warren's moved their premises. Several windows of the new building looked out on a busy street. "Bob Fagin and I," Dickens writes, "had attained to great dexterity in tying up the pots, I forget how many we could do, in five minutes." For the sake of light, the two boys worked together at one of the windows, "and we were so brisk at it, that the people used to stop and look in. Sometimes there would be quite a little crowd there. I saw my father coming in at the door one day when we were very busy, and I wondered how he could bear it." This is a puzzling little scene. It seems at once flat and over-intense; it is characterized by extreme, if unarticulated, ambivalence: pride in dexterity and shame over the work; pleasure in skillful performance before a crowd or "audience," yet anxiety and humiliation at being observed or seen; and of course an utter mélange of feelings about being seen by his father. Young Charles had hidden from Bob Fagin the fact that his father's home, and thus in a sense his own, was a prison; now, his father came publicly to his son's place of degradation and saw him exposed to full view in the company of Bob Fagin.

The sense one has of emotions so intense as to be almost incoherent is strengthened by what follows. Dickens's father apparently "could bear it," at least for a while. But "at last, one day," he writes, "my father, and the relative so often mentioned, quarrelled." It was by letter, which Charles carried, and the quarrel, he says, was very fierce. "It was about me. It may have had some backward reference, in part, for anything I know, to my employment at the window." This is the purest conjecture, as Dickens himself admits; but we should note that he is connecting this climactic scene with the previous one about being seen in the window. All Dickens was "certain of," he says, is that he gave his relative the note; soon after (how long? the same day? next week?) the relative told him that he was "very much insulted about me," and that Charles would have to leave the warehouse. At that the boy broke down: "I cried very much, partly because it was so sudden, and partly because in his anger he was violent about my father, though gentle to me." And then, "with relief so strange that it was like oppression, I went home." The incoherence of this memory, along with Dickens's unsupported but wishful association of it with the scene at the window, lead me to suggest that the entire incident and Dickens's memory of it are what is known in psychoanalysis as "over-determined": a multiplicity of meanings and motives converge upon an event, charging its separate elements with significances which refer elsewhere and to other things. This episode of young Charles, Bob Fagin, John Dickens and the window has, I believe, the character of what is called a "screen memory." But in order to discover what it is screening we must turn back to the novel.

There are two passages in *Oliver Twist* which have always struck me as being out of place in the sense that they do not emerge out of any inner logic or necessity of the story but seem to have been written by Dickens because what he was about to describe had some special private resonance. In both Dickens ceases momentarily to speak as the impersonal narrator and addresses the reader in a personal, essayistic, and almost musing voice; both act as preludes to a scene between Oliver and Fagin; both are connected with an experience of sleep; both also contain "illogical" or "false" details in the sense that something mysterious happens in each which Dickens fails subsequently to clear up. They are in fact the same scene, though they are separated by two hundred pages, and each contains elements which augment or complete the other.

The first of these scenes occurs on the morning after Oliver has first been introduced to Fagin's den. The boys have gone out, Fagin is boiling coffee for breakfast, and Oliver is on the point of waking, but is still half-asleep. Dickens goes on to describe this condition:

> There is a drowsy state, between sleeping and waking, when you dream more in five minutes with your eyes half open, and yourself half conscious of everything that is passing around you, than you would in five nights with your eyes fast closed, and your senses wrapt in perfect unconsciousness. At such times, a mortal knows just enough of what his mind is doing to form some glimmering conception of its mighty powers, its bounding from earth and spurning time and space, when freed from the restraint of its corporeal associate.

Dickens is representing what is now called a "hypnagogic" phenomenon, that condition between sleep and waking when the conscious mind and its censor relax and unconscious processes and impulses become more than usually accessible. Oliver is in that half-state, apparently asleep and yet able to see and hear Fagin. Fagin looks at him, calls him by name, and when the boy does not answer, locks the door, draws forth from the trap-door "a small box" which he lays on the table and then takes out of it gold watches, "sparkling with jewels," and "rings, brooches, bracelets, and other articles of jewellery," while he chuckles with pleasure over his late cohorts who hanged without "peaching" on him. He then takes out another trinket which seems to have "some very minute inscription on it," which he pores over "long and earnestly." Suddenly—

> his bright dark eyes, which had been staring vacantly before him fell on Oliver's face; the boy's eyes were fixed on his in mute curiosity; and although the recognition was only for an instant— for the briefest space of time that can possibly be conceived—it was enough to show the old man that he had been observed. He closed the lid of the box with a loud crash; and laying his hand on a bread knife which was on the table, started furiously up.

He questions Oliver about what he has seen, and whether he was awake an hour ago. Oliver, in his stupefaction or his innocence, has seen nothing or understands nothing of what he has seen, and the scene ends inconsequentially.

The second scene takes place two hundred pages later. Oliver has been rescued and restored by the Maylies; they have retired to the country where Oliver is learning to read better and to write, and has his own "little room" on the ground floor at the back of the house "in which he was accustomed to sit, when busy at his books." It looks out on to a small garden. One summer evening, Oliver sits at this window "intent upon his books. He had been poring over them for some time . . . he had exerted himself a great deal . . . [and] gradually and by slow degrees, he fell asleep." At this point Dickens enters upon a second explanation of the hypnagogic phenomenon: [Marcus quotes the passages that appear in this volume on pp. 66–67, from "There is a kind of sleep . . ." to ". . . who sat beside him," and on pp. 230–31, from "There—there— at the window . . ." to ". . . called loudly for help"].

These scenes have in common several elements: a boy in a state of sleep or half-sleep in which conscious and unconscious impressions, fantasies and realities, dreams and recollections, tend to be fused and confused; supervening on this an intense experience of watching and of being watched, which then gives way to emotions of threat and terror. In one scene there are the jewel box and the trinkets and the brandished knife; in the other the book and the window. I think that we are witness here to the decomposed elements of what Freud called the primal scene, to either a memory or fantasy of it: the child asleep, or just waking, or feigning sleep while observing sexual intercourse between his parents, and, frightened by what he sees or imagines, is either then noticed by the parents or has a fantasy of what would occur if he were noticed. The symbolism of the jewel box and the knife in the first scene are self-explanatory; for the window and the book we recur to the scene in the window at the blacking factory, and behind it, perhaps, to Dickens's earlier recollection of himself as a small boy on "a summer evening . . . sitting on my bed, reading as if for life."

Dickens's experience of desolation, fear and anguish during the months of his father's imprisonment and his employment at the factory had the effect of re-awakening and reviving in him similar emotions which he, like every child, experienced at an earlier age, the age when parents seem like gods, giants and demons. Indeed, the trauma of the London experiences was so acute that in a peculiar sense it seemed to absorb and obliterate his earlier life. Dickens was not, after all, a young child when he came to live in London—he was eleven years old. And yet it is an interesting fact that he was rarely able to write with conviction or credibility about life outside the city. "'The memories which peaceful country scenes call up," he says in *Oliver Twist*, "are not of this world, nor of its thoughts and hopes." However we may regard them, he goes on, "there lingers, in the least reflective mind, a vague and half-formed consciousness of having held such feelings long before, in some remote and distant time, which calls up solemn thoughts of distant times to come." The paradise or Eden of infancy which we all have known and out of which we create all our ideas of supernal happiness are, in other words, a foretaste of heaven; but Dickens seems uncertain whether these are memories of anything he ever actually experienced. It was almost as if the months in London had canceled or cut him off from the reality of his earlier life, even while they reactivated other emotions and memories from that same period.

The scene of young Charles and Bob Fagin at the window being suddenly seen by Dickens's father—to which Charles responded so strongly—acted as a screen for earlier thoughts of being suddenly seen in an exposed and dangerous situation; and very likely as a screen for memories of the reverse situation of suddenly *seeing* something that is dangerous. (The two cannot in fact be separated, as in *Oliver Twist* they are not.) It seems clear, therefore, that the Bob Fagin whose friendship contained the threat of exposure, and the father whose freedom was a fraud and an outrage while his son slaved in a window, coalesced in Dickens's mind. But they coalesced into an image which has its origin in an earlier phase of Dickens's development, a phase which the London experience re-awakened and which the scene at the window both refers to and conceals. This is the image of the father of infancy and earliest childhood. And it is at this point that Fagin, the terrible, frightening old Jew, becomes relevant. For the traditional popular mythology of the Jew as Devil and Anti-Christ, as the castrator and murderer of good little Christian boys, corresponds itself to this image of the terrible father of infancy and of our primal fantasies, and is indeed one of western culture's chief expressions of it.

The argument I have been proposing would be less convincing if these were the only examples from Dickens's writings of such scenes. But the fact is that variations of this scene recur in Dickens repeatedly; moreover, the image of being closely watched, stared at and suddenly surrounded by glaring eyes appears with obsessive frequency in Dickens's novels. There are, in addition, two other instances in *Oliver Twist*, both of which support the point I have been trying to make.

Before unconscious ideas or memories are permitted to emerge into consciousness, they are made to undergo certain disguises and distortions—such as condensation, decomposition, displacement, reversal or multiplication. In the two scenes from *Oliver Twist*, which I have discussed as expressing a primal fantasy or recollection of Dickens's, one thing seems missing. Except for a symbolic representation in the jewel box and the trinkets inside it which Fagin hoards and caresses, there is no direct representation either of the primal act itself or of the other partner in the act. In the mind of a very small child, we know, sexual intercourse is first apprehended as a form of violence, specifically of murder, inflicted by the male upon the female. There is such a scene in *Oliver Twist*, one of its most famous, the murder of Nancy by Bill Sikes—and in this connection, it is relevant to observe that Sikes kills her because he believes she has betrayed him out of her affection for Oliver. It is after he has clubbed her to death that the image of the staring eyes reappears. Sikes throws a rug over her corpse, "but it was worse to fancy the eyes, and imagine them moving toward him, than to see them glaring upward." He flees the city and wanders about the country all day, but is pursued by "a vision . . . as constant and more terrible than that from which he had escaped." Then follows one of Dickens's incomparable passages:

> Those widely staring eyes, so lustreless and so glassy, that he had better borne to see them than think upon them, appeared in the midst of darkness; light in themselves, but giving light to nothing. There were but two, but they were everywhere. If he shut out the sight, there came the room with every well-known object . . . each in its accustomed place. The body was in *its* place, and its eyes were as he saw them when he stole away. He got up, and rushed into the field without. The figure was behind him. He re-entered the shed, and shrunk down once more. The eyes were there, before he had laid himself along.

He flees again, "flying from memory and himself," but is pursued by the vision, and finally by that hydra-headed and argus-eyed great beast, the London mob. At the end, surrounded by "tiers and tiers of faces in every window," by people fighting each other "only for an instant to see the wretch," he tries to escape across the roof-tops and lower himself by a rope into a ditch. Suddenly he looks behind him, cries out, "The eyes again," loses his balance, is caught in the noose of the rope, and hangs himself. "He fell for five-and-thirty feet. There was a sudden jerk, a terrific convulsion of the limbs; and there he hung, with the open knife clenched in his stiffening hand." Without pausing to analyse, we can see how recurrent and how suggestive in their recurrence are the elements of these episodes.

The second additional instance is the great scene of Fagin's trial, and now it is Fagin who is the object of this frightful scrutiny.

> The court was paved, from floor to roof, with human faces. In-
> quisitive and eager eyes peered from every inch of space. From the
> rail before the dock, away into the sharpest angle of the smallest
> corner in the galleries, all looks fixed upon one man—Fagin. Before
> him and behind: above, below, on the right and on the left: he
> seemed to stand surrounded by a firmament, all bright with gleam-
> ing eyes.
> He stood there, in all this glare of living light, with one hand
> resting on the wooden slab before him, the other held to his
> ear. . . .

Sikes and Fagin, both of them figures who threaten to ruin, castrate and destroy Oliver, are now in Oliver's place; and the reader's emotions are enlisted in their terror, as they were in Oliver's. What has happened here is too intricate and compressed for simple analysis, but it is essential to note again the identification Dickens dramatically asserts between Oliver on the one hand and Fagin and Sikes on the other—and by inevitable implication between himself and his father. It is essential because otherwise we would be unable to understand how it is that Fagin, inhuman monster that he is, is also human and charming and an imaginative triumph. Part of the answer, I believe, has to do with the fact that at the deeper levels of his being Dickens maintained and had access to a feeling of identity with his father, even with that father who appeared to him as destroyer and betrayer of his son. His father was alive in him, as was Fagin, and in creating Fagin Dickens affirmed that fact as much as he negated it.

Two more bits of evidence and we are done. While Dickens was writing *Oliver Twist* he was afflicted with a return of his boyhood illness. The spasms came on him with particular severity while he was writing the final, climatic parts of the novel, and he understood this, he wrote, as "the penalty for sticking so close to Oliver." He was to pay one further penalty. Years later, toward the end of his career, Dickens embarked upon a series of public readings from his works. He was a superb actor and reader, and the accounts of these performances are uniform in their praise of his brilliance and power. He eventually decided to make some readings from *Oliver Twist*, choosing a series of scenes from it which ended in Fagin's betrayal of Nancy, the murder of Nancy, and Sikes's flight and death. He was at first reluctant to read these particular passages because he thought they might make too horrifying an impression on his impressionable Victorian audiences. And the impression they did make was from all accounts extravagant: women fainting and being carried from the auditorium "stiff and rigid" came to be a preposterous matter of course. But the impression they made on Dickens was more profound, and disastrous. They became an obsession with him; he read them more than any of his other selections; and he killed himself by means of them. After each reading of the scenes from *Oliver Twist* he was literally prostrated; his pulse would rise to 120 and above; it would take ten or fifteen minutes before he could utter a rational or coherent phrase. In already uncertain health, he was advised by his family, friends and physicians to stop this suicidal pursuit. Yet he would not and could not, and at last it killed him.

This culminating episode of Dickens's career has been much discussed; various explanations of it have been advanced, none of which is really satisfactory. I think that now we can understand it better. In returning at the end of his life to *Oliver Twist*, Dickens was returning to his first and most intense representation of the crisis of his young boyhood. But he was also returning to events in the still more remote past, events which had been re-aroused by the months of suffering in the blacking factory, and which were both expressed and concealed in his recollection of them and in *Oliver Twist*. These events we all experience, and most of us then forget them forever. It was part of Dickens's destiny as a genius, part of the pain as well as the glory, that it was not given to him to "forget" such things in the way it is to most. They recurred in him, they spoke through him, he wrote them out symbolically, he acted them out, and still they recurred, and still he was bitterly loyal to them—they were, after all, himself. Dickens is one of the heroes of literature, and if my interpretation of these events in his life is persuasive, it is possible to see something heroic even in his self-destruction. Blind and unknowing as his struggle was on the level of consciousness, he was at least struggling with the depths of his being—the same depths that exist in all of us. That he remained until death engrossed in his most primitive and vital conflicts may also add to our understanding of his extraordinary development as a novelist: to remain in touch with vital conflicts is to remain in touch with vital feelings, with one's roots in life.

What, then, have we accomplished? We have, I believe, accounted in some degree for the genesis of Fagin, demonstrating how various details of Dickens's experience were brought together in him. That the part of Fagin which is Jewish turns out to be not merely minor but almost fortuitous, or if not fortuitous then curiously unpremeditated in its mythological cast, and that Fagin's relations to Oliver are more paradoxical than might at first seem likely, is not really surprising. Similar things have been suspected before. But we have not accounted for the power of Fagin as an imaginative creation; we have not explained why this demonic, disgusting and monstrous old man should be so fascinating, so comic, even so winning in his abominable wickedness. It will not do to invoke genius, which in this context is a convenient way of avoiding explanation—though Fagin is nothing if not a creation of genius. Perhaps the closest we can come to an answer is to say that the boy who suffered passively in the blacking warehouse, who grieved in solitude and felt himself to be Oliver Twist, was also the boy who was not afraid to lie to protect his and his father's poor pride and shame, who acted out that lie with spirit and audacity, and who told stories to amuse and entertain his fellows in the warehouse. He went on lying and telling stories until he became one of the world's great masters of the art, and created those grand imaginative lies which in our perplexed condition somehow approximate the truth. Oliver Twist could never have imagined Fagin, and Dickens could neither have imagined nor created him had Fagin not been part of himself and had he been unable ever to affirm that part of himself with gusto and delight.

MONROE ENGEL

The Social and Political Issues†

Dickens learned about poverty in the least desirable way, by being a poor child. His interest in the poor thereafter was constant and passionate. The pity and the pain of their condition were always apparent to him, and part of the great obsessive center of his writing. In all his fiction, there was purpose in his portraits of the poor: "I have great faith in the Poor; to the best of my ability I always endeavour to present them in a favourable light to the rich; and I shall never cease, I hope, until I die, to advocate their being made as happy and as wise as the circumstances of their condition in its utmost improvement, will admit of their becoming." The "circumstances of their condition" ranged wide in his mind. He defended vanity and color in poor women's dress to Lady Burdett-Coutts as one of "the good influences of a poor man's house." He opposed the Sunday Law because he thought it discriminated against the amusements of the poor, and regretted the elimination of village sports and of shooting for the average farmer or villager for similar reasons. He believed that some measures meant to help the poor would

† From *The Maturity of Dickens* (Cambridge, 1967) 48–59. Reprinted by permission of Harvard University Press.

in fact do the reverse, and that the proposal of such measures showed an ignorance of the actual circumstances of the lives of the poor. Thus he refused in 1843 to support factory legislation to reduce the length of the working day, because he thought the poor could not afford the loss of income that would attend the shorter working day.

He had no soft ideas of the blessings of poverty, and the poor often seemed disgusting to him, particularly if they happened not to be the English poor. The dregs of the population of Naples he described to Forster as "mere squalid, abject, miserable animals for vermin to batten on; slouching, slinking, ugly, shabby, scavenging scarecrows." His long, often virtually daily correspondence with Lady Burdett-Coutts in regard to her reform home for prostitutes at Shepherd's Bush also shows this combination of concern and hard practicality, and at times distaste.[1] He habitually linked poverty with filth and disease, and the connections between poverty, sanitation, and disease provide perhaps the most exploited subject in both *Household Words* and *All the Year Round*. Crime, too, he sees as a product of poverty and its companion, ignorance. *Household Words* and *All the Year Round* are used repeatedly to publicize certain specific conditions of the poor, as well as their general plight. Typical subjects dealt with are inadequate housing and attempts to improve it, or conditions of women employed in factories, and how this contrasts with the conditions of women still working in home or cottage industries.

In the last twenty years of his life, one of Dickens' chief blows for the poor was his opposition to the Poor Law of 1834. Even in 1842 he had written: "Pray tell Mr. Chadwick . . . I *do* differ from him, to the death, on his crack topic—the New Poor-Law"; and it is likely that he was suspicious of the law from the very beginning. Yet it is probable too that in the genesis of his political ideas Dickens was much indebted to the rational reformism of Bentham, and that not until roughly the date of *Hard Times* (1854) had he clarified even for himself the grounds of his differences with the Benthamites. The Poor Law of 1834 applied the principles of political economy to the problem of the poor as stringently as common feeling and opinion could, under the circumstances, allow; and this Benthamite basis of the law may for a time have complicated Dickens' feelings against it. Certainly even when he conducted all-out war on the law, he concentrated his attack on the way it was administered, and in the postscript to *Our Mutual Friend*, he said of the law: "I believe there has been in England since the days of the STUARTS, no law so often infamously administered, no law so often openly violated, no law habitually so ill-supervised."

It is necessary to understand that the Poor Law of 1834 represented a break with the method of dealing with the poor that had been in

1. See above, pp. 381–83 [*Editor*].

operation since the time of Queen Elizabeth. Sidney and Beatrice Webb, in *English Poor Law Policy* [1910], give a useful account of the change produced by the Law of 1834; and even their prejudice on the subject, close in some ways to Dickens' own, helps to an understanding of Dickens' opposition. The Act of 1834 creates an administration but lays down no policy; it is the Report of 1834 that underlies the new policy. Central to the Report is the assertion made in the course of one argument, but never made as a recommendation, that the situation of the pauper should not be "really or apparently so eligible as the situation of the independent labourer of the lowest class." More plainly put, this asserts that pauperism must be made less desirable than the condition of people dependent for their subsistence on the most menial kind of work, or else it would soon be impossible to get people to do this menial work. In the course of the Report it is made clear that this applies to able-bodied laborers and their dependents, and not to orphans, or the aged, sick, or infirm.

If political economy had been strictly adhered to, the able-bodied would have had to work or starve, and the distinction between the pauper and "the independent labourer of the lowest class" would have been at its most persuasive. But popular sentiment would not have allowed this. The next best policy, then, was to keep the able-bodied pauper a scant distance from starvation, and thus make the undesirability of his situation clear. Of course there was another possibility—to improve the conditions of life of the menial laborer rather than lower the standards of the pauper. Dickens, or the Webbs, or humanitarians of many other descriptions would favor this alternative, but the Report of 1834 came out of the Benthamite climate.

The Report also recommended that responsibility for a policy in regard to paupers be taken from the individual parishes, to which it had been assigned during the reign of Elizabeth, and given to a central authority, which could then insure uniformity in the treatment of each class of destitute persons, reduce the shifting of paupers from one parish to another, prevent discontent among paupers, and bring the management more effectually under the control of Parliament. It recommended very strongly against the continuation of out-door relief (i.e., relief given outside a workhouse) for able-bodied laborers, because of the difficulty of discriminating according to merit in the award of such relief. It also set rules for "well-regulated workhouses."

But the principle of the Report of 1834 most heeded was that paupers not be treated too well. Treatment of paupers did not become as uniform as the writers of the Report had wished, varying a great deal from one workhouse to another; but the bad workhouses exceeded the good in number, and the total picture was certainly no encouragement to idle poverty. "Can any one wonder," Friedrich Engels asked, "that the poor decline to accept public relief under these conditions? That they starve rather than enter these bastilles?" The examinations of poor-law practice frequently published in *Household Words* and *All the Year Round* reflect a similar point of view, and in one of these pieces an almost identical statement is made: "The principle upon which relief is administered under the law that taxes us for succour of the poor appears to be, to make the help rendered so distasteful, that they must be far gone indeed in wretchedness who will apply for it; and the high-hearted poor will starve rather than take it, will die instead of coming on the rates." A few of these articles in the weekly periodicals merely describe the methods and problems of dealing with paupers, but most are directed against the Law of 1834, calling attention to such problems as overcrowding and actual lack of facilities in workhouses, particularly during hard winters, the inadequacy of medical help, the injustice of the residence requirements for relief, or the unfairness of having poor and rich parishes equally responsible for their own poor.

What Dickens and other observers found reprehensible in the operation of the New Poor Law was the combination of inefficiency and a basic lack of charity. The word "charity" has often introduced confusion into discussions of Dickens' social views. Some specific things can be said about his view of charity, however, that will enlighten rather than confuse. Even the Benthamite framers of the New Poor Law did not think the law would obviate the further need for almsgiving. They wanted such charity to be private, not public, however, and depended on charity to provide what the law, in order to be consistent, could not provide: "Where cases of real hardship occur, the remedy must be applied by individual charity, a virtue for which no system of compulsory relief can be or ought to be a substitute." Dickens' insistence upon charity, then, is far from singular. Where he breaks on principle with the writers of the Report of 1834 is in his belief that charity cannot be merely private but must enter also into any government plan for dealing with paupers, and in his belief in charity as a quality as well as an activity. He insists that duty without love is not enough. He is scornful also of charity that is not disinterested, and an unpleasant story in *Household Words* tells how a curate's use of alms to get the poor to attend church finally demoralizes an entire community.

Certain ideals of charity are indicated in the activities of an order of begging nuns whose work is inferentially compared to treatment of the poor by other agencies, and in those of a man who is an exemplar of individually conducted charity. Various charitable institutions are also described and commented on, most notably the first Children's Hospital in England. This hospital is reexamined ten years after its founding, and another hospital in Liverpool, modelled on the first one in London, is also described. Similar is the account of a visit to a foundling hospital in London. The need and justification for private charity is presented in "Houseless and Hungry," in which the inmates of a shelter for the houseless-hungry are cast against the arguments of the extreme Malthusians and plain sceptics that there is no reason for such charity. A similar strategy lies behind two accounts of charity-financed homes for working girls whose earnings, even when they were employed, were not sufficient to enable them to live decently.

But charity seemed to Dickens far more certainly a boon to the giver than to the receiver. He believed in self-help and independence and even perhaps in the salutary effect of work. He was a hard as well as vulnerable man who had pulled himself up with the aid of a great talent, to be sure, but also by terrible determination and labor; and he expected other people to exert themselves, also. "You can no more help a people who do not help themselves, than you can help a man who does not help himself," he said. Similarly, he told two men who had asked him to join in a movement on behalf of working men that any such movement would be pointless until working people had begun to move on their own behalf.

He liked to see men helping themselves, or men in a similar situation helping each other out of a sense of common interest. He gave publicity to examples of the poor banding together to help each other, and he supported any plan that would increase the economic independence of the poor or laboring family. He favored the formation of provident societies, and he argued their superiority to parish charities. He published an article in favor of post office savings banks; a recommendation of insurance as a joint social enterprise in which all take part for mutual protection; an appeal for some kind of sick insurance for railway clerks, who were early examples of underpaid white-collar workers.

In April of 1864, 1865, and 1866, *All the Year Round* printed articles in favor of a government plan to sponsor inexpensive insurance for workingmen, annuities for old age and sickness. Years before, an article in *Household Words* had suggested that taxes should be a kind of insurance paid voluntarily by all members of the nation to secure their rights and needs. Together, all these articles suggest the possibility of a nation that does not so much indulge in kindnesses toward those broken by life, as try to recognize and insure the rights of its citizens not to be so broken.

Dickens expected society to allow the workingman his self-respect. It is notable that the comedy of the working class characters in his novels does not often impinge on their dignity. When an article on workingmen's clubs was being prepared for *All the Year Round*, Dickens indicated the lines the article was to follow: that the men be trusted to manage their own affairs, including the problem of drunkenness among members, that they be neither babied nor patronized, and that social rest and recreation be made available to them as a needed respite without pretense of education.

JAMES R. KINCAID

Oliver Twist: Laughter and the Rhetoric of Attack†

One of the major questions is how such a dark novel can be so funny. It is probable that most critics often laugh while reading it; it is certain that when they are finished they write essays on its bleak effects. And they are right—in both cases. The reason for the paradoxical reaction is, I think, that Dickens uses laughter here to subvert our conventional reactions and to emphasize more dramatically the isolation of his young hero, indeed, the essential isolation of all men. In denying the possibility of a comic society and yet provoking laughter, the novel continually thwarts and frustrates the reader; for our laughter continues to search for a social basis, even when there is no longer any support for it in the novel. In other words, laughter is stirred, but the impulses aroused behind it are not allowed to collect and settle. Unlike the convivial atmosphere of *Pickwick Papers*, where our laughter finally provides us a place with Sam and with Mr. Pickwick, here there is no possibility of escape to a society sanctified by the expulsion of all the villains. Instead, laughter is used primarily as a weapon, to suggest that we are the villains. The selfishness and unfeeling cruelty which are a subconscious part of much laughter are here brought to the surface and used to intensify our reaction and our involvement. Laughter is a necessary part of the proper reaction to the novel, but in the end it is used against us, undercutting the comfortable aloofness we had originally maintained and forcing us into conjunction with the lonely and terrified orphan. This suggests that, just as in *Pickwick*, the basic attack is on detachment. But the comparison doesn't go very far. There are no comparable rewards for submitting to the attack in *Oliver Twist* and no comfortably stable scheme of values to which we can attach ourselves. We are left alone in a rootless and threatening world.

There is, of course, an apparently brighter world in *Oliver Twist*, and the plot of the novel seems to point us towards it. Even before the narrative reaches midpoint, Dickens has rescued his hero and placed him firmly in the protection of the Maylie group; the last half of the novel simply reinforces Oliver's 'safe' position, on the one hand, by methodically hunting down the threats to his safety and eliminating them (Fagin and Sikes) or converting them (Charlie Bates and Nancy), and, on the other hand, by securing the prospects of wealth for the hero

† From *Dickens and the Rhetoric of Laughter*. Copyright © 1971. Reprinted by permission of Oxford University Press. Pp. 50–66.

(through Monks's will) and eternal bliss for the rest of the good people (the marriage between Rose and Harry Maylie). Yet most commentators have found themselves untouched by this arrangement of events and have emphasized the novel's predominantly grim effect. This paradox has generally been explained by the argument that Dickens portrayed Fagin and his group with great vividness, that a part of him identified very closely with them, that he treated them with great 'sympathy'. In contrast, even Forster admitted that the Maylie-Brownlow group were so poorly realized, so completely unbelievable as to constitute 'the weak part of the story'. Graham Greene has merged these two contrasting impressions by describing the controlling view of the novel as 'Manichaean'; he argues that the power of the book comes from 'the eternal and alluring trait of the Manichee, with its simple and terrible explanation of our plight, how the world was made by Satan and not by God, lulling us with the music of despair.'[1]

But the problem really goes much deeper, and the novel really does not make such simple distinctions as are implied by these views. The fact is that there are two separate and conflicting dualisms: one social, between the individual and the institution, the second moral, between the respectable and the criminal. Arnold Kettle has described this conflict as that between the pattern and the plot of the novel.[2] For the first eleven chapters the basic pattern of the novel is developed: the evocation of the dark world of the poor and the engagement of our sympathy with them in their struggle against institutions. This pattern, he argues, is most deeply felt and continues throughout, though in the second half of the novel it tends to lose ground to the plot, a relatively superficial and conventionally formulated moralistic conflict. The basic problem, though, is not in the superficiality of the moral theme, but in its conflict with the more deeply-felt theme of institutional oppression. The 'good' people in the second half of the novel sometimes use the hated institution of the first half to fight not only the persecutors but the victims as well.

Laughter leads us to Oliver's side, but Oliver soon leaves us and heads for the enemy. As a result we are likely to be stranded. Our laughter has exposed us and isolated us along with Oliver, and it then deprives us of even his alliance. It is our response to this desolation, pushed on us by our laughter, that is at the core of the novel's one undoubted effect: discomfort. We not only have an uneasy aesthetic response to a thematically fractured novel, but an uneasy emotional response at being forced into the same isolation the novel portrays. In the end, *Oliver Twist* comes near to making orphans of us all by dislocating us from the world we are comfortable in, and displaying the full force of Mrs. Thingummy's bitter mockery of consolation.

1. See above, p. 431 [*Editor*].
2. Arnold Kettle, *Introduction to the English Novel* (New York, 1960) i.132.

I

The most obvious cause of this dislocation is the lack of consistency in the narrative personality. It is impossible to define the characteristics or moral positions of the narrator in this novel, for they are continually shifting. It is true that, as in most Dickens novels, the narrative voice provides a counterpoint to the story and gives oblique directions to the reader. But here the directions are generally misleading. We expect those obtrusive narrative commentaries at least to provide accurate sign-posts to a comfortable position we can take, but here Dickens exploits this very expectation to attack such smug confidence.

* * *

The same subversive technique illustrated by the author's comments and the point of view is utilized more fully and more subtly in the narrative itself. Though there are other important humorous appeals, particularly later in the novel, it is the dominant humour of the first half, focusing on the conflict between the novel's outcasts and its established society, which is most functional. The laughter called up by these situations to a large extent determines our reaction to the general world of the novel and to the social assumptions on which that world is built.

The humour attending these conflicts between the institution and the individual almost invariably calls for an ambiguous response. For example, in the second chapter, Oliver is told that 'the board had said he was to appear before it forthwith'. Oliver is confused by this report, 'not having a very clearly defined notion of what a live board was', and when he is ushered into the august presence of 'eight or ten fat gentlemen' and told to 'bow to the board', 'seeing no board but the table, [he] fortunately bowed to that'. This is both tactful and pointed; it could be very funny. Dickens manages to use Oliver's ignorance to make the point that his confusion is, after all, not so meaningless: the board does have all the flexibility and feeling of a thick plank. Given only these details and this perspective, the humour could well be successful. There are, however, other factors which work against laughter. First of all, the situation is under the control of Bumble, who at this point is an almost unrelieved villain. Second, we are disturbed by Oliver's reaction: he 'was not quite certain whether he ought to laugh or cry'. Finally, however, the boy's conflict is resolved; Bumble gives him so many 'taps' behind that he cries. The scene seems to be devised in such a way as to undercut the aloofness we have originally assumed in order to laugh and to force us into a closer identification with Oliver, adding by the way a penetrating glance into the underlying viciousness of such laughter. In order to laugh in the first place, the reader must remove himself slightly from the situation: he knows what a board is, Oliver does not. Oliver's ambiguous reaction, however, recalls the novel's earlier remarks

about institutions, workhouse institutions in particular; and the reference
to the possibility of crying similarly recalls us to a position of sympathy
for him. When he is finally forced by Bumble to decide against laughing
in favour of crying, we too must decide. In order to laugh, we must
identify ourselves with the board, and this is clearly impossible. Our
probable laughter at the beginning of the scene is cut off, perhaps denied,
but we are not likely to escape a recognition of the fact that, for a brief
instant, we had allowed ourselves to be members of the board, regarding
Oliver as an 'it'. The shock of recognition urges us closer to Oliver and
denies us the easy sanctuary of laughter.

* * *

There are, however, times when we *are* associated with Sikes, or with
any other victim, any other man who is hunted, frightened, or alone.
Dickens uses the technique of subversion so consistently and subtly that,
by the end of the novel, we are asked to react with the same combination of guilt, insight, and intense association with the victims,
even when there is no 'gentleman in the white waistcoat' to nullify
our temptation to laughter and even when the victim is an equivocal character at best. For instance, during Sikes's flight through the
countryside, he draws near two mail-coach guards to hear them talk of
the murder:

> 'Corn's up a little. I heerd talk of a murder, too, down Spitalfields
> way, but I don't reckon much upon it.'
> 'Oh, that's quite true,' said a gentleman inside, who was looking
> out of the window. 'And a dreadful murder it was.'
> 'Was it, sir?' rejoined the guard, touching his hat. 'Man or
> woman, pray, sir?'
> 'A woman,' replied the gentleman. 'It is supposed—'
> 'Now, Ben,' replied the coachman impatiently.
> 'Damn that 'ere bag,' said the guard; 'are you gone to sleep in
> there?'
> 'Coming!' cried the office keeper, running out.
> 'Coming,' growled the guard. 'Ah, and so's the young 'ooman
> of property that's going to take a fancy to me, but I don't know
> when. Here, give hold. All ri—ight!'
> The horn sounded a few cheerful notes, and the coach was gone.
> (XLVIII)

The joke clashes strongly with an atmosphere which is so controlled and
intense that it allows us no real interest outside Sikes; the brilliant jux-
taposition of the guard's slight and impersonal interest in the sensational
aspects of the crime with Sikes's obsession with the eyes that won't shut
is capped by the final unconsciously brutal witticism about 'the young
'ooman of property'. Since the focus has shifted only very briefly from
the killer, the only woman on our minds at the moment is the mangled

corpse of Nancy, who has been killed precisely because her 'fancy' for Bill would not allow her to desert him. Two orders of reality, connected only by a startling and accidental relevance of referents, are violently contrasted here: the order which contains the social world, easy jokes and thoughtlessness, and the horribly intense and torturous world of Sikes. By this point, the reader is most likely conditioned by Dickens's technique and has no real choice but to enter into the latter; the social world has consistently been shown to be cruel with the special cruelty of comfortable aloofness. The notes of the horn certainly are cheerful only to those who regard the fact that 'Corn's up a little' as equal in interest to the murder. The continual and subtle rhetorical insistence is that crimes of passion, no matter how brutal, are not nearly so pervasive as crimes of indifference.

The final goal of this technique is to pry us away from the normal identification we make with an aloof society and to force us to enter much more fully into the world of the terrified and alienated individual, who at various times is Oliver, Fagin, Sikes, Bumble, and the Artful Dodger. Laughter, the strongest expression of social identification, is brilliantly used as a weapon against our own safety, quietly urging us to assume, for the moment, the perilous position of the hunted and the trapped. Instead of providing for a comic society, our laughter is meant to deny society altogether and to force us to be as alone as the novel's victims. The novel's humour, in other words, maintains that the real conflict is between the outcasts and the establishment, even after the plot itself has introduced a new theme which seems to provide a sanctified society and which turns against the outcasts.

*   *   *

Thus Dickens again undermines any comfortable laughter and forces us beyond the rigid moral categories in which we may have taken refuge. The laughter is once more used as a weapon against our social as-sumptions, forcing us closer into the novel and into a closer identification not only with Oliver but also with Bumble, Fagin, and Sikes. By the end of this chapter, Bumble has been beaten, humiliated in front of the paupers, and driven to drink. But Dickens doesn't even allow him the traditional alcoholic solace of the henpecked; for in the bar he meets Monks, and in the later interview between Monks and the Bumbles, the former beadle is forced into the role of the pathetic, self-conscious buffoon:

> [Mrs. Bumble:] 'But I may ask you two questions, may I?'
> 'You may ask,' said Monks, with some show of surprise; 'but whether I answer or not is another question.'
> '—Which makes three,' observed Mr. Bumble, essaying a stroke of facetiousness. (XXXVIII)

His degradation is indeed complete.

*   *   *

The humour in the novel, then, seems to me to be consistently and brilliantly directed to these ends: to make us see how incomplete and hostile a reaction our laughter is, to force us by this recognition briefly to see in ourselves the shadow of Fang, Mrs. Corney, and the gentleman in the white waistcoat, and to direct us through this insight into a participation in the vital action of the novel which is, at once, more complete and much more intense.

But the 'vital action' of the novel supported by the rhetoric of laughter is not, as has been noted, coincident with the plot of the last half of the novel. The novel shifts its grounds to a concern with the simplistically defined good and bad, but we are already committed to a position which refuses to be so easily upset. In comparison with the problems suggested by Fagin and Mr. Bumble, the pivotal concern in the Maylie-Brownlow plot about 'stains' on one's honour, noble sacrifices of 'station', and recovered wills seems incredibly trivial. This means that when the novel switches to the conflict between the Fagin world and the Brownlow world, our laughter tends to tie us to the former, even when Oliver changes sides. Oliver may no longer be a victim (he almost, in fact, disappears from the novel), but there are plenty of victims around, and, in so far as the Maylies, Brownlows, Losbernes, and the like are relevant to this vital world of the thieves at all, they are enemies. The novel thus pushes us towards a position which it finally refuses to countenance, for all the concern with good societies at the end, when the thieves' society decays, the reader is left with no social possibilities. He is, in fact, as isolated as the young hero was at the beginning. This is one major reason why we react very intensely to *Oliver Twist* but still are likely to say that it is a bad novel. It lacks entirely the congruence of plot, theme, and emotion which was so marked in *Pickwick Papers*. But it accomplishes something perhaps as rare: it makes us live for a time with Fagin—and like it.

The opposition between the worlds of Fagin and Rose Maylie has often been discussed, and it seems clear that no one really likes, believes in, or remembers Rose and that everyone is somehow attracted to Fagin. Part of the reason for this has already been discussed: the rhetoric of laughter, which provides for a sympathetic alignment with the victims. But the social implications of these two worlds, the kinds of homes they provide for the reader, need to be investigated further.

As it is first introduced, Fagin's world is, in almost every way, a distinctly positive contrast to the one Oliver had known. It provides a release from misery, starvation, and, most important, loneliness. When the Artful Dodger crosses the street to say, 'Hullo! my covey, what's the row?' (VIII), there is no question that this is a new world, friendlier, freer, warmer. All sinister motives aside, the Dodger is the first person to express spontaneous and real concern for Oliver. He is the first to provide an alternative to the most horrifying part of the orphan's early life: its desolation. It is certainly better to be a thief than to be alone: the whole emotional force of the novel has made that clear. The Dodger's simple announcement, then, 'This is him, Fagin . . . my friend, Oliver Twist' (VIII), introduces us to a new and welcome environment. It hardly even matters that it is sinister.

More often than 'sinister' even, the words 'gentle' and 'soft' are associated with Fagin, and the over-emphasized and obvious satanic connections should not obscure the fact that there is something maternal as well about the recurring image of Fagin bending over the fire and about his favourite phrase, 'my dear'. Of course, these images are partly ironic, but, I think, only partly. In context, they are seen as relief from the workhouse and as an alternative to rigid system. Dickens makes the contrast pointedly. There is, first of all, no hint of starvation here; the thieves are constantly eating. Second, the thieves' life has a profusion and, paradoxically, an openness completely lacking in the pinched material and emotional life the workhouse allowed.

* * *

The one vigorous and persuasive life-force in the novel, in fact, is centred in Fagin. Both the workhouse and the Maylie group are associated with, if not dedicated to, death. The life celebrated at Fagin's is, in addition, of the kind that we associate particularly with a comic society. Like the Dodger, all Fagin's gang are adept at parody and speak a language which constantly makes fun of the petrified, respectable world. They are, further, extremely resilient and flexible, and they create a warm kind of conviviality through a life of the imagination[3] conspicuously absent at the Maylies'. Rose and Oliver, we gather, sit around for hours weeping at mental pictures of 'the friends whom they had so sadly lost' (liii). This gruesome faculty might be called the tombstone imagination. But the thieves' imagination is one of joy, of recapturing laughter from pain. For example, when Charley Bates is despondent over the Dodger's arrest, Fagin helps him to create an imaginative— and, as it turns out, accurate—picture of the trial. The vision of this 'regular game' allows Charley to escape from pain; he is transported by the humorous imagination:

> 'I think I see him now,' cried the Jew, bending his eyes upon his pupil.
> 'So do I,' cried Charley Bates. 'Ha! ha! ha! so do I. I see it all afore me, upon my soul I do, Fagin. What a game! What a regular game! All the big-wigs trying to look solemn, and Jack Dawkins addressing of 'em as intimate and comfortable as if he was the judge's own son making a speech arter dinner—ha! ha! ha!' (XLIII)

3. See Mark Spilka, *Dickens and Kafka* (Bloomington, 1963) 73, for the best discussion of Fagin's imaginative powers.

He sees that the Dodger's essential witty challenge is to society's (and the reader's) lack of compassion. He acts exactly as if he were our 'own son'. But it is perhaps the imaginative warmth generated by Charley and his fellow thieves that is most important. It is the only joy we find in the novel, defensive and often dark though it may be. It is the closest thing to Dulwich that *Oliver Twist* offers.

Even Oliver is affected by this joy and significantly laughs at Fagin's 'droll and curious' stories 'in spite of all his better feelings' (XVIII). Perhaps this phrasing suggests the real problem with this novel; the plot wants Oliver to drop the laughter in favour of his 'better feelings', but the central pattern, confirmed by the rhetoric, is all for ignoring these imbecilic and deathly 'better feelings' for ever. There is nothing more reminiscent of the freedom of *Pickwick Papers* than the wonderful parody games Fagin plays with his young charges, which make Oliver laugh 'till the tears ran down his face' (IX).

But Oliver deserts this life and us for games at the Brownlows' played 'with great interest and gravity' (XIV), and it is just this contrast which informs the emotional life of the last half of the book. The whole Maylie-Brownlow camp swim in a virtual bath of tears. Taking their lead from Rose, who cries at happiness, sorrow, disappointment, and hope, everyone, down to Brownlow, expresses himself with tears, and not the tears engendered by helpless laughter at a versatile and witty Fagin. Even 'delight', the central emotion of comedy, causes the dismals here: Mrs. Bedwin, 'being in a state of considerable delight at seeing [Oliver] so much better, forthwith began to cry most violently' (XII). It is perhaps perverse, but not ultimately inaccurate, to suggest that Mrs. Bedwin is really crying because Oliver did not, in fact, die. The Maylie-Brownlow group are in every way the antithesis of the comic dedication to life. Even Dickens seems hard pressed to imagine them doing anything (i.e. living), and we long for a touch of those 'continental frivolities' (XLIX) to which Monks's mother had apparently so abandoned herself. We want them even more because Mr. Brownlow is so ridiculously stolid and pompous in denouncing them.

The subversion, then, is complete and fundamental. The laughter of the reader and the characters is used as a weapon of self-exposure, and we are pulled toward the one isolated pocket of spontaneity in the novel, Fagin's den. When, with Fagin's execution, the last echo of unmalicious laughter dies away, we almost certainly feel a sense of regret. By this point, we have been encouraged to cast aside altogether our normal social identification by means of the most solid of all social gestures, laughter, and we are left without a society. Dickens has here used the technique of attack through our laughter with great intensity but without complete control. The experience of isolation is insisted upon and made real by our laughter, but this experience works against that 'little society' of nearly 'perfect happiness' which the entire second half of the novel has been somewhat desperately trying to establish. The novelist does work out a tactic here he will use in later novels, perhaps never with more startling effect but more in consonance with major theme˜ ˜nd patterns. Here the novel remains fractured. Most readers have some tendency, encouraged by their laughter, to rewrite it in their minds, though, and when Charley Bates says of Oliver, 'What a pity it is he isn't a prig!' (XVIII), we are tempted to respond, using the term without the thieves' irony, 'What a pity he *is*!'

MICHAEL SLATER

On Reading *Oliver Twist*†

Oliver Twist was the first Dickens novel I ever read (at the age of eleven) and, not long afterwards, I sat shuddering and laughing through a show-ing of David Lean's wonderful film of the story. Ever since, this book —such an extraordinary mixture of satire, nightmare, documentary, farce, melodrama and near-tragedy—has haunted and fascinated me.

It begins as satire in the Swiftian tradition ('my glance at the new poor Law Bill'). Just as the insanely sane *Modest Proposal* resulted from Swift's rage at the English Government's policy towards Ireland so the pres-entation of the workhouse in *Oliver Twist* results from Dickens's outrage at Malthusian chatter about the 'surplus population' and the Govern-ment's 'workhouse-as-deterrent' policy. The 'philosophers' who organise and run these establishments he portrays as deliberate exterminators, 'whose blood is ice, whose heart is iron', out to kill off, by any means short of shooting, the inconvenient hordes of the poor: 'they established the rule, that all poor people should have the alternative . . . of being starved by a gradual process in the house, or by a quick one out of it'. Oliver challenges them by actually getting himself born in a workhouse, thus ironically producing the opposite effect to that intended. Had he been surrounded, Dickens comments, 'by careful grandmothers, anxious aunts, experienced nurses and doctors of profound wisdom' he would certainly have died; but, just because he was born into such a brutal extermination camp he survived. Moreover, he reaches his ninth birth-day at Mrs Mann's baby-farm perhaps only because his 'good sturdy spirit' gets plenty of room to expand 'thanks to the spare diet of the establishment', and finally crowns his obstinate defiance of the philos-ophers by 'asking for more'. Dickens wonderfully dramatises the famous scene to make it seem that Oliver's request shakes the whole system to its very foundations: the master of the workhouse 'shrieks' for the beadle

† From *The Dickensian* 70 (1974): 71–81. Reprinted by permission.

and the latter rushes excitedly to the Board to announce the terrible news that Oliver has asked for more ('There was a general start. Horror was depicted on every countenance.'). After this the Board has no option—it cannot afford to wait for the fulfilment of the gentleman in a white waistcoat's prophecy that Oliver will eventually be hanged but must dispose of him more quickly:

> The board . . . took counsel together on the expedience of shipping off Oliver Twist, in some small trading vessel bound to a good unhealthy port; which suggested itself as the very best thing that could possibly be done with him; the probability being, that the skipper would flog him to death, in a playful mood, some day after dinner; or would knock his brains out with an iron bar; both pastimes being, as is pretty generally known, very favourite and common recreations among gentlemen of that class.

In the event, however, they pay the parish undertaker to take him away.

The world of the workhouse is embodied in that great satiric creation, Mr Bumble, whose chief business is to beat Oliver within an inch of his life, and who dominates the early part of the novel as Fagin dominates the later part. Bumble is totally identified with his institutional role; once he has ceased to be beadle, he dwindles into a stock figure of farce, the hen-pecked husband (a stock figure hilariously manipulated by Dickens, though) and an agent of the melodramatic plot. Oliver is the traditional symbolic satiric hero, like Candide or Byron's Don Juan, the innocent to whom the things that happen reveal the appalling nature of the world through which he is passing (Martin Chuzzlewit in America fulfils essentially the same role). As such he is the embodiment of the satirist's positive values—humanity, compassion, tenderness, loyalty, love—fiercely defending his dead mother against the taunts of Noah Claypole who, in his relations with Oliver, is a brutal forerunner of Mr Dorrit in his relations with Old Nandy, and very much a documentary or 'realistic' figure, showing us 'what a beautiful thing human nature sometimes is'. Modern readers find little difficulty with this scene because of the vivid realism of Noah but Oliver's parting with Little Dick is less acceptable because both the characters involved lack this kind of realism. Yet it seems to me that this scene effectively makes its point which is to show that no amount of cruelty can altogether dry up the springs of love and tenderness in human nature, to reassure us that, as he leaves Bumble's world, Oliver, humanity's representative, has not, after all, been ground down to that 'state of brutal stupidity and sullenness' that Dickens warns us, in Chapter 4, he was 'in a fair way' of being reduced to.

In these first seven chapters of the novel Dickens shows with devastating economy the failure, or worse than failure, of the institutions of society—Government, the Law, the Church. Existing to protect the weak against the strong they do nothing of the sort or, if they do, it is quite accidentally. Government, represented by Bumble is, in fact, sheer tyranny; the Church, represented by the clergyman at the pauper funeral, reading 'as much of the burial service as could be compressed into four minutes', is indifferent; and the Law, represented by the 'half blind and half childish' magistrate, saves Oliver from certain death at the hands of Mr Gamfield only by the accident of the ink-pot's not happening to be where the magistrate thought it was. This causes him to look into Oliver's face and see him for a moment as a human being—just as even Bumble is startled into doing in the next chapter—and he then has a human reaction ('Take the boy back to the workhouse, and treat him kindly. He seems to want it'). But, by and large, in this society those in power do not *see* the people they govern; they see only large abstractions such as 'the surplus population' or 'paupers'.

Oliver escapes from this society in chapter 8 only to be decoyed into the criminal underworld of London. A direct cause-and-effect link between social injustice and neglect and crime was always central to Dickens's thinking and the novel's Hogarthian sub-title, 'The Parish Boy's Progress', gives a clear enough hint of the way in which the novel will move. We might recall again the gentleman in the white waistcoat who so perseveringly proclaims his belief that Oliver will come to be hanged; society, Dickens is saying, is a great maker of such self-fulfilling prophecies. It creates and maintains conditions which will drive the poor into crime or, at the very least, encourage the criminal or anti-social tendencies of such a boy as Noah Claypole.

From chapter 8 onwards it seems to me that the novel ceases to be satirical and becomes a strangely powerful mixture of the fabular or visionary, with Oliver as 'the principle of Good surviving through every adverse circumstance', and of the documentary, showing criminals 'as they really are'. The London in which the action takes place is both the actual city of the 1830s—with all the respectable areas left out—and a dark and sinister labyrinth perpetually shrouded in night. The way Dickens describes Oliver's nocturnal entry into the city, escorted by the Artful Dodger, exemplifies this perfectly:

> They crossed from the Angel into St. John's-road; struck down the small street which terminates at Sadler's Wells Theatre; through Exmouth-street and Coppice-row; down the little court by the side of the workhouse; across the classic ground which once bore the name of Hockley-in-the-Hole; thence into Little Saffron-hill; and so into Saffron-hill the Great . . .

One can follow the route on a map but the overwhelming impression that this sentence leaves is not one of topographical exactitude but of the hapless Oliver's being drawn deeper and deeper into a dangerous maze.

At the heart of this maze is Fagin and indeed he *is* the London of *Oliver Twist*. He incarnates it, just as Bumble incarnates the workhouse and the Poor Law. At one point (chapter 19) he is described as though he were some kind of actual emanation from the black wet streets: 'the hideous old man seemed like some loathsome reptile, engendered in the slime and darkness through which he moved'. Fagin has his documentary aspects such as the way he runs his school for pickpockets, his professional jargon (the 'kinchin lay', etc.) and his Jewishness—as Dickens explained later to Mrs Davis most receivers of stolen property at that time were, in fact, Jewish, like the celebrated Ikey Solomons. But, as has long been recognized, he is differently conceived from all the other thieves in that he is *inexplicably* evil (one could no more imagine an innocent young Fagin than an experienced grown-up Oliver). He is, in fact, the Devil and London is the Devil's city. Confronted with Good in the shape of Oliver he must seek to destroy it as inevitably as Melville's Claggart must seek to destroy Billy Budd. At one point (the end of chapter 19) Fagin is temporarily checked simply by the powerful aura of Oliver's goodness and this is almost like the moment in Milton when Satan is staggered and rendered 'stupidly good' by his first sight of innocent Eve in Paradise. Fagin goes to Oliver to announce his impending delivery over to Sikes to assist in that crime which will make him Fagin's for ever ('Once let him feel that he is one of us; once fill his mind with the idea that he has been a thief; and he's ours! Ours for his life!'). But Oliver is asleep and spiritually radiant:

> . . . he looked like death; not death as it shews in shroud and coffin, but in the guise it wears when life has just departed; when a young and gentle spirit has, but an instant, fled to Heaven: and the gross air of the world has not had time to breathe upon the changing dust it hallowed.
> "Not now," said the Jew, turning softly away. "To-morrow. To-morrow."

Fagin must be motivated at the level of the plot, however, since this is not overtly a fable, and so he is provided with Monks, a conventional enough melodrama villain and a fit subject for Mr Carey's jesting,[1] though there is some resonance in his relationship to Oliver, I think, the child of socially-sanctioned hate bent on destroying the child of socially-condemned love.

How is it that Fagin emerges as this terrifying figure, 'the devil with a great-coat on'? By doing so he changes the essential mode of the novel from satire and also from documentary, pushing it towards the fabular mode of the *Christmas Carol* and puzzling even his author (Dickens told Forster that Fagin was 'such an out-and-outer I don't know what

---

1. Mr Carey observes in his *The Violent Effigy: A Study of Dickens' Imagination* (27) that on the only occasion when Monks attempts to strike Oliver he falls over.

to make of him'). The clue to what has happened lies, as John Bayley long ago pointed out, in the character's name:

> Dickens himself had been at Fagin's school—the blacking factory—and the boy who chiefly befriended him there was actually called Fagin. No wonder Fagin the criminal is such an ambivalent figure when the real Fagin's kindness had, so to speak, threatened to inure Dickens to the hopeless routine of the wage-slave. So passionate was the young Dickens's desire for the station in life to which he felt entitled, and so terrifying his sense that it was being denied him, that he must have hated the real Fagin for the virtue which he could not bear to accept or recognize in that nightmare world, because it might help to subdue him into it. The real Fagin's kindness becomes the criminal Fagin's villainy.[2]

One can go even further than Mr Bayley does here, I think. Dickens's chief retrospective fear for himself, as it were, was not that he might have been become a 'wage-slave' but that 'for any care that was taken of me I might have become a little robber or a little vagabond'. A little robber is, of course, just what Fagin intends to make of Oliver.

In contrast to Fagin, Sikes is essentially a 'documentary' figure. We must accept that he, like Noah Claypole, was once innocent even if he has since eagerly co-operated with society in his own corruption. Dickens says of him (in his 'Preface to the Third Edition'), 'I fear there are in the world some insensible and callous natures that do become, at last, utterly and irredeemably bad'. Notice the word 'become'; Fagin, on the other hand, has not *become* bad, he *is* bad from all eternity. Sikes is treated differently, however, during the description of the murder and its aftermath. Dickens is now attempting the tragic and the housebreaker's status must be raised accordingly to a Shakespearian level (Mr Bayley mentions the echoes of *Macbeth* and, in this number of *The Dickensian*, Professor Senelick draws our attention to the relevance here of *Othello*).

It was essential to Dickens to believe that petty criminals must be miserable (how many suicidal Marthas, moaning low into their shawls, actually arrived at Urania Cottage, one wonders?) since he saw them as victims of society and tended to be rather upset when they appeared to be enjoying themselves—in *Sketches by Boz* he describes the urchins in Newgate as a very 'disagreeable sight' when they merrily show off in front of visitors. Fagin is obviously happy in his work but then he is the Devil (not Milton's Satan, racked with inward torments, but the gleeful Devil of folklore), Nancy and Sikes are appropriately gloomy for most of the time, but what about the Dodger? He, it seems to me, is a case like Mrs Gamp—a marvellous, grotesque exaggeration of a type Dickens had observed (and, in the case of the Dodger, first reported on in the

---

2. *'Oliver Twist*: "Things as they really are" ' in *Dickens and the Twentieth Century*, ed. J. Gross and G. Pearson, 1962. [See above, pp. 461–69—*Editor*.]

sketch called 'Criminal Courts' in *Sketches by Boz*) which soon transcends the author's original intention, whether this be a matter of satire,
documentary or moral fable, and ends up as a 'free-standing' Dickens
character, exhibited and delighted in for its own sake. The Dodger exits
triumphantly from the novel in chapter 43 and one no more believes
that that sentence in the last chapter, '. . . far from home, died the
chief remaining members . . . of Fagin's gang', applies to him than one
believes that Mr Pecksniff degenerated into a 'squalid begging-letter
writer' after *his* comparably triumphant exit.

As for Nancy, her 'documentary' aspect ('I will not . . . abate . . .
one scrap of curlpaper in the girl's dishevelled hair') is rapidly eclipsed
by Dickens's interest in dramatising through her one of his deepest
beliefs, that of the beneficent moral influence on us of memories of our
own past wrongs and sorrows (cf. *The Haunted Man*). Nancy suddenly
sees in Oliver the image of her own past self and pities it: 'I thieved for
you when I was a child not half as old as this!' she screams at Fagin,
when defending Oliver from his blows, '. . . the cold, wet, dirty streets
are my home; and you're the wretch that drove me to them long ago'.
Just as Scrooge's heart is unfrozen by being shown a vision of himself
as a forlorn and lonely child so Nancy's humanity and goodness is
aroused by witnessing a re-enactment of her own undoing. Yet this, and
her pathetic loyalty to Sikes, the only object that her sordid and brutal
world gives her to love (a love in which she nonetheless takes pride like
her prototype in 'The Hospital Patient' in *Sketches by Boz*), leads directly
to her murder and brings her closer to true tragic status than any other
of Dickens's heroines. Lady Dedlock is too shadowy a figure in comparison though she perhaps comes nearest to Nancy in this kind (essentially a Shakespearian kind) of tragedy whilst Edith Dombey, Louisa
Gradgrind and Estella are perhaps closer to George Eliot's kind of tragedy, the sort that the heroine generally survives, a sadder and a wiser
woman.

What continuity is there between the satirically-presented social institutions of the first seven chapters and the London of Fagin? They are,
I think, thematically linked in a way that, for example, Dotheboys Hall
and the London of *Nicholas Nickleby* are not. The society we are shown
in the first seven chapters is one in which selfishness dominates
everything—each group and individual is out for his own interests but
there is a hypocritical pretence at a true society with institutions of
government, law and religion. Fagin's anti-society, eating out the heart
of the city, occupying ruined old houses deserted by 'respectable' society,
is by comparison 'honest' in that 'looking after Number One' is the
openly avowed principle on which it rests. It wickedly exploits people
by striking devilish bargains with them but it does not want to kill them
just for being born. Cruikshank's two plates, 'Oliver asking for more'

and 'Oliver introduced to the respectable Old Gentleman' are suggestive here. In each plate the child, in a begging posture, confronts a figure of power presiding over a supply of food. But what is bleak and hostile in the first plate is convivial and welcoming in the second. Fagin and his gang will (for a terrible price) give Oliver that food, warmth, shelter and companionship that 'lawful' society harshly denies him, so forcing him to seek it elsewhere.

The 'good' people in *Oliver Twist*—Brownlow, the Maylies and the rest—belong wholly to the fabular aspect of the book, the story of the 'principle of Good'. Dickens wills them into existence (helped in the case of Rose Maylie by his idealisation of his recently dead young sister-in-law, Mary Hogarth) to counterbalance the nightmare of Fagin, which had so nearly turned into terrible reality for him, and seeks desperately to give them some solidity by providing them with comic attendants such as Mr Grimwig and Dr Losberne. They are identified with a conventionally pastoral countryside (Brownlow's house may be said to be near Pentonville but it is really unlocalised, a state of being—Oliver has only to step outside its doors to be at once reclaimed by Fagin) and they are in no way part of, or responsible for, the atrocious society shown in the early chapters: Brownlow is powerless to cope with Mr Fang. Their only contact with Fagin's world is through the Abdiel-figure of Nancy who meets them in no-man's-land, on London Bridge or in a hotel. Sikes's invasion of their territory is a disastrous failure and Fagin can only leer in at the Chertsey window. At the end of the book they simply withdraw deep into the countryside with little Oliver, 'triumphing at last', leaving the world (Bumble's Mudfog[3] and Fagin's London) to its fate, and linking themselves together in 'a little society, whose condition approached as nearly to one of perfect happiness as can ever be known in this changing world'. Oliver, in fact, returns to Heaven after his season in Hell. He dies just as surely as Little Nell does at the end of *The Old Curiosity Shop*, even though we see no corpse. Graham Greene's famous description of the abiding impression made on him by *Oliver Twist* still seems to me the truest to my own experience of the book of all the critiques that I have read:

> . . . is it too fantastic to imagine that in this novel, as in many of his later books, creeps in, unrecognized by the author, the eternal and alluring taint of the Manichee, with its simple and terrible explanation of our plight, how the world was made by Satan and not by God, lulling us with the music of despair?[4]

---

3. Dickens originally gave the town in which Oliver was born the good satirical name of Mudfog, prophetic of the opening of *Bleak House*, but changed it to 'a certain town' for the first volume publication of the story.
4. See above, pp. 426–32 [*Editor*].

DENNIS WALDER

[*Oliver Twist* and Charity]†

* * *

The fundamental aim of *Oliver Twist* (1837–9) is to move us, as Mr Pickwick was moved in the Fleet, into sympathy and charity for the poor. * * * But the overall mood of *Oliver Twist* is more like one long, oppressive nightmare.

However, we should not be misled into detecting in this pervasive darkness of tone what Graham Greene called 'the eternal and alluring taint of the Manichee, with its simple and terrible explanation of our plight, how the world was made by Satan, and not by God.[1] It is true, as Greene points out, that this forbidding atmosphere is strikingly reinforced by the diabolic overtones surrounding the red-haired 'old gentleman' Fagin, Oliver's main antagonist, and by the comparatively weak depiction of goodness in his benefactors, Mrs Brownlow and the Maylies. But it is unlikely that Dickens should so soon—indeed, almost simultaneously—contradict the ultimately hopeful view of human destiny expressed in *Pickwick Papers*. More probably, the orderly, tolerant, finally *secure* world of *Pickwick Papers* has been overtaken by the novelist's awareness that reality is more varied and unstable, even frightening, than he was at first prepared to admit. Moments in which evil becomes terrifyingly close as a force in life are no longer relegated to interpolated tales, subsidiary fictions, but are made central to the main narrative itself. Evil is now directly faced, and by no means easily subdued. It is one of the abiding strengths of Dickens's vision of life that, unlike most of his great contemporaries in the English novel, such as Thackeray, George Eliot, or Trollope, he had a profound apprehension of evil which extended beyond the domestic or even social.

This is not to ignore (as Greene and later critics ignore) the fact that the hero of *Oliver Twist* is, finally, *saved*. He is saved by the sympathy and charity, the freely given loving aid of those good Christians (explicitly identified as such) into whose hands he is cast 'by a stronger hand than chance' (ch. xlix). If God permits evil to flourish in *Oliver Twist*—and there can be no denying the *initial* power of the parish authorities, of Fagin and his gang—then he also ensures its ultimate failure and destruction. The turning-point is quite clear: not only do we see Bumble, symbol of parish authority, reduced and humbled by his wife (ch. xxxvii), but Sikes and Nancy pale, cadaverous and ill (ch. xxxix), after Oliver's

---

† From *Dickens and Religion* (London: George Allen and Unwin, 1981) 41–59. Reprinted by permission.
1. See above, pp. 426–32 [*Editor*].

recovery with the Maylies. Thenceforward, evil is set on a downward path. It is too simple to be overwhelmed by Oliver's earlier suffering, and to forget that, far from sharing the fate of that other parish orphan, little Dick, he is to survive and flourish in the end. Dickens's intention is expressed in the 1841 Preface, the most extended defence of any of his works.[2] He 'wished to show', he said, 'in little Oliver, the principle of Good surviving through every adverse circumstance, and triumphing at last'. He continues to believe not only in the ultimately hopeful ordering of human affairs, despite the suffering of the poor and destitute, but also in the existence of good as a transcendental value, a 'principle' to be embodied in symbolic or 'romantic', rather than realistic form. In *Oliver Twist* Dickens moves towards the expression of both good and evil as forces having their origin beyond the material world, so that in reading the novel we are often aware of some metaphysical drama hovering about the events of the surface-narrative. In so far as *Oliver Twist* insists upon its importance in meeting the needs of the poor, the novel carries a more noticeably Christian hue than most of his fictional works, except perhaps the Christmas Books and the last novels. The term means more than the simple human virtue of benevolence, or giving alms to the poor; it implies the more general motive of Christian love, expressed as a love of God and one's neighbour. This distinction has been used to argue that Dickens's charitable characters are not strictly Christian in their performance of benevolent acts towards others, since these seem no more than spontaneous expressions of their good nature, rather than reflections of a will dedicated to God. But Dickens wishes to avoid the premeditativeness of doing good as a duty, as well as any hint of excess—or even merely open—piety, preferring a modest, self-effacing, yet direct goodness which emerges as the natural expression of the personality. He reveals virtue implicitly, in terms of the essential being of a character, rather than in terms of its motivation. If his good people love God—and he often implies that they do—this is revealed only implicitly, through imagery and action, and not by allotting characters overtly Christian motives.

For Dickens, charity is 'the one great cardinal virtue, which, properly nourished and exercised, leads to, if it does not necessarily include, all the others' (*Nicholas Nickleby*, ch. xviii). Nourishing and exercising charity involves other people: it is a social as well as a Christian virtue. St Paul (I Corinthians 13) provides a comprehensive account of it as an impulse directed primarily towards God, but Christ made it clear that we owe it to ourselves, and our neighbours too, as the objects of God's love (Matthew 22:37–40). Who exactly are our neighbours? Dickens pointedly alludes to the parable Christ used to supply the answer, when he has the parish beadle explain that the 'porochial seal' on the brass

2. See above, pp. 3–7 [*Editor*].

buttons embellishing his coat is a representation of the Good Samaritan 'healing the sick and bruised man' (ch. iv). The parable enjoins us to succour him who 'fell among thieves' (Luke 10:29–37). Oliver, plainly, falls among thieves. But his needs are evident before he does so: from the moment of his arrival in the world, a nameless, illegitimate orphan, he is left to 'the tender mercies of churchwardens and overseers' (ch. i). The opening chapters of the novel constitute a fiercely satirical attack upon those public authorities who signally fail to care for the poor in their charge, in direct contradiction to the message of their seal. The social dimension of this has been well accounted for, but the religious dimension has been largely ignored. This is despite Dickens's attempts to suggest it, by means of his allusion to the Good Samaritan, despite, too, the involvement of contemporary religious figures in the revision of the Poor Laws which was particularly the object of his attack.

To understand and respond to this aspect of *Oliver Twist*, it is essential to clarify the immediately topical, historical situation which inspired the opening chapters. It may seem that this has been sufficiently expounded by, for instance, Humphry House, whose very thorough analysis in *The Dickens World* has been adopted by most later critics. But there is more to Dickens's attack upon the Poor Laws than has so far been made apparent. Dickens was tapping a specific contemporary source in the newspapers of the time for the views, even, to some extent, the techniques, adopted in his anti-Poor Law satire; and the way in which he transformed fact into fiction has not been fully accounted for, much less the relation of all this to a growing distrust of the religious establishment.

It is generally assumed that Dickens, as a young parliamentary reporter, must have heard, and so drawn on for *Oliver Twist*, the debates on the New Poor Law. In fact, debates on this new legislation during the period when he was actually in Parliament (1834–6) were relatively slight, since the Whig government hurried the reform through in a mere six months early in 1834, and thorough parliamentary discussion began only with the motion (proposed by John Walter of *The Times*) in February 1837 for a Select Committee to inquire into the working of the new law. This was the month in which *Oliver Twist* began appearing in *Bentley's Miscellany*, which reveals in what sense exactly Dickens's 'glance at the new poor Law Bill' was topical. The early months of 1837 marked the extension of the New Poor Law into the London metropolitan area, arousing great popular controversy, as the pages of the *Morning Chronicle* or *The Times* testify. It seems likely that it was these events, rather than the early debates on, or even the actual passing of, the new law, which directly inspired the writing of the novel. Dickens must have been very soon aware of the broader implications of the Bill: he later recalled how he and the editor of the *Morning Chronicle*, John Black, used to quarrel about its effects, the paper having been acquired in 1834 by the Whig John Easthope in order to support the Bill. His views were much closer to those of *The Times* which, under Walter's direction, consistently opposed the Bill and its results, becoming a veritable 'compendium of poor-law crimes', not all of them based on real evidence. A typical leader of February 1837 refers to the 'BENTHAMITE cant' then current according to which the policy designed to produce *'the greatest happiness to the greatest number'* was 'unquestionably' the best, yet was 'most difficult to reconcile with Christianity or civilization.' This contrast between the utilitarian cant of the 'philosophers' and the claims of Christian civilisation runs right through *The Times*'s criticism, in leading articles, letters, even fiction—extracts from *Oliver Twist*'s opening chapters were published as soon as they appeared. Even if Dickens did attend some of the early debates on the new law, most of his information, as well as a confirmation of his basic position, was probably derived from *The Times*. The narrator who remarks of the members of the 'board' who bring in the new 'system' in *Oliver Twist* that they are 'very sage, deep, philosophical men' (ch. ii) shares the tone and attitude of the newspaper which opened its extracts from the novel with the same words.

At the same time, Dickens is careful to purge his work of specific dates, places, or names—even the fictional 'Mudfog', used for Oliver's place of birth, he drops after its first appearance. He tries to avoid the accusation of bias and sensationalism inevitable when dealing with such a live issue, by avoiding the explicitness of a journalist—or of a typical 'social problem' novelist such as Frances Trollope, who clumsily attempted to deal with the renewed New Poor Law in her *Jessie Phillips* (1843). Dickens could not entirely avoid such accusations—*The Examiner* criticised his 'unworthy' use of the 'bugbears of popular prejudice'—but he was successful in preferring symbolic generalisation to detailed analysis in his treatment of the law. His art is an art of implication, not explication.

This does not mean that our reading of the novel cannot be helped by teasing out some of its more specific implications—for instance, in relation to the bastardy issue, of obvious relevance to Oliver's plight. The new law set out to abolish the traditional duty laid on parishes since Elizabethan times to 'search for the father' of illegitimate children in their care. Oliver, it seems, is born before the passing of the new law, so 'the most superlative, and, I may say, supernat'ral exertions', if we can believe Bumble, have been made to discover 'who is his father, or what was his mother's settlement, name or con-dition' (ch. ii)—but in vain (a glance at the complicated unravelling of Oliver's family history towards the end of his story suggests a reason for this failure). However, the new 'system' which comes into being after Oliver's return from the branch workhouse introduces, in addition to the notorious dietary restrictions, regulations which 'instead of compelling a man to support his family, as they had heretofore done, took his family away from him, and made him a bachelor!' (ch. ii). Fathers need no longer be sought after, and so the 'natural' Christian ties between parents and children are denied. Dickens emphasises the sanctity of the family in such a way as to *include* illegitimate children such as Oliver—or Rose Maylie, who carries the 'shame' of illegitimacy despite the fact that, as we later learn, this was a mere slander (ch. li). When the truth about Oliver and Rose finally emerges, they share a 'sacred' embrace, for 'A father, sister, and mother, were gained, and lost, in that one moment' (ch. li). Dickens endorses Harry Maylie's sacrifice of parliamentary ambition in order to marry the apparently 'stained' Rose, just as he endorses Mr Brownlow's correction of Monks's use of the phrase 'bastard child' for Oliver, a reproach to those 'long since passed beyond the feeble censure of the world', reflecting 'disgrace on no one living, except you who use it' (ch. li). Not for Oliver or Rose—any more than for other illegitimates such as Esther Summerson in *Bleak House*—the stigma laid down by the Old Testament: 'A bastard shall not enter into the congregation of the Lord; even to his tenth generation shall he not enter into the congregation of the Lord' (Deuteronomy 23:2). Dickens consciously aligns himself against the contemporary puritan attitude to sexual morality which had developed since the seventeenth century, but which was given new force by the evangelicals, to the effect that children begotten in sin would inherit their parents' weakness. So he concludes *Oliver Twist* by having his two orphans visit a memorial stone 'within the altar' of the old village church, a stone hallowed to the memory of Oliver's mother, and where her 'shade' may hover, for all that she was 'weak and erring' (ch. liii).

The strength of contemporary feeling about the bastardy clause, and, indeed, about the whole attempt of the New Poor Law to 'break those bonds which naught but death should break', may be gauged from the complaint of 'Honest Jack' to John Gotch, first guardian elected under the new law in Northamptonshire, in a letter of 26 March 1838: it was difficult to understand, he wrote, 'how High Professors of the religion of him who went about doing good, can act like those brutal beings in the West Indies and tear asunder Fathers, Mothers, and Children the same time they read the command to love one another.' Most conspicuous of these 'High Professors' was Bishop Blomfield of London, since it was he who chaired the commission whose report into the Poor Laws recommended throwing out 'search for the father', and the separation of families in the new workhouses; it was he who, when it came to debate the new Bill in the House of Lords with fellow prelate Phillpotts of Exeter, argued as strongly as he could in favour of the report's original recommendations on bastardy, and against any compromise. As *The Times* reported, he was in favour of regulations which 'would make workhouses schools of moral reformation, and not of moral degradation.' Doubtless Blomfield had in mind the familiar horrors of the old 'general

mixed' workhouse, in which the sick, the elderly, the insane, the unemployed and children all lived together. For him, the old law regarding
illegitimacy put a premium on perjury and unchastity; the new law
would sweep all this away in a wave of righteousness. And he carried
the day, despite having roused so much feeling against himself that he
had his speeches corrected and published, hoping to explain to the
growing number of critics of the Church how he and several episcopal
colleagues could endorse the unChristian measure of driving mothers
to the workhouse to support their illegitimate children, thereby separating
the family from the father and ruining any future prospects for them.

　Blomfield was known to Dickens, who must have been aware that
his defence of the bastardy clause was only one facet of 'a continuing
campaign to pass legislation correcting the wanton and dissolute behaviour of the lower orders.' Although a High Churchman, Blomfield was
as dourly moralistic in his attitude to the behaviour of the poor as any
evangelical within or outside the Church. His prominence as a Sab-
batarian, for instance, earned him the ironic dedication of *Sunday Under
Three Heads*, which appeared two years after the clashes over the bastardy
issue in the Lords, and eight months before *Oliver Twist*. The dedication
concluded:

> That your Lordship would ever have contemplated Sunday recre-
> ations with so much horror, if you had been at all acquainted with
> the wants and necessities of the people who indulged in them, I
> cannot imagine possible. That a Prelate of your elevated rank has
> the faintest conception of the extent of those wants, and the nature
> of those necessities, I do not believe.

Dickens's suspicion of the religious establishment's attitude towards the
poor, whose spiritual guardian it was supposed to be, is clearly reflected
in *Oliver Twist*, where it is a *sin* as well as a crime for an illegitimate
pauper orphan to demand charity. Oliver's famous demand for more
is followed by a passage generally overlooked: 'For a week after the
commission of the impious and profane offence of asking for more,
Oliver remained a close prisoner in the dark and solitary room to
which he had been consigned by the wisdom and mercy of the board'
(ch. iii).

　'Impious', 'profane', 'wisdom', 'mercy': responsibility extends beyond
the politicians and administrators; it is evidently an offence *against
Christianity* to ask for more. Churchmen who nominally represented
the interests of the poor on the Poor Law Commission and in the House
of Lords were quite as eager as Benthamite 'philosophers' like Nassau
Senior or Edwin Chadwick to transform workhouses from refuges for
the needy and infirm into houses of correction in which unemployed
and able-bodied paupers were treated as if they were depraved criminals.

What happens to Oliver is an indication of wider social and religious attitudes, of the wider lack of sympathy and charity towards the poverty-stricken.

*   *   *

Dickens was critical not only of the New Poor Law as such, but of the whole structure of beliefs concerning the poor which underlay the legal system of his time: 'this ain't the shop for justice', as the Dodger remarks (ch. xliii). The link between the social philosophy of the utilitarian political economists and the religious outlook for the evangelicals, implicit in the new regulations, was forged long before their appearance, and not only among economists or evangelical ministers: it had long been the general conviction that the visible inequality of rewards was a part of the Providential plan; that vice and misery were God-given checks upon population growth; above all, that providing relief for the poor was simply interfering with the severe but necessary conditions for social, economic and moral progress. This is implicit in all that happens before the appearance of the board's new 'system'. Oliver's first cry in the workhouse advertises the fact of 'a new burden having been imposed upon the parish' (ch. i), a phrasing immediately suggestive of the prevailing attitude. Poverty is a vice to be cured by firmness, not compassion. Oliver's mother's death is brought about as much by the indifference of the authorities as by her fear of disapproval. Found lying in the street, and brought in by the overseer's order, her confinement has been attended by a pauper old woman 'rendered rather misty by an unwonted allowance of beer', and by the parish surgeon, who 'did such matters by contract' (ch. i). The ignorant inhumanity of the one, the uncaring professionalism of the other, are summed up in the surgeon's curt: 'It's all over, Mrs Thingummy!' (ch. i). Oliver's condition is that of a total outcast, illegitimate and naked, without identity; as such, he represents a fundamental challenge to the authorities to do something about him; they immediately ensure he is 'badged and ticketed' a 'parish child', henceforward to be 'despised by all, and pitied by none' (ch. i). Life at the branch workhouse to which he is farmed out confirms this prospect for him, as it does for the 'twenty or thirty other juvenile offenders against the poor-laws', rolling about the floor starving and naked (ch. ii). By appropriating the greater part of their weekly stipend for herself, the aptly named Mrs Mann proves herself 'a very great experimental philosopher', remarks Dickens, 'finding in the lowest depth a deeper still' (ch. ii).

The new Poor Law did not originate the practices it set out to further, any more than its underlying assumptions were limited to its acknowledged supporters. The only *entirely* new feature was the centralisation of poor relief, which does not concern Dickens in *Oliver Twist*, and the justice of which he may well have appreciated, given the chaotic state of public charity under the old laws (Dickens's opposition to utilitarian philosophy did not extend to its reformist implications; indeed, he warmly supported those such as his friend Dr Southwood Smith, formerly Bentham's private secretary, who were active in housing and public health). The workhouse, the board (as a local, not a national body), the closely watched diet, separation of the sexes, harsh treatment of children, especially the illegitimate—all were present before 1834. Even the abolition of 'search for the father' represents a continuation, rather than a reversal, of earlier attitudes and treatment. It is therefore misguided to assume, as Harriet Martineau and others have done, that Dickens is uncertain or confused, mixing the abuses of the old system with those of the new. Dickens's chronology is hazy, but he was quite clear about the abuses, specific and general, that he wished to attack, as well as about the way to attack them—by a heightening and intensification of reality, not by mere journalism. Nor did his concern subside once the immediate provocation was past: in 1849 he was quick to denounce the continuing inadequacies in the system highlighted by the Tooting baby-farm scandal, calling the place a 'disgrace to a Christian community', and to *Our Mutual Friend* he added a postscript condemning the Poor Laws from the time of the Stuarts onwards, after showing in Betty Higden's paranoid fear of public charity what a 'Christian improvement' had been carried out by making 'a pursuing Fury of the Good Samaritan' (bk 3, ch. viii).

*   *   *

Oliver is the touchstone for the lack of mercy and charity in society. His plight absorbs the main force of the narrative, at times to a profoundly moving extent, as when he expresses the agony of his childish grief on being brought away by Bumble from the wretched baby-farm, associated only with deprivation, but containing also his companions in misery: he is, he cries, 'So lonely, sir! So very lonely!' causing even Bumble to lose his composure (ch. iv). Isolated from those who can offer him the compassion and security for which he so desperately longs, Oliver is a pitiful and largely passive object. He lacks the vitality of Bumble or even Noah Claypole. But his primary function is to reveal the neglect and corruption of those around him.

*   *   *

Dickens's criticism of the inadequacy of religious as well as social institutions is more powerful and direct in *Oliver Twist* than in *Pickwick Papers*. Stiggins in the Fleet provides an easy scapegoat by comparison with the anonymous clergyman indicted above. Criticism of the Established Church and its representatives had already begun in Dickens, as his comments in, and dedication to, *Sunday Under Three Heads*, suggest; and there is also the peremptory behaviour of the clergyman in 'The Bloomsbury Christening', who has 'two churchings, three christenings, and a funeral' to perform in less than an hour. But the novelist seems to be becoming more aware of the Church's shortcomings. Of course, he was not alone: 'The Church as it now stands, no human power can save', cried Dr Arnold. Arnold, like Dickens, felt that the narrowness and rigidity of the Evangelicals who seemed to dominate the Church militated against its ability to fulfil the practical, saving role demanded of it by the gospels. He even contemplated addressing the poor directly, by means of a magazine, 'Cobbett-like in style—but Christian in spirit,' an ambition which, in a sense, Dickens fulfilled with the writing of *Oliver Twist* for *Bentley's Miscellany* (although its audience was the more literate middle class, rather than the poor themselves).

✳   ✳   ✳

This emphasis upon the offering of Christian charity—as distinct from the condemnation of a vengeful God—to fallen women such as Nancy reappears later in the depiction of Alice Marwood in *Dombey and Son* and Emily in *David Copperfield*. It also appears in Dickens's conduct of Miss Burdett Coutts's Home for Fallen Women, Urania House, over some ten or twelve years, his most prolonged involvement in any single charitable activity. Miss Coutts tended towards a sterner approach, but Dickens was quite clear about where he stood, and insisted that his views be followed, according to which the former prostitutes were to be, as he put it, *'tempted to virtue'*, not frightened off by reminders of their sinfulness and degradation; and in so far as they were to receive spiritual enlightenment, this was to be from 'the *New* Testament' (his emphasis), not by 'injudicious use of the Old'. What is meant by this appears in the treatment of Nancy, indicating that for Dickens, as for many of his contemporaries, charity operates on the assumption of original virtue: we are created in God's image, which is good, and so there will remain at least a spark of divinity in even the most depraved. Hazlitt wrote that 'even among the most abandoned of the other sex, there is not infrequently found to exist (contrary to all that is generally supposed) one strong and individual attachment, which remains unshaken to the last. Virtue may be said to steal, like a guilty thing, into the secret haunts of vice and infamy; it clings to their devoted victim, and will not be driven away. Nothing can destroy the human heart'; while Mrs Gaskell, in a similar context, held that 'the most depraved have also their seed of the Holiness that shall one day overcome their evil' (*Mary Barton*, 1848, ch. 8). Nancy is as important to Dickens as Oliver, perhaps more so, since she reflects this belief. Hence his passionate defence of her against those who, like Thackeray, found her improbable and sentimental: 'From the first introduction of that poor wretch', he wrote,

> to her laying her bloody head upon the robber's breast, there is not one word exaggerated or over-wrought. It is emphatically God's truth, for it is the truth He leaves in such depraved and miserable

breasts; the hope yet lingering behind; the last fair drop of water at the bottom of the dried-up weed-choked well. (1841 Preface)[3]

Special pleading, perhaps; but Nancy is a little more interesting than the usual easy dismissal of her implies. She first reveals her 'soul of goodness in things evil' in the chapter to which Dickens gave this running title in 1867, chapter xvi: there she emerges, astonishingly, as the defender of the boy Oliver, whom she has just helped recapture for Fagin. The only real moral battle in the novel is the one which takes place within her (it is also one of the earliest instances in Dickens of a 'change of heart'). At first she is merely one of a couple of young 'ladies' Oliver meets when he enters Fagin's 'school' of hopeful young thieves, seeming to the innocent Oliver 'remarkably free and agreeable' in manner (ch. ix); she seems as callously disposed towards him as Sikes, to whom she reports that 'the young brat's been ill' (ch. xv); and when she finds him on his errand for Brownlow, she puts on a superlative act as his long-lost sister to get him back into Fagin's clutches (ch. xv). But when Oliver is then tormented by his captors into breaking loose, shrieking, with Fagin, the Dodger and Charley Bates in pursuit, she springs to the door crying, 'Keep back the dog, Bill', to Sikes's amazement, 'the child shan't be torn down by the dog, unless you kill me first' (ch. xvi). It is as if some pent-up former self has emerged, with a shock that turns her almost insane, 'not speaking, but pouring out the words in one continuous and vehement scream' (ch. xvi). Apparently Oliver has reminded her of herself as a child, 'not half as old as this', swept up into evil ways by Fagin, as the old devil hopes to sweep up Oliver; and hardened until only the impact of seeing the child threatened with being torn to pieces can bring back the recollection of what she once was. This is a typically Romantic notion, which Dickens ensures we will interpret in Christian terms: Oliver's arrival begins the erosion of Nancy's former, depraved self, leading eventually to the climax of her dying cry to Sikes, as he batters her down after her attempt to save the child has threatened her lover: 'It is never too late to repent' (ch. xlvii). Her words echo Rose Maylie's, and the martyrdom is complete when she draws out Rose's white handkerchief, emblem of unspotted virtue, holding it up 'in her folded hands, as high towards Heaven as her feeble strength would allow', breathing 'one prayer for mercy to her Maker' (ch. xlvii).

Nancy's death reveals 'God's truth', that good will come out of evil; this is further borne out by the events which follow it, her murder leading to the death of Sikes and the disruption and dispersal of Fagin's gang. It is not made clear what, precisely, Fagin is condemned to death for, but in terms of narrative logic, it is for his part in the corruption and death of Nancy, as well as in the attempted corruption of Oliver. It is the power of Providence, rather than the character of Brownlow, the

3. See above, pp. 3–7 [Editor].

Maylies, or Nancy, which ultimately ensures the triumph of charity and goodwill over evil; our sense of this is created by moments such as that in which Oliver, awaiting delivery to Sikes for the Chertsey robbery, prays to 'Heaven': 'if any aid were to be raised up for a poor outcast boy, who had never known the love of friends or kindred, it might come to him now: when, desolate and deserted, he stood alone in the midst of wickedness and guilt' (ch. xx); at once Nancy arrives and, seeing him, feels confirmed in her secret, instinctual determination to save the boy, despite her fears for herself and Sikes: 'God forgive me', she cries, 'I never thought of this' (loc. cit.).

Thus prayer is answered, and charity offered, even when this involves some fairly obvious (realistically considered) plot manipulation. Oliver must be brought into the bosom of that cosy 'little society, whose condition approached as nearly to one of perfect happiness as can ever be known in this changing world' (ch. liii), and individual, private benevolence, even at the cost which Nancy must suffer, will serve this end. Paradoxically, Dickens seems to endorse Bentham's view that one will only sacrifice individual interest to others when those others are such with whom one is 'connected by some domestic or other private and narrow tie of sympathy', since Brownlow and the Maylies all turn out to be related to Oliver; but Nancy provides the sacrifice which is absolute.

BURTON M. WHEELER

The Text and Plan of *Oliver Twist*†

Oliver Twist poses unique problems for Dickensian scholars. While there is general agreement that it is a work of remarkably evocative power, there is substantial disagreement about its coherence. This study maintains that the disagreements stem in large part from mistaken assumptions about the genesis and development of the novel. It advances the hypothesis, based on the text as it first appeared in *Bentley's Miscellany*, that "The Adventures of Oliver Twist, or, The Parish Boy's Progress" was begun as a short serial, that Dickens had already published four installments before deciding to convert it into a novel, and that its plot did not take shape even in general form until he had published yet another three installments.

Determining to meet one of his commitments to Richard Bentley by extending the serial into a novel, Dickens decided to rescue Oliver from

† From *Dickens Studies Annual*, ed. M. Timko, F. Kaplan, and E. Guiliano, 12 (1984): 41–58. Copyright © 1984 AMS Press, Inc. Reprinted by permission.

a representative "Parish Boy's Progress," that is, from workhouse to criminal associates to deportation or the gallows. He then settled upon Nancy as the character who, replacing Oliver as the central focus of the work, could sustain the theme that private benevolence must rescue children from the corruptive forces of society. Only later, to achieve a semblance of unity, did he graft on the melodramatic plot replete with lockets, wills, villains, and bucolic conclusion. Efforts to represent *Oliver Twist* as a unified, planned work are, I think, misbegotten, a misrepresentation of the nature of Dickens' early genius.

* * *

The best available evidence indicates that the first chapters were not completed before January, 1837. Richard Bentley's aide and accountant, E. S. Morgan, prepared a "brief retrospect" of his associations with Henry Colburn and Bentley in July, 1873. Although Morgan ends his recollections with an apology for his "enfeebled powers of brain" and "this imperfect sketch" after a thirty-six year lapse, his evidence is, unlike Forster's, first-hand. Morgan recalls:

> It had been at first intended that the Miscellany should open with the Story of 'Oliver Twist', but this was frustrated by the illness of Mr. Dickens. He had been attacked by influenza, then raging as an epidemic, and I remember calling upon him at his then lodgings at Furnivals Inn for Copy, when he explained to me the cause of the delay, promising that the opening chapter should be delivered in time for the 2nd Number, to appear on the 1st of February, 1837.

Morgan's evidence does not provide assistance in determining the scope and proposed length of "Oliver Twist," but it appears to preclude earlier composition than 1837. Further, the prospectus for *Bentley's Miscellany* gives no indication that a lengthy serial or novel would be a feature. Morgan, who claims to have prepared the prospectus, recalls that the *Miscellany* was "to be devoted to humorous papers by popular writers." The proposed title, "The Wit's Miscellany," emphasized that expectation. A copy of the prospectus in Dickens' own hand contains the statement: "These papers will be the exclusive copyright of Mr. Bentley. They will be found nowhere else, and will never be collected in any other form." Within a matter of months, Dickens would accept neither of these conditions.

* * *

Throughout the correspondence of 1837–1838 Dickens refers to having just completed copy or to his need to finish an installment. Although most of these comments are of limited significance, several are particularly relevant to the question of when Dickens' plans for *Oliver Twist* took shape. In a letter dated October 13, 1837 by the editors of the Pilgrim *Letters*, Dickens wrote to Morgan requesting a copy of Volume

I of the *Miscellany* (containing the issues of January through June, 1837), indicating "I have distributed all I had of that part, and have nothing to refer to for that portion of Oliver's history." Dickens was then in the process of writing Chapters XVI and XVII in which he takes the reader back to Oliver's birthplace. Dickens' failure to retain a copy of the early portions, even in manuscript, may have been sheer carelessness, of course, but raises the possibility that he had not anticipated any need to refer to the details of the first chapters. My hypothesis is that only as he was writing the November installment after extracting the new agreement from Bentley did the details of his plot take sufficient shape to require review of the early issues.

Three weeks after the request to Morgan, Dickens wrote the often quoted letter (November 3) to Forster: "I am glad you like Oliver this month [the reference is to Chapters XVI and XVII]—especially glad that you particularize the first chapter. I hope to do great things with Nancy. If I can only work out the idea I have formed of her, and of the female who is to contrast with her." Rose Maylie does not appear until Chapter XXIX (April, 1838), but it seems likely that Dickens' objective was now clear although the details of his achieving it were as yet uncertain. Dickens' phrasing also implies that his conception of Nancy is a recent one.

In mid-March, 1838, Dickens wrote to Frederick Yates about unauthorized stage productions, indicating that he felt no anxiety about premature revelations: "I am quite satisfied that nobody can have heard what I mean to do with the different characters in the end, inasmuch as at present I don't quite know, myself." Not until July 10, 1838 does he declare in a letter to Bentley: "I have planned the tale to the close." In mid October he completed the final chapter.

*   *   *

The first interruption, surely primarily occasioned by Dickens' grief [at the death of his sister-in-law, Mary Hogarth], follows Chapter VIII and immediately precedes Oliver's delivery into the care of Mr. Brownlow in the following installment. The second occurs following Chapter XV, preceding the first intervention by Nancy on Oliver's behalf and the return to the town of Oliver's birth and Bumble in the November, 1837 issue. The third interruption occurs in the middle of Chapter XXXIX, preparatory to Nancy's conversation with Rose in the October, 1838 issue. The interruptions of the serial publication of *Oliver Twist*, whatever their causes, came at times when Dickens was working out critical areas in the novel's development. That the interruptions occur at such significant points is consistent with the hypothesis here advanced: Dickens first determined to reverse the typical course of a "Parish Boy's Progress" in order to extend the serial and subsequently found in Nancy a new focus for the novel Bentley reluctantly agreed to accept in partial fulfillment of the August, 1836 contract.

*   *   *

Revising in 1838, Dickens deleted or emended more than 260 passages that had appeared in the *Miscellany* in the first eighteen installments. Most of these changes were minor adjustments in word order, punctuation, or language of the "underworld" characters, changes which do not affect the meaning of passages. Some, like the change in the Artful Dodger's height from a dwarfish three feet, six inches to a more respectable four feet, six inches are mere curiosities. A number are related to Dickens' never resolved difficulties in controlling the time frame of the novel.

The most striking changes are those in the divisions of the novel. At the end of the January, 1838 number of the *Miscellany*, which concludes with Chapter XXII, "The End of the First Book" appears. To the reader of the *Miscellany* surely the statement occasioned no surprise. Considered from the perspective of the hypothesis advanced in this essay, what is surprising is the absence of "Book the First" at the beginning of the February, 1837 issue where only "Chapter the First" appears. *   *   * The absence of the designation "Book the First" in the *Miscellany*, unless one argues that it is an undetected printer's error, establishes the fact that Dickens significantly altered his plans for *Oliver Twist*. At the very least the introduction and then subsequent deletion of book divisions of unequal length indicates how shapeless were his plans for the work during the early months of composition. Other changes in the text effected for the 1838 edition indicate that the alteration of plans went substantially beyond the question of book division.

The most important changes made for the 1838 edition are the deletions. Some of these have been noted by other critics, others ignored, but no one has suggested that there is a pattern to the deletions which require attention. There are fourteen significant deletions. By significant I mean a deletion of more than several words or a deletion which alters the meaning. Five of these fourteen deletions bear explicitly on the hypothesis that Dickens did not think of *Oliver Twist* as a novel until sometime after Mary Hogarth's death in May, 1837 and did not work out his basic plan or plot details before October of that year. Four of the passages provide circumstantial evidence for the thesis. One provides concrete support. All five passages appear in the first eight issues, the last one appearing in Chapter XVII (the November issue). The deletions will be discussed in the order of their appearance in the *Miscellany* text.

The first such deletion occurs in the first line of the first chapter. The 1838 three-volume edition and all subsequent editions read: "Among other public buildings in a certain town, which for many reasons it will be prudent to refrain from mentioning, and to which I will assign no fictitious name . . ." The *Miscellany* reads: "Among other public buildings in the town of Mudfog. . . ." Dickens' only contributions of substantial length to the *Miscellany* other than *Oliver Twist* were three

"Mudfog" papers. Robert Colby notes that the use of "Mudfog" at the beginning of the *Miscellany* text suggests "a continuation of *The Mudfog Papers*," but he does not pursue the point.[1] Dickens' exclusion of the name "Mudfog" from the 1838 edition at least indicates his desire to disassociate the novel from those more satiric and topical pieces. It lends credence to the hypothesis that when he began "The Adventures of Oliver Twist" in the *Miscellany*, he was thinking of it as a serial related to that set of papers. Writing as late as February, 1838, he wrote in the manuscript "the Mudfog peasantry" but corrected it before publication in the *Miscellany*. In the course of one year he had concluded that he did not want to associate Oliver's birthplace with Mudfog.

The second deletion relevant to the hypothesis has greater weight. At the conclusion of Chapter II, the text of the *Miscellany* reads: "I should perhaps mar the interest of this narrative (supposing it to possess any at all), if I ventured to hint, just yet, whether the life of Oliver Twist will be a long or a short piece of biography." Subsequent editions read: "whether the life of Oliver Twist had this violent termination or no." Clearly a three volume novel entitled *Oliver Twist* containing the original passage would appear absurd. One may argue that the line, initially, was a teaser for the serial reader. Yet the phrasing and the subsequent deletion of the passage raises the question whether or not Dickens had himself determined the length of his "biography."

The third deletion is perhaps the most revealing. It conceals a reversal in design which has gone unnoticed. Chapter VII in the *Miscellany* (May, 1837) concludes: "The blessing was from a young child's lips [Dick] but it was the first that Oliver had ever heard invoked upon his head; and through all the struggles and sufferings of his after life, through all the troubles and changes *of many weary years* he never once forgot it." For the 1838 edition Dickens rewrote the sentence, omitting the phrase I have italicized. The deleted phrase stands in direct contradiction to the version of Oliver's life that Dickens began developing in the July, 1837 issue following the interruption of *Oliver Twist* in the June issue. In a period of only a few months, Oliver is twice freed from Fagin's grasp and is happily secured in the Maylie household to await passively the discovery of his fortune. The presence of "many weary years" in the original text provides strong support for the thesis that Dickens initially intended Oliver to fulfill a typical "Parish Boy's Progress."

The fourth deletion occurs at the beginning of Chapter XV, one of the pivotal points in the novel's development. The chapter appears in the issue of September, 1837, a month preceding the omission of an installment of *Oliver Twist*. It was written while Dickens was battling for the acceptance of *Oliver Twist* as the second novel of the August, 1836 agreement. From the time of his letter of July 14, 1837, in which

---

1. Robert Colby, *Fiction With a Purpose* (Bloomington, 1967) 324.

he first made the proposal, to the middle of September Dickens used every weapon at his disposal to force a revised contract from Bentley. In a letter to Forster, dated 24 September, his exhilaration in the heat of battle is evident. Describing a new offer from Bentley that apparently promised additional payment, Dickens wrote: "Of course we refused it —a new agreement and copyright, being the War Cry." A letter of August 18, probably written just following the completion of the September installment indicates that Dickens was angry enough to break off all personal contact with Bentley.

The passage deleted from the *Miscellany* text of Chapter XV is given in its entirety in the Clarendon edition. The bulk of the passage is devoted to a rather tiresome, sardonic discussion of the folly of benevolence. Had it come nearer the end of an installment, one might suspect that it was "filler" to meet the sixteen-page contractual obligation, but it comes at the very beginning of the chapter, at the mid-point of the installment. Only the introductory sentence is directly relevant to the hypothesis. I quote it only in part:

> If it did not come within the scope and bearing of my long-considered intentions and plans regarding this prose epic (for such I mean it to be,) to leave the two old gentlemen sitting with the watch between them long after it grew too dark to see it, and both doubting Oliver's return, the one in triumph, and the other in sorrow, I might take occasion to entertain the reader with many wise reflections on the obvious impolicy of ever attempting to do good to our fellow creatures where there is no hope of earthly reward. . . .

The passage continues at length concluding: "I shall not enter into any such digression in this place: and, if this be not a sufficient reason for this determination, I have a better, and, indeed, a wholly unanswerable one, already stated; which is, that it forms no part of my original intention so to do." It is a curious passage in its entirety, in the part not quoted here stylistically similar to the early chapters of the novel satirizing parish officials. Dickens' mockery of self-interested philanthropists may relate to his own indignation at being treated, as he thought, ungenerously by his publisher. The opening lines here quoted, particularly the parenthetical "for such I mean it to be," sounds very like a throwing down of the gauntlet before Bentley, a declaration that he *is* writing a novel, a warning that Bentley must capitulate.

Mrs. Tillotson draws different conclusions from the same passage. Advancing her contention that the inception of *Oliver Twist* may have been as early as 1833, she states,

> There are certain other references that indicate a long incubation for the novel. In chapter XV he speaks, not necessarily ironically, of his "long-considered intentions and plans regarding this prose

epic"; and in the Introduction of 1841 claims that the "conduct and character" of Nancy has been "suggested to [his] mind long ago—long before I dealt in fiction—by what I often saw and read of, in actual life around me."[2]

These two references are the only textual ones Mrs. Tillotson cites for her "long incubation" theory and they are cited, of necessity, conditionally. The "Introduction" passage argues only for the accuracy of the portrayal of the "conduct and character of the girl." Whether Dickens' assertion in Chapter XV that his plans were "long-considered" is ironic or not is but one of the questions we need to ask. More importantly, how long must Dickens have considered his plans to justify such a claim? To a young writer of twenty-five, four months may meet his requirements for honesty as well as four years. In any event, the declaration that his plans were "long-considered" is less significant than the fact that in the seventh installment of his serial, Dickens chose to declare to his readers (and perhaps Bentley) that *Oliver Twist* was to be a "prose epic."

The fifth deletion is from Chapter XVII which appeared the following month (November, 1837). It is part of an unusually lengthy explanation for leaving Oliver, upon his recapture, in the hands of Fagin while the narrator returns to Oliver's birthplace. In the midst of the third paragraph of the chapter, while addressing his readers on the custom of leaving characters in various dilemmas at the end of each chapter, the narrator adds, "this brief introduction to the present one [chapter] may perhaps be deemed unnecessary." In the *Miscellany*, the text continues:

> But I have set it in this place because I am anxious to disclaim at once the slightest desire to tantalise my readers by leaving young Oliver Twist in situations of doubt and difficulty, and then flying off at a tangent to impertinent matters, which have nothing to do with him. My sole desire is to proceed straight through this history with all convenient despatch, carrying my reader along with me if I can, and, if not, leaving him to take a more pleasant route for a chapter or two, and join me again afterwards if he will. Indeed, there is so much to do, that I have no room for digressions, even if I possessed the inclination; and I merely make this one in order to set myself quite right with the reader, between whom and the historian it is essentially necessary that perfect faith should be kept, and a good understanding preserved. The advantage of this amicable explanation is, that when I say, as I do now, that I am going back directly to the town in which Oliver Twist was born, the reader will at once take it for granted that I have good and substantial reasons for making the journey, or I would not ask him to accompany me on any account.

2. *Oliver Twist*, Clarendon Dickens, ed. Kathleen Tillotson (Oxford, 1966) xv.

The last sentence, in revised form, was retained. The remainder of the paragraph was deleted for the 1838 edition.

The transparent pose of the historian proceeding straight through Oliver's history "with all convenient despatch" is at best an awkward explanation of Dickens' intentions. Subsequent returns to the town of Oliver's birth are not marred by such self-conscious, mechanical transitions. The declaration "there is so much to do" suggests Dickens' awareness of the complexities before him now that he has extracted the new agreement from Bentley and returned Oliver to the machinations of Fagin.

Chapter XVII, which reintroduces Bumble, must have been written sometime after October 12, 1837, shortly after Dickens requested Morgan to send the first volume of the *Miscellany*. Within the following two weeks, Dickens responded to Forster's praise of the November installment with the previously quoted letter setting forth his expectations for Nancy. That letter, when considered together with the deletions from the *Miscellany* text, would seem to establish the approximate date by which Dickens knew clearly how his serial, now converted into a novel, could achieve a sustaining focus. The deletion from Chapter VII indicates that not until sometime after April did he decide to rescue Oliver from the course on which he had first set him. Not until he was writing the section on Nancy during October, however, does he seem to have been certain that he had a satisfactory character through whom he could express his concern about the cost of public indifference to neglected children. Once Dickens had settled upon Nancy as his principal character for the latter portion of the novel and upon her contrasting figure, Rose Maylie, he was faced with the problem of tying together the disparate strands he had already spun in the *Miscellany*. He may have concocted his melodramatic solution soon after writing to Forster, but there is no allusion to Monks before Chapter XXVI (March, 1838) and no reference to the locket until Chapter XXXVIII (August, 1838).

Of the remaining nine significant deletions from the *Miscellany* text, several lend themselves readily to explanation. A passage in Chapter XXVI, which describes Fagin's behavior upon hearing Toby Crackit's report of the abortive Chertsey "crack," was possibly deleted because it is astonishingly similar to the passage describing Nancy's reaction to the conversation between Monks and Fagin. Six other deletions seem to have been made to tone down dialogue or descriptive passages. These include the bathetic lines of Oliver to which G. H. Lewes objected, a trivial thrust at Fang, an irrelevant comment on the weather, and three passages dealing with Nancy. In the latter Dickens apparently wished to mute suggestions of vulgarity or excessively melodramatic behavior.

Two other deletions are not easily explained. One in Chapter XXI (January, 1838) details the journey of Sikes and Oliver toward Chertsey. For the 1838 edition "Twickenham" and the crossing "of a little bridge" are deleted. In further rewriting after the 1841 edition, the name of the "Red Lion Inn" was dropped. That this passage received a strangely disproportionate attention is further evidenced by an addition to the 1838 edition: "here they lingered about in the fields for some hours."

The second curious deletion is in Chapter IX (July, 1837). While Oliver watches drowsily, Fagin inspects his hoard, muttering to himself about capital punishment. The line omitted, "The prospect of the gallows, too, makes them hardy and bold," seems in keeping with the remainder of the passage which Dickens retained: "Ah, it's a fine thing for the trade! Five of 'em strung up in a row; and none left to play booty, or turn white-livered!"

While the deletion of the one line from Fagin's mutterings serves no obvious purpose, the passage is interesting for another reason. It exemplifies a method which Dickens utilized effectively as he extended the serial into a novel. Between June and September as he wrote *Oliver Twist* he prepared several passages with open options to which he could return, if necessary, as he worked out the plot. Among the items which Fagin examines as Oliver watches is a "trinket" with "Some very minute description on it. . . . At length he put it down, as if despairing of success." The 'trinket' anticipates the locket of Oliver's mother. Fagin also examines with particular care a "magnificent gold watch, sparkling with jewels." The passage was written in June, 1837, just before Dickens demanded the new agreement from Bentley. The passage provides pegs upon which he could hang a plot, but is not so explicit as to limit him.

One such passage, however, was too binding, yet Dickens failed to detect it when revising for the 1838 edition. In Chapter XIV (September, 1837) when Mr. Brownlow addresses Oliver in a quite intimidating tone for the purpose of getting the truth about the boy's history, he admonishes: "Speak the truth; and you shall not be friendless while I live." The text of the *Miscellany* and of the 1838 edition contain the clause "if I find you have committed no crime." This clause was not deleted until the careful revision for the 1846 edition. The reason for the deletion seems clear. When writing Chapter XIV, and Chapter IX discussed above, Dickens had not yet conceived of the Leeford will which contains the stipulation that Oliver "in his minority . . . should never have stained his name with any public act of dishonour, meanness, cowardice, or wrong." The first reference to the will does not appear until Chapter XLIX, written sometime after October 2, 1838. At the time of Brownlow's warning to Oliver in Chapter XIV and in the hoard of Fagin of Chapter IX, Dickens may well have had other plans for disclosing Oliver's parentage and developing the theme of virtue triumphant. Brownlow's warning is appropriate to the context of the passage in Chapter XIV, but, in the light of the Leeford will, Dickens must have considered it an awkward tautology.

Another such multiple option passage in Chapter XII (August, 1837) led Dickens into a contradiction which he could have corrected only with difficulty. According to Brownlow and Mrs. Bedwin, Oliver's features are identical to those of the portrait of his mother: "its living copy. The eyes, the head, the mouth; every feature was the same. The expression was, for the instant, so precisely alike, that the minutest line seemed copied with startling accuracy." In the chapter heading of the *Miscellany*, Dickens called further attention to the likeness by including "WITH SOME PARTICULARS CONCERNING A CERTAIN PICTURE," which he did not delete until the 1846 edition. Unfortunately, the reader must also conclude that Oliver looks exactly like his father. The source is Nancy's report to Rose: "That Monks . . . had seen him accidentally with two of our boys on the day we first lost him, and had known him directly to be the same child that he was watching for." Monks has never seen a picture of Oliver's mother nor has he at the time traced Oliver to the workhouse, but, amid all the urchins of London, he knew him "directly." Although Dickens committed such blunders throughout his career, the mistake here was forced on him by the later introduction of the suppressed will and the paranoid, epileptic half-brother. He had so bound himself in the first chapter in which Oliver's mother dies unidentified and in the second chapter where Bumble reports that the Parish offer of a reward for information has gone unanswered that he had no ready means to account for Monks' swift recognition of Oliver.

Another scene to which Dickens did not return also has all the characteristics of the multiple-option method. Any frequent and careful reader of Dickens will find the passage one which whets anticipation. In Chapter XIII (August, 1837), in his first appearance Sikes charges Fagin with being an informer, but is sharply interrupted. Sikes then performs a dumb show of a hanging before he is calmed with liquor. The charge of informing and the dumb show could refer back to Fagin's mutterings in Chapter IX or forward to the hangings Nancy anticipates in Chapter XVI. Because of the confused chronology, it is not clear whether both passages allude to the same hangings. The introduction of the gallows and the return to the hangings twice suggest that Dickens intended to do more with the passages than merely cast a spectre of death over the world of Fagin and his cohorts. This possibility is reinforced by Cruikshank's illustration for the issue. The illustration and the passages lead to the conjecture that between June and September, 1837 he anticipated using the hangings as a vehicle for plot development and subsequently rejected that idea.

The emphasis given here to the several multiple-option passages is intended to demonstrate the number of loose ends evident in the chapters written during the summer and early fall of 1837 as Dickens struggled to develop a plan for his novel which could accommodate the earlier chapters. While their existence *proves* nothing with regard to the evolution of the novel, the hypothesis that Dickens fundamentally altered his plans for the "Parish Boy's Progress" seems a more satisfactory explanation for them than a charge of carelessness.

*   *   *

The assumption that *Oliver Twist* was conceived as a full-length novel offers no satisfactory answer to four insistent questions: 1) Why does no hint of mystery surround Oliver's parentage in the first ten chapters? 2) Why is the conspiracy between Monks and Fagin so long withheld and so implausible when finally established? 3) Why does the focus shift so drastically from Oliver to Nancy in the latter portion of the work? 4) Why is there such a pronounced alteration in narrative mode following the opening chapters? The hypothesis here advanced offers reasonable explanations.

In Chapter I, although Oliver's mother momentarily arouses the curiosity of the parish surgeon, she is no more than a vehicle for delivering Oliver to the tender mercies of the parish. She dies telling no secrets, delivering no locket, and making only one plea—to be allowed to see her child and die. The presence of the parish surgeon throughout her childbirth and death and the surrounding details of Oliver's birth quite simply do not allow for the conversation which "Old Sally" reports to Mrs. Corney in Chapter XXIV. Had Dickens expected to return to the scene, he surely would not have constricted himself so severely. The plot, perhaps especially because of its elaborateness, appears to be an afterthought, a rejection of the original plan to develop Oliver as a representative ward of the parish in favor of making him heir to a fortune.

The conspiracy between Monks and Fagin is the other element of the plot that does not bear close scrutiny. The suppressed will and the malevolent half-brother subvert the novel more than Dickens could have anticipated. His fascination with the criminal but human qualities of Sikes, Nancy, and Fagin produces extraordinary power and genuine insight which he could not bring to his stage villain, Monks. Although the will was intended to provide the motivation for Monks' absurd and unnecessary attempt to corrupt Oliver, it did not unleash Dickens' creative powers. The contention that the Monks-Fagin relationship was conceived late in composition is supported by the absence of any early scenes foreshadowing the conspiracy first revealed in Chapter XXVI (March, 1838).

According to Nancy's report to Rose in Chapter XL, Monks made inquiries about Oliver after seeing him on the day he is taken before Fang, a scene which appeared in July, 1837. Not until Chapter XXVI (March, 1838), however, does Nancy or the reader know that Fagin's interest in Oliver is rooted in what he blurts out to Nancy: "the boy's worth hundreds of pounds to me." When Oliver is returned to Fagin in Chapter XVI (November, 1837), Fagin greets him with mock graciousness, losing his temper only when Oliver tries to escape. Fagin's behavior does not suggest Oliver's value. Even the anxiety to recapture

Oliver depicted in Chapter XIII (August, 1837) arises from his concern that Oliver might provide information to authorities. A person rereading the novel may attribute Fagin's eagerness to the conspiracy with Monks, but a careful reading shows that nothing in Chapter XIII or Chapter XVI supports that assumption. Nancy's intervention in defense of Oliver in Chapter XVI marks the turning point of Dickens' interest in her as principal character, but even in the succeeding issue (December, 1837) there is no certain indication that Dickens has worked out a relationship between Fagin and Monks.

The hypothesis here advanced does not justify Dickens' use of so threadbare a plot, but by accounting for it as a late and hastily considered addition, the hypothesis helps to explain why the plot was so incidental to Dickens' purposes. For all its complexities and coincidences, the plot generates little force in the novel. It is not organically related to any of the novel's principal themes. Once introduced, however, it acts on its own like the Sorcerer's Apprentice, leading Dickens into improbabilities and absurdities such as Monks entrusting his father's will, for "better security," to the safekeeping of Fagin. In spite of the strain the plot places on the reader's credulity, it serves one effective purpose. It enables Dickens to proceed to the portrayal of the generous impulse, the self-lessness, and loyalty of Nancy without doing absolute violence to the early chapters of "A Parish Boy's Progress."

Dickens turned his attention from Oliver to Nancy because she alone could exhibit what Dickens was later to call, in the Preface to the 1841 edition, "the principle of Good surviving through every adverse circumstance." There, of course, he attributes the illustration of the principle to Oliver. Oliver's untutored prayer life, his foreknowledge of how long it will take him to reach the bookseller's shop when he has not been out of Brownlow's house since his arrival there unconscious, his ready preference of death to crime, and total blandness with the Maylies make him an impossible vehicle for what Dickens proclaimed in 1841. In turning to Nancy, Dickens apparently lost all interest in plausibly developing Oliver. As H. M. Daleski argues effectively, the true instrument for revealing the "principle of Good surviving through every adverse circumstance" is Nancy.[3]

The problem of the alteration of the narrative mode of *Oliver Twist* has been discussed by many critics, most recently William Lankford.[4] In the opening scenes, Dickens assumes an intimate relationship with his reader which provides the greatest opportunity for sardonic authorial comments. The narrator's presence is obtrusive, often marked by heavy-handed irony. Only after Oliver flees Sowerberry's establishment is the narrative presence muted. The authorial intrusions which characterize

3. H. M. Daleski, *Dickens and the Art of Analogy* (London, 1970) 72–73.
4. William T. Lankford, "The Parish Boy's Progress: The Evolving Form of *Oliver Twist*," *PMLA* 93 (January 1978): 20–32.

the early chapters disappear, with rare exception, after Chapter XVIII. The narration of the early chapters is akin to portions of the Mudfog articles. Dickens' shift in narrative mode coincides with the decisions which I have argued Dickens made between June and September, 1837 to extend his story into a novel and to turn his focus to Nancy and her contrasting figure, Rose Maylie.

To argue that *Oliver Twist* is the product of a radical change of plans is not to belittle Dickens. The work is, after all, that of a novice, a uniquely talented and ambitious young writer determined to overcome his own "adverse circumstances." James R. Kincaid notes that the reader of *Oliver Twist* is left "with the uneasy suspicion that the book is powerful despite all that Dickens could do to make it conventional and safe, that it represents a triumph of unconscious forces over conscious intentions."[5] With regard to the characterizations of Sikes and Fagin, Kincaid is quite likely correct. The evidence advanced here, however, indicates that many of the problems with which critics of *Oliver Twist* have been occupied are the result of radical and conscious alterations in Dickens' plan for the work. The paradoxes of Dickens the man and the writer continue to astound us. If the hypothesis I advance is valid, it is surely remarkable that he could erect a novel's structure on the foundation of a short serial with such precocious dexterity that those of us who admire his work have found more grist than our mills have been able to grind.

JANET LARSON

[*Oliver Twist* and Christian Scripture]†

Although *Oliver Twist* is not a religious novel, it is a book, as Steven Marcus puts it more precisely, "conceived under substantial pressure of the Christian sentiments and language which were the received culture of Dickens's time."[1] * * *

* * *

Steven Marcus has placed *Oliver Twist* within the English parabolic tradition of morality plays, homiletic tales, and Bunyan.[2] In fact, *Oliver Twist* is three parables. * * * The most prominent is the fable Bunyan claimed to write "in parables" like his Master: Dickens announces it in the novel's subtitle, "The Parish Boy's Progress," and recalls it in a running headline for Chapter 8 ("The Young Pilgrim's Progress," added

5. See above, pp. 500–508 [*Editor*].
† Reprinted by permission from *Dickens and the Broken Scripture* (Athens: The U of Georgia P, 1985) 47–67. Copyright © 1985 by the University of Georgia.
1. Steven Marcus, *Dickens from Pickwick to Dombey* (New York: Simon and Schuster, 1965) 76. John Bunyan, *The Pilgrim's Progress* (1684).
2. Marcus, *Dickens from Pickwick to Dombey*, 67–68. I am indebted to Marcus' fine discussion of the Bunyan parallel.

in 1867), where "Oliver Walks to London, He Encounters on the Road, a Strange Sort of Young Gentleman" when the hero is nearly "dead upon the king's highway." This echo of Bunyan's "such robberies [of faith] are done on the King's highway" calls to mind the other story engaged in *Oliver Twist* as a subtext with wide relevance: the parable of the Good Samaritan. The motif of providential rescue is there in Bunyan's allegory as well as in Jesus' exemplary tale; but the latter's predominance in *Oliver Twist* requires the redefinition of the Bunyan hero as a passive sufferer for Good Samaritans to assist—a redefinition that attenuates the spiritual impact of the revised Puritan classic and clouds the "truth within a fable" Dickens would, like his precursor, convey. (Here is an early instance of Dickens' privileging one religious subtext, which modifies the perspective of another.) On the other hand, the Good Samaritan subtext is relevant to more of Dickens' novel and, within its own limits, is more imaginatively engaged by Dickens as parabler.

A literary allusion is a medium of vision, as Herman Meyer describes it, "permitting another world to radiate into the self-contained world of the novel."[3] *The Pilgrim's Progress* as subtext invites the reader to see behind the adventures of Oliver's story an archetypal struggle between the forces of good and evil for the hero's soul. Yet since its "other world" is two centuries removed (and in signal ways alien to Dickens' temperament), the Bunyan text must be revised for a later time. One way Dickens secures spiritual issues in a set of nineteenth-century conventions is to assimilate this Bunyan design to melodrama; its signs also gesture toward a subsurface Manichean battle, and in its plot a moral universe among men is at length vindicated. While Bunyan defends his use of parable to convey spiritual truth in "The Author's Apology for His Book," Dickens' famous apology opening chapter 17 argues for the natural truth of melodrama's conventional aim to "present the tragic and the comic scenes, in as regular alternation, as the layers of red and white in a side of streaky, well-cured bacon"; such "sudden shiftings of the scene," besides, are "sanctioned in books by long usage," and although Dickens did not name it in his 1841 preface, *Pilgrim's Progress* is one of those books. Superficially, with its dramatic changes of fortune, Bunyan's story lends itself to melodramatization—not surprisingly, since melodrama's roots can be found in the same morality tradition that Bunyan drew upon. Alternating between radical peril and dramatic rescue, his hero's journey is "sometimes up-hill, sometimes down-hill," as Honest says; "we are seldom at a certainty" about the soul's destination until the glorious end. Dickens exploits this apparent uncertainty with melodramatic suspense: Which way will Oliver go?—toward the "tragic" hell of urban crime and poverty or the divinely "comic" heaven he

3. Herman Meyer, *The Poetics of Quotation in the European Novel*, trans. Theodore and Yetta Ziolkowski (Princeton: Princeton UP, 1968) 6.

dreams about and miraculously discovers on earth in the society of Mr. Brownlow and the Maylies?

But of course Dickens' Oliver is not Bunyan's more active wayfaring Christian, nor a Christian in any other orthodox sense. If the borrowed paradigm suggests that life is a stage on which the drama of salvation is enacted and the faithful matured as well as tested by adversity, Dickens actually precludes any real moral drama, undercuts this paradigm, and belies the notion of "progress" in his subtitle. For his hero already embodies the "incorruptible" goodness that Christian seeks, as the preordained "principle of Good surviving through every adverse circumstance, and triumphing at last" (1841 preface). In consequence Oliver is what Bumble calls him, "a artificial soul and spirit" (7), not the "human boy" even Chadband in *Bleak House* finds Jo. At this stage in his career, Dickens apparently needed an unsullied image of his child-self as well as proof definitive of a God who takes care of his own, in what he already knew was "a world of disappointment: often to the hopes we most cherish" (51). Thus he embodies a Romantic version of Puritan election in his innocent child, while stoutly rejecting what was the logical counterpart for many of his contemporaries—the predestined damnation voiced by the gentleman in the white waistcoat and Mr. Grimwig (Oliver's "A bad one!" 41). As Dickens' melodrama drives toward the revelation of the hero's pure identity and the expulsion of evil in a public spectacle, Oliver must remain a passive victim of the inexorable logic of the plot in order to prove God's all-powerful providence.

Bunyan's allegory also starts with the premise of election; but his story has brought comfort and inspiration to generations of embattled Christians because his hero enacts their struggles in ways that Oliver's so obviously preordained goodness never allows him to do. Unlike the episodic mishaps of the static Oliver, Christian's plot of spiritual growth takes him through the entire Puritan psychology of conversion; and even after he loses his burden at the foot of the Cross and receives assurance of his election, he must beat back an army of spiritual temptations, wrestle for the truth of Scripture texts, and hold onto the promises of eternal life. Oliver, in contrast, dressed in rags and with no burden on his back but the unmerited curse of his illegitimacy and poverty, runs from Dickens' City of Destruction crying for physical survival, the first thing needful for his "Good" to survive; instead of the truth Christian seeks, the utterly lonely Oliver wants only an arbor to rest in and a family identity. In this beginning, Dickens is already setting the scene for his Good Samaritan parable, which requires Oliver not to fight the good fight of faith but to lie in literal and figurative ditches awaiting rescue, "a poor outcast boy . . . alone in the midst of wickedness and guilt" (20).

Through Sloughs of Despond, Valleys of the Shadow of Death and

Valleys of Humiliation, up Hills of Difficulty, and into Vanity Fairs (for Oliver, a Rag-Fair), both protagonists travel; both are met by allegorical personages and confront demons at hell's mouth. But Christian does heroic battle with creatures like Giant Despair who personify his inner doubts, while Oliver's enemies are strictly external menaces, and he seems never seriously to be tempted. Resting in an arbor at the Maylies' country retreat, he momentarily loses his "scroll" (his proof of election) like Christian sleeping, when the evil of Fagin and Monks at the window impresses itself on his consciousness; but it is only a moment, before all traces of them and their influence vanish. This disappearance is the more incredible because the reader *is* powerfully impressed by the real menace of the evil characters—as the Bunyan subtext would require, with its lesson that we must never underestimate the powers of darkness. It is, significantly, in the context Dickens has himself created that the notion of Oliver's inherent goodness seems as much a piece of folly as the self-delusion of Bunyan's Ignorance, who has stifled his conviction of sin because his "heart" has told him he is good. Bunyan knows better: Ignorance misses entering the Celestial City by a hair's-breadth; Oliver, on the strength of Dickens' new Pelagian heresy, finds himself already in.

Because being spiritually saved is not enough, Dickens diverges even further from the Bunyan model in his final disposition of affairs. Turning away from whatever divine grace has been implied in Oliver's deliverances, Dickens lands his hero at length in Bunyan's eschewed Village of Morality under the care of Legality and his son Civility to "live by honest neighbours, in credit and good fashion." Ordering this ending, Dickens becomes Mr. Worldly-Wiseman, "the eternal bourgeois trying to tell a social inferior which way he should go."[4] As bourgeois rewards of being good replace Christian ones and the "inheritance incorruptible" becomes the father's money and the father's name, Oliver's intimations of the heavenly are realized in Brownlow's "little society, whose condition approached as nearly to one of perfect happiness as can ever be known in this changing world" (53). Dickens' last phrase is disingenuous; we have left that world behind for another Eden, like Pickwick's final retreat. The other heaven, after all, is "a long way off; and they are too happy there, to come down to" earth, as Oliver says (12). If in this Dickens retreats from affirming the "Heavenly Home" that was Christian's reward, the Victorian writer's earthly paradise is curiously deathlike nonetheless. * * * Cruikshank's last plate, "Rose Maylie and Oliver," is appropriate to this deathlike close of their stories: in a church reduced to its function as mausoleum, the two gaze solemnly at Agnes' memorial stone, their faces grown too old (as Dickens himself noticed) as though their lives are already over. (The picture also resembles the preceding

4. Roger Sharrock, Introduction to *The Pilgrim's Progress*, 15.

illustration of Fagin's death cell, with stained glass replacing his gaol window.) We have arrived at the other pole of Oliver's predetermined "claustral universe," where the novel's obsessive fears of suffocation, which J. Hillis Miller has noted, are associated not only with baby farms, chimney sweeping, hanging, and the close dens of thieves,[5] but also with the stifling domestic interiors, funereally perfumed with flowers, of the Maylie household—and with the church, a place of the dead. In the irreversible logic of events, this is the artificial Elysium where Oliver, victim as much as beneficiary of his predestination, has no choice but to go.

If Dickens attenuates the power of his Bunyan model by eliminating or displacing much of its spiritual drama, in depositing his hero at this House Beautiful he misses another form of dramatic tension and progression in *The Pilgrim's Progress*. Dayton Haskin has argued that Bunyan presents a drama of interpretation in which Christian, a lonely figure burdened with a Book whose texts initially menace his peace of mind and render him impotent, must "lear[n] to interpret for himself, making his way through the wilderness of the world."[6] Growing in his understanding of Scripture at the House of the Interpreter and later at the House Beautiful, Christian becomes ever more adept, even playful, at quoting a saving and clarifying text for the situations that arise on his journey, and correcting the misinterpretations of the tempters put in his way. Bunyan would foster a similar growth in his reader. Arguing in the "Author's Apology" for "The use of parables; in which lay hid / That gold, those pearls, and precious stones that were / Worth digging for," Bunyan assigns to his reader the "travail" of puzzling out readings, that the burden of interpretation eventually lighten and reading become a source of "delightful things to see," comfort, and self-knowledge. Enticing his reader at the threshold of this story into the serious textual play, Bunyan concludes his catalog of the many pleasures to be found in this work with a challenge to his participating reader:

> Would'st read thyself, and read thou know'st not what
> And yet know whether thou art blest or not,
> By reading the same lines? O then come hither,
> And lay my book, thy head and heart together.

When Oliver Twist comes to his House Beautiful, like Christian he reviews his adventures, receives religious instruction, and glimpses the Delectable Mountains that will be his by the tale's end. Having been earlier prepared at Brownlow's House of the Interpreter—where he had been ministered to by "soft-hearted psalm-singers" (16) and an old

---

5. J. Hillis Miller, *Charles Dickens: The World of His Novels* (Bloomington: Indiana UP, 1958) 38–39.
6. Dayton Haskin, "The Burden of Interpretation in *The Pilgrim's Progress*," *Studies in Philology* 79 (Summer 1982): 278.

woman with "a small Prayer Book and a large nightcap" (12)—Oliver now can "read a chapter or two from the Bible: which he had been studying all the week." Rather than bringing the multiple delights and puzzles Bunyan celebrates, however, reading the Bible is for Oliver "the performance of [a] duty," which makes him feel "more proud and pleased, than if he had been the clergyman himself" (33). Clearly Oliver is not "pleased" by the pleasures of the text, for no imaginative engagement is required, no difficulties of interpretation arise; learning to read the Bible is assimilated rather to his pleasure of acquiring a higher station in life, even that of the clergyman. Never puzzling over the application of the right texts to life situations, Oliver also never cites any specific verses; the text Oliver's narrator often comes closest to quoting for him is not from Scripture at all but Wordsworth's *Intimations of Immortality* ode (see 30, 32). Goodness in his world seems as transparently readable as the words of the Book, provoking nothing but a blank of reflection in this artificial soul.

In this early novel, like Oliver, Dickens is not wrestling with the simple biblical texts he chooses for his story; and in his interpretation of Bunyan's classic, founded on shoals of Scripture texts, he smooths all the rough places in their theology and dispenses finally with its Christian message. Nor, with one important exception, does he impose on his readers the burden of interpretation that becomes the serious play of allusion in his later books. Passively we are to receive the Bunyan parallel in the subtitle, without inquiring too far into it; no labor is required to dig out the meaning of other religious allusions, such as the association of Monks and Sikes with Cain (46, 48) or the use of "Pharisee" for the religious hypocrite. Like Oliver, we too can be complacently "proud and pleased" with these confirmations of our common heritage, rather than challenged to read for ourselves. In the early Dickens, the reading and application of Scripture is in general unproblematic—or meant to be.

The important exception anticipates, on a small scale, some of the more interesting ways Dickens uses the Bible in his later fiction. If his readers are challenged at all to more active critical reading of themselves and their world, it is not through the Bunyan fable but the parable of the Good Samaritan. One of the few of Christ's parables that sets forth a clear moral for earthly action, and thus appropriate for a Victorian fable that ends in the Village of Morality, this story radiates into the world of Dickens' novel to illuminate where duty lies. At the same time, Dickens' depiction of much social suffering draws attention to the darker places in Oliver Twist's world and in human nature, insoluble enigmas Good Samaritans address in vain. Thus, unlike the Bunyan melodrama, which expels evil with the triumph of good on earth, Dickens' application of Jesus' parable does not solve all the problems it illuminates and is unevenly matched against the forces of the third, darker "parable"—in

Kermode's sense[7]—that *Oliver Twist* also tells through its nightmarish visions of the Victorian urban hell.

From a pragmatic point of view, it might seem perfectly obvious why Dickens used the parable of the Good Samaritan: at a time when he was trying to build up his public, he appealed to biblical knowledge the most commonly shared among his readers, thereby gaining credibility while he "flattered their moral feelings" (as Humphry House writes more generally of the religious Dickens and his public).[8] But such an analysis slights both Dickens' serious intention and the biblical story itself. Some consideration of what Jesus' parables are and how Dickens acts as parabler in his Master's tradition will be useful at this point.

Jesus' parables were heuristic devices adapted to specific audiences of his day: through the experience of a story, he intended to make his hearers see a new reality, moving "from 'what is' to 'what might be.' " While the story of the Good Samaritan in Luke 10:25–37 is not metaphorical like most of Jesus' parables, like others it is both dialogical and dialectical. Usually Jesus' teaching stories emerged out of debate; this one begins in Jesus' dialogue with a "certain lawyer" who "tempt[s] him, saying, Master, what shall I do to inherit eternal life?" and, when Jesus urges him to love God and "thy neighbour as thyself," asks further, "And who is my neighbour?" Out of such dialogues the parable emerges, engaging the hearers' ordinary social categories, prejudices, pious beliefs, and conventional expectations at the outset of the tale. But as the parable begins to reveal the kind of story it is, John Dominic Crossan writes, the listeners draw back: "I don't know what you mean by that story," they think, "but I'm certain I don't like it."[9] The dialectical thrust of the parable is to the story the hearers expected to hear, often with polar reversals (poor become rich, rich become poor) that revolutionize the way reality is perceived. Turning on a surprise, the parable draws in the hearers as critical participants: through their participation, the kingdom "comes" in the transformed hearts of those who have ears to hear—or they reject the parable and effectively exclude themselves from the kingdom.

Although the Good Samaritan parable does not illustrate this process as clearly as the Prodigal Son story, for example, Jesus does transform the expectations of his hearers on several key points. In expanding the definition of the "good neighbour" as the one "that sheweth mercy" to the outcast (v. 37), Jesus removes all limits on the duty of love—some-

7. In *The Genesis of Secrecy: On the Interpretation of Narrative* (Cambridge: Harvard UP, 1979), Frank Kermode discusses the New Testament parables as unstable and enigmatic stories, "narratives that mean more and other than they seem to say, and mean different things to different people." Such a biblical text is "dark" because the reader can never be fully "inside" its latent meaning, although one may glimpse it from "outside" as a momentary "radiance" (25, 23, 28).

8. Humphry House, *The Dickens World*, 2d ed. (London: Oxford UP, 1942) 42.

9. John Dominic Crossman, *The Dark Interval: Towards a Theology of Story* (Niles, Ill.: Argus Communications, 1975) 56.

thing his hearers were quite unprepared to accept. Jesus does not exclude the pious priest and the Levite, whom the audience would expect not to help since handling a dead man would have made them ritually unclean, from the injunction to act charitably toward anyone in need. Most tellingly, in making the good neighbor one despised by the Jewish community, to whom "Good Samaritan" would be "a contradiction in terms . . . the impossible, the unspeakable," Jesus forces those who would "Go and do . . . likewise" (v. 37) to acknowledge the integrity of the traditional enemy and even to identify with the outcast-hero of the story. Entering the radically new world of these unforseen relationships, the hearer enters the kingdom the parables proclaim.

With its implicit social criticism, its exposure of the legalism and hypocrisy of religious officialdom, its dramatic counterpointing of indifference and spontaneous generosity, and its challenges to conventional seeing—both of the wretched and of those who imagine themselves charitable—the Good Samaritan parable is just the sort of story Dickens would have felt impelled to recast again and again for new nineteenth-century conditions. Throughout his career, like Matthew Arnold using "lines and expressions of the great masters" to discover "the truly excellent,"[1] Dickens used his Master's moral example story often as a touchstone for distinguishing the truly virtuous—those who *act* upon their faith—from pretenders to virtue. * * * Dickens' strategy, however, was not only to embed such little parabolic moments in his narrative, which may merely call up stock responses by themselves, but so to detail and populate his novel that his readers might newly see the "vast outlying mass of unseen human suffering" as well as reconceive their conventional duties. As Dean Stanley observed in his memorial sermon in Westminster Abby the Sunday following Dickens' funeral there, it was this "dramatic power of making things which are not seen be as even though they were seen" that made Dickens the parabler "the advoca[te] of the absent poor." By combining pathetic and horrific social documentation with the Good Samaritan story, Dickens wanted to recall his readers to a fresh sense of what the officially current values of a Christian country should mean in the actual urban setting. The desolate parish boy is his test case.

If Oliver is a pawn in the Bunyanesque spiritual melodrama, he is equally passive in this second parable; but his being little more than an "item of mortality" (1) throughout the story is a mark of his desolation in itself impressive, quite apart from the other reasons Dickens needed him to remain such a blank. Oliver comes into the world with his mother's legacy, "the old story"—*she* "was found lying in the street" (2), rescued by the parish only to die giving birth in the workhouse. Although Oliver lives, his rescue by these bogus Samaritans is hardly

---

1. Matthew Arnold, "The Study of Poetry" (1880), in *Essays in Criticism*, 2d ser., ed. S. R. Littlewood (New York: St. Martin's Press, 1958) 10.

the happy conclusion of the parable, which turns into a satiric version of itself. Dickens drives his stable satire home by having Bumble explain the emblem on his "very elegant button": "The die is the same as the porochial seal—the Good Samaritan healing the sick and bruised man. . . . I put it on, I remember, for the first time, to attend the inquest on that reduced tradesman, who died in a doorway at midnight." "Died from exposure to the cold," Sowerberry adds, "and want of the common necessaries of life" because "the relieving officer had——" ("refused him," the reader adds silently, readily completing Dickens' point; 4). When the beadle calls the troublesome Oliver "a dead-weight, a mill-stone, as I may say; round the porochial throat" (21), he condemns himself, as Dennis Walder has observed, by echoing Christ's words, "But whoso shall offend one of these little ones which believe in me, it were better for him that a millstone were hanged about his neck, and that he were drowned in the depth of the sea" (Matt. 18:6; the board also decides to send Oliver to sea, 23).[2] To "offend" the little ones is to sin not only by cuffing and starving them in the workhouse, but also, as Dr. Arnold explains in one of his sermons on this favorite theme, by "leading them into evil" or hindering them from doing right[3]—as this "porochial" gang would Oliver, were he not under the protection of a Higher Power.

Dickens assimilates other biblical satire to this central situation, in a parish where the practice of baby farming has caused more than one infant to be "summoned into another world, and there gathered to the fathers which it had never known in this" (2). When Oliver is apprenticed to the undertaker, he "Forms an Unfavourable Notion of His Master's Business" (title, chap. 5)—"business" hardly spiritual, though concerned with one of the Four Last Things. Here Oliver meets another charity boy named Noah (who "could trace his genealogy all the way back to his parents"), a cruel survivor in whom all the violence of the world before the Flood seems concentrated against the outcast boy "everybody lets . . . alone" (27). The subject of taunts and even prayers against "the sins and vices of Oliver Twist" (3), Oliver is only "half-baptized" by the parish (6); it is no wonder he is considered demonic by those who have failed to complete the Christian ritual of exorcism.

* * *

In Dickens' later fiction, the satiric and ironic biblical allusions accumulate to expose the inefficacy of the religious models themselves in a culture where "civilisation and barbarism walked this boastful island together." But in *Oliver Twist*, the satire appeals to Scripture as the still-recognized ground of order against which modern practices are judged. Thus, despite his inventiveness with these biblical texts, Dickens' satire is an art of closure, allowing his reader some imaginative engagement

2. Dennis Walder, *Dickens and Religion* (Boston: George Allen and Unwin, 1981) 53.
3. Dr. Thomas Arnold, *Sermons* (London: B. Fellowes, 1844) 2:65.

with Scripture but directing that play toward stable moral interpretations. When we later meet the serious counterparts of these Samaritan pretenders, who treat Oliver "with a kindness and solicitude that knew no bounds" (12), we are in the even less imaginative realm of the "type." Cruikshank drives the point of the parable home by hanging a religious print of the Good Samaritan over Brownlow's fireplace in his illustration, "Oliver recovering from the fever." After Oliver has been left by the housebreakers badly wounded and "lying in a ditch" (25; compare Fagin's "Poor little child. Left in a ditch," 26.), Cruikshank pictures "Oliver Twist at Mrs. Maylie's door" "half dead," a wretched subject indeed for rescue. In every respect these goodly Samaritans counter the bad ones; and unlike the parish authorities, they teach Oliver to pray so that now, with his child's eloquence, he can offer up praise of his benefactors, echoing their own (as Mrs. Maylie says, "may mercy be shewn to me as I shew it to others!" 27).

The problem with these types, of course, is that they evoke no critical participation from the reader but merely call up appropriate responses; and a sentiment automatically induced makes no parabolic impact on conventional ways of seeing. Nor do Dickens' respectable Samaritans challenge the hearer to new and surprising identifications. Where the New Testament subtext does become more provocative to the reader's moral imagination is precisely on Jesus' most disturbing point: the identity of the rescuer as outcast, whom the hearer is bid to imitate. In counterpoint to the ideal behavior of the Maylies and the "respectable old gentleman" Brownlow, Dickens also offers the unstable example of the thieves who take Oliver in.

On his way to London, Oliver nearly falls "dead upon the king's highway" when he is "roused" by a boy "surveying him most earnestly" (8). Although this "young gentleman" is dressed like a parody of the respectable grown-up male rescuers Oliver will come to know, and his mode of discourse confesses itself "playfully ironical," the Dodger is as spontaneously generous as it is possible for an Artful lad to be, buying food and offering Oliver free lodging in London with "a 'spectable old gentleman as lives there, wot'll give you lodgings for nothink, and never ask for the change; that is, if any genelman he knows interduces you." Despite the ironic play anticipating the thieves' duplicity soon to be revealed, surely no reader can be insensible to the impact of this aid and comfort upon the lonely Oliver, the Dodger's "new pal." Cruikshank's famous illustration, "Oliver introduced to the respectable Old Gentleman," may contain stable irony in its title but visually it is unstable: there is the devilish Fagin with the boy-sized pitchfork by the fire, but there is also the food and drink, warmth, comfortable smokes, and companionship Oliver has craved. The real attractions of this underground society offset Dickens' efforts to make it a demonic inversion of the other respectable old gentleman's world, indeed, to some readers, like J. Hillis Miller, the thieves' self-conscious parodies of this daylight realm instead "bring into the open the inauthenticity of what is imitated."[4] Unlike Bumble's unconscious parody of Good Samaritanism, the criminals' deliberate equivocal imitations make them hard to judge and may subtly call in question the righteous rescuers of the tale, even if their sentimental form of goodness is not in itself enough to subvert our belief in them.

"Mr. Fagin," who sometimes falls into biblical cadences as cover for his identity as the "Old Gentleman" of folklore, soon turns out to be the Bad Samaritan most to be feared. Like the workhouse authorities, he reads Oliver "a long lecture on the crying sin of ingratitude" and lays "great stress on the fact of his having taken Oliver in, and cherished him, when, without his timely aid, he might have perished with hunger." Fagin also does not fail to follow this with another parable, "the dismal and affecting history of a young lad whom, in his philanthropy, he had succoured under parallel circumstances, but who, proving unworthy of his confidence, and evincing a desire to communicate with the police, had unfortunately come to be hanged at the Old Bailey one morning" (18). The effect of these parables is not to transform but to transfix Oliver, his blood running cold. When Sikes falls ill, Fagin poses as Good Samaritan again, but Sikes knows better and punctures the pose. In this underworld, mutual aid is subject to the thieves' Golden Rule, as Fagin explains "the catechism of his trade" (18): each must look out for number one, but "You can't take care of yourself, number one, without taking care of me, number one," for "a regard for number one holds us all together, and must do so, unless we would all go to pieces in company" (43). Still, this ambiguously self-interested kind of Samaritanism is a way of surviving, offering more comfort and expressing more social energies than the cold indifference of the parish authorities or the hostility of the "good citizens" Oliver meets.

It is good enough to evoke Nancy's curious loyalty to the band: "there are many of us who have kept the same courses together," she explains to Rose, "and I'll not turn upon them, who might—any of them—have turned upon me, but didn't, bad as they are" (46). It is her commitment to their culture and its rules warring with some contrary sentiments of her "woman's heart" that makes her an equivocal Samaritan, even though the Bunyan parable would have her, more simply, be the "Soul of Goodness in Things Evil" (1867 running headline for chapter 16). She tends Bill in his illness with all solicitude, but she also risks bruising for Oliver's sake. Early on she saves him (with a "God Almighty help me" on her lips; see 16); later, even while pointing out what she has borne for his sake, she delivers Oliver up to Bill Sikes (with a "God

---

4. J. Hillis Miller, "The Fiction of Realism: *Sketches by Boz, Oliver Twist,* and Cruikshank's Illustrations," in *Dickens Centennial Essays,* ed. Ada Nisbet and Blake Nevius (Berkeley and Los Angeles: U of California P, 1971) 113.

forgive me!" this time, 20) as his accomplice in the robbery. It is this
sequence that leads to Oliver's being left for dead in a ditch by the fleeing
housebreakers. Nancy's curiously indifferent, even brutal response to
this reported plight is meant to shock: "The child is better where he is,
than among us . . . I hope he lies dead in the ditch, and that his young
bones may rot there" (26). Nancy, too, looks out for Number One: "I
can't bear to have him about me. The sight of him turns me against
myself, and all of you." While helping the indigent is easy for the
Maylies, Nancy represents the Samaritan ensnared in a morally ambiguous place—not simply "right or wrong," as Dickens says of her in the
1841 preface—caught between conflicting imperatives of help, and between them both and her own need to survive.

In Nancy's case we see how the simple moral lesson of the Good
Samaritan parable begins to run aground in *Oliver Twist*, given Dickens'
attempt to apply it to the realities of a social scene too complex
and indeterminate to fit his understanding of the Bible's scheme.
H. M. Daleski has identified this general problem with Dickens' contradictory, unstable book in his argument that *Oliver Twist* is really "two
novels"—its story-plot "affirm[ing] a moral belief in virtue triumphant"
is inconsistent with the imaginative social problem novel.[5] Daleski does
not observe that the other moral story Dickens tells, the Good Samaritan
parable, is meant to unite these two worlds of Bunyan and the city:
charity is the virtue triumphant that is to solve the social problem. But
like the revised Bunyan plot, the use of Jesus' parable confers only a
spurious unity on Dickens' novel and is inadequate to contain the potential chaos of his social observation—of the third, dark parable he is
constrained to tell.

Dickens' "two novels"—in general, the religious tale with its two
diverging parables and the realistically detailed story of poverty and
crime—arose out of contradictory intentions voiced in his 1841 preface.
* * * Dickens first proclaims to his readers that he wanted to draw "a
lesson of the purest good . . . from the vilest evil" and has set Oliver
amid criminal "companions" in order to prove that Good can triumph
over the most "adverse circumstance." But as he describes his "aim"
(he uses the singular) in depicting these companions' "miserable reality,"
he already begins to create sympathy for figures who are not merely
pawns in a moral fable or proofs of Oliver's election, but people grounded
in social concretions Dickens claims to know well (from "long ago"
having "tracked [them] through many profligate and noisome ways"):
he aims "to paint them in all their deformity, in all their wretchedness,
in all the squalid poverty of their lives; to shew them as they really are."
The rest of the preface abandons altogether the initial point of
discussion—the "lesson of the purest good"—for self-defense against the

5. H. M. Daleski, *Dickens and the Art of Analogy* (London: Faber and Faber, 1970) 49. I am
    indebted to Daleski's discussion of the conflicts in *Oliver Twist*.

charge of having portrayed so much vice. He concludes by discussing Sikes in his "circumstances" "becom[ing], at last, utterly and irredeemably bad" (but no agent of the Devil here) and the equivocal case of Nancy: "It is useless to discuss whether . . . [she] seems natural or unnatural, probable or improbable, right or wrong," he declares, for her portrait is "TRUE." This preface thus makes a telling circuit: the novelist introduces himself as one committed to absolute values and closes by confessing his deeper interest in particular conditions and in what is "a contradiction, an anomaly, an apparent impossibility, but . . . truth" in all its moral awkwardness and murky circumstantiality.

Oliver Twist, then, has its divergent roots in both an explicit moral intention and a commitment to circumstantial truth-telling that declines to name the moral. In her introduction to the Clarendon edition, Kathleen Tillotson traces the novel's most important antecedents to Dickens' 1834–35 sketches (such as "The Old Bailey"), his professional reporting of the police courts and Parliament in 1834–36, and the period in his early life when criminality impinged upon poverty for this "small Cain."[6] "I know," Dickens memorably told Forster, "that I have lounged about the streets, insufficiently and unsatisfactorily fed. I know that, but for the mercy of God, I might easily have been, for any care that was taken of me, a little robber or a little vagabond." This often-quoted passage expresses both the personal experience behind the circumstantial truth-telling of *Oliver Twist* and its need for a moral pattern illustrating "the mercy of God" if also some reason to question God's providence. While one implication of this statement is that the religious patterns in Dickens' thinking cannot be summarily dismissed, the other is that they maintain a precarious hold in fictions directed by his most passionate drive to tell the dark parable. This uneasy coexistence can be observed in the incompletely dialogized relations between *Oliver Twist's* three parabolic stories, which sometimes seem to know about each other and at other times do not.[7]

The tale of social observation subverts the Bunyan fable because while the latter requires the exclusive moral coordinates of Good and Evil, the Saved and the Damned, the former shows that these structures of belief are as rotten as the tottering houses of the poor. The victims of starvation so starkly presented in Dickens' opening chapters belie these conventional categories of the moral life: these creatures are neither good nor bad, although they already suffer the torments of the damned. With such conditions as theirs in mind, James Anthony Froude's Markham Sutherland in *The Nemesis of Faith* wants to minister to the poor but

---

6. Tillotson, Introduction to the Clarendon *Oliver Twist*, xi–xvi.
7. In *The Dialogic Imagination: Four Essays* (ed. Michael Holquist, trans. Caryl Emerson and M. Holquist [Austin: U of Texas P, 1981]), Mikhail M. Bakhtin explains that the throng of social voices in an artistically-constructed novel "know about each other (just as two exchanges in a dialogue know of each other and are structured in this mutual knowledge of each other). . . . A potential dialogue is embedded in [these voices], one as yet unfolded" (324).

will preach "no hell terrors, none of these fear doctrines": "No, if I am to be a minister of religion, I must teach the poor people that they have a Father in heaven, not a tyrant. . . . What! am I to tell these poor millions of sufferers, who struggle on their wretched lives of want and misery, starved into sin, maddened into passion by the fiends of hunger and privation, in ignorance because they were never taught, and with but enough of knowledge to feel the deep injustice under which they are pining; am I to tell them, I say, that there is no hope for them here, and less than none hereafter?"[8] Neither can the conventional message of Virtue Tried by Adversity inform a social vision adequate to these horrors, for as many Victorian sermons on Joban patience could illustrate, this moral formula fosters indifference to suffering and, with its injunction to endure unto the end to be saved, vitiates the will to change the conditions that cause distress. The larger general problem with this set of moral ideals in the Bunyan subtext is the inadequacy of applying standards of individual morality to systemic, institutionalized evils. But from such monstrous wrongs, neither can individual acts of Good Samaritanism save—the rescue from "vice and infamy" of one small boy is the right moral gesture of a certain philanthropic sort, but hardly a social program.

With the triumph of charity in the first Brownlow rescue, the Samaritan narrative tries to banish Oliver's past wretchedness and his voices of temptation as "a long and troubled dream." But the eerie reality of this dark parable is what we most remember (in contrast to the bland dreamworld of bourgeois respectability). Stretching to all points of the compass, suddenly looming up in the narrative's path, menacing the borders of the happy episodes, the "neighborhoods" (if such they may be called) of the poor compel the reader's imagination like a recurring nightmare: [Larson quotes the passage that appears in this volume on p. 47, from "A great many . . ." to ". . . hideous with fame."] "You'll get used to it in time, Oliver," says the undertaker. "Nothing when you *are* used to it, my boy." But that is precisely what Dickens as dark parabler refuses to let us do: we must see this world invisible to conventional minds over and over again. Near the end of the book the narrator conducts his reader to yet another such locality, "the filthiest, the strangest, the most extraordinary" of all, Jacob's Island: [Larson quotes the passage that appears in this volume on pp. 331–32, from "To reach this place . . ." to ". . . desolation and neglect."] How these passages operate parabolically is more complex than at first appears. The signs Dickens bids us read are enigmatic, inviting interpretation of their latent meaning. Ostensibly, the precise detailing of social reality here would seem to teach a simple moral lesson for those who have eyes to see: "every imaginable sign" points to "desolation and neglect"; hence,

---

8. James Anthony Froude, *The Nemesis of Faith*, 2d ed. (London: John Chapman, 1849) 17–18.

we must not neglect the poor. Repeatedly erupting in the narrative, what such scenes come to register, however, is Dickens' discovery that a dark, unstable parable has replaced this more transparent one.

At first the narrator seems to promise parabolic clarity by taking his reader in hand to "penetrate through a maze": he will make this outsider an insider by showing him the shocking sights, challenging his conventional ways of seeing, and bringing him into a new sense of the real. Following this parabolic program, these two passages move again and again from "appearance" to "reality": what look like shop fronts are in fact "fast closed"; what at first appear to be people, with occupations and sexual identities, lose all human definition, becoming assimilated to their physical environment ("refuse of the river," mere "offensive sights and smells"); what look like ruins "falling into the street" are really homes; the signs of human entrance and exit are merely places of disappearance, for no one appears in this scene but the rats, "hideous with famine," who have metonymically replaced the humans. Even metonymy is an illusion, for it has a literal meaning after all: the contiguity of rats and people in this close neighborhood menaces human life; bearing disease, a community of rats literally replaces the other one. By moving from appearance to reality in a series of surprises, Dickens defamiliarizes the familiar terms in which his reader normally sees and thinks ("house," "shop," "human"), inviting him to reflect on his ordinary processes of interpretation and giving him a new vision of what is really here.

But this is not the new world and unforeseen relationships in which Jesus' parables terminate: we are left with "what is," not with "what might be." Moreover, Dickens' detailing the surface of the enigma does not "penetrate" it. This is the crux of interpretation through which the Dickensian observer moves, turning this parable from a moral example story into a dark enigma or even, perhaps, a mere muddle. Promised he will "penetrate through a maze," the visitor finds only, when he does come to Jacob's Island, an even more bewildering labyrinth of slums; this locale, as Kermode describes obscure narratives, is "a treacherous network rather than a continuous and systematic sequence"[9]—like Dickens' text as contrasted to the clarifying story it had promised to be. The visitor remains an outsider, seeing without perceiving, and so does the narrator: for such scenes are incomprehensible, like the seven ragged paupers, "dumb, wet, silent horrors," which Dickens described to Forster as "sphinxes set up against that dead wall, and no one likely to be at the pains of solving them until the General Overthrow." Even here, while Dickens seems to suggest there is an answer if only someone took the "pains," these sodden bundles of rags seem more like a muddle than a riddle, and they dramatize a dark parable indeed to the would-be

9. Frank Kermode, The Genesis of Secrecy, 126.

parabler, rebuffing the Samaritan and shutting out this interpreter on
the outside of their meaning. * * * Over such scenes in this early work,
however, no God of mercy or judgment presides; starved innocents and
good-hearted prostitutes as well as brutal criminals like Sikes are indis-
criminately driven to death by the social forces that have made them
what they are. Dickens' dark parable in *Oliver Twist* thus explodes
religious categories as well as theories of political economy, literary
conventions, and familiar ways of seeing: none of the received formulas
can make sense of such anarchic "desolation."

FRED KAPLAN

[The Creation of *Oliver Twist*]†

* * *

Dickens' August 1836 agreement to write two novels for Richard Bentley was still operative, though John Macrone continued to claim that
he had the rights to *Barnaby Rudge*, the second of the two. In January
1837, Dickens protested to Bentley about liberties that he felt the publisher had taken with one of the contributions. Working regularly on
Pickwick, writing for the *Miscellany*, selecting, revising, and proofread-
ing articles and corresponding with authors, he became "extremely un-
well" toward the end of January, "half dead with fatigue." In spite of
an infant and a depressed wife at home, he began work on his weekly
contribution to the magazine. "I have thrown my whole heart and soul
into Oliver Twist, and most confidently believe he will make a feature
in the work, and be very popular." With the exception of June and
October 1837 and September 1838, an installment appeared every
month from February 1837 to April 1839.

Soon it became crucial, as a matter of self-esteem, that Bentley accept
Oliver in lieu of one of the two novels Dickens had pledged himself to
write in the agreement of the previous August. By midsummer 1837,
Dickens began to pressure Bentley to have *Barnaby* count as the first
contracted novel and the ongoing *Oliver* as the second. The publisher
resisted. In August, Dickens responded by finding an excuse not to write
an installment for the September *Miscellany*, perhaps on John Forster's
advice. Having negotiated the agreement between Dickens, Macrone,
and Chapman and Hall, Forster [Dickens' intimate friend] had become
his adviser on all such matters, much to the annoyance of Bentley, who
exaggerated both his role and his influence. Using his objection to

† From *Dickens, A Biography*. Copyright © 1988 by Fred Kaplan. Reprinted by permission of
William Morrow & Company, Inc. Pp. 95–96, 101–3, 532–33, 538.

Bentley's contractually permissible editorial interference as his justification, Dickens raised the stakes in September. Claiming that he had
been "superseded" in his position as editor, he resigned abruptly.

Bentley immediately retreated. Dickens resumed his editorship and
the novel. Late in September, the publisher reluctantly agreed that *Oliver*
would count as the second novel, with the new, later delivery date of
October 1838 for *Barnaby*. Dickens then proposed that *Barnaby* appear
in the *Miscellany* rather than that he be obligated both for it and for a
substantial contribution to the magazine. In January 1838, he edited
for Bentley, for the flat fee of one hundred pounds, the *Memoirs of
Grimaldi*, with the help of [his father] John Dickens, who mostly took
dictation. It was partly a sentimental nod in the direction of the theatrical
fantasies of his childhood. By the spring, Dickens was furious with the
publisher, though Bentley had made all the concessions, for deducting
small sums from his fees for the installments of *Oliver* because they were
shorter than had been agreed upon. Having been ground down by Dickens, Bentley expressed his resentment in this and in other petty ways,
such as not keeping appointments. In September, author and publisher
signed a new agreement, basically repeating the provisions of the earlier
contracts, though slightly more financially favorable to Dickens and with
the stipulation that *Barnaby* appear in the *Miscellany* after *Oliver*. In
January 1839, Dickens peremptorily insisted that there be a further delay
in *Barnaby*, that the financial provisions be renegotiated, "for I do most
solemnly declare that morally, before God and man, I hold myself
released from such hard bargains as these." Forster advised prudence
and reconsideration. But Dickens had had enough of Bentley, of the
frustration that must have been all the more difficult to bear because of
his need to suppress the obvious fact that he was fully responsible for
the contracts he had signed. With an aggressiveness characteristic of
him when he was even partly, let alone fully, in the wrong, he castigated
the publisher as a prelude to halting all communication with him. "I
do *not* . . . I will *not* consent to extend my engagements with you.
. . . If you presume to address me again in the style of offensive im-
pertinence . . . I will from that moment abandon at once and for ever
all conditions and agreements that may exist between us, and leave the
whole question to be settled by a jury as soon as you think proper to
bring it before one."

At the end of the month, he again resigned as editor of the *Miscellany*.
For a full day Dickens, Forster, and [William Harrison] Ainsworth [a
novelist and a friend of Dickens] sent notes to one another and to Bentley,
attempting to persuade the publisher to appoint Ainsworth the new editor
under favorable terms. Reluctantly, he agreed, though both Dickens
and especially Forster felt that Ainsworth had bungled his negotiations,
settling for less money and editorial control than he could have gotten.

Dickens turned over to his lawyer his negotiations with Bentley, who accepted his resignation and agreed to pay him two thousand pounds on the delivery of the manuscript of *Barnaby Rudge*, which was to be published only in book form, and another two thousand pounds if the sales should be strong. In fact, after the completion of *Oliver* in April 1839, Bentley was never to publish anything of his again. Represented by [his lawyer, Thomas] Mitton, and with Forster as his literary spokesman, Dickens had burst the self-imposed "Bentleian bonds."

* * *

Dickens' response to [Mary Hogarth's] death[1] had an additional focal point in the novel that he had begun to write in January 1837, the month of the birth of his first child, "a son and heir," Charles Culliford Boz Dickens. In a sense his first novel, *Oliver Twist*, unlike *Sketches* and *Pickwick*, was conceived as a fiction unified by a plot, which he had the idea for as early as December 1833. Years later, Cruikshank, who did the illustrations, claimed that the notion of presenting the story of an orphan among London thieves had been his. *Oliver Twist* is so powerfully autobiographical that the "illustrious" George's claim seems irrelevant. Written almost entirely in the year and a half after Mary's death, the novel dramatizes some of Dickens' deepest emotional patterns. It is a successful inward voyage of reconciliation of a sort that he was to make much more readily and regularly in his fiction than in his life. His own experience had made the child figure central to his imagination, the sensitive youth whose sense of his worth is assaulted by a hostile world from infancy onward. The assault precedes adolescence, and adolescent experience is a late stage of the reenactment of early-childhood loss. The most powerful expression in his fiction of such loss and deprivation is to be born an orphan or near orphan, as are Oliver, Pip, Little Nell, David Copperfield, and Esther Summerson, or to have lost one parent, like Nicholas Nickleby, Florence Dombey, and Amy Dorrit. In the first of his fictional child heroes, he contrasts the emotional impact of his own mother's distance and rejection with the absence of Oliver's, as if to say that a dead mother is preferable to a deadening one. Unlike his own, Oliver's mother dies while giving birth to her son. It is a tragic sacrifice that Dickens provides as an expression of the unqualified love of the perfect mother for her only son. Like Mary, she dies "Young Beautiful And Good," and her angelic presence at crucial moments in the novel provides Oliver with both an assurance of his self-worth and, since it is she he resembles, a visible connection with the world of love, benevolence, and innate moral values.

Neither an obstacle nor an enemy, his father has been removed considerably before Oliver's birth. That convenience allows Dickens to focus

---

1. Mary Hogarth (1819–37), the young sister of Dickens' wife, Catherine, who lived with the Dickenses, died suddenly in May 1837. Dickens idealized her youth, beauty, and goodness.

on his relationship with his idealized mother and on the conflict between potential substitute fathers, the benevolent Mr. Brownlow and the devilish Fagin. In providing Oliver with a vicious brother, his father gives him the opportunity to demonstrate that he is innately good and Monks innately bad. Dickens may have found it emotionally attractive to identify with the father's good son, to create a drama of alternate children, or of the one child divided into two children, in which the child whom he believes himself to have been shows himself worthy of love and respect. In Mr. Brownlow, Oliver eventually finds a loving father, who fills "the mind of his adopted child . . . his own son . . . with stores of knowledge" of the sort that Dickens fantasied about when he believed that he would grow up to be a learned man. Father and son "were truly happy."

In the beautiful seventeen-year-old Rose Maylie, conceived a little more than a year after Mary's death, he created an elegiac representation of his lost but ever-present sister. Like Mary, Rose seems made for heaven. "Cast in so slight and exquisite a mould; so mild and gentle; so pure and beautiful; that earth seemed not her element. . . . The very intelligence that shone in her deep blue eye, and was stamped upon her noble head, seemed scarcely of her age or of the world." Unlike Oliver's mother or Mary Hogarth, Rose is destined for fulfillment and happiness here on earth. She "was in the lovely bloom and spring-time of womanhood . . . the smile; the cheerful, happy smile, were made for Home; for fireside peace and happiness." In the reconciling magic of fictional representation, he both elegizes Mary and affirms that she is alive. "In all the bloom and grace of early womanhood," Rose Maylie marries and becomes "the life and joy of the fire-side circle and the lively summer group."

*   *   *

In the late summer, in preparation for his farewell [reading] tour from October 1868 to May 1869, Dickens created a new reading, based on one he had fashioned in 1863 but had decided against using, a version of Bill Sikes's murder of Nancy in *Oliver Twist*. He wanted something fresh and extraordinary, partly an expression of the showman's search for novelty, partly of his need to find a new challenge. Practicing outdoors at Gad's Hill [his country home in Kent], he frightened those who overheard him rehearsing his most demanding, most exhausting, performance. Though worried that it might prove too upsetting, even revolting, to his audiences, he loved the experience of being absorbed in it, of acting it out, of being both murdered and murderer. Finding it difficult to distinguish between himself and his text, after each rehearsal, as he walked the streets, he had the "vague sensation of being 'wanted.' " When he began the tour, he had not yet decided whether to include it. The old formula worked well enough. The enthusiastic crowds at the inaugural reading at St. James's Hall [London], and in Manchester and Liverpool later in the month, "were beyond all former experience." A thousand people were turned away. In London, the demand was so great that "it seems as though we could fill St. Paul's." But the same problems he had experienced while reading in America surfaced quickly, weariness, hoarseness, sleeplessness, and frenetic, pulse-racing exhaustion after each performance.

In mid-November, he read the "Murder of Nancy" as an experiment to an audience of over one hundred invited guests. The opinion of his friends confirmed his desires. "The verdict of ninety of them was: 'It must be done.' So it is going to be done." There were warnings in the form of compliments and compliments in the form of warnings. A doctor said, "My dear Dickens, you may rely upon it that if only one woman cries out when you murder the girl, there will be a contagion of hysteria all over this place." A well-known actress replied, "Why, of course, do it. . . . Having got such an effect as that, it must be done. . . . The public have been looking for a sensation these fifty years or so, and by Heaven they have got it."

Through the late fall and winter of 1868–69 in England, Scotland, and Ireland, he went on "murdering Nancy" with a regularity that became addictive. Worried, [his business manager and friend Charles] Dolby began to advise him to read it less often. The constant railway journeys made Dickens' nerves tremble, his lips turn white. He looked additionally haggard, the illusion of health with which he had returned from America long gone. He clung, though, to the new reading stubbornly, passionately. In mid-February 1869, his foot, the left one this time, to his surprise, "turned lame again," forcing him to cancel a reading. He had known "for some days that the inflammation was coming on; but it is impossible to guard against it when that amount of standing in a hot place has to be encountered for months together." A well-known Edinburgh doctor disparaged Dr. Henry Thompson's previous diagnosis, laughing away contemptuously the suspicion that it was gout and attributing it instead to fatigue and walking in the snow. The enforced withdrawal was even more painful than his swollen foot, and he felt "as restless as if [he] were behind bars in the Zoological Gardens." If "I could afford it, [I] would wear a part of my mane away as the Lion has done by rubbing it against the windows of my cage."

*   *   *

His fascination with murdering Nancy, "continually done with great passion and fury," was also partly self-portraiture in which he played both victim and victimizer. Nancy resonated with his vision of the innately good women in his life. In her murder he enacted the lives and deaths, both physical and emotional, of Mary Hogarth, Little Nell, Little Em'ly, his sister Fanny, and the emotional sacrifices of Georgina

Hogarth and Katie Dickens,[2] the ideal vision of moral purity embodied in the life of a prostitute who by her very nature must love and help the deprived child. Some of his terror in presenting her murder derived from his knowledge that the murderer was not only Bill Sikes but also her author and creator. When he enacted Sikes's killing of Nancy, he created the stage illusion that he was Sikes, that his will and his heart were committed to the crime. They were. In repeatedly murdering her, he expressed himself with displaced violence against the horrible women of his life, his mother and his wife. Perhaps he also expressed some of his occasional ambivalence about what he had done to Georgina and Ellen.[3] In murdering Nancy, he committed a crime of vengeance and self-assertion available to him only within fiction. So powerful was his identification with Sikes that not even Sikes's death could free him from the emotional grip of that identification. An unworthy criminal still prowled on the loose, within himself. After the reading, when he left the theatre, he almost expected to be arrested in the streets. He looked over his shoulder to see who was pursuing him.

ROBERT TRACY

"The Old Story" and Inside Stories: Modish Fiction and Fictional Modes in *Oliver Twist*†

Very early in *Oliver Twist* we meet a connoisseur of stories and a projector of stories. The connoisseur is the workhouse doctor who delivers Oliver. He recognizes the child and his nameless mother as figures from a familiar narrative. " 'The old story,' " he remarks, examining the dead woman's hand; " 'no wedding ring, I see.' " He reads her story in her circumstances and comments on that story's lack of novelty. And, though we must wait until the very end of *Oliver Twist* to hear the story in detail, the doctor is quite right. A young woman trusted a lover too far, found herself pregnant, and ran away with her guilty secret. But when we do hear the story of Oliver's parentage, of Edwin Leeford's loveless

2. Katie (Kate Macready) Dickens (1839–1929) was Dickens' eldest daughter. "Mary Hogarth": see above, p. 554, n. 1. "Little Nell": the main character of Dickens' *The Old Curiosity Shop* (1841). "Little Em'ly": a character in *David Copperfield* (1850). "Georgina Hogarth": another Dickens sister-in-law (1827–1917), who, after Mary Hogarth's death, joined the Dickens household and gradually took over many of the domestic responsibilities of Dickens' wife, Catherine. When Dickens separated from his wife in 1858, Georgina continued to make her home with her brother-in-law.
3. Ellen Lawless Ternan (1839–1914), an actress, became Dickens' mistress about 1860. They maintained separate residences but traveled and sometimes lived together until Dickens' death in 1870.
† From *Dickens Studies Annual*, ed M. Timko, F. Kaplan, and E. Guiliano, 17 (1988): 1–33. Copyright © 1988 AMS Press, Inc. Reprinted by permission.

marriage and his affair with Agnes Fleming, it does not really seem to have very much to do with the novel we have been reading. Indeed, these revelations even cancel out the novel's title and subtitle: we have, it seems, been reading "Oliver Leeford" or "Oliver Fleming" all along, and the story moves backward in time, belying the "Parish Boy's Progress" we have been promised.

The projector of stories is Mr. Bumble, whose duties include the naming of the parish orphans. Like a novelist who must name a character in a way that will reinforce that character's fictional identity, Bumble names Oliver to become the hero of a certain story. " 'I inwented' " his name, Bumble tells Mrs. Mann:

> "We name our fondlins in alphabetical order. The last was a S.— Swubble, I named him. This was a T.—Twist, I named *him*. The next one as comes will be Unwin, and the next Vilkins. I have got names ready made to the end of the alphabet, and all the way through it again, when we come to Z."
>
> "Why, you're quite a literary character, sir!" said Mrs. Mann.
>
> "Well, well," said the beadle, evidently gratified with the compliment; "perhaps I may be. Perhaps I may be, Mrs. Mann."(2)

Like Bumble, Fang, Grimwig, and Bolter, the alias Noah Claypole chooses for himself after he runs away, the names Bumble "inwents" predict certain temperaments and fates for their bearers: Swubble rhymes with trouble and Unwin is a loser's name, both probable enough destinies for parish boys, while Vilkins recalls the lugubrious/comic cockney ballad of Villikins and his Dinah. Twist is full of implications. To twist is to eat heartily, and a twister is a very hearty eater, appropriate for the boy who is to ask for more and whose probable appetite makes Mrs. Sowerberry apprehensive. To twist is also to hang, and represents an all-too-likely end for a parish boy. The gentleman in the white waistcoat thrice prophesizes that fate for Oliver (2; 3), responding perhaps as much to the implications of his name as to the sociological odds, and a protracted stay with Fagin can have no other ending. Finally, in nineteenth-century naval parlance, a twist is a yarn, a story, as Dickens, son of a naval clerk, would have known—in the January 1838 *Bentley's*, "Father Prout" (Francis Sylvester Mahony) praises Boz for "the yarn you spin concerning Oliver Twist." Oliver's true destiny is to feature in a story. In standard English, twist has connotations of perversion, appropriate to the atmosphere of Fagin's gang and to the Monks plot, which would pervert Oliver into a criminal. As for Oliver, it is the highwayman's and the burglar's slang term for the moon: perhaps Bumble, like Dickens, had read Edward Bulwer's *Paul Clifford* (1830) or William Harrison Ainsworth's *Rookwood* (1834), where the term is often employed. Here, combined with the hanging implications of Twist, it helps to suggest a criminal career for Oliver.

The doctor and Bumble both think they can tell the story of Oliver Twist. But that story evades their categories. Dickens refuses to satisfy their (or our) expectations. The story he tells us also consistently evades its own categories. There are sudden and drastic changes of plot and purpose as the novel develops. It is made up of four different plots, which are not exactly combined—they are, rather, stitched together to create a book-length narrative. It is a tribute to Dickens' extraordinary skill and energy that we can overlook the uncertain progress of the story when we read *Oliver Twist*.

Dickens' subtitle, "The Parish Boy's Progress," suggests that Oliver is to grow and develop, but he does not really do so. Apart from three moments early in the novel, when he asks for more, knocks Noah Claypole down, and runs off to London, Oliver hardly acts at all. On one later occasion he decides to take the initiative by alarming the Maylie family during the burglary, "whether he died in the attempt or not" (22). But he has no chance to do this. Though he passively resists efforts to make him perform criminal acts, he is controlled and manipulated by others throughout the novel.

Nor does the plot of *Oliver Twist* really progress or develop. Instead, on at least three occasions Dickens drastically shifts both the mode and the direction of his story, in such a way as to suggest that he was improvising rather than following a plan already worked out. Oliver's uncertain progress reflects the uncertain process by which he is written. *Oliver Twist* begins as a sardonic account of a child's life as a ward of the Parish, describing Oliver's upbringing, the mean calculations of public charity, his near apprenticeship to Mr. Gamfield as a chimney sweep, and his service with Mr. Sowerberry the undertaker. This section includes the satirically presented figure of Bumble, and the bleak portrayal of a pauper death and funeral. Dickens' tone is ironic, and he often addresses the reader directly, to underline the evils and the parsimony of the workhouse system. But the workhouse theme, and Oliver's specific identity as a Parish Boy and so a victim of a meanly conceived theory of public charity, ends in Part IV (chapters 7–8, May 1837), with Oliver's departure for London.

Oliver Twist may not originally have been intended as a novel at all. When the first installment appeared in *Bentley's Miscellany* (February 1837), the opening sentence specified "Mudfog" as the town of Oliver's birth, suggesting that Oliver was not to figure in a novel, but in some of the "Mudfog Papers" that Dickens contributed to *Bentley's* in 1837–38. These were aimed at contemporary abuses and absurdities. Their slightly labored sarcasm is echoed in the novel's early chapters. Dickens' subsequent dispute with Richard Bentley, publisher of the *Miscellany*, over Bentley's unwillingness to accept *Oliver Twist* as the second of two novels for which Dickens had signed a contract (the first, as yet unwritten, was *Barnaby Rudge*), is further evidence that *Oliver Twist* had not originally been planned as a novel; Bentley argued that *Oliver Twist* had already been paid for as a series of papers in the *Miscellany*.

Oliver's story veers completely away from the workhouse theme when he meets the Artful Dodger and Fagin in Part IV (chapter 8), and the second plot, with its criminal theme, begins. This is not necessarily at variance with what has gone before—a "Parish Boy's Progress" may very well bring him into the dens of thieves and through them to the gallows. But we hear nothing more about the workhouse as an institution, and when Bumble reappears he is being groomed for another role, as a criminal, albeit an ineffectual and comic one. Dickens' personal comments are more general, as in his remarks about the human passion "for *hunting something*" (10), or more specific, as in his hostile portrayal of the real Magistrate Laing (11) as the impatient Mr. Fang.

Once the Artful Dodger and Fagin appear, *Oliver Twist* becomes a study of criminal life in London at its lowest level, emphasizing its poverty, discomfort, and brutality. This theme persists through Part X (chapters 20–22, January 1838). Dickens records Oliver's first stay with Fagin, his arrest and appearance before Mr. Fang, his rescue by Mr. Brownlow, his recapture, and his enforced participation in Bill Sikes' attempt to burglarize Mrs. Maylie's house. Fagin, at once attractive and repellent, dominates this part of the book.

Early in these criminal chapters, there is an abortive movement toward yet another plot. In Part V (chapters 9–11, July 1837), Oliver, half awake, watches Fagin draw out his treasures from a hole in the floor and examine them, especially a trinket "so small that it lay in the palm of his hand. There seemed to be some very minute inscription on it; for the Jew laid it flat upon the table, and, shading it with his hand, pored over it, long and earnestly. At length he put it down, as if despairing of success" (9). Presumably Dickens at one point intended that this trinket have something to do with Oliver, but we never hear of it again; it is later superseded by the "little gold locket: in which were two locks of hair, and a plain gold wedding-ring" with "Agnes" engraved on the inside and a blank left for the surname, then a date "within a year" before Oliver's birth (38).

The burglary ends Oliver's criminal career, and any active role for him in the novel. He disappears for two whole numbers (XI and XII: chapters 23–27, February and March, 1838), and once he is settled with the Maylies, he becomes a static character; events occur around him, but he has no real part in them.

As the story appeared in *Bentley's*, Dickens headed Part XI (chapters 23–25, February 1838) with the words "Book II," although he had commenced his narrative with no indication that it was to be divided into books, that it was to be a tale of novel length. Part XI also represents another drastic change in direction for the plot, with the intimation that Oliver is no ordinary parish boy but some sort of dispossessed heir. Part

XI—or Book II—opens with Mr. Bumble's wooing of Mrs. Corney, interrupted by her interview with old Sally and the first mention of some mysterious gold object which might have gained Oliver better treatment, had Sally not stolen it from his mother's corpse. This episode is clearly an afterthought, a completely new idea. Dickens' initial account of Oliver's birth and his mother's death left no room for her dying speech and the presence of identifying jewelry. It seems clear that Oliver was originally intended to be an ordinary parish boy who undergoes the vicissitudes and neglect of his lot. Dickens decided much later to make him of gentle though illegitimate birth, the hero of a conventional melodramatic plot of dispossession.

The three chapters of Part XI prepare the reader for the new plot concerning Monks, his hatred of Oliver, and his plot to prevent the boy from inheriting the money left to him by Edwin Leeford—their mutual father—both by concealing his identity, and by arranging with Fagin for Oliver's involvement in some criminal act: Edwin Leeford's will stipulated that his second son would inherit only on condition that " 'in his minority he should never have stained his name with any public act of dishonour, meanness, cowardice, or wrong' " (51). The atmosphere of the story changes from the sometimes jolly, sometimes brutal atmosphere of the thieves' den to one of mystery and spying, or to the sentimentality of the Maylie household. We are far from the sardonic treatment of workhouse life and public charity with which the story began, and Fagin's practical motives for making Oliver a criminal have been replaced by Monks' fantastic hatred.

Monks himself appears in the first chapter of Part XII (chapters 26–27, March 1838). Now Oliver is threatened, not by public neglect or the temptations of the criminal life, but by an insane fraternal vindictiveness, which Dickens improvises in a retroactive effort to impose a specific plot and direction upon his novel. He does this at considerable risk to the plausibility of the story, as when Monks allegedly recognized Oliver by sight on the day he went out with Charley Bates and the Dodger (26), and was wrongfully accused of picking Mr. Brownlow's pocket. Monks' " 'suspicions were first awakened by' " Oliver's resemblance to his father (49), according to Mr. Brownlow, but Brownlow also noted the boy's " 'strong resemblance' " (335) to his mother's portrait, painted by Edwin Leeford, and old Sally recalls that " 'The boy grew so like his mother . . . that I could never forget it when I saw his face' " (24).

Before old Sally's deathbed confession in chapter 24, there is really nothing in *Oliver Twist* to prepare us for the plot involving Monks and Oliver's parentage. Dickens seems to have added this new plot as a way of stretching his story to novel length. In doing so, he abandons the satire of the early chapters, and the realistic drama of the Fagin chapters, for melodrama. Though Monks and Fagin continue to menace Oliver, they are not able to touch him. They are excluded from the Maylie world of calm domesticity, and their adventures essentially diverge from those of Oliver. And Dickens introduces yet another plot, the not very interesting love story of Harry and Rose Maylie, its weakness emphasized by Rose's nearly fatal illness and Harry's nearly thwarted courtship.

With the virtual disappearance of Oliver, Nancy emerges as the principal character in and after Part XII (chapters 26–27, March 1838), a development foreshadowed by her passionate defence of Oliver after his recapture (16). "I am glad you like Oliver this month—especially glad that you particularize the first chapter," Dickens wrote to Forster on 3 November 1837, referring to the chapter in which Nancy defends Oliver. "I hope to do great things with Nancy. If I can only work out the idea I have formed of her, and of the female who is to contrast with her." She becomes the chief opponent of Monks and Fagin by eavesdropping on them in chapter 26, the very chapter in which the Monks plot begins. Her emergence as heroine and eventually as victim in the second half of the book, coupled with Oliver's disappearance, strongly suggests that she has superseded Oliver as the representative of "the principle of Good surviving through every adverse circumstance" which Dickens later declared to be his subject, in his 1841 preface to the third edition. When he turned her into a heroine, Dickens had to go back and suppress certain references to her vulgarity as he revised his text for book publication—for example, he strips her of the "red gown, green boots, and yellow curl-papers" (13) which she wore when she first appeared in the pages of *Bentley's*.

Nancy's conversion, or the emergence of her suppressed better self, is more interesting and psychologically more believable than Oliver's instinctive virtue and gentlemanly ideals, apparently genetic in origin, spontaneously developed, and preserved throughout his years in the workhouse. Nancy offered Dickens a greater opportunity for sustaining and developing his story. In his 1841 preface,[1] he saves his strongest defence for his treatment of Nancy, and with it concludes that preface:

> It is useless to discuss whether the conduct and character of the girl seems natural or unnatural, probable or improbable, right or wrong. IT IS TRUE . . . From the first introduction of that poor wretch, to her laying her bloody head upon the robber's breast, there is not one word exaggerated or over-wrought. It is emphatically God's truth, for it is the truth He leaves in such depraved and miserable breasts; the hope yet lingering behind; the last fair drop of water at the bottom of the dried-up weed-choked well. . . . I am glad to have had it doubted, for in that circumstance I find a sufficient assurance that it needed to be told.

1. See above, pp. 3–7 [*Editor*].

In representing Nancy's devotion to the brutal Sikes, Dickens may be drawing on an actual experience of his own. He is certainly drawing on his own earlier work. One of the most moving of the *Sketches by Boz*, "The Hospital Patient," describes a dying girl, savagely beaten by her lover, who refuses on her deathbed to identify him as her assailant, because she loves him.

There are two other factors which contribute to the changes of direction which characterize *Oliver Twist*. One of these is Dickens' increasingly strained relationship with George Cruikshank, his illustrator and would-be co-author. The other is his awareness of contemporary modes of fiction, and his simultaneous effort to imitate, parody, and transcend those modes, which led him to begin a grim tale of workhouse life, transform it into an account of petty criminals and their methods, then move into a story of a lost heir and a fiendish brother, to conclude with the genuine horror of Nancy's death and Sikes' self-execution, intermixed with the sentimentality of the Maylie love story and the happy life it seems to initiate. In effect, Dickens explored virtually every aspect of his new profession while writing—or teaching himself to write— *Oliver Twist*. And he also began to examine that uneasiness with the act of fiction, with the novelist's ability to form and manipulate his characters, that is a persistent theme in much of his later work. These factors may further explain the uncertain development of *Oliver Twist*. They also seem to have worked to create the novel's most memorable character, Fagin.

Like Cruikshank, Fagin has his own ideas about how Oliver is to develop, what his story is to be. In Fagin's hands, that story seems initially to be a novel of crime, of the sort that Dickens' contemporaries called "Newgate" novels; later, when Fagin joins forces with Monks, the projected story of Oliver as criminal turns into a story of Oliver as dispossessed heir and as victim of terror, traditional elements in the equally popular Gothic novels of the day. In the role of Fagin, Dickens internalizes Cruikshank's efforts to control the novel. Fagin also internalizes the ways in which Dickens' awareness of popular fictional modes threaten his novel by offering models to which it might conform, and so become an example of a type rather than the highly original work it is. Since Fagin's efforts to shape Oliver's story are criminal efforts, Fagin also represents Dickens' uneasiness about writing fiction.

George Cruikshank was twenty years Dickens' senior, and the most popular illustrator in England, when the two men first met, in November 1835. They had been brought together by the publisher John Macrone, who had engaged Cruikshank to illustrate *Sketches by Boz* for book publication. Dickens was delighted at the prospect of working with Cruikshank, whose work he admired. He even proposed that Cruikshank receive equal billing on the title page, suggesting "Sketches by Boz and Cuts by Cruikshank" or "Etchings by Boz and Wood Cuts by Cruikshank."

Cruikshank was already a student of London's odd corners, and was particularly gifted at picturing scenes of grimness and despair, as his plates for *Oliver Twist* prove. He seems to have had some effect on Dickens' choice of topics for those sketches written after they had met. Dickens begins to write of prisons and prisoners, starting with "The Prisoners' Van," which appeared in *Bell's Life in London* on November 29, 1835, twelve days after his first encounter with Cruikshank; later we have "Gin-shops," "The Pawnbroker's Shop," "Criminal Courts," "A Visit to Newgate," and "The Hospital Patient." Although Cruikshank illustrated only the first, second, and fifth of these, they may well have been chosen at his suggestion as promising subjects for his special skills. Most of them have some later echo in *Oliver Twist*: "The Pawnbroker's Shop" and Cruikshank's plate for that sketch contrast a refined young woman and a prostitute, anticipating the contrasting yet connected roles of Nancy and Rose Maylie; the Artful Dodger's cheeky behavior at his trial is foreshadowed in "Criminal Courts"; "A Visit to Newgate" describes the condemned cell, where Dickens and Cruikshank will place Fagin on the eve of his execution; Nancy, as we have seen, owes something to the victim in "The Hospital Patient," and in Cruikshank's plate to illustrate that sketch, "A Pickpocket in Custody," we can spot the first appearance of Bill Sikes. The artist has also added Dickens himself, observing Sikes with great interest.

Despite these tokens of Cruikshank's importance as a partial collaborator for at least some of the later *Sketches*, by October 1836 Dickens was already weary of the artist's constant suggestions and his eagerness to offer "any little alteration to suit the Pencil" for the text of *Sketches*, Second Series. "I have long believed Cruikshank to be mad," Dickens told Macrone. "If you have any further communication with him, you will greatly oblige me by saying *from me* that I am very much amused at the notion of his altering my Manuscript, and that had it fallen into his hands, I should have preserved his emendations as 'curiosities of Literature.' Most decidedly am I of opinion that he may just go to the Devil; and so far as I have any interest in the book, I positively object to his touching it." Dickens was angry enough to propose substituting "Phiz"—Hablot Browne—as illustrator.

Nevertheless, Cruikshank apparently offered suggestions about the development of *Oliver Twist*, and was rebellious about the subjects to be illustrated, throughout the writing and publishing of the novel. The time needed to prepare a plate, and Dickens' inability to provide the completed text of a number before the printer's deadline, made it impossible for Cruikshank to read what Dickens had written and then illustrate it appropriately. Since Cruikshank disliked written instructions from an author, he preferred to meet with Dickens, be told what was to occur in the next number, and then negotiate about the subject of each plate. Well aware at each meeting that Oliver's next adventure had not yet been written, he seems to have been full of ideas about how the story should develop.

Because of these meetings, we have few written records about the way the novelist and the illustrator worked together. At first, Dickens was enthusiastic. "I think I have hit on a capital notion for myself, and one which will bring Cruikshank out," he wrote Bentley, while preparing the first installment of *Oliver Twist*—as indeed it did, in the famous plate "Oliver asking for More". But Cruikshank's frequent suggestions, and his apparent wish to control the enterprise, eventually annoyed Dickens. William Harrison Ainsworth, whose novels were also illustrated by Cruikshank, later described the artist as "excessively troublesome and obtrusive in his suggestions. Mr. Dickens declared to me that he could not stand it, and should send him printed matter in future." Dickens' declaration must refer to the period of *Oliver Twist*, since he never worked with Cruikshank again. There were frequent disputes about the subjects for plates, the direction of the story, and even about Oliver's name—Cruikshank wanted him to be called "Frank Foundling or Frank Steadfast." He forced Dickens, "with the greatest difficulty," to provide a scene in the condemned cell at Newgate. Dickens insisted that "the scene of Sikes's escape will not do for illustration. It is so very complicated, with such a multitude of figures, such violent action, and torchlight to boot, that a small plate could not take in the slightest idea of it". But Cruikshank proved him wrong by brilliantly depicting the scene in "The Last Chance." A final crisis occurred when Dickens returned to London on November 8, 1838, and saw for the first time Cruikshank's last plates for *Oliver Twist*, which had already been engraved and bound. He apparently objected to several of them, notably "Sikes attempting to destroy his dog" and the last plate, the so-called "Fireside Plate," which showed a comfortable parlor with Oliver, Rose, Harry Maylie, and Mrs. Maylie seated around the fire. Forster immediately notified Bentley that both plates constituted "a vile and disgusting interpolation of the sense and bearing of the tale" and claimed that he had "had some difficulty in prevailing with Mr. Dickens to restrict the omissions to these two" —an intimation that Dickens did not like "The Meeting" (Nancy with Mr. Brownlow and Rose Maylie, while Noah Claypole eavesdrops) nor the extremely effective "Fagin in the condemned cell." Dickens wrote more mildly to Cruikshank the next day, objecting only to the "Fireside" plate and asking for a new design. Though Cruikshank tried to improve the plate, Dickens insisted on a substitution, the drawing of "Rose Maylie and Oliver" which all subsequent editions have contained. "But when done, what was it?" Cruikshank later exclaimed bitterly. "Why, merely a lady and a boy standing inside of a church looking at a stone wall!"

Cruikshank later claimed to have been the originator of most of the

characters and incidents of *Oliver Twist*, and to have shaped several of
Ainsworth's novels. E. S. Morgan, Bentley's accountant at the time
Oliver Twist first appeared, long afterwards remembered that Cruikshank
"stated to me emphatically in the course of many conversations I had
with him on the subject, in the course of business that it was to him,
Mr. Dickens had been indebted for his introduction to many of the
characters that served as prototypes of prominent personages in Oliver
Twist: Fagin, the Artful Dodger etc. etc.; as well as for many suggestions
as to the incidents that figure conspicuously in that work." In 1847
Cruikshank told a similar story to Robert Shelton Mackenzie, who published a slightly confused account in *The Round Table* (Philadelphia)
on November 11, 1865, two years before Dickens' last tour of the United
States, and five years before Dickens' death. Mackenzie's story, repeated
in his *Life of Charles Dickens* (1870), was that he had seen in Cruikshank's house a portfolio of drawings representing the criminal gang in
Oliver Twist, and that Cruikshank had told him these had originally
been intended "to show the life of a London thief by a series of drawings
engraved by himself, in which, without a single line of letter-press, the
story would be strikingly and clearly told"—that is, a pictorial "Progress"
in the tradition of Hogarth's *The Harlot's Progress* (1732) and *The Rake's
Progress* (1735), or of Cruikshank's own "The Sailor's Progress" (1819)
and "The Progress of a Midshipman exemplified in the career of Master
Blockhead" (1835), as well as his later pair of series, *The Bottle* (1847)
and *The Drunkard's Children* (1848). According to Cruikshank, Dickens
had "ferreted out that bundle of drawings" and decided to change the
plan of *Oliver Twist* to bring Oliver among a band of London thieves.

Forster denied this story in the first volume of his *Life of Charles
Dickens* (1871). Cruikshank replied with a letter to the *Times*, which
appeared on December 30, 1871, in which he took full responsibility
for the substance of Mackenzie's story—"I am the originator of 'Oliver
Twist,' and . . . all the principal characters are mine"—but indicated
that the story about the portfolio of pictures was not quite right. In a
separate letter to Mackenzie he reminded him that what he had seen
was a "*list* . . . of the proposed illustrations for 'The Life of a London
Thief'—with some of the sketches—all of which were done when
Charles Dickens was a little boy—some 15 years before I ever saw or
heard of him." Cruikshank later repeated his claim at greater length in
a pamphlet, *The Artist and the Author* (1872), in which he also took
credit for many of Ainsworth's characters and scenes. This provoked a
sharp denial from Ainsworth and another denial from Forster in the
second volume of the *Life of Charles Dickens* (1872). Nevertheless,
Cruikshank's assertions about his contributions to some of Ainsworth's
novels have been to a considerable extent substantiated by recent
scholarship.

Cruikshank claims that after the appearance of "Oliver asking for more" (Plate 1), he drew Dickens' attention to the deaths of some workhouse children in London, and urged him to write about workhouse abuses of children; "and I earnestly begged of him to let me make Oliver a nice pretty little boy, and if we so represented him the public—and particularly the ladies—would be sure to take a greater interest in him." Cruikshank points out that Oliver's "appearance . . . is altered after the two first illustrations." The Oliver of "Oliver plucks up a spirit" (Plate 3) is very different from the Oliver of "Oliver asking for more," in which he is portrayed as what Cruikshank called "rather a queer kind of chap." We can see the beginnings of the change to "a nice pretty little boy" in "Oliver escapes being bound apprentice to the Sweep" (Plate 2).

This change certainly anticipates shifts in the direction of the story. Oliver's sad appearance moves the old gentleman in the tortoise-shell spectacles to pity him and save him from becoming one of Mr. Gamfield's sweeps (3); a little later, Mr. Sowerberry, the undertaker, is struck by the " 'very interesting' . . . 'expression of melancholy in his face' " and decides to make Oliver a mute (5). Whether he was partially agreeing with Cruikshank's advice or not, Dickens does seem to be changing his concept of Oliver and of his story, presumably changing him from the limited role of parochial victim to a larger role as an honest boy fallen among the colorful thieves of London, allegedly the objects of Cruikshank's special studies.

Cruikshank may well have suggested the shift of the story to London, though Dickens himself had clearly exhausted the workhouse theme, and a change was necessary if he was to go on. Dickens hardly needed Cruikshank's advice. The departure to London to seek one's fortune was an obvious move. But he may well have received that advice, a commodity that the artist seldom spared. As for the introduction of the criminal gang, Dickens had plenty of precedents in Newgate fiction. Nevertheless, Cruikshank's long-cherished project for a series of plates, "The Life of a London Thief," was a reality and did predate his relationship with Dickens. Furthermore, long before he met Dickens, Cruikshank had published drawings which contain figures who seem to be the prototypes for Fagin, Bumble, and many other characters from *Oliver Twist*. Apparently he simply redrew these figures, with some variations, when illustrating *Oliver Twist*, but they were already part of his repertory. We cannot be sure that Dickens knew these earlier drawings, or that they played any role in the literary—as opposed to the pictorial—development of his novel. But in view of the great popularity of Cruikshank's work, and Dickens' long admiration for it, he probably did know at least some of them.

Cruikshank's own statement of his role in the development of the criminal theme in *Oliver Twist* is as follows:

I suggested to Mr. Dickens that he should write the life of a London boy, and strongly advised him to do this, assuring him that I would furnish him with the subject and supply him with all the characters, which my large experience of London life would enable me to do. My idea was to raise a boy from a most humble position up to a high and respectable one—in fact, to illustrate one of those cases of common occurrence, where men of humble origin by natural ability, industry, honest and honourable conduct, raise themselves to first-class positions in society. And as I wished particularly to bring the habits and manners of the thieves of London before the public (and this for a most important purpose, which I shall explain one of these days), I suggested that the poor boy should fall among thieves, but that his honesty and natural good disposition should enable him to pass through this ordeal without contamination, and after I had fully described the full-grown thieves (the "Bill Sikes") and their female companions, also the young thieves (the "Artful Dodgers") and the receivers of stolen goods, Mr. Dickens agreed to act on my suggestion, and the work was commenced, but we differed as to what sort of boy the hero should be. Mr. Dickens wanted rather a queer kind of chap. . . .

Cruikshank then refers to the workhouse abuses to which he drew Dickens' attention, and the resulting change in Oliver's appearance by Plate 3. He also claims "to have described and performed the character" of one of the Holborn Hill "Jew receivers, whom I had long had my eye upon" for Dickens and Ainsworth; "and this was the origin of 'Fagan' " (sic). We can doubt Cruikshank's estimation about the importance of his own role but not his eagerness to control the story's development. One piece of evidence that suggests that Dickens at one point intended to follow Cruikshank's plan is the last sentence of chapter 7, as it appeared in *Bentley's Miscellany*: when Oliver says goodbye to little Dick, and the child blesses him, Dickens comments, "through all the struggles and sufferings of his after life, through all the troubles and changes of many weary years, he never once forgot it" (7). Dickens altered this for book publication, since Oliver is still a boy when we leave him. But the "many weary years," like the earlier uncertainty—removed for book publication—as to whether Oliver's life "will be a long or a short piece of biography" (2), argue that at some point Dickens intended to bring Oliver to manhood, probably to have him avoid the temptation to crime and raise himself to a "first-class position in society."

To suggest that Fagin, who creates criminals and controls their stories by informing on them, is partly based on Cruikshank's efforts to control Dickens' novel, is not necessarily to endorse Cruikshank's claims about his role in the composition of *Oliver Twist*. According to the illustrator's own account, Dickens did not really follow Cruikshank's suggestions, or did not follow them very far. The differences between *Oliver Twist*

as Cruikshank wanted it written and the novel Dickens actually wrote
are in fact evidence that Cruikshank's story is essentially true. Had
Cruikshank been lying or hallucinating, he presumably would have
claimed to have suggested the existing plot of *Oliver Twist*, not the plot
as it might have been. What we can believe is that Cruikshank made
frequent suggestions about the development of the story; that Dickens
sometimes followed these, but more often ignored or drastically altered
them; and that they contributed to the character and behavior of Fagin,
who tried to shape Oliver's destiny as a novelist shapes the destiny of a
fictional character.

Like Cruikshank, Fagin recognizes the commercial possibilities in "a
nice pretty little boy" as opposed to ordinary boys, whose " 'looks convict
'em when they get into trouble. . . . With this boy, properly managed,
my dears, I could do what I couldn't with twenty of them' " (19). He
is determined to make Oliver's life that "Life of a London Thief" which
Cruikshank urged Dickens to make the plot of *Oliver Twist*, though
Fagin's version would have a grimmer ending. Something of Fagin's
eagerness to shape and control Oliver's destiny seems to reflect Cruikshank's efforts to control Dickens' book, an irritation which Dickens has
brilliantly transformed into his novel's chief source of energy. To hint
at this, Dickens, near the end of his tale, has Fagin become absorbed
in an artist   Cruikshank?—"sketching his face in a little notebook"
during his trial. "He wondered whether it was like, and looked on when
the artist broke his pencil-point, and made another with his knife" (52).
As for Cruikshank, he had partly modelled Fagin's features on his own,
and when he came to draw the penultimate plate, "Fagin in the condemned cell," he posed himself before a mirror and copied what he
saw. Chesterton sensed Cruikshank's identification with Fagin when he
remarked that "In the doubled-up figure and frightful eyes of Fagin in
the condemned cell there is not only a baseness of subject; there is a
kind of baseness in the very technique of it. It is not drawn with the
free lines of a free man; it has the half-witted secrecies of a hunted thief.
It does not look merely like a picture of Fagin; it looks like a picture by
Fagin." In later life, various witnesses report, Cruikshank often imitated
Fagin's speech and movements as a kind of performance, and in self-
caricatures exaggerated his own features into Fagin's.

Even without Cruikshank, contemporary literature offered Dickens
an abundance of hints and models for continuing Oliver's adventures
among the criminal classes, and once he had made the decision to shift
the story to London, Dickens immediately began to imitate and yet
repudiate these models. With the appearance of the Artful Dodger,
Dickens brings us, not quite yet into the world of criminals, but into
the world of the dandy who prided himself on his knowledge of London
low life and on his ability to converse in the "flash" language of the
underworld. Here his literary prototype was Pierce Egan's enormously

popular *Tom and Jerry* (1821), or, in full, *Life in London; or, The Day and Night Scenes of Jerry Hawthorn, Esq., and his elegant friend Corinthian Tom, accompanied by Bob Logic, the Oxonian, in their Rambles and Sprees through the Metropolis.* Egan's book is a kind of light-hearted guide to the fashionable pleasures available in London, which are about equally divided between excursions into high society and slumming expeditions. It was, incidentally, illustrated by Cruikshank and his brother, Isaac Robert Cruikshank. Egan, as author, was properly deferential to his artist collaborators. Each episode leads up to a culminating moment which a plate depicts, and Egan's text carefully points out the beauties and details of the plate. He even describes one plate as "equal to anything in HOGARTH's collection; it may be examined again and again with delight: and the author thinks, that his readers will agree with him, that he has not travelled out of his way to thank the artist for the powerful talents he has displayed in portraying such a scene." It is not surprising that Cruikshank, accustomed to this sort of treatment from the writers he worked with, should have resented Dickens' assumption that the artist's role was subordinate to the author's.

*   *   *

Fagin himself is a creator of fiction in a variety of ways. Apart from planning the literary destinies of his gang, he is a gifted story-teller, able to tell "stories of robberies he had committed in his younger days: mixed up with so much that was droll and curious, that Oliver could not help laughing heartily, and showing that he was amused in spite of all his better feelings" (18:120). He can act an absent-minded old gentleman to perfection (9:54–55), and endow Nancy with the props to turn her into a respectable girl (13: 80). Fagin seems to have read Fielding's *Jonathan Wild*, and to have savored its ironies, when he urges Oliver to make the members of the gang, and especially the Dodger, his models. " 'He'll be a GREAT MAN himself; and will make you one too, if you take pattern by him. Is my handkerchief HANGING out of my pocket, my dear?' " (9; caps added). In *Jonathan Wild*, Fielding uses GREAT MAN, usually in caps, when he refers to Wild, well aware that in contemporary usage GREAT MAN almost invariably meant Sir Robert Walpole. Fielding considered the corrupt Walpole to be as great a rogue as Wild, a thief and informer. But Walpole is honored, Wild is hung. Fagin's apparently accidental shift from "great man" to hanging suggests his subconscious awareness that a great man, in the sense he is using the term, will end on the gallows.

At once the thieves' former and informer, Fagin both contributes to and derives from the *Newgate Calendar*. He can also be identified with the devil. He has red hair (8) and a red beard, which were then popularly believed to be traditionally Jewish characteristics—in the eighteenth and early nineteenth centuries, Shylock was always played with red hair. But red hair is also associated with the devil. Fagin's touch reminds

Sikes of " 'being nabbed by the devil. . . . There never was another man with such a face as yours, unless it was your father, and I suppose *he* is singeing his grizzled red beard by this time, unless you came straight from the old 'un without any father at all betwixt you; which I shouldn't wonder at, a bit' " (44). Fagin first appears as a kind of shabby devil, with a cooking fire for the fires of hell and a toasting fork for the traditional pitchfork, but he is truly diabolic in his efforts to corrupt and pervert. Dickens also endows him with something of his own creative energy. After all, Fagin too is a contriver of stories, of plots, and in depicting him, Dickens—who would have known that his own name was a euphemism for the devil—perhaps exorcises some of his own persistent guilt about creating characters in rivalry with God, and then determining their fates.

With the robbery, and Oliver's acceptance among the Maylies, Dickens shifts away from the Newgate novel mode, although he returns to it from time to time as the story reverts to the doings of Fagin's gang. He even introduces a miniature Newgate novel in Mr. Blathers' account of Conkey Chickweed (31). In his treatment of criminal life, and his simultaneous use of and parody of some of the Newgate conventions, Dickens may almost be credited with the destruction of the Newgate novel as a literary form, though he himself may not have realized this —he returns to the charge, at least symbolically, in *Barnaby Rudge* (1841), a novel in gestation during the writing of *Oliver Twist*. *Barnaby Rudge* is, in a sense, the Newgate novel to end all Newgate novels, for in it Dickens destroys Newgate itself. "I have just burnt into Newgate, and am going in the next number to tear the prisoners out by the hair of their heads," he exultantly wrote Forster of the scene in which the jail is destroyed, and a week later, "I have let all the prisoners out of Newgate, burnt down Lord Mansfield's, and played the very devil. . . . I feel quite smoky when I am at work."

For the remainder of *Oliver Twist*, Dickens shifts primarily to another popular mode, the Gothic novel, a shift signalized by the advent of Monks in chapter 26. In combining the Newgate mode with the Gothic, or developing one out of the other—and thus concocting that romance which he wished Mrs. Fry, the prison reformer, had written as a substitute for one of Mrs. Radcliffe's Gothic novels—Dickens had been anticipated by Ainsworth, who had merged the two forms in *Rookwood*. In his preface, Ainsworth describes himself as the heir of Horace Walpole, Monk Lewis, Mrs. Radcliffe, and Maturin—the major Gothic novelists—but suggests that he has improved on their imperfections and inharmonies by adding "a warmer and more genial current"—presumably the vigor of Dick Turpin and his friends.

Rookwood opens in a funeral vault and is rich in crypts, a ruined friary, secret passageways, supernatural portents, a sinister Jesuit, and a real ghost. There is even a band of gypsies. Secret passages and half-

ruined buildings, often of a monastic nature, are the characteristic settings of the Gothic novel, from the half-ruined castle of Otranto in
Walpole's novel of that name (1764) and the half-ruined abbey of Mrs.
Radcliffe's *Romance of the Forest* (1791) through the labyrinthine mon-
asteries of her *The Mysteries of Udolpho* (1794) and "Monk" Lewis's *The
Monk* (1796) to those described in Charles Robert Maturin's *Melmoth
the Wanderer* (1820). Among the other components of the Gothic are
ghosts and demons (real in most Gothic novels, elaborate contrivances
in Mrs. Radcliffe's); a dark protagonist, who is ultimately both doomed
and damned; a passive heroine-victim, threatened sometimes by rape,
sometimes by death, but always by the loss of her rightful fortune and
estate. *Rookwood* showed Dickens how these elements could be combined with the Newgate mode, and so gave him the basic recipe for the
second half of *Oliver Twist*.

The ruinous and labyrinthine settings of Gothic novels and of *Rookwood* are metaphors for the elaborate plots and deceits which the evil
forces in these books use to accomplish their aims. They reappear,
diminished, in *Oliver Twist*, in the half-ruined tenements where Fagin
and his gang lurk, and in the labyrinthine streets surrounding those
tenements—metaphors for the schemes and the twisting minds of Fagin and Monks. Those tenements and streets begin as sordid but
eventually—with the advent of Monks—become evil and haunted, as
the criminal theme gives way to the demonic malevolence that directs
Monks's efforts at moral fratricide.

Monks's name, his malevolent nature, and even his appearance indicate his origins in Gothic fiction. Gothic novels were almost always
set in the Catholic countries of southern Europe, and their villains were
often monks or priests. Such villains were invariably dark, pale, and
haggard. Walpole's Manfred, Mrs. Radcliffe's Montoni and Schedoni,
"Monk" Lewis' Ambrosio, and Maturin's Melmoth all share these physical traits, as do their Byronic cousins, Manfred and Childe Harold, and
such later descendants as Dracula. Monks comes with the appropriate
black cloak, pale face, dark hair and eyes, gnashing teeth, " 'lurking
walk' " (33; 46). He even has a peculiar scar or mark round his throat,
" 'A broad red mark, like a burn or scald' " (46), suggesting that he has
somehow survived hanging or is the ghost of a hanged man.

Monks's association with Fagin recalls the association of villain and
demon or tempter often found in Gothic novels, especially in Monk
Lewis' *The Monk*, where Ambrosio is tempted and then destroyed by
a demon, and in *Melmoth the Wanderer*, where Melmoth has sold
himself to the devil. Though Fagin is identified with the devil, Dickens
blurs the role of tempter and tempted after Monks's appearance in the
story: Fagin describes himself as " 'bound . . . to a born devil' " (26),
and he becomes less a scheming criminal and more a kind of supernatural

terror once he is allied with Monks. When he appears with Monks outside of the room at the Maylies in which Oliver has fallen asleep—the subject of one of Cruikshank's most striking plates—and Oliver wakes and raises the alarm. Monks and Fagin escape, leaving no footprints or any other sign of physical presence. No one in the neighborhood has seen them (34–35).

Monks's supernatural aura brings about a distinct change in the atmosphere of the novel; the sordid world of the thieves becomes one of hauntings and terror. Monks's black-cloaked figure establishes a new mood of nocturnal meetings, portents, apparitions, that eventually pervades the book and touches most of the characters; Nancy thinks of death and shrouds and coffins before her meeting with Mr. Brownlow and Rose Maylie, and a ghostly coffin passes her in the street (46); Sikes is pursued by Nancy's eyes after he has murdered her. Even Mr. Brownlow's rhetoric is affected: " 'Shadows on the wall have caught your whispers, and brought them to my ear' " (49), he tells the thwarted Monks.

When Fagin and Monks gaze into that window, Oliver has become a different kind of victim—not a social victim of the workhouse, nor of the poverty which can lead to a life of crime, but the object of a specific individual malevolence very different from society's general indifference and scorn. That malevolence governs through terror, and the Gothic novel is about terror. Its villains terrorize their intended victims, and its authors tried to terrify their readers. The victim, usually female and passive, is physically and often sexually threatened. She is to be frightened into surrendering herself and her fortune—the Gothic novel is almost invariably about the exploitation or intimidation of a woman through fear. Oliver's role as Gothic victim conforms to this tradition. Monks and Fagin want to possess him, in order to corrupt his very soul, to mark him with that "poison which . . . would blacken it" (18: 120), a metaphor for both moral and sexual possession. Ambrosio in *The Monk* and the hero of *Melmoth* are both possessed and corrupted in that way, by tempting demons; Monks would turn Oliver into a criminal, not merely for gain, as Fagin would do, but to destroy him. Oliver's passivity, his captive state, his youth and prettiness associate him with the Gothic heroine (Oliver has often been played by an actress on the stage). Like her, he is a potential victim of sexual exploitation, though Dickens cannot say so—Humphry House comments on the use of prostitutes in recruiting for such gangs as Fagin's, and adds that "the whole atmosphere in which Oliver lived in London would have been drenched in sex."[2] The introduction of Rose Maylie and her nearly fatal illness, and Rose's association with and contrast to Nancy, seem to suggest Dickens' partial

2. Humphry House, *The Dickens World* (Oxford, 1941) 217.

recognition of these aspects of his tale. Like Gothic heroines, Oliver is also heir to an estate, and for Monks, to destroy Oliver morally is to gain that estate under the terms of Edwin Leeford's will.

Dickens does interestingly vary the formulae he had inherited in his final explanation about Oliver's identity. In *Paul Clifford, Rookwood,* and many Gothic novels, the identifying tokens—those lockets and rings and documents—not only identify an heir or heiress but prove legitimacy. As Dickens manipulated the conventions, his readers could reasonably have expected that Oliver too will prove to be legitimate, and that his mother's reputation will be rehabilitated. Instead, Dickens excuses her fall—a serious business for nineteenth-century readers—by stressing the loveless nature of Edwin Leeford's marriage to Monks's mother, and the vindictiveness of that woman and her son. The liaison with Agnes Fleming is not exactly justified, and Agnes suffers the traditional punishment of a fallen woman, but she is not condemned. Dickens, as he exploits the conventions of the Newgate and Gothic novels, also deliberately thwarts them. He uses these forms as models, but is determined to transcend them and create a novel that defies easy categorization.

Here again he has internalized his own problems as a novice writer whose enterprise is threatened by the attractive modes of popular successes. If Fagin wished to write Oliver's story by making him the hero of a Newgate romance, Monks is eager to make him the protagonist-victim of a Gothic thriller. Dickens' novel develops out of this clash or mixture of novel types, and these internal efforts by characters in the novel to write Oliver's story comprise the story of Oliver Twist.

DAVID MILLER

[*Oliver Twist* and the Police]†

One reason for mistrusting the view that contraposes the notions of novel and police is that the novel itself does most to promote such a view. Crucially, the novel organizes its world in a way that already restricts the pertinence of the police. Regularly including the topic of the police, the novel no less regularly sets it against other topics of surpassing interest—so that the centrality of what it puts at the center is established by holding the police to their place on the periphery. At times, the limitations placed by the novel on the power of the police are coolly taken for granted, as in the long tradition of portraying the

† From *The Novel and the Police* (Berkeley and Los Angeles: U of California P, 1988) 2–10. Copyright © 1988 The Regents of the University of California. Reprinted by permission.

police as incompetent or powerless. At others, more tellingly, the marginality is dramatized as a gradual process of marginalization, in which police work becomes less and less relevant to what the novel is "really" about.

Even in the special case of detective fiction, where police detectives often hold center stage, the police never quite emerge from the ghetto in which the novel generally confines them. I don't simply refer to the fact that the work of detection is frequently transferred from the police to a private or amateur agent. Whether the investigation is conducted by police or private detectives, its sheer intrusiveness posits a world whose normality has been hitherto defined as a matter of *not needing* the police or policelike detectives. The investigation repairs this normality, not only by solving the crime, but also, far more important, by withdrawing from what had been, for an aberrant moment, its "scene." Along with the criminal, criminology itself is deported elsewhere.

In the economy of the "mainstream" novel, a more obviously circumscribed police apparatus functions somewhat analogously to define the field that exceeds its range. Its very limitations bear witness to the existence of other domains, formally lawless, outside and beyond its powers of supervision and detection. Characteristically locating its story in an everyday middle-class world, the novel takes frequent and explicit notice that this is an area that for the most part the law does not cover or supervise. Yet when the law falls short in the novel, the world is never reduced to anarchy as a result. In the same move whereby the police are contained in a marginal pocket of the representation, the work of the police is superseded by the operations of another, informal, and extralegal principle of organization and control.

Central among the ideological effects that such a pattern produces is the notion of *delinquency*. For the official police share their ghetto with an official criminality: the population of petty, repeated offenders, whose conspicuousness licenses it to enact, together with the police, a normative scenario of crime and punishment. To confine the actions of the police to a delinquent milieu has inevitably the result of consolidating the milieu itself, which not only stages a normative version of crime and punishment, but contains it as well in a world radically divorced from our own. Throughout the nineteenth-century novel, the confinement of the police allusively reinforces this ideology of delinquency. We may see it exemplarily surface in a novel such as *Oliver Twist* (1838). Though the novel is plainly written as a humane attack on the institutions that help produce the delinquent milieu, the very terms of the attack strengthen the perception of delinquency that upholds the phenomenon.

A large part of the moral shock *Oliver Twist* seeks to induce has to do with the *coherence* of delinquency, as a structured milieu or network. The logic of Oliver's "career," for instance, establishes workhouse, apprenticeship, and membership in Fagin's gang as versions of a single experience of incarceration. Other delinquent careers are similarly full of superficial movement in which nothing really changes. The Artful Dodger's fate links Fagin's gang with prison and deportation, and Noah Claypole discards the uniform of a charity boy for the more picturesque attire of Fagin's gang with as much ease as he later betrays the gang to become a police informer. Nor is it fortuitous that Fagin recruits his gang from institutions such as workhouses and groups such as apprentices, or that Mr. and Mrs. Bumble become paupers "in that very same workhouse in which they had once lorded it over others." The world of delinquency encompasses not only the delinquents themselves, but also the persons and institutions supposed to reform them or prevent them from forming. The policemen in the novel—the Bow Street runners Duff and Blathers—belong to this world, too. The story they tell about a man named Chickweed *who robbed himself* nicely illustrates the unity of both sides of the law in the delinquent context, the same unity that has allowed cop Blathers to call robber Chickweed "one of the family." Police and offenders are conjoined in a single system for the formation and re-formation of delinquents. More than an obvious phonetic linkage connects the police magistrate Mr. Fang with Fagin himself, who avidly reads the *Police Gazette* and regularly delivers certain gang members to the police.

In proportion as Dickens stresses the coherence and systematic nature of delinquency, he makes it an *enclosed* world from which it is all but impossible to escape. Characters may move from more to less advantageous positions in the system, but they never depart from it altogether—what is worse, they apparently never want to. With the exception of Oliver, characters are either appallingly comfortable with their roles or pathetically resigned to them. An elsewhere or an otherwise cannot be conceived, much less desired and sought out. The closed-circuit character of delinquency is, of course, a sign of Dickens's progressive attitude, his willingness to see coercive system where it was traditional only to see bad morals. Yet one should recognize how closing the circuit results in an "outside" as well as an "inside," an "outside" precisely determined as *outside the circuit*. At the same time as the novel exposes the network that ties together the workhouse, Fagin's gang, and the police *within* the world of delinquency, it also draws a circle around it, and in that gesture, holds the line of a *cordon sanitaire*. Perhaps the novel offers its most literal image of holding the line in the gesture of *shrinking* that accompanies Nancy's contact with the "outside." "The poorest women fall back," as Nancy makes her way along the crowded pavement, and even Rose Maylie is shown "involuntarily falling from her strange companion." When Nancy herself, anticipating her meeting with Rose, "thought of the wide contrast which the small room would in another moment contain, she felt burdened with the sense of her own deep shame, and shrunk as though she could scarcely bear the presence of her with whom she had sought this interview." Much of the proof of Nancy's ultimate goodness lies in her awed recognition of the impermeable boundaries that separate her from Rose Maylie. It is this, as much as her love for Bill Sikes (the two things are not ultimately very different), that brings her to say to Rose's offers of help: "I wish to go back. . . . I must go back." Righteously "exposed" in the novel, the world of delinquency is also actively occulted: made cryptic by virtue of its cryptlike isolation.

Outside and surrounding the world of delinquency lies the middle-class world of private life, presided over by Oliver's benefactors Mr. Brownlow, Mr. Losberne, and the Maylies. What repeatedly and rhapsodically characterizes this world is the contrast that opposes it to the world of delinquency. Thus, at Mr. Brownlow's, "everything was so quiet, and neat, and orderly; everybody was kind and gentle; that *after the noise and turbulence in the midst of which [Oliver] had always lived*, it seemed like Heaven itself"; and at the Maylies' country cottage, "Oliver, *whose days had been spent among squalid crowds, and in the midst of noise and brawling*, seemed to enter on a new existence" (italics added). No doubt, the contrast serves the ends of Dickens's moral and political outrage: the middle-class standards in effect, say, at Mr. Brownlow's dramatically enhance our appreciation of the miseries of delinquency. However, the outrage is limited in the contrast, too, since these miseries in turn help secure a proper (relieved, grateful) appreciation of *the standards themselves*. It is systematically unclear which kind of appreciation *Oliver Twist* does most to foster. Much as delinquency is circumscribed by middle-class private life, the indignation to which delinquency gives rise is bounded by gratitude for the class habits and securities that make indignation possible.

The "alternative" character of the middle-class community depends significantly on the fact that it is kept free, not just from noise and squalor, but also from the police. When this freedom is momentarily violated by Duff and Blathers, who want to know Oliver's story, Mr. Losberne persuades Rose and Mrs. Maylie not to cooperate with them:

> "The more I think of it," said the doctor, "the more I see that it will occasion endless trouble and difficulty if we put these men in possession of the boy's real story. I am certain it will not be believed; and even if they can do nothing to him in the end, still the dragging it forward, and giving publicity to all the doubts that will be cast upon it, must interfere, materially, with your benevolent plan of rescuing him from misery."

The police are felt to obstruct an alternative power of regulation, such as the plan of rescue implies. Not to cooperate with the police, therefore, is part of a strategy of surreptitiously assuming and revising their functions. Losberne himself, for instance, soon forces his way into a suspect dwelling in the best policial manner. In a more central and extensive pattern, Oliver's diabolical half-brother Monks is subject to a replicated version of a whole legal and police apparatus. There is no wish to prosecute Monks legally because, as Mr. Brownlow says, "there must be circumstances in Oliver's little history which it would be painful to drag before the public eye." Instead Brownlow proposes "to extort the secret" from Monks. Accordingly, Monks is "kidnapped in the street" by two of Brownlow's men and submitted to a long cross-examination in which he is overwhelmed by the "accumulated charges." The Bumbles are brought in to testify against him, and the "trial" concludes with his agreement to render up Oliver's patrimony and sign a written admission that he stole it.

We would call this vigilantism, except that no ultimate conflict of purpose or interest divides it from the legal and police apparatus that it supplants. Such division as does surface between the law and its supplement seems to articulate a deeper congruency, as though the text were positing something like a doctrine of "separation of powers," whereby each in its own sphere rendered assistance to the other, in the coherence of a single policing action. Thus, while the law gets rid of Fagin and his gang, the amateur supplement gets rid of Monks. Monks's final fate is instructive in this light. Retired with his portion to the New World, "he once more fell into his old courses, and, after undergoing a long confinement for some fresh act of fraud and knavery, at length sunk under an attack of his old disorder, and died in prison." The two systems of regulation beautifully support one another. Only when the embarrassment that an initial appeal to the law would have created has been circumvented, does the law come to claim its own; and in so doing, it punishes on behalf of the vigilantes. A similar complicitousness obtains in the fate of the Bumbles. Although the reason for dealing with Monks privately has been to keep the secret of Oliver's parentage, it is hard to know on what basis the Bumbles are "deprived of their position" at the end, since this would imply a disclosure of their involvement in Monks's scheme to the proper authorities. Even if the confusion is inadvertent, it attests to the tacit concurrence the text assumes between the law and its supplement.

The two systems come together, then, in the connivance of class rule, but more of society is covered by the rule than outsiders such as Fagin or monsters such as Monks. Perhaps finally more interesting than the quasi-legal procedures applied to Monks are the disciplinary techniques imposed on Oliver himself. From his first moment at Mr. Brownlow's, Oliver is subject to incessant examination:

> "Oliver what? Oliver White, eh?"
> "No, sir, Twist, Oliver Twist."

"Queer name!" said the old gentleman. "What made you tell the magistrate that your name was White?"

"I never told him so, sir," returned Oliver in amazement.

This sounded so like a falsehood, that the old gentleman looked somewhat sternly in Oliver's face. It was impossible to doubt him; there was truth in every one of its thin and sharpened lineaments.

However "impossible" Oliver is to doubt, Brownlow is capable of making "inquiries" to "confirm" his "statement." The object of both interrogation and inquiry is to produce and possess a *full account* of Oliver. "Let me hear your story," Brownlow demands of Oliver, "where you come from; who brought you up; and how you got into the company in which I found you." With a similar intent, when Oliver later disappears, he advertises for "such information as will lead to the discovery of the said Oliver Twist, or tend to throw any light upon his previous history." It is clear what kind of narrative Oliver's "story" is supposed to be: the continuous line of an evolution. Not unlike the novel itself, Brownlow is seeking to articulate an original "story" over the heterogeneous and lacunary data provided in the "plot." It is also clear what Oliver's story, so constructed, is going to do: it will entitle him to what his Standard English already anticipates, a full integration into middle-class respectability. Another side to this entitlement, however, is alluded to in Brownlow's advertisement, which concludes with "a full description of Oliver's dress, person, appearance, and disappearance." The "full description" allows Oliver to be identified and (what comes to the same thing here) *traced*. And if, as Brownlow thinks possible, Oliver has "absconded," then he will be traced *against his will*. To constitute Oliver as an object of knowledge is thus to assume power over him as well. One remembers that the police, too, wanted to know Oliver's story.

The same ideals of continuity and repleteness that determine the major articulations of this story govern the minor ones as well. The "new existence" Oliver enters into at the Maylies' cottage consists predominantly in a routine and a timetable:

> Every morning he went to a white-headed old gentleman, who lived near the little church: who taught him to read better, and to write: and who spoke so kindly, and took such pains, that Oliver could never try enough to please him. Then, he would walk with Mrs. Maylie and Rose, and hear them talk of books; or perhaps sit near them, in some shady place, and listen whilst the young lady read: which he could have done, until it grew too dark to see the letters. Then, he had his own lesson for the next day to prepare; and at this, he would work hard, in a little room which looked into the garden, till evening came slowly on, when the ladies would walk out again, and he with them: listening with such pleasure to all they said: and so happy if they wanted a flower that he could

climb to reach, or had forgotten anything he could run to fetch:
that he could never be quick enough about it. When it became
quite dark, and they returned home, the young lady would sit down
to the piano, and play some pleasant air, or sing, in a low and
gentle voice, some old song which it pleased her aunt to hear.
There would be no candles lighted at such times as these; and
Oliver would sit by one of the windows, listening to the sweet music,
in a perfect rapture.

This "iterative" tense continues to determine the presentation of the
idyll, whose serenity depends crucially on its legato: on its not leaving
a moment blank, or out of consecutive order. "No wonder," the text
concludes, that at the end of a very short time, "Oliver had become
completely domesticated with the old lady and her niece." No wonder
indeed, when the techniques that structure Oliver's time are precisely
those of a domesticating pedagogy. Despite the half-lights and soft kindly
tones, *as well as by means of them*, a technology of discipline constitutes
this happy family as a field of power relations. Recalling that Blathers
called Chickweed "one of the family," conjoining those who work the
police apparatus and those whom it works over, we might propose a
sense—only discreetly broached by the text—in which the family itself
is "one of the family" of disciplinary institutions.

* * *

JOHN O. JORDAN

The Purloined Handkerchief†

The topic of this essay is a small but revealing aspect of Dickens' *Oliver
Twist* (1837–39): namely, the motif of pocket-handkerchiefs in the book.
The title, "The Purloined Handkerchief," aims not only at the scenes
of pocket picking and handkerchief thieving in the novel but also, somewhat more obliquely, at Edgar Allan Poe's celebrated detective story of
1845, "The Purloined Letter," and at the important body of critical
commentary that Poe's story has received in recent years, notably in
essays by Jacques Lacan, Jacques Derrida, and Barbara Johnson. The
term "purloined" derives largely from this critical tradition. The verb
"to purloin" (from the Anglo-French *pur* + *loigner*) means to set aside
or delay and hence, by extension, to steal; but as Lacan insists with
respect to Poe, the word should properly retain something of its original
sense of retardation and displacement in addition to the more straight-

† From *Dickens Studies Annual*, ed. M. Timko, F. Kaplan, and E. Guiliano, 18 (1989): 1–
17. Copyright © 1989 AMS Press, Inc. Reprinted by permission.

forward notion of theft, and it is with this broader sense of its meaning that the word is used here. Like the letter in Poe's story, the handkerchiefs in *Oliver Twist* are displaced from their original location and made to circulate through the text and illustrations of the book along a complex network of communication and exchange. To describe some of the features of this network, its circuitry so to speak, will be a principal goal of this paper.

Pocket-handkerchiefs abound in *Oliver Twist*. Nearly every major character in the book handles, carries, or wears some form of handkerchief during the course of the narrative. Over fifty separate instances of the word "handkerchief" or its near-synonyms ("neckerchief," "cravat"; also the slang terms "fogle" and "wipe") occur in the text, and if we include references to other woven materials such as veils, shrouds, curtains, blankets, coverlets, and so forth, then the number is even greater. In addition, handkerchiefs figure prominently in Cruikshank's illustrations to the novel. At least half of the twenty-four plates in the book contain or suggest the presence of a handkerchief. Moreover, the novel appears at times deliberately to flaunt its preoccupation with handkerchiefs, presenting them not just singly but in astonishing profusion.

The abundance of pocket-handkerchiefs in *Oliver Twist* is of course in large part a function of the plot and of Dickens' decision to place his young protagonist in Fagin's gang of juvenile London pickpockets, for whom the theft of handkerchiefs represents a chief source of livelihood. The importance of handkerchiefs in the thieves' domestic economy is evident in the description of Oliver's first arrival at Fagin's den.

> [Fagin] was dressed in a greasy flannel gown, with his throat bare; and seemed to be dividing his attention between the frying pan and a clothes-horse: over which a great number of silk handkerchiefs were hanging. . . .
>
> "We are very glad to see you Oliver—very," said the Jew. "Dodger, take off the sausages; and draw a tub near the fire for Oliver. Ah, you're a-staring at the pocket-handkerchiefs! eh, my dear? There are a good many of 'em, ain't there? We've just looked 'em out, ready for the wash; that's all. Oliver; that's all. Ha! ha! ha!"

Oliver finds many things to wonder at in his new surroundings, but, as Fagin observes and as Cruikshank's illustration for this scene also suggests, what astonishes him most is the profusion of handkerchiefs. The reader immediately recognizes what Oliver fails to understand: namely, that the handkerchiefs are stolen. Oliver's failure to grasp this fact reveals more than just his naiveté, however. Ignorance here is a sign of goodness. Because his heart and mind are innocent, the idea of theft never occurs to him. Indeed, it is only much later, when he actually witnesses a crime, that the meaning of the handkerchiefs becomes clear. Until then, they remain morally neutral objects in what he mistakenly construes as a game.

A few chapters later, in a companion scene to the one just cited, the narrative follows Fagin through the streets of London to another point along the route traced by handkerchiefs through the text of the book.

> Near to the spot on which Snow Hill and Holborn Hill meet, there opens: upon the right hand as you come out of the city, a narrow and dismal alley leading to Saffron Hill. In its filthy shops are exposed for sale huge bunches of second-hand silk handkerchiefs, of all sizes and patterns; for here reside the traders who purchase them from pickpockets. Hundreds of these handkerchiefs hang dangling from pegs outside the windows, or flaunting from the doorposts; and the shelves, within, are piled with them. Confined as the limits of Field Lane are, it has its barber, its coffee-shop, its beer-shop, and its fried-fish warehouse. It is a commercial colony of itself: the emporium of petty larceny: visited at early morning, and setting-in of dusk, by silent merchants, who traffic in dark back-parlours; and who go as strangely as they come. Here, the clothes-man, the shoe-vamper, and the rag-merchant, display their goods, as sign-boards to the petty thief; here, stores of old iron and bones, and heaps of mildewy fragments of woolen-stuff and linen, rust and rot in the grimy cellars.

Here we have the documentary urban journalist at work, the Dickens of *Sketches by Boz*, describing a real London street—Field Lane—for the benefit of middle-class readers who have presumably never seen it. Unlike Oliver in the preceding passage, the narrative voice here has no difficulty grasping the significance of the many handkerchiefs on display. They are "sign-boards" that advertise to both buyer and seller the particular form of commerce conducted within. As such, they belong to a larger class of cultural signs that the narrator records and interprets in conjunction with his project of documenting city life. As in the earlier passage, the very excess of pocket-handkerchiefs in the text calls attention to their status as signifiers in need of interpretation and thus reinforces the handkerchief motif in the book.

In addition to documenting a particular class of petty criminals, the handkerchiefs in *Oliver Twist* are themselves part of a specific social and historical formation. During the 1820s and 30s, when the action of *Oliver Twist* presumably takes place, handkerchiefs continued, as they had throughout the eighteenth century, to be an important fashion accessory for well-to-do persons of both sexes. Fine handkerchiefs were considered articles of luxury, hence their value to thieves and receivers of stolen goods such as Fagin. Preferably made of silk, but also of cambric and fine muslin, dress handkerchiefs frequently bore the "marks" or initials of their owners embroidered into the fabric. Women's handkerchiefs were usually white, often with fancy lace borders and other examples of fine needlework, while men's handkerchiefs, especially snuff handkerchiefs, were more likely to be dark and to bear a printed pattern or design.

Men's handkerchiefs of the period were quite large by modern standards, averaging more than thirty inches square; women's handkerchiefs, though somewhat smaller, also tended to be large. Since the eighteenth century, men generally carried handkerchiefs in the pockets of their trousers, waistcoats, or topcoats, bringing the term pocket-handkerchief into common parlance as a result. Ladies carried their handkerchiefs in a bag or reticule tied round the waist on top of the skirt. From a pickpocket's perspective, the most easily accessible place from which to take a handkerchief was probably the tail-pocket of a gentleman's long-tailed coat. It is from this location, as we see in Cruikshank's illustration, that the Artful Dodger and Charley Bates lift a handkerchief from the distracted Mr. Brownlow, while Oliver looks on in horrified amazement.

In addition to dress handkerchiefs of the kind I have been describing, the late eighteenth and early nineteenth century saw an increase in the use of handkerchiefs by people of the lower classes. The power loom and the availability of cheap cotton from America, together with improved dyeing techniques, made it possible for relatively inexpensive cotton handkerchiefs to be owned by all but the poorest members of society. Thus, although there are no handkerchiefs in the workhouse, when Oliver runs away from the undertaker's house, he does have a handkerchief in which to tie up his few articles of clothing. Likewise, the charity boy Noah Claypole arrives in London with his belongings tied in a handkerchief. Servants also have handkerchiefs. For example, we are told that Giles, the butler in Mrs. Maylie's house, wipes his eyes "with a blue cotton pocket-handkerchief dotted with white spots." This distinctive pattern identifies it as a "belcher" handkerchief, so named in honor of the early nineteenth-century prize fighter, Jim Belcher, who wore neckerchiefs of this design.

The thieves also carry handkerchiefs—ordinary cotton ones worn characteristically around the neck rather than carried in the pocket. Bill Sikes, for example, wears "a dirty belcher handkerchief round his neck"; flash Toby Crackit wears an orange neckerchief; and Charley Bates explains the slang term "scragged" to Oliver by giving a "pantomimic representation" that involves holding the end of his neckerchief in the air and dropping his head on his shoulder so as to indicate "that scragging and hanging were one and the same thing." Only Fagin, whose throat is bare, lacks the distinctive neckerchief that is virtually a badge of membership in the gang. Thus, although they steal silk handkerchiefs, the thieves do not normally wear them, the one exception to this rule being the occasion when Fagin dresses up like an old gentleman in order to teach Oliver the pocket-handkerchief "game." Fagin's own handkerchief, however, is an old cotton one in which he ties up his gold coins.

What begins to emerge from these examples is something like a rudimentary dress code in the book with respect to handkerchiefs. Silk handkerchiefs, carried in the pocket, are the property of the upper classes. Ordinary cotton handkerchiefs, often worn about the neck, belong to the lower classes, especially the thieves. Thieves wear neckerchiefs, the neckerchief being an article of working-class attire used for protection against the sun and for wiping away sweat. Sailors, agricultural laborers, and boxers wear neckerchiefs; gentlemen wear "neckcloths" and "cravats," ancestors of the present-day necktie. This code perhaps helps to explain why Mr. Bumble, a lower-class character whose role as beadle aligns him politically with the upper classes, should have two handkerchiefs: one in his pocket, which he daintily spreads over his knees when he takes tea with Mrs. Corney so as "to prevent the crumbs from sullying the splendour of his shorts"—a parodic imitation of upper-class gentility; and another that he takes from inside his hat to wipe his brow. There are, of course, exceptions to the handkerchief code. Both Grimwig and Monks, two upper-class characters, wear neckerchiefs, though the case of Monks is complicated by his close association with the thieves and by the special reason he has for covering his throat.

One other aspect of early nineteenth-century handkerchief history deserves mention at this point: a development that I shall call the "textualization" of the handkerchief. The invention of the roller or cylinder printing machine by Thomas Bell in 1785 was of tremendous importance for the British textile industry at the turn of the century. Printed handkerchiefs, which had previously been relatively difficult and expensive to manufacture, now became mass-produced articles. In addition to decorative patterns such as the blue and white belcher design, one finds an increasing number of utilitarian, commemorative, literary, and political motifs represented upon nineteenth-century handkerchiefs. Maps, statistical tables, poems, political caricatures, and scenes depicting important social and historical events appear with regularity. Handkerchiefs thus become texts as well as textiles, objects to be read and interpreted as well as used in connection with some bodily function.

The "textualization" of handkerchiefs of course begins long before the nineteenth century with the use of embroidered initials, names, and decorative motifs (like the strawberry pattern in *Othello* [III.3.435]), but it is not until the industrial age that this practice becomes so elaborate or widespread. Dickens was well aware of these new developments in handkerchief production, as he was of nearly every commercial and technological innovation of the age. In *Nicholas Nickleby* (1838–39), for example, the novel that immediately followed *Oliver Twist*, he describes one of the boys who is about to leave with Squeers for Dotheboys Hall as sobbing and "rubbing his face very hard with the Beggar's Petition in printed calico." Likewise, in *Dombey and Son* (1846–48), a decade after *Oliver Twist*, he mentions something called "the Strangers' Map of London, . . . printed (with a view to pleasant and commodious reference) on pocket handkerchiefs." Although *Oliver Twist* contains no references to printed handkerchiefs of this sort, I believe that the idea of the handkerchief as a printed document or text is implicit in the novel and shall return to this point later in the paper.

From the examples already cited, it will be clear that *Oliver Twist* is full of handkerchiefs to an extent that both reflects the tremendous increase in handkerchief production around and after the turn of the century and at the same time exceeds the requirements of any documentary or mimetic realism on Dickens' part. As they reappear and pass from one context to another, handkerchiefs take on increasing thematic and figural significance in the novel. Thus, although their importance as a commodity is evident, they seem as well to have symbolic or exchange value in the book, circulating like a form of currency in the thieves' underground economy. As we have seen, handkerchiefs also function as indicators of social class and gender in the book. Their distribution follows a semiotic system or dress code that may owe something to the philosophy of clothes elaborated in Carlyle's *Sartor Resartus* (1833–34) but that lends itself as well to analysis in terms of Roland Barthes' *Système de la mode*.

That Dickens was attempting to develop some kind of philosophy of clothing in the book is evident from a passage at the end of the opening chapter, in which the narrator moralizes upon the newly born Oliver's first entry into clothes:

> What an excellent example of the power of dress, young Oliver Twist was! Wrapped in the blanket which had hitherto formed his only covering, he might have been the child of a nobleman or a beggar; it would have been hard for the haughtiest stranger to have assigned him his proper station in society. But now that he was enveloped in the old calico robes which had grown yellow in the same service, he was badged and ticketed, and fell into his place at once—a parish child—the orphan of a workhouse—the humble half-starved drudge—to be cuffed and buffeted through the world—despised by all, and pitied by none.

Several important points concerning the "power of dress" emerge from this passage. First, clothes are a powerful way of marking social distinctions in a class society; second, power itself is often vested in clothing or social roles rather than in the person, as we see later on in the book from the example of Mr. Bumble, who loses every vestige of authority when he takes off his beadle's cocked hat, laced coat, and cane; and finally, dress codes function not just as a differential system of classification but as a means of social control whereby institutions like the workhouse identify and regulate ("badge" and "ticket") members of the lower classes. The exercise of this control begins in the workhouse with the naming, dressing, and subsequent selling of parish orphans as apprentices; it takes its ultimate form in the power of the state over life and death—that is, in the operation of the gallows, which, as Fagin notes, changes "strong and vigorous men to dangling heaps of clothes."

Not surprisingly, then, in a book so preoccupied with handkerchiefs, the power of the state in *Oliver Twist* extends to the absurd length of an attempt by the workhouse board of governors to forbid the possession of pocket-handkerchiefs by any inmate. When the gentleman in the white waistcoat predicts that one day Oliver will come to be hung, the narrator responds with the following ironic comment:

> It appears, at first sight, not unreasonable to suppose, that, if he had entertained a becoming feeling of respect for the prediction of the gentleman in the white waistcoat, he would have established that sage individual's prophetic character, once and for ever, by tying one end of his pocket-handkerchief to a hook in the wall, and attaching himself to the other. To the performance of this feat, however, there was one obstacle: namely, that pocket-handkerchiefs being decided articles of luxury, had been, for all future times and ages, removed from the noses of paupers by the express order of the board, in council assembled: solemnly given and pronounced under their hands and seals.

The connection between pocket-handkerchiefs and hanging that appears in this passage is another important aspect of the handkerchief motif in the book. The thieves of course all live in constant fear of the gallows. Their nervousness on this score is evident in their frequent joking references to public execution and in the colorful figurative language they use in order to avoid pronouncing the word "hanging." Instead, they say things like "scragged" and "dance upon nothing." Bill Sikes, who has more to fear than anyone at the hands of "Jack Ketch," betrays his anxiety by means of hostile attacks on other people's throats. He threatens to "stop [Oliver's] windpipe," takes his knife to Fagin's throat, and leaves bruises on Nancy's "neck and arms." "Wolves tear your throats!" is his most violent oath in the book, and he attempts to drown his dog by tying a stone to its throat with a handkerchief and throwing them in the river.

As these and other examples indicate, the throat is an extremely sensitive part of the anatomy in *Oliver Twist* precisely because it is the focus of so much physical and verbal aggression. It is little wonder then that the thieves make such efforts to protect their throats by wearing handkerchiefs around the neck. These neckerchiefs perform a double and almost contradictory function, however. In addition to protecting a sensitive part of the body, they also serve as a constant reminder of the noose that is figuratively always around the thieves' necks: the "cravat," as Fagin sardonically calls it at one point. Fagin's bare throat suggests his greater vulnerability to the danger that threatens them all, a danger reinforced linguistically throughout the novel by the pun lurking in the first syllable of the word "handkerchief." If handkerchiefs are "*hang*-erchiefs" and if petty larceny is a capital crime (as it was within recent memory, until the Larceny Act of 1808), then the game to which Oliver is introduced at Fagin's and in which Dodger and the other boys are old hands is one where they are invited to play with their own mortality.

The association between handkerchiefs and hanging is confirmed both verbally and visually in *Oliver Twist*. In the passage already discussed describing Oliver's first arrival at Fagin's den, the silk handkerchiefs are said to be "*hanging*" (emphasis mine) over a clothes-horse, and in the companion scene-describing Field Lane they "*hang dangling* from pegs outside the windows" (emphasis mine). The hanging motif is further reinforced in the illustration that accompanies the first of these scenes. On the wall adjacent to the cascade of handkerchiefs we can recognize a small popular print in which three bodies are shown hanging from a gallows. The hang/handkerchief pun is also apparent in Charley Bates's dumb-show explanation of the word "scragged." Here again, Cruikshank's illustration for the scene repeats and thus corroborates the evidence of the verbal text.

The thieves' obsessive fear of hanging may point toward other anxieties as well. Dianne Sadoff, for example, has argued that the thieves' tenderness about the neck represents the displacement upward of a repressed castration anxiety that structures the entire novel.[1] For Sadoff, metaphors of castration at once repress and repeat Oedipal fantasies that underlie Oliver's story. Handkerchiefs and neckerchiefs can thus be understood as signifiers that mark the place of a conspicuous absence in the text—that of the phallus. Likewise, handkerchief stealing can be viewed as a defensive strategy whereby the original conflict is displaced but in which the substitute symptom—pocket picking—repeats in symbolic form the conflict it was intended to resolve.

Castration anxiety is not the only motive for narration in *Oliver Twist*. If handkerchiefs signal a conspicuous absence in the text, then we should consider them as well in relation to Oliver's status as an orphan. Oliver's lack of parents, or rather the lack of any evidence as to their identity, is of course a central mystery that the plot works initially to obscure but ultimately to clear up to achieve narrative closure. The search for parents and for parental substitutes is thus an important motivating force behind the story. It is perhaps too much, however, to say that Oliver himself engages actively in this search. Indeed, he remains remarkably passive

---

1. Dianne F. Sadoff, *Monsters of Affection: Dickens, Eliot, and Brontë on Fatherhood* (Baltimore, 1982) 212–14.

throughout the book, ready to attach himself to almost any adult figure that the plot tosses his way, but hardly ever an active participant in initiating such attachments. The search for his father, for example is carried out on Oliver's behalf by a committee of (mostly) older men, all of them aligned in various ways with the paternal order and the rule of law. The place of Oliver's missing father is marked in the text by a series of written documents—the will, the letter, and the ring given by him to Oliver's mother with her name inscribed inside. All of these, along with other unnamed "proofs," have been either stolen or destroyed by Monks and his mother in their effort to conceal Oliver's paternal origin. They constitute what we might call the "purloined letters" of the novel, and they must be recovered before the plot can come to a close.

The place of Oliver's missing mother is marked in the text not so much by documents and inscriptions, although these exist, as by a series of woven materials such as blankets, curtains, shrouds, and of course handkerchiefs, that appear regularly throughout the novel. These materials are similar but not identical to what the psychoanalytic literature calls "transitional objects"—that is, objects that take the place of the absent mother and help the child to master the trauma of separation from her. Typically these include such things as the child's teddy bear or blanket—soft, malleable objects that recall the maternal breast and that the child can use as a comforting substitute when the mother is away. The transitional objects in *Oliver Twist* do not always provide comfort, however, but serve instead as reminders or premonitions of the mother's death.

The trail marked by these reminders of maternal death begins in the workhouse with the "patchwork coverlet" thrown over the body of his dying mother and continues with the "old blanket" that covers the corpse of the poor woman whose home Oliver visits in the company of the undertaker. It includes the curtain from behind which Mrs. Bedwin's "motherly" face appears at Mr. Brownlow's house, as well as the figurative "dusky curtain" or "shroud" that hangs over Brownlow's memory and keeps him from recognizing the resemblance between Oliver's face and the portrait of Agnes Fleming hanging on the wall. The portrait itself, painted on "canvas," is another instance of the motif, as is the rug that Bill Sikes throws over the body of the murdered Nancy. Less obvious examples include the wallpaper in Brownlow's house, whose "intricate pattern" Oliver traces with his eyes in the still of the night as if attempting to make out on the wall the image of his lost mother's face, an image that materializes for him the next morning when he sees the portrait. The white handkerchief that passes from Rose Maylie, who almost dies, to Nancy, who holds it up in an effort to ward off Bill Sikes' murderous assault, is another instance of the motif, the handkerchief here serving as a link among the three "sisters"—Rose, Nancy, and Agnes—each of whom briefly occupies the place of Oliver's mother in the book.

The signifying chain that unites these various examples comes to an end in the concluding image of the novel: the white marble tablet with the name "Agnes" inscribed upon it. White like the handkerchief and positioned like the portrait and the wallpaper patterns on the wall, the tablet achieves a permanency that the other objects lack and that promises therefore to bring the chain of substitutions to a close. The fact, however, that the inscription is incomplete—like the ring, it lacks a second name—and that it marks a grave without a corpse may indicate that the tablet is only a temporary resting place in the endless process of signification. Indeed, the closure achieved here seems not only unstable but also transparently ideological in its motivation. The marble tablet enshrines Agnes Fleming safely within the bourgeois order that prevails at the novel's end. It thus prevents the search for Oliver's mother from going back to the anonymous pauper's grave at the workhouse where her body presumably lies, and in this way it helps to shield the institution—as well as Oliver's dead father—from any charge of responsibility or neglect in the matter of her death.

Among the many pocket-handkerchiefs that dot the text of *Oliver Twist*, none is so distinctive as the one that Nancy holds aloft at the moment when Bill Sikes bludgeons her to death. Nancy's handkerchief is memorable on several accounts, not the least of which is the strong contrast it presents to the phallic violence of Sikes. Hers is specifically a female-gendered handkerchief—white, as if to suggest that the purity of her womanly "nature" remains unstained despite the sordid conditions in which she lives. Moreover, since it comes from Rose Maylie, the handkerchief signifies the sisterly bond that unites two women of different social classes who are nevertheless alike in their devotion to Oliver. The handkerchief also seems imbued with religious significance, for as she lifts it "towards Heaven" Nancy "breathe[s] one prayer for mercy to her Maker."

It is important to recall that Nancy acquires the handkerchief from Rose Maylie not as a simple gift but in exchange for the information about Oliver that she provides to the Maylie group. Nancy will not sell her story, refusing the money that they offer as a reward, but requests from Rose instead some personal memento—a glove or handkerchief. The fact that it is exchanged for a story suggests that the handkerchief has story value of its own, as a female subtext or intertext in a narrative ostensibly about the progress of a parish boy. When Sikes strikes through the handkerchief with his club, he is attempting to cancel the woman's story, but he succeeds only in driving it underground. He represses it (just as he covers Nancy's body with the rug), but it will not stay hidden. The story dogs him, literally, in the form of the mongrel that follows and finally betrays him to the mob. Even the handkerchief returns to haunt him. In Cruikshank's illustration of the scene in which Sikes falls to his death, we see not only the belcher handkerchief around his neck and the hangman's noose that awaits his fall, but in the background, hanging from a pole, a large white square cloth, mentioned in the text only as an absence—"the linen that is never there"—but traceable nonetheless back to Nancy and to Rose. Although repressed, the female subtext returns to assert its power in the end.

One further suggestion concerning Nancy's handkerchief merits consideration at this point. The scenes between Sikes and Nancy in the final one-quarter of the novel represent, I believe, Dickens' attempt to retell the story of *Othello*, with Bill Sikes in the role of the murderer, Nancy as Desdemona, and Fagin as the cunning, manipulative Iago who drives Sikes to commit the deed. "You won't be—too—violent, Bill?" he says after confronting Sikes with the evidence of Nancy's betrayal. The handkerchief that Nancy lifts toward Heaven in the murder scene is thus, I would suggest, an intertextual allusion to the lost or purloined handkerchief that serves as the focus of Othello's sexual jealousy. Nancy's unexpected and futile gesture with the handkerchief has its motive partly at least in Shakespeare's play, in Desdemona's equally futile wish to prove her innocence by returning to her husband the missing object that has come to symbolize for him her sexual infidelity.

The hypothesis that Dickens may have been attempting a Newgate *Othello* in *Oliver Twist* is not entirely without foundation. Dickens was of course familiar with all of Shakespeare's work, both as a reader and as a theater-goer. His friend Macready often played the part of Othello and was in fact performing it in 1838, just as Dickens was putting the finishing touches to his novel. Moreover, Dickens appears to have taken a particular interest in *Othello* during the 1830s. We know that in 1833, for example, at the age of 21, he wrote and produced a burlesque theatrical version of *Othello* entitled *O'Thello*, in which his father took a leading role. Only a few manuscript fragments of this burlesque have survived. Similarly, the satirical sketch of 1834 entitled "Mrs. Joseph Porter," reprinted two years later in *Sketches by Boz*, deals with the hilarious and unsuccessful attempt to mount an amateur theatrical production of *Othello*. The scenes between Sikes and Nancy in *Oliver Twist* thus may well be another effort to revise Shakespeare's tragedy, this time as melodrama rather than burlesque or farce. If this hypothesis is correct, it may also help to explain the shift in narrative perspective that takes place toward the end of the book, when the novel's point of view moves inside the guilty consciousness of Sikes, creating greater sympathy for him and making him, if not a tragic hero, at least briefly the protagonist of a Victorian melodrama.

Finally, and at the risk of giving an overly figural reading to the book,

I would submit that Oliver himself is a purloined handkerchief circulating through the text of the novel and waiting to be claimed by his rightful owner. To view Oliver in this way is to consider him not so much a character as a narrative function—a small but valuable piece of portable property shuttled about the story by forces outside of his control, including the narrator, until he settles more or less permanently in the Maylie household.

Certainly, from the hour of his birth onward, Oliver is treated more like an object than a human child. " 'You needn't mind sending up to me, if the child cries, nurse' said the surgeon. . . . 'It's very likely it *will* be troublesome. Give it a little gruel if it is!' " The narrator himself ironically adopts the language of the workhouse in order to satirize its treatment of people as commodities, calling Oliver an "item of mortality" and "an article direct from the manufactory of the Devil himself." If at times Oliver figures as a small piece of manufactured goods, he is also, in Bumble's delightfully mixed metaphor, a strange species of neckerchief: "a porochial 'prentis, who is at present a dead-weight; a millstone, as I may say; round the porochial throat."

Like a handkerchief, Oliver seems at first to be little more than a blank space on which others can inscribe their mark of ownership. Bumble gives him the memorable name by which he is known, using the arbitrary, impersonal rule of the alphabet as one guide and his own inadvertent talent for metaphor as another. The police officer who brings Oliver before Mr. Fang, the magistrate, gives him his other name: Tom White. Both names reflect in different ways the namegiver's attempt to classify the boy and insert him in a narrative. "Twist" suggests the hangman's rope and thus the often-repeated prediction that "this boy will be hung." "Tom White" is of course a generic name (recalling Tom Jones), used here to indicate obscure origin and social inconsequence. At the same time, the name suggests that whiteness is an important quality in the boy. Its connotations include both moral purity and genteel birth, both of which Oliver turns out to possess in ample amounts, as well as the inviting and somewhat feminized blankness that leads so many characters to try and leave their mark on him. White, we recall, is also the color of women's handkerchiefs.

Fagin too attempts to impose an identity on Oliver, but not by giving him a name. Rather, he seeks to inscribe a narrative of crime on Oliver's blankness by telling him exciting stories about robbery and giving him the Newgate Calendar to read. In this way he hopes to "blacken" Oliver's soul—an echo of Dickens' blacking factory experience, perhaps. Oliver appears to be a *tabula rasa* unmarked by experience, and he is often described as having a face of perfect innocence. His body is physically unmarked as well. The proof of his identity does not depend, like that of Fielding's Joseph Andrews, on the discovery of a strawberry mark upon his breast. Instead, it his brother Monks who bears the identifying mark, in this case of evil—a birthmark located, significantly, on his throat.

Although he seems at first to be a blank handkerchief, Oliver in fact turns out to be a printed one. In the opening chapter of the book, Oliver's mother "imprint[s] her cold white lips passionately on [his] forehead" only a moment before she dies, and this mark apparently remains with him through the rest of the novel. A crucial scene for this reading of Oliver's character is the one in which he is set to work by Fagin "picking the marks out of the pocket-handkerchiefs." The task that Fagin assigns him is in fact the same one that Fagin is engaged to perform upon the boy—to remove the mark of origin from his soul. Oliver is a pocket-handkerchief that bears the mark of its owner, the dead mother whose spirit serves as Oliver's guardian angel. The question of whether that mark is indelible or can be effaced and another printed in its place is raised by the terms of the father's will. Oliver can inherit only if it can be shown that in his minority he should never have "stained" his name with any public act of dishonor, meanness, cowardice, or wrong.

The question of "marks" and "stains," of genetic traits and environmental determinants, arises in connection with other characters in the book. Rose, Nancy, Sikes, and Monks are all "marked" characters in one way or another. Indeed, the novel seems to revert at times to an almost literal understanding of the idea of "character" as a graphic sign or glyph. For example, the female pauper who announces the death of Old Sally in the workhouse has a face that "resembled more the grotesque shaping of some wild pencil, than the work of Nature's hand." Character in this sense is something written or printed on the body, a textual effect like the designs and patterns printed upon nineteenth-century handkerchiefs.

The handkerchiefs in *Oliver Twist* belong both to a material economy of production and exchange and to a symbolic economy of representation. I have tried to show the presence of both economies in the book as well as some of the connections between them. The history and sociology of handkerchiefs in Britain from the eighteenth through the early nineteenth century provides a useful context for understanding the different kinds of handkerchiefs that appear in the book. In particular, the dramatic increase in handkerchief production at the end of the century, brought about by the new industrial technology, may help to explain the presence of so many handkerchiefs in *Oliver Twist* as well as their availability for the complex thematic treatment that Dickens gives to the handkerchief motif.

Handkerchiefs are integral to the plot and to the narrative project of documenting London's criminal classes. They carry a range of thematic significance, especially in relation to hanging and to issues of power and social control. They are also one of the chief means by which the novel represents its own text-making practice. The circulation of handkerchiefs, like the regular displacement of the letter in Poe's story, is a figure for the process of narration itself. So long as handkerchiefs remain in circulation, the story continues. When they stop, the story ends.

In his "Seminar on 'The Purloined Letter,' " Lacan draws the conclusion that "a letter always arrives at its destination." One might argue similarly with respect to *Oliver Twist* that a purloined handkerchief always reaches its destination as well. Indeed, the story of Oliver suggests that a handkerchief usually ends up back in its owner's pocket. The story of Oliver's mother, however, suggests otherwise. If the marble tablet on the church wall provides a fitting emblem of closure and containment, refiguring Rose Maylie's white handkerchief after its violent passage through the scene of Nancy's murder, this image of reconciliation is offset by the figure of Agnes Fleming's restless "shade" hovering about the church, and even more so, in the final words of the novel, by the narrator's memory of the living woman as "weak and erring." Despite his evident wish to recover and redeem the fallen woman, the narrator's language here recalls the transgressive sexual desire that generated the entire story as well as the weary, footsore vagrant who gives birth to Oliver in the novel's opening chapter. "Erring"—that is, wandering— she remains an outsider to the final scene of domestic bliss.

The novel's effort to reach closure thus contains the elements of its own undoing, an undoing that Derrida would attribute to the process of "dissemination" and that he views as inherent in the structure of the signifier. To paraphrase Derrida's reformulation of Lacan, it is not that the handkerchief never arrives at its destination, but that it belongs to the structure of the handkerchief to be capable, always, of not arriving. In *Oliver Twist*, the handkerchief that arrives, but at the same time does not fully arrive, is female.

GARRY WILLS

The Loves of *Oliver Twist*†

1

Boy's Book

One of the first novels Dickens conceived, *Oliver Twist* is both his most knowing and his most innocent book. It is a Newgate School "thriller," lurid enough to provoke Victorian censors. It is also the classic "boy's

† Reprinted with permission from *The New York Review of Books* 36.16 (Oct. 26, 1989): 60– 67. Copyright © 1989 Nyrev, Inc.

book," written to a formula he put his stamp on forever. When Mark Twain and Robert Louis Stevenson use the formula they are imitating him, without ever surpassing him.

The formula has these basic elements: a boy separated from his family (usually by being orphaned) finds a mentor in some social outcast. Deprived of "normal" socialization, the boy is forced to cope with society as an outsider, partly taking on the critical attitude of his abnormal guide. He learns from an "eccentric" before he acquires real experience of the center. The formula not only provides the child with perilous adventure but throws a questioning light on those social ties the boy has been deprived of (or delivered from).

Once the formula is described, examples of it spring to mind—in Stevenson, Jim Hawkins and Long John Silver, or David Balfour and Alan Breck; in Twain, Huck and Jim. Stevenson made a less successful use of the formula when he paired Dick Shelton with the outlaw Ellis Duckworth (in *The Black Arrow*), as did Twain when he made the banished Miles Herndon protect his prince disguised as a pauper. Tom Sawyer fails, among other reasons, because Tom merely keeps running across Injun Joe in the commission of improbable nocturnal crimes, instead of being forced into a sustained companionship with him. Variations on the formula can be traced from Kipling's *Captains Courageous* to such light entertainment as Patrick Dennis's *Auntie Mame*. Graham Greene, a particular admirer of *Oliver Twist* and a distant relative of Robert Louis Stevenson, tried out the formula in several short stories before making it the basis of his late and comparatively minor novel *The Captain and the Enemy*. E. L. Doctorow brings the scheme back to triumphant life in *Billy Bathgate*.

The action in most of these novels takes place at night, when the child's imagination comes most alive to danger. The books breathe an air of adult secrets only half heard or understood, portentous words that come to an eavesdropping child when he is supposed to be asleep. Jim Hawkins catches his first hint of the sinister when, hiding in the ship's apple barrel, he overhears Long John talking to his confederates. And Oliver, watching through half-waking eyes while Fagin goes over his secret treasure, is first threatened by Fagin's knife when it becomes clear that he has seen what he should not have. Graham Greene created an intense vision of evil—primarily of the innocent's power to bring about evil consequences—in his story "The Basement Room," where the boy misunderstands his idolized butler's insignificant adultery.

But for a complete exploration of the formula's possibilities, one must go to Dickens, who had a special gift for understanding childhood despair at the encounter with adult cruelty or obtuseness. This is the organizing principle for *Oliver Twist*; and it is a subordinate theme in the other novels, especially the "autobiographical" ones—exemplified in the tie

between David Copperfield and the socially irresponsible Wilkins Micawber, or in that between Pip and such socially marginal characters as
the secluded Miss Havisham and the fugitive Abel Magwitch.

In *Oliver Twist*, Dickens deliberately set out to shock his audience.
He succeeded well enough that Lord Melbourne denounced the novel's
"bad; depraved, vicious taste," and Thackeray accused Dickens of making
his audience "expend our sympathies on cut-throats, and other such
prodigies of evil." The book was listed in police reports among other
contributors to crime, and theatrical adaptations of it were banned by
the Lord Chamberlain. Under the novel's surface decorum, there lurk
feverish visions of life in the underworld of London, brutal visions of a
sadistic murderer and a masochistic prostitute, of a pederastic "fence"
who has a small harem of assistants, and—last and most shocking—of
a legal workhouse system that is even worse than the underworld from
which it purports to save those trusted to its care.

Who are the real criminals, Dickens is asking, Fagin and Bill Sikes
or Oliver's workhouse persecutors, Beadle Bumble and Mrs. Mann?
Where is Oliver's spirit crushed more abjectly, in the workhouse or in
Fagin's "ken"? Oliver is more frequently admonished that he will be
"hung" in the ordered world of law (if the Poor Law's regime deserves
that name) than he is in the company of whores and catamites. Among
the latter, at least, he has the energy to laugh. When Fagin theatrically
"rehearses" street thefts with his protégés, he does it "in such a very
funny and natural manner, that Oliver laughed till the tears ran down
his face." It is the first time he laughs in the novel.

Admittedly, Oliver does not yet understand the criminal intent of
these antics; but even after he is recaptured by Fagin's "family," he
experiences a camaraderie that had not existed in the workhouse:

> At other times, the old man would tell them stories of robberies
> he had committed in his younger days: mixed up with so much
> that was droll and curious, that Oliver could not help laughing
> heartily, and showing that he was amused in spite of all his better
> feelings.

In the workhouse system, Oliver had only one friend—Dick, who is too
weak to run away with him. Undernourishment drains from the wards
of the state all their initiative—except for the devisings of a cannibalistic
desperation. Oliver is forced, in the famous dining hall scene, to ask
for "more" (having secretly drawn straws with the others), because his
fellow workhouse inmates are as frightened by each other as by their
masters:

> Oliver Twist and his companions suffered the tortures of slow star-
> vation for three months; at last they got so voracious and wild with
> hunger, that one boy; who was tall for his age, and hadn't been

used to that sort of thing, (for his father had kept a small cook's shop): hinted darkly to his companions, that unless he had another basin of gruel *per diem*, he was afraid he might some night happen to eat the boy who slept next him, who happened to be a weakly youth of tender age. He had a wild, hungry, eye; and they implicitly believed him.

Even Fagin's associates, for all their fear that one of them will inform ("blow") on the others, are never reduced to such antisocial degradation as this. David Lean's post-World War II movie version of *Twist* caught perfectly the bleak atmosphere of the workhouse by using images of Nazi prison camps.

"Normal" socialization for Oliver means promotion from the workhouse to indenture, another form of slavery. The apprentice, at the bottom of the trade ladder, is primarily to be taught that there *is* a ladder, and that his place is the lowest on it. Noah Claypole, confirming the law that the lower the office the greater is the officiousness, catechizes Oliver on his social rank:

> "Yer don't know who I am, I suppose. Work'us?" said the charity-boy, in continuation: descending from the top of the post, meanwhile, with edifying gravity.
> "No, sir," rejoined Oliver.
> "I'm Mister Noah Claypole," said the charity-boy, "and you're under me."

Fagin's "ken" is attractive because such a nest of rebels, having rejected the stratifications of respectable society, allows for a degree of familiarity suggesting egality. Rank and degree are jumbled. Fagin's form of address—"My dear"—echoes, at the bottom of society, the easy terms used within the charmed circles of gentility (the Brownlow and Maylie homes) Oliver will be taken into. There is a freedom at the top and the bottom of the social world that is squeezed out of those struggling for place in the middle, and Oliver only reaches the freedom of the upper world by falling first into the lower one.

It is not often enough remembered that Oliver was a criminal even before the Dodger found him on the streets of London. By running away from the undertaker's shop, Oliver has broken his indenture. (The rebellious apprentice would be a symbol of larger revolutionary forces in *Barnaby Rudge,* which Dickens was planning as he wrote *Twist*). Oliver has the classic criminal excuse—society made him an outlaw. He broke the rules because the rules were dehumanizing. His sense of human dignity, preserved in the ideal image he has formed of his mother, makes him resist the system, as much by his attitude as by any acts. He cannot be blamed or credited for the appeal against short rations, since others forced him into that. But Beadle Bumble rightly sees nonconformity in Oliver's very carriage, his shrinking from authority, his struggle against indenture to the brutal chimney sweep, his refusal to adopt the proper terms of submission:

> The accounts of his ferocity, as related by Mrs. Sowerberry and Charlotte, were of so startling a nature, that Mr. Bumble judged it prudent to parley, before opening the door. With this view, he gave a kick at the outside, by way of prelude; and then, applying his mouth to the keyhole, said, in a deep and impressive tone:
>
> "Oliver!"
>
> "Come; you let me out!" replied Oliver, from the inside.
>
> "Do you know this here voice, Oliver?" said Mr. Bumble.
>
> "Yes," replied Oliver.
>
> "Ain't you afraid of it, sir? Ain't you a-trembling while I speak, sir?" said Mr. Bumble.
>
> "No!" replied Oliver boldly.
>
> An answer so different from the one he had expected to elicit, and was in the habit of receiving, staggered Mr. Bumble not a little. He stepped back from the keyhole; drew himself up to his full height; and looked from one to another of the three bystanders, in mute astonishment.
>
> "Oh, you know, Mr. Bumble, he must be mad," said Mrs. Sowerberry. "No boy in half his senses could venture to speak so to you."
>
> "It's not Madness, ma'am," replied Mr. Bumble, after a few moments of deep meditation, "it's Meat."
>
> "What!" exclaimed Mrs. Sowerberry.
>
> "Meat, ma'am, meat," replied Bumble, with stern emphasis. "You've overfed him, ma'am. You've raised a artificial soul and spirit in him, ma'am, unbecoming a person of his condition. . . ."

It is Oliver's "artificial soul"—roused not by Mrs. Sowerberry's "wittles" but by Noah Claypole's challenge to the image of Oliver's mother— that makes Oliver escape the "condition" prescribed him by society. Oliver escapes by an act as deliberate as Huck Finn's. Huck feigns his own death to get beyond the brutal reach of his "Pap." Oliver walks over eighty miles to make himself invisible in the disreputable streets of London. Later, he will try to regain visibility in those same streets, only to be trapped when Nancy and Bill, pretending to respectability, rail at Oliver as an unnatural rebel who has deserted his mother.

2

Fagin

Oliver, though frightened by Fagin, is also fascinated by him. Indeed, the power of Dickens's most lurid novel lies in his ability to make Fagin and Sikes *charismatically* creepy, the more so as we understand their vileness. Sikes comes most vigorously to life when we see him commit the most vicious murder. And Fagin intrigues us precisely because of his sexual dominance over children. No wonder Thackeray accused Dickens of rousing admiration for "prodigies of evil."

Dickens does not, it is true, call Fagin a pederast directly—as he nowhere calls Nancy a prostitute. Yet Nancy's prostitution clearly underlies all her outbursts of grievance against Fagin, who put her on the streets; and Fagin's pederasty as clearly underlies much of Oliver's fear and fascination. "As he glanced timidly up, and met the Jew's searching look, he felt that his pale face and trembling limbs were neither unnoticed, nor unrelished by that wary old gentleman." The hostile distance between Fagin and Sikes is created in part by the latter's brutal heterosexuality, contemptuous of Fagin's silken charms. In the pub that serves as the criminal "flash house," the flash (knowing) talk about Fagin's boys is a staple:

> "Wud of Bister Fagin's lads," exclaimed Barney [the keeper of the flash house], with a grin.
> "Fagin's 'eh!" exclaimed Toby [Crackit], looking at Oliver. "Wot an inwalable boy that'll make, for the old ladies' pockets in chapels. His mug is a fortun' to him."
> "There—there's enough of that," interposed Sikes; impatiently; and stooping over his recumbent friend, he whispered a few words in his ear: at which Mr. Crackit laughed immensely, and honoured Oliver with a long stare of astonishment.

What astonishes Toby? Not the fact that Oliver is one of Fagin's boys. That was taken for granted in his first remark. The only thing that would astonish him is that Oliver had *not* done what was taken for granted. Fagin's method is one of seduction, not force—he usually leaves the force to Bill Sikes: and Oliver has refused to be seduced. On the level of overt action, this means that Oliver refuses to become a thief. He rebels against Fagin's system as he had against the more respectable institutions of society. Fagin, we learn in time, has been hired by Oliver's unknown half-brother ("Monks") to debase Oliver so thoroughly that he will not dare, later in his life, to lay claim to the family estate in the West Indies. Monks resorts to this indirect way of eliminating Oliver's claims since he feels the taboo against actual fratricide. His demands on Fagin explain the pederast's panic at the thought that Sikes would risk the boy's life, putting Monks's bribes in peril:

> "Once let him feel that he is one of us; once fill his mind with the idea that he has been a thief; and he's ours! Ours for his life! Oho! It couldn't have come about better!" The old man crossed his arms upon his breast, and, drawing his head and shoulders into a heap, literally hugged himself for joy.
> "Ours!" said Sikes. "Yours you mean."

"Perhaps I do, my dear," said the Jew, with a shrill chuckle. "Mine, if you like, Bill."

"And wot," said Sikes, scowling fiercely on his agreeable friend, "wot makes you take so much pains about one chalk-faced kid, when you know there are fifty boys snoozing about Common Garden every night, as you might pick and choose from?"

"Because they're of no use to me, my dear," replied the Jew with some confusion, "not worth the taking."

Fagin speaks with confusion because he cannot tell Sikes about the bargain with Monks. Instead, he invents a reason for his solicitude that Oliver not be killed—the boy's innocent look is useful for gulling victims of the gang's theft.

When I first read *Oliver Twist*, in my own childhood, I did not know that Sikes's lover Nancy is a prostitute; and it is safe to bet that Queen Victoria, enthusiastically following the novel as it appeared in serial numbers, did not realize that Fagin is a pederast. Did Dickens expect his knowledgeable adult readers to understand this fact, as important to Fagin's speeches as her prostitution is to Nancy's? There are many things, within the novel itself as well as in Dickens's other works, to indicate that he did expect such understanding. Fred Kaplan notes that "Dickens's knowledgeability about sexual relationships between males (particularly between older men and young boys) can hardly be doubted."[1] His good friend and fellow mesmerist Chauncy Hare Townshend had a boy subject for his hypnotizing sessions who seems to have been his catamite.

Nor was Dickens's awareness of homosexuality confined to male lovers. In *Little Dorrit*, the relationship of Miss Wade to Tattycoram is clearly lesbian. Miss Wade describes a girlhood experience that seems to have set the pattern for her later emotional experiences. As a girl of twelve, she was obsessed with a "chosen friend" at school, a friend who humiliated her by acts of kindness to Miss Wade herself and to all others, acts (Miss Wade is convinced) meant deliberately to contrast with her own suspicion and jealousy:

> I so loved that unworthy girl, that my life was made stormy by my fondness for her. I was constantly lectured and disgraced for what was called "trying her"; in other words, charging her with her little perfidy and throwing her into tears by showing her that I read her heart. However, I loved her, faithfully; and one time I went home with her for the holidays.
>
> She was worse at home than she had been at school. She had a crowd of cousins and acquaintances, and we had dances at her house, and went out to dances at other houses, and, both at home and out, she tormented my love beyond endurance. Her plan was, to make them all fond of her—and so drive me wild with jealousy.

1. Fred Kaplan, *Dickens and Mesmerism: The Hidden Springs of Fiction* (Princeton, 1975) 197.

To be familiar and endearing with them all—and so make me mad
with envying them. When we were left alone in our bedroom at
night, I would reproach her with my perfect knowledge of her
baseness; and then she would cry and cry and say I was cruel, and
then I would hold her in my arms till morning: loving her as much
as ever, and often feeling as if, rather than suffer so, I could so
hold her in my arms and plunge to the bottom of a river—where
I would still hold her, after we were both dead.

When Miss Wade finds Tattycoram chafing under her service at the
Meagleses', she recruits her to a sisterhood of resentment. Tattycoram's
break with the Meagleses resembles Miss Wade's angry departure from
her childhood friend's house. Tattycoram has grown increasingly jealous
of "Pet," the Meagleses' child, who is in love with a young man. On
the night she leaves the house, Tattycoram denounces the family in
words that Mr. Meagles recalls: "When we pretended to be so fond of
one another, we exulted over her; that was what we did; we exulted over
her, and shamed her." Tattycoram runs off to join Miss Wade, who
establishes a passionate hold over her. When Mr. Meagles fails in his
appeal to Tattycoram, Miss Wade claims her prize:

> Miss Wade, who had watched her under this final appeal with that
> strange attentive smile, and that repressing hand upon her own
> bosom, with which she had watched her in her struggle at Mar-
> seilles, then put her arm about her waist as if she took possession
> of her for evermore.

This is the bond that Meagles had feared, giving a special emphasis to
his words with Miss Wade: "If it should happen that you are a woman,
who, from whatever cause, has a perverted delight in making a sister-
woman as wretched as she is (*I am old enough to have heard of such*),
I warn her against you, and I warn you against yourself" (italics added).
   Miss Wade takes Tattycoram captive, as Fagin is supposed to subjugate
Oliver, in a way that will make it impossible for the victim to rejoin
respectable society. So Tattycoram, even when she is beginning to rebel
against her thralldom to Miss Wade, rejects the idea that she could ever
go back to the Meagleses. "You know very well that I have thrown them
off, and never can, never shall, never will, go back to them." When
she does go back, proving the depth of kindness in the Meagleses, it is
with an almost hysterical self-abasement:

> "Oh! I have been so wretched," cried Tattycoram, weeping much
> more, after that, than before; "always so unhappy, and so repentant!
> I was afraid of her, from the first time I ever saw her. I knew she
> had got a power over me, through understanding what was bad in
> me, so well. It was madness in me, and she could raise it whenever
> she liked."

A closer parallel to Oliver's situation at Fagin's is to be found in *Dombey and Son*. Indeed, Dickens seems deliberately to have gone back to *Oliver Twist*, in this novel, to "update" its themes in one of his larger social tales. Thus Florence is kidnapped by "Good Mrs. Brown," stripped of her fine clothes and dressed in rags, like Oliver after Nancy and Bill bring him back to the ken. But the more important parallel is between Oliver's tutelage and that of Robin Toodle ("Rob the Grinder"). Rob may in fact be considered an Oliver who does not escape the snares of the criminals he deals with. Sent to a charity school, where he is beaten and brutalized, he joins a street gang fencing its goods to Mrs. Brown, and then falls into the literal clutches of James Carker, who immediately shows his repressed violence by almost strangling the young boy of fifteen. Despite this harsh first encounter, or because of it, Rob becomes abjectly devoted to Carker, constantly fixing on him "eyes, which were nailed upon him as if he had won the boy by a charm, body and soul." Dickens describes the boy's "stupor of submission," his "reverie of worshipful terror," in terms that would perfectly express Oliver's bondage to Fagin if he had surrendered to him:

> [Rob] could not have quaked more, through his whole being, before the teeth [of Carker], though he had come into the service of some powerful enchanter, and they had been his strongest spells. The boy had a sense of power and authority in this patron of his that engrossed his whole attention and exacted his most implicit submission and obedience. He hardly considered himself safe in thinking about him when he was absent, lest he should feel himself immediately taken by the throat again, as on the morning *when he first became bound to him*, and should see every one of the teeth finding him out, and taxing him, with every fancy of his mind. Face to face with him, Rob had no more doubt that Mr. Carker read his secret thoughts, or that he could read them by the least exertion of his will if he were so inclined, than he had that Mr. Carker saw him when he looked at him. The ascendancy was so complete, and held him in such enthralment, that, hardly daring to think at all but with his mind *filled with a constantly dilating impression of his patron's irresistible command over him, and power of doing anything with him*, he would stand watching his pleasure, and trying to anticipate his orders, in a state of mental suspension, as to all other things.
>
> [italics added]

Aside from these passages in other works, the text of *Oliver Twist* itself points to something heinous in Fagin's activities when the crowd reacts in frenzy to the discovery of his gang. In technical terms, the worst that Fagin is guilty of—and the charge on which he is hanged—is being an accessory before the fact to Nancy's murder. It is hard to imagine that the mob hunts him down because of this indirect form of guilt, of which it has had little time to be informed. (The charge is so little inflammatory that Dickens does not even specify it in the dramatic chapter on Fagin's trial.) The people hounding Fagin show the same indignation that the American public has recently shown over cases of child abuse. The most disgraceful thing about the man is his circle of corrupted boys.

Dickens's narrator expresses this revulsion, out of proportion to the offenses he is permitted to make explicit by the code of the novel's decorum. The revulsion expressed is clearly meant to be shared by the reader:

> The mud lay thick upon the stones: and a black mist hung over the streets; the rain fell sluggishly down: and everything felt cold and clammy to the touch. It seemed just the night when it befitted such a being as the Jew, to be abroad. As he glided stealthily along, creeping beneath the shelter of the walls and doorways, the hideous old man seemed like some loathsome reptile, engendered in the slime and darkness through which he moved: crawling forth, by night, in search of some rich offal for a meal.

The loathsomeness of Dickens's first and most frightening villain was completed by the author's collaboration with Cruikshank in the illustrations. Chesterton, who began his own career as an art student and critic, catches the spirit of Cruikshank:

> It was a strange and appropriate accident that Cruikshank and not "Phiz" should have illustrated this book. There was about Cruikshank's art a kind of cramped energy which is almost the definition of the criminal mind. His drawings have a dark strength: yet he does not only draw morbidly, he draws meanly. In the doubled up figure and frightful eyes of Fagin in the condemned cell there is not only a baseness of subject; there is a kind of baseness in the very technique of it. It is not drawn with the free lines of a free man; it has the half-witted secrecies of a hunted thief. It does not look merely like a picture of Fagin; it looks like a picture by Fagin. Among these dark and detestable plates there is one which has, with a kind of black directness, struck the dreadful poetry that does inhere in the story, stumbling as it often is. It represents Oliver asleep at an open window in the house of one of his humaner patrons. And outside the window, but as big and close as if they were in the room, stand Fagin and the foul-faced Monks, staring at him with dark monstrous visages and great white wicked eyes, in the style of the simple devilry of the draughtsman. The very naivete of the horror is horrifying: the very woodenness of the two wicked men seems to make them worse than mere men who are wicked. But this picture of big devils at the window-sill does express, as has been suggested above, the thread of poetry in the whole

thing; the sense, that is, of the thieves as a kind of army of devils
compassing earth and sky crying for Oliver's soul and besieging the
house in which he is barred for safety.

Many critics have concentrated on the last-described scene, of Oliver's
half-waking vision of Fagin at the window, as one of the eerier moments
in all of Dickens's fiction. Fred Kaplan finds in it a description of the
hypnotized person's sleeping consciousness, induced by the mesmeric
eyes and repeated phrases of Fagin. Graham Greene notes the way
Dickens is able to make of the novel a "closed Fagin universe":

> Fagin has always about him this quality of darkness and nightmare.
> He never appears on the daylight streets. Even when we see him
> last in the condemned cell, it is in the hours before the dawn. In
> the Fagin darkness Dickens's hand seldom fumbles. . . . It is with
> a sense of relief that at last in twilight we see the faces of the Jew
> and Monks peer into the cottage window between the spray of
> jessamine. At that moment we realize how the whole world, and
> not London only, belongs to these two after dark. [2]

Of course, some people think the frenzy of the mob against Fagin, and
the narrator's horror of him, and even Cruikshank's touch of the diabolic
in his portrait, all stem from the fact that Fagin is a Jew. The demonic
forces Dickens has loosed are the simple but deep ones of anti-Semitism.
This is a misunderstanding for which Dickens was, as he came to realize,
guilty. The popular anti-Semitism he assumed in his audience, and
shared with it, in the 1830s was one of the "covers" for the pederastic
story he was telling.

　　He first conceived it as a blind for the censors. The reaction to a child
abuser would be "explained," on the story's literal level, by the resentment at Jewish fences. Fatally convenient for his purpose lay the trial,
in the preceding decade, of a criminal named Ikey Solomons, whose
fame had carried him into the popular arts of his time—and into Dickens's own *Sketches by Boz*, where a Solomon Jacobs, with his assistant
Ikey, keeps one of those lock-up houses where debtors could settle their
accounts before trial by the payment of extra fees. Dickens's later attempts
to calm the passions he aroused over Fagin show that he miscalculated
the dangerous feelings he was playing with. Instead of merely "covering"
the real subject, those feelings extinguished it. Thus there were artistic
as well as moral reasons for his effort at erasing Fagin's Jewishness,
partially in later numbers and editions of the novel and entirely in his
stage readings of it. There is no reference to Fagin's being a Jew in his
reading text, where he is introduced simply as "Fagin the receiver of
stolen goods." His vivid impersonation of Fagin had, we are told, no
suggestion of the "stage Jew" at all.

---

2. See above, pp. 430–32 [*Editor*].

It is clear from Dickens's dramatization of his own text that modern adaptations of the story for the theater should not make Fagin a Jew, repeating an artistic mistake that Dickens rectified on the stage. Correspondingly, it is clear that modern interpreters of Fagin's role should go farther than Alec Guinness did, in the David Lean film of 1948, to indicate that Fagin is a pederast (Guinness merely gave him a lisp). The 1966 BBC production for television, though it was explicitly violent enough in the depiction of Nancy's murder to prompt calls in Parliament for censorship, was too delicate to make clear the sexual climate of Fagin's ken.

Without a clear recognition of Fagin's pederasty, the intensity of Dickens's assault on the workhouse and indenture systems cannot fully be appreciated. Better Fagin than Bumble, Dickens continues to insist, even after we know that Fagin is a child abuser. Better a crippled or twisted love than no love at all. The workhouse was emotionally as well as physically starved. Oliver resisted Fagin, but he also laughs with him. He is emotionally involved with him. That is why he is taken to see him in his cell at the end. The plot motivation for this is to let Oliver learn where Fagin has hidden the papers he took from Monks, papers that establish Oliver's identity. But the emotional reason is for Oliver to express his sympathy with Fagin, along with his continuing fear of him, and his forgiveness. He asks Fagin to pray with him—not, pointedly, in any Christian form. The narrator has already told us that Fagin rejected the attempts of rabbis to have him pray in the Jewish forms. Dickens's Christians, unlike Shakespeare's in *The Merchant of Venice*, do not try to convert the Jewish villain. Dickens's cruelly thoughtless anti-Semitism of the 1830s was a social prejudice, not a religious one.

3

Nancy and Bill

The possibility of real love even in the seamy world of Fagin is the point of Nancy. Not that the love she has for Bill is ennobling. That is a degrading addiction—as Dickens indicates by ranking her devotion with that of Bull's-eye, the kicked dog who comes back and back to Sikes, and even throws itself off the rooftop to follow him in death. Nancy's genuine love is expressed not in her relationship with Bill, but in her self-sacrifice for Oliver. Only after she pretends to be acting for his mother during the kidnapping scene on the street does Nancy begin to protect him in the thieves' ken, slamming the door so the dog cannot get at him, wrestling the club from Fagin's hand when the latter yields to an uncharacteristic fit of violence. The respectable people who feigned a motherly care for Oliver in the workhouse system were acting in their own interest, exploiting the child while they claimed to be caring for him. Oliver's idealized image of his mother finds its most dramatic fulfillment in a whore masochistically submissive to a thug.

Nancy, more than any other character but "Little Nell," demonstrates the shift of taste that has occurred between Dickens's time and our own. We find it difficult to take Nancy seriously; yet Wilkie Collins wrote, in 1890: "The character of 'Nancy' is the finest thing he ever did. He never afterwards saw all sides of a woman's character—saw all round her." What measures our distance from the past is that most people today find it hard to accept Nancy's goodness, the proverbial golden heart in her tart's breast. What Dickens's contemporaries found incredible was her badness, her return to Bill when she has been offered not only escape but respectability. In terms of rational morality, her return to Bill is suicide—which Dickens does not defend on any grounds but clinical observation: "It is useless to discuss whether the conduct and character of the girl seems natural or unnatural, probable or improbable, right or wrong. IT IS TRUE. Every man who has watched these melancholy shades of life knows it to be so" (preface to third edition).[3]

He made the same defense of his truthfulness to character in the similarly masochistic prostitute of *Dombey and Son*, Alice Marwood. Alice is a Nancy morbidly attached to a far subtler villain than Sikes, to James Carker, whom she both loves and hates. Alice, too, shows some motherly feeling toward Florence; but not the redeeming kind that Nancy is allowed. Dickens could create subtler women characters in his later work—but none that he seems to have felt more deeply than Nancy. Despite the vitality he gave to Fagin and Sikes in his final public readings, many in the audience found that the most moving passage in the whole performance was his delivery of Nancy's final speech to Bill.

Another obstacle to our appreciation of Nancy is the importance of class difference in Dickens's time. Nancy seems too self-abasing before the social superiority of Rose Maylie, just as Rose seems too condescending to Nancy. We underestimate the social abyss that kept a Victorian woman from contact with prostitutes. Nancy fully expects to be prevented from the interview with Rose on which Oliver's life depends. She is proportionately grateful when Rose countermands the efforts of her servants to keep this unworthy thing from their mistress's view. After Rose hears what prompts Nancy, she tries to give her more concrete evidence of her affection than the handkerchief that Nancy will lift up as she dies, the emblem of her bond with a gentlewoman. As usually happens in Dickens, women are able to transcend social barriers by their concern for a child. Not fraternity but maternity is the principle of equality in Dickens's world.

3. See above, pp. 3–7 [*Editor*].

The gift of one's own handkerchief was a particularly intimate exchange for Victorian women. That is why Dickens puts such mysterious weight on Esther Summerson's reception of Lady Dedlock's gift before Esther knows that Honoria Dedlock is her mother. That handkerchief travels conspicuously through the plot of *Bleak House*, as a symbol of the literal implication of people in one another's lives. The symbol is more important than any parallel gift would be today because of the intrinsic value of Victorian handkerchiefs made of silk and because of the special designs created to express the owner's identity. In *Dombey and Son* we learn that "Sir Barnet Skettles expressed his personal consequence chiefly through an antique gold snuff-box, and a ponderous silk pocket-handkerchief, which he had an imposing manner of drawing out of his pocket like a banner." We know from Henry Mayhew that there was a heavy traffic in stolen handkerchiefs; and the value of individual ones is indicated by Fagin's care to remove identifying initials from them. The thieves' elaborate exercises in extracting handkerchiefs from unwilling victims is contrasted with Rose's free gift, the pledge that Nancy lifts up in her bloodied last moment as Cyrano lifts his plume. Dickens cut, from his public readings of the novel's last scenes, most of the details that depend on knowledge of what went before, but not the handkerchief.

The crowning proof that love can exist in the depths of Fagin's world is, astonishingly, Sikes. Dickens claimed, in his "Author's Preface to the Third Edition," that Sikes has no redeeming qualities. But his own artifact confutes him. Many have noted the paradox that Bill is an entirely unsympathetic character until the moment when he should forfeit our sympathy. Yet Bill, an animal much less worthy than the one he punishes throughout the book, becomes a man only after he has killed a woman. John Bayley goes so far as to describe Sikes's murder as a metaphysically transmuting act, and to compare it with Raskolnikov's murder of the woman in *Crime and Punishment*.[4] But Sikes does not consciously commit a crime as an experiment upon himself. All his life has been one continual series of criminal acts, including (Fagin hints repeatedly) prior murders. It is not as a connoisseur of guilt that Sikes wins our compassion. What haunts him in his flight is the unshakable vision of Nancy's form and face and—particularly—eyes. He is still brute enough to attempt further killings—of his dog on the road and of Charley Bates in the Jacob's Island ken. What the murder of Nancy stirs in the inert stuff of Sikes is belated recognition of his love for her. Killing her was not one of his ordinary acts of cruelty. Fagin, knowing this would be the case, had screwed him up to the act with a series of hypotheticals: Would he kill *this* person for blowing? Would he kill *that*

---

4. See above, pp. 461–69 [*Editor*].

one? In a carefully graduated series of "thought experiments," Fagin builds Sikes's fury to a crescendo before revealing (and skewing at the same time) the things that Noah Claypole heard Nancy reveal to Mr. Maylie.

The wrench of Nancy's loss leaves Sikes bewildered by the beginnings of human feeling in him. He sits guilty wake upon the body, trying to dispel the visionary eyes by taking the cover off the real eyes wide open in her beaten face. But he cannot, as in the past, ignore or accept the stark evidence of his violence. He flees, seeking solitude. Even the dog is unwelcome company now, not only as an identifying mark to others but as an accusing witness of the crime. Then, in the most psychologically powerful scene of the book, Sikes tries to find human company in a crowd that is fighting fires in the village of Hatfield, where his flight has taken him. He throws himself into a frenzy of rescue. Only in the spontaneous responses to communal disaster can he blot out, for a moment, the insistent eyes:

> There were people there—men and women—light, bustle. It was like new life to him. He darted onward—straight, headlong— dashing through brier and brake, and leaping gate and fence as madly as the dog, who careered with loud and sounding bark before him. . . . Women and children shrieked, and men encouraged each other with noisy shouts and cheers. The clanking of the engine-pumps, and the spirting and hissing of the water as it fell upon the blazing wood, added to the tremendous roar. He shouted, too, till he was hoarse; and, flying from memory and himself, plunged into the thickest of the throng.
>
> Hither and thither he dived that night: now working at the pumps, and now hurrying through the smoke and flame, but never ceasing to engage himself wherever noise and men were thickest. Up and down the ladders, upon the roofs of buildings, over floors that quaked and trembled with his weight, under the lee of falling bricks and stones, in every part of that great fire was he; but he bore a charmed life, and had neither scratch nor bruise, nor weariness nor thought, till morning dawned again, and only smoke and blackened ruins remained.

But as soon as the excitement dies down, Bill feels himself isolated again. "He looked suspiciously about him, for the men were conversing in groups, and he feared to be the subject of their talk." He slinks off with Bull's-eye, hoping not to be noticed. When he struggles back to the Jacob's Island hideout, even his former comrades try to exclude him.

At the very moment when he has come to feel the need for human community, there is none to receive him. He is like a moral astronaut, blasted off from the atmosphere of human things, who has a permanent reentry problem. The cohesion of the community he has violated thickens to resist him. Even in the low conviviality of the tavern Sikes stops at, a peddler terrifies him with the chanted slogans for his cleanser—takes out "water-stains, paint-stains, pitch-stains, mud-stains, blood-stains." He realizes that everyone is talking about him because they are talking about the homely ordinary world he cannot share. Everything human was killed for him in the one thing recognizably human, even to him, that he has slain. He killed the world, and cannot reenter what he has destroyed. He cannot bear the one form of companionship still vouchsafed him, that of Bull's-eye. All the traces of the human that still cling to him turn against him, becoming tracks that his pursuers can follow.

Two years after Dickens wrote the searing end of his tale, Poe, who was following Dickens's writings very carefully at this stage, wrote "The Man of the Crowd," in which a narrator follows a man of strikingly troubled aspect all night long, as the man rushes from one crowded human scene to another, always seeking the presence of others but remaining anonymous in their midst. At last the narrator leaves him, at dawn, convinced that his secrets are so dreadful that a mercy keeps him unreadable (*er lasst sich nicht lesen*) [he doesn't allow himself to be read].

Dickens felt the compulsion to mingle in reassuring crowds. He compulsively reenacted Sikes's crime in his days of waning health and haggard need for new audiences. Fired up at the end of a performance, he sometimes wanted to begin the ordeal all over again. When his friends restrained him, he wandered out alone, through the streets, feeling wanted for some crime of his own. He felt exalted downward, lifted out of himself by a lowering of his mind into Sikes's hyperconsciousness of everything denied him. Chesterton's detective, Father Brown, says he must commit a crime in his own mind, *become* the criminal, in order to find the criminal. Dickens not only did that, but draws his readers into doing it. Sikes is not, as Bayley thought, experimenting with crime in the story; Dickens is experimenting with crime in Sikes. As Chesterton wrote of *Twist*, "Characters which are not very clearly conceived as regards their own psychology are yet, at certain moments, managed so as to shake to its foundation our own psychology." We are frightened by Fagin, and join in sympathy with those who hunt him down. But we are frightened *with* Bill Sikes, and shy away from those who bay for his life. Sikes is the dark aspect of ourselves that we are surprised to find within us, and that gripped Dickens so firmly as simultaneously to draw him into crowds and drive him from them. The Victorian censors were right to feel troubled by this novel. It opens moral trapdoors under us.

Charles Dickens: A Chronology

1812   Born February 7 in Portsmouth to John Dickens, a clerk in the Navy Pay Office, and Elizabeth Barrow. He is the second of eight children.

1817   Family moves to Chatham, near Rochester in Kent. Dickens attends a local school and reads widely in his father's library.

1822   Father transferred to London; family moves to Camden Town and then Bloomsbury. Charles not enrolled in school.

1824   John Dickens imprisoned for debt. Charles sent to work as a laborer at Warren's Blacking Factory. Later in the year, John Dickens obtains his release from the Marshalsea, and sometime thereafter Charles is removed from the blacking factory.

1825   Attends Wellington House Academy.

1827   Clerks for two London lawyers and considers a career as an attorney.

1828–29   Learns shorthand and works as a freelance reporter at Doctors' Commons.

1830   Falls in love with Maria Beadnell.

1831–34   Works as a parliamentary reporter.

1833   Publishes his first story.

1834   Becomes a reporter on *The Morning Chronicle* and publishes six stories.

1836   Marries Catherine Hogarth. Collects the stories he has been writing into his first book, *Sketches by Boz*. Resigns as reporter.

1836–37   Writes *Pickwick Papers*.

1837   Edits *Bentley's Miscellany* where *Oliver Twist* is published serially from February 1837 to April 1839. The first of his ten children is born. Death of Mary Hogarth in May.

1838–39   Writes *Nicholas Nickleby*.

1840–41   Writes *The Old Curiosity Shop*.

1842   Visits America and publishes *American Notes*.

1842–43   Writes *Martin Chuzzlewit*.

1843   Publishes *A Christmas Carol*.

1844   Lives in Italy with his family until early 1845.

1846   Edits *The Daily News* and lives part of the year in Switzerland and in Paris.

1846–48   Writes *Dombey and Son*.

1847   Supervises the creation of a home for homeless women at Urania Cottage.

1849–50   Writes *David Copperfield*.

1850   Founds and edits a weekly journal, *Household Words*.

1852–53   Writes *Bleak House*.

1853   Gives his first public reading of his works for charity.

1854   Serializes *Hard Times* in *Household Words*.

1855   Lives in Paris from October 1855 to March 1856.

1855–57   Writes *Little Dorrit*.

1856   Purchases Gad's Hill Place, near Rochester in Kent.

1857   Meets Ellen Ternan, who is to become his mistress.

1858   Gives his first public reading for his own profit and legally separates from his wife.

1859   Creates and edits a new journal, *All the Year Round*, in which he publishes *A Tale of Two Cities*.

1860   Serializes *Great Expectation* in *All the Year Round* and gives up his London residence for Gad's Hill Place.

1861   Undertakes the first of an intensive series of readings in London and in the provinces, which he does regularly for the next eight years.

1862   Maintains his official home at Gad's Hill and spends periods living with Ellen Ternan at other residences in England and in France until 1870.

1864–65   Writes *Our Mutual Friend*.

1865   Suffers minor injuries and serious trauma in a railway accident in Kent.

1867   After a reading tour in England and Ireland, visits America, to earn money giving readings, where he remains until April 1868.

1869   Suffers a series of minor strokes.

1870   Begins *The Mystery of Edwin Drood*, half of which he completes; gives a series of farewell readings in London; dies in June at Gad's Hill of a cerebral hemorrhage.

Selected Bibliography

BIOGRAPHIES

John Forster's *Life of Charles Dickens*, 2 vols. (1876), has the majesty, intimacy, and limitations of a biography written by one of Dickens' closest friends soon after Dickens' death. There are three modern biographies: Edgar Johnson's *Charles Dickens*, 2 vols. (1952), which contains the fullest account of the factual details of Dickens' life; Fred Kaplan's *Dickens: A Biography* (1988), which emphasizes psychological portraiture and relationships, and Peter Ackroyd, *Dickens* (1990). *Charles Dickens, Interviews and Recollections*, 2 vols. (1981), ed. Philip Collins, provides fascinating accounts of the impression Dickens made on many of his contemporaries. For Dickens' involvement with hypnotism and its role in *Oliver Twist*, see Fred Kaplan, *Dickens and Mesmerism, The Hidden Springs of Fiction* (1975). The best source for Dickens' self-revelations are his own words, in the Pilgrim Edition of *The Letters of Charles Dickens*, six volumes of which have been published (1968–88).

BIBLIOGRAPHIES

There is an excellent bibliographical volume devoted entirely to *Oliver Twist*, David Paroissien's *"Oliver Twist," An Annotated Bibliography* (1986). Four sources provide ongoing annual bibliographies of current work on Dickens and, of course, on *Oliver: The Dickens Quarterly*, *Dickens Studies Annual*, *Victorian Studies*, and the annual bibliographical issue of *PMLA* (*Publications of the Modern Language Association*); the back volumes of these bibliographies are valuable sources for modern articles and books on Dickens. Volume 3 of *The New Cambridge Bibliography of English Literature* (1969) contains an excellent primary and secondary bibliography of Dickens. Two very readable, annotated, general bibliographical essays on Dickens exist: Ada Nisbet's in *Victorian Fiction, A Guide to Research*, ed. Lionel Stevenson (1954), and Philip Collins in *Victorian Fiction, A Second Guide*, ed. George Ford (1978). David Paroissien's *Companion to "Oliver Twist"* (1991) provides chapter-by-chapter, detailed annotations, ancillary material, and an extensive bibliography.

CRITICAL STUDIES

There is a vast shelf of critical studies of Dickens, and many of the volumes contain sections on *Oliver Twist*. Most of the best such studies (with the exception of H. M. Daleski's chapter on *Oliver* in *Dickens and the Art of Analogy* [1970] and Kathleen Tillotson's "Oliver Twist" in *Essays and Studies* [1959]) are contained in the volumes from which I have selected excerpts for the Criticism section of this edition, where full citations appear. But a number of other books warrant mention: *Dickens, The Critical Heritage*, ed. Philip Collins (1971), contains early reviews; Humphry's House's *The Dickens World* (1941) and Fred Kaplan's *Sacred Tears, Sentimentality in Victorian Fiction* (1987) are helpful on the subjects of benevolence and the moral sentiments in *Oliver*; Alexander Welsh's *The City of Dickens* (1971) provides a perceptive guide to Dickens' labyrinthine depictions of London; Kathleen Tillotson's introduction to the Clarendon Edition contains an excellent history of the critical reception of the novel, and George Ford's *Dickens & His Readers* (1955) a full-scale account of the audience reception of all of Dickens' novels; Dickens' complicated relationship with the illustrator of *Oliver*, George Cruikshank, is fully detailed in Robert Patten's forthcoming biography of Cruikshank.

611

FIC
DIC

Dickens, Charles,
1812-1870.

Oliver Twist.

$17.95

16789020002150
09/23/1995

DATE			